GLENN CURTISS: Pioneer of Flight

C. R. ROSEBERRY

GLENN CURTISS
Pioneer of Flight

 SYRACUSE UNIVERSITY PRESS

Syracuse University Press Edition 1991
17 18 19   8 7 6

This book was originally published in 1972 by Doubleday and Co., Inc.

∞ The paper used in this publication meets the minimum requirements of the American National Standard for Information Sciences—Permanence of Paper for Printed Library Materials, ANSI Z39.48-1992.

For a listing of books published and distributed by Syracuse University Press, visit our website at SyracuseUniversityPress.syr.edu.

ISBN: 978-0-8156-0264-4

Library of Congress Cataloging-in-Publication Data

Roseberry, Cecil R.
    Glenn Curtiss. pioneer of flight/C. R. Roseberry.—Syracuse University Press
    ed.
        p. cm.
    Reprint. Originally published: Garden City, N.Y.: Doubleday, 1972.
Includes bibliographical reference (p.   ) and index.
    ISBN: 0-8156-0264-2 (alk. paper)
1. Curtiss, Glenn Hammond, 1878-1930. 2. Aeronautics—United States—
    Biography. I. Title.
    [TL540.C9R67   1991]
    629.13'0092—dc20
    [B]

Manufactured in the United States of America

CONTENTS

List of Illustrations   vii

1. SPEED CRAVING   1
2. THE HELL-RIDER   18
3. A DALLIANCE WITH DIRIGIBLES   35
4. CHANUTE AND THE BROTHERS   59
5. "TO GET INTO THE AIR"   67
6. RED WING   83
7. WHITE WING   96
8. JUNE BUG   102
9. TOM SELFRIDGE   119
10. SILVER DART   136
11. GOLD BUG; ALIAS GOLDEN FLIER   163
12. GLORY AT RHEIMS   183
13. FUMBLE AT GOVERNORS ISLAND   204
14. WESTERING WINGS   223
15. HERRING NON GRATA   237
16. RETURN TO THE RIVER   261
17. THE EXHIBITIONISTS   281

18. WATER FLYING   308
19. FEUD WITH THE WRIGHTS   332
20. ATLANTIC FANTASY   363
21. FLYING THE *LANGLEY*   381
22. A FORTUNE OF WAR   394
23. ATLANTIC REALITY   411
24. FLORIDA YEARS   424
25. KEUKA SUNSET   448

APPENDIX   457
    Notes   459
    Concerning Sources   485
    Bibliography   489
INDEX   493

LIST OF ILLUSTRATIONS

following pages 84, 180, 324, and 420:

1. Glenn H. Curtiss in 1912
2. The Curtiss home on Castle Hill in Hammondsport, New York
3. Two stars of the Hammondsport Boys racing group: Tank Waters and Glenn Curtiss
4. Lena Neff and Glenn Curtiss in a betrothal portrait
5. Curtiss the "hell-rider"
6. Lena Curtiss trying out one of her husband's sidecars
7. The monstrous 8-cylindered motorcycle
8. Curtiss's first experience in the air, in the dirigible *California Arrow*
9. A Baldwin dirigible ascending
10. Shop building of the Curtiss Manufacturing Company
11. The earliest powered military aircraft in the United States
12. Beinn Bhreagh Hall, the summer home of Alexander Graham Bell
13. An experimental, propeller-driven boat
14. Dr. Alexander Graham Bell and his wife
15. Curtiss's earliest known sketch of a proposed flying machine
16. Members of the Aerial Experiment Association
17. The tetrahedral kite *Cygnet*
18. The *Cygnet* being towed for its first, and last, flight
19. Experimental glider
20. The "ice-cycle" as a test-bed for the *Red Wing*
21. The *Red Wing*'s air-cooled engine
22. Drome Number 1 of the A.E.A. prior to its successful flight

23. The battered *Red Wing* after its first flight
24. The *White Wing*
25. Alexander Graham Bell and Casey Baldwin
26. The "Wind-Wagon"
27. A meeting of the A.E.A. at Hammondsport
28. I. Newton Williams' experimental helicopter
29. Glenn Curtiss at the controls of the *June Bug*
30. *June Bug* aflight
31. Orville Wright and Lieutenant Tom Selfridge
32. The *Silver Dart*
33. The *Silver Dart* as a two-man machine
34. The *Loon*
35. The *Loon* on Keuka Lake
36. Glenn Curtiss with the *Silver Dart*
37. A horse-drawn sleigh pulling the *Silver Dart*
38. The *Cygnet II*
39. First flight of the *Gold Bug*
40. The *Gold Bug* at Morris Park racetrack
41. The Gordon Bennett Trophy racer
42. Glenn Curtiss at Rheims
43. The Curtiss racer at Rheims
44. A French postcard illustrating the famous flight
45. The Gordon Bennett Trophy
46. French Pilot's license "Number Two"
47. Alexander Pfitzner in his monoplane
48. Louis Paulhan visits Curtiss
49. Augustus M. Herring
50. The *Hudson Flyer* at Governors Island
51. Banquet honoring the Hudson River flight
52. Charles K. Hamilton, the original Curtiss exhibition pilot
53. Lincoln Beachey
54. Beachey flight under the bridge at Niagara Falls
55. J. Lansing Callan
56. Julia Clarke, an early pilot
57. Captain Thomas Baldwin
58. A handbill of a Curtiss exhibition
59. Glenn Curtiss and Billy Sunday
60. Eugene Ely's first landing aboard the cruiser *Pennsylvania*
61. Ely taking off from the *Pennsylvania*
62. Curtiss's first hydroplane

63. Curtiss's hydroplane being hoisted aboard the *Pennsylvania*
64. Navy Pilot Number 1, Lieutenant "Spuds" Ellyson
65. Experimental triplane
66. Aero Club of America's Number 1 license
67. The *Triad*
68. Beaching facilities at Keuka Lake
69. Lieutenant John H. Towers
70. Curtiss and Ellyson experiment with new launching device
71. Curtiss aviation school at North Island
72. Early aeroboats on Keuka Lake
73. Curtiss Aviation School at Hammondsport
74. Curtiss with Lieutenant John Towers
75. Proud parents with Glenn H. Curtiss, Jr.
76. The Langley Medal awarded to Curtiss
77. Orville and Wilbur Wright
78. Henry Ford and Glenn Curtiss
79. Lincoln Beachey
80. Beachey's plane hitting a tent
81. A family group
82. Christening of the *America*
83. Glenn Curtiss, Jr., astride the prow of the *America*
84. The *America* in a trial run on Keuka Lake
85. The Langley aerodrome being assembled
86. The *Langley* ready for launching
87. Glenn Curtiss in the *Langley* cockpit
88. The *Langley's* successful first flight
89. A later flight of the *Langley*
90. The Curtiss plant
91. A Curtiss JN-4
92. The Curtiss plant in Garden City, New York
93. The Curtisses on Long Island
94. The remarkable tail of the NC-1
95. The NC-4 after takeoff
96. The crippled NC-3
97. Streamlined triplane developed at Garden City plant
98. Mr. and Mrs. Curtiss on their return from Europe—1919
99. The Curtiss Florida home
100. City Hall of Opa-Locka
101. Curtiss and his streamlined Aero-Car trailer
102. The *Scooter*

103. Glenn Curtiss, Jr., and his father
104. Last formal portrait of Glenn Curtiss
105. The Curtisses at the twentieth anniversary celebration of the Hudson River flight

GLENN CURTISS: Pioneer of Flight

1. Speed Craving

By the turn of the century, bicycles had grown so numerous in Hammondsport as to pose a traffic hazard. Up to then, they were the most popular and liberating private vehicle yet invented. The village board in 1901 adopted an ordinance requiring cyclists to dismount when meeting or passing pedestrians on the public walks; the penalty for violation was a fine of $2. It did not occur to the civic fathers to ban wheels from the public walks.

In defense of bicycles, it could have been argued that they were not noisy and did not emit evil fumes. The nice, staid, and close-knit community cherished its tranquillity. Who would have suspected that a harmless bicycle might one day turn into a monster and rend the genteel calm to tatters? Or that, when it had so done, the village would not be the same again for a long, exciting time to come?

Hammondsport, Steuben County, New York, U.S.A. . . .

Population 1169 by the 1900 census. Locus, the head of Keuka Lake on whose sapphire surface steamboats plied the 21 miles to Penn Yan and back. Hillbound mart of trade for a lush vineyard region styled "Grape Bowl of the East." Economic mainstay the juice of the grape, fermented and bottled in a dozen wineries. Four or five modest hotels, an opera house, church spires thrusting from trees, a few saloons, a Civil War monument, a small lakefront depot of the nine-mile Bath & Hammondsport Railroad.

Taken all in all, Hammondsport was not the sort of town where anything of the least historic moment was likely to happen.

A certain summer's day of 1901 started out as serenely as days invariably did. Merchants as usual opened their stores facing the shady rectangle of Pulteney Park. Familiarly called the Park Square, or simply the Square, this gracious space served double duty as village green and hub of commerce. The canopied trees were maples. Walks from corner to corner formed an "X" at the center, and benches were set at intervals beside them. In the grassy triangle of the western side was a roofed bandstand with scrollwork at the eaves. Doctors, lawyers, dentists kept offices upstairs over the stores. Horses tethered at curbs switched their tails at tormenting flies. Clerks came out and lowered awnings in pace with the sun.

Beneath the routine of this day, however, ran a lambent flicker of expectancy. Everyone around Pulteney Park knew that Glenn Curtiss was ready to try out his lunatic bicycle with a gasoline engine. Whether it would function or flop was a moot question among the villagers. Naturally there were scoffers, one of whom predicted that Glenn might conceivably get as far as the post office—if he pedaled hard enough.

The youthful proprietor of the bicycle shop over on Pulteney Street, the north edge of the square, was afflicted with a lust for speed, and he had become a local celebrity as a champion bike racer of Steuben and several adjacent counties. A good cyclist could still ride circles around most automobiles in 1901. Suddenly Glenn Curtiss had conceived the notion that he could make a bicycle go faster by giving it engine instead of leg power. The idea was not original with him, to be sure. He had been reading about it in the cycling periodicals to which he subscribed, and knew that gasoline motors were at last being developed which were small and light enough to put into a bicycle. Such motors were not very successful as yet, but he determined to give one a try. By mail order, he purchased an advertised set of engine castings from a firm in Buffalo.

The shop where he both sold and repaired "wheels" was cramped into a one-story frame building so narrow that it usurped only twelve feet of frontage on Pulteney Street. The sign on the awning said: G. H. CURTISS—BICYCLE SUPPLIES—SPORTING GOODS. During the year he had been at this stand, he had earned the respect of his neighbors not only for a clever mechanical talent, but for persistency and business acumen as well. Lean, muscular, soft-spoken, laconic, he appeared older than his twenty-three years. A thick dark mustache contributed to the illusion, but even more so did his serious and sober demeanor.

There being few secrets on the Park Square, people had been dropping by the Curtiss shop, watching him tinker with the uncouth engine, trying as best he could to improve it. The thing did not even come equipped with a carburetor, and so he made one out of a tomato can and a gauze screen. More tin cans were soldered into service for other uses, attached "wherever there was a place for them to hang," inspiring bystanders to dub the peculiar machine the Happy Hooligan (the reference was to a cartoon-strip character, a likable hobo who wore an inverted tin can for a hat). Curtiss later described it as "a remarkable contrivance."

Finally came the moment of truth. The Happy Hooligan was trundled into the street as stores and offices emptied to the sidewalks. Glenn's plan was to pedal the transmogrified bicycle up to a speed where the motor could be started by engaging the transmission belt. He pedaled strenuously around the perimeter of Park Square without coaxing a grunt from the engine. Some onlookers were commencing to giggle. Reaching the post-office corner, he paused for breath, monkeyed with the spark and the tin-can carburetor, remounted and headed downgrade on a street sloping to the waterfront. Of a sudden the engine sprang to life. Glenn sped exultantly down the hill as residents gaped from their porches. To avoid running into Lake Keuka, he ditched the Hooligan and leaped for safety.

Thus, with a volley of ear-splitting bangs, the era of the internal combustion engine dawned upon Hammondsport. The bemused villagers had no premonition of what this portended for the future of their treasured tranquillity.

Glenn Curtiss immediately ordered a larger set of engine castings.

*   *   *

It is a truism that geography often lends direction to the affairs of men. From that viewpoint, the influence of Keuka Lake upon the career of Glenn Curtiss invites consideration.

He knew it first as Crooked Lake, the descriptive if prosaic title pinned on it by early settlers. It was Crooked Lake in whose cool embrace he became an adept swimmer and upon whose winter lid he learned to skate. He was nine years old when a local crusade succeeded in getting it officially rechristened with the prior Indian name, translated by some authorities as "lake with an elbow." Keuka is the maverick among Finger Lakes. Where the others are uniformly linear, as the Iroquois Divinity imprinted them on the land with his outspread fingers, Keuka is shaped like a boy's slingshot. The crotch of the fork is held apart by a singularly handsome promontory, Bluff Point. At the base of the Y, a landward extension of the steep-walled glacial trough bends west by south. So entrancing was this prospect to the pioneers that they called it Pleasant Valley.

Where valley meets lake, Lazarus Hammond, in 1807, paid $10 for 140 acres, taking it off the hands of another man who had acquired it in a tax sale. With the advent of steamboats a few years later, his purchase bloomed into a lake port with a link to the Erie Canal. An Episcopal clergyman gave destiny a different quirk by bringing some grapevine cuttings with him from the Hudson River Valley; they throve amazingly in the rectory yard. Before many more years elapsed, the shoulders of Crooked Lake were mantled with vineyards. Charles Champlin founded the Pleasant Valley Wine Company in 1860, with U.S. winery license number one, and soon surprised the market with the first American-made champagne. More wine cellars rapidly ensued. Expert vintners from France were grafted into the community.

Early in the 1870s, the village awakened to the potential of yet another natural asset: the Glen, a deep cleft with fifteen waterfalls, debouching within a stone's throw of Pulteney Park. A few years prior, a smart promoter had opened Watkins Glen to the public, and it was reaping profits hand over fist, acclaimed as a scenic wonder of the world. Watkins was just across the hills at the head of Seneca Lake, and the example bestirred Hammondsport capital to follow suit. The Glen was developed along similar lines, with walks, stairs, railings, and an admission fee. Excursionists were diverted from their boat rides to visit it.

Such was the attractive setting which two Curtiss couples found emphatically to their liking when they arrived in the year 1876, under the auspices of the Methodist Episcopal Church.

* * *

For the Reverend Claudius G. Curtiss and his stoical wife, Ruth, it looked like the end of the rainbow after a weary succession of smalltown pastorates in western New York. The Methodist Conference believed in shifting its ministers around. For their son Frank and his bride, Lua, it seemed a heaven-sent spot to begin married life and put down roots.

Well into his fifties, the Reverend Claudius was a large and weighty man, of more than ample girth. The long road had begun for him in Niagara County, where he was born of Connecticut Yankee ancestry.[1] Surmounting a bare minimum of schooling to enter the ministry, he "uttered thoughts that breathed and words that burned," to quote a churchly eulogist. Two sons came of his union with Ruth Bramble, a tall, black-haired, durable farm girl. They were Claudius Adelbert and Frank Richmond. Along the path of the family peregrinations, the younger boy, Frank, picked up the trade of harness-making.

In 1873, the Reverend Claudius Curtiss was called (a euphemism for ordered) to the pulpit of Jasper, a village tucked away in the hilly folds of southern Steuben County. The organist of his church was Lua Andrews, a lissome, airily imaginative damsel who caught Frank's eye. Daughter of Henry B. Andrews, a grocer and drug dealer, Lua had a musical and artistic bent. She sang, played piano, dabbled at watercolors, decorated chinaware. She claimed to be a great-grandniece of Samuel F. B. Morse, who, to remind listeners who missed the point, she would casually remark had been a portrait artist of some note before tackling the telegraph.

Three years was above average for a Curtiss stay at any one post, and the next call came in 1876, to the Methodist Church of Hammondsport. By that time Frank and Lua were ripe for matrimony, and they gladly accepted the invitation to accompany his parents and share the parsonage roof until he could get established in a harness shop. The older son stayed in Jasper, rounding out his life as a farmer and carpenter.[2]

Never before had any pastorate provided so congenial an environment for the Curtiss clan. Frank found a ready market for harness-making, while Lua joined the Methodist choir and was appointed church organist. Lua took delight in roaming the Glen and painting its scenes. Though rated "an able and earnest temperance worker" by church colleagues, the Reverend Claudius seems not to have been unduly disturbed by the fact that many, perhaps most, of his parishioners owed their livelihood to wine-making. No record survives of his preaching a sermon on the text: "Look not on the wine when it is red."

On the 21st of May, 1878, in the Methodist parsonage on Orchard

Street, Lua Curtiss gave birth to a son. The weekly Hammondsport *Herald* reported: "It is a boy and weighs 8 pounds—Harness is cheaper and Curtiss is happy."

Choosing a name for the infant was the next order of business. It was out of character for Lua to let anything be commonplace if she could possibly help it. The same edition of the *Herald* remarked: "Our beautiful Glen has been for the past few years slowly but surely winning its way into public favor." The Glen Wigwam, a rustic shelter for dancing and refreshment, was to be dedicated the following week. In short, the Glen was right then on the tip of Hammondsport tongues.

Lua Curtiss made up her mind to identify her son indelibly and for all time with his birthplace. She named him Glenn, for the gorge she had so much enjoyed; adding the extra "n" for more imposing effect. For a middle name she chose Hammond, in tribute to the founder of the village.[3]

Hence: Glenn Hammond Curtiss.

*   *   *

Presently the young parents discovered a house which could be had at a bargain, but they were unable to swing its purchase alone. This was a large, elderly homestead perched on a terrace of the hillside, over-looking and slightly aloof from the village proper. They understood it to have been built by Lazarus Hammond as his own home, and its commanding position would seem to support that thesis. A long flight of stone steps led up to a veranda crossing the front; while an addition at the rear made it adaptable to two families. A goodly bonus came with it: a sizable vineyard climbing the slope behind. The terrace on which it stood was known as Castle Hill, and was a glacial lake delta of the Glen creek.

The house was obviously too roomy for one couple. Presumably thinking ahead to retirement, the elder Curtiss made the down payment and took title, Frank engaging to keep up the mortgage payments. In this way did the minister of the gospel become titular proprietor of a vineyard. In after years, Glenn's mother wrote that she and Frank "went to housekeeping in one of the first houses built in Hammondsport"; boasting of the "fine vineyard" in which the grapes were Catawbas, Concords, and Agawams. (Catawbas were deemed the "backbone" of the champagne and white wines made in the district.)

Doubtless the Reverend Claudius knew he was about due for

another call, and it came in 1879. He was transferred to Cambria, a hamlet in his native Niagara County; a year later to Sparta, Livingston County.

Between the harness shop and the vineyard, the younger Curtisses made ends meet. If a faint shadow crept over their connubial bliss, it was the fact that Frank began to develop a taste for the demon rum. Possibly this weakness was magnified in village gossip because he was "a minister's son." But he made no denial, once saying: "I don't know why I do it. I know I am a fool, but it just seems as if I have to drink." Nothing indicates, however, that either his business or his family suffered unduly.

A girl was born on February 15, 1881, christened Rutha Luella. It is easy to guess that Frank wished his daughter to be his mother's namesake, and that Lua, with her incurable itch for embellishment, tacked on the "a."

Meanwhile, the always robust health of Claudius began to crumble, and Frank urged him to give up preaching and come on home. The Methodist Conference granted him retirement status in the summer of 1881, and he returned gratefully to Hammondsport, moving in with the young folks. There he felt better, puttering in the vineyard and relishing the view from the veranda. Unhappily, he was allotted but a scant year in which to enjoy his surcease. During a steamboat excursion with friends on the lake, he was felled by a stroke, taken home, and died in August 1882.

Henceforth, Mrs. Ruth Curtiss was the strong-minded matriarch of Castle Hill. The next census report cited her as owner of the property and a "vineyardist." Lua, with a chronic distaste for the mundane chores of housekeeping, was content to hand over the reins to her mother-in-law; the arrangement permitted her more time for music and her other aesthetic interests.

A malign fate struck a far more grievous blow to the domestic scene five months later. In a strangely sudden attack of illness, Frank Curtiss died at the hour of midnight on January 30, 1883. He had not yet attained the age of twenty-eight. The only clue to cause of death appeared in the *Herald*'s obituary notice: "inflammation of the stomach." (Vital statistics were not yet being kept by the town.)

And so it came about that Glenn Curtiss was deprived of both father and grandfather while he was a child of four. As a result, women were to be the arbiters of his boyhood and adolescence.

Now two widows were in mourning together on Castle Hill. Instead of returning to her Jasper kinfolk, Lua elected to remain with her mother-in-law. The stock of the harness shop went into storage. The vineyard was providential, and they marketed grapes to the local wineries and shipped out purple Concords for table use. Glenn was taught to tie and prune the vines and help with the harvest, and townsfolk would remember seeing the small boy driving grapes to the depot in a pony cart for express shipment. To piece out the income, Lua gave piano lessons to a class of ten pupils, while retaining her post as church organist.

Of the two children, the boy was his grandmother's favorite, and he in turn held for her a deep and abiding affection. Her influence on his upbringing was more profound than Lua's; indeed, there seems never to have been a really close tie between Glenn and his mother. As might be expected, Ruth Curtiss indoctrinated her grandson in the moral precepts of Methodism, and yet she was much more to him than a spiritual superintendent. She it was who allowed him to erect a home-made incubator in an upstairs room and have baby chicks overrunning the house. Once she gave him a birthday party at which she bewildered his playmates by serving corned-beef-and-cabbage because Glenn especially fancied that dish.

Before he was of school age, Grandmother Curtiss often read to him, and one literary curiosity which he never tired of hearing was *Darius Green and His Flying Machine*. This humorous poem, lampooning man's efforts to fly, was having a vogue at the time, in booklet form with comic illustrations. Ruth Curtiss told her wide-eyed grandson that she had personally known its author, John T. Trowbridge, when she was a girl in Ontario County. The verses narrated how a gangling farmer lad decided that if birds could fly, so could he; how he built a device of "wings strapped to his arms, and a tail." When he tested it from the hayloft window of his father's barn, he hit the ground hard, and concluded:

> "Wal, I like flyin' well enough,"
> He said: "but the' ain't sich a thunderin' sight
> O' fun in 't when ye come to light."

Glenn and his grandmother regarded the misadventures of Darius Green as hilarious, and they laughed together, sharing the universal skepticism of the day about flying experiments. In time to come, J. T. Trowbridge, when an aged man, would make a trip into Boston to see Glenn fly. It seems a shame that Ruth Curtiss did not live long enough to know this.

A boy is a boy, and this one had the normal amount of fun, even if he was a bit of a sobersides. He would "sit for hours down on the lake shore watching the sea gulls," to quote a chum. He climbed trees to collect birds' eggs, and entered into a partnership with Harry Genung to breed blue-ribbon rabbits. Perhaps the earliest symptom of his zest for speed was the skating sail he rigged up with a bamboo fishpole, which made him the fastest skater of his gang on Keuka Lake. As a newsboy, he won his first bicycle as a prize offered by the Hammondsport *Herald* to the carrier who rode it to cover the delivery route in the shortest time. Coming into the home stretch, his momentum ran him into the curb and flung him forcibly to the sidewalk. As he told it from adult memory: "One of our compositors, a big Irishman, gathered me up in his arms and I heard him say, 'The poor little devil's dead ez me hat, but he's winner.' I knew no more, but the thrill of joy that ushered me into unconsciousness has never been duplicated in my experience. I wasn't hurt seriously, only badly shaken and in a state of nervous collapse. In half an hour I was well enough to mount my wheel and scud for home."

A trait which early manifested itself was that of the Yankee tinker. The Curtiss boy was handy at "fixing things." Somehow he gleaned a rudimentary understanding of electricity at a time when telephones and electric lights were just coming in, and he went around town armed with a screwdriver repairing doorbells. He pored over magazines like *Popular Mechanics*, and his playmates had a saying that: "Glenn would think half an hour to do fifteen minutes' work."

*   *   *

The nemesis that hovered over Castle Hill had one further parcel of ill fortune to deliver. When Rutha was six years old she fell victim to meningitis. Although she recovered from the malady itself, her hearing was destroyed and she was in danger of becoming a deaf-mute. Glenn was a solicitous brother who learned finger-spelling along with her and practiced precise movements of the lips and tongue when speaking, in order to assist her with lip-reading.

Lua Curtiss heard of the Western New York Institution for Deaf Mutes, in Rochester. This progressive school had been started just lately by Zenas F. Westervelt whose technique was noted as the "Rochester Method." Embattled against the "deaf-mute mind," he ruled out sign language, advocating instead manual spelling, lip-reading, and as much speech as the patient could retain. In this approach, Westervelt was in full agreement with Dr. Alexander Graham Bell, with whom he corresponded. Bell had been a teacher of the deaf before inventing the telephone, and had married a girl who was deaf, Mabel Hubbard of Boston.

Rutha Curtiss was enrolled as a pupil in Westervelt's institution in 1889, and her mother moved to Rochester with her, taking lodgings in a boardinghouse. Glenn remained with his grandmother, having three grades yet to go in the Hammondsport Union Free School. Probably his help was needed in the vineyard, the profits of which now must stretch to cover at least partial support of the Rochester half of the family.

As a student, Glenn was no better than average, except in mathematics which was his best subject. He finished the eighth grade in 1892, just past his fourteenth birthday, and that was the end of his formal education. The high school certificate he received was never put to use, as Lua wished him to join her in Rochester and go to work. In other words, his sister's deafness and the decision to give her special training marked an early limit to his own schooling. But it did afford him the experience of a fairly large city in his adolescent years.

In Rochester, Glenn readily found a job with the Eastman Dry Plate and Film Company (soon to be reincorporated as the Eastman Kodak Company). George Eastman was expanding his Kodak Park plant to meet the demand for his roll film, hiring large numbers of teen-age boys to stencil numbers on the paper backing of the film. For this sort of drudgery Glenn was paid $4 a week. His reaction was characteristic: to figure out a better way of doing it. At home he built a rack with a hinged-brush device which would stencil one hundred strips of film at a stroke, then suggested to his foreman that the work might move faster if the boys were put on a piecework basis, at 25 cents per one hundred strips. The foreman thought it a capital idea. Next morning Glenn smuggled his machine into the plant and began stenciling 2500 strips a day, instead of the usual 250. As soon as the foreman caught on, the company adopted the device but cut the piecework rate; even so, the boys were able to earn more money.

Eastman's six-story camera works, the State Street Plant, was erected in 1893 and Glenn was transferred there. Learning the fundamentals of camera construction, he made one for himself from a cigarbox, and undertook a serious study of photography.

Missing the lake and hills, it is plausible to suppose that he found factory employment irksome. At all events, as soon as he could afford a bicycle he switched jobs, becoming a Western Union messenger. Immediately his horizons and his recreations expanded. In off-duty hours, he joined other messenger boys in impromptu races wherever they could find a good stretch of asphalt. Also, he began taking weekend bicycle trips back to Hammondsport, a distance of 70 miles, where a lonely grandmother welcomed him with open arms. He had spun up into such a gandershanks that she hardly recognized him.

Lua Curtiss by now had a suitor, an acquaintance from the past. She had first known J. Charles Adams as a singer in the church choir at Hammondsport, when he was living in the vineyard country bordering the lake. Considered something of a "dandy" and a ladies' man, he capitalized on a good tenor voice by joining choruses and singing societies over a wide radius. Since that time, Adams had been twice married and transferred his place of residence to Rock Stream, a small town on the hill above the west beach of Seneca Lake, near Watkins Glen. There, in a speculative venture, he had purchased a considerable acreage of steep hillslope which he planted to vineyards and fruit trees. A local farmer's daughter who became his second wife soon died. Ascertaining the whereabouts of the Curtiss widow, he now paid court to her, and they were married in Rochester on April 1, 1895. The bride was age thirty-seven, her groom forty-two. Apparently Adams divided his time between Rochester and Rock Stream for the time being. Since his vineyards were prospering, circumstances were suddenly easier for Lua and her brood.

During one of his revisits to Hammondsport, Glenn was riding his bike around the Park Square when a young fellow, watching from the curb, signaled him to stop. Introducing himself as Leonard Waters, nicknamed Tank, the stranger asked where he had learned to ride so well. Waters was a newcomer since Glenn left town, a clerk in James H. Smellie's pharmacy and the ringleader in a team of bicycle racers known as the Hammondsport Boys. Smellie had taken on a bicycle agency as a sideline of his drugstore and was a patron of the racers. Near the same age, Tank and Glenn found they had much in common. Early next morning, Curtiss appeared at Champlin's racetrack for an initiatory ride with the Hammondsport Boys and was invited to join their ranks.

Harry M. Champlin, a son of the founder of the Pleasant Valley Wine Company, was by hobby a breeder and exhibitor of trotting horses. Two miles out the valley, on the flats overscanned by the winery, he maintained Stony Brook Farm, with a huge red barn and a half-mile oval training track for his horses. Ever the sportsman, Champlin allowed the use of his track to the bicycle racers for practice. He little dreamed what this precedent would lead to.

With an inborn love for the sheer physical sensation of rapid motion, and endowed with long legs that were like a pair of muscular pistons, Glenn Curtiss caught racing fever. His jaunts to Hammondsport grew more frequent as he worked out with Tank Waters and his cronies. Before long he was accompanying them to racing meets at county fairs, field days, and the like. More often than not, the Hammondsport Boys returned with cash prizes which they divided, share and share alike.

Jim Smellie recognized Curtiss as a comer and determined to "put him in a race that would make him." George Lyon, the jeweler, who was Smellie's main competitor as a bicycle agent, was organizing a five-mile race around the Pleasant Valley circuit of buggy roads. Plotting a surprise, Smellie made a quick trip to the Stearns factory, ordering a special racing model which weighed but 17 pounds. When it arrived at the B.&H. station, he told Glenn to unpack it secretly and ride it home after dark through back streets. The day of the race, Glenn showed up to enter. Lyon took one startled look at the slick Stearns racer and ruled that such a bicycle was unfair, and so disqualified him. When Smellie heard this, he sent Glenn back to protest that the race had been advertised as a free-for-all, and therefore he could not legitimately be debarred. After a huddle with his committee, Lyon called off the race. Whereupon Smellie arranged a five-mile road race of his own, and when it was over bragged that Curtiss was "home eating his dinner when the rest of the crowd got in."

Through Smellie's deal with the company, Glenn was enabled to purchase the $100 bicycle for $50, on the installment plan, for the publicity value of having him ride it. "I felt as if I were stealing it," Curtiss confessed. Thenceforward, the yellow Stearns racer, with Glenn astride, led the pack in many a Southern Tier race. Its very appearance in a starting lineup became a symbol of almost certain victory. When Tank Waters left town to seek fortune in Buffalo, Curtiss inherited the captaincy of the Hammondsport Boys.

Concerning Glenn's prowess of the racetracks, Jim Smellie said: "He had tremendous endurance. He was never a quitter. He would do anything that was fair to win." A quality which was manifest throughout his racing career was a strong competitive instinct, with a corollary dislike for defeat that verged on the traumatic. "What is the need of racing," he said, "unless you think you are going to win? And if you are beaten before you start, why take a chance?"

*   *   *

The Curtiss youth, at the age of eighteen, probably had no inkling that Darius Green was being vindicated. The steps taken in aerial experimentation had minimal newspaper exposure, to be sure. In 1896, for example, a significant scene was enacted on the Potomac River off Quantico, Virginia, and no reporters were among the tiny group of spectators.

Two bearded men stood tensely together on the roof of an anchored houseboat. One was Dr. Samuel P. Langley, distinguished secretary of the Smithsonian Institution, an astrophysicist famed for his researches in solar radiation; the other, Dr. Alexander Graham Bell, inventor of the telephone, whose major interest now was in the possibility of human flight. These two were friends of long standing, and Langley had visited Bell at his summer estate in Nova Scotia and watched his experiments with large box kites. In return, Langley invited Bell to witness his attempt to fly a model of a steam-powered aircraft which he designated as an aerodrome (this usage was a combination of two Greek words denoting "runner of the air").

The aerodrome was Langley's Model Number 5, scaled to one-fourth the size of a machine he hoped to produce later, designed to transport a man. It had four wings in tandem, in the manner of a dragonfly, with a wingspan of 14 feet; and a small steam-engine which spun dual propellers. A spring catapult was to vault it into the air from the top of the houseboat. The launching was successful and the model flew along evenly for 3000 feet, settling gently on the river when the steam ran out. Retrieved from the water, it was brought back and flew a second sortie.

Dr. Bell was enthusiastic, and he wrote: "The sight of Langley's steam aerodrome circling in the sky convinced me that the age of the flying machine was at hand." Back in Nova Scotia that summer, he redoubled his work with the kites.

In a surge of optimism, Dr. Langley returned to his laboratory in Washington and constructed Model Number 6 of his aerodrome. In tests that November, again over the Potomac, it flew better than Model Number 5, staying airborne for as much as 4200 feet. For the time being, however, Langley was without funds to move ahead to a man-carrying machine.

In that same year an exhaustive series of glider trials was being conducted at Dune Park, a strip of rolling sand hills on the Indiana shore of Lake Michigan. The sponsor of these tests was Octave Chanute of Chicago, a retired civil engineer who had made a modest fortune building railroads and bridges, including the first bridge across the Missouri. Studying the experiments with gliders in Germany by the Lilienthal brothers, Otto and Gustav, Chanute set about following their lead in America. His primary motive was to solve the problem of lateral stability. He wrote a scholarly little book, *Progress in Flying Machines*, which won him recognition as this country's best authority in the field. Many varieties of gliders were tried out among the windy dunes, ranging from biplanes to a monstrosity with twelve wings. A select few young men assisted Chanute at his camp, and one of these was Augustus M. Herring, who had worked briefly for Langley at the Smithsonian.

Meanwhile, the Lilienthals were continuing their attempts to imitate the flight of birds in the Stollerier Mountains, not far from Berlin. There, on August 9, 1896, Otto Lilienthal left the ground in a monoplane glider testing a new stability device for "raising the wings at the tip." In a sudden lull of wind, the glider plunged by the nose and he was killed.

In Dayton, Ohio, the Wright brothers, Wilbur and Orville, were running a bicycle shop. Reading the news of Lilienthal's death, they decided to take up a study of aeronautics, and wrote hither and yon for literature on the subject.

✿   ✿   ✿

In Rochester, New York, Mrs. J. Charles Adams found herself in a state of pregnancy, and agreed with her husband that the child should be born in Rock Stream. Rutha Curtiss, having reached the age of sixteen, could be left alone as a boarding student at the Institution for Deaf Mutes. When the move was made in 1897, Glenn accompanied them, did some work for Adams in the vineyards and assisted him in building two or three houses, but this was not for long. From Rock Stream, it was a mere twenty miles over the hills to Hammondsport, and the pull of that village was like a magnet to him. Later that year, his half brother, G. Carl Adams, was born.

Until lately, Glenn had been girl shy. Nobody could recall his ever having a schoolboy crush. On one of his long rides from Rochester, he was hot, tired, and very thirsty. Nearing Hammondsport, he saw a nice-looking girl picking grapes beside the road, and stopped to inquire where he could get a drink of water. Obligingly, the girl hastened to a nearby house and came back with a bucket of cold spring water. He observed that she was rather small, well formed, had wavy brown hair and brown eyes, and was both friendly and ladylike. In brief, before getting back on his bicycle Glenn Curtiss had bashfully made a date, which led to many future dates.

The girl was Lena Pearl Neff, whom he had not before known because she was a relative newcomer to Hammondsport. Two years younger than he, Lena had been born in Wheeler, some ten miles west of the village, the only child of Mr. and Mrs. Guy L. Neff. Her father, a lumberman, moved the family to Hammondsport in the early '90s, when he became superintendent of a sawmill on the outskirts. At the time Glenn met her, she was working as a grape packer, a seasonal employment that was customary for the young ladies of Hammondsport; the job involved packing table grapes in baskets in so careful a way that they would not be bruised in shipment. Acquaintances spoke of her as "just an ordinary country girl."

When Glenn left the Neff home one evening after going through the ritual of asking parental consent for the hand of their daughter, Mrs. Neff voiced her mild misgivings lest he was too young for marriage. Said Guy Neff: "That boy is going places, and he will put her in a brick house some day." Many years later, Lena used to tell of the episode, and laughed that she "never did get that brick house."

They were married on March 7, 1898, in the Presbyterian parsonage at Hammondsport. On the Register of Marriages, Glenn stated his age as twenty-one. In reality, he was nineteen, going on twenty. The only reasonable surmise as to why he falsified his age is that, as a minor, he lacked his mother's consent. (Relatives afterward said that Mrs. Lua Adams more than once tried to break up the marriage.)

More truthfully, the bridegroom set down his occupation as "photographer." A married man, after all, needed a steadier source of income than bicycle racing. The study of photography begun as an Eastman employee had not been abandoned, and he now went to work for

Saylor's studio in Hammondsport. His forte was the out-of-town assignments, which he could cover handily on his bicycle, and he took many
pictures of rural family groups, horses, and barns. Between-times, he
continued racing and did bicycle repairs on the side for Jim Smellie.

The newlyweds moved in with his grandmother on Castle Hill. Mrs.
Ruth Curtiss was more than receptive to the marriage and the bride. Age
was catching up and her sight was failing. In fact, she was scheduled
soon to undergo surgery for removal of cataracts from both eyes.

Glenn chose the time of his marriage to grow the mustache which
stayed with him through life. It imparted an air of maturity which
before he lacked.

*   *   *

The pharmaceutical trade of Jim Smellie was expanding so that, in
1900, he offered to turn over all his bicycle repair and spare-parts business to Curtiss. This tipped the scales. Glenn made his decision to drop
photography and open a bicycle shop. Mrs. Malinda Bennitt gave him
the rent-free use of the narrow building on Pulteney Street. Mrs. Bennitt
was the elderly widow of an attorney who had left her well-fixed, and
she had been a co-founder of the Hammondsport *Herald*. Watching
Glenn grow up, she always spoke of him as "my boy," and she now
took pride in helping him get a foothold in business.

Cannily, Curtiss seized the opportunity to unload the leftover stock
of his father's harness shop. One of his early advertisements in the
Herald said: "Curtiss' Harness Store. Felt-Less Sweat Pads. Fly Nets,
Dusters, Brushes, Whips and Everything in the Harness Line." There
was a vacant barn behind the bicycle shop, and this appears to have
been the location of the harness department.

Acetylene gas was the common mode of lighting stores around Park
Square, before electricity. When the gas generator of a neighboring
shop went out of kilter, Curtiss volunteered to fix it. In so doing, he saw
a way to augment its capacity with a double-drip system of feeding water
into the carbide lumps; two tomato cans and a few dabs of solder turned
the trick. From this experience, he made an acetylene plant to illumine
his own shop, and then several more for other stores. It taught him the
utility of tin cans and made him a little money.

Noting the large margin of profit realized by manufacturers of
bicycles for which Smellie held the agencies, Curtiss resolved to create
a brand of his own. Sketching out some design ideas, he contracted

with a machine shop in Addison, New York, to make bicycles to his order, and trademarked them the Hercules. While underselling other makes with the Hercules, he was able to pocket twice the profit. Soon he opened a branch of the firm, now called the Curtiss Bicycle Stores, in Bath, the county seat, placing Will Damoth, a former racing companion, in charge.

In June of 1901, Jim Smellie took the full step of getting out of the bicycle trade entirely, transferring his agencies to Curtiss. Brand names which were thereupon advertised by Curtiss, to be "closed out at greatly reduced prices," were: Stearns, Columbias, Clevelands, Nationals, and Racycles.

*   *   *

A glow of happiness suffused the house on Castle Hill when it became apparent that Lena was going to have a baby. The glow was replaced by a pall of gloom when the child, a boy, was delivered in March 1901. He was born a blue baby—that is, with a congenital heart defect which deprived the bloodstream of the proper amount of oxygen. In those days there was no such thing as open-heart surgery to correct that condition.

They named him Carlton, and had him for only eleven months. Then a small grave was dug in Pleasant Valley Cemetery.

So desolated was Lena Curtiss that she took a vow never to bear another child. She feared that if she did, it would have the same incurable ailment.

2. The Hell-Rider

Intrigued as he was with speed, it was inevitable that Glenn Curtiss would attempt to motorize a bicycle, although as yet he knew little if anything about internal combustion engines. When he did so in 1901, it was by installing a crude mail-order motor in one of his own bicycle frames. At that time, by his own word, he had seen only one such vehicle, the Thomas Auto-Bi, and had heard about just one other type, the Orient, made in Waltham, Massachusetts.

The Thomas Auto-Bi, reputedly the first practical motorcycle in America, was introduced in 1900 by the E. R. Thomas Company of Buffalo, which was already making automobiles. Curtiss ordered his set of engine castings from that company in response to an advertisement in a trade periodical. The Pan-American Exposition opened in Buffalo in May 1901, and Curtiss was among the earliest Hammondsporters to visit the fair. It is logical to guess that he saw the Auto-Bi on that occasion.

There is a legend that Curtiss made up his mind to build a motorcycle in reaction at being humiliatingly beaten by professionals in a bicycle race at the New York State Fair at Syracuse in 1900. This story does not stand up under scrutiny. In the first place, the State Fair had no bicycle races on its program in 1900—only horse racing. On Labor Day, after the fair was over, the track was given over to a series of bike races, with amateur teams entered from Syracuse, Rochester, and other nearby cities. There was no team from Hammondsport, and the name of Glenn Curtiss does not appear anywhere in the lists of entries which the Syracuse papers printed in full. When the racing was completed, a Stearns motor-bicycle was exhibited as a novelty in two runs on the track. A year later, Curtiss said he had seen only a Thomas Auto-Bi. Thus it would appear that he was stimulated into building a motorcycle by nothing more dramatic than his inborn desire to go faster.

The fact remains that Glenn was not always the victor in his races, as indicated by his later admission: "I didn't like being beaten."

When the engine castings arrived from the E. R. Thomas Company, he was disconcerted to find that they were rough-cast (that is, not machine-polished), and were unaccompanied by an instruction sheet. Also, they came without a carburetor. He could hardly have been blamed had he refused delivery. Instead, he set about making an engine of the chunks of metal, with the convenient aid of his wife's uncle, Frank F. Neff.

Neff had recently risen to be a figure of some prestige in Hammondsport by inventing the wire hood for capping champagne bottles (hitherto, the corks, under pressure of carbonation, had been held in by waxed twine). The key to Neff's device was the mechanism with which the hood was automatically clamped on as the bottle was corked. He obtained international patents, established a plant at the lakefront, and soon even French wineries were among his customers. As a result, he owned the machine tools with which to help his nephew finish off and assemble his rough castings.

The Happy Hooligan took form by trial-and-error. Glenn did not propose to imitate the Thomas Auto-Bi. A knotty question was on which wheel to apply the power; after trying both, he settled on the rear wheel. The simple belt-and-pulley transmission of the Thomas Auto-Bi invited slippage; instead he adopted a V-shaped leather belt passing through grooved pulleys. Dry-cell batteries did not provide a hot enough spark to suit him for the ignition. The family physician, Dr. Philias Alden, helped out with the loan of a spark coil from a gadget with which he administered mild electric shocks to patients, on the theory that these were beneficial to health.

After the Happy Hooligan's brief and hectic career, Glenn obtained the largest set of castings the Thomas Company was able to supply. Again with the aid of Frank Neff they were machined, and the assembled motor weighed 180 pounds. When mounted in a bicycle, it was "a terror"; to further quote Curtiss, it "exploded only occasionally, but when it did it almost tore itself loose from the frame." In the initiation, he was considerate enough to head directly out of the village, steering up the steep hill highway through North Urbana and roaring into Wayne, where the gasoline gave out.

At this juncture, Curtiss reached the conclusion that he could make a better engine himself than any which were to be bought. This was the most crucial decision of his life, as time would demonstrate.

With speed as his guiding star, he etched into his mind the criteria for any engine he was to create: maximal horsepower with minimal weight. From this formula he never wavered.

The nearest machine shop with a minor foundry attached was at a mini-place called Taggart's, halfway along the road to Bath. Its owner was John Kirkham, a farmer-carpenter who had moved down from the hill country not long before to purchase a woodworking and planing mill; he had since added the machine shop as an afterthought. Glenn entered into a transaction with Kirkham to cast engines for him, in accord with designs which he (Curtiss) was to supply.[1]

The earliest mention of a motorcycle to find its way into the columns of the Hammondsport *Herald* appeared in the issue of January 22, 1902. It said:

"Glenn H. Curtiss is using the second motor cycle made by him during the past few months. The first was rather heavy and carried too much power for this region. The one he is now using appears to be a perfect success, demonstrating, as a manufacturer recently wrote Mr. Curtiss, that he has the principle down fine and can now manufacture, should he care to, with no fear of failure."

Evidently the *Herald* did not consider the Happy Hooligan worth counting. The next clue comes with the reopening of his Bath branch on March 15, 1902, with the announcement that he would now specialize in motorcycles. The paper added: "He has sold the second machine he built to a Pennsylvania man, and will soon commence a moto-tandem."

In May 1902 Curtiss opened his second branch agency in Corning, the metropolis of Steuben County, and marked the occasion with "the first moto-cycle tandem trip" in the county. A. W. Stanton was his rearward passenger as he bounced the 30 miles from Hammondsport to

Corning. The tandem machine was promptly snapped up by a Corning customer. The *Herald* was now starting to blare the trumpets:

"Mr. Curtiss has experimented extensively in the building of moto-cycles, and has many original ideas which are in advance of anything on the market in this section. He hopes and reasonably expects to attain considerable notoriety for the superiority of his moto-cycles."

The bicycle tradename, Hercules, was extended to both the motors and the motorcycles. Soon the orders for engines outnumbered those for complete machines.

Indicative of the young manufacturer's rapidly growing stature in the community is the frequency of personal items about him appearing in the local weekly, such as this: "Glenn H. Curtiss has ordered telephones for his store and residence. One by one the business men are putting in these convenient time savers." Or this: "Glenn H. Curtiss received a special delivery registered letter, the first ever received in the Hammondsport postoffice."

He was appointed county sidepath commissioner for Hammondsport. The duties of that office entailed seeing to the maintenance and improvement of a cindered riding path for bicyclists which paralleled the roadway from Hammondsport to Bath. The commissioner also was responsible for distributing the 50-cent license tags required for use of the path. Curtiss announced that the tags were on sale at his bicycle shop, at the Pleasant Valley Wine Cellars, and at the Kirkham machine shop. (He was still sidepath commissioner as late as 1906.)

* * *

The mushrooming demand for his engines and motorcycles caught Curtiss by surprise. In designing motors with a higher ratio of horsepower to weight, what he was basically after was more speed—but the market was hungry for just such a motor. He didn't know it yet, but especially so were the aviation experimenters.

To feel out the possibilities of the Hercules, he took to the dirt highways out of Hammondsport. It was considered quite a feat when he completed a 200-mile circuit touching Dansville, Geneseo, Bergen, Rochester, Palmyra, and Canandaigua. And indeed it was, considering the dusty condition of the roads at the time.

Nothing short of racing, however, was going to satisfy this competitive man, now that he had achieved a dramatically better instrument of speed. For his first gasoline-powered race he chose a meet sponsored by the New York Motorcycle Club at Queens Boulevard, Brooklyn, on Labor Day, 1902. Although failing to win any of the events, he scored second place in a time race and third place in a finish race. The *Herald's* account of this foray said: "Mr. Curtiss was complimented on every hand for the excellence of his machine, and had he known more of the requirements of the race and stood in with the management a little closer, there is no doubt he would have been a dangerous rival for first position. As it was, he gave them a race for their lives."

The public debut of the Hercules at Brooklyn was sufficiently impressive to spawn a wave of orders, compelling the shop to enlarge its facilities and hire more help. One customer was "a New York aeronaut," unidentified in print but more than likely a balloonist. The news in October was that: "Glenn H. Curtiss has disposed of his harness business to make room for the manufacture of motorcycles."

The shoestring on which Curtiss had been operating would stretch no further. Working capital suddenly became a crying necessity. A feeler for a loan seems to have been rejected by the Hammondsport Bank. A very few townsmen came to the rescue with modest investments in a firm which now began styling itself the G. H. Curtiss Manufacturing Company. The bravest plunger was J. Seymour Hubbs, a wine financier, with $1000. Victor Masson and Lynn D. Masson, sons of Jules Masson who had sailed from France to direct champagne making in Pleasant Valley, came in to the tune of $500 each. George H. Keeler, who was both mayor and postmaster of the village, was another charter investor. In his future successes, Curtiss was never forgetful of those who had helped him at the outset.[2]

Shipments of motorcycles were soon ranging as far afield as California, while inquiries were received from Nova Scotia, New Zealand, and South Africa. Curtiss issued a small catalog. Spring found him running three months behind orders, and due to this backlog he discontinued his Corning branch. A workshop annex was built on the sidehill back of the store and barn—a temporary expedient, at best. Curtiss was later to refer to the bicycle shop as his "industrial incubator."

To cope with the influx of correspondence, he had no typewriter, much less a stenographer. The town's leading attorney, Monroe Wheeler, county surrogate, had both and made them available to him. Once or twice a week, Curtiss dropped in at Wheeler's office to dictate letters and have them typed. As a director of the Bank of Hammondsport, it was Wheeler who aided him in finally obtaining bank credit.

Every time he turned around these days, it seemed, G. H. Curtiss (whom old acquaintances never ceased addressing as Glenn) provided a fresh sensation for the village. In December 1902 he became the first person to own an automobile in Hammondsport. He accepted it in trade for a Hercules motorcycle. It was a steam-propelled car which he described as "a very swift machine and one of the best makes on the market." Overnight, he was an automobile enthusiast, owning a steady succession of cars from then on and habitually altering them to suit himself. In January 1903 he attended the Automobile Show in New York, and this became an annual ritual, as he thereafter entered motorcycles and motors in the exhibits.

As a matter of fact, Curtiss obtained the Hammondsport agencies for several makes of automobile, starting with the Orient Motor Buckboard and later including such as the Frayer-Miller and the Ford. Lynn Masson was his first customer for an Orient Buckboard, and together, as a test of its quality, they "ascended the hill to Mount Washington known as the Winding Stairs in the machine without a stop."

❋   ❋   ❋

Too much time had elapsed since Glenn last tasted victory on a racetrack. Before challenging professionals again, however, he was determined to have a more powerful engine, and the surest way of getting it was with two cylinders. Up to then, all motorcycle engines were one-cylindered. Sketching out a way to accomplish this, he went to John Kirkham and had the casts molded. In the bench test, the new motor rated 5-horsepower. It required a sturdier frame, of course, and he installed roller bearings.

So equipped, Curtiss was loaded for bear when he entered the next meet of the New York Motorcycle Club, held at Riverdale Park on Memorial Day, 1903. The Indian motorcycles, with chain drive and a built-in reputation, were obviously what he had to beat. The opener was a hill-climbing event, and the course was up a devilish grade on Riverdale Hill. The macadam paving was pockmarked with holes and wet from sprinkling.

An "old pro" from the Indian factory, Oscar Hedstrom, shot over the crest of the hill on his battle-scarred steed, took a sharp turn to the finish line, and was assumed momentarily to be the winner. His regular racing partner, Charles Gustafsen, clipped his time by three seconds.

The crowd guessed it to be, as usual, a clean sweep for the Indians. But then came the man from Hammondsport roaring over the rise, glued flat to the frame in his unique style. The stopwatch said he crossed the finish line several seconds inside Gustafsen's timing. The gold medal was awarded to Curtiss, while sportsmen gave his Hercules a closer scrutiny.

The day was still young and Curtiss had further plans. Remounting, he rode a few miles upriver to the Empire Race Track, in Yonkers, where the National Cycle Association was running off its first championship tournament. There he proceeded to win the 10-mile event with no trouble, and was suddenly the American motorcycle champion. At the same time he set a world's speed record of 56⅔ seconds for the mile.

Back in Hammondsport, the *Herald* pulled out the stops:

"The first hall-marked American Motorcycle Champion has appeared . . . Mr. Curtiss is certainly to be congratulated. From the most modest beginning, unaided by experts in motor building or skilled mechanics in bicycle work, he has developed a motorcycle which probably outranks for roadwork and speed any and all others.

"With humble and unpretentious surroundings, he has put upon the market this year twenty cycles and has many orders yet to fill . . . Fifteen men are now employed in the manufacture of Hercules Motorcycles, and with the proper facilities, the output can be greatly increased . . . The result of these Memorial Day victories will doubtless give the Hercules a great boom."

And so it did. But the widespread publicity also brought a notification from an obscure California firm that it held priority on the trademark Hercules. A hasty conference was called to discuss a substitute, and company colleagues insisted that nothing could serve the purpose better than his own name. Curtiss surrendered to their urging only with some reluctance, it was said. Henceforward, the single word, *Curtiss*, in scroll lettering which suggested his signature but actually was not, appeared as the trademark on all his products.[3]

*   *   *

While her husband was moving up in the world, Lena Curtiss had carried out the role of homemaker, briefly a mother, and of companion and caretaker to Glenn's grandmother. The latter task had grown more exacting as Mrs. Ruth Curtiss yielded to the infirmities of age, being now seventy-nine. For the last two years she had been almost totally blind. Lena seems to have been genuinely devoted to her, recalling her as a "lovely, gentle, and kind" person.

While groping about the house one day in September 1903, the old lady opened the wrong door and fell down the cellar stairs, suffering a brain concussion from which she never regained consciousness. Death came a few days later.

Glenn Curtiss was the heir to Castle Hill—house, grounds, and vineyard.

Earlier that year Lena had lost her father, Guy Neff. With the passing of Mrs. Ruth Curtiss, she invited her widowed mother, Jennie Neff, to join their household. A trained nurse by vocation, Jennie (Mary Jane) Neff was a pleasant, extroverted woman, quite popular in the town. It was afterward said that "everyone in the village liked Jennie better than they did her daughter." This was not to infer that Lena was disliked; only that some people thought her rather "cold and withdrawn."

Unquestionably, Lena and Glenn were a well-matched couple in tastes, personality, and social characteristics. The prevailing impression of him, at least on first acquaintance, was one of aloof reticence. Among friends, he was genial enough, though always a better listener than a talker. He seemed to be perpetually mulling over some problem in his mind. Husband and wife were alike in avoiding pretension, preferring simplicity, and shunning social functions. In entertaining, they clung to a small coterie of trusted and loyal friends, and this was a tendency they never outgrew. The marital bond was close, and they disliked being separated, even for short intervals. At a future date, a Supreme Court judge would define this mutual devotion in more legalistic phraseology: "Their relations were harmonious, and she was disposed to and did aid him whenever, and as best she could."

When the capable Jennie Neff moved in, she shouldered the major housekeeping responsibilities, freeing Lena for more direct assistance to her husband. At that point, Mrs. Curtiss took charge of the office routine of the G. H. Curtiss Manufacturing Company. She went daily to the shop, doing the bookkeeping, handling the mail, and making herself generally useful.

❊   ❊   ❊

If he was an attentive reader of the Hammondsport *Herald*, Glenn Curtiss would not have overlooked the following page 1 dispatch of July 22, 1903:

"Professor S. P. Langley's new airship was towed down the Potomac River from Washington on a houseboat to a secluded point on the lower Potomac where it will be given its initial trials as soon as some few details can be arranged.

"Professor Langley was not in the party that left on the houseboat but will go by rail to a point near the spot selected for the test. It is believed that this will take place near Widewater, Va., where the Potomac has a width of five or six miles and is quite shallow except in the channel.

"Professor Langley, who is head of the Smithsonian Institution, in planning his airship, it is stated, studied the movements of the buzzard and tried to develop a machine that would have strong pinions and be capable not only of soaring but of beating the air with one or both wings."

Anyone familiar with Langley's prior achievements would have spotted the monstrous error in that story: he had no idea of "beating the air" with the wings, which were rigidly fixed in the tandem dragonfly configuration. Perhaps the reporter was not too blameworthy, as Langley once again was trying to maintain utmost secrecy. The press was obviously unaware that the "new airship" was only a scale model of the man-carrying aerodrome he was preparing to try out several weeks later.

For the renewal of his aerial experiments, Dr. Langley was much beholden to the Spanish-American War. When the battleship *Maine* was blown up in Havana Harbor, certain Army and Navy officials, aware of Langley's successful models of 1896, wondered if aircraft might be quickly developed for use in the looming war. A joint board of officers investigated Langley's work and recommended the financing of further experiments; that the War and Navy Departments should allot him $25,000 each. The war had been fought to its swift conclusion by the time the report was submitted, but President William McKinley ordered the project undertaken, nonetheless. The Navy backed down on its share of the expense, whereupon the Army's Board of Ordnance and Fortification made up the full $50,000 to underwrite construction of a man-carrying aerodrome. Before the machine was finished, Langley dug into his private funds for an additional $25,000.

Dismissing steam power as impractical for aerial use, Langley sought vainly for a lightweight gasoline engine. Finally he signed a contract with a New York machinist, Stephen M. Balzer, who had designed and built the first automobile to run in the streets of New

York. The vehicle was powered by a 3-cylinder rotary engine (that is, the engine itself revolved around its shaft); Balzer was striving for financial backing to market his automobile. At the same time, Dr. Langley asked the dean of the Cornell School of Engineering to recommend the best young engineer he knew to become his assistant, and was sent Charles M. Manly, on the very eve of his graduation from Cornell. Shuttling between Washington and New York, Manly worked closely with Balzer in developing the motor, which fell far behind contract schedule.

Balzer's pattern was a 5-cylindered rotary engine, the cylinders arranged radially, like the points of a star. It was to be air-cooled. When it was finally up to testing, this motor could produce no more than 8-horsepower, when the contract called for a minimal 12-horsepower. Balzer was allowed more money and more time, while Langley and Manly combed Europe for a suitable engine or at least ideas for one. Both became convinced that the rotary principle was wrong. Finally Langley paid Balzer the full amount of his contract ($1500) and had the incomplete engine shipped to the Smithsonian, where he set Manly to work on altering it. The first thing Manly did was to convert it from a rotary to a static radial engine. The power picked up instantly. He made it water-cooled and gave it lighter pistons, along with other refinements. Ultimately the engine Manly installed in Langley's "aerodrome" produced 52.4-horsepower for a weight of 120 pounds. It was by far the most advanced and powerful aviation engine in the world in the early part of the century. When critics in later years protested that Manly had only made improvements on an engine already designed by Balzer, the Smithsonian was fair enough to designate it as the Balzer-Manly engine.

Meanwhile, the airframe to receive it had been meticulously constructed at the Smithsonian Institution. Langley took elaborate precautions to preserve secrecy, even allowing the grass to grow knee-high around the carpenter shop to create the illusion that nothing was going on. In defense of this policy, he said: "It is the practice of all scientific men, indeed of all prudent men, not to make public the results of their work until they are certain." Still, rumors leaked and prying reporters took offense. Langley started getting a "bad press" even before the trials of 1903 were launched.

The preliminary test with the scale model took place on August 8. It flew 1000 feet and then hit the water because of a defect in the steering gear. Manly said it had supplied all the data for which it was designed, and preparations went forward to fly the man-sized aerodrome.

The irritation of newsmen increased because the houseboat was stationed in a remote part of the river, with no provision for their presence. They had to rent rowboats and maintain a daily watch.

The date of the first attempt, with Manly as the pilot, was October 7. The full-scale machine, like the models before it, was launched by catapult, hurled from the houseboat roof by a powerful spring. Again, Curtiss must have read what happened, in the columns of his hometown paper:

"The immense airship sped rapidly along its 70-foot track, was carried by its own momentum for a hundred yards and then fell gradually into the Potomac River, whence it emerged a total wreck.

"Professor Charles M. Manly, Langley's chief assistant, made the ascent and escaped with a ducking. At no time was there any semblance of flight, the initial momentum, the lightness of the machine and the sustained surface of the wings furnished the conditions which account for the hundred yards transit."

A projection had fouled the kingpost, causing the front pair of wings to collapse just as the machine left the catapult. The reporters now had their revenge, jeering at the "Flying Machine Fiasco." One New York editorial observed that Manly had "prudently clothed himself in a cork jacket—doubtless because cork is a good non-conductor and would tend to keep the wearer warm in the rarefied strata of the upper atmosphere in which he perhaps expected to cruise." The writer drew a comparison to the long evolution of birds, suggesting that the aerial machine "which will really fly might be evolved by combined and continuous efforts of mathematicians and mechanicians in from one to 10 million years."

From a tented camp amid the sand dunes of Kitty Hawk, North Carolina, Wilbur Wright wrote his faithful correspondent, Octave Chanute: "I see that Langley has had his fling, and failed. It seems to be our turn to throw now, and I wonder what our luck will be."

When the Wright brothers asked Chanute for advice on a place for glider experiments, he told them to seek dunes along the southern Atlantic coast where they would have steady sea breezes. Following this counsel, they adopted the lonely Kitty Hawk barrier beach, and there they had spent several autumnal weeks annually since 1900. They succeeded better than Langley in attaining secrecy; the press had no inkling of what they were up to. And now they had come to the verge of mounting an engine in one of their gliders. The possibility that Langley's aerodrome might fly before they got off the ground had been holding them in nervous suspense.

Wilbur and Orville were unaware that Dr. Langley was repairing his machine for a second try, which was made on December 8. The houseboat was anchored closer to Washington, just downriver from the Anacostia Navy Yard. Again the motor was started, the two propellers whirled, the catapult spring was triggered. The clearest account of the ensuing debacle was given in the report of an officer observer for the Board of Ordance and Fortification:

"The rear guy-post seemed to drag, bringing the rudder down on the launching ways, and a crashing, rending sound, followed by the collapse of the rear wings, showed that the machine had been wrecked in the launching . . . The fact remains that the rear wings and rudder were wrecked before the machine was free of the ways. Their collapse deprived the machine of its support in the rear, and it consequently reared up in the front under the action of the motor, assumed a vertical position, and then toppled over to the rear, falling into the water a few feet in front of the boat. Mr. Manly was pulled out of the wreck uninjured."

The unfriendly press now bayed in a full chorus of ridicule. The New York *Herald* said nastily: "Prof. Langley's disappointment was almost overshadowed by his anxiety for Mr. Manly." The New York *Times* wound up an editorial guffaw with these comparatively polite words: "We hope that Prof. Langley will not put his substantial greatness as a scientist to further peril by continuing to waste his time, and the money involved, in further airship experiments."

The Hammondsport *Herald* did not even bother to report Langley's second humiliation; nor did it make the slightest mention, either before or after the event, of what the Wrights did nine days later.

On Thursday, December 17, at Kill Devil Hills, near Kitty Hawk, with a handful of local spectators gathered, the brothers alternated in four brief lifts of their powered glider. The machine took off into the teeth of a fairly brisk wind, from a 40-foot monorail track elevated 8 inches above the level sand. No catapult device was used, though the Wrights later adopted one. Their piloting posture was lying prone across the lower wing—an innovation on their part, as previous gliding experimenters had hung by the elbows, with feet dangling. For control

of lateral stability, they warped, or twisted, the wing margins; this
effect was achieved by moving the hips within a swivel. Orville made
the first hop at 10:35 A.M., remaining airborne 12 seconds, rising less
than 10 feet, and covering about 100 feet before striking the sand a
sharp whack due to trouble with the front rudder. After minor repairs, Wilbur did the second flight at 11:20 A.M., distance about 175
feet. Orville took his second turn at 11:40, roughly matching Wilbur's
in length and undulating as high as 12 or 14 feet. At noon, Wilbur
climaxed the series with a flight lasting 59 seconds and measuring
852 feet; this ended in another pitch to the ground which broke
the front rudder frame. The plane was carried back to camp where its
wrecking was completed by a gust of wind. The Wrights then returned
to Dayton.

The events of the day were not so unnoticed as legend would
have it, but the scorn heaped upon Langley's attempts had engendered
a mood of public skepticism which enveloped the Wrights as well.
A telegraph operator at Norfolk, who relayed Orville's telegram reporting the success to their family, tipped off a newspaper friend.
Unable to get direct information, the reporter manufactured a story
which was grotesquely fictitious, but which appeared in a number of
papers, including the New York *Tribune*. Before leaving Kitty Hawk,
the brothers already were besieged with offers for exclusive rights to
the story and pictures. They ignored these feelers, but on January
5, 1904, issued a short statement to the Associated Press for the purpose
of setting the facts straight, and many papers used it.

Apparently Glenn Curtiss did not encounter any of these reports.
In after years, he said he could not remember exactly when he first
heard of the Wrights' achievement; that, if he knew about it when
it happened, "It didn't make a lasting impression on me." He admitted: "It is quite likely that I was skeptical, like almost everybody
else."

Langley had every intention of restoring his aerodrome and continuing the tests, but the Army refused further funds. The Board of
Ordnance and Fortification "deemed it advisable, largely in view of
the adverse opinions expressed in Congress and elsewhere, to suspend
operations in this direction." The wreckage was stored away at the
Smithsonian Institution, with a view to revival of the experiments after
the public furor died down.

Dr. Langley was heartbroken at being denied the chance to vindicate his creation, and he brooded over the barrage of mockery. When he died of a stroke in 1906, it was widely reported that his death had been hastened by the mental anguish he had undergone.

* * *

Meanwhile, Curtiss was pouring his energies into making motorcycles and racing them. The fame he won as a racer was the best conceivable advertising for his machines. Sports writers by now had dubbed him "the hell-rider," for his speed and daring. Another newspaper phrase was "that amazing Mr. Curtiss." According to Jim Smellie, he "took awful chances sometimes," but his expert skill as a rider should not be underestimated. "He figured things out in advance, and gained over rivals in tight places." What seemed to onlookers as reckless abandon—as when he swooped high on a curving embankment —was actually calculated risk. Not surprisingly, he took an occasional spill, netting cuts and bruises.

Curtiss made his discovery of Florida in January 1904. Ormond Beach was a favorite speedway for automobiles, with its 30 miles of level sand which was like a pavement when the tide ebbed. By this time motorcycle events were being admitted to auto race programs. With an improved machine, Curtiss streaked along Ormond Beach to establish a new world's speed record for the 10-mile straightaway: 8 minutes, 54⅖ seconds. That was a record which stood for more than seven years.

More and still more orders flooded the shop, and in May of that year Curtiss met with the Board of Trade and Business Men's Association of Owego, New York. This was the first hint to his fellow townsmen that it was possible for them to lose the promising industry. The *Herald* recorded: "They made him a very flattering offer to remove his motorcycle works to that place, which he is considering. Very little effort on the part of the business men of Hammondsport will keep the industry here. Mr. Curtiss is not desirous of moving from here, but cannot well afford to let pass such desirable propositions as this and others which he has received."

The publisher of the Hammondsport *Herald*, Llewellyn H. Brown, had become a virtual press agent for Curtiss; and, as befits a small-town editor, he was a first-class village booster. His nudge to the business leaders seemingly brought results. Instead of accepting the Owego overture, Curtiss thrust his roots deeper into his native soil with a striking decision. He started in to construct a motorcycle plant adjacent to his home on Castle Hill.

Few people would care to have a factory in their dooryards. It was typical of Curtiss not to mind the proximity. A real plant had become imperative, and this solved the problem of a site without a purchase of real estate. His work was his recreation, and vice versa, as friends often said, and this solution would make his work all the handier. Since Lena was now functioning as his office assistant, it was similarly convenient for her, and neither of them gave a fig for social considerations. The dimensions of the new structure were 60 by 20 feet, and it had two stories. It was occupied by November. A second building was added a year later, a third in 1906.

So close did the vineyard grow to the factory that vines were seared when a fire in one of the buildings burst through rear windows. Fortunately, a workman wielded an extinguisher to good effect.

Curtiss always referred to his plant as "the shop," no matter how large it grew. "The word 'factory' was not in his vocabulary," a later acquaintance recalled. The atmosphere of the "shop" in those early days was one of camaraderie and cooperation, in which the workers found their employer easy to talk with, open to any suggestion, dirtying his hands alongside them. They recognized that he was always thinking, and were alert for whatever fresh idea he might hatch next. One day, while standing outside talking with a customer, Curtiss idly twisted a rubber grip on the handlebar of a motorcycle. Cutting short the conversation, he dashed into the shop, beckoned a mechanic, and invented the handlebar throttle control on the spur of the moment.

Before long, Glenn was reunited with his old pal and racing partner, Leonard (Tank) Waters, who had married while in Buffalo. Waters returned to Hammondsport, bringing with him the stock of his Buffalo Bicycle Supply Company, for which Curtiss turned over his bicycle shop. As time went on, Tank worked for the Curtiss company in varied capacities, and, as might be expected, he was quickly mounted on a motorcycle and filling race dates.

There was a 25-mile handicap road race at Waltham, Massachusetts, which may serve as an example of the kind of dazzling performance Curtiss usually put on. The race was run on a tricky 5-mile course infested with sharp bends. The Boston *Globe* reported that Curtiss "simply outclassed the others"; that he made "terrific speed" on the straight stretches to compensate for time lost on the turns; that when he completed his fifth circuit, none of his rivals had yet finished their

fourth. The enthusiastic sports writer said that Curtiss "dashed away
like a race horse . . . went down the road like a shot . . . flashed
into view like a high-speed locomotive . . . passed the tape so fast that
his number could not be seen." The same reporter, however, could not
resist an innuendo: "It was regretted that Curtiss was the only man to
start on a two-cylinder machine. The New Yorker in that way had
an advantage over the others, who used ordinary single-cylinder stock
motorcycles."

Meanwhile, the large fairs of the country came around to tolerating
motor vehicle racing on tracks which had always been sacrosanct to
the hoofs of thoroughbred horses. The New York State Fair at Syracuse
let down the barrier to automobiles in 1901, turning over the track
on the final day when the horse racing was finished. The first big
year for motorcycles at the Syracuse Fair was 1905, and Glenn Curtiss
was the star performer of that occasion, setting three new world's
speed records before the day was over. In the event for one-cylinder
motorcycles, a sports writer reported, he was "so far ahead that no
interest attached." He proceeded to break the 1-mile record; then,
in the 2-mile race, he smashed two world records. In the 5-mile open
for motorcycles, he was "another easy victor"; the Syracuse *Post-Standard*
said that, after a couple of warm-up miles, "when he nodded for
the starting shot, he was fairly shooting on his own account." A
dispatch to the Hammondsport *Herald* asserted: "His competitors in
every instance were so far outclassed as to be hopelessly out of the
running." In fact, that day at Syracuse, Curtiss was more of a sensation
than Barney Oldfield, the most famous automobile race driver of the
time, who was on hand with his *Green Flash*. While Oldfield demonstrated well, he failed to establish any new record.

In October, Curtiss set forth on a tandem motorcycle, with J. Seymour Hubbs perched behind, to attend automobile races at Garden
City, Long Island. Upon their arrival, Glenn was appointed patrol
judge of the races. Immense throngs jammed the grounds and a
dangerous situation developed when spectators pressed too close to the
track. Curtiss was shocked at seeing two men killed by race cars.

✿   ✿   ✿

Despite the new plant on-the-hill, orders continued to outstrip capacity. Boards of trade in Rochester, Elmira, and other cities made
"flattering offers" of financial help if Curtiss would relocate the in-

dustry. Lew Brown again sounded the alarm, scolding that there seemed to be "little or no disposition on the part of Hammondsport capitalists and business men to retain this promising industry"; and that "Mr. Curtiss much prefers to remain here, but the inducements offered by the Rochester people will probably locate him there unless some encouragement is extended here." Pointing out that the present payroll ranging from eight to sixteen men would soon need to be doubled, the editor wrote: "It would seem that this is too important an industry to be regarded indifferently."

The journalistic prodding again had the desired effect. Several "liberal subscriptions" were immediately forthcoming, and these resulted in the filing at Albany, on October 19, 1905, of incorporation papers for the G. H. Curtiss Manufacturing Company, Inc. The purpose of the corporation was stated to be the manufacture and sale of motors, motorcycles, motor vehicles, "and other vehicles and motors of various kinds"; also attachments and parts for such vehicles; and to "generally carry on any other manufacturing business which can conveniently be carried on in conjunction with any of the matters aforesaid."

Capital stock of the corporation was $40,000, and five directors were listed: Glenn H. Curtiss, Lynn D. Masson, Aaron G. Pratt, Judge Monroe Wheeler, and G. Ray Hall. Curtiss was elected president and manager; Masson secretary and treasurer. The stock consisted of 400 shares of common, 400 shares of preferred. Curtiss held all 400 shares of common stock, while the preferred stock was distributed among the other directors, with five shares allotted to Lew H. Brown, publisher and editor of the Hammondsport *Herald*.

The company announced that it would increase its labor force to thirty or forty men, and begin the manufacture of its motors exclusively in Hammondsport. Hitherto the Kirkham shop had continued making engines for Curtiss. Meantime Charles Kirkham had taken charge of that concern, joined by his brothers, Clarence and Percy, and moved the shop into Bath. With loss of the Curtiss business, the Kirkham brothers launched into the manufacture of motors for automobiles.

The president of the new corporation on Keuka Lake was only twenty-seven years of age. And Lew Brown, now a stockholder, had this to tell his readers:

"It is pleasing to the people of Hammondsport that Mr. Curtiss has decided to permanently remain here. He was born and bred in Hammondsport and . . . it seems fitting that the locality where Mr. Curtiss's friends are legion should have the benefit of his ingenuity."

3. A Dalliance with Dirigibles

In the early summer of 1904, Curtiss received a telegram from San Francisco. It was an urgent order for a 2-cylindered motorcycle engine. The impatient buyer signed himself Captain Thomas Baldwin. Having no loose engine available at such short notice, Curtiss yanked one out of a used motorcycle, polished it up and shipped it. As of that moment, he was ignorant of Baldwin's identity or the purpose for which he desired the motor.

The version of how Baldwin discovered the Curtiss motor which seems to have the best claim to authenticity runs as follows:

Captain Baldwin was at a California ranch, nursing along the latest of his many attempts at a dirigible balloon and having no more success than usual. Cowhands loafed about, cracking jokes, as he started his dinky engine time and again, only to have it die when he tried to leave the ground. "Put the spurs to that buckin' cloud-jumper o' yourn," the ranchmen bantered. Of a sudden they all heard the "rhythmical drumming noise" of a gasoline engine and saw a dust-cloud approaching. "It's Harry White," a bystander drawled, "on his new-fangled motorcycle he's just got from the East."

Harry White sped up to join the group watching the would-be aeronaut, and was barely halted when Baldwin crouched to examine the hot engine. Spotting the scroll trademark on the gas tank, Baldwin demanded: "Where is this Curtiss outfit?"

The rider fished out of his pocket a small, cheaply printed catalog and pointed to the words: "G. H. Curtiss Manufacturing Company, Hammondsport, N.Y." Thumbing through the catalog, Baldwin saw a picture of Curtiss zooming up the Riverdale hill on his motorcycle. He turned to his aides and hollered: "Boys, dump the gas out of the bag and chuck that old junk pile of a motor. Mash it, bust it, sell it for old iron—but get rid of it. I've found the motor we need."[1]

Back at his San Francisco office Baldwin fired off the telegram ordering an engine like the one he had seen in the motorcycle.

*   *   *

Captain Thomas Scott Baldwin was the most colorful and well-liked figure to stride the stage of early American aeronautics. (His rank was about as militarily authentic as that of a Kentucky colonel). A graduate of the circus big top, he came into aviation by way of balloon ascents and parachute jumps, but his breezy theatricality masked a genuine interest in the problems of flight. From his global travels, he was known to millions as Captain Tom. Now he was forty-nine years old, a robust, hearty, and genial showman.

As a child in Missouri, he had seen his father and mother shot down by Civil War raiders. Bound out as an orphan, he ran away at the age of fourteen and became a railroad brakeman. A natural athlete, he was turning handsprings atop a moving freight car when the manager of a circus train standing on a siding offered him a job as an apprentice acrobat. He worked up to the high trapeze. A circus which later employed him featured an act with a hot-air balloon which rose to the peak of the tent with an acrobat clinging to a trapeze bar beneath. Baldwin so daringly embellished the contortions of the man on the trapeze that he became a star of the show. After acquiring a hydrogen balloon of his own, he quit circus life and, joined by his brother Sam, went free-lancing the fair circuits. Adding tightrope walking to their act, they made a number of world tours. Captain Tom hit national headlines in 1885 by walking a tightwire stretched 70 feet above the raging surf between San Francisco's Old Cliff House and the offshore Seal Rocks.

The Baldwin brothers set about inventing a parachute, testing their designs with sandbags from cliffs and high buildings. It was Tom who finally substituted himself for a sandbag in America's first successful parachute jump. This was followed by the pioneering public jump from a balloon, 1000 feet in the air, at Golden Gate Park on January 30, 1887. The Baldwins did not apply for a patent on their parachute; as Tom said: "We never supposed anybody else would care to try it." The novel profession of balloon parachutist was a lucrative one. Baldwin's customary fee was $1 per foot of the height of his jumps, with 2000 feet as minimum.

Free balloons were always at the mercy of the winds, and Captain Baldwin could not dismiss from his mind what a controllable, steerable (i.e., dirigible) balloon would do for his public performances. As early as 1894 he began his efforts to devise a balloon driven by an engine and propeller. The chief problem was to find a lightweight engine which would turn the trick. A motor obtained from Paris lacked the necessary power. A Pierce-Arrow automobile motor was too heavy for the gas bag to lift. While Baldwin continued "looking the field over" for the right engine, he was exasperated to learn that dirigible balloons were already being flown in Europe.

Alberto Santos-Dumont, the frail son of a wealthy Brazilian coffee planter, living in Paris on his father's largess, made a semicontrolled flight with his first powered airship in 1898. In Germany in 1900, Count Ferdinand von Zeppelin was aloft over the Boden See with his cigar-shaped LZ-1, progenitor of a long line of zeppelins. Santos-Dumont created a global sensation in 1901 by circling the Eiffel Tower and returning to his point of departure, thereby winning a prize of 100,000 francs. This feat prompted an offer of $20,000 for an airship flight around the Statue of Liberty in New York Harbor, in the name of something called the Aero Club (the Aero Club of America was not founded until 1905). Santos-Dumont was lured into going after this prize, and brought his famed dirigible Number 6 to New York in July 1902. The balloon was housed in a large shed at Brighton Beach where crowds paid 25 cents per head to view it. After a month of this, Santos-Dumont realized that the $20,000 for the prize was nonexistent; that the promoter, General Francis Kerr, was the whole "Aero Club," including its "Board of Directors." The dapper little Brazilian sailed for France in disgust.

News of such doings stimulated Captain Baldwin into a trip abroad to study at first hand the machines of both Zeppelin and Santos-Dumont. He came home more determined than ever to construct a dirigible, without directly copying either of the European models. By now there was a fresh goad to urge him on—a grand prize of $100,000 for the best demonstration by an aircraft of whatever kind during the Louisiana Purchase Exposition of 1903 at St. Louis. This world's fair was to celebrate the centennial of the purchase of Louisiana Territory. Its directors proposed to make a feature of the latest advances in human flight, to which end both Octave Chanute and Alberto Santos-Dumont were appointed to an aeronautical advisory board.

Chanute, who was privy to the gliding activities of the Wright brothers, confided the preliminary plans to them in January 1902, and asked: "Would you be inclined to compete?" Wilbur replied: "Whether we shall compete will depend much on the conditions under which the prizes are offered. I have little of the gambling instinct, and unless there is reasonable hope of getting at least the amount expended in competing I would enter only after very careful consideration . . . However we shall see about the matter later."

Although the St. Louis Exposition duly opened in April 1903, with President Theodore Roosevelt reviewing the parade, the aeronautical program did not shape up for that year. The fair was extended through 1904, and then interest quickened in the aerial prize money. The Kitty Hawk success had meanwhile altered the outlook of the Wrights. A month after that, Wilbur informed Chanute: "We are at work building three machines with which we shall probably give exhibitions at several different places during the coming season. We may decide to enter one at St. Louis, and have written for copy of the revised rules & regulations . . . If we find that the objectionable features of the original rules have been eliminated we may decide to make a try for it."

"I am greatly pleased," Chanute answered, "that you now contemplate entering your machine at St. Louis. I trust that you will develop it in sufficient time and that you will carry off the main prize." Within a few days, Chanute made a trip to Dayton in hope of getting a commitment, but Orville again found fault with the rules; the brothers felt, for one thing, that these were slanted to favor dirigibles, perhaps because Santos-Dumont was on the advisory board. Certainly the Exposition was anxious to have Santos-Dumont for a drawing card. The Wrights went so far as to visit St. Louis to look over the grounds, but "found things even less favorable than we anticipated." Wilbur then complained to Chanute: "As there are no consolation prizes for flying machines, like those provided for airships, we would have to win the grand prize or get nothing. It is a tough proposition . . . The conditions are such that we wish to know that we will win before we decide to go for it. If we enter, it will be for the purpose of winning, not for the purpose of seeing how close we can come to it." To this Chanute replied with a roguish touch: "You are mistaken . . . as to there being no 'consolation' prizes for flying machines. There are three of them if you can contrive to go slow enough."

A fortnight later Chanute relayed the word that Santos-Dumont would definitely enter for the $100,000 prize. In another letter, he added: "No other man with the least chance of winning has yet entered the lists at St. Louis." Wilbur wanted to know if the deadline for entries was positively to be June 1, saying: "We wish to enter but not just yet." The brothers had begun experimental flights to improve their machine at Huffman's pasture, 8 miles outside Dayton, and were meeting more problems than anticipated, even though the newspapers left them entirely alone. On June 25 Chanute advised them that "in order to give contestants a chance to perfect their apparatus, the time for formal entries will be extended from time to time clear up to September 1st"; adding that there were some ninety applications to date, "but none of them seem to me to stand any show against Santos-Dumont."

The Brazilian's airship Number 7 was delivered at the Exposition in three large boxes, and he proposed to give it a trial flight on July 4. The boxes were left overnight with nails drawn. When the gas envelope was taken from its crate in the morning, Santos-Dumont was infuriated to find that it had been slashed repeatedly by a knife. (Almost the identical kind of damage had been done the year before to his Number 6, when it was unpacked in London for exhibit at the Crystal Palace.) The police began by interrogating the members of his own crew, which angered him the more; then they hinted that Santos-Dumont was himself largely to blame for not properly guarding his property. The mystery of the sabotage was never solved. (Curiously, two days later the bellows of a huge pipe organ being installed at the Exposition was vandalized by the cutting of long gashes.) Santos-Dumont took his wounded gas bag to Paris, ostensibly to have it repaired; then cabled St. Louis that the repair would take too long, and so he withdrew from the contest.

Chanute was unhappy about the reluctance of his Dayton friends, writing them in mid-August: "Aeronautics are languishing at St. Louis.

Even those who have paid their entrance fees are not coming forward with their machines." The aerial panoply still looked like a fizzle
on October 5, when Wilbur wrote: "It seems that every aeronautical
feature of the Exposition has been a failure to date. It seems a real
pity, yet as we have done little ourselves for success I do not know
that we have the right to blame anyone else. Possibly there would have
been more show, if the conditions attached to the various prizes had
been less exacting." An unspoken reason why the Wrights held back,
presumably, was the resolution they had formed not to reveal the
structure of their machine in public; Wilbur closed the letter with
these words: "As we have decided to keep our experiments strictly
secret for the present, we are becoming uneasy about continuing them
much longer at our present location. In fact, it is a question whether
we are not ready to begin considering what we will do about our
baby now that we have it."

*   *   *

People who had crossed off the aviation program of the Louisiana
Purchase Exposition as a complete washout were reckoning without
Captain Thomas S. Baldwin and the secondhand motorcycle engine he
had procured from Glenn H. Curtiss.

At his San Francisco balloon plant, Baldwin installed the engine
toward the rear of the spruce keel which was suspended, like a catwalk,
by cords from a net surrounding the bag of his newest hopeful dirigible.
The rather shapeless non-rigid bag, 52 feet long by 17 feet in diameter
when inflated with hydrogen, was made of varnished Japanese silk.
By means of a long shaft of steel tubing, the engine drove an 8-
foot propeller mounted at the front to drag the craft through the air.
The propeller was an oak framework covered by fabric. The pilot's
seat was far aft, and behind him was a vertical rudder operated by
tiller ropes. Uptilt or downtilt was managed by the pilot's moving
forward or aft on the keel. Such was the rude contrivance to which
Baldwin gave the proud name, *California Arrow*, and it was the first
successful dirigible to fly in the United States.

Baldwin initiated the *Arrow* with ascents at Idora Park, Oakland,
on July 29 and August 3, 1904. On the latter date he made a
circle out over San Francisco Bay and back to his starting point. Not
before had any aircraft completed a circuit in this country. (The
Wrights did not succeed in doing so until September 20, 1904.) There

was one drawback to Baldwin's elation: his excess bodily weight proved a handicap to the machine.

After more trials and improvisations, Baldwin notified the St. Louis fair that he was entering for the grand prize. With no competition at all, he had clear sailing when he appeared with the *California Arrow* toward the end of October. Right away he spotted a slim young chap, A. Roy Knabenshue, from Toledo, who was already at the fairgrounds making balloon ascents. Fearful that his poundage was going to hinder his chances, Baldwin invited Knabenshue to be his pilot and partner in case he should need him. Roy had his own hydrogen plant for inflating his balloons—a barrel containing iron filings over which he poured sulphuric acid; with this he generated the hydrogen to fill the *Arrow*. Baldwin stepped on the frame for a trial flight, and she would not rise. Turning to Roy, he said: "Son, I guess you are elected." Knabenshue long afterward entertained a congressional committee with an account of his baptism in dirigible flying.

"I knew nothing about managing an airship. I had had some experience steering a yacht, which I believe came in handy . . . The time came to fly it and a great crowd was assembled and we took it outdoors. The engine was improperly timed which caused the frame to vibrate so that it was difficult to stand on it. I was told to stand in a certain position and when Tom bawled out to let go, we were off. It was a harrowing experience. For the first few minutes we narrowly missed the fence and then headed straight for the Brazilian building and missed it by inches, then headed straight for the center of the Ferris wheel and I had visions of my sliding down one of the spokes. By experimenting with the tiller rope I found it was possible to steer . . . I then described a very wide circle and headed back toward the grounds . . . When I got back to within 1000 feet of the starting place, the engine just coughed and died and then we became a balloon ascension. It became a free balloon and drifted across the city and landed over in Illinois."

In subsequent flights, Knabenshue handled the craft more skillfully and the Curtiss engine behaved better. Out of twenty-three ascents, he completed nine returns to starting point. The decisive flight for the prize was made on October 31 when Roy circled at 2000 feet, covered 3½ miles in 28 minutes, and returned to the starting point "in an imposing manner." A tidal wave of cheering spectators swept around the *Arrow*, hats were tossed in air, and Knabenshue was carried around the concourse of the Exposition on the shoulders of a mob.

After the tumult subsided, the wry aftermath which the public never knew was that Baldwin and Knabenshue had no prize money to collect. A governmental unit (probably municipal) had advanced money as a loan to help finance the Exposition, and the fair ended up in the red. The fund for aerial prizes was among the assets impounded toward repayment.

Nonetheless, Captain Baldwin boasted: "I am now convinced that I have a wonderful airship." In Dayton, Wilbur Wright took note: "The newspapers report a little whirl of excitement at St. Louis. The performance of the Baldwin machine is creditable though not remarkable." And in Hammondsport the *Herald* reported: "The mysteries of aerial navigation seem to have been partially solved. The recent test of the Baldwin air ship at the World's Fair was perhaps the best exhibition of the feasibility of aerial navigation yet made."

Strangely enough, neither Lew Brown nor Glenn Curtiss had yet awakened to the fact that a Curtiss engine propelled the *California Arrow.* They would soon find out. After taking the prize-winning airship to Los Angeles where he left it in charge of Knabenshue for exhibition flying, Baldwin entrained for the East and an out-of-the-way town called Hammondsport.

The B.&H. Railroad deposited the illustrious Captain Baldwin at the tiny lakefront depot on or about November 23. The visitation was a thunderclap to the village. He was a celebrity—the American equivalent of what Santos-Dumont was in Europe. Moreover, he immediately spread the news that he and Knabenshue had salvaged the aeronautical prestige of the St. Louis Exposition with a Curtiss engine.

Baldwin was mildly astonished at the unpretentious building that was pointed out to him as the motorcycle factory, but more so by the man he met inside. He had expected to see a substantial, mature, well-dressed executive type seated in a decently furnished office; instead, he found himself face-to-face with a disarmingly young man, reticent almost to the point of shyness, informal, working in shop clothes alongside his employees. "I am Glenn Curtiss," this individual said, wiping a hand on a wad of waste so it could be shaken.

For his part, Curtiss was more than a little taken aback by the florid, jovial, extrovert character who came barging into his plant. In spite of the differences in age and personalities, however, the two men took an instant liking to each other and a warm friendship was kindled which went on for many years. During the several days of his stay, Baldwin was a house guest at the Curtiss home.

The Hammondsport *Herald* pounced gleefully upon Baldwin's tidings, and said: "The most recent notoriety for the Curtiss motor came as a surprise even to Mr. Curtiss." In aftertime, Curtiss recalled: "When we heard that he [Baldwin] was using that motor, we offered to improve it for him and adapt it to his requirements."

Baldwin supplied the local weekly with photographs of his *California Arrow* in action, and in the feature spread was included a picture of him standing beside the Curtiss tandem motorcycle on which he had just ridden. He was quoted as believing that "navigation of the air is as practicable as navigation of water"; also as saying "the Curtiss motor is absolutely perfect." He announced that he was planning a larger airship, and that he had ordered two more Curtiss engines. What he did not yet divulge was that he had made a long-term compact with Curtiss about motors for a whole series of *California Arrows.*

The eyes of Glenn Curtiss were well opened to the prospect for human flight by this visitor, although as yet he was viewing it only in terms of an unanticipated and welcome new market for his motors. It is likely that Baldwin at that time told him something of what the Wrights had done; in trying to recall when he first heard of them, Curtiss said it was possible that Baldwin had informed him.

❀   ❀   ❀

When he got back to California, Captain Tom found that Roy Knabenshue had "really learned to fly" the *Arrow* in his absence and was showing symptoms of independence. Starting to build the second and larger airship, Baldwin telephoned Curtiss to make him an engine with an external flywheel.

As the St. Louis Exposition ended, Portland, Oregon, picked up the ball and prepared to sponsor the Lewis and Clark Exposition in 1905, marking the centennial of the exploration which opened up the Louisiana Territory. The Portland world's fair followed the lead of St. Louis in offering liberal prize money for aerial performing, and Baldwin registered his new dirigible for entry, naming it the *City of Portland.* Long before the fair opened, however, he was compelled to seek another pilot. Knabenshue quit him in a "disagreement" and fared forth as a free-lance flyer in dirigibles built by himself, using Curtiss motors. (As in the case of the parachute, Baldwin did not trouble to patent his airship.)

The replacement Baldwin found was Lincoln Beachey, who also

hailed from Toledo and had been doing ascents in free balloons. Besides being a slender lightweight, Beachey had the advantage of being a born daredevil in the air. That summer he gave Portland its money's worth, making the airship do practically everything but turn somersaults. He guided it low through narrow streets and settled it down on the roofs of office buildings. His final score was twenty-five flights with twenty-three returns to base. Everyone recognized that the motor was the determining factor which had made Beachey's gyrations possible, and the gratified authorities of the Portland fair placed it in a special exhibit. At the end of the Exposition season, the judges awarded the gold medal to the G. H. Curtiss Manufacturing Company for best motor of the show. Besides the medal, the company received "a handsome banner with the award inscription" and this was displayed in the window of a Hammondsport store.

Indeed, the Curtiss engine—with its low ratio of weight in proportion to horsepower—had made a breakthrough for dirigibles, and there ensued a rush of venturesome young men to operate them and cash in on fat exhibition fees. Lincoln Beachey shortly left Baldwin and joined Knabenshue as his assistant working out of Toledo. The nation's capital thrilled to see him circle the Washington Monument and the Capitol dome and land on the White House lawn. Congress adjourned to meet him. In the summer of 1906, Beachey made his introductory appearance at Hammondsport to order a special-built engine for an airship he was designing at Pittsburgh; he said he was using Curtiss motors "exclusively."

On July 4, 1905, at Coney Island, New Yorkers had their first glimpse of a dirigible balloon in flight. Leo Stevens of Hoboken, New Jersey, was demonstrating Baldwin's *California Arrow*. For the holiday crowds, he circled it around the Brighton Beach racetrack, soared along Manhattan Beach, and returned "in perfect safety." A few weeks after that, Roy Knabenshue brought his airship to New York and sailed it from Central Park southward over the city as far as the Flatiron Building. "All Manhattan went airship mad," the papers reported.

While the *California Arrow* was at Brighton Beach, two air-smitten chaps, Charles K. Hamilton and Israel Ludlow, came out from the city to look it over. Hamilton, who wore a sombrero and a rattlesnake belt and claimed to have flown something or other in Texas, was allowed to give the *Arrow* a whirl, and thus became infected with dirigible fever.

In reality, Charles Hamilton's hometown was New Britain, Connecticut, and he was in New York assisting Israel Ludlow in trying to loft a series of flying-machine models, each of which ended in a smashup. Ludlow, an attorney, had been working with large box kites in which he hoped to install an engine. His method was to tow them into the air by automobile, using a sandbag for ballast. One day Hamilton, who stood only one inch over 5 feet tall and barely tipped the scales at 100 pounds, turned up and volunteered to man the models for him. As Ludlow evolved his kites toward wings, Hamilton showed an uncanny talent for surviving crashes. Ludlow's model number 19 was towed by a tugboat on the Hudson River in an effort to impress the Navy (the fleet was in). It actually got up 100 feet before the line snapped. Hamilton was fished out of icy water, blue with cold, chattering: "H-h-however, it was a s-s-s-successful flight."

A great deal more would be heard of Charley Hamilton.

❀   ❀   ❀

The motorcycle factory kept on growing and Curtiss kept on racing. To him, the dirigible trade which had fortuitously dropped in his lap was a "sideline." Once he let slip the rather tactless remark: "I get twice as much money for my motors from those aviation cranks."

The demand for Curtiss motorcycles increased steadily, especially among the racing fraternity. While the "name" motorcycles of the era were Indians and Harley-Davidsons, mainly due to lavish advertising, these makes were heavy by comparison. The great advantage of the Curtiss was its powerful, lightweight motor, on which its originator continuously made improvements. Curtiss maintained that he always resented being called an inventor; that in those days inventors were looked upon in small towns as "wild-eyed crackpots." But to have developed so superior an engine that the world beat a path to his door was undeniably a matter of invention, coupled with a pragmatic engineering talent.[2]

The walls of the early Curtiss shop were covered with his pencil sketches of mechanical designs. Meticulous engineering drawings did not concern him. Instead, he would step to the nearest wall and rapidly rough out a sketch, saying to the workmen: "Here is how I think it should be." Moreover, he had inherited something of his mother's artistic flair, as his sketches were considerably better than crude. If he happened to be outdoors when discussing a point, he would squat down and draw a diagram in the dirt with a stick. A habitual stance when talking with someone was to lean against a building, looking down, and absently kicking the sand with the toe of his shoe.

Ultimately the Curtiss plant was working day and night shifts and still could not keep abreast of demand. A California dealer sent an order for three carloads of motorcycles and Curtiss could squeeze out only one carload. Further additions were made to the factory.

At Fourth of July races sponsored by the Rochester Motor Club in 1906, Curtiss won a 5-mile speed contest by a margin of 300 yards. Again he came in ahead in the 1-mile contest, while Albert Cook, a loyal henchman and hot rider from the bicycle days, took third place on a Curtiss motorcycle. "The Indians were there in force," said a news account, "and but for the accidents to the Curtiss machines they would not have been in the running."

Between races, it was not unusual for Curtiss, wearing his inevitable battered old cap and goggles, to hop on a motorcycle to keep a distant business appointment. Once he made what was hailed as a record trip to Albany (some 250 miles) and return: leaving Hammondsport on a Tuesday night, he spent 10 hours on Wednesday repairing and adjusting a motorcycle for a customer, and was home in time to begin work at 7:00 A.M. Thursday. This had meant traveling in the dark over unpaved highways, without rest.

Around this time, Curtiss made a conspicuous alteration in the family homestead. Calling in carpenters, he had a rectangular cupola affixed in the middle of the roof, calling it The Annex. This was uniquely an expression of the Curtiss personality—his version, perhaps, of an ivory tower. The room it enclosed, lighted by windows all around, was fairly large, with dimensions of 12 by 16 feet. It had no access from any other room in the house. Its individual stairway was entered by a separate outside door from the side porch, locked by its own key. The cupola was not intended as an architectural furbelow, nor did it look like one. For Curtiss, it served the purpose of an office in his home, a private retreat where he could be alone to think, or to which he could bring privileged visitors to talk undisturbed.

While Lena pursued faithfully her self-assumed clerical duties and her mother took care of the house, the business had mushroomed so that Curtiss sorely needed an office manager. For this position he preferred an individual whom he knew intimately and could trust implicitly. He contacted his old friend Harry Genung. Harry had left town and was working in an executive capacity for a firm in Elmira, but a signal from Glenn brought him running to cast his lot with the Curtiss industry. The Curtisses took him into their home as a boarder, but Harry's mind was not entirely on his work. He confided in Glenn that he was engaged to a girl in Elmira, but that marriage would have to wait until he could afford a house in Hammondsport. Curtiss solved this impasse neatly by hiring the girl as his secretary and placing the rear wing of his house at the disposal of the newlyweds. (Genung remembered one slight hitch about the arrangement: now and then the couple would be awakened in the dead of night by Curtiss banging on their door, summoning Harry to a conference on a factory problem which was nagging at him and would not wait until morning.)

Glenn's comparative youthfulness for the presidency of a corporation was not so much a handicap as might be imagined. He appeared to be older than his age. The moustache, dark and bristly, contributed to the illusion, abetted by shaggy brows and an aspect of perpetual frowning. His smiles were rare. The frown was not really a scowl, and no ill-nature was involved. It was more the result of persistent concentration. "He was always thinking," the villagers understood. Lena was downtown walking through Park Square one day and passed her preoccupied husband without his giving her a sign of recognition. When he came home that evening, she playfully chided him: "So! You aren't speaking to me these days!" He was dumbfounded.

His lankiness gave an impression of tallness, when in reality he was of no more than medium height. His forehead was high and the straight dark hair began to recede at an early age. The blue eyes gazed steadily and keenly, without shifting as he spoke. The lips were firm, the chin determined. An interpreter of character by the reading of hands would have found his interesting: the fingers were long and tapering, akin to those of a surgeon or an artist, while the thumbs were broad and flattened like those of a mechanic.

*   *   *

The Aero Club of America was organized in October 1905 as an offshoot of the Automobile Club of America. Its roster contained such redoubtable names as Harry Payne Whitney, Colonel John Jacob Astor, O. H. P. Belmont, and William K. Vanderbilt, Jr. For its public debut, it planned an aeronautical show to be held in conjunction with the annual Automobile Show scheduled for January 1906 in the 69th Regiment Armory, New York City. The Curtiss Corporation prepared its customary exhibit for the Auto Show, with particular emphasis on the engines it was now making for dirigible balloons. Glenn Curtiss arranged to attend, as he always did.

Four dirigibles, including Baldwin's latest *California Arrow*, were suspended from the armory ceiling. The exhibits committee appealed to Dr. Samuel P. Langley, Octave Chanute, the Wright brothers, and Dr. Alexander Graham Bell for examples of their work. The Smithsonian supplied an early Langley model aerodrome, and Chanute responded with one of his gliders. The Wrights sent the crankshaft and flywheel of their 1903 engine and a few gliding photos, explaining: "It would interfere with our plans [i.e., to get some financial return for their efforts] if we should make public at once a description of our machine and methods."

Alexander Graham Bell, the burly, tweedy inventor of the telephone, in the majesty of his bushy white whiskers, appeared in the flesh with one of his "famous flying tetrahedral kites." The kite was a large, bright red structure, honeycombed with five hundred tetrahedral cells. Bell had been experimenting with kites for years at his summer estate in Nova Scotia, and was now near the point of powering one of these with an engine.

No one at the first Aero Show stirred a bigger ripple or was more in demand than Alexander Graham Bell. Addressing the banquet of the Automobile Club, he declared: "The age of the flying machine is not in the future. It is with us now." He said that the Wright brothers had flown as far as 25 miles at Dayton, and predicted that the time was not far off when the Atlantic could be crossed in twenty-four hours. Bell was the main attraction also at the annual dinner of the Transportation Club, where the toastmaster drew laughs by quoting from *Darius Green and His Flying Machine*. Dr. Bell told this audience that he had built a kite "as big as a house" in Nova Scotia, and then found that it needed a gale to lift it. "The gale came," he continued in his sonorous tones, "but nobody could be found who was willing to go up in that tugging, roaring kite. So, in order not to disappoint astronomers and country folks, we made a dummy of a man and attached it to the kite. Then the hurricane did the rest. The kite went away and the country folks in the neighborhood of its start are still asking: 'What became of that poor man?' . . . Seriously, I think the kite is the safe medium of aerial navigation. I think, too, that it is coming very soon."

Between these two speeches, Bell was plainly inferring his belief that the Wrights, though they had flown, did not have the ultimate solution; and that he was on the verge of a better answer. Stability, to his mind, was more important than speed, and he was convinced that his tetrahedral cell structure would be stable. Around this period, he set down the thought that "first flights to be safe should be done slowly and deliberately until experience has been gained regarding propulsion and steering . . . Better to crawl safely than to run full speed to destruction."

Whether or not Curtiss heard Bell's talks in New York, it is a certainty that these two men, whose lives were to be fatefully interwoven, met for the first time at this Aero Show. Seeking an engine for his next kite, Bell inspected the Curtiss exhibit. Back home in Washington, he scribbled in his diary: *A 15 horsepower motor can be obtained from the Curtis Motor Cycle Company—weighing 125 lbs— (double cylinder) and can probably be considerably lightened. Safe to say 150 lbs for motor fittings, oil, etc. at outside figures.*

Soon thereafter he ordered such a motor expressed to Baddeck, Nova Scotia, near his summer home, for propeller experiments on a catamaran boat.

* * *

That April a great earthquake devastated San Francisco and fire followed in its wake. Captain Baldwin's balloon plant went up in smoke, together with his third dirigible. His office and equipment lay in ashes, with records and data representing years of research. Fortunately he had shipped the gas envelope of a fourth *Arrow* to Hammondsport for mechanical completion there. Already he had realized that it was awkward to improve power transmission when the airship itself was built on the West Coast and the engine in the East.

For his third dirigible, which he called the *20th Century*, Baldwin had asked Curtiss to supply him with a more powerful motor, as he intended increasing the hydrogen capacity to 9000 cubic feet. Perhaps his trouble in keeping a pilot had some bearing on that decision; he resolved to be his own pilot, hence would need a ship able to uphold his weight. Curtiss obliged by doubling the number of cylinders in a "V" arrangement. Thus Baldwin was at least partly responsible for the origination of the Curtiss 4-cylinder motor. In flights here and there in California, the *20th Century* chalked up a record of fifty-one returns out of fifty-three starts before the quake ended her career.

Baldwin hove into Hammondsport a few days after the earthquake, glum but buoyant as one of his balloons. His next step was indicated when he said he regarded that village as "an ideal spot for aerial experiments." After a meeting with Curtiss, the announcement was given out that the Baldwin balloon business was being transferred to Hammondsport and would henceforth operate in close harmony with the motor works. This was quite the most exciting thing which had yet happened to the town on Keuka Lake. Abruptly it found itself thrust into the aeronautical spotlight of America. It could look forward to the daily spectacle of dirigibles floating over Pleasant Valley, while the factory on Castle Hill was turning out the motors for every airship that flew in the United States. Baldwin erected his plant at the mouth of the Glen and used its entrance amphitheater as a roofless hangar for his ships. Its high rock walls provided shelter against the wind.

World's fairs trod on one another's heels in that euphoric decade, and each tried to outdo the last in the aeronautics department. The next one coming up was the Jamestown Tercentenary Exposition of 1907, commemorating the settlement of Jamestown, Virginia. Baldwin was not going to skip that, and his first Hammondsport balloon was designed for this purpose, with a 4-cylinder engine upped to 16-horsepower. The major innovation was a pair of propellers, rotating in opposite directions, to solve the problem of torque (i.e., the tendency of the ship to veer from a straight course with a single propeller).

To assist Baldwin in the improvement of propellers, Curtiss invented his immortal wind-wagon, or horse-scarer. This device consisted of a simple framework on a tricycle carriage of bicycle wheels, with an engine and propeller mounted behind the driver. With Glenn at the helm, it went skittering around the rural highways at a rate of speed which was hard to control. So many buggies and wagons got in the way that an automobile was sent on ahead to clear the road, but the wind-wagon quickly overtook the auto. Farmers stormed angrily into town with the complaint that the wind-wagon was scaring their horses and causing runaways. Merchants supported their protest, saying it made the roads unsafe and was "bad for business generally." Bowing to the clamor, Curtiss retired the horse-scarer from the public highways, but transferred the concept to a boat on the lake and an ice-boat in winter.

The United States Army evinced its earliest recorded interest in what was going on at Hammondsport when, in the fall of 1906, the War Department ordered a Curtiss motorcycle for use with a portable wireless telegraph apparatus.

*   *   *

Curtiss took on the agency for the Frayer-Miller touring car, which was manufactured in Columbus, Ohio, and promptly made a sale to J. Seymour Hubbs, a stockholder in the G. H. Curtiss Manufacturing Company. Incidentally, Hubbs was the business man for whom Curtiss had repaired the acetylene gas plant when he was new in the bicycle shop. Curtiss had no show-room and no Thayer-Miller in stock, and Hubbs decided to go to Columbus and pick up his purchase in person. The trip turned into a minor expedition, as he was accompanied by Curtiss, George H. Keeler, and Lynn D. Masson. Bethinking himself that Columbus was only 60-odd miles from Dayton, Curtiss evidently had the idea of fishing for added business while in Ohio. Under date of May 16, 1906, he addressed a letter to the Wright brothers in Dayton, and this was his first contact with them. The typist errors in that letter suggest either an incompetent stenographer, or that he tapped it out himself by the hunt-and-peck method. He wrote:

> Dear Sirs:- We have read of your success with the Aeroplane and thinking we might be of service to you in getting out a light and powerful motor with which to carry on your work we take the liberity of writing you on the subject.
>
> We have built a large number of motors for aerial purposes. We have sold motors to Stevens, Knabenshue, Tomlinson and others: while Capt. Baldwin has used ours exclusively for the last two years, as you doubtless know has made some twenty-three success return flights at Portland, Ore.
>
> Of course we under stand that your work is of a some waht different character, but we mention these to prove that our motor has great power and reliability, as it is proved that much power is required to drage a big gas bag through the air at 15 miles an hour.
>
> We recently shipped to Dr. Bell's Nova Scotia Laboratory a motor designed for Aeroplane work, and we hope that this experience will be service to you.
>
> The writer will be in Columbus next Sunday, and if you

are interested would be willing to go on the Dayton and take
up the matter further with you. Address, me c/o Oscar Lear
Auto, Co.,

> Yours truly,
> G. H. Curtiss Mfg. Co.
> Per   G. H. Curtiss

An inference seemingly warranted by this letter is that Curtiss
was already aware of the relative inadequacy of the self-made Wright
engine; otherwise he would scarcely have had the temerity to approach
them in this matter. The chances are that he had been told this by
Dr. Bell, who in turn had it from Dr. Langley. The Wrights had not
yet flown publicly. (Many years later, Orville Wright admitted that their
engine was "one of the poorest parts of our plane.") At all events,
the brothers had no intention of using anyone else's motors. Not long
after the Curtiss feeler, Wilbur remarked to Chanute: "We have never
considered light motors the important point in solving the flying problem."

Instead of sending their reply in care of the Lear automobile firm,
as requested, the Wrights mailed it to the Hammondsport address given
on the company letterhead, where it arrived after Curtiss's departure.
Finding no reply awaiting him in Columbus, Curtiss wired the Wrights
from there: IF CONVENIENT LIKE TO TALK WITH YOU SIX O'CLOCK BELL
PHONE. That evening he called and reached one of the brothers who
evidently discouraged him from expecting an engine deal but left the
door ajar for a visit if he cared to make the side trip.

The automobile party omitted Dayton and drove home by way of
Cleveland, Buffalo, and Rochester. Curtiss then wrote his second communication to the Wrights:

"On my return I find your letter. Trust I did not cause you any
inconvenience in getting you to the phone . . . Was delayed a day in
Columbus and thought of going over to see you. Am glad, however, to
have made your acquaintance and hope to meet you at some future
time."

That hoped-for meeting transpired three months later, when Baldwin took Curtiss with him to nurse the motor for a week's contract at
the Dayton Fair. The Wright brothers attended the fair to see Baldwin
perform, and ran across fields to help haul the dirigible back to the
fairgrounds when, on two successive days, the wind carried it far
astray. "Captain Baldwin is at the fair at Dayton this week," Wilbur

wrote Chanute on September 4, "but the wind has been too strong for
him to attempt a flight . . . Mr. Curtiss, who is building the motor for
Prof. Bell's experiments this fall, called to see us. He thinks the report
of wireless experiments is without foundation."

By this time the Wrights had suspended their flights altogether, to
avoid prying eyes, and were earnestly seeking a market for their invention in Europe. Baldwin and Curtiss visited them at the Wright Cycle
Company and had conversations with them at the fairground. These
talks naturally dwelt on aeronautics, particularly on propellers, which
were as yet in an embryonic stage. The visitors were not allowed to see
an airplane, but were shown photographs of the Wright "flyer" off the
ground at Huffman's Prairie.

Once again, upon his return to Hammondsport, Curtiss showed a
desire to keep up a correspondence with the Wright brothers, in a letter
dated September 22:

Gentlemen:—

This is my first opportunity to write you since getting back
from Dayton . . . This week have been with Baldwin at Elmira,
where he has made a successful flight each day, so far.

It may interest you to know that we cut out some of the
inner surface of the blades on the big propellor, so as to reduce
the resistance and allow it to speed up, and it showed a remarkable improvement. The same accident which occurred
in Dayton, that is, the ship coming down to the ground when
starting and striking the propellor, put the small one out of
business and twisted off the shaft, so that it made it necessary
to use the large one. Having some time to spare while I repaired the shaft, Mr. Baldwin cut a panel out, and we were all
greatly surprised to see the way it pulled the ship around when
ascension was made. It was late and he did not leave the Fair
Grounds, but a person could not keep under him as he circled
about the center field and track. I think he must have been
making 12 miles an hour in all directions . . .

We are getting well started on the 8-cylinder motor for
Jones. It certainly looks good on the drawings. Will let you
know how it pans out as to power etc.

So detailed a review of the Dayton affair is warranted because of
the attention to be focused on it in the controversy of later years.

The Wrights and their partisans repeatedly cited it as evidence that Curtiss attempted to pick their brains at their first meeting. The passage about the altered propeller in the foregoing letter has often been singled out as proof of unethical intent. For example, an editor with an obvious anti-Curtiss bias[3] says in a footnote: "That technical information furnished by the Wrights was promptly utilized by Curtiss is evident from his letter to them of Sept. 22, 1906, in which he describes how the performance of the propeller . . . was markedly improved by cutting away part of the blades' 'inner' surfaces." A dispassionate reading of that paragraph in the letter does not indicate that the Wrights had proposed reducing the size of the blades; it suggests no more than a candid attempt to pass on information about a subject which they had discussed together. Even if the brothers had advised the change, it was Baldwin's own aircraft which was involved and Baldwin personally did the cutting. If Curtiss had been underhandedly pirating an idea, it hardly stands to reason that he would have immediately notified them of the fact.

There is not a scrap of evidence that Curtiss, at that time, had the least thought of going in for aviation himself.

*   *   *

The "8-cylinder motor for Jones" refers to an unexpected order Curtiss had received while in Dayton. Just a few days before his arrival, Wilbur had mentioned "experiments by a Mr. Jones of Dayton." No such thing as an 8-cylinder engine yet existed for aerial use, hence the Wrights would naturally have been interested in the outcome.

Charles Oliver Jones, formerly a Cincinnati engraver, had taken up a study of aeronautics while touring the West as a Socialist lecturer. Appearing at Dayton in 1903, he had organized a stock company to promote his plans for a flying machine which someone depicted as "a combination aeroplane and wing-flapper." Because of its size and weight, he felt the need of a super-engine, and therefore asked Curtiss if he could supply one with 8 cylinders. When Curtiss accepted the proposition, Jones moved his family, unfinished airplane, and base of operations to Hammondsport. As it eventuated, his machine was too unwieldy for flight, and he turned to building a dirigible instead, a variant from Baldwin's *Arrows*. He called his balloon the *Boomerang*.

Another patron for an 8-cylinder engine showed up simultaneously with Jones. This was "a man from Detroit" whose name Curtiss could not recall when relating the incident long afterward; probably he meant a certain Captain Mattery, who was soon claiming to have "the largest airship in the world." The Detroiter submitted a sketch of the machine, and Curtiss "didn't think much of the idea," saying that it was on the general scheme of a length of stovepipe; that it was supposed to produce suction at the front for lift, expulsion at the rear for thrust. Upon investigation, the customer's credit proved to be good and his order was accepted. Presumably it was buyers like Jones and Mattery to whom Curtiss referred as "aviation cranks." (Roy Knabenshue testified that Curtiss could get twice as much money for an aeronautical engine as for a complete motorcycle.)

In any event, these two "aviation cranks" performed a notable service to aeronautics: they got Curtiss launched on the 8-cylinder waters. While meeting their desires, he fell to wondering what so powerful an engine would do in a motorcycle. The temptation was too much to resist. His workmen had their moment of doubting his sanity when he instructed them to start building an oversized motorcycle to receive an 8-cylinder engine. While carrying out his orders, they muttered that it would be suicidal to ride such a monstrous machine, and that its speed would be far too great for any known racetrack. The frame itself exceeded 7 feet in length and contained enough bracing for a lion's cage. The rear wheel was so large as to require an automobile tire. Since no chain or belt could convey that much power without breaking, a transmission shaft connected with the rear hub by beveled gears. The V-shaped engine protruded on both sides so that it could not be straddled; to overcome this obstacle, the handlebars were made preposterously long and the rider's seat was pushed away back over the wheel.

One of the rare occasions when Curtiss was known to lose his temper occurred while this project was under way. In tightening a cylinder-head bolt, hurriedly and a bit carelessly, a youthful mechanic broke off one of the encircling flanges which helped to cool the engine. This meant the delay of getting another cylinder casting, and the boss gave the unfortunate workman a tongue-lashing which, according to those who heard it, was heavily punctuated with swear words. The man picked up his tools and quit his job on the spot. The use of profanity was not a customary trait of Curtiss, but at least he seems to have known the vocabulary.

When the engine was ready for its test run on the block, all employees gathered around curiously. They were amazed by its smooth purring, so different from the nervous chug-bang to which they were accustomed in small motors. It tested up to 40-horsepower. Manifestly there could be no practical use or market for a motorcycle of so much power. At best it would be a colossal freak, and Curtiss knew this, but he was resolved to find out, once and for all, what would happen. And he knew exactly where to make the trial: he had already filed his entry for the regular motorcycle races at the Florida Speed Carnival, scheduled at Ormond Beach for January 1907. There was no official race in which such an outsized behemoth could be entered, but he planned to spring it as a surprise.

In December 1906 the annual Automobile Show recurred, this time in New York's Grand Central Palace, and with it the second Aero Club exhibit. More than ninety makes of automobiles were shown, and attention focused on the Marmon, the first practical 8-cylindered motorcar (even a Rolls-Royce in the show boasted of its 6 cylinders). While new models of automobiles overflowed onto the Lexington Avenue sidewalk, the Aero Club held undisputed sway on the skylighted top floor where three of Baldwin's *California Arrows* dominated the scene.

Glenn Curtiss was there again, presiding over his exhibit of motors and motorcycles, to which had been added the wind-wagon, or horsescarer (a few copies of this novelty were actually sold). Once more, Alexander Graham Bell sought him out and they grew better acquainted, talking of engines and kites. Presumably it was on this occasion that Bell placed an order for a 4-cylinder motor. While the 2-cylinder job had served well enough for propeller testing, a good deal more power would be needed to hoist a kite with a man in it. On learning of the impending trip to the motorcycle races at Ormond Beach, Bell invited Curtiss to be his guest in Washington en route.

The Aero Show exhibit netted Curtiss an "armful" of orders. To help fulfill them, construction of a new machine shop was begun in the rear of his home; this necessitated the sacrifice of a portion of the vineyard. Then all his energies were centered on finishing up the incredible giant motorcycle. The prototype 8-cylinder engines were duly delivered to their purchasers; while a third one was mounted on wheels and went on to its peculiar fame.

Captain Baldwin and Tank Waters accompanied Curtiss to Florida to see the sport. The Speed Carnival was primarily for auto racers. The day came when the beach was relinquished to motorcycles, and Curtiss started off by winning the 1-mile speed race on his standard machine, setting a new world's record of 46⅖ seconds. When the scheduled program was over, he wheeled out his nonesuch. The word had spread afar, and the crowd lining the shore was larger than it had been on any day of the meet. Since there was not another motorcycle like it in the world, the freak could not be registered for a record, but the race officials agreed to time it anyway.

In every race he rode, there was an element of risk, but in this non-race, which was really an escapade, he was literally gambling his life. His costume consisted of a leather jacket and a protective helmet of his own design, but no goggles. As a precaution against being blown off by the wind, he buckled a strap around his back. A starting run of 2 miles was agreed upon to allow him full speed. Baldwin and Waters ran alongside pushing until he could engage the clutch and start the engine. The rest was, for the rider, a streak of beach, a blur of waves, a roar of wind. He was flattened to the frame as if a part of the machine. At one point the course ran beneath a pier and he remembered instinctively pulling his elbows in close to his sides to avoid its widely spaced posts.

The stopwatches proved he had traveled a mile in 26⅖ seconds, or 136.3 miles an hour. This made him incontestably "the fastest man in the world," the title which newspapers bestowed on him. The lead on the story in the Chicago *Daily News* read: "Bullets are the only rivals of Glenn H. Curtiss of Hammondsport." No human being traveled faster until 1911, when an automobile racer made 141.7.

As for Curtiss, he said: "It satisfied my speed-craving."

On his return to Hammondsport, the night shift of the plant was relieved from duty while Curtiss entertained his entire work force with what was for him an extremely unusual procedure—a speech lasting over an hour in which he related his adventure with the jumbo motorcycle. While they listened and chuckled, the men ate fresh oranges their employer had brought from Florida.

The Chicago Automobile Show was held just then, and it displayed the 8-cylinder engine out of Captain Mattery's "airship," placarded as a duplicate of the one which had made Curtiss the "fastest man in the world."

Although the big motorcycle was never ridden again, Curtiss preserved it as a keepsake, storing it in his home. More than a decade

later, it was accorded the position of honor on a pedestal in the lobby
of his new plant at Garden City, Long Island.[4]

About its engine, Curtiss afterward said: "That was our first aeronautical motor."

*   *   *

Ever since Captain Baldwin set up shop in Hammondsport, Glenn
had been watching his ascents, traveling about to fairs with him,
helping to improve the performance of the airships—but with no temptation to go up in the air personally. Nor had Baldwin thought of him in
terms of a potential pilot. There came a day when Curtiss made up
his mind to stop being a timid groundling.

Each time Baldwin had a new *California Arrow* ready for test flying, a virtual village holiday was declared in Hammondsport. So it was
on June 28, 1907, when Baldwin was testing his latest model at the
Kingsley flats, down by the lakefront. Besides at least half the village
population, a number of out-of-town aeronautical "experts" were on
hand to watch the proceedings. After Baldwin had made two or three
circles over the valley, proving that the ship was airworthy, Curtiss
quietly hinted: "I think maybe I could get the idea better if I tried it
myself."

"Sure," Captain Tom grinned, "take her up if you want to, son."

The best surviving account of what happened next may be found
in the files of the Hammondsport *Herald*:

"He shot into the air to the height of several hundred feet and then
proceeded to do a little speeding. Sailing about leisurely after he had
demonstrated perfect control of the ship was too tame for this holder
of many world's records, and so he registered 20 miles an hour in this
wonderful invention of Captain Baldwin's, something unprecedented. He
alighted where he started, enthusiastic over the sensation of airship sailing.

"Someone asked Mr. Curtiss what the sensation was while driving
through the air and he replied: 'It is delightful, only there is no place
to go.' He said there was not the slightest fear of falling."

On that day Glenn Curtiss—manufacturer and motorcycle speed
champion—broke the bonds tying him to terra firma. His immediate reaction was the thought of more speed.

4. Chanute and the Brothers

Wilbur Wright first sought the cooperation of Octave Chanute in a letter dated May 13, 1900, in which he set forth his and Orville's plans to experiment in the field of flight, and said: "I believe no financial profit will accrue to the inventor of the first flying machine, and that only those who are willing to give as well as to receive suggestions can hope to link their names with the honor of its discovery. The problem is too great for one man alone and unaided to solve in secret."

Chanute, himself an altruist in his aeronautical researches, who favored the free pooling of knowledge in order to reach a solution, liked Wilbur's approach and responded that he was "quite in sympathy with your proposal to experiment; especially as I believe like yourself that no financial profit is to be expected from such investigations for a long while to come." At the same time, Chanute answered Wilbur's request for advice on a good location for glider flying in fall and winter weather, recommending a survey of the Atlantic coasts of South Carolina and Georgia.

With that began an extraordinary relationship between youth and age; the most voluminous and valuable correspondence in the annals of aviation. Octave Chanute was sixty-eight years of age, a resident of Chicago, still a consulting engineer but deriving his income chiefly from a chain of wood-preserving plants. He was a man of high character, meticulous honesty, and devotion to scientific method. At the turn of the century, he ranked with Lilienthal and Langley in having brought heavier-than-air flight to the brink of reality.

Wilbur Wright did most of the letter writing for both brothers. In his second letter to Chanute, he said: "It is important that more persons should be intelligently interested in this subject . . . What one man can do himself is but little. If however he can stir up ten others to take up the task he has accomplished much. I know of no man in America so well fitted as yourself to do this missionary work." The like attitude was echoed in 1901, when Chanute was about to visit the Kitty Hawk camp and be joined there by two protégés for whose reliability he vouched: "The labors of others have been of great benefit to us in obtaining an understanding of the subject and have been suggestive and stimulating. We would be pleased if our labors should be of similar benefit to others. We of course would not wish our ideas and methods appropriated bodily, but if our work suggests ideas to others which they can work out on a different line and reach better results than we do, we will try hard not to feel jealous or that we have been robbed in any way."

Chanute assisted the brothers unceasingly, with both personal counsel and documentary material, including the computations of his own glider experiments. In turn, they kept him minutely informed of their results. He visited them at Dayton and for three intervals at Kitty Hawk. He first suggested to them, in May 1902, that they ought to take out a patent, "not that money is to be made by it, but to save unpleasant disputes as to priority." Again he pressed the point: "I think you had better patent your improvements." Then, too, it was Chanute who escorted Augustus M. Herring to their camp, and later regretted doing so.

Herring, to recall, was one of Chanute's assistants in his glider experiments at Dune Park, Indiana. Friction had arisen between them, and Herring left in 1897 to seek another backer who would allow him to mount an engine on a glider (Chanute did not feel that the problem of stability had yet been adequately solved). A wealthy citizen of Elmira, New York, Matthias C. Arnot, became his "angel," and in 1898 Herring had a glider equipped with a small compressed-air motor among the Lake Michigan dunes near St. Joseph, Michigan. There he claimed to have made the first powered flights of history, dangling by his elbows with his feet barely off the ground. A sparsity of witnesses was his trouble about proving it, although he asserted afterward that there were two. He went to the office of the Detroit *Daily News* and volunteered an account of having flown 50 feet; the *News* printed the story, and apparently was the only paper to do so. Then Herring invited Chanute to St. Joseph to see him repeat the flight. When Chanute came, Herring was unable to get the machine in the air. One of his later flights that year covered 72 feet, Herring would subsequently maintain.

By 1902 Arnot was dead and Herring, out of work, came to Chanute with a proposal to rebuild some of their gliders for further study. Chanute allowed him to reconstruct a multiple-wing glider and got the consent of Wilbur Wright to bring Herring to Kitty Hawk to experiment with it. While there, Herring watched glides of the Wright brothers and even helped keep the records. But he could not make his own glider perform. Disillusioned, Chanute wrote to Dr. Langley: "I have lately got out of conceit with Mr. Herring, and I fear that he is a bungler . . . When the machine was tried by him in North Carolina, it proved a failure, and he said that he did not know what was the matter."

Evidently Herring made no great point, while at Kitty Hawk, of his claim to have flown in 1898. If he had, it would presumably have turned up in the Wrights' correspondence or diaries, or in Chanute's commentaries.

Within a few days after the Wrights' successful flights of December, 1903, Herring wrote them an impudent proposal—namely, that they take him into partnership. Reminding them belatedly of his purported flights five years earlier and hinting that he held patents, he magnanimously offered to settle for only one-third interest in the company, allowing them two-thirds. There was the veiled threat of a patent infringement suit if they did not acquiesce. Wilbur forwarded a copy of this letter to Chanute and did not dignify it with an answer.[1]

*   *   *

A wisp of cloud, no bigger than a boy's kite, now appeared on the horizon of friendship between the Wrights and Octave Chanute. The brothers' prepared statement to the press on the triumph at Kill Devil Hill embodied this phrase: ". . . all the experiments have been conducted at our own expense, without assistance from any individual or institution." Chanute snatched this up and inquired: "Please write me just what you had in your mind concerning myself when you framed that sentence that way." Wilbur replied that they had found "there was a somewhat general impression that our Kitty Hawk experiments had not been carried on at our expense, &c. We thought it might save embarrassment to correct this promptly."

Chanute detected something else—the symptom of a subtle change in outlook—and commented on it to another correspondent: "The Wrights are immensely elated. They have grown very secretive, and nobody is to be allowed to see the machine at present."

The Wrights, heeding Chanute's urgings, already had applied for a patent on the essential principle of their glider: i.e., the wing-warping method of stability control. Now they consulted a patent attorney who advised letting that application stand instead of filing a new one on the powered machine, "in order to avoid necessity of demonstrating operation of machine before examiners" (as Orville put it). The Patent Office long had a standing rule against recognizing applications on either perpetual motion machines or flying machines, so pestiferous had these become. After Langley flew his models, however, the stricture was relaxed to admit flying machines to consideration, provided the device was demonstrated to a board of examiners. The Wrights did not propose to let even the patent people see their "flyer." Consequently the U.S. patent finally granted them in May 1906 applied solely to the glider of 1903, which they demonstrated for examiners in a return trip to Kitty Hawk. (Overseas, the Wrights secured patents in seven countries.)

The crux of the patent was in these words: ". . . it is possible to move the forward corner of the lateral edges of the aeroplane [i.e., wing] on one side of the machine either above or below the normal planes of the aeroplane, a reverse movement of the forward corners of the lateral margins on the other side of the machine occurring simultaneously." As this wing-warping induced a turning of the machine, the method required an interrelation with the vertical rear rudder to hold it on a straight course: ". . . the construction is such that the rudder will always be so turned as to present its resisting-surface on that side of the machine on which the lateral margins of the aeroplane present the least angle of resistance."

The sweepingly broad reach of the patent was couched in this clause: "We wish it to be understood . . . that our invention is not limited to this particular construction, since any construction whereby the angular relations of the lateral margins of the aeroplane may be varied in opposite directions with respect to the normal planes of said aeroplanes comes within the scope of our invention."

The brothers did not move to get an updated patent on their motorized plane. As Wilbur explained in 1907: "We have a patent on our early gliding machine, but have not applied for protection on any of our work of the past five years. We have generally been informed that secrets were worth more to governments than patented articles. For that reason we have taken out no patents since we found there was any practical use in our invention."

When Professor Langley died in February 1906, as the result of a stroke, Wilbur Wright paid him tribute in a letter to Chanute: "The knowledge that the head of the most prominent scientific institution of America believed in the possibility of human flight was one of the influences that led us to undertake the preliminary investigation that preceded our active work. He recommended to us the books which enabled us to form sane ideas at the outset. It was a helping hand at a critical time and we shall always be grateful . . . I think his treatment by the newspapers and many of his professed friends most shameful. His work deserved neither abuse nor apology."

The Wrights ceased their flying experiments altogether at the end of the 1905 season, to protect their secret and look for a source of monetary return. At the swampy meadow east of Dayton, they had made a total of 160 flights, averaging one mile per flight. All of these were done with the pilot lying prone, to minimize air resistance. Their machines had skids instead of wheels and were launched from a monorail track. The launching impulse came from the dropping of a weight in a derrick. (The Wrights never used wheels before 1910, and then in combination with skids.)

Envisioning their best chance of a market to be with a government, for military purposes, the brothers made an overture to the War Department through the Congressman from the Dayton district, early in 1905. The response from the Bureau of Ordnance and Fortification was a brush-off: ". . . as many requests have been made for financial assistance in the development of designs for flying-machines, the Board has found it necessary to decline to make allotments for the experimental development of devices for mechanical flight." It added that whenever the Wright machine was brought to a stage of "practical operation," the Board "would be pleased to receive further representations from them in regard to it." The ever-sensitive Wrights took umbrage at this turn-down, and at once put out feelers in the direction of Europe.

France was the nation which came nearest to making a deal with them. The price they asked was $200,000 for an initial machine. Chanute gently warned them that they might be setting their sights too high, especially when French experimenters were making rapid strides toward practical aircraft. Santos-Dumont, Henry Farman, and Louis Blériot were in the vanguard abroad.

Besides being disturbed by the plain signs that the Wrights were out in pursuit of large money, Chanute worried about their cessation of flying and did not hesitate to let them know it. Wilbur was irritated by his needling, and pointed out that price was a relative matter; that if governments knew there was no way to obtain a practical airplane in less than five or ten years, then $200,000 would be considered cheap. He wrote in October 1906, soon after Curtiss and Baldwin had been at Dayton: "If it were indeed true that others would be flying within a year or two, there would be reason in selling at any price but we are convinced that no one will be able to develop a practical flyer within five years. This opinion is based upon cold calculation. It takes into consideration practical and scientific difficulties whose existence is unknown to all but ourselves. Even you, Mr. Chanute, have little idea how difficult the flying problem really is. When we see men laboring year after year on points we overcame within a few weeks, without ever getting far enough along to meet the worse points beyond, we know that their rivalry and competition are not to be feared for many years. When the distance is known and the speed is known a reasonable estimate of the time required can be formed. It is many times five years. We do not believe there is one chance in a hundred that anyone will have a machine of the least *practical* usefulness within five years."

In other words, the Wrights had convinced themselves that the threat of their being overtaken could be reduced to a mathematical formula. Chanute replied:

"You are quite correct in saying that it is not the amount of money involved but the possibility of buying your machine cheaper which causes your clients to hesitate. The value of an invention is whatever it costs to reproduce it, and I am by no means sure that persistent experimenting by others, now that they know one success has been achieved, may not produce a practical flyer within five years.

"The important factor is that light motors have been developed . . . I cheerfully acknowledge that I have little idea how difficult the flying problem really is and that its solution is beyond my powers, but are you not too cocksure that yours is the only secret worth knowing and that others may not hit upon a solution in less than 'many times five years'? It took you much less than that and there are a few (very few) other able inventors in the world. The danger therefore is that others may achieve success."

Wilbur continued argumentative: "The one thing that impresses me as remarkable is the shortness of the time within which our work was done. It was due to peculiar combinations of circumstances which might never occur again . . . We look upon the present question in an entirely impersonal way. It is not chiefly a question of relative ability, but of mathematical probabilities. The fact that lightning strikes once in some particular spot is no evidence that it will strike there again soon."

Five days before Wilbur put these words on paper, Alberto Santos-Dumont, in a Paris suburb, had kept an ungainly contraption called his *Number 14 bis* in the air for about 60 meters' distance. The thing seemed a hodgepodge of box kites, but its performance was enough to stampede the French public into a belief that Santos had made the first heavier-than-air flight in history (so little was the accomplishment of the Wrights known abroad). A headline in Paris proclaimed: L'HOMME A CONQUIS L'AIR! Chanute directed Wilbur's attention to this news, which at first said he had flown a kilometer or more, and observed of Santos-Dumont: "I fancy that he is now very nearly where you were in 1904." He went on: "I suppose that you can do no better than to await the result, for the outcome will depend not only upon the 'mental ability' which you misunderstood me as constituting the sole cause, but upon mechanical instinct and that conjunction of circumstances which is sometimes called luck."

Wilbur's reaction to the Santos-Dumont danger signal was instantaneous: "This report gives such an excellent opportunity for exercising our powers as prophets that I cannot resist making a forecast before the details arrive. From our knowledge of the subject we estimate that it is possible to *jump* about 250 ft., with a machine which has not made the first steps toward controllability and which is quite unable to maintain the motive force necessary for flight . . . From our knowledge of the degree of progress that Santos has attained we predict that his flight covered less than $\frac{1}{10}$ of a kilometer, and that he has only jumped . . . When someone goes over three hundred feet and lands safely in a wind of seven or eight miles it will then be important for us to do something. So far we see no indication that it will be done for several years yet. There is all the difference in the world between jumping and flying."

The debate was a recurring theme in the letters which passed back and forth between the flying pioneers and their counselor. "I still differ with you," Chanute would say, "as to the possibility of your being caught up with if you rest upon your oars. It is practice, practice, practice which tells and the other fellows are getting it." And Wilbur: "Fear that others will produce a machine capable of practical service in less than several years does not worry us. We have been over the course and understand how much yet remains for them to do."

Oddly enough, the thought does not seem to have occurred to either party in the running dispute that a rival airplane might be developed in America. All their talk centered upon what the foreigners were doing, especially the French. Chanute was undoubtedly thinking of the Curtiss engines, however, when he mentioned that "light motors have been developed."

In June 1907, while Wilbur was on his first trip abroad, Chanute communicated to Orville his hope that "Wilbur's views will be modified by his journey." He was now convinced that "the Europeans are catching up with you more rapidly than I had believed." And Orville was as ready as his brother to bat the ball back: "Of course there is always a possibility that some unheard-of investigator may come into the light with a machine far in advance of any machine of known inventors, but we have always considered this a remote possibility."

As late as January 1, 1908, the elder brother was writing to Chanute: "I note from several remarks in your recent letters that you evidently view the present situation in aviation circles with very different eyes from what we do. I must confess that I still hold to my prediction that an independent solution of the flying problem would require at least five years . . . I have confidence that our prediction will stand solid after the scythe of time has reaped several fresh crops of French predictions."

At that precise moment the Aerial Experiment Association was going into action at Hammondsport, New York.

5. "To Get into the Air"

Availing himself of Dr. Bell's invitation, Curtiss stopped over in Washington on his way to the Ormond Beach races and was agreeably surprised at the wholehearted warmth of his reception. Through billows of pipe smoke, Bell poured forth the story of his kite researches and of the dramatic stride he confidently hoped to achieve with the more powerful Curtiss motor. This time there was a mutual exchange of invitations: Bell urged Curtiss to follow the engine to Nova Scotia that summer and observe for himself what was going on; Curtiss invited Bell to be his guest in Hammondsport and look over his "shop."

Quite the pleasantest aspect of his stay in the hospitable mansion on Connecticut Avenue was the gracious and sensitive charm of his hostess, Mrs. Mabel Bell. He had been forewarned that she was deaf. A bond of empathy was quickly forged between them, owing to Glenn's prior experience with the unhearing and the ability he had cultivated to enunciate distinctly for lip-reading. Mabel Hubbard had lost her hearing to scarlet fever when a small child, as Rutha had lost hers to meningitis. Like Rutha, too, she had been protected from "deaf-mute psychology" by not being allowed to learn the sign language, and she retained the faculty of speech in fair degree. Mabel Hubbard's parents had sought the counsel of Dr. Bell, who at that time had been an educator of the deaf in Boston; although the girl was not actually enrolled as a pupil of Bell's.

Up to now, Glenn's acquaintance with aeronautics was confined to Baldwin's dirigibles and the propeller testing he had done for them with his wind-wagon. Beyond that, he had not been especially curious; attempts at flight offered a wider market for his engines, and that sufficed. For Bell's part, he had no idea of venturing personally into the air, but was deeply interested in making it possible for younger men to do so. In his sixtieth year, he was much overweight with a bulk which was due in part to a diabetic tendency.

Like everyone else, Curtiss required an explanation of what a tetrahedral kite really was, though he had seen a model at the Aero Show in New York. Bell related how, in the early 1890s, he had started experimenting with kites on his private mountainside in Nova Scotia, with the aim of eventually developing a super-kite, stable and sizable enough to receive a motor and be operated by a man as a flying machine, for which he had adopted Langley's word "aerodrome." His wealth from the telephone made it possible to maintain laboratories and a staff of assistants for these and a variety of other experiments; Bell's was an incessantly inquiring brain. In quest of the ideal geometric shape for the cellular bracing and liftability of such a kite, he had finally settled on the tetrahedron, a four-faced pyramid. For Glenn's benefit, he illustrated a tetrahedron in his customary way: by laying three matches on the table to form a triangle, then propping three more matches upright from the angles with their tips joined. Aluminum frames of this shape were encased in red silk, and hundreds of these cells were fitted together between the plane surfaces of a kite, somewhat like a honeycomb. The color of the silk was chosen for its photogenic quality; as a lesson learned from his agonizing patent litigations, Bell insisted on a good photographic record of all his later experiments. From his background as a photographer, Curtiss readily appreciated this point.

*   *   *

Born in Scotland in 1847, Alexander Graham Bell was brought in 1871 to Ontario by his parents as a youth in delicate health, followed his father's footsteps as a speech specialist, later became a citizen of the United States. After his brilliant success as an inventor, he made his home in Washington, D.C., where both he and his wife disliked the summer humidity. During a holiday cruise, they happily discovered the Bras d'Or Lakes of Cape Breton Island; these are not truly lakes, but ramifying inland branches of the ocean, bordered by low mountains and picturesque headlands. The scene, thus penetrated by arms of salt water, reminded Bell of his native heath. The resort village of Baddeck gazed across its bay at a long peninsula jutting into the Little Bras d'Or, with a sightly hill at its tip, locally known as Red Head. Enamored of this promontory, the Bells selected it as their haven of refuge from the heat of Washington, bought up a thousand acres of its land, and erected on its point an imposing summer home, substantial enough for winter use if need be. Its architecture ran to gables and porches, corner towers with conical roofs, and tall stone chimneys. Bell named the estate Beinn Bhreagh (pronounced "ben vree-ah"), Gaelic for "mountain beautiful." Here his restless imagination found free rein, but the kite investigations came in time to dominate all others.

Aeronautical science was no sudden whim of Bell's. Thomas A. Watson, his aide in the invention of the telephone, recalled: "From my earliest association with Bell, he discussed with me the possibility of making a machine that would fly like a bird. He took every opportunity that presented itself to study birds, living or dead . . . I fancy, if Bell had been in easy financial circumstances, he might have dropped his telegraph experiments and gone into flying machines at that time."

Letters passed between Bell and Octave Chanute at the same time Chanute was advising the Wright brothers. Chanute sent a photograph of his "ladder kite," and Bell reciprocated with a pamphlet on tetrahedral structure. In the summer of 1903, Bell wrote to thank Chanute for a copy of Wilbur Wright's pamphlet, *Experiments and Observations in Soaring Flight*, describing the early gliding experiments at Kitty Hawk, which he had given as a lecture to the Western Society of Engineers.

By the end of 1905, Bell had a kite capable of lifting a man off the ground, and it was this which led directly to his ordering the first engine from Curtiss. In December of that year, the kite was lofted in celebration of a wedding at the Beinn Bhreagh estate. Arthur McCurdy, a native of Baddeck, was Bell's secretary and photographer and a virtual member of the family. McCurdy had a daughter and two sons. When the daughter, Susan, was betrothed to Walter Frost, the Bells insisted that the nuptials be performed in their big house. As soon as the couple were pronounced man and wife, Dr. Bell christened his new kite the *Frost King* in their honor.

The wedding party adjourned to Kite Hill and watched the *Frost King* ride high on the wind. When it was at greatest altitude, Lucien McCurdy, a brother of the bride, climbed the rope hand over hand, flung both legs over it, and remained suspended five feet off the ground as long as he could hold on. Lucien weighed 149 pounds. The episode was reported by the Halifax *Herald* and the Washington *Times.* In all likelihood, Bell told Curtiss about this when they met at the Aero Show two weeks later.

The following summer, the "Curtiss Number 1" motor was mounted in a catamaran at Beinn Bhreagh for propeller testing, and simultaneously the Bells were notified of the birth of a grandson in Washington. The baby was baptized Alexander Graham Bell Fairchild. In his telegram of congratulations to Mr. and Mrs. David Fairchild, Bell included a morsel of Nova Scotia news: A MOTORBOAT EQUIPPED WITH AERIAL PROPELLERS . . . YESTERDAY SUCCESSFULLY MADE HER FIRST TRIP ON THE WATERS OF BEINN BHREAGH HARBOR DURING HARVEST HOME FESTIVAL. WE HAVE NAMED HER THE UGLY DUCKLING AND HOPE SHE WILL TURN OUT TO BE A SWAN.

The wire which bounced back from Washington was addressed TO THE UGLY DUCKLING, and said: PROUD TO BE YOUR TWIN. MY FATHER THINKS I'LL TURN OUT TO BE A SWAN TOO. ALEXANDER GRAHAM BELL FAIRCHILD.

Such family jocularity foreshadowed the name of the kite which was destined to soar with a man aboard. It was called the *Cygnet,* (i.e., young swan), and the *Ugly Duckling* was to serve as its launching platform.

The second McCurdy son, Douglas, was at home on vacation from his science studies at the University of Toronto, bringing with him a college friend who was anxious to meet Bell and see his kites in action. The guest, just graduated as a mechanical engineer from Toronto, was Frederick W. Baldwin, better known as Casey, a nickname picked up in prep-school baseball. These youths showed such enthusiasm for the project that Bell invited them to be his volunteer assistants after McCurdy's graduation in 1907, at which time he proposed to have the *Cygnet* kite about completed.

*   *   *

Shortly after Curtiss's Washington visit, Bell received a call from an Army officer who sought an interview regarding the kite experiments.

Lieutenant Thomas E. Selfridge of the 1st Field Artillery, four years out of West Point, explained that he had been making an intensive study of everything so far known about human flight. Convinced that the Army would soon begin taking military aviation seriously, he intended to be well prepared for that branch of service. Bell took an instant liking to Selfridge, finding him a remarkably personable and earnest fellow. When Selfridge mentioned that he would like to observe some of the kite work, Bell replied: "Come along. We want the War Department of the United States to know what we are doing, so that, if there is any benefit, the United States may share in it as well as Canada."[1]

If he were to spend any time at Baddeck, Selfridge would need special orders. Bell was a friend of President Theodore Roosevelt, to whom he addressed a letter urging the desirability of such a step for the Army and endorsing Selfridge's application for temporary duty in Nova Scotia. The President pushed a button and Selfridge received orders to proceed to Baddeck "for the study of aeronautics in general and of aviation, meaning heavier-than-air craft, in particular." (On July 1, 1907, the War Department established an Aeronautical Division in the Office of Chief Signal Officer, and Selfridge was assigned to that division.)

A plan was gradually crystallizing in Bell's mind, and circumstances seemed to be conspiring with him toward putting it into execution: a program to gather around himself a team of bright, dedicated young men to help him over the final hurdle of putting a mechanical kite in the air, at the same time becoming indoctrinated in the art so they could carry on the torch. Now he had three promising candidates for the team, but he lacked the key person of all—an engine specialist. He considered Glenn Curtiss "the greatest motor expert in the country," but could hardly expect a man with an established industry to walk out on it for a quixotic adventure in kite-flying. The first step must be to arouse his interest. Sometime that spring Bell went to Hammondsport with a view to pinning Curtiss down for a trip to Nova Scotia. On the score that his men needed instruction in the operation and maintenance of the new engine, Bell offered him a stipend of $25 a day, plus travel expenses, and Curtiss accepted.

This much achieved, Bell and his wife packed for a roundabout voyage back to Nova Scotia by way of London, where he went to receive an honorary degree from Oxford University. While in England, he stated: "The actual problem of the navigation of the air has already been solved by the Wright brothers"; but he hoped to add materially to

that knowledge with experiments he was continuing at Cape Breton
Island. His objective was to propel a kite with "a specially constructed
engine of 15 horsepower"; he did not expect the kite to travel faster
than 10 or 15 miles an hour, but "Man must learn to go slow before he
goes fast." Prophetically, if a little off in timing, he added: "The developments of the next few months will be unprecedented."

❊   ❊

Putting in his appearance at Baddeck in mid-July, Curtiss was inducted into a congenial circle at Beinn Bhreagh Hall, where Doug
McCurdy, Casey Baldwin, and Tom Selfridge had preceded him. He
was ushered to the choice guest apartment—a circular room in one of
the corner towers, with windows commanding a superb view across the
Little Bras d'Or at Washabuck Mountain. If at first he was a trifle uneasy with a gathering in which he was the only person not a university
graduate, the open friendliness and high spirits soon allayed the feeling.
In a tour of the estate, he was shown the finely equipped laboratories
and the Kite House, and saw some tetrahedral kites in flight. The Kite
House was a long, narrow building without partitions, in which the
huge kites were suspended from rafters during construction. One side
wall opened on rollers to let a kite escape when finished. Work was
under way on the frame of the *Cygnet,* and women hired in Baddeck
were sewing red silk over the many cells.

Daytimes, Glenn joined McCurdy, Baldwin, and Selfridge in running propeller tests with the *Ugly Duckling,* on which the "Curtiss
Number 2" engine was mounted, tutoring them in handling the motor.
Evenings were relaxing, with lively talk sessions and song fests. Bell
had an excellent singing voice, and both he and Mabel played the
piano. Not before had Curtiss encountered so stimulating a social atmosphere.

Bell lost no time in broaching the subject uppermost in his mind, for
which primarily he had lured Curtiss to Nova Scotia. Some of the
discussions took place in a houseboat moored offshore, a retreat where
the inventor liked to work undisturbed. The tenor of these confabs
may be sensed from Bell's entries in his journal, which he designated
as "Home Notes." On July 19, 1907, he jotted:

"The experiments at Beinn Bhreagh point to an early conclusion of
the problem of aerial flight." Noting the recruitment of two Canadian
college graduates, one a mechanical engineer, he expressed his pleasure

that an officer of the U. S. Army had now joined them as "an onlooker and adviser"; and appended: "I have also called to my assistance Mr. Glenn H. Curtiss of Hammondsport, N.Y., as a well known expert in the construction of light gasolene motors as I felt that his knowledge and experience with such motors will be invaluable—and indeed necessary to the successful conclusion of these experiments."

The pen scratched on: "Now it appears to me that in the above personnel we have an ideal combination for pursuing aerial researches . . . For many years my laboratory experiments have been directed mainly along lines leading up to aerial flight as a logical conclusion. I now have associated with me gentlemen who supplement by their technical knowledge my deficiencies; and in this combination I now feel that we are strong, where before we were weak. I think, therefore, that the progress of the experiments will be greatly promoted and the world benefited if these young men . . . can be given some personal inducement to continue cooperating together in accomplishing the great object we have in common—to get into the air."

Such inducements, he speculated, might be: for each man to have an opportunity of "making a name and reputation for himself as a promoter of aviation or mechanical flight"; and, in the event of "any pecuniary emolument," for each to share in the profits. But: "The chief inducement that can urge us to keep together is the actual accomplishment of aerial flight and the honor and glory that will attach to those who succeed."

Some formula by which they might be welded into a cohesive group "is a problem which we are now discussing together." Mrs. Bell had suggested "that we should copy the plan adopted when the Volta Laboratory Association was formed."[2] Her idea was an association, financed by a guaranteed working capital, to promote aerial experiments. For the working capital, Mrs. Bell offered to invest $20,000 which she could obtain from the sale of a corner lot she owned in Washington, a gift from her father. In case that ran out, Bell might agree to supply an additional $10,000 himself, and that total "ought to suffice to put our first machine successfully in the air." If any patentable features resulted, the association could be converted into a company, with a trustee at the helm.

The very mention of patents stirred odious memories and misgivings for Bell, and he gave his daybook the information that the American Bell Telephone Company, in its early struggles for survival, had spent more than $75,000 a year on patent litigations. "There never had been in the world," he wrote, "more litigations over an invention—but it will be as nothing should successful flying machines be the result of our efforts."

The proposal did not have clear sailing, and Bell came close to a change of heart at one stage. Plainly, he was thinking no further than getting a tetrahedral kite, or an aircraft of its general type, in the air. The idea that his protégés might wish to ride off in a different direction had not fully dawned on him, it seems. If an association were to be formed, he insisted that a few of his veteran employees, who had helped him to evolve the kites, deserved to be taken in as members. When the young men objected to this, he was irked: "This is the first snag I have struck, but there are others." He was dictating the diary entry to Doug McCurdy when he said:

"These young men come in, not at the beginning, but near the conclusion of a long series of experiments to which they have contributed nothing. We come together, not to develop a flying-machine (which is probably their point of view), but to complete a flying-machine which has already been developed, without their aid, up to the threshold of success. I feel confident that with the Curtiss Number 2 and with the propellers we have, we could actually put into the air and sustain in the air any one of several structures already contemplated—built of cells—and support a man as well. I could give orders today for construction of a machine that would fly—with the means we already have. It is not a question of creating a flying-machine that confronts us, but a question of selection of the best of several models and of its improvement in actual construction. The only problem that demands invention before actually constructing the machine is the problem of alighting safely . . . In one word—flotation."

His youthful friends, he observed, probably looked upon the $20,000 offered by Mrs. Bell as the "total capital involved," without knowing how much he had already spent in the prior experiments, which he estimated at $100,000 over a period of fifteen years. By the same token they did not perceive why the faithful efforts of his long-term aides should be rewarded. "I must not make an arrangement now that would fetter me in recognizing these services later on. I am beginning to be a little doubtful whether the suggested association plan might not fetter me more than it could help me. As outlined so far it would practically deprive me of the control of my own laboratory and the disposal of my own capital. The point I have had mainly in mind has been how to secure the continued interest of these young men and how to give them a financial interest in any profits that might arise. In trying to deal justly by them I fear that I am not dealing justly towards myself and towards the persons who have for so many years given me their assistance . . . Maybe the simplest plan would be for me to go to these young men and say:—I want to engage you as my assistants in concluding these experiments for at least one year. I will pay you, Curtiss, $5000 a year; you McCurdy $1000, Baldwin $1000, Selfridge $1000; and you will agree to remain with me for one year. I will give you each a 5 percent interest of whatever I receive as a result of the Beinn Bhreagh experiments. Why is this not enough? I would then be free to give an interest to others as I saw fit . . . I would be free to dispose of my own capital as I saw fit."

Obviously, Bell was vexed; how serious he may have been about backtracking is problematical. Perhaps he was only feeling them out. He told McCurdy to show what he had written to the others and invited their comment. Casey Baldwin was outspoken, replying that, even as a random thought, "it hit hard right at the vitals of the machine. If you still entertain this thought seriously, by all means give the whole scheme up." Curtiss apparently was silent. At all events, Bell emerged from his quandary with a fresh formula: that the new men were not entitled to the fruits of previous labors, nor the veterans to the profits of future work. "The past belongs to the past and the future to the future—The Association to deal only with the future."

Curtiss was obliged by other commitments to return home before anything was settled, leaving it to the others to thresh out details and draft a formal covenant. On July 26, he sent word from Hammondsport: "I have given the Association plan considerable thought and am very favorable toward it."

In a series of conferences the Baddeck group reached agreement on the terms of a charter for an Aerial Experiment Association, and these were forwarded to Curtiss with the request that he return at the earliest possible moment for an organization meeting. Bell came around to a compromise whereby his man-carrying kite would not be the sole device to be worked on during the year, although the *Cygnet* was given priority; after it had its tryout, each other member was to be allotted authority over a machine designed in accordance with his own ideas.

If Lieutenant Selfridge were to be a participating member in such an organization, he would need a special dispensation from the Army; this kind of duty, in alliance with civilians, was manifestly outside the bounds of normal military routine. For permission, he had to reach high in the chain of command, and again Dr. Bell brought his influence to bear. Bell wrote President Roosevelt, setting forth the association plan and asking that Selfridge be detailed as a member for one year. "Money is not our object," he emphasized, "but simply to get into the air." He directed a similar letter to the Secretary of War, William Howard Taft. The request was approved and new orders were cut for Selfridge.

Afterward, Bell credited Selfridge with having coined the slogan: "To get into the air."

*   *   *

A pressing reason why Curtiss was unable to remain through the formative sessions of the association was another motorcycle race. The Federation of American Motorcyclists was to open a five-day meet on July 31 at Providence, Rhode Island, where he was booked as a competitor, with Albert D. Cook again as his partner. Cook started off a string of victories for them by winning a diamond medal in a cross-country endurance contest from New York City to Providence. Curtiss chalked up a new world's speed record for 1-cylinder motorcycles, a mile in 52⅖ seconds, with Cook right behind in second place. Next came a hill-climbing fray in which the unbeatable team again finished in that same order. A sports writer reported that they scored "fresh laurels for the Curtiss motorcycles."

The meet continued, and Glenn led the pack all the way in a free-for-all hill climb over a wicked course. At the crest of the hill, just before the finish line, was a tricky bend. Curtiss took the turn in his characteristic style, faster than most racers dared, but it caught him a trifle off balance. Wobbling, he crossed the goal as winner, but his machine then went out of control and threw him. It was one of the worst spills he ever took, landing him in the hospital for repairs. One knee was severely injured and there were deep wounds on a hand. Internally, he seemed to be intact, though badly shaken up. Incapacitated for the following day's events, he forbade Cook to take any further part, declaring the course too dangerous.

When Lena Curtiss greeted home a battered and bandaged husband, she questioned if the time had not come for him to renounce racing and devote himself to the business. Whatever thoughts she had, pro or con, about the aerial monkeyshines brewing in Nova Scotia are not on record. She had long since learned that this man she married was deliberate in making up his mind, but once he had done so he stuck stubbornly to the decision. Manufacturing engines for flying machines did not necessarily signify that he was going to want to fly the things. Besides, he had probably communicated to her his doubt that the kites would travel. From the outset, he felt that the cells would present too much air resistance.

Leaning on a cane to favor his bad knee, he managed to limp around the shop, and was glad to see how well his new foreman, Henry Kleckler, was fitting into the picture. Here was a person to be relied upon in his absences. A native of Hammondsport, four years younger than himself, Kleckler had gone afield before the Curtiss industry started rolling, and worked for a carpet mill in Thompsonville, Connecticut. Hearing of the rapid expansion of the motorcycle plant, he came home in 1906 and applied for a job just when Curtiss was embarking on his 8-cylinder phase. Put on as night foreman, he did a piece of work so ably that Curtiss transferred him to the day shift. Kleckler quickly displayed a knack with gasoline motors. Equipped with no more technical education than his superior, he was cut from the same piece of cloth as a born "practical" engineer; they spoke the same language, and Kleckler soon was Curtiss's right-hand engine man. To his employer he was always "Henny." As far as Kleckler was concerned, those were "the best years of my life," and Curtiss was "one of the finest men I ever worked for or with."

Satisfied that production was in capable hands without his constant attention, and he could at least afford to see what the Bell proposition was all about, Curtiss did some checking with Captain Baldwin at his neighboring dirigible plant. There a new balloon was being constructed along experimental lines laid down by Curtiss, who was convinced he could make a dirigible go faster. Captain Tom was willing to humor him. He learned that Baldwin, too, would be in Nova Scotia the first week of October, having an engagement for dirigible flights at Halifax. Perhaps the people at Baddeck would be interested . . .

* * *

The tang of Canadian autumn was in the air when Curtiss returned to Beinn Bhreagh, and the maple trees were gaudy earlier than those he had left behind. Logs blazed in the cavernous stone fireplace, and the warmth they threw out felt good after brisk hours in the wind of Kite Hill and the scud of choppy water on Baddeck Bay. A reunion was held around a tea table before the fire, as Mabel Bell poured and her husband stoked his omnipresent pipe.

There ensued a ceremonial reading of the articles of agreement for an Aerial Experiment Association which had been hammered out while Curtiss was absent, bearing the imprint of Bell's style. By the terms of this document, Bell agreed to lend his assistance "to these gentlemen in carrying out their own independent ideas relating to aerial locomotion, and all working together individually and conjointly in pursuance of their common aim 'to get into the air' upon the construction of a practical aerodrome driven by its own motive power and carrying a man." Bell pledged the free use of his laboratory. The Beinn Bhreagh estate was designated as headquarters, with a proviso that "on or before the first of January 1908, the headquarters of the Association shall be removed to some place yet to be determined within the limits of the United States." The sense of the latter clause was that, because of the rugged Nova Scotia winters, work could better be continued in a more temperate latitude, after which a return to Baddeck was envisioned. The *Cygnet* kite was taking longer to complete than anticipated, and Bell wanted its tryout to be held before moving south.[3]

An informal vote gave unanimous approval to the agreement on the spot, but it had yet to go through the legal formality of being signed and notarized. Curtiss advised his colleagues of Captain Baldwin's forthcoming booking at Halifax, and someone came up with the inspiration that the organization meeting be held in that city, some 230 miles distant from Baddeck. In that way their charter would gain the dignity of being ratified in the capital city of the Province, while at the same time they could all have the experience of seeing a dirigible in flight. The entire group, Mrs. Bell included, boarded a train for Halifax.

The organization meeting of the Aerial Experiment Association took place in the Halifax Hotel on September 30, 1907, making it effective October 1. Besides a notary public, Bell arranged to have the signing witnessed by the U. S. Consul to Nova Scotia, David F. Wilder. First to affix his signature was Alexander Graham Bell; second, Glenn H. Curtiss.

In a subsequent session, Mabel Bell expressed her happiness in a written note, saying she would be glad to advance funds "from time to time," up to the amount of $20,000; her initial check was for $2000. A motion was adopted to accept her offer, providing that, for each $1000 she contributed, she would be assigned a 1 percent interest in any proceeds resulting from the work of the Association. Officers elected were: chairman, Dr. Bell; secretary, Tom Selfridge; treasurer, J. A. D. McCurdy. The officers then appointed Curtiss as director of experiments and F. W. (Casey) Baldwin as chief engineer.

Curtiss was voted a salary of $5000, which he accepted on condition that he would receive only half-pay whenever he was "not actually at the scene of operations or headquarters of the Association." Casey Baldwin's pay was set at $1000 and the same amount for McCurdy, whose duties also covered those of assistant engineer in special charge of photographic records. On his own motion, Selfridge would receive no salary, since he was on full pay from the Army. Dr. Bell refused to accept any payment, "as he did not wish to measure the value of his services by receiving a salary."

One of Selfridge's first secretarial acts was the reading of a prepared statement by Curtiss:

"In the first place I must say that I am thoroughly in accord with the plan and feel honored to have an opportunity to associate myself with Dr. Bell and the men who constitute the Association; and also express my admiration for Mrs. Bell who conceived the idea and made the Association possible.

"When Mrs. Bell first made known her proposition, I was not in a position to devote much time to the scheme, owing to my rather rapidly growing business, which I felt would not be made to pay without my personal and constant attention. In talking over my plans with Messrs. Bell, Baldwin, McCurdy and Selfridge, I stated that I believed arrangements could be made whereby I could give a large part of my time to the undertaking. A plan was formed in which I could give an active part and receive a salary of $5000 per year. With this in view I carried on negotiations to transfer my business to a new company which, however, necessitated my giving up a large part of my interest in business, but enabled me to absent myself much of the time by turning over the brunt of my business to others.

"As to the Association, my plan is to devote myself entirely to its interest, with the exception of the time required to handle important matters of my company. I shall be at the 'scene of action' as much as possible, but when not, I shall be constantly working to further the interests of the organization.

"Aside from the actual necessity of my continued identity with the Curtiss Company, I think it is quite desirable that the 'A.E.A.' be in touch with such a company backed by prominent men with plenty of capital which could take hold of the commerical end of the Association's achievements."

What Curtiss meant by the mention of transferring his business to a new company is not clear. As of that time, no new company was in the offing; perhaps he had explored the possibility of a reorganization while in Hammondsport, but thought better of it.

At the earliest opportunity, the Baddeck delegation went out to the Halifax fairgrounds where Captain Baldwin was performing. There the two Baldwins who played so large a role in Curtiss's career were introduced to one another (for some time to come, newspapers had difficulty untangling Tom Baldwin and Casey Baldwin). As if for the particular benefit of the group, Captain Tom gave an exceptionally good demonstration that day. Bell expressed himself as "delighted" with the first flight by man he had ever witnessed.

That evening, the balloon Baldwin joined the others for "a pleasant little dinner" which Dr. Bell hosted at the Halifax Hotel in celebration of the birth of the A.E.A. In an impromptu program, Bell jovially awarded two "loving cups" he had dug up in Halifax. The first was presented to Curtiss for being "the fastest man in the world" and for having built the engine which made Baldwin's balloon soar so well; the second to Captain Tom Baldwin for the excellence of his flight that afternoon, for having been an aeronaut for thirty-two years, and for being the first man to jump in a parachute "this side of the Atlantic Ocean."

✼   ✼   ✼

Once again, Curtiss was obligated by a prior engagement to curtail his stay at Beinn Bhreagh. While his associates went forward with completion of the *Cygnet*, he entrained back to Hammondsport, whence he proceeded to St. Louis in company with Tom Baldwin for a unique, if frustrating, episode.

His experience in flying the *California Arrow* had imbued him with the ambition to give a dirigible better speed. When he mentioned that he would like to design an airship of his own, Captain Tom not only humored him but offered to take him along for an aeronautic carnival in St. Louis where the new ship could be entered in competition.

There was no denying that Baldwin's gas bags were bulky and cumbersome. It was Curtiss's idea to make a streamlined envelope of lesser hydrogen capacity and to power it with an 8-cylinder motor. Such a craft, he figured, ought to go twice as fast as the *Arrows*.

At St. Louis he was in for disillusion. With its reduced buoyancy and the weight of the heavier engine, the one and only "Curtiss dirigible" never rose from the ground. Baldwin was too good-natured a man to rub it in, and Curtiss had cleared his decks for a different form of action in the air.

*   *   *

The Aerial Experiment Association had letterheads printed in Baddeck and a supply came to Hammondsport. In an upper ear of the sheet were listed the members, with "G. H. Curtiss, Director of Experiments" just beneath Alexander Graham Bell. In using one of these instead of his company letterhead to revive contact with the Wright brothers, Curtiss may have thought to impress them with his entry into the aeronautical field and his alliance with Bell. At any rate, he now offered to *give* them one of his engines, free of charge. The letter, dated December 30, 1907, said:

Dear Mr. Wright:—

Although I have been endeavoring to keep track of your movements by the newspapers, I am not sure which of the Brothers is in Dayton. Therefore, address you as above.

I just wish to keep in touch and let you know that we have been making considerable progress in engine construction. We are now turning out in addition to the 15, 20, 30 and 40 H.P. air cooled engines, a 4-cylinder vertical 5×5 water cooled and an 8-cylinder V 5×5 water cooled which we rate at 50 and 100 H.P. respectively. [Note: This is the earliest indication that Curtiss was starting to make watercooled motors.]

These engines embody the same design as our cycle motors which, as you may have heard, develop more power for the cylinder capacity than any others . . .

The 50 H.P. engine will weigh about 200 lbs. and the 100 about 350 lbs. We would be glad to furnish you with one of these gratis, providing you are in the market for engines, as we have great confidence in them. This proposition you will appreciate is not at all regular and is made you confidentially.

The writer has been getting rather deeply mixed in Aeronautics and Hammondsport is getting to be quite a headquarters for this class of work . . .

I understand from Gen. Allen [Chief of the Army Signal Corps], with whom I had a talk the other day in Washington, that the department are anxious to know more about your machine and will take steps which may lead to your giving a demonstration.

The specifications, a copy of which Dr. Bell read at our last meeting, seemed to me to be rather difficult to fulfill. You, of course, are the only persons who could possibly come any where near doing what is required and I sincerely hope you will be able to do business with the Government.

I should like very much to have you come to Hammondsport at any time you can find it convenient, not only that we may talk engine, but we would feel honored to make you our guests as long as you would care to stay.

The Wright brothers accepted neither the proffered gift nor the invitation. In his reply of January 17, 1908, Wilbur was coolly restrained and avoided mention of the A.E.A. Inasmuch as he had so lately reaffirmed to Chanute his prediction that nobody could possibly catch up with them in less than five years, he certainly had no fear of what the A.E.A. might accomplish; probably he assumed that it was concerned only with Bell's kites. He wrote:

Your very interesting letter of December 30th has been received. We thank you for your offer to us of your powerful motors for use on our flyer. We believe, however, that our own motor of 25 to 30 h.p. will be sufficient to meet all the requirements of the specifications of the U. S. Signal department, though it will not leave us much surplus. Our present machine is designed for 40 miles. Naturally we would prefer to use as small power as is possible and meet the requirements, since this would demonstrate a high efficiency in the designing of the aeroplane. We are expecting to make a bid.

We remember your visit to Dayton with pleasure. The experience we had together in helping Captain Baldwin back to the fair grounds was one not soon to be forgotten.

6. Red Wing

Under the program adopted by the Aerial Experiment Association, five "aerodromes" were to be created and hopefully flown during the year at its disposal—that is, one for each member. After Bell's tetrahedral had its opportunity, there was to be a pooling of ideas, although the man to whom a machine was nominally assigned would have the final word on matters of its design. As things worked out, the four "dromes" on which the younger members worked closely together adhered to the same general biplane pattern, each being an improvement over its predecessor.

Curtiss did not retrace his steps to Baddeck for the debut of the *Cygnet*. His services were of greater value in preparing facilities of his plant for whatever the A.E.A. involvement might demand of it; particularly so by placing in production the 8-cylinder engine which was to be his original airplane motor. No one doubted that Hammondsport would be the site chosen for winter quarters. The director of experiments had done all he reasonably could for the *Cygnet*, advising on the propeller and engine mounting. On his last trip he had solved a difficulty which his associates had been having with the "Curtiss

Number 2" engine: they could not induce it to run evenly with the single carburetor. He brought back with him four separate carburetors, attaching one to each cylinder, with favorable results.

The *Cygnet* was a rather graceful if not precisely swan-like edifice, containing 3393 silken tetrahedral cells in open latticework through which the air could pass with at least some freedom. Its unmanned weight was 208 pounds. Length at its ridgepole was 42½ feet, and from there the structure sloped outward to a fairly wide base while tapering in at the ends. It stood twice the height of a man. In the exact center, an open space or crawlway was provided amid the honeycomb of cells where the pilot was to lie prone on his stomach. At the rear entrance of this crawlway the engine and propeller were expected to be installed. On the underside were rubber floats for landing on water.

The schedule planned for the *Cygnet* was a preliminary motorless flight, under tow by a steamboat, with a man aboard; if all went well, then power would be added for the main test. Lieutenant Selfridge volunteered for the privilege of being first man in the air for the A.E.A. and Bell granted his wish; perhaps feeling it significant that an American Army officer should have the historic honor of initiating the pioneer man-carrying kite.

The moment arrived on December 7. Mabel Bell christened the kite with a cup of Beinn Bhreagh water poured over its bow. The *Cygnet* was lashed to launching arms on the raft, *Ugly Duckling*. Selfridge took his position in the crawlway with some meteorological instruments. Because of the chance that he might be plunged in the icy water, he was clad lightly in oilskins, without boots, and wrapped himself in rugs for warmth. The Victoria Steamship Company of Baddeck lent the use of its excursion vessel, the *Blue Hill*, for the towing.

The *Blue Hill* gradually got up speed on the Bras d'Or Lake, pulling the raft behind. The *Cygnet* was unleashed and rose prettily into the air at the end of a line unreeled from the stern. She climbed to an elevation of 168 feet and sailed along steadily for seven minutes. Then, in a change of wind, she settled back on the water so gently that Selfridge, with red silk cutting off his view on both sides, did not realize that he was down and failed to drop the towline in time. Just then a curtain of smoke drifted between the kite and the *Blue Hill*'s pilot house, so that the steamer kept churning full-speed ahead, dragging the *Cygnet* through waves. The fragile kite began to rip apart

1. Glenn H. Curtiss in 1912.
FROM THE J. LANSING CALLAN
COLLECTION.

2. The Curtiss homestead on Castle Hill, as it was around the turn of the century. FROM
PHOTO ALBUMS OF HENRY KLECKLER. COURTESY OF MRS. BLANCHE KLECKLER.

3. Two stars of the racing group known as the Hammondsport Boys. Mounted on the bicycle is C. Leonard (Tank) Waters, being given a shove by Glenn Curtiss. FROM THE J. LANSING CALLAN COLLECTION. COURTESY OF MRS. FREDERICK B. DOWNING.

4. Lena Neff and Glenn Curtiss make an attractive couple in this betrothal portrait. COURTESY OF GLENN H. CURTISS, JR.

5. Curtiss the hell-rider, after winning one of his many motorcycle racing victories. The track is perhaps in Riverdale, New York. COURTESY OF GLENN H. CURTISS, JR.

6. Lena Curtiss trying out one of her husband's early sidecars. Her driver is Tank Waters. COURTESY OF GLENN H. CURTISS, JR.

7. The monstrous 8-cylindered motorcycle which made Glenn Curtiss "fastest man in the world" at Ormond Beach, Florida. NATIONAL AIR AND SPACE MUSEUM.

8. Curtiss's first experience in the air. Captain Tom Baldwin permitted him a frolic with his newest *California Arrow* in June 1907. FROM A HENRY KLECKLER PHOTO ALBUM. COURTESY OF MRS. BLANCHE KLECKLER.

9. With buildings of Hammondsport for a backdrop, another Baldwin dirigible balloon ascends. The slim silhouette of the pilot suggests that he may have been Curtiss. If so, this was not his maiden flight. The defoliated trees indicate either early spring or late autumn. NATIONAL AIR AND SPACE MUSEUM.

10. Shop building of the G. H. Curtiss Manufacturing Company, probably in 1907. The odd vehicle at right is the "wind wagon," or "horse-scarer," devised by Curtiss to experiment with propellers for Baldwin's airships. COURTESY OF GLENN H. CURTISS, JR.

11. Built at Hammondsport, this was the earliest powered military aircraft in the United States. Captain Thomas Baldwin won the contract for Army Dirigible Number 1 and Curtiss was responsible for its engine. The picture shows one of the acceptance trials at Fort Myer, Virginia, with Baldwin at left on the catwalk and Curtiss up forward tending the motor. U. S. SIGNAL CORPS PHOTO IN THE NATIONAL ARCHIVES.

12. Beinn Bhreagh Hall, the summer home of Alexander Graham Bell in Nova Scotia, as it appeared in the early part of the century. PHOTOGRAPH BY GILBERT H. GROSVENOR, COURTESY AND COPYRIGHT, THE BELL FAMILY AND THE NATIONAL GEOGRAPHIC SOCIETY.

23 *Taken 1907 July 18 G.H.* *Dv. 1907 July 20 ?*

13. During his introductory visit to Beinn Bhreagh, Glenn Curtiss tried out on Baddeck Bay a novel boat which Bell's laboratory staff had built for propeller experiments. It was powered by a motorcycle engine he had shipped earlier. PHOTOGRAPH BY GILBERT H. GROSVENOR. COURTESY AND COPYRIGHT, THE BELL FAMILY AND THE NATIONAL GEOGRAPHIC SOCIETY.

14. Dr. Alexander Graham Bell and his wife, Mabel, strolling on their Nova Scotia estate. PHOTOGRAPH BY CHARLES MARTIN. COURTESY AND COPYRIGHT, THE BELL FAMILY AND THE NATIONAL GEOGRAPHIC SOCIETY.

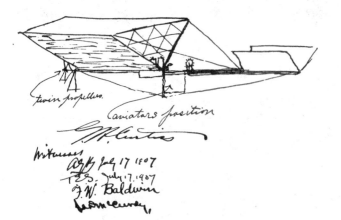

15. Curtiss's earliest known sketch of an idea for a flying machine. While at Beinn Bhreagh in the summer of 1907, he made this drawing on a page of Dr. Bell's *Home Notes*. Obviously, it was his conception of how engine power might be applied to a tetrahedral kite. The sketch was witnessed by Bell, Lieutenant Thomas E. Selfridge, F. W. Baldwin, and J. A. D. McCurdy. COURTESY AND COPYRIGHT, THE BELL FAMILY AND THE NATIONAL GEOGRAPHIC SOCIETY.

16. The members of the Aerial Experiment Association, lined up in the rose garden at Beinn Bhreagh at the time of organizing in 1907. They are, in order: Glenn H. Curtiss, Frederick W. (Casey) Baldwin, Dr. Bell, Lieutenant Thomas E. Selfridge, and J. A. D. McCurdy. PHOTOGRAPH BY GILBERT H. GROSVENOR. COURTESY AND COPYRIGHT, THE BELL FAMILY AND THE NATIONAL GEOGRAPHIC SOCIETY.

17. The tetrahedral kite *Cygnet* being readied for its trial ascent with a man (note the figure lying prone in the central aperture). Dr. Alexander Graham Bell stands at right of the dock. The house on the hill is the Lodge, Bell's original home at Baddeck. PHOTOGRAPH BY J. A. D. MCCURDY. COURTESY, THE BELL FAMILY. COPYRIGHT, NATIONAL GEOGRAPHIC SOCIETY.

18. In the wake of the *Cygnet* being towed by the steamer *Blue Hill* for its one and only trip aloft. Seen in black silhouette in the pilot's cell is Lieutenant Thomas Selfridge. PHOTOGRAPH BY JOHN MC NEIL. COURTESY AND COPYRIGHT, THE NATIONAL GEOGRAPHIC SOCIETY.

19. Experimental glider of the Aerial Experiment Association at the start of a run on a Hammondsport hillside. The rider is unidentified, but the assistant at right is obviously Augustus M. Post, observer for the Aero Club of America. NATIONAL AIR AND SPACE MUSEUM.

20. With his ice-cycle on frozen Keuka Lake, Glenn Curtiss tests both motor and propeller for the *Red Wing*, winter of 1908. NATIONAL AIR AND SPACE MUSEUM.

21. The air-cooled engine built by Curtiss for the *Red Wing*, which also served the *White Wing* and the *June Bug*. Note sheet-metal blades of the propeller, also individual carburetors for each cylinder. COURTESY AND COPYRIGHT, THE BELL FAMILY AND NATIONAL GEOGRAPHIC SOCIETY.

22. Drome Number 1 of the A.E.A., better known as the *Red Wing*, stands ready to make aviation history, March 12, 1908. Observe the sled runners for ice takeoff. COURTESY AND COPYRIGHT, THE BELL FAMILY AND NATIONAL GEOGRAPHIC SOCIETY.

23. The *Red Wing*, somewhat battered, after completing the first public flight by an airplane in the United States. J. LANSING CALLAN COLLECTION.

24. The *White Wing* held two valid distinctions: she was the first airplane in the United States to employ ailerons, also the first to take off on wheels. Doug McCurdy was on crutches because of a crackup with a Curtiss motorcycle. J. LANSING CALLAN COLLECTION.

25. Dr. Bell, who proposed the aileron concept, returned to Hammondsport for the *White Wing* trials. Here he talks it over with Casey Baldwin, who designed the ailerons in accord with his written suggestions. COURTESY OF MRS. BLANCHE KLECKLER.

26. With a modified version of his "wind-wagon," Curtiss experimented with propellers and wing surfaces for the A.E.A. aerodromes. COURTESY OF MRS. BLANCHE KLECKLER.

and Selfridge dove. He was picked up by a following motorboat and given liberal libations of a stimulant.

The *Cygnet* was a total loss, and thus never had her chance with an engine. Bell consoled himself by declaring that her behavior in the air had been "eminently satisfactory," and at once began planning for a *Cygnet II*, which would require many months to build. In the meanwhile the A.E.A. might proceed with another aerodrome, perhaps two, he ruled.

At an emergency meeting that night, Bell asserted that, by risking his life in the kite, Selfridge had earned the right to the next machine. This would now be designated as Drome Number 1. The members so voted. As a forerunner to that, and to give them some advance training in flight, Selfridge proposed that they commence with "a gliding machine modelled after the machines that have been successfully used in America and France." A resolution was adopted that such a glider be built at Hammondsport "under the direction of Mr. Curtiss," along such lines as Selfridge might recommend.

The Bells preferred to spend Christmas at Beinn Bhreagh, and the others remained until then. On Christmas Eve the A.E.A. held a meeting just long enough to pass a resolution transferring headquarters to Hammondsport "for the present."

*   *   *

After dispersing for the holiday week, the league of would-be aeronauts converged on the new seat of operations, Dr. and Mrs. Bell being the last to arrive. All took up residence in the Curtiss homestead, imparting to that commonplace house a sudden luminescence of gaiety, wit, and fellowship. The presence of the renowned inventor created a stir in the community, and every move he made was a matter of vital concern to the townsfolk. The grapevine carried the intelligence that he habitually studied and wrote in his room most of the night, then slept until noon. Mirth rippled through the village at the tidbit that Bell could not stand the jangling of the telephone, muffled its bell with paper, and grumbled: "Little did I think when I invented this thing that it would rise up to mock and annoy me!"

Following Selfridge's diagrams, Curtiss had a glider ready for use when the A.E.A. moved in. It was a simple affair of bamboo poles and white sheeting, patterned after the biplane gliders used by Octave

Chanute on the sand dunes of Lake Michigan. (As Bell was wont to say: "Any schoolboy could build a flying machine from Chanute's handbook.") The novices did their practice gliding on a snowclad flank of Washington Mountain, over on the eastern side of the valley. To get airborne, they ran down a slope and rode the wind as far as possible, dangling by their elbows from a hatch in the lower wing. These exercises continued over a period of two months, replacing one glider with another and toying with variations in tail and wings. Full reports and drawings of previous gliding experiments in both America and Europe were in their hands. One usage they did not bother to try was wing-bending. Having studied a copy of the Wright patent while in Baddeck, they were aware that any flexing of the surfaces would amount to infringement. More than that, however, they were unanimous in disliking the Wright method, considering it structurally unsound and therefore potentially dangerous. There had to be other ways of controlling a flying machine, and the greatest challenge facing them was to discover one to suit their purposes.

Of course, Bell took no personal part in the strenuous days of gliding, but he poured the vigor of his intellect into nightly after-dinner conclaves in a rear wing which Curtiss had called The Annex, but which the A.E.A. members rechristened as their "thinkorium." In these conferences, the plan for Drome Number 1 began to take form as a biplane with wings tapering, birdlike, to the tips; the engine mounted to the rear of the pilot and driving a pusher propeller. The idea was advanced, probably by Curtiss who was familiar with the local seasons, that it might be constructed in time for trials on runners from the ice of Keuka Lake. Those were evenings of animated conversation which often strayed to topics apart from aeronautics: once they talked about methods by which sound might be added to motion pictures.

As the accepted authority on aeronautical history because of his deep researches, Tom Selfridge held a leading role in these deliberations, and it was he who phrased the overall policy of the Association: ". . . to walk in the footprints of those who had gone before, and then advance beyond." In a sense, he conducted a seminar on aviation for his fellow members as they delved into a comprehensive study of the existing literature and of all aerial apparatus heretofore devised, including (in Bell's words) "what little was known or surmised of the machine of the Wright brothers, who were then working in secret and allowed very little information to leak out."

Selfridge was not convinced that the Wrights had been the first to fly, and passed on to his associates what he construed as the facts; at least, he wrote for their benefit a lengthy paper on the history of aerial experimentation in which he referred to Augustus M. Herring as "the first man, so far as we know, to have made a flight in a power driven machine." In this essay, he gave credence to Herring's claim of having left the ground twice with a compressed air engine at St. Joseph, Michigan, back in 1898. Going on to Kitty Hawk, he qualified the Wrights as "the second men in the world to get in the air in a dynamic flying machine."

As secretary of the A.E.A., Selfridge took it upon himself to query various experts for background material, in the tradition of the time by which experimenters usually exchanged information for the progress of the art. On January 15, 1908, he applied to the Wright brothers, not for any secret of their airplane but for some pointers on glider building:

"I am taking the liberty of writing you and asking your advice on certain points connected with gliding experiments, or rather glider construction, which we started here last Monday.

"Will you kindly tell me what results you obtained on the travel of the center of pressure both on aerocurve and aeroplanes?

"Also, what is a good, efficient method of constructing the ribs of the surfaces so that they will be light and yet strong enough to maintain their curvatures under ordinary conditions, and a good means of fastening them to the cloth and upper lateral cords of the frame?"

In all probability, Selfridge would have read aloud, in the "thinkorium," Wilbur's reply of January 18, which was reasonably cooperative: "The travel of the center of pressure on aeroplanes is from the center at 90 degrees, toward the front edge as the angle becomes smaller" (by "aeroplanes" meaning wings). He gave some other data relating to gliders, and referred Selfridge to certain documents, including their patent, which the A.E.A. already had seen. "The ribs of our gliders," he added, "were made of second growth ash, steamed and bent to shape." (The Wrights would not afterward let the world forget that Selfridge asked for this information at the outset of the A.E.A. work.)

As one who was openly critical of the Wrights' secrecy, Dr. Bell swung the pendulum to the opposite extreme with the A.E.A.: he courted the fullest publicity, and invited anyone and everyone to come and watch. The move to New York State brought the activities within

easier range of coverage for major newspapers, and the Associated Press
was alerted. The Aero Club of America quickly located Hammondsport
and delegated its secretary, Augustus M. Post, to keep a close eye
on what was transpiring there. Post was on the spot even before the
Canadian contingent arrived, and he became for many months a virtual
resident of the village. A handsome chap in his mid-thirties, flaunting
a carefully groomed black beard, Post was independently wealthy and
an active sportsman-balloonist, later to win an international balloon
race.

Unfortunately, the Bells were prevented from staying the winter in
Hammondsport. By the end of January, Mabel Bell was stricken with
a serious illness. Regretfully, Dr. Bell decided that he must get his
wife back to their Washington home and remain with her there until
she was improved. Thus he was unavoidably absent while Drome Number 1 was being produced.

*   *   *

Meanwhile, Curtiss had become implicated in a government contract of extreme significance. The United States Army at last had come
around to purchasing one dirigible balloon and one aeroplane. Signal
Corps Dirigible Number 1 was destined to be the first powered aircraft to enter military service anywhere in the world, and Curtiss was
committed to manufacturing and installing the engine for it, which
meant that he would also be its engineer during the acceptance demonstrations. Although the contract belonged to Captain Thomas S. Baldwin, Curtiss was in effect a partner to it.

The sequence of events had begun at the St. Louis air carnival
of the previous October, for which Curtiss had rushed back from Nova
Scotia. Brigadier General James Allen, Chief Signal Officer, had been
in attendance, watched Baldwin's flights with interest, and talked with
him about building a dirigible for the Army. If this were to be feasible,
General Allen made clear, the balloon would have to be larger and
more durable, capable of carrying two men and of making a speed
of 20 miles per hour. During that autumn, Baldwin and Curtiss made
trips to Washington for further conferences with Allen and his staff.
What the Army desired was an airship which could soar for two hours
at a time, and this requirement ruled out an air-cooled motor ("the
engine must have suitable cooling arrangements, so that excessive heating will not occur"). No aircraft had yet flown with water cooling,

which, of necessity, would add weight. Curtiss thought he could meet the demand by converting a 4-cylinder motor. This development accounts for the fact that he was abruptly going in for water-cooled engines, as he had revealed in his letter to the Wright brothers at the end of 1907.

Baldwin conceived an airship about double the capacity of his latest *California Arrow*, and his next hurdle was the fabric for the envelope. The Army would not settle for the usual varnished silk, which deteriorated too rapidly and leaked gas. Baldwin went to the Hodgman Rubber Company and asked if it would be practical to seal a layer of rubber between two layers of Japanese silk. The company . ran off a sample, and this hastily invented rubberized silk satisfied the Army. With such behind-the-scenes arrangements in advance, it was assured that the Signal Corps would hand the contract to Baldwin, although it was necessary to go through the formality of asking bids. Baldwin entered a bid of $6750, deliberately losing money on the deal (Roy Knabenshue said) in order to make certain of being low. None of the eight other bids even came close, nor could any other dirigible have matched the specifications. The contract was awarded to Baldwin on February 24, 1908. Deadline for delivery was 150 days.

Hammondsporters were able to divert their attention from what Bell's Boys were up to long enough to exult over this heartening news affecting two local industries. The *Herald* went out on a limb to clarion: "The Baldwin craft will be the nucleus of an aerial war squadron."

As Wilbur Wright had told Curtiss in his letter declining the gift of an engine, he and Orville intended to submit a bid to the Signal Corps for a military airplane. While nursing the grievance at having been cold-shouldered in their early overtures to Washington, the Wrights had striven in vain for a military contract with some European nation. At last, through the intercession of the Aero Club, a negotiation was opened in 1907 between them and the U. S. War Department, only to founder on their stiff demand for $100,000 for a single plane which they did not propose to let anyone see in advance of signing a contract. The Board of Ordnance and Fortification did not have that kind of funds to play with, and was still smarting from the criticism it had taken for spending $50,000 on the Langley plane. Thus stood the situation when Wilbur returned from Europe late in November and was invited to Washington for a talk with the Board, which resulted in the more rational figure of $25,000; Wilbur agreeing to supply a machine which would carry two men, stay airborne for at least an hour, and attain a minimal speed of 40 miles per hour. Specifications were drawn to this effect.

Again the Signal Corps must go through the formality of advertising for bids, even though it was committed to the Wright plane. In forty-one proposals opened on February 1, 1908, only three bidders purported to meet the specifications: the Wrights, at $25,000; Augustus M. Herring, at $20,000; and James F. Scott of Chicago, at $1000. The Army could not legally ignore the two bids which were lower than the Wrights', and so was faced with a dilemma; this was resolved by a hasty juggling act permitting it to accept all three of the low bids. Scott soon let the War Department off the hook by admitting he was in no position to fulfill the contract, but Herring hung on doggedly.

*   *   *

Before the A.E.A. sprouted wings, it was necessary to have wheels. A Peerless 4-cylinder automobile was purchased for transport of the members around town. The Curtiss plant being already crowded beyond its limit, an "aerodrome shed" was erected down on the Kingsley Flats, near the lakefront east of town; in summer this patch of filled land served as both a cow pasture and a diamond for the Curtiss Baseball Team, which was challenging other industrial teams.

The shaping of Selfridge's Drome Number 1 was begun in the "aerodrome shed" before the end of January. Construction details were in charge of William F. Bedwin, superintendent of the Bell laboratories in Nova Scotia. (Bedwin was the chief of those loyal retainers whom Bell had wished to make members of the A.E.A.) Curtiss resurrected his "ice-cycle" on the frozen lake for testing of the engine and propeller. A metal propeller was decided upon, consisting of flapper-like blades of sheet steel riveted to tubular frames; it was to be driven direct from the engine shaft.

"Drome Number 1" was too ordinary a title to suit so venturesome a machine and so imaginative a crew; besides, Bell had set a precedent with his *Cygnet* for pinning fanciful names on the A.E.A. creations. Selfridge had no trouble finding a label for his "drome." For its fabric, a supply of the red silk used in Bell's kites had been brought from Baddeck. Thus bedizened, the *Red Wing* practically named herself.

It cannot be said that one man more than another fashioned the *Red Wing*, since there was a meshing of minds. To the extent that

Tom Selfridge held the ultimate whip hand over its design and did not hesitate to inject his own ideas, he shed an influence over all four of the Hammondsport productions, which bore a family resemblance to one another. But Casey Baldwin, who took seriously and merited his title of chief engineer, patently had much to do with its configuration. Of course, Curtiss was almost solely responsible for the power plant. A good deal of careful thought and discussion went into it. The A.E.A. machines were "designed, not just thrown together," J. A. D. McCurdy emphasized at a time when he was the last survivor of the group. This was not a matter of rough sketches on a wall, but of calculated stresses and precise engineering drawings; as well as learning from mistakes as one machine led to another.

The most vivid imagination could not have pictured the *Red Wing* as an imitation of anything that ever flew before.[1] Not one of the five had ever seen an aeroplane. Its form was nothing if not original, apart from being a biplane. Selfridge sanctioned, if he did not personally originate, the radical departure from horizontally parallel wings. These wings were arched outward one from another, like a sidelong pair of parentheses, and tapered toward the ends. The upper wing, a trifle longer than the lower, actually came to pointed tips. The theory behind this peculiar configuration was that it would facilitate turning in the air, while at the same time making for lateral stability. There was no other device at all for stability control. The ruling aim was to achieve a minimum of air resistance. A vertical rudder panel jutted behind on fishpole outriggers. "We used a lot of bamboo in those A.E.A. planes," Henry Kleckler would recall. (Possibly the bamboo idea originated with Curtiss, whose memory harked back to the fishpole masts of his skate-sails as a boy on the lake.) Because the weather was apt to be cold for the trials, the *Red Wing* had the ancestor of all airplane cockpits: a wedge-shaped enclosure stuck out in front to shield the pilot's legs. They hoped it would fly the length of the lake.

Among its numerous flaws, there was one defect about the *Red Wing* which was almost comical: in their anxiety to get in the air, they hadn't given much thought to getting down again. The ignition switch was placed beneath the seat, and the pilot could not let go of the controls to reach it before landing.

Not quite all of the time that winter was spent in gliding, study, and constructing the *Red Wing*. Bell's Boys (as they were now often called) were socially popular in the community, and the doors of the wine aristocracy were opened to them. During February, Mrs. Harry

Champlin, whose husband was owner of the Stony Brook Farm race-track, was hostess for a fashionable soirée at which dancing continued into the small hours. Selfridge, Baldwin, and McCurdy were lions of the occasion.

*   *   *

Curtiss warned his confrères that they should have the *Red Wing* ready for trial by the first of March. Any time after the middle of that month the break-up could come on Keuka Lake. In fact, there was already three miles of open water at the south end of the lake when March blew in, and preparations were made to have the *Red Wing* ferried to the margin. The state of Mabel Bell's health was still such that her devoted husband did not feel justified in leaving her side for the momentous event.

Selfridge was keyed up to be the first of the A.E.A. men to "get into the air" with an airplane, as he had been with the kite, but weather conspired with the Army to cheat him of the privilege. A remorseless wind whipped out of the north for days on end, and before it ceased he was compelled to obey a military summons for business in Washington. As might have been predicted, the wind promptly died down overnight, leaving a calm, biting cold in its wake.

It was March 12, 1908. The three members remaining at Hammondsport had no choice but to take advantage of the weather while they had it. Feeling a trifle guilty about supplanting Selfridge, they drew lots to determine which would fly the *Red Wing* first. Casey Baldwin was the winner.

The fact that the *Red Wing* was about to try her pinions was freely announced in Hammondsport and flashed on the wires. Defiant of cold, a major share of the population trooped down both shores of the lake and many walked out on the ice to have a nearer view. A tugboat, the *Springstead*, bore the airplane down the lake on its deck. Because the receding ice margin was thin at the edge, there was considerable difficulty with the unloading. During this operation, Tank Waters managed to tumble overboard and was fished out of icewater.

Casey Baldwin perched on the narrow ledge forward of the engine and shoved his legs inside the shield. Henry Kleckler strongarmed the prop. While the motor was warming, the "ground crew" held the wings fast. At a signal, they let go and the *Red Wing* skittered over the ice "like a scared rabbit." After a run of 200 feet she "jumped into the air" and spectators raised a cheer. At an altitude of between 10 and 20 feet, she flew levelly for a long, breathless moment, then slipped off sidewise. A wing ticked ice and the machine spun around. The wing telescoped and the tail frame bent, but Baldwin stepped forth undamaged.

Curtiss and McCurdy came dashing with a tape to measure the distance over which the runners had left no trace in the snow. It was 318 feet, 11 inches. "We were jubilant," Curtiss said. "We knew now that we could build another machine that would fly higher and longer."

What the *Red Wing* had succeeded in doing was hailed then and ever afterward known as the first public flight by an airplane in the United States. It was also proclaimed the longest first trial yet accomplished by a heavier-than-air machine. Incidentally, the flight had been done by a citizen of Canada.

That the Wright brothers resented the "first public flight" claim was revealed by Wilbur in a letter to the editor of the *Scientific American*. "In 1904 and 1905," he said, "we were flying every few days in a field alongside the main wagon road and electric trolley line from Dayton to Springfield, and hundreds of travelers and inhabitants saw the machine in flight. Anyone who wished could look. We merely did not advertise the flights in the newspapers." (On second thought, he struck out this paragraph before the letter was published.)

*   *   *

The *Red Wing* was barged back to town for repairs and another try.

Two nights later, the Aero Club of America held its second annual banquet at the Hotel St. Regis in New York, with Dr. Alexander Graham Bell as the reluctant hero of the evening. Bell came from Washington on the stipulation that he would not be called on to speak. Not having been at the scene, he was annoyed because the newspaper reports of the *Red Wing* flight referred to it as "Bell's Aerodrome." The other A.E.A. members were seated at the same table as guests of honor.

The 250 banqueters gave Bell such an ovation that he was finally forced to respond. "I really had nothing to do with the success of the aeroplane," he said, "except my interest in the experiment. The machine did better than anyone expected, but the credit for its success was due to G. H. Curtiss of Hammondsport, F. W. Baldwin, J. A. D. McCurdy. Mr. Curtiss, who may be called the motor expert of America, produced an engine developing 40-horsepower, weighing but 145 pounds, for the machine.

"In the company of experimenters, I must include the names of Lieutenant Selfridge of the U. S. Army and Mrs. Bell, who supplied the capital for the scientific experiments to get the machine in the air. This is the first time in America that a woman has taken an active part in making an experiment in aeronautics a complete success."

Bell took the occasion to praise the attainments of the Wright brothers, but "deprecated their secrecy in not making public the nature of their experiments."

                              *   *   *

The second and valedictory flight of the *Red Wing* took place on St. Patrick's Day, and Casey Baldwin wore a green necktie as he once again took the pilot's seat. The good saint seems to have been looking the other way. The weather outlook was anything but good. By this time the ice had disintegrated so far that the tugboat had to steam 8 miles down the lake to find a solid margin. In a letter describing the occasion, Curtiss wrote to Mrs. Bell: "We saw some very good samples of flying machines on the way down. The edge of the ice which had been broken up was completely lined with gulls, wild duck and wild geese. While trying to land, it began to snow and then rain." The silken fabric was so drenched that he estimated the moisture added 50 pounds to the weight of the plane, and that most of this weight was back of the center of gravity, "which, I believe, had something to do with the accident."

Nonetheless, Baldwin took off "in the teeth of a 10-mile wind" and lifted unevenly from the ice after 50 feet. The right runner came up first and the aircraft continued tilting to the left in a cross-wind. Casey struggled in vain to head back into the wind. Instead, he crashed on the tip of the left wing. The crumpling of the wing cushioned the shock for both him and the engine. The length of the flight was 40 yards.

Tom Selfridge arrived back in town next day to find his beloved *Red Wing* a tangle of "matchwood and rags." A fellow passenger on the train up from New York was Augustus M. Herring, coming to scan the wreckage and scout for a means of getting his foot in the door of the A.E.A. A day or two later, Selfridge wrote Herring "to take advantage of your generous offer to make a few suggestions should we decide to rebuild." After detailing how the smashup occurred, he concluded: "We have decided to rebuild immediately and would be more than glad to receive any suggestion you might care to make."

7. White Wing

By the logic of events, Casey Baldwin was in line for the proprietorship of Drome Number 2. As Selfridge had taken his gamble in the kite, so Baldwin had risked his neck in the *Red Wing* and been the first of the group to qualify as an "aviator." The engine was intact and could be used again. But they had run out of red silk, which was ritzy stuff, anyway, for a rough-and-tumble flying-machine. And so, for wing fabric, they turned to white muslin nainsook, which predestined the name of the second "drome": *White Wing.*

As they surveyed the ruins of the *Red Wing*, the copartners reminded each other: "We've got to have lateral stability."

Mulling over the reports sent him in Washington, Bell was struck with the same thought, and told Casey that a decision had to be made at once on "how to improve the lateral stability to prevent sliding off on one side." Bell's suggested remedy was "moveable surfaces at the extremities of the wing piece," and he added: ". . . it might be worth while considering whether the protruding ends might not be made moveable and be controlled by the instinctive balancing movements of the body of the operator . . . In voluntary control by moveable surfaces what we want to do is reef one wing and extend the other."

In those words Alexander Graham Bell clearly enunciated the fundamental concept of the aileron (nowadays better known as wing-flaps). It can hardly be gainsaid that the aileron was the turning-point for aviation, whoever its originator. (The wing-warping of the Wrights, to be sure, obtained about the same effect, though less efficiently. The visual fact remains that the aileron was a separate and distinct device. As Curtiss once said, if the Wrights had thought of it they would have incorporated it in their patent.)

All evidence points to Bell's having arrived at the idea quite independently, although it had been minimally used before in France. Robert Esnault-Pelterie, in glider experiments in 1904, began by trying out the Wrights' wing-warping and then discarded it as "dangerous"; he substituted "two independent horizontal rudders, one placed at either extremity of the aeroplane."[1] Santos-Dumont in 1906 adapted the same artifice to his *Number 14 bis,* in the form of two octagonal surfaces mounted between the outer wing struts and moveable by the pilot.

The rock-ribbed integrity of Dr. Bell was an outstanding characteristic. If he had picked up the aileron inspiration from a European source, he would have been the first to say so. What he did say on the subject later that year (in the *A.E.A. Bulletin*) was this: "I do not know exactly the circumstances that led to the adoption of the moveable wing tips as I was in Washington at the time; but if, as I have reason to believe, their adoption was due to a suggestion of mine that moveable wing tips should be used, contained in a letter to Mr. Baldwin, I may say that this suggestion was made without any knowledge upon my part of anything the Wright brothers may have done. They had kept the details of construction of their machine secret." (Of course, the twisting of forward margins was in their patent.)

A piece of Curtiss testimony on this point was subsequently heard: "Lateral balance was often the subject of discussion [by the A.E.A.]. We were familiar with the warping wing system of the Wrights and we hoped to develop some other system of balance . . . The second machine was fitted with what we afterwards called ailerons. We called them at the time wing tips . . . I personally favored controlling these surfaces, but some of the others thought there might be sufficient inherent stability in the machine to be able to fly it, and they thought we couldn't handle so many controls at once."

A radically differing version was given by Augustus Herring who, on a witness stand years afterward, arrogated the credit to himself. When Selfridge welcomed suggestions from him, he proposed the "auxiliary surfaces for lateral stability," he testified. Herring claimed to have had ailerons on a glider in 1894 (but did not explain, when specifically asked, why he never put them on a later machine). According to him, he advised Selfridge also on how to make a better propeller.

* * *

At all events, the *White Wing* holds the honor of having been the first airplane in America to be controlled by ailerons. The success achieved and the publicity reaped, by this and its A.E.A. successors, brought ailerons to the world's attention and sparked their universal adoption. But it was some time before Bell's Boys even heard the French word (which means "pinion" or "little wing").

The actual designing of the moveable tips fell to the lot of Casey Baldwin, to whom Bell tossed the idea. He produced triangular, sharply pointed flaps on hinges beyond the ends of both top and bottom wings. They were moved up or down, differentially, by means of cords attached to the pilot's body, as he leaned right or left in reflex to the plane's tilting.

* * *

Because the next flying would need to be done from land, the *White Wing* acquired another valid distinction: she would be the first airplane on wheels this side of the Atlantic. (Again, the French were ahead.) The A.E.A. never considered the monorail-and-weight-dropping to which the Wrights clung. Aside from motors, Curtiss was in an ideal position to supply wheels. His motorcycle works turned out three wire-spoked wheels, with pneumatic tires, a trifle smaller than the standard cycle size, for the tricycle landing gear of the new "drome." In most other respects, she followed the general style of her red-winged sister, although she was favored with a laminated spruce propeller. The "cockpit" enclosure for the pilot was enlarged as more of a windshield, and a horizontal elevator stuck out in front.

Flat, dry fields were at a premium in Pleasant Valley. Where to fly the *White Wing?* Probably Curtiss had this question answered well in advance. It would have been strange if he had not thought of the racetrack of his bicycling days. Although Harry Champlin still bred trotting-horses, he cheerfully offered the use of his oval track at Stony Brook Farm for the benefit of aeronautics. In this way the officials and employees of the Pleasant Valley winery got a grandstand seat for whatever prodigies were about to transpire on the flats overlooked by their hillside doors and windows.

Curtiss placed motorcycles at the disposal of his young colleagues, and McCurdy and Baldwin went spinning in all directions on the rural highways, even racing each other around Keuka Lake. "McCurdy used to give us daily demonstrations of how to fall off a motorcycle scientifically," Curtiss remembered.

Having missed the *Red Wing* act completely, Dr. Bell had his heart set on seeing the *White Wing* initiated. Happily, his wife's health was improved sufficiently so that he was able to leave her for a few days, and was in Hammondsport to observe the completion and the first few test hops of Drome Number 2. Chatting with newsmen, he pointed out that "every known type of flying machine" was now represented there, saying: "In no other locality on earth is there such an assemblage of genius along the line of aerial work as Hammondsport can now boast of, being attracted hither by the Curtiss motors, acknowledged to be the lightest and strongest motors made."

Oliver Jones was finishing his dirigible, *Boomerang*, and planning next to tackle a large monoplane. Someone had brought a so-called ornithopter to town. A Hungarian ex-officer from Budapest, Lieutenant Alexander L. Pfitzner, was on the scene building a light monoplane around a Curtiss engine. Especially intriguing to the men of the A.E.A. was an experimental helicopter being nursed along by I. Newton Williams, an elderly typewriter manufacturer from Derby, Connecticut. Prudently, Williams kept it tied down with ropes, but its rotors lifted it a foot or two off ground.

At Stony Brook Farm, a tent was pitched as shelter for the *White Wing*. The raised sides of the horse track scraped the lower wing of the plane, and so she was tried on the grassy infield, only to break the wheel supports on rough sod. Harry Champlin was so cooperative as to order the track widened by plowing up marginal ground and having the sides rolled flat.

When the machine showed reluctance to lift during dry runs, it was realized that the nainsook was porous to air. Bell suggested varnishing the cloth, which proved a big help.

On May 18, the "drome" became airborne to a height of 10 feet, with Casey Baldwin piloting. It touched down after 93 yards because the lower wing surged up and fouled the propeller. Dr. Bell was so exuberant that he gave a mass interview to the press, saying: "We had the first very promising spring into the air today, showing that the machine will fly. It was not very much in itself, but a very great thing as showing what it may do in the future . . . We will go slowly about the matter. We are not trying to exhibit an aerodrome for popularity. We are trying scientific experiments . . . One object in having Glenn H. Curtiss associated with us is to lead him to develop a lighter and stronger motor, suitable for flying machines. He has already beaten America in producing light motors."

On the following day, an officer of the U. S. Army flew an airplane for the first time in history. Tom Selfridge finally had his inning. In fact, he then made two hops in rapid succession. The first was off ground only 100 feet, aborting because a loose guy wire caught in the propeller. The second was "a beautiful and steady flight of 240 feet," at 20 feet altitude, even though it ended in a plowed field, damaging the forward wheel. A reporter found it "an inspiring spectacle"; that Selfridge "soared as gracefully as a bird"; and that "There was no apparent reason except the inexperience of the operator to prevent the continuation of the flight indefinitely."

For the next turn, McCurdy deferred to Curtiss on the score that it was his engine. Before he would make the attempt, Glenn asked permission of the others to remove the "cloth covering" in front—that is, the pilot's windshield, which obstructed the view. Curtiss wanted the nose to be "entirely open so that the aviator can see the ground and better gauge distances." Meanwhile the nose wheel had been made steerable when they discovered that the rear rudder was not going to do the job for them on the ground. A fourth wheel was added beneath the tail. "We soon learned that it was comparatively easy to get the machine up in the air," said Curtiss, "but it was most difficult to get it back to earth without smashing something. The fact was, we had not learned the art of landing an aeroplane with ease and safety."

Bell did not see Curtiss make his debut as an airplane pilot, having returned to Washington. This occurred on May 21, by coincidence Glenn's 30th birthday. It was reported by Selfridge in a telegram to Charles F. Thompson of the Associated Press in New York:

G. H. CURTISS OF THE CURTISS MANUFACTURING COMPANY MADE A FLIGHT OF 339 YARDS (1017 FEET) IN TWO JUMPS IN BALDWIN'S WHITE WING THIS AFTERNOON AT 6.47 P.M.

IN THE FIRST JUMP HE COVERED 205 YARDS THEN TOUCHED, ROSE
IMMEDIATELY AND FLEW 134 YARDS FURTHER WHEN THE FLIGHT ENDED ON
THE EDGE OF A PLOUGHED FIELD. THE MACHINE WAS IN PERFECT CONTROL
AT ALL TIMES AND WAS STEERED FIRST TO THE RIGHT AND THEN TO THE
LEFT BEFORE LANDING. THE 339 YARDS WAS COVERED IN 19 SECONDS OR 37
MILES PER HOUR.

People in the outskirts of Hammondsport were thrilled at seeing the
white bird in the air above the racetrack fences. In his very first experience in flying an airplane, Curtiss had performed the best and longest
flight to date for the A.E.A. This meant, of course, that he had also
made the longest public flight yet in America. He expressed his own
reaction with an economy of words: "I felt very much elated."

Two days later the brief but happy career of the *White Wing* was
ended by Doug McCurdy. After four hops by the "veterans," she was
turned over to the Canadian who had proved so accident-prone on a
motorcycle. Failing to use the ailerons properly to correct for a "quarter-
ing wind," he careened and struck the right wing. The plane pivoted
on its nose and flipped, ending on its back with wheels up. Somehow,
in the maneuver, McCurdy was "deposited gently" on the ground. He had
covered 183 yards, nonetheless.

The Wright brothers may have shrugged off the *Red Wing* as having
merely "jumped," but they could not ignore the *White Wing*. On June 7,
Orville Wright concluded a letter to Wilbur, who was in Europe getting
ready to make their own introductory flights in the public eye: "I see by
one of the papers that the Bell outfit is offering Red Wings for sale at
$5000 each. They have got some nerve." The thought continued to
rankle, and on June 28 he wrote again: "Curtiss et al. are using our
patents, I understand, and are now offering machines for sale at $5000
each, according to the Scientific American. They have got good cheek!"

Considering their habitual distrust of the accuracy of the press in
relation to their own affairs, it seems strange that one of the brothers was
so ready to accept at face value such a manifestly fictitious report. What
the *Scientific American* did indeed print, in the windup to its glowing
account of the *White Wing*'s exploits, was this: "The builders will duplicate this machine for anyone desiring one for $5000, delivery to be made
within 60 days."

The origin of that unfounded assertion remains a mystery. No person connected with the A.E.A. could legitimately have said it.

8. June Bug

The *White Wing* could have been salvaged and flown some more. In fact, the first impulse after McCurdy's crackup was to do this, with an estimate of two weeks for repair. Once again the engine had come through unscathed, as had the propeller.

But a mood of exultation now gripped the men of the A.E.A. Beyond their wildest hopes and sooner than expected, they had succeeded in getting into the air, and in a really persuasive manner. With their second throw of the dice, they had made the breakthrough to lateral control. They knew that this machine could be quickly improved upon. Then why loiter?

Especially was Curtiss caught up in this mood because the Association had allocated Drome Number 3 to him. Moreover, now that he had tasted the sensation of flight, he liked it enormously. A new world was opening before him. The route to real speed, he could see, lay in the air. He had tried and failed to make a speedier dirigible. Now he understood that the machine with wings was the vehicle to defy limitations.

Besides, the old competitive instinct of Glenn Curtiss was simul-

taneously aroused. A year earlier the *Scientific American*, a weekly periodical which was ardently plugging aeronautics, had deposited in the
custody of the Aero Club of America a large and beautiful silver trophy.
It was the first reward for a feat of heavier-than-air flying ever dangled
in the United States. Initially put forward as bait for a contest at the
Jamestown Tercentenary Exposition of 1907, it drew only a couple of
feckless entries, and failed to lure the Wrights out of hiding. No doubt
Curtiss had seen and admired the trophy at the Aero Club rooms on
42nd Street in New York, where Tom Baldwin had introduced him. The
collecting of trophies was, so to speak, a hobby of his. This specimen
was no ordinary loving cup but more like a piece of sculpture. Grouped
around its green onyx base were silver-winged horses with riders bearing
olive branches. Rising from the pedestal amid argentine swirls of cloud
was a silver cartouche upholding the globe of Earth. Langley's dragonfly
airplane was in flight at last, pinned like a brooch to the bosom of the
sphere. Perched atop the pile was the American eagle, a wreath of victory clamped in his beak. The silver alone was valued at $2500, but
money was not the measure of its worth.

Under the rules, an individual must win this resplendent object at
least once in three separate years in order to gain its permanent possession, pending which time the Aero Club retained custody and the name
of each year's winner was to be engraved in the silver. The first leg
called for a straightaway flight of one kilometer (3281 feet). After that
the terms were to be toughened for each remaining leg, to accord with
advances in aviation.

In brief, Curtiss coveted that trophy. He proposed that the damaged
White Wing be scrapped and that his Drome Number 3 be built as
soon as possible with the deliberate intent of going after the Scientific
American Trophy. His confrères heartily agreed and were equally impatient to get on with it. As for Dr. Bell, he had already changed his
schedule, due mainly to his wife's slow convalescence but partly to the
amazing progress at Hammondsport. Instead of transferring the A.E.A.
back to Nova Scotia in June to start work on his next kite, *Cygnet II*, he
notified his young friends to go ahead with Drome Number 3 as an
improvement over the *White Wing*. In order to be on hand for its
first trials, he arranged a later and more leisurely itinerary to Baddeck
via Hammondsport and Toronto. The tetrahedral kite would have to wait.

So far as Curtiss was concerned, time was urgent for a reason other
than the trophy. He was committed to seeing Captain Baldwin's Army
dirigible contract through to a finish, and this entailed his acting as

the engineer in its demonstration flights during August. Meanwhile
he was dividing his time, helping Baldwin finish the balloon with
special reference to its new type of water-cooled engine. Tom Selfridge,
incidentally, was designing the propeller for the dirigible.

With the go-ahead for his "drome," Curtiss switched priorities for
the nonce. There were certain fresh ideas of his own to be incorporated.
The group had been talking about a double propeller for the next
machine (that is, two propellers on the same shaft). But the making
of an extra prop would consume too much time, so Curtiss contented
himself with the same one used on the *White Wing*, cutting down its
length by three inches. The same varnished nainsook served for
wing fabric, but the wing surface area was considerably reduced. The
wing-tip ailerons were larger and longer, the tail smaller.

The main point Curtiss strove to make with this machine (and Bell
later credited him almost exclusively with its "special features") was
that an airplane would be more controllable with greater speed and
steerage way. Cutting air resistance wherever possible, he lengthened
the central body structure, pushing the pilot's perch two feet forward
and the engine five inches backward. The front elevator went farther
ahead and the wedge-shaped nose was left uncovered. The tricycle
wheel-base was extended two feet. Switch and spark controls were placed
conveniently on the steering wheel instead of under the seat.

For the lay observer, the most obvious innovation was the shoulder
yoke, replacing the cords for control of the ailerons. This was a U-shaped
fork fitting around the pilot's shoulders, moving as he leaned, and it
became a hallmark, next to ailerons themselves, on early Curtiss aircraft

Drome Number 3 was finally assembled and ready for testing at
Stony Brook Farm. Before doing another thing about it, Curtiss drove
his Stoddard-Dayton automobile around to the home of Mrs. Malinda
Bennitt and invited her to ride out and see his new bird. Mrs.
Bennitt was the elderly widow who had given him the rent-free use
of his original bicycle shop. Of late years she had been living with
sons in Joliet, Illinois, but returned to occupy her Hammondsport
house each summer.

Curtiss pulled up beside the "drome" and, while she was voicing
her admiration, he announced: "Mrs. Bennitt, I reserve for you the
privilege of naming this aeroplane."

Mrs. Bennitt was flustered, and for the life of her could not think
of an appropriate name. "My old head just wouldn't work," she recalled.

Consequently, Dr. Bell coined the name for the most immortal of the A.E.A. machines: *June Bug*. The fat flying beetles known as june bugs were out in full force, bumbling around the village every evening, and Bell had scrutinized them with a scientist's eye. He noticed that their heavy outer wings were held stiffly out from their sides during flight, while the actual work of moving them through the air was done by more delicate under-wings fluttering beneath. The insects reminded him of the way their "dromes" operated, with rigid wings and pusher propeller.[1]

If the christening had been delayed a few days longer, it may conceivably have been the *Yellow Wing*. The varnish filler of the wing fabric, the A.E.A. discovered, quickly cracked in the summer heat. They substituted a mixture of turpentine, paraffin, and gasoline, adding yellow ochre for coloring to show up better in photographs. (This was the first use in America of what later came to be known as "wing dope.")

On June 21, 1908, a telegram went to Thompson of the Associated Press saying that the *June Bug* had made three successful flights with Curtiss at the controls: the first covering a distance of 456 feet; the second, 417 feet; and the third 1266 feet at 34½ miles per hour. The message concluded: THIS LAST FLIGHT IS THE LONGEST YET MADE IN PUBLIC IN AMERICA, AND IS ONLY MR. CURTISS'S FOURTH ATTEMPT. GRAHAM BELL.

Having seen the *June Bug* merrily on the wing, Dr. Bell and his wife resumed their unhurried journey to Nova Scotia, after arranging a schedule of way-points where telegrams could be sent them en route. For the sake of Mrs. Bell's health, they were to travel by steamboat from Toronto across Lake Ontario, thence down the St. Lawrence to Prince Edward Island.

The first telegram, signed by McCurdy, reached Bell at his Toronto hotel on June 25: JUNE BUG MADE RECORD FLIGHT EARLY THIS MORNING, 725 YARDS AT AN ELEVATION OF 40 FEET . . . TIPS WORKED BEAUTIFULLY AND MACHINE UNDER PERFECT LATERAL CONTROL . . . SURFACES HAVE BEEN REVARNISHED AND COLORED YELLOW, STRETCHING THEM TIGHT AND ABSO-LUTELY AIR PROOF.

That afternoon the Bells boarded the steamer *Toronto,* bound for Montreal, and the telegram wired that night caught up with them as the boat docked at Kingston: CURTISS FLEW 1140 YARDS, 3420 FEET, IN 60 SECONDS THIS EVENING ABOUT 7:30. WE HAVE TELEGRAPHED AND TELEPHONED SECRETARY AERO CLUB OF AMERICA THAT WE ARE NOW READY TO TRY FOR THE SCIENTIFIC AMERICAN CUP. HURRAH. SELFRIDGE.

The distance covered in that flight was about 140 feet farther than the kilometer required for the trophy.

Selfridge elaborated in his dispatch to the AP: THE FLIGHT WAS STOPPED ON ACCOUNT OF THE TREES AND A FENCE WHICH LIMIT THE PRACTICE GROUND. THIS PERFORMANCE IS THE MOST REMARKABLE RECORD, BEING ONLY THE SEVENTH FLIGHT OF THE MACHINE AND THE EIGHTH ATTEMPT BY THE AVIATOR . . . ALL CREDIT IS DUE TO THE MARVELLOUSLY EFFICIENT EIGHT-CYLINDER CURTISS AIR-COOLED MOTOR WHICH HAS NEVER GIVEN THE SLIGHTEST DIFFICULTY, AND TO THE WONDERFUL APTITUDE SHOWN BY THE AVIATOR, MR. CURTISS. THERE WERE SEVERAL HUNDRED SPECTATORS.

The *Scientific American* reported the two *June Bug* showings of that day as being the longest flights "ever accomplished by a heavier-than-air flying machine in America at any accessible place"; and that the 40-foot altitude of the morning flight was "quite a considerable height for one of these machines, being about four times as high as they usually fly abroad."

*   *   *

The secretary of the Aero Club, Augustus Post, instantly notified Charles A. Munn, publisher of the *Scientific American*, that the A.E.A. was asking for a crack at the trophy. Evidently the news caught Munn a trifle off balance, for he had been trying hard to coax Orville Wright into going for the trophy and was reluctant to give up. As recently as June 4, Munn had written asking Orville if he would make the attempt in a meet at Washington as soon as the upcoming trials of his Army contract machine were over. Now Munn, without a moment's delay, wrote Orville another letter (dated June 25) informing him of the A.E.A. application and offering to put Curtiss off, if Wright would reconsider. In order to qualify, Orville would need to substitute wheels for skids, as the rules required a takeoff from level ground. Orville replied:

"I have not been able to think of any way of changing our machine so that it could compete for the Scientific American Trophy within the next month or two. All of our machines have been designed for starting from a track. The changes necessary would require more time than we can give, till after we are through with the trials at Fort Myer, which will begin in August.

"Personally, I think the flying machines of the future will start from tracks, or from special apparatus. The system of pneumatic wheels, now used in Europe, has not proved satisfactory except on very large fields, and it will probably be easier to provide small tracks than large fields. Of course wheels can be applied to our machine as well as to others, so that the rule regarding starting does not absolutely prevent us from competing; but it does put us to great inconvenience. At the first opportunity we will fit up one machine to start without a track."

As Orville's negative response was dated June 30 and Munn could not well have received it before July 1, the indication is strong that Munn employed delaying tactics on the Curtiss entry. The A.E.A. had asked to have the trial on July 4 at Hammondsport, to coincide with the traditional Independence Day celebration of that village. The *Scientific American* and the Aero Club's officers argued against this on the score that an event of such magnitude ought to be conducted in proximity to a large center of population. Curtiss and Selfridge went to New York on July 1 to thresh out the matter. They were able to point to a clause in the regulations which specified that a contestant might choose the location of his trial. The publisher of the *Scientific American* and the affluent officials of the Aero Club had no choice but to give in and consult time-tables. Thus Curtiss was able to keep the promise he had made his fellow townsmen upon boarding the train: "We'll fly the *June Bug* on the Fourth of July. Advertise it. Invite everybody interested in flight. Draw a crowd to Hammondsport and prove to the world that we can really fly."

It was July 2, however, before McCurdy could wire Dr. Bell at the Victoria Hotel in Charlottetown, Prince Edward Island: ARRANGE-MENTS MADE WITH AERO CLUB FOR TROPHY TRIALS JULY 4 AT HAMMONDS-PORT.

The *Scientific American* publicly explained the situation by stating that Curtiss was "the first aviator to come forward with a practical aeroplane and request a trial." But it also conceded that "of all the efforts being put into the development of flying machines in America, none has been more systematic and thorough than that of the members of Dr. Alexander Graham Bell's Aerial Experiment Association."

*   *   *

The Fourth of July dawned glowering over Pleasant Valley. Rain threatened and a wind was working up. Undeterred, people began flocking into town from all directions, by train, by automobile, by horse carriage, and afoot. Some family groups with picnic hampers arrived as early as 5:00 A.M., staking out plots along the grassy embankment of the valley's north flank. The B.&H. Railroad scheduled a special train to shuttle out from Hammondsport to Rheims, the winery depot.

An Aero Club delegation of twenty-two members, headed by Alan R. Hawley, acting president, journeyed up from New York overnight. Charles M. Manly was official starter for the contest committee. Others of the contingent were the two Augustuses—Post and Herring. All in all, it was an imposing array of notables who had bowed to Curtiss's stubborn demand that his native town in the upstate hinterlands be favored with the spectacle of the first airplane flight ever to be officially observed, timed, recorded, and rewarded on the American continent. The train from Bath also disgorged a bevy of newsmen and photographers, even a motion picture camera crew. The *June Bug* was about to have the additional honor of being the first winged aircraft in this country to perform in a movie.

The behavior of the weather precluded an early takeoff and the crowd settled in for a tiresome wait. Curtiss would take no chances in a wind stronger than a zephyr. The machine on which so much depended was resting snugly in her tent. About midforenoon the harbinger of a series of thundershowers gave down. Umbrellas popped open all over the hillslope, while people not so equipped scrambled for the shelter of trees. Still there was no exodus. If anything, the numbers grew, and Hammondsport was close to being a deserted village. The Pleasant Valley Wine Company hereupon made a magnanimous gesture which was not soon forgotten. It threw open the winery doors and invited in the multitude for a buffet luncheon, washed down with generous samples of its potable products.

The afternoon lengthened with more splashes of rain. Lena Curtiss was spending this damp and anxious day in the agreeable company of Mr. and Mrs. David Fairchild, a young pair up from Washington. Mrs. Fairchild was Marian, the second daughter of the Bells (called Daisy in the family); and her husband was a brilliant botanist and "plant explorer" in service of the federal government. In order to gain as close a view as possible for the flight when it eventually happened, these three picked for their vantage point an old log on the far side of Champlin's potato patch. David Fairchild started off the day immaculate in a white suit, but persisted in roving about so much in mud and wet shrubbery that he "came back a sorry sight," quoting Daisy.

Late in the afternoon, the sky cleared and the wind died. Around six o'clock the *June Bug* was wheeled out of her tent, carefully checked over, the tail attached, the motor revved up and switched off to cool again. Charles Manly, with ample volunteer help, proceeded to measure off the course—no enviable task after all the rain. (This was the same Manly who twice survived a ducking in the Potomac River with Langley's ill-starred aerodrome.) The starting line was on the track beside the big horse barn. A vineyard loomed across the route 200 yards from start, and he measured straight through the vines; the A.E.A. flights had always swerved around the margin of this vineyard, and the trophy rules were modified to permit Curtiss to do the same, though it meant extra distance for him. Manly tramped on across the potato field, through knee-high clover, brambles, and swale holes. He made the course 3300 feet (20 feet more than the kilometer) and marked the finish line with a red flag on a post.

As official starter, Manly then assumed his stand at the starting line. The timer at the finish was Alan Hawley, a wealthy Wall Street broker who was a racing balloonist by hobby. The *June Bug* was rolled around to the line at 7 o'clock.

Any attempt to describe a long-ago scene such as was now enacted, in terms meaningful, and not absurd, to a generation inured to jet airliners streaking overhead, would be an exercise in futility. The impact of it on a 1908 audience can best be recaptured through the eyes and the emotions of people who were there. What David Fairchild saw, for example, was this:

"On an old race track a hundred yards away was a big thing of yellow cloth stretched on sticks and stayed by wires. Our eyes were riveted on it and in breathless expectation we waited for it to move . . . To stand in the gathering dusk of a mountain valley in your own country and wait to see, not only a man but a man whom you have been interested in for years fly over you, is the experience of a lifetime . . . Mixed with the expectation was an anxiety lest something happen . . . lest you should be on the point of seeing a tragedy with all that your near association with the man and your admiration for him would mean . . .

"Suddenly the group of people around the machine scattered into the fields. Curtiss climbed into the seat in front of the yellow wings, the assistant turned over the narrow wooden propeller, there was a sharp loud whirr and a cloud of dust and smoke as the blades of the propeller churned in the air . . . The men holding the gigantic bird let go. It started down the track on its rubber-tired wheels going faster and faster. Then, before we realized what it was doing, it glided upward into the air and bore down upon us at the rate of 30 miles an hour. Nearer and nearer it came like a gigantic ochre-colored condor carrying its prey. Soon the thin, strong features of the man, his bare outstretched arms with hands on the steering wheel, his legs on the bar in front, riveted our attention. Hemmed in by bars and wires, with a 40-horsepower engine exploding behind him leaving a trail of smoke and with a whirling propeller cutting the air 1200 times a minute, he sailed with 40 feet of outstretched wings 20 feet above our heads."

Actually, this was a false start. The *Bug* kept rising unaccountably until it was at an elevation of 40 feet. "Oh, why does he go so high?" Lena Curtiss cried out. "Do you think he's going to make it?"

The pilot was fighting the craft to check its rise, finding it necessary, as he explained, "to depress the forward plane to keep the machine on an even keel." The tail had been attached and detached so often that it had acquired "a slightly negative angle." As a last resort he retarded the ignition and settled in a field 1000 feet short of the finish post. Swarms of men came running through the clover and rapidly pushed the machine back to the start, where she was found to be undamaged. The tail angle was corrected and the second takeoff was signaled by Manly at 7:30. This time "she flew like a real june bug," in Curtiss's phrase.

David Fairchild continued: "What a moment for the vivid imagination. The thing is done. Man flies! All the tedious details of perfecting a practical passenger-carrying machine are forgotten. Even the previous successes of which you have seen reports mean nothing, and with one leap the imagination builds, on this one positive fact which your eyes are seeing, a whole superstructure of world locomotion. You remember the flights of homing pigeons that cover 500 miles in eleven hours, and these suggest strange visions of great fleets of airships crossing and re-crossing both oceans with their thousands of passengers. In short, we cast aside every pessimism and gave our imaginations free rein as we stood watching the weird bowed outline pass by . . .

"The machine which was 20 feet or more above our heads seemed to slowly descend until it was not more than 10 or 15 feet high, but it did not go lower. Directly over the stake it steered, rising higher as it went, and away it soared over the fences, turning to the left and settling gently down in a pasture over a mile away from where it left the race course. Yells and cheers and screams from the groups of spectators announced the fact that the trophy was handsomely won, and then, over potato fields, through vineyards and oat fields, and down the railroad, crowds of men ran to cheer the successful navigator and to bring back to its tent the uninjured *June Bug*.

"In one minute and 40 seconds Mr. Curtiss had ridden witch fashion astride a motor-driven broomstick, as it were, 80 feet more than a mile through the air and used up in the flight less than a quart of gasoline."

Fairchild's wife Daisy added: "As Mr. Curtiss flew over the red flag that marked the finish and way on toward the trees, I don't think any of us quite knew what we were doing. One lady was so absorbed as not to hear a coming train and was struck by the engine and had two ribs broken . . . We all lost our heads and David shouted, and I cried, and everyone cheered and clapped, and engines tooted."

Fairchild was among those who ran to where the landing took place. Walking beside Curtiss and helping to push the *June Bug* back, he asked him if it had not been nervous work and if he weren't exhausted. Curtiss answered: "It's no more nervous work than running a motorcycle and I don't feel any unusual exhaustion, and in still air I don't think there is any more danger; but I don't know enough yet to handle it in a breeze. There is no special difficulty in landing if I can keep up my headway, and this time I came down on all three wheels as easily as anyone could wish to."

What he had actually done was to stretch the kilometer into more than a mile, crossing three fences and "describing a letter S." The speed added up to 39 miles per hour. An associate enthused: "The long flight could have been continued at the will of the operator had he cared to rise over the trees which bounded the field." (This was an exaggeration, as the engine heated too rapidly for much more distance.)

The day which had begun so inauspiciously ended up in wild jubilation. The Champlins had their wine cellars opened again that evening and champagne flowed freely for all comers.

As for the modest hero, he wrote Dr. Bell: "The affair of July fourth went off very nicely." He explained the continuation of the flight beyond the requisite kilometer in this way: "Just on account of Mr. B——[H. M. Benner?], who was standing at the finish with a camera to photograph the machine in case I fell short on the distance, I flew the machine as far as the field would permit, regardless of fences, ditches, etc."

The Fourth of July having fallen on a Saturday, the Aero Club contingent remained for the weekend. Together with the A.E.A. members, they were guests of the village for a Sunday steamboat excursion and luncheon on Keuka Lake. Upon its return, the boat was greeted at the dock by a brass band and a vociferous turnout of celebrants. As Curtiss moved toward the gangplank, he was seized by Selfridge, Baldwin, and McCurdy, who carried him ashore on their shoulders, to his considerable embarrassment.

There was nothing he could do about it. The news wires had suddenly made Glenn H. Curtiss a famous man. Neither of the Wright brothers had yet flown in public. More than any other aircraft up to that moment, the *June Bug* convinced the world of the reality of human flight.

It had also convinced Curtiss that he was henceforth an aviator. As a close friend said: "The *June Bug* whetted his appetite for flying."

The inscription which forthwith appeared on the Scientific American Trophy at Aero Club headquarters was not, however, the name of Curtiss; it was "Aerial Experiment Association."

When the New York *World* asked Curtiss for a statement of his views on aviation, he wrote: "We have reached the conclusion that a curved surface is vastly more efficient than a flat surface"; and added a prediction: "The aeroplane of the future will furl and reef its plane surfaces, much the same as a ship's sails are adjusted to the conditions of the weather."

The motion picture of the flight had its premiere in New York City "with great success," Curtiss heard. It was entitled *The Great American Aeroplane, "June Bug," Winning the American Trophy July 4, 1908.* By an unfortunate oversight, the subtitles made no mention of either the A.E.A. or Hammondsport. When the film was later screened in Hammondsport, Curtiss pronounced it "very good indeed," and told Mrs. Bell: "A very touching incident was the lifelike appearance of

Tom and his dog Jack . . . The village urchins' grinning faces show up in the foreground greatly to the delight of the audience."

*   *   *

On that Fourth of July, Dr. and Mrs. Bell were in a hotel at Charlottetown, Prince Edward Island. When a telegram from Douglas McCurdy was delivered, Bell tore it open and read: CAPTURED TROPHY TODAY BY FLYING DISTANCE OF ONE MILE IN 1 MINUTE AND 42 SECONDS. FLEW FULL DISTANCE OF VALLEY. CAME DOWN ON ACCOUNT OF TREES, MAKING BEAUTIFUL LANDING. MACHINE UNDER PERFECT CONTROL AND EVERYBODY HAPPY.

The reaction of Dr. Bell was galvanic. That Sunday he kept the telegraph office busy. First he wired the law firm of Mauro, Cameron & Lewis, solicitors of patents, Washington, D.C.: PLEASE SEND SOMEONE TO HAMMONDSPORT, N.Y., AT ONCE AT MY EXPENSE TO EXAMINE THE AERODROME OF THE AERIAL EXPERIMENT ASSOCIATION WHICH HAS JUST WON THE SCIENTIFIC AMERICAN TROPHY FOR HEAVIER-THAN-AIR MACHINES. WE WANT TO KNOW WHAT PATENTABLE FEATURES THERE MAY BE ABOUT THE MACHINE. SEE MR. CURTISS AND REPORT BY MAIL TO ME AT BADDECK, NOVA SCOTIA.

To Curtiss sped the message: ACCEPT OUR HEARTIEST CONGRATULA-TIONS UPON YOUR MAGNIFICENT SUCCESS; at the same time informing him of the action he had taken relative to a patent investigation.

McCurdy received this admonition: I RECOMMEND POSTPONING FUR-THER EXPERIMENTS UNTIL MACHINE HAS BEEN EXAMINED BY PATENT EXPERT. IMPORTANT TO KEEP MACHINE UNINJURED UNTIL THEN.

As a matter of fact, the *June Bug* already had sustained some injury when McCurdy received the telegram. Having clinched the trophy, Curtiss thought there could be no harm in "a little experimenting." His next ambition was to fly a complete circle (without his knowledge, the Wright brothers had circumnavigated their Dayton field on September 20, 1904). As a farewell treat for the Aero Club delegates on Sunday, he went up, attempted a circle, managed to get turned around and headed back; then, making another swing to avoid the vineyard, he lost so much speed that he was forced to land. The impact broke a wheel and a wing strut.

On Monday, the 6th, the Bells reached Pictou, Nova Scotia, and he had done more thinking while ferrying across Northumberland Strait. A fuller telegram went to the A.E.A. as an entity:

IF MCCURDY WISHES TO FOLLOW ON LINE OF JUNE BUG, I RECOMMEND
THAT MCCURDY'S MACHINE BE NOW BUILT AT HAMMONDSPORT AND HEAD-
QUARTERS BE RETAINED THERE FOR THE PRESENT. IN MEANTIME DON'T RUN
ANY RISK OF INJURING JUNE BUG UNTIL AN APPLICATION FOR A PATENT
HAS BEEN PREPARED. WOULD LIKE BALDWIN TO HELP ME IN BADDECK AS
SOON AS POSSIBLE, AND WHEN WE ARE READY FOR MOTOR WOULD LIKE
ALL TO COME TO BADDECK.

WOULD SIMPLY LET IT BE KNOWN THAT AT MY REQUEST FURTHER
TRIALS OF JUNE BUG WILL BE POSTPONED UNTIL AERODROME HAS BEEN
COMPLETED SO THAT IN CASE OF ACCIDENT TO ONE MACHINE ANOTHER
WILL BE AVAILABLE FOR EXPERIMENTS. WOULD SAY NOTHING ABOUT PATENTS
OUTSIDE AS THIS WOULD ONLY STIR UP OTHER INVENTORS TO FORESTALL
US IN THE PATENT OFFICE.

A partner of the Washington law firm, Sheldon Cameron, lost little
time in getting to Hammondsport, where he arrived on July 8. Curtiss
made flights for his benefit, and Cameron found several patentable
features in the *June Bug*. Among these were the wing-tips (ailerons);
the shoulder-yoke control of the ailerons; the tricycle landing gear; and
the combination steering of front ground wheel and rudder.

No sooner had Cameron pinned down these points than Curtiss
resumed his experimental flying. On July 10, after his eighteenth flight
in the *June Bug*, he wired Bell exultantly: MADE COMPLETE TURN.

The absent A.E.A. members communicated with Mrs. Bell almost
as frequently as with her husband. Casey had called her "the little
mother of us all," and that is how they thought of her. Curtiss answered
her letter of congratulation on the trophy flight:

"I am greatly pleased myself that we were successful in accomplishing what we set out to do. I am satisfied that our machine is equal,
if not superior, to any of the foreigners. I note in Mr. Farman's contract
that he specifies absolutely smooth fields, with no fences or ditches,
and with grass cropped short. We have been working at a considerable
disadvantage in this respect so that, if we can fly a mile at a time, picking
our way as we do, we could surely make a good showing over a
perfect course where landing could be effected anywhere."

*   *   *

The *June Bug's* feat jolted the complacency of the Wright brothers.
From Le Mans, France—where he would not be ready for his first public
flight until August 9—Wilbur advised Orville on July 10:

"It might be well to write to Curtiss that we have a patent covering broadly the combination with wings to right and left of the center of a flying machine which can be adjusted to different angles of incidence, of vertical surfaces adjustable to correct inequalities in the horizontal resistance of the differently adjusted wings.

"Say that we do not believe that flyers can be made practical without using this combination, and inquire whether he would like to take a license to operate under our patent for exhibition purposes. I would not offer any manufacturing rights."

Orville replied on the 19th: "I had been thinking of writing Curtiss. I also intended to call the attention of the *Scientific American* to the fact that the Curtiss machine was a poor copy of ours; that we had furnished them the information as to how our older machines were constructed, and that they had followed this construction very closely, but have failed to mention the fact in any of their writings."

It is significant that, in the foregoing exchange, the brothers referred to Curtiss personally, and not to the A.E.A., the actual owner of the *June Bug;* or to Alexander Graham Bell, chairman of the A.E.A. Similarly the letter which Orville wrote on July 20 was addressed to Curtiss as an individual, and that sounded an ominous note of warning:

"I learn from the *Scientific American* that your *June Bug* has moveable surfaces at the tips of the wings, adjustable to different angles on the right and left sides for maintaining the lateral balance. In our letter to Lieutenant Selfridge of January 18th, replying to his of the 15th, in which he asked for information on the construction of flyers, we referred him to several publications containing descriptions of the structural features of our machines, and to our U. S. Patent No. 821,393. We did not intend, of course, to give permission to use the patented features of our machines for exhibitions or in a commercial way.

"This patent broadly covers the combination of sustaining surfaces to the right and left of the center of a flying machine adjustable to different angles, with vertical surfaces adjustable to correct inequalities in the horizontal resistances of the differently adjusted wings. Claim 14 of our patent No. 821,393 specifically covers the combination which we are informed you are using. We believe it will be very difficult to develop a successful machine without the use of some of the features covered in this patent.

"The commercial part of our business is taking so much of our time that we have not been able to undertake public exhibitions. If it is your desire to enter the exhibition business, we would be glad to take up the matter of a license to operate under our patents for that purpose.

"Please give Capt. Baldwin my best wishes for his success in the coming government tests."

Orville mailed a copy of this letter to Wilbur. A few days later he sent off a postscript: "I have a reply from Curtiss saying that he is not intending entering the exhibition business as has been reported by the papers, and that the matter of patents has been referred to the secretary of the Aero. Experiment Assn."

*   *   *

In the wake of the *June Bug* furor, the coming of Henry Farman,[2] rated as the current paragon of European aeronauts, proved an anti-climax. His contract with a syndicate, carrying with it a guarantee of $24,600, called for a tour of several American cities, starting at the Brighton Beach racetrack, in the course of which he engaged to make at least fifteen flights. A highspot of his visit was to be an aeronautical show at St. Louis, and now the promoters of that meet were anxious to add the *June Bug* to their program, offering the A.E.A. $10,000 for a single flight. If Curtiss would agree to enter in a race with Farman, they were prepared to pay beyond that amount.

The younger A.E.A. members were eager to accept this challenge, but Dr. Bell slapped them down. Through the medium of the *Bulletin,*[3] Bell said it was "tempting" to race the *June Bug* "for the honor and glory of America and the A.E.A., and incidentally to make some money for the Association. Such propositions, however, cannot be entertained by us." He reminded them that they were organized for experimental purposes only, and that they had unfinished experiments on their hands. "If we authorize public exhibitions of our aerodromes involving pecuniary transactions or emoluments, we at once lay ourselves open to attack from numerous inventors who will claim that we are infringing their patents, and we will be obliged to defend ourselves. The letter from Orville Wright . . . indicates clearly what would happen, and the Wright Brothers would not be the only aggressors . . . So long as we are an Experiment Association carrying on experiments, not for gain but simply to promote the art of aviation in America, there can be no possible ground for legal action of any kind. But the moment we begin to make money, look out for trouble." Bell knew whereof he spoke.

Curtiss was elected a member of the Aero Club of America right after the *June Bug* flight, and was one of a committee named by the club to arrange for entertaining "the great Farman." He went to New York on July 29 to participate in the welcome, proceeding thence to Fort Myer for the dirigible tests. Farman disembarked with his wife, five mechanics, and two large Voisin-built biplanes with box-like tails for rudders. Impressive with his pointed dark beard and athletic physique, he was interviewed by reporters at the pier. In an oblique thrust at the Wrights, he said: "It is better for others to see what you are doing, and for you to see what they are doing, each improving by the mistakes of the other."

Only one of his planes was assembled at Brighton Beach and Farman made three brief hops, at ground-hugging altitude, which drew public notice as being the first in the New York metropolitan area. On hand to observe them for the A.E.A. were McCurdy and Selfridge. McCurdy wrote Mabel Bell that "Farman's attempts were very disappointing indeed." In conversing with Farman, they described how the wing-tips functioned on the *June Bug*, and he broke in: "Ah, ailerons!" So far as known, this was the first time the word "ailerons" was heard in the United States. Farman hinted that he was thinking of adopting the same system himself.

Farman went no farther than Brighton Beach on his projected tour. His sponsors had paid him $7500 in advance on his contract, and when he asked for more, nothing happened. Charging that the syndicate had forfeited the contract, he packed up his planes and sailed for France, in an indignant manner reminiscent of Santos-Dumont.

* * *

In accordance with Bell's suggestion, McCurdy's Drome Number 4 went into construction—a much advanced version of the *June Bug*. In mid-July, Casey Baldwin and his bride left for Baddeck to assist Bell with the new tetrahedral. (Casey married a Toronto girl while the *June Bug* was being built.) The A.E.A. was consequently divided between Nova Scotia and Hammondsport, linked together by means of the weekly *Bulletin*.

It was now agreed that the purely experimental phase was over, and that steps toward commercial development should be foreshadowed with Drome Number 4. As McCurdy put it, they had gone beyond the "minutes" stage of flying, and now proposed to go into the "hours." In order to do this, they must graduate from the quick-heating air-cooled engine to one that was water-cooled. Curtiss started in production an 8-cylinder water-cooled motor, before leaving for Fort Myer to aid Captain Tom Baldwin with the Army dirigible trials.

At this point, McCurdy and Selfridge seriously set about learning how to fly the *June Bug*, which nobody but Curtiss had flown before. "I think that watching Curtiss fly so often," said McCurdy, "has instilled into our minds the motions to be gone through with in handling the machine from just talking things over, and I was surprised myself at the ease with which I could manipulate the controls . . . Mr. Bell, I had perfect control of the machine and could have steered her any-where. Please don't consider this as a brag. I only put it that way to try and convince you that we have absolutely mastered the control of the machine."

Alternating at the controls day after day, Selfridge and McCurdy made scores of sorties and became fairly proficient as pilots. And then their fun together was abruptly terminated. Selfridge received Army orders to report in Washington at the end of August. "I suppose we have lost him for the rest of the summer," Curtiss wrote Mabel Bell at Beinn Bhreagh.

From the wording of that remark, it appears that Curtiss already knew the reason behind the orders.

9. Tom Selfridge

At Stony Brook Farm, while Selfridge and McCurdy were enjoying their fine sport with the *June Bug*, an insurance agent named Holcomb was among the onlookers who came and went. This person also happened to be a trustee of the local hospital. In a bantering way, but with serious undertone, he warned: "You must be careful, Selfridge, or we will need a bed for you in the hospital."[1]

"Oh, I am careful all right," Tom retorted as he moved off to take another round with the *Bug*. That evening he laughed about the incident during a session with Curtiss and McCurdy in the "thinkorium."

If any member of the A.E.A. was a favorite with Mabel Bell, it was Tom Selfridge. She depicted him as "one of the most loveable boys I have ever known, good, true, gentle, and affectionate." And: "Nothing escaped those bright brown eyes of his." She was deeply touched by a singular thing he did just before they departed Nova Scotia for Hammondsport the previous December.

One twilight she came down the broad staircase to join the customary gathering before the fireplace in the great hall of Beinn Bhreagh. Tom awaited at the lower landing and escorted her to an armchair behind which he had carefully arranged the floorlamps. When she was seated, he signaled the others, "Be quiet, boys." He knelt beside the chair where the lights shone clearly on his face so that she would have no trouble reading his lips. Then he spoke an eloquent little speech saying he wished to thank the Bells for all they had done to make him so happy as a guest beneath their roof, and especially for having permitted him to be the one to ride the kite. He wanted her to know how much they all appreciated her being the "little mother" of the Association. Tears welled in her eyes as she reached to touch his hand.

*　　*　　*

On July 6, 1908, General Allen appointed a five-man Aeronautical Board to conduct the performance trials of the Baldwin-Curtiss dirigible, the Wright aeroplane, and the Herring aeroplane; and to rule on whether they met the contract specifications. When Lieutenant Selfridge reported in Washington a few weeks later, he was added to that Board. It is probable that the Signal Corps, fully informed of the work he was doing, had left him in Hammondsport until the last available minute.

Selfridge, at the early age of twenty-six, was unquestionably the best-qualified officer in the U. S. Army for duty with this Aeronautical Board. Not only had he made the most comprehensive study of the subject, but he had been on special assignment for the past year as a participating member of the only organization in the United States and Canada which was carrying on sustained experiments with aviation. The activities of that organization had been crowned with a resounding success. Selfridge was the first and only officer in the Army to have flown an airplane, and to have genuinely learned how to fly. Of late, propellers were his specialty, and he had designed the prop for the Army dirigible which was to undergo its proving. This had occasioned an intimate collaboration with Curtiss, the maker of the engine. It was for the very purpose of developing an officer who would be knowledge-able about aeronautics that the War Department had sent him to Nova Scotia and Hammondsport, and now the time came to make use of the background he had accumulated. By all indications, Selfridge was headed for important rank in the germinating air service he had foreseen and for which he had so assiduously prepared himself.

Another young lieutenant assigned to the Aeronautical Board, on the strength of a thesis he had written for graduation from the Signal School, was Benjamin D. Foulois.[2] Though he had no prior experience of aircraft, Foulois was put in charge of the Balloon Detachment at Fort Myer just in time to watch the assembling of the dirigible. He was introduced to Curtiss, Captain Baldwin, and Lieutenant Selfridge. Primarily interested in the motor, he spent most of his time with Curtiss, whom he found to be "a serious man who had nothing but engines on his mind."

When Foulois reported to him for duty, Curtiss surveyed his spic-and-span uniform with a frown of exasperation. The look was translated into words when Curtiss told him that, if he expected to work with him, he would have to provide himself with five items: a suit of coveralls, a screwdriver, a pair of pliers, a wad of cotton waste, and a bar of soap. All the while the airship was being rigged, inflated, and tested, Foulois hung around. As he said in his memoirs: "I asked hundreds of questions of Baldwin and Curtiss, and probably made myself obnoxious to them looking over their shoulders every time they tightened and tinkered and turnbuckled."

The dirigible was delivered at Fort Myer a month ahead of the Wright airplane, hence its official trials preceded those of Orville Wright. As for the Herring contract, it called for delivery by August 15, but he requested a month's extension on the plea of an odd accident. His tale was that, during a bench-test of his motor, a counterweight fell off, setting up a vibration that shook the engine to pieces; in his frantic effort to replace the weight he caught a finger in the machinery and "painfully injured it." Herring was quoted as saying he would *fly* his airplane from New York to Washington, instead of shipping it. Before the postponed deadline fell due, he was granted another month's reprieve to complete his new engine, which he promised would weigh a mere one pound per horsepower. Curtiss continued to hold a high opinion of Herring as an aeronautical scientist, and told his associates: "I believe he employs gyroscope, and I think there are great possibilities in this line. I see no other solution to automatic stability."

Meanwhile, the Fort Myer trials struggled along without Herring's presence, arousing keen public interest. Never before had any army conducted tests of powered aircraft with a view to purchase. Owing to the military implications, observers from several foreign embassies haunted the scene. The Signal Corps had intended the trials to be conducted in private, but the newspapers raised such a clamor that the War Department took the lid off. Daily throngs crossed the Potomac from nearby Washington, including governmental bigwigs, cabinet members, Congressmen, and socialites.

Since the dirigible must carry two men and the water-cooled engine, its hydrogen capacity was 20,000 cubic feet, making it the largest balloon so far seen in the United States—over twice the size of the biggest *California Arrow*. The suspended platform, or "car," was 66 feet long and had canvas seats for its crew. The pilot, Baldwin, was stationed aft, manipulating rudder and stabilizer. As engineer, Curtiss sat well forward to be with his motor, and also operated front elevator planes for altitude control.

Baldwin and Curtiss commenced practice flights on August 4 and continued them, as weather permitted, until the 12th when they notified the Signal Corps of their readiness for the official trials. In the early rehearsals the airship "rode like a cantering horse," due to the piling up of air in front of the bag, which periodically reared up to climb over a gob of pressure. On the downslope of each such hurdle, the nose became a trifle deflated and tended to droop. Sensing the danger that it might foul the propeller, Curtiss throttled back the engine at every dip. Away off to the rear, Baldwin did not grasp the reason for this maneuver, and he beamed a torrent of lurid profanity at the back of Curtiss's head, to no avail. Now Captain Tom, though usually an amiable and well-spoken individual, bore a reputation for being capable, when it became absolutely necessary, of swearing for six hours running without repeating himself. This struck him as being that kind of emergency. The trouble was that Curtiss, with the engine in his lap, could not hear a word he said, while the multitude down below heard quite distinctly. The ground audience gave Baldwin high marks for a masterful performance.

During one of the preliminary cruises over Virginia fields and woodlands, once the "cantering" difficulty was cured, Curtiss had so little work to do that he sketched a map of the terrain passing underneath, which he presented to Army officers as an example of what might be done by way of aerial mapping.

At the showdown, Signal Corps Dirigible No. 1 passed her inspection with ease. On August 15 she fulfilled the culminating two-hours endurance requirement with eight round trips over a measured course, staying aloft ten minutes overtime. Curtiss later confided to the homefolk that the flight "could have been continued with the fuel on board for two hours more, and a trip to Washington and return would probably have been made except for the fact of darkness coming on."

When the Aeronautical Board notified Baldwin that his airship had met specifications and was accepted by the U. S. Army, a representative of the German government who had been hovering about Hammondsport for some time took quick action. He ordered an exact duplicate to be shipped to Berlin, and this was the first American aircraft ever exported to Europe. (Since the huge rigid zeppelins were coming along nicely by this time, the reason for the purchase on behalf of the German Imperial Army, already being groomed for World War I, may be surmised.)

One further contract stipulation remained for Captain Baldwin to carry out: the instruction of two Signal Corps officers. He made it three for good measure, giving lessons to Tom Selfridge, Lieutenant Foulois, and Lieutenant Frank P. Lahm (the trio, as Foulois expressed it, "who had gotten our hands dirty helping them get their ship in the air"). While these tutorial ascents were in progress, Orville Wright put in his appearance at Fort Myer and began assembling his contract "flyer."

*   *   *

Not surprisingly, when it became known that the government was in the market for an aeroplane, possibly two, many people remembered that the Army still owned the wrecked Langley machine upon which it had expended $50,000. A number of scientists had been urging that it be resurrected and given the fair trial of which they felt it had been cheated. Now nicknamed *The Buzzard*, it was locked in the carpenter shop behind the Smithsonian Institution where it had been stored, not as a historic heirloom, but with a view to further experimentation some day when the hubbub of ridicule had died away.

Pressure mounted for tearing off the "veil of secrecy" which had shrouded *The Buzzard*, and for having the Signal Corps give it a fresh chance while trying out experimental aircraft. The press, which had been so vitriolic four years earlier, bored in with questions. General James Allen, Chief Signal Officer, finally issued a statement that if the Wrights and Herring should fail to carry out their contracts, "it is not at all unlikely that we will bring out the old Langley machine for the purpose of conducting experiments." The Smithsonian unlocked the carpenter shop, brushed off the cobwebs, and admitted reporters to write their impressions of the crippled dragonfly which someone had since mistaken for a buzzard.

Popular anticipation of the forthcoming performances by Wright was even greater than it had been for the dirigible. These were to be the first open flights by either brother in their native land, and would mark the public debut of their machine about which they had been so secretive. Wilbur was creating a sensation abroad with his flights near Le Mans, France. The length of time he was able to stay airborne and the maneuverability of his "flyer" caught Europeans by surprise. The French machines could not compare.

It is abundantly clear that Orville Wright was irritated at finding Selfridge a member of the Aeronautical Board which was to render the decision on his own showing; and that he particularly had no stomach for taking Selfridge as a passenger. The Signal Corps expected him to give each Board member a demonstrational flight. Doubtless Orville was aware that Selfridge had recently flown both the *White Wing* and the *June Bug*. Nor could it have escaped his notice that Tom was the only Army officer yet to operate an airplane, and that he was one of that small, select handful of men in the entire world who could be termed aviators. Inevitably, he knew that, if Selfridge flew with him, he would be silently comparing the wing-warping system with the aileron flanges used by the A.E.A.

Then, too, the appearance of Curtiss on the field was no balm to Orville's emotions. The dirigible's engine took to misbehaving in the forepart of September and Curtiss was recalled to Fort Myer to rectify it. Not only did he watch Orville's practice flights for two days running, but he went out of his way to converse with him. Orville wrote to Wilbur on September 6 that: "Curtiss was here Thursday and Friday. They have not been able to make the motor on the dirigible run more than a minute or two without missing about half its explosions. Ours runs without a miss. Selfridge has been trying to find out how we do it!"

In the same letter he commented: "Lieutenants Selfridge and Foulois are detailed to operate the dirigible at St. Joseph, Mo. the latter part of the month. Lieut. Lahm will stay here. I like Foulois very well, but I will be glad to have Selfridge out of the way. I don't trust him an inch. He is intensely interested in the subject, and plans to meet me often at dinners, etc. where he can pump me. He has a good education, and a clear mind. I understand that he does a good deal of knocking behind my back."

To his sister, Katharine, he wrote: "I will probably take a passenger on board in a few days. I would like to take Lieut. Lahm, but I am afraid it will cause jealousy among the young officers. Selfridge is doing what he can behind our backs to injure us."

At the identical time, Curtiss was mailing to Dr. Bell, in Nova Scotia, what appears to have been his only firsthand appraisal of the Wright airplane on record:

"The first flight was rather short as Mr. Wright said he was unaccustomed to the machine and the levers seemed awkward for him. He made a wrong move and headed for the tent, which necessitated immediate landing . . . The next day he did better, however, and made as fine a landing as you would make on wheels. The launching device, which includes a derrick, and a big weight which drops the pulleys and rope to give the initial velocity, does not seem to be very well liked, and I believe that all who have seen our machine and the Wrights' prefer our method of starting on wheels, to skids.

"I had some talk with Mr. Wright and nothing was said about his patents on adjustable surfaces. He has nothing startling about his machine and no secrets. The front control has a new action. The ribs are flexible and bend. I cannot see there is any advantage in the movement, however. The propellers are also odd. They are very flat at the hub, presenting great resistance as they revolve. The blades are wider towards the ends, perhaps three times the width at the hub . . . The engine is the same they had four years ago, being rather crude and not exceptionally light. Mr. Wright sits to the left of the engine just inside of the front surface on a little cushioned seat, which is large enough for two.

"Mr. Wright told me they intended to use but one propeller hereafter, presumably to simplify. This double-chain transmission they have weighs 100 pounds more than the single propeller would.

"Selfridge has been ordered to St. Joseph, Missouri, to fly the Government airship at the coming maneuvers. After that he will probably fly the Wrights' machine."

As they said, the Army had promptly given its new aerial showpiece an inaugural assignment to appear at the Missouri State Fair in St. Joseph, with Lieutenants Foulois and Selfridge as its operators. Foulois, with a ground crew of eight enlisted men, proceeded to St. Joe to get the airship assembled. Selfridge remained at Fort Myer to round out his duty as a judge of the qualifications of the Wright "flyer," and was to join Foulois in time for the opening of the fair on September 21.

In the meantime, Dr. Bell was ruminating about the fate of the

A.E.A., whose postulated year of existence was due to expire on September 30. He called for a meeting at Baddeck not later than that date to decide what was to be done, noting that Selfridge was still tied down and "It is hoped that he too may be able to visit Beinn Bhreagh before the 30th of September." If it looked as if he could not be there, Selfridge was "specially requested to communicate his views concerning the future of the Association by letter to the Chairman"; to send his proxy vote and turn over the secretary's records to Curtiss.

Through the medium of the *A.E.A. Bulletin,* Bell expressed his thoughts on the problem to the other members: "We cannot stop although the object of the Association at its inception has been attained. The limit of our desire in the beginning was to 'get into the air' by hook or crook, and in any sort of a heavier-than-air machine." Since then four members had flown and the organization was near the end of its funds. He felt that its purpose ought now to be rephrased as: "to get into the air by new means of a patentable nature." Pending the patent report, the next step should be the appointment of a trustee to whom patents and commercial rights, if any, would be turned over. "Mr. Curtiss has closer affiliations with business men than any other member of the Association and perhaps he may be able to suggest the name of a suitable person to act as Trustee." One possibility was to broaden the Association with an increase of membership, then "to go to the public for donations and bequests in aid of experimental work." Bell was willing to donate to such an Association, "and Mrs. Bell and others would probably contribute." In this way, the A.E.A. might "promote the progress of aviation generally in America." An alternative plan was to continue the Association as it stood for a limited period, "arranging with Mrs. Bell for continued financial aid."

On September 17, Bell set out for Washington, accompanied by Casey Baldwin, to consult with the patent attorneys. They had gone only as far as Grand Narrows, Nova Scotia, when shattering news overtook them in a message from Mabel Bell.

*   *   *

The major specifications for the Wright "flyer" were that it must carry two men, make a speed of 40 miles per hour, and be able to remain in the air at least one hour. When Orville Wright settled down to business on September 9, his initial efforts were directed at topping the one-hour mark. That day he established a world's endurance record, then broke it himself: in the morning, 57 minutes, 31 seconds; in the afternoon, 1 hour, 2 minutes and a fraction.

Upon landing from the latter flight, he discovered that one of the twin propellers had developed an 18-inch split. He replaced it before taking up his first passenger, who was, as he had hoped, Lieutenant Frank Lahm. Next day the split propeller was repaired by nailing down the loose piece and glueing it with cloth.

Among the laudatory messages which poured in upon Orville was a telegram from Dr. Bell: ON BEHALF OF THE AERIAL EXPERIMENT ASSOCIATION, ALLOW ME TO CONGRATULATE YOU UPON YOUR MAGNIFICENT SUCCESS. AN HOUR IN THE AIR MARKS A HISTORIC OCCASION.

On Saturday, September 12, Wright increased the endurance record to one hour, 14 minutes, 20 seconds. He also took up his second guest, Major George O. Squier, president of the Aeronautical Board, who probably informed him then that Lieutenant Selfridge was slated to be his next passenger. Much as he disliked the prospect, there was no legitimate way he could refuse to accept Selfridge.

Because of their devout upbringing, neither of the Wright brothers would ever fly on Sunday, and so that was a day's respite. On Monday, Tuesday, and Wednesday, Selfridge stood by, but a persistent wind ruled out any flights. On Thursday, the 17th, conditions came right, and Orville had a pair of untried propellers attached. Two thousand spectators were milling on the field and the mounted cavalry forced them back. Doffing hat and jacket, Selfridge took his seat beside Orville at the front edge of the lower wing, acting eager as a schoolboy and curious to find out what the Wright plane was like. The weight in the derrick dropped at 5:14 P.M. and the "flyer" shot along its monorail and into the air. At 150 feet of altitude, Wright began circling the parade ground.

As the aircraft was going into its fourth circuit, its occupants heard a light tapping sound in the rear, followed by two solid thumps which shook the machine alarmingly. Orville cut the engine and managed to get headed back toward the derrick. One of the new propellers had cracked lengthwise allowing a blade to flatten out and lose thrust. The resulting imbalance set up a vibration so strong that the other propeller fouled a stay wire leading to the tail, the broken wire then wrapping itself around a blade and snapping it off. Orville found the tail rudder inoperative and worked hard at his levers trying to control the descent. Witnesses saw the plane lowering in a gentle glide, then it nosed up, lost speed, and went into a nearly vertical plunge.

Up to this time, Selfridge had not uttered a word. After a hasty glance behind, he turned once or twice to look into Orville's face, as if to discern his thoughts. As the plane pitched downward, he murmured "Oh! Oh!" in a scarcely audible voice.

A thick cloud of yellow dust arose where the plane struck. Spectators surged over the sidelines. Cavalry galloped in and its commanders shouted: "If they won't stand back, ride them down."

Both men were terribly injured, pinned in the wreckage, and Selfridge was unconscious, choking in his blood; the engine and fuel tank were partly on top of him. Extricated by soldiers, they were rushed to the nearby Army hospital. Wright had four broken ribs, a fractured thigh, and a dislocated hip. Besides internal injuries, Selfridge sustained a fracture at the base of the skull and a depressed forehead fracture for which he had emergency surgery. Despite this, he died three hours after the crash without regaining consciousness.

In such a way did Tom Selfridge attain the melancholy distinction of being the first person in the world to lose his life in an airplane. Deep sorrow was felt by his A.E.A. associates, and especially by Mabel Bell who was well-nigh inconsolable. Even the German emperor, Wilhelm II, cabled his condolences to the family. The Army buried Selfridge with full military honors in Arlington National Cemetery. A memorial monument was erected at West Point. Selfridge Air Force Base at Mount Clemens, Michigan, commemorated him, and with that the military aviation arm established the precedent of naming bases for flyers killed in line of duty. The loss to the Army of its able pioneer airman was incalculable.[3]

Upon his arrival in Washington, Bell was interviewed by newsmen about the tragedy. He blamed the design of the Wright airplane, saying that the two propellers should have been operated on one shaft; that if they had not been mounted separately, the crackup would not have occurred.

In his account of the accident to his wife, Bell said: "In his excitement, Wright evidently raised the front control too much, or too quickly, causing the head to rise with danger of sliding backwards, and this caused the machine to lose its headway."[4]

For the next issue of the *A.E.A. Bulletin*, Mrs. Bell penned Selfridge's most touching eulogy:

"On Thursday, September 17, the beautiful bond of companionship which we called 'the A.E.A.' was broken, when Tom Selfridge sealed his devotion to our common cause with his life . . . All over the world true hearts are sorrowing for the brave young life so suddenly cut down in its brilliant beginning . . . Others will place on record what Lieutenant Selfridge was as patriotic soldier, earnest worker in the struggle to win for mankind the highway of the air . . . To the mother of the Association it may be permitted to speak of him as he was in the family . . . [Always] he showed me the gentlest, most thoughtful consideration. None more quick than he to see what was wanted for my comfort or pleasure . . . The same quiet kindliness characterized his bearing to every other woman he came in contact with, so that today they cannot speak of him without tears . . . He was so quiet it seems strange how large the place is he left vacant . . . Tom was so simple and remote from display that at first it comes with almost a shock to think of him in connection with the pomp and circumstance of the military funeral he is receiving."

Curtiss and McCurdy hastened down from Hammondsport and a quick meeting of the A.E.A. was held at Bell's home on Connecticut Avenue, where it was resolved: "That we place upon record our high appreciation of our late Secretary, Lieutenant Thomas E. Selfridge, who met death in his efforts to advance the art of aviation. The Association laments the loss of a dear friend and valued associate. The United States Army loses a valuable and promising officer; and the world an ardent student of aviation who made himself familiar with the whole progress of the art in the interests of his native country."

Another resolution was addressed to Wright: "Resolved: That the members of the Aerial Experiment Association herewith extend to Mr. Orville Wright their deepest sympathy for his grief at the death of their associate, Lieutenant Selfridge. We realize in this pioneering of the air the unforeseen must occasionally be disastrous. We hope sincerely that Mr. Wright will soon recover from the serious injuries he has sustained, and continue, in conjunction with his brother, Mr. Wilbur Wright, his splendid demonstration to the world of the great possibilities of aerial flight."

Douglas McCurdy was elected secretary of the A.E.A. to succeed Selfridge. The meeting sanctioned a note which Dr. Bell sent to President Theodore Roosevelt proposing that the War Department detail another officer in place of Selfridge as observer with the A.E.A.

The Aero Club of America appointed Bell chairman of a committee to represent the club at Selfridge's funeral, but Bell declined on the ground that he wished to appear solely as chairman of the A.E.A. His suggestion that Octave Chanute be named instead was approved by the club. Honorary bearers were designated from the Army, the Navy, and the Aero Club. All four surviving members of the A.E.A. were honorary bearers, although Curtiss did not attend the funeral; the pressure of business matters compelled his return to Hammondsport for a few days.

The interment waited on the arrival from San Francisco of Selfridge's father and twin brothers. It took place on September 25, culminating with three rifle volleys fired over the grave and the traditional lone bugle playing Taps.

The Signal Corps substituted Lieutenant Lahm to join Lieutenant Foulois in carrying out the dirigible flights at St. Joseph.

*　　*　　*

Taking leave from her position as a high school teacher in Dayton, Katharine Wright hurried to her brother's bedside. They were soon greatly disturbed by a report which some tale-bearer brought to Orville's attention.

The morning after Curtiss's departure, Dr. Bell, McCurdy, and Baldwin went over to Fort Myer with the idea of paying a sympathy visit to the patient. Upon being told at the hospital that Mr. Wright was not well enough to receive visitors, they left their cards and walked across the parade ground to the building where the wreckage of the airplane was stored. There they were politely welcomed by a Sergeant Downey, in charge of the guard, and permitted to look around. Most of the machine had already been packed for shipment back to Dayton, but a large case containing the wings was still uncovered. The rumor carried to Wright's sickbed said that Bell had taken measurements of the wings.

Thence the three went to the receiving vault at Arlington Cemetery to view Selfridge's casket; after that, returning to Sergeant Downey's tent to copy details of Orville's Fort Myer flights from the official log, they found Octave Chanute on hand for the like purpose. Chanute went back to Washington with them for lunch and spent the whole afternoon in their company. This seems to have been Chanute's first personal contact with the A.E.A.

When Chanute later called on Katharine Wright, she asked him to look into the purported incident for them. Having done so (and probably consulted Bell himself about it), Chanute sent this note to Katharine:

"I am inclined to believe that the account which reached you was greatly exaggerated. I met Sergeant Downey after I left you and spoke to him about the occurrence.

"He says that Dr. Bell went in the shed after almost everything was packed up, but there was no cover on the aeroplane box. That a dispute arose about the width of the wing and Dr. Bell said, 'Well, I have a tape in my pocket and we will measure it.' That this was the only measurement taken is what I gathered, but you had better see Sergeant Downey when opportunity serves and get an understanding of what occurred."

Chanute helped Miss Wright draft a request to Major George Squier for a nine-months extension in fulfilling the contract with the Signal Corps. This was granted, setting the postponed deadline at June 28, 1909. (Meanwhile, Herring made a gesture of offering to fly a replacement machine for the Wrights at Fort Myer, in case Wilbur could not return from Europe to do so.)

Katharine finally brought Orville home from the hospital, in a wheelchair, on November 1.

*　　*　　*

On September 26, Curtiss arrived back in Washington and a full-scale meeting of the A.E.A. convened at Bell's home to consider the future of the Association as it was affected by Selfridge's death. Octave Chanute sat in on this session as a guest and was introduced to Curtiss. Tom's father, Edward A. Selfridge, attended on behalf of his son's heirs. Bell opened the proceedings by saying: "It may be possible that some day or other our work may be found to be of value after all, in which case the heirs of Lieutenant Selfridge will be entitled to his share of the proceeds."

By resolution, Mr. Selfridge was recognized as the legal representative for his son, with the right to attend meetings and to vote in Tom's name. His first vote was then cast in favor of continuing the A.E.A. for an additional six months. Bell announced that his wife had authorized him to say she would provide more money, up to the amount of $10,000, if they voted for the continuance.

On motion of Curtiss, the A.E.A. appointed as trustee Charles J.

Bell, president of the American Security & Trust Company, a cousin of
Alexander Graham Bell; he was married to a younger sister of Mabel
Bell. It would be his function to receive and administer any patents
and profits growing out of the association's work.

At one point, as Bell sketched the history of the A.E.A. and was
touching on the prospect of future litigations, Mr. Selfridge asked: "You
may be trespassing on some other person's property?"

"Exactly," Bell replied. "We do not know what other people have
done . . . An examination is now being made to see whether we have
got anything to patent . . . Of course, it may be possible that we
are making a mountain out of a mole hill, but I cannot forget the
early days of the telephone when business people said there was
nothing in it. There may be nothing in *this*, but we are not going
to take any chances about it. We shall proceed as though it were
the most valuable thing in the world and make due preparations."

The Signal Corps was distressed and not a little worried at the
delay in obtaining its airplane, just when European governments were
finally awake to the potentiality. Bell pondered this fact after returning
to Nova Scotia, and put the question to Curtiss:

"Now why cannot the A.E.A. offer its services at this juncture?
We are not in any sense competitors of the Wright brothers in the
matter of their contract with the government . . . One of the reasons
for associating Lieutenant Selfridge with us was that the U. S. Army
should have the benefit of our experiments through an officer especially
detailed to observe them. We now have two aerodromes (Numbers 3
and 4) ready to fly, and why should we not offer the War Department
the use of these aerodromes for experimental purposes while they
are waiting for Orville Wright to recover? . . . I can say that we are
their friends, and not their competitors, and will not do anything that
would interfere with their contract with the government."

Curtiss wired back: THINK WELL OF YOUR IDEA. ALL HERE WITH
YOU IN ANY ACTION YOU TAKE.

Bell thereupon wrote to President Roosevelt, reminding him that
Selfridge's death "has deprived the U. S. Army of the services of the
only officer acquainted with the work of the A.E.A."; and "We shall
be very glad to give any information concerning our work to some
other officer of the U. S. Army if desired." The *June Bug*, he added,
would soon be joined in the air by the *Silver Dart;* and these machines,
together with two tetrahedral kites partly completed, would be turned
over for experiments "to any officer properly detailed."

The answer came from Assistant Secretary of War Robert Shaw Oliver, who promised that the War Department would assign a Signal Corps officer to Hammondsport as observer when the first test flights of the *Silver Dart* were scheduled. The proffer of all the A.E.A. machines for military experiment was evaded.

                                        *   *   *

Herring's postponed deadline date was October 13, and on the 12th he showed up at Fort Myer to make what he called a "technical delivery." Accompanied by an assistant to help with the lugging, he brought parts of the machine in two suitcases and a wardrobe trunk— "only enough to convince them," as he said. The Signal Corps, still hopeful that one of its flying machines would come through, allowed itself to be convinced sufficiently that it did not cancel Herring's contract on the spot.

An interesting theory which may help to explain Herring's ruse was advanced by Orville Wright: namely, that Herring had purposely made his bid $5000 under the $25,000 which he knew the Wrights were going to bid; expecting then to be awarded the contract and engage the Wrights to carry it out. The Army's acceptance of three bids, instead of only one, "put a crimp in his plans." Nevertheless, in the pinch, he did go to Dayton and make the proposition that they build the airplane for him. "We refused to help him out in the matter and that is the reason he was compelled to make the ridiculous 'technical delivery' of his machine."

A taxicab deposited the two men and their queer baggage at the balloon shed, and from the articles in the trunk Herring set up the center section of a small biplane, explaining that it was to be controlled in flight by twisting the struts adjacent to the pilot's seat. Out of the suitcases emerged fragments enough for the partial assembly of an engine which Lieutenant Lahm considered "a beautifully built 5-cylinder, air-cooled radial." After inspecting the samples, the Aeronautical Board accepted the "technical delivery" and gave Herring another month's extension to complete the machine for the acceptance trials. This time he assured the Signal Corps that the aircraft could fly from New York to Chicago.

Herring immediately dismantled the parts and packed them up, refusing to let newsmen have a peek. When they backed him into a corner, he said: "The parade ground at Fort Myer is too small for swift

aeroplane flight. My machine travels with express-train speed and I
prefer a longer straightaway in which to practice control . . . I prefer
to hold its preliminary flights in secret."

A reporter asked: "Have you ever flown in a powered machine?"

"Of course I have," Herring snapped. "I would be foolish to come
down here with a flying machine if I had never flown. But I don't like
publicity, and I don't have any more of it than I can help."

Pressed for some description of his plane, he merely declared that
he was "carrying all the details and figures in his head."

Late at night, he and his aide went to the balloon shed, collected
their impedimenta, and boarded a train for New York; as one news
account had it, he "stole away as silently as he came."[5]

The newspapers opened up with their artillery of ridicule, referring
to him as: "Modest Mr. Herring, the man who wants all his trials in
secret and doesn't want the bad newspapermen to learn anything about
his machine or to take pictures of it." The New York *Herald* observed:
"The Herring airship is packed in a suit case. This is the safe way to use
it." Another paper wisecracked: "Mr. Herring, the ambitious would-be
aviator, denies that he received his inspiration from flying fish."

Now the fresh deadline of November 13 loomed ahead. On October
28, according to his story, he went alone out to Hempstead Plains on
Long Island at early dawn to test his plane in privacy. As in the case of
his purported 1898 flights in Michigan, he later sought out a newsman
and volunteered an account, with no one to substantiate it. He said he
had put the plane together hastily and that some important parts were
"lacking altogether." Even so, he claimed a flight of 300 feet at an
altitude of three feet, which ended in a "considerable smashup" of the
machine, from which he escaped uninjured but "much disheartened."
After the wreck, he looked about to see if anyone had witnessed his
chagrin, and, seeing no one, concluded he was alone with his grief. Later
he learned that "one person" had seen it from a distance, but he had no
name to offer.

When quizzed on a witness stand in future as to the identity of that
person, he said it was "a neighbor's boy—or somebody else." How far did
he fly? "Oh, not quite as far as across the street, I don't think." How
high? "I shouldn't say it was more than the height of a table." Finally he
sidestepped: "I don't think I have got a very good memory."

So now Herring, like the Wrights, would have to start from scratch
and build a new airplane to fulfill his contract. The brothers had been

granted an extension of nine months because of Orville's accident. When Herring requested nine months for a similar reason, the Signal Corps could not consistently deny him the same privilege, even though it had no proof of the calamity he claimed.

10. Silver Dart

With Selfridge's death, much of the boyish verve, the sheer fun, drained out of the A.E.A. It came as a grim reminder that what they were involved in was not child's play; that the law of gravity had not been repealed. A crumb of consolation was the fact that the tragedy did not strike in one of their own machines. The Association at any rate had a martyr as it turned, sorrowing, back to the unfinished task.

The shock was compounded for Hammondsport residents by the nearly simultaneous death of Oliver Jones in a dirigible. Jones's *Boomerang* had not panned out very well and, needing money, he accepted an exhibition date in Maine for a Toledo promoter. His wife was in the crowd when the propeller fouled the gas-bag and the hydrogen burst into flame. Jones was killed by falling atop the engine. He was the father of three small children.

The Curtiss abode was reduced to only one boarder, J. A. D. McCurdy, and the Hammondsport wing of the A.E.A. had full control in the design of his Drome Number 4. Hence the team of John and Glenn was welded into a closer partnership than had previously been the case, while a similar orientation, though of a father-son type, was taking place in Nova Scotia between Bell and Baldwin. McCurdy confided that he preferred his first name, John, to the "Douglas" which Dr. Bell always used because of its Scottishness. Curtiss respected his wish, and took to calling him John even in messages to Bell. (McCurdy's surplus initial stood for Alexander.)

An early decision about Drome Number 4 was for a change of wing fabric. The *June Bug's* wings, despite the yellow "dope," tended to leak air. Captain Baldwin helped out by getting the rubber company to make up a thinner variant of the rubberized silk used in his Army dirigible: silk on top, rubber beneath. When Mrs. Bell heard that McCurdy had christened his "drome" the *Silver Dart*, she asked why, and he elucidated: "Well, the surfaces are silvered on one side, that suggested the 'Silver'; and the word 'Dart' will explain itself. Also the combination of the two sounded rather attractive to me . . . She certainly is a beauty."

Indeed, the *Silver Dart* was accorded more loving care and craftsmanship than had gone into the prior three A.E.A. machines, and Curtiss likewise referred to her as "a beauty." He wrote Mrs. Bell that Drome Number 4 was being "built 'like a watch,' and looks like business throughout. The parts are well finished, the result of knowing what we want and not having to change as in the previous machines." There was "no home-made appearance." As for mechanical improvements, Carl Dienstbach, the German writer, who made a special trip to look her over, declared that the A.E.A., with the *Dart*, had reached "fully the level of the Wright flyer."

The main handicap of the *June Bug*, as all recognized, was the brevity of her flights due to rapid heating of the engine. Above all else McCurdy wanted his "drome" to have a water-cooled motor. Reporting to Bell on progress up to September 1, Curtiss said: "As we have become more proficient in handling flying machines, and desire to make longer flights, it is thought advisable to fit the Number 4 with an engine having a surplus of power, and a positive cooling system. Such a type of engine would ultimately be necessary on all successful machines . . . Our shops are running night and day on this motor."

And McCurdy told Mrs. Bell: "We are staking a lot on the Silver Dart's future with the new engine. It will be such a satisfaction to have the engine maintain its power indefinitely so that you can come down only when you want to."

The *Dart* was originally intended to be a two-man vehicle, the passenger to sit tandem behind the pilot. With this in mind, she was also to have dual propellers, mounted coaxially on the same shaft. That was the idea before the Fort Myer tragedy: After that, Bell put his foot down against the double plan in a letter to Curtiss:

"The temptation is strong to attempt to carry two men in the *June Bug*, or the *Silver Dart*, because Orville Wright, Wilbur Wright, Farman and Delagrange have done it. I do not want you, or any of you, to attempt it. It has already been done by others, and of course we know we can do it too, but I do not think that we have any right to run unnecessary risks . . . Orville Wright, the most experienced aviator of the world, and probably the best, has lost poor Selfridge. Do not let us, with less experience, run any risks of this kind . . . Remember Selfridge."

Accordingly, the twin propellers were dismissed. Construction details were supervised by Kenneth Ingraham, Bell's mechanical foreman sent down from Baddeck in place of Bedwin. The *Herald* was ecstatic about the *Dart*, reporting: "All the woodwork is carefully varnished and polished, metal work enameled and the entire mechanism finished like an up-to-date automobile."

From his experience with the *June Bug*, Curtiss suggested that the wing-tip ailerons be enlarged and lengthened for stronger lateral control. As a matter of fact, the trusty old *June Bug* took on the role of guinea-pig for her successor. To try out modifications, Curtiss and McCurdy made repeated and risky hops in the *Bug*. In this way they found it possible to dispense with a tail altogether, and that the craft was then speedier and more sensitive to control. "John and I both flew tonight with nothing behind but rudder; no tail," Curtiss wired Bell. The *Silver Dart*, in consequence, was tailless. To make up for the lack, she was given a really imposing front elevator, in biplane form, which jutted forward 17 feet on bamboo longerons.

During one of those *June Bug* tests, Curtiss had an experience he considered worth reporting to Bell. The breaking of a fuel line caused four cylinders to cut out and he seized the opportunity to see "how near I could come to flying" with only half an engine. "To my surprise, I kept on going and I made a good half mile, including quite a turn."

Still another innovation in the *Silver Dart* was a power transmission arrangement, the propeller being set higher than the motor instead of rotating directly on the shaft. McCurdy settled for a chain transmission with sprocket wheels after multiple belts did too much slipping.

One evening Harry Champlin, out for an autumnal stroll with his pointer, stopped by at the tent to see how the new "drome" was coming along. The dog was inquisitive, too, and took a notion to leap on the wing. A large hole in the fabric was the unhappy outcome of this visit, but the *Herald* was amused: "H. M. Champlin's pointer tried out the flying machine, *Silver Dart*, the other night in the tent on Stony Brook Farm. It failed to support him, even on the ground. He did not confine himself to the aviator's seat, but climbed out on the wings, the silken surfaces of which were not sufficiently strong at one point to support his weight. He then fell through and abandoned further experiments."

*   *   *

Meanwhile, scarcely a month elapsed after Curtiss won first leg on the Scientific American Trophy when the conditions for second leg were made known. Owing to the rapid strides of French aviation, explained the Aero Club, the new requirement would be a flight of 25 kilometers (15.5 miles), with a rounding of the starting point for a complete circle. The Aero Club took it for granted that the A.E.A. would defend its grip on the trophy, but also had some reason to hope for a contest this time. General Allen, Chief of the Signal Corps, indicated that either or both of the Army contract machines (that is, the Wright and the Herring) would be permitted to compete if delivered soon enough. The date was set for the coming Labor Day, September 7.

McCurdy picked up word of it when he stopped off at the Aero Club on the way back from a Washington trip. Notifying Bell of the conditions, he asked wistfully: "Do you think we ought to enter?" McCurdy very much yearned to be the A.E.A. man to clinch second leg on the trophy with his *Silver Dart*. Plainly, the *June Bug*, with its quick-heating engine, did not stand a chance of doing 25 kilometers. Bell's reply, while not arbitrary, was negative enough: "Not advisable I think to enter for Scientific American Trophy September under new conditions without some reasonable prospect of success and without competitors, but do as you think best."

The trophy committee intended to make certain that the next trial would be in or near the city of New York, and specified Morris Park as the place. Morris Park, high up in the Bronx, was an erstwhile horse track which the Automobile Club of America had used for auto racing. Now a newly formed Aeronautic Society of New York (an inner circle of the Aero Club) had leased it as a flying ground for machines made by its own members, none of which was able to fly.[1] The Curtiss Manufacturing Company placed two engines on loan there for use by the experimenters.

Failing to drum up a trophy contestant for Labor Day, the Aero Club and its splinter Society continued to put pressure on Curtiss and McCurdy to make the try with the *Silver Dart*, and they were itching to do so. Unfortunately the making of the engine, with larger cylinder bore than any previous, ran into difficulties and took far longer than expected. On October 22, Curtiss went to New York to consult with Charles Manly of the contest committee and look over Morris Park "to be sure of our ground there." He found the track and infield suitable for size, but reported a number of fences they should insist be removed if they went. On the final day of October the engine was installed in the *Dart*, but Curtiss was obliged to wire the Aeronautic Society: MORRIS PARK IM-POSSIBLE. NO FLIGHTS HERE YET. VERY SORRY INDEED. Still the Aero Club people would not give up, and McCurdy informed Bell: "Mr. Post assures us that we can have a trial whenever we wish."

Tribulations with the *Silver Dart*, especially in adjusting the engine with the new style of transmission, combined with the onset of cold weather to rule out a trophy trial before spring.

*   *   *

By this time, Dr. Bell was showing signs of impatience at the delay with the *Silver Dart* and at the obvious tendency on the part of his protégés to be more interested in airplanes than in his tetrahedral kites. In truth, the *Cygnet II* was getting the short end of the stick. Theoretically, the headquarters of the A.E.A. had been transferred back to Nova Scotia as of October 1, on a motion by Curtiss himself at the Washington meeting; and here was half of the Association lingering at Hammondsport, paying so much homage to the *Silver Dart* that the engine for the new kite was not yet in production. Even Casey Baldwin, at Baddeck with him, was off on a new tack, striving to make an aircraft that would rise from water. Little could Bell be blamed for reminding the others that, after all, his kites had been the root of the Association.

During the six-months grace period of the A.E.A., the chairman suggested that its activity be restricted, insofar as possible, to "the utilization of tetrahedral structures in practical aerodromes, and subordinate other plans until we have succeeded in placing a tetrahedral structure in the air." This had been the original object, he pointed out; and besides they would have "no difficulty in securing good patents upon aerodromes embodying tetrahedral structures. So much work has been done by other people upon plans for aerodromes having the general features of our first four aerodromes . . . that it is extremely doubtful whether patents of any great value can be obtained to represent our work at Hammondsport." This pessimistic view seems at variance with his initial reaction to the *June Bug.*

Bell's theorizing was in sharp contrast to Curtiss's ingrained practicality. (Curtiss once remarked that he never saw a man less handy with tools than Bell.) The aging inventor used the *Bulletin* often to expound his theories on aeronautics. "I look upon the kite as a flying machine at anchor, and the flying machine as a free kite; and between these two conditions we have a vast field for exploration with engines and propellers operating under the actual conditions of flight, the whole being supported in the air by the wind whether the engine should prove self-supporting or not." Again: "I have no doubt that from the viewpoint of efficiency horizontal surfaces are superior to oblique, but they are very unstable in the air . . . Automatic stability is the great feature of the pure tetrahedral construction, so that I feel that this feature must not be sacrificed for any other consideration."

So far as known, Curtiss did not openly argue the divergence of views with Bell, as Casey Baldwin evidently did at Baddeck, but he was capable of innuendo to get his point across. For instance, in a letter to Bell he said he had found the summary of latest experiments on tetrahedral aerodromes "most interesting and instructive"; then added: "The recent flight of the 'June Bug' with but four cylinders running, Mr. Wright's flights of an hour alone and shorter time with Mr. Lahm aboard, furnish data as to the power required in aerodromes of this type. By making deductions, required power for the tetrahedral-cell structure may be obtained with reasonable accuracy."

Stubborn as he was about his kites, it must not be inferred that Bell's theorizing was all impractical. The aileron concept, after all, had been injected by him. In October 1908 he tossed into the pool another idea in advance of its time: "Should not the front control be at the rear instead of the front? . . . Would it not be better to use a horizontal tail at the rear? The natural action of the wind of advance upon the front control is to upset the whole machine upwards or downwards so as to make a complete somersault . . . Whereas the natural action upon a horizontal tail at the rear is to keep the longitudinal axis of the machine parallel to the line of advance and prevent any deviation up or down excepting by the will of the operator."

Dr. Bell had never gone up in an airplane and never would. Nonetheless, he sensed that the long "heads" which were carried by practically all early planes (those of Curtiss and the Wrights included) were implausible as well as potentially dangerous.

In a memorandum to the attorneys handling the A.E.A. patent application, Bell set forth a lucid analysis of the differences between the Wright planes and those of the A.E.A.; in substance, a brief for defense in an infringement suit if the Wrights should see fit to start one. The Wright framework was flexible, of necessity, in order to permit of wing-warping. The A.E.A. framework was stiff and rigid. "We do not twist our aeroplanes, or any portion of them, for any purpose whatsoever; indeed, we look upon this kind of action as distinctly detrimental from a structural point of view, and our form of truss is specially designed to prevent it."

The Wrights' wing-twisting, he submitted, was not enough in itself to accomplish the result they were after, and so: "They require to combine, with the twisting action of the aeroplane, a steering movement of the vertical rudder at the rear. Our lateral rudders [ailerons] by themselves accomplish the desired result without any cooperation with the vertical rudder . . . Even though it should be held that the twisted aeroplanes of the Wright Brothers machine act as lateral rudders or are lateral rudders themselves, still it is obvious that they are not the equivalent of *our* lateral rudders, for an additional element is required in the Wright combination (the vertical rudder) to produce our result.

"Moving the 'lateral marginal portions of the surfaces' is then the essence of the Wright method. The one essential ingredient of their combination. If we do this we infringe their patent according to their own declaration [in the words of their patent]. But if we do not, do we infringe? Here we have the utmost scope of their invention defined in their own words; and yet it seems to me they do not cover our own case. In our machine we do not move 'the lateral margins of the aeroplanes' at all; and could not move them, even if we so desired, on account of the rigid nature of the trussing employed.

"Of course, we must anticipate an attempt to show that our lateral rudders are the lateral margins of the aeroplane.

"I think we can show clearly that our lateral rudders are quite distinct from 'the lateral margins of the aeroplanes' . . . Our lateral rudders are mere appendages.

"I am decidedly of the opinion that our invention is not covered by the Wright Brothers patent."

On November 18, 1908, Bell received from his attorneys copies of a proposed application for patent on the Hammondsport airplanes, and forwarded one to Curtiss and McCurdy. It was entitled "A new and useful Improvement in Flying Machines." Twenty-eight claims were cited, Number 1 of which was a pair of "lateral balancing rudders"; the word "aileron" does not appear in the text of the patent. Claim Number 1 is stated thus: "In a flying machine, the combination of a supporting surface having a positive angle of incidence, a pair of lateral balancing rudders, one arranged on either side of the medial fore and aft line of the machine connections between said balancing rudders, means normally supporting said lateral rudders at a zero angle of incidence, and means operating to shift said balancing rudders to equal and opposite angles of incidence."

In general, the patent provided for "rigid non-flexible supporting surfaces," as opposed to flexible wings, and stated: "Any suitable form of rigid non-flexible supporting surfaces may be employed, and there may be one or a plurality of such surfaces arranged in any desired relation to each other"; the essential point being that they "shall not be constructed to be warped or flexed for the purpose of restoring the lateral balance." The ailerons were preferably to be arranged so as to be automatically operated by movements of the aviator's body. The total structure was to be "supported on wheels, one of which serves as a steering wheel to control the forward line of movement of the machine when it is on the ground."

The main A.E.A. patent, No. 1,011,106, was granted December 5, 1911, but its issuance was delayed until 1913 by an interference action. Two separate patents, covering claims on inventions made under the A.E.A., were issued to Baldwin and Bell, respectively.

*   *   *

The notion of a water airplane cropped up spontaneously in each wing of the A.E.A.; although this was not, of course, a new idea in the world. A few European attempts had been made in that direction, and the Wrights had tried a pontooned plane unsuccessfully on the Miami River in Ohio. With spacious expanses of water at both Hammondsport and Baddeck, it would have been surprising if Bell's Boys had not thought of putting them to some aeronautical use.

Baldwin was the first to do something about it, writing McCurdy in August 1908 that they were beginning at Baddeck to develop "an aerodrome of the water-fowl type—start off as a boat, lift out on hydroplanes, and then be a free flying machine." (By "hydroplanes," he meant what later came to be known as hydrofoils, ladder-like steps of tilted blades fastened to the keel of a boat; he likened them to a Venetian blind.) "We have retackled the old problem of speed on water," he said. "It has always seemed to me that the hydroplane was worthy of a lot more consideration than it is getting."

A week later, Curtiss expressed himself on the same subject without mentioning hydrofoils: "The scheme of starting a flying machine from and landing on the water has been in my mind for some time. It has many advantages, and I believe it can be worked out. Even if a most suitable device for launching and landing on land is secured, a water craft will still be indispensable for war purposes, and if the exhibition field is to be considered, would, I believe, present greater possibilities in this line than a machine which works on land . . . I do not think the problem is difficult."

On Baddeck Bay, Baldwin conducted towing experiments with a specially built boat hull designed to become the body of an aircraft if it could be made to leave the water riding on hydrofoils. When a workman spoke of this boat as a "dhonnas beag," Gaelic for "little devil," that became its formal name: the *Dhonnas Beag*. Bell denominated it Drome Number 6, anticipating a modified tetrahedral kite superstructure akin to a heavily braced triplane. After many frustrations in obtaining a lift out of the hydrofoils, Baldwin had the satisfaction of making the *Dhonnas Beag* rise a foot above the surface under its own power with an aerial propeller. This did not, however, make it a hydroaeroplane, and Drome Number 6 never broke out of its chrysalis.

The Hammondsport partners fussed and fumed with the *Silver Dart* all during November, and Bell grew a mite testy, asking for news. "I have not written before," Curtiss reacted on the 24th, "as I had nothing good to report. Most people don't like excuses. Cylinder blew on the Loon. Other mishaps. Water got on distributor and caused engine to skip.—Plant working 22 hours a day.—We have read so much of the Wrights and others flying, not to mention the fact that we should have been through here long ago, that we are getting very uneasy."

Bell answered through the *A.E.A. Bulletin*: "The only criticism I have to offer is that our Hammondsport members seem inclined to report only their successes and look upon accidents as failures instead of experiences to be profited by. What we want to know from Hammondsport is the answer to the question: 'What are you doing?' . . . Silence does not give us any information . . . The delay in completing the new engine affects us all, for it is needed at Beinn Bhreagh as much as at Hammondsport. We all have confidence in Curtiss, however, and feel sure that out of his troubles will come triumph and a better and more reliable engine than we have had before. Go ahead, Curtiss, and don't get too blue. Your letter of Nov. 24 sounds like a wail. Baldwin had his ups and downs, too, but he is on top today—so will you be, too. Go ahead and good luck to you."

One thing Curtiss and McCurdy had been doing behind the curtain of their silence was taking an impromptu fling at water flying according to their own lights, neither being enthusiastic about Baldwin's hydrofoils. To that end, the *June Bug* was transformed into something Curtiss liked to call a "water bug," but which McCurdy promoted into a bird by naming the *Loon*. They built two canoe-like boats of California redwood, 20 feet long, covered with rubber oilcloth, and attached them "catamaran-like" to the *June Bug*'s underside. When this was done, Curtiss informed Bell, half apologetically: "Perhaps we have taken too much liberty in trying this experiment, but we thought no time was being lost and it would be fine to know what chances there are of raising from the boats."

Still they did not trespass on the *Silver Dart*'s legitimate time to try out the *Loon*, which they planned to do with the *Dart*'s powerful engine. At the tag-end of November, when McCurdy finally decided on a chain transmission to replace the slipping belts, they seized the chance while that was being built to transfer the motor over to the *Loon*. Keuka Lake was then introduced to her first pontooned aircraft, with McCurdy piloting and Curtiss observing from a motorboat. After a 400-yard run without a rise, the propeller shaft was sheared off. Repairs were made, and next day McCurdy forced the *Loon* a mile up the lake and back, clocked at 27 miles per hour, but could not get unstuck from the surface. "The experiment makes it apparent that it will take a great amount of power to get these boats out of the water," Curtiss reported to Baddeck. "Those hydroplanes you have been building begin to look good to us. We have not given up, however." In fact, even as the motor was restored to the *Silver Dart*, they began preparing a wide set of wooden hydrofoils for the *Loon*'s next experiment.

*   *   *

Winter cracked down abruptly on the Finger Lakes, with snow and blow and more troubles for the *Silver Dart*. A vicious wind slashed rips in the sheltering tent, and Harry Champlin allowed them to nail up a jerry-built shed against the side of his barn. With a water-cooled engine, some kind of anti-freeze fluid was necessary. A solution of calcium chloride was tried, but it made the water heat quickly and a hose burst. The anhydrous chemical drew moisture. The chain transmission did not function well and they reverted to a belt drive.

Despite bad weather, McCurdy broke in the *Silver Dart* with three "preliminary canters" on December 6, and rejoiced: "She seems so light and buoyant." Meteorology was friendlier on the 14th, and he made four flights of significant length, duly reported to Mrs. Bell: "Balance and control satisfactory. Feels to king's taste."

Contrary to habit, the Bells were remaining at Beinn Bhreagh for the winter in order to see the remaining A.E.A. experiments through to a finish, and it was heartening news that Drome Number 4 was at long last in the air. By this time Dr. Bell was in Washington for a meeting of the Regents of the Smithsonian Institution. He had previously written to Dr. Charles D. Walcott, secretary of the Smithsonian: "The Wright Brothers are being deservedly honored in Europe. Cannot America do anything for them? Why should not the Smithsonian Institution give a Langley Medal to encourage aviation?" This letter was read at the meeting and sparked a resolution creating such a medal for "specially meritorious investigations in aeronautical science." The Regents then voted its first award to the Wright brothers.

Having set the ball rolling for honors to the Wrights, Dr. Bell turned his attention to the new A.E.A. "drome" which Dienstbach judged had caught up with them. He invited three influential aviation specialists to accompany him to Hammondsport and see what had there been wrought: E. L. Jones, editor of *Aeronautics;* James Means of Boston, editor of the *Aeronautical Annual;* and Wilbur R. Kimball, secretary of the Aeronautic Society of New York. The delegation arrived too late for that good flying day and put up at the Hammondsport Hotel, hoping for another day of the same kind.

Meanwhile, General Allen notified Bell that the Signal Corps would be unable to send an officer to Hammondsport to observe the *Silver Dart* trials, "due to pressure of public business."

Time was short, what with the holidays coming on, and Bell insisted on being back at Beinn Bhreagh for Christmas with his wife. On the 20th, weather relented enough for an attempt, though a brisk wind was blowing down the lake, and north was the only direction in which takeoff was possible at Stony Brook Farm. McCurdy made three runs downwind but was unable to get airborne; Bell took this failure as an indication that the Hammondsport machines were growing too heavy. He inspected the *Loon* and shook his head at the 9-foot width of its hydrofoils. On the 21st, the weather turned wretched again, and the visitors left town without witnessing a flight. Bell told Curtiss and McCurdy that he wanted a full meeting of the A.E.A. at Baddeck right after New Year's.

While dismantling the *Silver Dart* for shipment to Nova Scotia, the two lagging members snatched the opportunity to give the *Loon* a farewell try with the hydrofoils, the southern end of the lake not yet being locked in. The *Dart's* engine was mounted anew in the *Loon*. On January 2, 1909, late in the day, McCurdy gunned the "water-bug" back and forth, and the hydrofoil blades lifted her barely enough for a little open space to show between pontoons and water.

After that, they jacked her up and sawed off the hydrofoils for a last go with the bare pontoons. By then the sun was gone, but a bright moon rode the sky. In pulling away from the dock, McCurdy felt a jerk but ignored it. In fact, the sternpost of a pontoon had fouled the pier and been ripped out. After an unfruitful run up the lake and back, he taxied slowly abreast of the dock as water poured into the damaged pontoon. The *Loon* listed and sank humiliatingly sidewise in 12 feet of water.

Like mischievous boys, McCurdy and Curtiss jointly signed a telegram to Bell: GAVE VAUDEVILLE PERFORMANCE TONIGHT BY MOONLIGHT WITH LOON. FIRST HYDRO TEST SUCCESSFUL, SECOND AERODROME TEST FAIRLY SUCCESSFUL, THIRD SUBMARINE TEST MOST SUCCESSFUL OF ALL. EXPERIMENTS ENDED.

* * *

On the 8th of January, McCurdy appeared alone at Beinn Bhreagh, bringing with him Curtiss's proxy vote for the appointed meeting. Curtiss sent word he would be detained longer in Hammondsport because of a directors' meeting of his company "and other important business." Bell's annoyance growled in a telegram to Curtiss on the 12th: YOUR PRESENCE NECESSARY TO DETERMINE THE NAMES TO BE SIGNED TO THE APPLICATION FOR A PATENT. NO PROXY WILL MEET THE CASE. PLEASE COME IMMEDIATELY AFTER YOUR DIRECTORS' MEETING IF POSSIBLE.

A hint that Curtiss did not feel obligated to jump when Bell cracked a whip may be sensed in the fact that he let three days lapse before answering, and then did so by letter: "I appreciate the importance of the patent matters, but I am sure it is also important to get the power plant of the tetrahedral aerodrome number 5 ready to ship so that there will not be any delay when we are ready to take her out on the ice." The Bras d'Or being icebound, the *Cygnet II* was being fitted with metal runners.

In returning to his "Douglas" identity, McCurdy found the Canadian wing of the A.E.A. in a glum mood. (Bell mirrored this in the *Bulletin:* "We have had our ups and downs, and we have now arrived at a point where we are, all of us, decidedly down.") Perhaps the bleak Nova Scotia winter was partly to blame, perhaps the lack of progress; Bell thought the main headache was "a difficulty of propulsion." The power problem of the big kite was yet unsolved. Buoyant by nature, McCurdy jumped in and gave the atmosphere an upbeat by starting to construct an ice-cycle, such as Curtiss had used on Keuka Lake, to test out propellers for the *Cygnet*. Soon this rig was scooting about Baddeck Bay with the 4-cylinder engine they had at hand.

Further word came from Curtiss that his stockholders' meeting had been belatedly held, that the new engine was being set up for bench-test, and that he would start north as soon as the test-runs were completed. Mrs. Curtiss, he added, would accompany him for her first visit to Beinn Bhreagh after long-standing invitation.

Owing to the vagaries of railroad express service, the *Silver Dart* reached its destination by installments. When the first crate was unloaded at Baddeck station, the villagers, suddenly smitten with aviation fever, took up cudgels to have the shipment exempted from customs duty. As the outcome of a spontaneous mass meeting, they wired the Minister of Customs at Ottawa: CITIZENS OF BADDECK VERY ANXIOUS THAT YOU ALLOW FREE ENTRY ON EXPERIMENTAL FLYING MACHINE AND APPARATUS FOR DR. GRAHAM BELL WHICH ARRIVED LAST NIGHT. The Minister obliged, but with a proviso that the machine be returned to the United States within two years (an academic point, as it eventuated).

A lengthy train ride through Canada's wintry wilderness brought the Curtisses to Baddeck by January 29. Bundled in robes, they enjoyed the adventure of a sleigh ride across the bay to Red Head Point, where their hosts proclaimed an "old home week" in their honor. The maestro of motors was back in the fold—or so it seemed. Huge logs blazed in the fireplace and there was animated talk in their glow. High in the scale of conversational topics was the burgeoning of trophies and financial rewards for exhibition flying, all tempting to these young men who so lately had found wings.

Nobody questioned that McCurdy was entitled to enter his *Silver Dart* for second leg on the Scientific American Trophy when spring came again. But what about the tantalizing cash prize offers now popping up in Europe? Lord Northcliffe, the British publisher, was dangling his London *Daily Mail* prize of £1000 for a flight across the English Channel, with no takers yet; Wilbur Wright had considered going for it the previous autumn, but backed down. The A.E.A. airmen were confident the *Dart* could span the Strait of Dover without half trying. The newest prize, just announced, was the Gordon Bennett Trophy, carrying with it $5000 cash, for the best speed by an airplane at an international air meet to be held somewhere in France that summer of 1909; the donor of this was James Gordon Bennett, Jr., flamboyant publisher of the New York *Herald* and its Paris edition (he lived self-exiled in Paris). Whoever won the Bennett race would axiomatically be aerial speed champion of the world. Yet another possibility mulled over was the forthcoming Hudson-Fulton Celebration, for which the State of New York had recently established a commission; the program for this was to embrace demonstrations of American progress in the air, and both the Aero Club and the Aeronautic Society were collaborating with the commission to decide exactly what.

Apart from the fireside circles, the A.E.A. lost no time diving into business sessions on the urgent patent matter. The members reached agreement that the application should include twenty-five claims in all, and that Casey Baldwin, as chief engineer, was responsible for the subject matter of fifteen of these. Accordingly, they approved a separate patent for Baldwin on his claims; while all members were to share alike in the other ten claims, of which the ailerons made one.

Shortly after reaching Beinn Bhreagh, Curtiss dropped a postcard to the editor of the Hammondsport paper, saying that parts of the *Silver Dart* were still held up by the express company, and: "Ice on the Bras d'Or Lakes is thick enough to build a house on. Eighteen below zero this morning. Dr. Bell's tetrahedral ready for engine. Been experimenting with propellors on motor ice boat."

Pending arrival of the *Dart's* motor and the new one for the powered kite, there was little for Curtiss to do except join the ice-cycle capers. The triangular platform was large enough for three men. On the 8th of February, they ran far down the harbor, making the fastest time to date. Bedwin manned the engine, McCurdy took instrument readings on the propeller, and Curtiss was at the steering wheel. The runners had no provision for braking. On the return, Bedwin did not cut the engine soon enough and the craft hit the landing of the motorboat shed with such force that all three men were thrown violently forward, but Curtiss was the only one injured. His lower lip was nearly torn off when his chin struck the rim of the wheel. Suffering from shock and loss of blood, he was helped to the house while McCurdy sped across to the village in an ice sailboat, bringing back a doctor and a nurse. Dr. McIver stitched the lip back on and diagnosed no internal injury, although the iron rod of the steering-post was bent by the impact.

Weak and dizzy, Curtiss spent the ensuing two or three days in bed, and the A.E.A. held meetings in his room. While the wound was healing, he was unable to shave over it, so that for several months to come he wore a small tuft of goatee. A conspicuous scar across his chin was a permanent souvenir of that accident, and for the remainder of his life his lower lip was numb.

*   *   *

The A.E.A. now centered its efforts upon how best to perpetuate and exploit its findings. The chairman was unwilling for Mrs. Bell to put up any additional funds for a continuance beyond March 31, and at the same time leery of litigation if they should take the easy path of raising money by exhibitions of the *Silver Dart* and *June Bug*. A proposal was seriously considered to place on the market a flying toy for children. One thing Bell made plain: "I am very much averse to attempting to make money under our present organization, or under any organization that would throw the financial responsibility on me alone, for I am the only member of the Association that could be touched in the matter."

It would be difficult to raise capital by a stock issue without the protection of patents, and the Patent Office would require time to pass on their applications. Bell had come around to thinking they should organize an American Aerodrome Company with Curtiss as manager, and said: "I would therefore ask Mr. Curtiss what he thinks would be the minimum amount of money required for the first year, considering the fact that we have already two aerodromes completed that can be used for exploitation purposes. He should also include in the estimate the manufacture of at least one other aerodrome at Hammondsport.

Then let us consider how far it would be possible to raise this amount of money and a sufficient amount more to pay the expenses of a moderate amount of litigation."

The estimate Curtiss arrived at was $10,000 as working capital to support running expenses for one year. He went beyond with his personal appraisal of commercial possibilities for the immediate future, starting from the premise that practically all aeroplanes up to then had been purely experimental. "Little or no revenue has been derived from their use except for the winning of a few prizes. Farman made one unsuccessful attempt at exhibition work and the U.S. government have let two contracts which, as yet, have not been filled. Government contracts and exhibition work seem to be the two most promising sources of revenue. There are no prospects of the U.S. government placing further orders for some time to come, and when they do the Wrights will no doubt be in on the 'ground floor.'" He thought the A.E.A. might try to get the Canadian government to invest in one or two machines, and went on: "There are now several cash prizes offered in America and still more abroad. But when you play for these big stakes you play against big odds and 'there is many a slip, etc.' However, these cash prizes look very alluring. I think prize chasing and exhibition work should go hand in hand . . .

"Probably by another year the machines will become more standardized and a certain amount of business may be expected from private parties for machines for sport. Perhaps an Aerial Development Company could be formed to look after Government contracts, prizes, etc., and get in shape to handle the large volume of business which is bound to come later."

The company idea firmed up in Bell's mind until, at a conference on February 19, he submitted details of his scheme. These were generally favored in the discussion, although no vote was taken. He proposed converting the Association into a joint-stock company to be known as "The American Aerodrome Company," chartered under the laws of New York State, with headquarters at Hammondsport. This company would have a nominal capital of $100,000, divided either into 1000 shares with par value of $100, or 10,000 shares with par value of $10. The A.E.A. was to transfer all its property and inventions to the company, receiving in return the amount of money it had expended on experiments, in the form of fully paid-up shares at par. Mrs. Bell would be given 1 percent of the Association's shares for each $1000 she had contributed; the rest to be divided equally between Bell, McCurdy, Baldwin, Curtiss, and E. A. Selfridge. The remainder of the nominal capital, in undistributed shares, would go into the company treasury, to be sold for working capital as needed.

* * *

While taking part in deliberations of this nature, Curtiss was carrying on an exchange of telegrams with Augustus M. Herring[2] in New York. Had his colleagues known the content of these messages, it would have given quite a different complexion to their planning.

Only two days prior to the above conference, Herring had wired: BEST POSSIBLE BACKING. SMALL COMPANY, FIRST. WAY CLEAR TO MILLION EACH. BETTER COME HERE NOW.

Curtiss replied: PROPOSITION AGREEABLE.

On the day that Bell submitted his plan of organization, another telegram came to Curtiss: CAN CLOSE $90,000 BASIS, 50 STOCK, $25,000 CASH, $15,000 PURCHASE MONEY MORTGAGE. WILL CASH MORTGAGE. SALARY $5000. WE CONTROL COMPANY. I KEEP FOREIGN PATENTS. GIVE INTEREST TO YOU. HELP WORK MEN. WIRE IF ACCEPTED. HERRING.

The answer was: BOTH MESSAGES RECEIVED. I SHOULD HAVE 50 CASH AS PER LETTER. HOW ABOUT 30 CASH, 20 GOOD MORTGAGE, 40 STOCK. IF THIS IS AGREEABLE, WILL COME FIRST OF WEEK. GLENN H. CURTISS.

Herring responded with alacrity: ACCEPT ON BASIS YOUR TELEGRAM. CAN YOU PERSUADE DR. BELL ONE OF OUR INCORPORATORS? ALL OTHERS BIG NAMES. BIG FUTURE.

Curtiss well knew what Bell's reaction would be to such a proposition. In this instance, he replied by letter, saying: "I do not think Mr. Bell would consider making any connection with this company as he has a plan for a big organization, and I think best not to mention this at present; however, if I should come with you I think the other scheme would be given up."

A tiny warning signal seems to have flashed in the back of Curtiss's ordinarily cautious brain, when he remarked: "I don't know the value of your patents but I assume they are fundamental and strong." (At a future time, under oath, Herring would say: "I didn't have any patents, but I had some applications." He would admit that he did not write to Curtiss to set him straight on the supposed patents, or inform him when next he saw him.)

The meaning of the foregoing long-distance dialogue is that Herring was roping Curtiss into accepting him as a quasi-partner in the formation of an aeronautical company, in which Curtiss was to surrender his Hammondsport plant and property, including the motorcycle business. From the content of the messages, it may be judged that the negotiation had not progressed far before Curtiss left for Nova Scotia, but that he had at least received the overture. As later became known, Herring laid his groundwork with Captain Thomas Baldwin in talks at the Aero Club, making Baldwin his intermediary. He told Baldwin that he had some new discoveries which, if applied to the A.E.A. type of airplanes, would "control the world's market"; that any machine without them would become practically valueless. These purported inventions (as Herring afterward declared) were "in automatic devices to produce stability" and "surfaces that were of a high degree of efficiency." Furthermore, he informed Baldwin in strict confidence (except for Curtiss's ear) that he had gained access to a large amount of investment money and had "very responsible people" behind him.

Worldly-wise though he was, Captain Baldwin was taken in enough to pass the idea on to Curtiss. Further consultations took place while Curtiss was in Nova Scotia, in some of which the two were joined by Cortlandt Field Bishop, millionaire president of the Aero Club. A factor in Baldwin's gullibility may have been Herring's pledge to create a dirigible division of the company and install him at the head of it.

Somewhere along the line, if Herring's testimony is to be trusted: "Mr. Curtiss stated that he thought the others [of the A.E.A.] were unprogressive, particularly Dr. Bell, and that he couldn't see that there was much of a future to him in the A.E.A.; that he thought there was more money outside of it, operating independently."

At all events, Curtiss was thrust into a quandary. Abruptly, he stood at a crossroad in his career, and it was embarrassing that this should happen while he was a guest under the roof of his great friend and benefactor. Obviously, he decided against burning any bridges until he examined the Herring proposition at close range and found out how bona fide his financial backing might be.

* * *

The Curtisses remained long enough for the maiden trial of the kite, *Cygnet II*, and the Canadian debut of the *Silver Dart*. One engine had finally been delivered. The *Silver Dart*'s engine was installed in the *Cygnet II*, while they awaited arrival of the newer motor. Most of the populace of Baddeck village swarmed over the ice on skates, in sleighs, in iceboats.

At last Bell had a power plant in a tetrahedral kite, and the *Cygnet II* was pushed out easily onto the frozen surface of the Bras d'Or on February 22. McCurdy was elected her pilot. The laboratory staff were all on skates, and there was an unforeseen difficulty about this. When the propeller whirred, the men were expected to hold the machine firm until signaled to let go. This did not work out because their skates slipped on the ice, and the kite got away from them for a short skate of her own. At the second try, the *Cygnet* had run only a hundred feet or so when the engine died. At the third, she was gathering good speed, without lifting, when the propeller shaft sheared off. The propeller was broken to bits in striking the ice, and spectators scrambled for splinters as souvenirs.

On the following day the *Silver Dart* held the stage. She was to take off from the ice on wheels, rather than runners. There was no question about who should fly her. McCurdy was not only her sponsor but a Canadian citizen—and no airplane had yet flown in Canada. (In fact, McCurdy was the only man who ever flew the *Silver Dart*.) Curtiss made the last-minute checkup of the motor and stepped aside. Charles R. Cox, correspondent for the Washington *Star*, described what happened next:

"Everyone stood dumb-founded, and before they could realize that they had actually witnessed the first flight of a heavier-than-air machine in Canada, Mr. McCurdy was compelled to shut off the current and glide to the ground [sic], owing to the long stretch of land and trees in front of him. Just as he was about 10 feet from the ground he noticed two little girls skating in front of the machine, and if it wasn't for his presence of mind, and his complete control of the machine, a serious accident might have occurred. Gracefully did he steer to one side of them, making a beautiful landing on the ice."

The Board of Commissioners of the Town of Baddeck convened in special session to take note of the flight, placing a resolution on its records officially declaring it "an event of historic importance," not only the first flight in Canada, but in the British Empire. The signatures of 145 witnesses were taken and preserved, among them those of Mr. and Mrs. Glenn H. Curtiss. The secretary of the town commissioners, H. Percy Blanchard, wrote Bell: "This means a great deal for Baddeck. We cannot help but share in the fame of this event. We can at least express our appreciation and congratulations, as well as our admiration of the courage and nerve displayed by Mr. Douglas McCurdy."[3]

On the 24th, McCurdy went "circumdroming Baddeck Bay" (in

Bell's characteristic phrase) and sent a thrill of excitement pulsing across the Dominion of Canada which was echoed in the press of England. He reeled off a distance of 4½ miles, the longest flight yet made by a machine of the A.E.A. "It now became obvious that the whole country had become flying-machine crazy," reported a Canadian newsman. "People were awe-stricken and looked on even with their mouths open when the machine soared through the air, and in much better control than were the eye-witnesses." A flurry of questions and debate sprang up in the Parliament at Ottawa, as a few MPs argued that the Dominion should begin acquiring aeroplanes for military experiment.

"The Curtiss Number 3 engine worked beautifully," McCurdy enthused. "Not a skip all through the flight." The *Dart* being slightly damaged in landing, its engine and propeller were promptly transferred to the *Cygnet II*. (It appears that the separate engine for the *Cygnet* had not come). In the dusk of the winter's evening, the kite made three more starts without a lift-off.

The following day the Curtisses were driven to the station on their way home via New York, and this was destined to be Glenn's farewell to Beinn Bhreagh. Did he leave without giving his associates at least an inkling of his alternative prospects? If such were the case, his conduct would be hard to condone. Documents written or printed fail to bridge the gap. There is a temptation to clutch at straws in defense of his ethical behavior at this point. The last clue in the *A.E.A. Bulletin*, six days earlier, has him evincing his approval of an American Aerodrome Company to be based at his plant in Hammondsport, while other sources show that he was privately trading telegrams with Herring. The fact that Bell did not push his carefully thought-out plan to a vote before Curtiss departed, which would have been logical, suggests strongly that Curtiss told him something—perhaps suggested holding off until he had explored the Herring situation. It is further indicative that Bell, a stickler for integrity, continued friendly relations with Curtiss afterward. Yet another piece of circumstantial evidence in Curtiss's favor is the telegram he sent Douglas McCurdy a few days after his arrival in New York: BISHOP AGREES FOR CUP TRIAL . . . MADE HERRING PROPOSITION WHICH HE VERBALLY ACCEPTED. TOOK ORDER FOR AEROPLANE FROM AVIATION SOCIETY.

McCurdy must have already known what he meant by a "Herring proposition." He certainly knew what was meant by the Aero Club president's agreement to a "Cup Trial"; that it was all right for McCurdy to fly the *Silver Dart* for the Scientific American Trophy. He wired back: ARRANGE WITH OFFICIALS FOR TRIAL OF TROPHY AS SOON AS POSSIBLE. About taking an order for the "Aviation Society," Curtiss was referring to the Aeronautic Society of New York, which asked him to build a plane for the flying instruction of its members at Morris Park.

During the final month of the A.E.A.'s existence, Bell wished to concentrate on the *Cygnet II* (or Drome Number 5); his primal motive from the outset was still hanging fire. McCurdy kept on flying the *Silver Dart*, pending the kite's new propeller, and made two flights which were longer than eight miles. Motor trouble was recurrent, due partly to the frigid climate, and Bell commented: "I feel our only chance of winning the Scientific American Trophy lies in the weather, unless at least Mr. Curtiss should be able to be present. He has only to look at the engine to get it to run well."

The tetrahedral, riding on three tubular ice runners, received its 9 foot propeller on March 2 and the *Dart's* engine was transferred back. In a series of tries by McCurdy over the next several days, *Cygnet II* still could not rise. Bell suspended the effort and was said to be "heartbroken." In aftertime, he would never admit any fault in the efficiency of the tetrahedral structure; he said the kite had been "successful," only underpowered. There were indeed times when the engine power dropped low, and Bell wired Curtiss for help. "Conditions require presence engine man," Curtiss replied, and was on the verge of sending Alexander Pfitzner, "who tested engine and can be absolutely depended on to correct." Only the timing was off, as it turned out, and Bell telegraphed: DISCOVERED TROUBLE. GETTING 31 HP TODAY. KEEP PFITZNER AT HOME.

This exchange took place after Bell knew that Curtiss had succumbed to the wiles of Herring.

❁   ❁   ❁

As part of the web he was spinning, Augustus Herring planted hints in newspapers that no less than three European syndicates (in France, Germany, and Belgium) were after him with offers of $100,000 to quit the United States and build his planes abroad; that he had all but decided to accept one of these proposals. When Tom Baldwin was not within earshot, he carried on confidential chats at the Aero Club with Cortlandt Field Bishop,[4] assuring him that he practically had Glenn Curtiss in his pocket, needing only some extra capital to

close the deal. Bishop, who shared the prevalent illusion that Herring
was a species of aeronautical wizard, grew interested.

When Herring, Bishop, and Baldwin got their heads together, painting the rosy picture they would have ready to lay in front of Curtiss
when he came from Nova Scotia, they hatched an inspiration: Why
not send Curtiss to France to compete for the Gordon Bennett Trophy?
Bishop already had felt out the Wrights, finding them unreceptive.
The Aero Club was determined to have an American representative
in the race, and Bishop had only to say the word. Moreover, if Curtiss
should go and win the trophy, it would be a fine feather in the cap
of the company they were contemplating. Bishop volunteered to pay
the travel expenses if they could induce Curtiss to enter; he also
suggested they promise Curtiss that he could keep for himself any
cash prizes he might collect in Europe. All agreed that this would be
the fair thing for the flyer who would be building the plane and taking
the risks.

Captain Baldwin was so carried away by the outlook that he
met the Curtisses at Grand Central Station as the bearer of great
tidings. He told them Bishop had consented to be the principal financier
and organizer of the company, investing $21,000 and rounding up other
Wall Street capitalists; that Herring would kick in a substantial sum of
money along with the rights to all his patents. The only other investors
turned out to be Bishop's brother, David, with $16,000; and a friend,
James M. Deering,[5] with $1000. (The best final estimate on Herring's
cash outlay was $650.)

A press conference was summoned at the Aero Club rooms on
March 3, to announce formation of the Herring-Curtiss Company, the
first aeroplane industry in America. This combination, Cortlandt Bishop
said in his prepared statement, would enable the "two manufacturers
to work together in the building and improving of their aeroplanes
and motors." It would retain Herring's genius for the U.S.A.: "We
have lost the Wright brothers [rumor had them planning to establish
their factory in Europe] and we do not intend to let the foreigners
take everyone else of prominence in developing aerial flight. If Congress
will offer no incentive to inventors to remain in their own country,
the next best thing is to keep them here by private enterprise . . .
This matter of air navigation, especially with aeroplanes, is no longer
a fad or a joke, and wide awake men in New York with means realize
that fact."

The press releases asserted that the Herring-Curtiss Company would be capitalized at $360,000, with 3600 shares of stock at $100 par value. Its manufacturing plant would be at Hammondsport, and was to embrace an airship division headed by Captain Thomas Baldwin. Herring told the reporters, in all humility: "The idea originated with Mr. Bishop." And Curtiss reassured the hometown paper: "This deal will mean much to the industrial growth of Hammondsport."

The reaction at Beinn Bhreagh was somewhat jaundiced, to judge from a report Casey Baldwin wrote for the *A.E.A. Bulletin* (in the knowledge that Curtiss would read it):

"The sensation of the week is the formation of the Herring-Curtiss Company. Presumably the object of this Company is to manufacture heavier-than-air machines on the Herring patents. Mr. Curtiss disposes of his motor-cycle manufacturing plant to the new company and assumes the managership of it . . . The papers have given themselves rather a free rein in outlining the immediate program for the new company, according to some accounts. One hundred aerodromes a week is to be the output of the Hammondsport works until a larger factory can be built.

"That level-headed American business men should back Mr. Herring has created quite a furore in aeronautical circles. It probably means that Mr. Herring has some more convincing arguments than he has ever made public, or—is it really the Curtiss Company with Mr. Herring's patents to flourish in the eyes of bewildered capitalists? So far as we actually know, the Herring patents are only talking points at present."

The news broke in morning papers of March 4, 1909, the day William Howard Taft was inaugurated as the 27th President of the United States. Bell waited two days and then wired Curtiss: PLEASE WRITE FULLY CONCERNING YOUR ARRANGEMENT WITH HERRING AND HOW IT AFFECTS YOUR RELATIONS WITH THE A.E.A. The letter in which Curtiss obliged ran as follows:

"I found Mr. Herring quite anxious to close up the deal with me, and I finally made him an offer, which he verbally accepted. He has promised to come to Hammondsport at once and make final arrangements. The announcement was made at the Aero Club Wednesday evening of the consolidation. Mr. Bishop represented the moneyed interests, and I understand that Mr. [Alan R.] Hawley and Mr. Cooper Hewitt are among the others.

"Mr. Herring showed me a great deal, and I would not be at all surprised if his patents, backed by a strong company, would pretty well control the use of the gyroscope in obtaining automatic equilibrium. This seems to be about the only road to success in securing automatic stability in an aeroplane.

"If the deal goes through, I will be manager of the company and everything will go on just as it has, except that we will have Mr. Herring's devices on the machines which we may build; which, by the way, recalls the fact that I accepted an order from the Aeronautical Society for an aeroplane to be delivered in the spring at Morris Park, New York. I did this on my own responsibility with the idea that if the consolidation was made with Herring it would be turned over to the new company, or if a commercial organization succeeded the Experiment Association the order could be turned over to them. If neither of these materialized, the Curtiss Company would endeavor to fill the order itself.

"I am planning to go to Washington to see Mr. Charles Bell as soon as I am sure of the outcome with the Herring proposition. There is no reason why the Aerodrome Company should not be formed if the Herring deal goes through, unless the members of the Association would care to come into the Herring combination. This would please Mr. Herring, I am sure, and I don't know but that it would be just as well for the Association. Mr. Herring was intending to write to you about the matter."

Obviously, no Aerodrome Company could be organized with the Hammondsport plant as its base; this remark seems to imply that the A.E.A. had previously discussed the possibility of a Canadian Aerodrome Company, should Curtiss cast his lot with Herring. At all events, the other members did not choose to join the "Herring combination."

The Herring-Curtiss Company was incorporated by the State Department at Albany on March 19, for the wide-reaching purpose of manufacturing and purveying "motors, motorcycles, motor boats, motor vehicles, electric generators, balloons, aeroplanes, airships, flying machines of any and all types and kinds, now or hereafter devised, and any and all other motor vehicles and equipment and forms of transportation, by land or in the air, or on the water." Its officers were: president, Monroe M. Wheeler, county court judge of Steuben County; vice-president and general manager, Glenn H. Curtiss; vice-president and director, Augustus M. Herring; secretary-treasurer, Lynn D. Masson. Directors in addition to the officers were Cortlandt Field Bishop and Thomas S. Baldwin. Both Curtiss and Herring were allotted salaries of $5000.

For the sum of $60,000, a portion of which was accepted as a mortgage, Curtiss signed over to Herring all assets, property, and good will of the G. H. Curtiss Manufacturing Company; not only these, but all his real estate holdings, upon which stood both his factory and his home; not only these, but all patents and inventions in which he might have patentable rights (including his share in the A.E.A. patent application). He was assigned 160 shares of Herring-Curtiss preferred stock, 400 shares of common stock. Herring retained for himself a voting majority of the stock, more than $200,000 of the $360,000 paper value.

Accountants appraised the real value of the properties which Curtiss signed away at $82,272.11. The G. H. Curtiss Manufacturing Company at the moment had one hundred employees on its payroll, and had netted a profit of $120,000 in 1908.

*   *   *

Whether or not there had been an advance agreement to this effect, Bell moved without delay in the direction of a Canadian Aerodrome Company, in which he would personally finance Baldwin and McCurdy to get started; leaving the commercial exploitation of the A.E.A. developments to Curtiss in the United States. This arrangement seems to have been mutually amicable, and the Canadians appear to have considered it fair, especially as their aspirations extended to supplying the aircraft needs of Great Britain as well as the Dominion. Bell set down his reasoning in his daybook on March 21:

"One of the first duties of an Aerodrome Company should be to secure patents if possible in other countries than the United States. If not—no reason why they should not manufacture in Canada and Great Britain without any reference to the Aerodrome Company, which would represent the interests of the A.E.A. That Casey and McCurdy should have an understanding with Curtiss—say for two years—to pay the Aerodrome Company some definite royalty. Then if the Aerodrome Company got patents in the United States, Canada, and Great Britain, it would license Curtiss in the United States and McCurdy and Baldwin in Canada and Great Britain.

"With such an understanding, Curtiss in the United States and Baldwin and McCurdy in Canada would be free to go ahead and make what they could by the manufacture of aerodromes. Any such understanding, however, would be a matter between them and all the interests concerned in the A.E.A.

"The public need know nothing more than that Curtiss is manufacturing aerodromes in the United States and McCurdy and Baldwin in Canada. In approaching Canada, point out that Curtiss desires to enter commercial field in U.S. and they in Canada—that Curtiss already had backing but they did not. Would it not be proper for the Canadian government to assist them in founding a new industry in Canada by placing an order with them for one or more aerodromes of the *Silver Dart* pattern?" Bell considered a price of $15,000 for the first machine, $10,000 for the second. This could well lead, he speculated, to their supplying the needs of the British Army, while Canada benefited by having the industry. Moreover, it could be to England's advantage, Bell thought, to have its airplane industry at a safe distance in Canada in the event of war in Europe, which the German Kaiser seemed to be fomenting.

Bell was invited to address the Canadian Club of Ottawa on March 27, and seized the occasion not only to make a public appeal for government support of the Canadian Aerodrome Company he proposed, but to enter a closed-door conference with the Governor General of Canada, Earl Grey, and Premier Sir Wilfrid Laurier. To the Canadian Club he said: "Mr. Curtiss intends to carry on the manufacture of aerodromes in Hammondsport, New York. Mr. McCurdy and Mr. Baldwin are a little different. They say they are Canadians, and they want to go into the practical manufacture of these machines. But they say: 'Cannot we do anything for the Canadian government?'" Emerging from his talk with the two top officials of Canada, he predicted that "important developments of the greatest consequence to the members of the A.E.A. will result."

*   *   *

March 31 was doomsday for the Aerial Experiment Association, which had fulfilled its historic destiny. Ten days before, Bell sent Curtiss a telegram peremptory in tone: HAVE YOUR BUSINESS ARRANGED SO AS TO BE HERE 31ST SURE. VERY IMPORTANT AND YOU WILL REGRET IT ALL YOUR LIFE IF NOT. There is reason to believe that Curtiss actually intended to be there and made a start. The Hammondsport *Herald* on March 31 carried this item: "G. H. Curtiss went to New York yesterday and expects to go to Baddeck probably for two weeks." Something obviously happened to detain him in New York, for he did not attend the "wake," after all.

In the evening of the last day of March, "a pathetic little group" gathered before the fireplace in the great hall of Beinn Bhreagh and watched the clock go round. Three men of the original five were present: Bell, McCurdy, and Baldwin. Keeping them company in the melancholy vigil were Mrs. Bell, Mrs. Casey Baldwin, Miss Mabel McCurdy, and the Washington *Star* correspondent, Charles R. Cox. A resolution of gratitude and appreciation to Dr. and Mrs. Bell was voted by Baldwin and McCurdy. Then: "It was reluctantly moved by Mr. Baldwin and regretfully seconded by the Secretary that we dissolve, so by the stroke of 12 (midnight) the A.E.A. as an association was no more."

Dr. Bell penned a valedictory which appeared in the final issue of the *Bulletin:*

> The A.E.A. is now a thing of the past.
>
> It has made its mark upon the history of aviation and *its work will live.*
>
> Every success to the commercial organization that will succeed it, and to the individual members of the Association in their future careers, is the earnest wish of
>
> Your Editor
>
> ALEXANDER GRAHAM BELL.

In the division of material assets of the A. E. A., the *Silver Dart* remained in Canada, along with Bell's latest kite and the engines which were there. The *June Bug* was apportioned to Curtiss, although he never used it again. When he offered it to the Smithsonian a short while later, that Institution had no place to exhibit it. Finally, the *June Bug* simply rotted away in a loft storage place at the Keuka lakefront.

11.   Gold Bug; alias Golden Flier

On taking leave of the A.E.A., Curtiss was "filled with ideas and plans for future flying," in the words of Harry Genung, his office manager and closest confidant, who also still shared his home. Motorcycle racing was banished from his mind. As yet no winged vehicle could begin to match a motorcycle in speed, but he knew this was only a matter of time. The witchery of movement off the ground had already caught him in its skein; the spell would prompt him to say later on: "I would fly for the mere sport if I were not in the business, for there is a fascination about flying that it is unnecessary to explain and difficult to resist."

Neither could he resist the challenge of designing a better, faster, and more practical craft than he had seen. Curtiss had determined to embark on airplane manufacture at a moment when no such industry existed in America and no real market was in sight. Undoubtedly he would have done this in collaboration with his A.E.A. comrades had not the Herring scheme interposed with its promise of abundant capital. Bell had made it crystal clear that he was not about to become the moneybags of the American Aerodrome Company; also that he did not intend to be the only party to that enterprise who might be held responsible for monetary damages in a patent suit. He had his fill of litigations. While Bell was a wealthy man, he was by no means the colossus of finance imagined by the public in the inventor of the telephone. Although he did not actually think the Wrights had a case in the aileron issue, he was treading cautiously.

In essence, Curtiss's quandary lay in making a choice between Bell and Herring. Weighed in the balance was Bell's continuing preoccupation with tetrahedral kites, which Curtiss saw for the dead-end they were. On the Herring side of the scale was an apparent pipeline to Wall Street finance, an illusion bolstered by Cortlandt Field Bishop. Unquestionably, the man from Hammondsport thought he saw his chance to get in on the ground floor of a new industry for which the sky would indeed be the limit.

Money was not the sole consideration in his choice. Curtiss was utterly persuaded of Herring's aeronautical genius. The fact that the U. S. Army had awarded Herring a contract, alongside the Wright brothers, added greatly to his luster. Moreover, the resolve to manufacture and sell airplanes was taken in the face of an implied threat of patent warfare. Curtiss believed that Herring held patent claims antedating those of the Wrights, and Herring promised to make these claims part of his contribution to the Herring-Curtiss Company, with the assurance that they would checkmate any such lawsuit. If Curtiss was naïve in this belief, so were Bishop and Tom Baldwin.

The cornerstone of Curtiss's resolution, of course, was his flourishing plant which was producing the most suitable engines in the United States for aeronautical use; a plant already partly tooled for the making of airplanes, and whose personnel had absorbed some know-how in that line. The factory was his trump card, whichever turn he took. In a status report drawn up for Herring, he said his company expected, in the calendar year 1909, to build 1000 motorcycles, 50 to 100 aero engines, and 8 or 10 aeroplanes. He asserted: "The Curtiss Company's motorcycle business not only earns handsome profits now but is bound to grow. Our old agents are doubling their orders and, with several thousand machines on the road, the 'small parts and repair department' is showing a good profit." Genung put the situation in a nutshell: "We had a front-row seat in the motorcycle business when aviation came along and pushed the business out the back door."

At this fateful crossroads of his career, Glenn Curtiss was just under thirty-one years of age. Barely a decade had elapsed since he was racing bicycles, but his name now was a trademark known from coast to coast. By the nature of his personality, his sobriety, the seriousness of his motives and thought processes, his devotion to work, he had skipped over the normal transition from youth to maturity. He had been a full-fledged industrialist in his twenties, and social relaxation was not in his makeup.

That brand of success held a strong appeal for the people among whom he had grown from childhood; who could remember him driving grapes to the press in a pony cart, peddling newspapers, repairing doorbells. Everyone in town still addressed him as Glenn. Only those of later acquaintance, perhaps awed by his importance, adopted the stilted "G.H." usage from the title of his company. Add to local liking and pride his prominent trait of loyalty to the village which had nurtured him, and particularly to persons who had befriended and aided him on the way up, and it is small wonder that in Hammondsport he had no enemies.

A widespread concept of him as being cold and taciturn was a distortion. Unsmiling photographs, with a perpetual frown and black brows, contributed to this fiction. There was nothing picturesque about this man, no swagger, no daredeviltry. It was reserve rather than taciturnity which underlay his quiet bearing. In reality, he was affable and friendly enough among acquaintances, but decidedly not the loquacious type. His employees found him approachable and "easy to talk to." Henry Kleckler described him as "always serious, but he smiled once in a while." One of his early flyers, Beckwith Havens, thought him "rather austere," and recalled: "He didn't laugh out loud very much." J. A. D. McCurdy, reminiscing, said: "Glenn was a most outstanding personality. There was a naturalism about him which was wonderful."

Though of abstemious habit, Curtiss was no prude or spoilsport. Lynn Bauder, a factory foreman in those days, recollected one sultry summer night when a few men volunteered to work overtime with him, reconditioning an engine that was needed in a hurry. Taking pity on their sweltering, Bauder went downtown for a case of beer and was carrying it up the hill on his shoulder when Curtiss met him. "What have you got there, Lynn?" the boss asked.

"Whatcha think?" Bauder replied. "I've got a box of wildcats."

"Don't you know it's against the rules to bring anything to drink into the factory?"

"When was those rules made?"

"You know very well."

"Now listen," Bauder bridled. "Those boys was good enough to come back to help me out. They're overhauling that motor and they're working on their own time—and it's awful dry up there on Number 1."

Curtiss reflected a moment, then said: "Twenty-four bottles for four or five guys working a night like this? Why, I could drink them all myself." Fishing out a bill, he gave it to Bauder with the command to go back and fetch another case.

*   *   *

On March 2, 1909, Lee S. Burridge, president of the Aeronautic Society of New York, announced that the society had placed an order for an aeroplane with Glenn H. Curtiss, who was tarrying in New York City on his way home from Nova Scotia. This would be the first flying machine ever sold commercially in the United States. The price tag was $5000, on which the society made a down payment of $500. The contract called for delivery at Morris Park, the society's headquarters, and the instruction of two members in how to fly it. This was strictly a personal deal with Curtiss, negotiated just prior to the formation of the Herring-Curtiss Company. (The society had previously considered a Wright plane, as indicated by Orville's query to Wilbur in December 1908: "Some of the members of the N. Y. Aero Club have been raising some money to buy a flyer. What price shall I ask?")

The press conference foreshadowing the Herring-Curtiss combination was held the day following. In talking informally with newsmen at that time, Herring said that the forthcoming Gordon Bennett Trophy contest in France was a factor they should not overlook in writing of the new company; that the Aero Club had asked him to build a plane for entry in that race, but he had declined for lack of facilities. Curtiss had the requisite facilities, Herring pointed out. An additional reason why he could not take on the job, said Herring, was his busy involvement in fulfilling the Army contract.

As usual, Curtiss did not have much to say to the reporters, but he did drop a hint that either Herring or himself might make a try for the English Channel prize in the near future.

The first order of business on his return to Hammondsport, a fortnight before the incorporation of Herring-Curtiss, was to launch production of the Aeronautic Society machine. For some time, he and Henry Kleckler had been mulling over how they would go about designing a plane if they were freed from the A.E.A. pattern. The Aeronautic Society's order came at exactly the right moment for him to put fresh ideas into practice, when he was severing one tie and before he had forged the next. Knowing that Herring himself had established a precedent, he felt justified in reserving this contract as his personal project, without interference.

During the preliminary stages of his maneuver, Herring had told Bishop that, if the company should materialize, he intended to exempt from the agreement his Signal Corps contract machine and one other which, he said, had been ordered privately. In other words, pre-existing orders for aircraft were not to be considered property of the company. Curtiss frankly informed Herring that, by the same token, he was reserving the Aeronautic Society contract from the deal, and he thought this was accepted as a quid pro quo. Thus he was taken aback when Herring later began suggesting changes in design of the machine under construction. By his testimony, Curtiss told Herring to go ahead and build his government plane as he pleased; and that "it was only fair that I build this Aeronautic Society machine after my own plans, particularly in view of the fact that I had to fly it and demonstrate it."

First and foremost, Curtiss intended to get rid of the arched wings which typified the A.E.A. "dromes." Both he and Kleckler felt (in Henry's phrase) that the tapered wings with their negative dihedral "amounted to nonsense," besides being tedious and expensive to construct. Hence Curtiss made the break directly into straight, untapered wings, with little more than half the span of the *June Bug* and the *Silver Dart*. The second drastic innovation was mid-wing, or inter-wing ailerons. These sensible, efficient flaps were between the upper and nether wings, fastened to the two outer trailing-edge struts. By divorcing the ailerons altogether from the wings, Curtiss probably had something more than utility in mind; this device might nullify the Wrights' viewpoint that wing-tip ailerons were merely an extension of the wing surfaces, consequently an infringement of their patent.

With this smaller, simpler, and altogether handier design, it is obvious that Curtiss was aiming for more speed, his constant desideratum. The power he put into it was a 4-cylinder water-cooled engine, an improvement over the type created for the Army dirigible.

For wing fabric, Baldwin supplied more of the lightweight rubberized silk used on the *Silver Dart*, but in this instance the silk was not left with its silvery sheen. It was doctored with the yellow ochre which had tinted the wings of the *June Bug*, while yellow varnish was brushed on the struts and other woodwork. The purpose of all the golden yellow was to make the machine more photogenic.

Precisely who it was around the Curtiss shops, or outside them, who dreamed up the name *Gold Bug* may never be known; but to anyone familiar with the *June Bug* it was a logical, not to say poetic, sequel.

The factory designation for this machine was *Curtiss Number 1* but the picturesque *Gold Bug* tag was a natural for popular appeal, finding its way here and there into print, so that historical writers have since perpetuated it. An oblique reference to Poe's mystery yarn, *The Gold Bug*, could scarcely be overlooked. Curtiss, however, did not presume to dictate a preconceived name to the purchaser, and the fact that the Aeronautic Society chose to label it instead the *Golden Flier* has sown confusion and debate ever since.[1]

*   *   *

As McCurdy requested, Curtiss had filed entry of the *Silver Dart* for a crack at second leg on the Scientific American Trophy. The A.E.A. asked for the trial to be held at Baddeck. From its experience in the *June Bug* case, the Aero Club had since amended the rules to require the contestant to pay the expenses of the club's official observer for travel beyond a 25-mile radius of New York City. Bell volunteered to meet this cost out of his own pocket, and McCurdy started casting about for a field to fly from in that hilly countryside. McCurdy by this time had made more open flights than any other flyer on the American continent, and was supremely confident of knocking off the 25 kilometers for the trophy.

After accepting the entry, the Aero Club enacted an abrupt further switch in the rules: the prize would now go to the pilot covering the greatest distance in excess of 25 kilometers during 1909, and the award would not be given until after the end of the year. Bell irately protested and McCurdy had his say: "From the standpoint of true sporting principles they are to be severely criticized for making a change in the competitive rules after an application for trial has been filed and accepted." Bishop explained to Bell that the club had no intent of discriminating against the A.E.A., but simply opted to follow European precedent: "We felt that the rapid development of aviation made it necessary to increase the interest and give the Trophy to the machine which had done the best work during the calendar year." Even Augustus Post, the club secretary, disliked the action, and wrote Bell with tongue-in-cheek: ". . . it would seem to produce the result of having all the machines held down to their very lowest distance until midnight December 31st, when all would have a race by moonlight to see which would fly the furthest before the New Year." Bell canceled the entry, refusing to pay the travel expenses under such conditions; he said the "status of the Association" would be lowered and that "We would be entering into a racing match in competition with others."

The withdrawal of the *Silver Dart* set Curtiss thinking about going for second leg on the trophy himself, using the *Gold Bug* if the Aeronautic Society would consent. As holder of the first leg, he felt as if he had a prior claim, and perhaps already was looking ahead to the third leg which would give him permanent possession of the elegant cup.

In the meantime, Bishop was exerting pressure on Curtiss to enter for the Gordon Bennett speed trophy as the Aero Club's representative. Curtiss objected that the machine he was building was too small (that is, underpowered) for such a speed trial against Europe's best, and Bishop argued: "You cannot tell unless you try. You would have a better chance than the Wrights." As Curtiss recalled: "He [Bishop] talked with the Wrights and he talked with me, and I wasn't very enthusiastic about it at the time." It was conceivable he did not care to play second fiddle to the Wrights.

Bishop sailed for his customary summer abroad without a commitment from Curtiss, leaving Captain Baldwin to carry on the persuasion. Friction was already arising between Curtiss and Herring, and one sore spot was that Herring thought 4-cylinder engines were big enough. Under Baldwin's urging, Curtiss began to capitulate: "I told Mr. Baldwin that I did not want to go into this race with the small-powered machine which the Herring-Curtiss Company was building; but that if I would be permitted to build a larger motor I would be willing to go to France and enter the race, and would pay my own expenses and the expenses of my assistants, and would take whatever chances there were in the matter for the prizes I would receive; understanding at the same time that if the prizes did not amount to enough to cover the expenses, that Mr. Bishop would pay said expenses or any difference between the prize and the expense."

Bishop had deputized his elderly secretary, Arthur W. Gilbert, to serve in his stead on the board of directors of the Herring-Curtiss Company. Baldwin and Monroe Wheeler thought Curtiss's point was fair enough, and Gilbert agreed. Even Herring grudgingly assented. Curtiss then told Gilbert: "I have decided to build an 8-cylinder motor, and with this greater power I may have a chance to win the Gordon Bennett race. I want you to communicate this to Mr. Bishop, but keep the fact that we have an 8-cylinder motor a secret, that our competitors think we are coming over with the same machine we have been using. I know we would have no chance of winning with the little machine and the small motor with which I have been flying. My only chance is to build a larger motor, and I think the company should have a larger motor, as the performance of the aeroplane is almost directly in proportion to the power. Mr. Herring is satisfied with small motors. He thinks we have plenty of power, but I disagree with him."

Gilbert responded: "Mr. Bishop will be glad to know this, and I am glad you are going over to enter this race. I hope you win a good share of the prizes."

Immediately on receipt of a cablegram from Gilbert, Bishop registered the entry of Curtiss as the American competitor for the Gordon Bennett Trophy in the world's first international air meet. The location by this time had been selected: Rheims, France.

Curtiss started building an airplane especially for that purpose before the *Gold Bug* was completed.

✿   ✿   ✿

Bishop arrived in France just in time to encounter the Wright brothers before they sailed for home with the plaudits of Europe ringing in their ears. While Wilbur had done the flying and taught three pilots for the French syndicate organized to market their planes, Orville, now able to limp without a cane, shared in the hero-worship. But they still had to demonstrate their new Army contract machine at Fort Myer. The talks he had with the brothers were upsetting to Bishop, and he wrote Monroe Wheeler, president of the Herring-Curtiss Company:

"I have seen a good deal of the Wrights before they left for New York. They have completely decided to begin legal action against the company and against Mr. Curtiss. They told me certain things which, if true, put matters in a very bad light, both on moral and legal grounds, and if the facts are as they state them I shall regret having anything

to do with the aeroplane part of the business. Of course I want to hear
both sides before making up my mind, and until I do I shall keep my
mind in suspense. There are certain phases of the subject which I hope
will be kept out of the papers for the sake of all of us. I have great
respect and esteem for the Wrights and for Curtiss and I hope that we
will all be discreet and not talk to the reporters . . .

"And right off comes the question of defending the suits which the
Wrights are going to bring at once. I certainly will not put up more
money nor will my brother. The Wrights have ample funds and unlimited backing and we would have no chance."

Aside from outlining to Bishop how they thought the aileron controls infringed their wing-warping, the Wrights must have related the
episodes on which they were later to place great emphasis: how Herring
had visited their Kitty Hawk camp and seen their gliders; the Dayton
visit of Curtiss, with Captain Baldwin, when they suspected him of
picking their brains; the request from Selfridge for pointers at the outset
of the A.E.A. experiments; Curtiss's supposed assurance to Orville that
he had no thought of exhibition flying. Now here was Curtiss building a
plane for sale to the Aeronautic Society.

Uneasy about his investment, Bishop felt obliged to maintain a
neutral stance as president of the Aero Club, of which the Wrights
were members. His embarrassment is understandable.

The Wrights returned to face with reluctance a lavish two-day
homecoming "carnival" in Dayton, and to scurry about accepting honors,
including the Langley Medal from the Smithsonian Institution. They
were far from being unsung prophets in their native land, as legend
would have it.

*   *   *

Morris Park was situated within the metropolitan limits and accessible by subway trains and trolleys, and the Aero Club had it in mind as
a place where large crowds could be drawn for the next assault on the
Scientific American Trophy. It embraced a field of 325 acres, from which
the fences had been removed as Curtiss recommended when he scouted
it. The automobile track was an oval of one and one-half mile circuit
and a diagonal straight track cut across the infield. Freakish would-be
aircraft built by Aeronautic Society members were stored about in sheds.
The society's secretary, Wilbur R. Kimball, was experimenting with a

foot-powered helicopter, and also had on the grounds an unflyable, airplane with eight propellers and a wire-rope drive. Balloons, gliders, and a wind-wagon rounded out the array.

Into this strange aerial menagerie on June 16, Glenn Curtiss introduced his *Curtiss Number 1, Gold Bug,* or whatever it might come to be called. The Aeronautic Society wanted him to perform a series of exhibition flights prior to acceptance of the machine, for which it could charge admission and prove to New Yorkers that flying was not a joke. Curtiss, who had not previously flown outside Hammondsport, was anxious to know if the plane was worthy of trophy-chasing. After getting it assembled, he made three short flights, then beckoned Kleckler aside. "Henny," he said, "we've got a winner this time for certain. These new ailerons work much better than the old type and give me the positive control I need."

"Well, it looked fine from where I stood," Kleckler assented, "and you seemed to have quite a bit more speed than with any of our other machines. But wasn't she a little slow rising from the ground?"

"Yes, she was. So far that's the only thing wrong. It needs a bit more power for getting off, and that extra power will probably give us even more speed in the air. Let's think about this some more."

Over the next ten days, they doctored up the engine. The Aeronautic Society had scheduled its first public exhibition and tournament for June 26. In the interim, onlookers hovered about most of the time, hoping to witness one of the occasional test hops, and the papers sent reporters to cover the event.

The 26th of June was the hottest day of the year for New York, and some 5000 spectators paid $1 per head for admittance to Morris Park, overflowing the grandstand onto the lawn and the paddock. This was to be Curtiss's first exhibition work before a really large audience; at the same time the first genuine flying ever seen in the New York City region (the short hops of Farman at Brighton Beach the previous summer hardly counted). The mass adulation, the ogling by the ladies, and demands for autographs were unnerving to him.

The society's dirigible balloon had been eliminated from the exhibition by a storm during the night, but among the apéritifs served up were Israel Ludlow's man-carrying kite towed aloft by a car; gliders catapulted by a weight in a derrick; and a wind-wagon racing itself around the track. Curtiss then supplied the climax. After two straightaway flights and perfect landings, he went up again and made a complete, tight circuit of the racetrack. Spectators were in a frenzy, cheering and applauding vociferously all during the two minutes it took him to do it. This stunt was acclaimed as the first circular flight around a racetrack, but what it proved for Curtiss was the good control he had achieved with the mid-wing ailerons and the compact design of the aircraft.

More flights ensued over the next several days, and on July 6, with an audience of 10,000, his largest yet, Curtiss had a different sample of New York mob behavior. The day was windy, and he kept putting off flying: "The wind is not just right. We must wait a while." Instead of the generous aerial program advertised, the society rang in a card of motorcycle races. Angry people yelled: "Get something in the air! . . . Where is Curtiss?" By 8 P.M. most of the huge crowd had gone home in disgust. With twilight the wind abated and the birdman made two short flights before dark, almost unobserved.

What Curtiss really had in mind was not the pleasing of crowds but edging up to his second trial for the Scientific American Trophy, and beyond that getting in some practice for the Rheims affair. The racetrack in the Bronx was not favorable to either objective. Because of the "rather poor ground at Morris Park," he said, "the flights were not entirely satisfactory to me or to the Society. I stated that if we could find some better grounds, which I thought I could do on Long Island, if they would permit me to use the machine in the trial the second year for the Scientific American Trophy, I would be glad to fly it in that manner." The society was happy to oblige, not having yet paid for the plane; and the Aero Club was impatient to have the trophy trial run off.

From attending automobile races at Garden City in 1905, Curtiss well remembered the level, sandy reaches of southern Long Island, especially the area known as the Hempstead Plains, yet uncluttered by suburbia. From what he heard of the champagne country around Rheims, it was similar, and he wanted experience in flying over unobstructed, flat land as training for what lay ahead. The anniversary date of his *June Bug* victory was spent reconnoitering the Hempstead Plains, in company with A. Holland Forbes, chairman of the Aero Club's contest committee, and Alan R. Hawley who had been timer at the finish post at Stony Brook Farm. They found exactly what they wanted, a broad field north of the Mineola Fairgrounds, and were able to arrange its rental.

On returning from that fruitful excursion, he told reporters he had decided, on request of the Aero Club, to enter the Gordon Bennett

Trophy contest, for which he would employ a "Herring-Curtiss aero-plane" already under construction at Hammondsport. So saying, he jumped the gun on the Aero Club itself, which issued the announcement five days later that its board of directors had chosen Curtiss as its entrant for the Rheims tournament.

In the meanwhile, Curtiss had sandwiched in a trip to Washington and Fort Myer where he saw the new Wright plane for the Army in preliminary action. Possibly he hoped for a talk with the Wrights about the patent matter; if so, he was disappointed. Both brothers were at Fort Myer this time, though Orville did all the flying. Indications are that Curtiss was there on July 1, since that was the date when three fairly good flights were made. On the 2nd, Orville came close to another disaster. His motor died in air, and in the glide for a landing he grazed a dead tree behind the "aeroplane shed," ripping the canvas and fractur-ing seven wing ribs. "Machine fell heavily, breaking skids," says the entry in the Signal Corps log. Orville escaped unhurt.

On July 10, Curtiss arrived at Mineola to commence his Long Island workouts, and that same day he mailed a letter to the Wright brothers at Fort Myer, revealing that the threat of a patent suit weighed on his mind. "I wish to express my admiration," he opened, "for the fine exhibition of flying I witnessed at Fort Myer and only regret that you should have had motor trouble." In the tone of a friendly hint, he suggested they try a different type of magneto with which he was obtaining good results, and went on: "I got in a couple of small flights for the Society at Morris Park last Saturday, of which you have probably heard. The exhibition, however, did not pan out well and they have not as yet taken the machine. We have seized the opportunity to secure some trials on Long Island where there are better grounds. We have not before made any attempts at long flights and I am anxious to experi-ment on these lines."

And then he came to the actual point of the letter: "In regard to patent matters, I want to suggest that if you contemplate any action that the matter be taken up privately between us to save if possible annoyance and publicity of lawsuits and trial."

*   *   *

The aircraft was sheltered in a large tent opposite the Mineola Fairgrounds and was a magnet to the curious. Long rows of automobiles were parked along adjacent roadways. Members of both the Aero Club and the Aeronautic Society were in evidence almost continually. So was Augustus Herring, as he had been at Morris Park, while professing to be sorely cramped for time to meet the deadline on his Army contract. A young Columbia University engineering student, Grover Cleveland Loening, virtually camped on the field, so enthralled was he with the lure of aviation.

On July 12, Curtiss began regular trials while Captain Tom Baldwin held a stopwatch. The *Times* gave him choice page one position for a 2-mile "circular flight," the longest yet seen in the vicinity of New York. Spectators gasped when a gust of wind tilted the plane at a "dangerous angle" and a wing tip brushed tall grass; but the intrepid aviator righted his vehicle and "sailed down the field" to a safe landing. "It was the easiest and most satisfactory flight I ever made with the new machine," he said. "I felt sure of my ground all the time, for the long flat expanse of the Hempstead Plains presents ideal conditions for aviation."

Among the witnesses was a wrinkled ancient, born in 1821 when steamboats were young on the Hudson River and the pioneering steam locomotive had yet to roll on rails. "This is a day I will always remember," he quavered. "I have lived eighty-eight years to see one of those curious flying machines and I now feel satisfied."

The favorite time for flying was early morning when the cooled air was "thicker" and had fewer "bumps." Two days later, with a 5:30 A.M. takeoff, Curtiss bettered his record with a circular 5-mile flight at 43 miles per hour, and remarked: "Things went so smoothly that if I had carried an orange with me I would have been glad to eat it." Next morning the *Gold Bug* was wheeled out at 4:30 A.M. in a Long Island fog. Undaunted, Curtiss took off into the mist for two flights totaling 8 miles, and said: "It is like flying through the clouds. Forty feet above the earth it is practically impossible to see anything and the moisture is like rain flying in my face." On the 16th, in a deliberate practice flight for Rheims, he circled ten times for a total 15 miles in 23 minutes—his longest and best performance to date. He also reached his highest altitude, 50 feet. So well under control was the plane that he took his hand from the wheel to wave at spectators.

It is another sign of enduring good feeling between him and the people at Baddeck that Curtiss telegraphed Bell from Mineoola: FIRST LONG FLIGHT THIS MORNING, 15 MILES. And that Bell promptly wired back: HEARTIEST CONGRATULATIONS FROM ALL. HOPE THIS MEANS THE

SCIENTIFIC AMERICAN TROPHY FOR YOU. BALDWIN AND MCCURDY WILL SOON
TRY TO RIVAL YOUR ACHIEVEMENT IN THEIR NEW AERODROME, BADDECK
NO. 1, WHICH HAS BEEN SENT TO PETAWAWA.[2]

There could be no debate that the *Gold Bug* was the lightest and
fleetest airplane yet built in America. In the flying of it, Curtiss learned
how to bank sharply and to describe tighter circles than had hitherto
been achieved by anyone.

Curtiss notified the Aero Club he was ready for the trophy attempt.
Charles Manly, again the official judge, paced off a triangular course
one and one-third miles around, planting a stake with a flag at each
corner. Twelve circuits would make the required 25 kilometers. Rules
stipulated that a contestant must land within 100 meters of his takeoff
point. The date was set for the very next morning, July 17. Simultaneously he filed entry for the Cortlandt Field Bishop Prize of $250. Bishop
had posted four such awards for the first Aero Club members to fly a
distance of one kilometer.

Spectators began assembling soon after sunup on Saturday, and an
audience of 3000 was on hand when Curtiss lifted off at 5:15. Fashionable Long Islanders came by auto and on horseback. Summer cottagers
of Garden City and Westbury set their alarm clocks. Many club members spent the night on the Island. The airman wore a short black
topcoat and borrowed a cap from one of his mechanics. It took him one
circuit and a couple of minutes to win the Bishop Prize, after which he
landed to pin that one down.

A flip of the propeller and he was off again at 5:23 A.M. for the big
event, with three gallons of gasoline sloshing in the tank. Round and
round the course he buzzed, at an average altitude of 15 to 25 feet. A
reporter noted his banking speed on the turns was "a spectacular and
inspiring sight." Each time he passed the starting stake, Manly's sister
held up a placard bearing the number of the circuit. When the figure
was "12," signifying that the trophy was his, a loud chorus of cheering
arose. Curtiss waved his hand and kept right on. During the seventeenth
lap he was seen reaching up to tap the overhead tank; this was the only
fuel gauge he had. At the end of nineteen laps he came down, having
covered 24.7 miles. Finding two quarts of gas remaining, he said he
could have continued another ten or fifteen minutes, but "I thought I
had done pretty well as it is." Bucking a slight wind, he felt it "not
prudent" to risk running out of fuel at the far end of the field and thus
failing to land within the prescribed limit. Should anyone exceed his
distance before the end of the year, he declared he would go out to win

back the record. Nobody else even tried, and the name Glenn H. Curtiss was inscribed on the Scientific American Trophy in January 1910.

With an already famous plane technically its property, the Aeronautic Society was not inclined to grant its further use to Curtiss. The truth was that he wanted to take it with him to France as a spare in case accident should befall the primary racer. His French rivals, he knew, would have extras in reserve. In fact, Bishop had registered him for two airplanes at the Rheims meet. When he had to go with only one, Curtiss explained that the Aeronautic Society had claimed delivery of its machine "and refused to allow us to retain it at any price."

Under the sale contract he had the final obligation of teaching two members to fly the machine which the Aeronautic Society promptly christened the *Golden Flier*. In view of the Rheims date, he wished to lose no time fulfilling this agreement, and the lessons were scheduled to begin the next morning. The men put forward for instruction were Charles F. Willard and Alexander Williams. They and a group of onlookers were on deck at 5:00 A.M. Sunday.

To make sure the plane was in trim and at the same time perhaps inspire his first pupils, Curtiss went up, described a figure-8, and set a new altitude record for himself, 150 feet. Willard, a young automotive engineer, then won a coin toss for the sequence of their lessons. Curtiss explained the controls, gave what pointers he could on the ground, and Willard was on his own. The novice showed aptitude, touching ground once, taking off a second time, and making an acceptable landing. "Well done," Curtiss commended. "It was better than my first flight."

Williams was one of those members who had been striving in vain to build his own plane at Morris Park. He was nervous about the lesson, had slept little, and came to the field without breakfast. To screw up his courage, it was said, he tossed off a glass of benedictine at the last minute. When his turn came, he went up at a steep angle, swayed, took too sharp a turn, lost flying speed, slipped off on one wing, and landed upside down, the motor still throbbing. Williams was pulled out of the wreck unconscious, with a broken arm and thumb, and after recovery decided that flying was not his dish.

Curtiss diagnosed the *Golden Flier* and said: "It is nothing but what can be repaired in a little time." The wings were messed up, and the steering gear and front wheel smashed. With some relief, he left for Hammondsport to obtain replacement parts and put his plant on a day-and-night basis for completion of the Rheims racer. The 8-cylinder for this was being rushed behind locked doors, but somehow the security was breached, for his chief French competitor was forewarned and forearmed.

*   *   *

While Long Island was being discovered as ideal flying territory, European aviators were zeroing in on Lord Northcliffe's prize for an English Channel flight. This was still in Curtiss's mind for future reference in case it was not captured by the time he was through at Rheims. Any dream the boys at Baddeck had entertained of going after it was shelved, as both the *Silver Dart* and the *Baddeck Number 1* were shipped to the Canadian Army's cavalry and artillery practice camp at Petawawa, Ontario; the Department of Militia and Defense had encouraged them to make demonstration flights, in the slim hope that Parliament might yet appropriate some aviation funds.[3]

Three French flyers had their sights set on the Strait of Dover: Louis Blériot, Hubert Latham, and Count Charles de Lambert, the latter with a Wright plane (he was Wilbur's first trainee). Blériot and Latham actually got poised on the French coast, waiting for a lull of wind. Latham, in an Antoinette monoplane, beat Blériot to the draw on July 19, swooping from the chalk cliff at Sangatte, and was 12 miles out when he killed his ailing motor and glided gently into the waves. He was rescued by the destroyer pacing him, sitting in the "saddle" above the wings, calmly puffing a cigarette.

Blériot, with one of his own feathery monoplanes, literally caught Latham napping at 4:35 A.M. on July 25 when he took off from Calais without so much as a compass in his pocket. He reached the white cliffs of Dover, nosed into a cleft between them where someone was waving a French flag, was swung entirely around by a strong wind, and made a safe if rough landing. Covering 25 miles in 37 minutes, he collected both the *Daily Mail*'s $5000 and a $2500 prize from a wine company, and became the first man to fly across a stretch of water from one nation into another. By this blazing feat, Blériot emerged as the chief foe Curtiss would have to face at Rheims.

*   *   *

Back in Hammondsport, Curtiss checked up on factory affairs before departing for his maiden trip to Europe. A new machine shop and other buildings being erected at a cost of over $18,000, in anticipation of the Herring-Curtiss boom, were nearing completion, but he wasn't sure how they were going to be paid for. Herring's working capital seemed to be in a category with his other promises. At the organization of the company, Monroe Wheeler had asked Herring: "What are you going to do for working capital—money to run the business?" Herring replied that he had made provision for that: he planned to sell some of his stock to raise it.

Curtiss was increasingly disillusioned with Herring, who, four months since the incorporation, had yet failed to produce the least evidence of patents or to inform anyone in the company what his patents were. Neither had he delivered the jigs and patterns from his shop in New York. (Herring said later he did not do this because Curtiss said he had no use for them, which was perhaps true, at least after he learned they could serve no purpose.) Herring made various suggestions on motors, motorcycles, and airplanes, some of which were tried and abandoned, others of which were simply ignored. For example, he proposed putting landing skids on the *Gold Bug*. In most cases (to quote from a court decision), "they involved nothing about which Mr. Curtiss was not already well informed." Thus, by the early summer of 1909, Curtiss had become convinced "and expressed his conviction to others connected with the business, that Mr. Herring had brought nothing of value to it [the company]." Moreover, Herring was widely credited with a "captious spirit and fault-finding disposition."

A symptom that aeronautics had indeed begun to elbow motorcycles "out the back door" of the Herring-Curtiss plant appears in the incorporation at this time of the Marvel Motorcycle Company, which Curtiss helped organize and finance. This was formed in unison with his old friend C. Leonard (Tank) Waters. A factory building for its use was commenced on the sidehill below the Herring-Curtiss plant. Waters merged his Equipment and Supply Company (bicycle and motorcycle) into the Marvel Company, which contracted with the Herring-Curtiss Company for 500 motorcycle engines and other parts. Kleckler designed an engine especially for the Marvel.

Herring afterward raised strenuous protest about Curtiss's role in the Marvel Motorcycle Company as having fostered competition with the Herring-Curtiss Company. Simultaneously, however, he was keeping under wraps his own side involvement with W. Starling Burgess, a well-known yacht and sailboat builder of Marblehead, Massachusetts, who had conceived an interest in aircraft manufacture. He contracted to design a Herring-Burgess aeroplane employing controls and devices which, he assured Burgess, were much better than Curtiss's, but which Curtiss scorned to use. Burgess testified later that Herring asked him to keep the contract "as secret as possible" and said "he shortly expected to obtain for himself entire control of the Herring-Curtiss Company." By Herring's own telling: "I signed the contract individually, agreeing to use my majority stock to enforce its being taken over after the annual meeting in January by the Herring-Curtiss Company." In other words, he planned to make Herring-Burgess a division of Herring-Curtiss. The Herring-Burgess model which emerged at Marblehead, equipped with Herring's idea of controls, was promptly smashed by that individual in a jump lasting about five seconds. Its successor capsized in testing. Burgess thereupon canceled the contract "in consideration of buying Herring's tools."

What with one thing and another, it is hard to figure how Herring was devoting much time to his Army contract plane, the postponed deadline for which was July 1, 1909. The Wrights had the same deadline, and their machine, with changes from the year before but the same engine which had killed Selfridge, arrived at Fort Myer on June 18. Owing to unforeseen troubles, climaxing in Orville's encounter with a tree, they were given another month's grace. The final test was passed on July 27 and the Army accepted their plane for $30,000, a bonus of $5000 being allowed for attaining a speed two miles above the specified 40 miles per hour.

The fine success of Curtiss's *Gold Bug*, in whose design Herring claimed a hand, led the Army to expect great things in the plane he was scheduled to deliver. In the absence of any word from him, it was rather anticipated that he would appear with a surprise package at the final hour. On July 1, General Allen, the Signal Corps Chief, waited in his office until 4:00 P.M., closing time for the War Department on Fridays. Still no Herring, and the general declared the contract forfeited. Within a few days, Herring mailed Allen an alibi, saying he had asked Curtiss to call on him in June and "explain the situation," and presumed he had done so; but that Curtiss had been so busy preparing for the Rheims meet that he had neglected to perform the mission. "I have been working 20 hours a day," he averred, "with a force of mechanics to get the machine ready and thought perhaps I would get the same extension given the Wrights. However, except for the criticism that will follow the failure to show up at Fort Myer, I do not care very much

27. A Hammondsport get-together: Seated on the grass is Dr. Bell, conversing with William F. Bedwin, superintendent of his Nova Scotia laboratory; behind them, Glenn Curtiss; standing are Captain Thomas Baldwin, Casey Baldwin, I. Newton Williams (the helicopter man), Doug McCurdy, and Tom Selfridge. COURTESY AND COPYRIGHT, THE BELL FAMILY AND NATIONAL GEOGRAPHIC SOCIETY.

28. Bell's Boys took time out to assist I. Newton Williams with his helicopter experiments. Williams, in the black skull cap, at left, brought his machine from Connecticut to work with Curtiss engines. COURTESY OF MRS. BLANCHE KLECKLER.

29. Glenn Curtiss at the controls of his aerodrome, to which Bell gave the name *June Bug*, for the flying beetles then abundant in the locality. NATIONAL AIR AND SPACE MUSEUM.

30. *June Bug* on the wing for the *Scientific American* Trophy. CULVER PICTURES.

31. Orville Wright, leaning backward, ready for the takeoff at Fort Myer, Virginia, with Tom Selfridge as passenger. The monorail from which the plane was catapulted may be discerned between the skids. NATIONAL AIR AND SPACE MUSEUM.

32. McCurdy's Aerodrome Number 4, the *Silver Dart*, being groomed on Champlin's racetrack at Stony Brook Farm, autumn 1908. COURTESY, ROLAND K. ALEXANDER.

33. The *Silver Dart*, with a more powerful water-cooled engine, was planned as a two-man machine, but Bell vetoed its use in that way after Selfridge's death. Seated tandem in this photograph are McCurdy and Curtiss. COURTESY AND COPYRIGHT, THE BELL FAMILY AND NATIONAL GEOGRAPHIC SOCIETY.

34. With half of the A.E.A. back in Nova Scotia, Curtiss and McCurdy decided on a brief water-flying experiment. With canoe-like pontoons, they altered the *June Bug* into a would-be hydroplane and called it the *Loon*. COURTESY AND COPYRIGHT, THE BELL FAMILY AND NATIONAL GEOGRAPHIC SOCIETY.

35. The *Loon* in action on Keuka Lake. She was unable to break loose from the surface. COURTESY OF MRS. BLANCHE KLECKLER.

36. After initiation at Hammondsport, the *Silver Dart* was shipped to Baddeck. In an ice-cycle accident there, Curtiss had his lower lip severely gashed, which explains the bandage around his chin. FROM THE HENRY KLECKLER ALBUMS.

37. A horse-drawn sleigh pulled the *Silver Dart* out upon the ice of Baddeck Bay. She was the first airplane to fly in Canada. PHOTOGRAPH BY H. M. BENNER. COURTESY AND COPY-RIGHT, THE BELL FAMILY AND NATIONAL GEOGRAPHIC SOCIETY.

38. Bell's kite, the *Cygnet II*, had an engine and metal runners for takeoff from ice; also a front elevator, in the style of the *Silver Dart*'s. Curtiss witnessed its first trial, a failure. FROM THE HENRY KLECKLER ALBUMS.

39. Curtiss trying out the first airplane which was entirely of his own design, using mid-wing ailerons. At Hammondsport, this was called the *Gold Bug*. NATIONAL AIR AND SPACE MUSEUM.

40. The *Gold Bug* being exhibited by Curtiss at Morris Park racetrack in the Bronx. After its acceptance, the Aeronautical Society of New York christened it the *Golden Flier*. NATIONAL AIR AND SPACE MUSEUM.

41. The trim and powerful racing plane Curtiss built for his try at the Gordon Bennett Trophy. Pictured at Hammondsport, presumably after the return from France. J. LANSING CALLAN COLLECTION.

42. For some time after the ice-boat mishap at Beinn Bhreagh, Curtiss wore a small goatee because he was unable to shave over the healing wound. This is how he looked in France. The ornament on his cap was a sort of good-luck charm which went with him on many flights. J. LANSING CALLAN COLLECTION.

43. The Curtiss racer on the field at Rheims, France, one of the grandstands, or "tribunes," in the background. FROM THE HENRY KLECKLER ALBUMS.

44. Reproduced from a French postcard Curtiss mailed to his mother, the photo shows him in the air, with the Farman of his English rival, George Cockburn, on the ground. The message penned on the back of the card said: "You see I am 'flying high.' Am now on the road to Italy via auto. Head for America Sept. 15. Best love. G. H. Curtiss." COURTESY, GLENN H. CURTISS, JR.

45. The Gordon Bennett Trophy. COURTESY, MRS. BLANCHE KLECKLER.

46. In recognition of his Rheims victory, the French pilot's license Number 2 was issued to Curtiss. Number 1 was held by Louis Blériot. Note that his given name was written as "Herring," then crossed out, in confusion over the title of the Herring-Curtiss Company. COURTESY, GLENN H. CURTISS, JR.

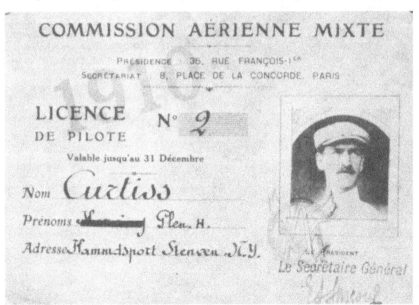

47. Alexander Pfitzner with his monoplane, built at Hammondsport and tried from the ice of Keuka Lake. FROM THE HENRY KLECKLER ALBUMS.

48. Louis Paulhan visits the Curtiss tent at the Los Angeles Air Meet, January 1910. J. LANSING CALLAN COLLECTION.

49. Augustus M. Herring (right) on the way to make "technical delivery" of his Army contract airplane at Fort Myer, Virginia. The two suitcases carried by his assistant contained the parts of the motor. FROM HARPERS WEEKLY.

50. The *Hudson Flyer* after landing at Governors Island from Albany. Notice the flotation gear beneath. COURTESY, OWEN S. BILLMAN.

51. Scene in the banquet hall of the Hotel Astor, at the dinner honoring Glenn Curtiss for his Hudson River flight. Curtiss sits fourth from left at the speakers' table. NATIONAL AIR AND SPACE MUSEUM.

about the government contract. We have more than we can do to carry out our present plans aside from government work."

General Allen was more than patient, and, without a direct request, extended Herring's time limit to August 1. When that date came and went with no sign of Herring, the Signal Corps notified him there would be no further extension, that the contract was null and void. Herring later maintained that he asked for release from the contract. Even after that, he told reporters that the plane was about ready and he would be taking it to Mineola for trials; then, if the Army didn't want it, he would sell it to a foreign government at a better price. No one ever saw the alleged airplane. Herring wrote: "It would be difficult to prove that it was a success for it was too delicately and expensively built and would not have been successful unless rebuilt and strengthened at the joints. There was, however, absolutely nothing wrong with it in theory." Under cross-questioning later, he confessed he had never finished it, giving as his excuse that he had tied up all his money in the Herring-Curtiss Company. "I can't say whether I had it in mind to deliver to the government or not," he said. "I may have."

*   *   *

Curtiss was booked to sail for France on August 5. He came down to New York two days early in order to bring the repair parts for the *Golden Flier* and put it back together. This done, he gave it a thorough tryout at Mineola and pronounced it fit for delivery. The Aeronautic Society, which had made him a second part-payment of $2000 at Morris Park, now handed him a check for the balance and took possession.

Charles Willard at once began flights and drew crowds to the Hempstead Plains, quickly acquiring mastery of the plane. In fact, Willard established an American cross-country record of 12 miles, flying over wires, railroads, and trees, and "caused much excitement in that part of the island." Thereupon the Society organized the Aeronautic Exhibition Company and sent Willard on tour to fulfill engagements with the *Golden Flier,* making him the pioneer exhibition pilot of the country. The company letterhead carried a photograph of the *Golden Flier* in flight and advertised it as "Smallest, Fastest, and Most Beautiful Aeroplane in the World."

One more potentially important business transaction arose for Curtiss before he embarked. He was waylaid in New York by James M.

Beck, chairman of the aeronautics committee of the Hudson-Fulton
Commission, with a proposition to do some flying in connection with
that grandiose celebration in the latter part of September. The field
was to be on Governors Island in New York Harbor, and flying over
water would be involved. He hadn't much time to consider, and seemingly signed a tentative agreement, subject to consultation with Bishop
after his arrival in France. The Rheims meet was getting under way
when Beck announced receipt of a contract signed by Wilbur Wright,
and that he had Curtiss's promise to participate. A complete circuit of
Manhattan Island might be made during the flights, Beck intimated.

12. Glory at Rheims

Without sensing what it would mean to his life, Glenn Curtiss read an item in his copy of the *A.E.A. Bulletin* in the November of 1908, while he and McCurdy were converting the *June Bug* into the *Loon*. It reprinted a dispatch out of the New York *Tribune*: "Paris, Oct. 22.—The Aero Club of France has decided to organize a big aeroplane meeting in the autumn of 1909, when the Grand Prix d'Aviation will be competed for. The value of this prize is $2000 and there will be other awards. The course will be laid out over the flat country in the Champagne or Beauce region. The flights will be judged for both speed and duration."

The next week's issue of the *Bulletin* relayed another choice bit of aero intelligence—namely, that the town of Brescia, on the Lombardy plains of northern Italy, was planning a Concour Internationale d'Aviation for the month of September 1909, also dangling cash prizes for bait. Bell's Boys were interested to see how the rash of aviation fever was breaking out all over Europe. Similarly affected were a certain trio of gentlemen in Paris whose primary concern up to then had been with ballooning: James Gordon Bennett, Jr., Cortlandt Field Bishop, and Comte Henri de la Vaulx.

The Count was president of the Fédération Aéronautique Internationale and had made ascensions in America, under the auspices of the Aero Club, at West Point and Pittsfield, Massachusetts. Bishop was official delegate of the Aero Club of America to the F.A.I. Between them they had cooked up an idea which they now conspired to impress upon Bennett.

The flamboyant and impulsive James Gordon Bennett had inherited from his father the New York *Herald* and its Paris edition, which was as much a gold mine as it was a newspaper. For some years Bennett had been an expatriate in Paris, partly because he enjoyed it there, partly because his scandalous behavior had made him the recipient of icy stares but no further invitations from New York high society. Like Curtiss, he had a lust for speed. When younger, he doted on driving four-in-hand coaches at a gallop through the streets of New York, careening around corners to the affright if not actual peril of the commonalty; on one memorable occasion balancing himself on the coachman's seat without a stitch of clothing. Again, he won a madcap yacht race across the Atlantic Ocean in midwinter. In his somewhat mellower age, Bennett was the leading patron of daring sports in Europe. In 1906, he established the Coupe Internationale des Aeronauts (better known as the Gordon Bennett Cup) for annual balloon races which quickly won world renown. The third of these events was a large success at Berlin in October 1908, and it was soon thereafter that the triumvirate were lunching together in a Parisian restaurant.

The discussion turned upon the international flying meet just announced by the Aéro Club de France, and the time was ripe for Bishop and Count de la Vaulx to propound their inspiration to Bennett: namely, that he set up a trophy, along with a cash prize, for a yearly airplane race, as he had previously done for balloons. Bennett required little suasion. Then and there, they roughed out the details over the lunch table, and Bishop went with the publisher directly to his newspaper office where an announcement of the Coupe d'Aviation Gordon-Bennett was issued and cabled to New York. This trophy, "emblematic of the world's championship in the sport of flying," was to be awarded in three successive years for "the best speed record by an airplane over a closed course"; the first presentation was timed for the international air meet of 1909. The silver trophy itself, to be designed later, would be valued at $2500; the money reward going with it was $5000.

Bishop's part in instigating the Gordon Bennett Trophy helps to account for his ardor in finding an American entrant for the first running of the race; perhaps it also had a bearing on his readiness to invest in the Herring-Curtiss Company.

*　　*　　*

Preparing for his overseas adventure, Curtiss was struck by a singular parallel of place names; a superstitious person might have imagined in this a favorable omen. Talking with newsmen at the gang-plank, he remarked: "I ought to find myself quite at home in Rheims, for it happens by odd coincidence that the place where I conducted some of my first experiments in flying near Hammondsport is also named Rheims. It is, too, a vineyard region, very much like that, perhaps, of the champagne country around Rheims, France."

The tiny railroad depot at the foot of the wine-cellar hill did indeed bear the name, Rheims, on its sign; and a Rheims postoffice was located in the central building of the Pleasant Valley Wine Company. Nearby, at the Pleasant Valley crossing of the B.&H., was a hamlet of Rheims where a few winery employees lived; entertainments were held in its Grange Hall; stickfuls of Rheims "personals" appeared regularly in the *Hammondsport Herald.* By local legendry, the place received its name from early vintners imported from Rheims, France, because it reminded them (actually, there is no resemblance) of home.

The plane was finished barely soon enough for shipment—"the greatest rush job I have ever undertaken," said Curtiss. There was no time at all for a trial flight, and the engine merely got a brief test run on the block. She was trim and dainty, closely akin to the *Golden Flier* but a few inches shorter in the wingspan. Wings were khaki-colored. No one attempted to pin a name on this one; after the event she was spoken of usually as the French plane, the Rheims racer, or "the Curtiss." The engine was the thing. All brains and energies the factory could muster had gone into making this the most advanced and powerful 8-cylinder yet built in America. A fresh talent who assisted with some of its fine points was A. L. Pfitzner, the towering Hungarian engineer from Budapest who was sojourning in Hammondsport to build his own monoplane. While rated at 50 horsepower, it perhaps actually delivered 35. "My own personal hopes lay in my motor," Curtiss would reiterate.

His traveling companions were Tod Shriver, an excellent mechanic loaned for the excursion by Captain Tom Baldwin (probably Henry Kleckler's presence was necessary in Hammondsport to keep the shop going); and Ward Fisher, a friend since bicycle-racing days in Rochester, who now held the Curtiss motorcycle agency in that city.

His valedictory words upon boarding the French liner *Savoie* were these: "The only contestants I fear at all are the men with the monoplanes. The machine I am taking with me I believe to be the fastest aeroplane in the world of the biplane model. If the monoplanes of Blériot and Latham can make 55 to 60 miles an hour as reported, they will doubtless keep us biplane chaps very busy. So far as I know, there are no biplane speed records much better than 42 or 43 miles an hour."

In truth, this was the gist of the matter as Curtiss set forth in pursuit of the world's speed record: it would be essentially a showdown between biplane and monoplane. The French flyers who were out in front were oriented to the light, graceful, and relatively fleet monoplanes. Indirectly, however, he was asserting that he knew he could beat the Wright biplanes, five of which were entered at Rheims.

A new trophy in this country, inspired by Curtiss, was announced just as he departed. Frank N. Doubleday, president of the Doubleday, Page Publishing Company, had seen one of Curtiss's best flights at Mineola and talked with him. As a result, he gave an order to Tiffany's for a "valuable trophy" to be offered as an encouragement to American aviators.

Cortlandt Bishop took it upon himself to act as Curtiss's European manager, so to speak. Without delaying for the flyer's consent, he booked him to fly at the Italian air meet which was to follow on the heels of the one at Rheims. Upon docking at Le Havre, Curtiss found this message from Bishop: I HAVE ENTERED YOU FOR BRESCIA TO SAVE THE FEES. ENTRIES CLOSED TODAY. I HAVE INSURED YOU FOR FIRE AND ACCIDENT. (A penalty would have been imposed for tardy entry.) Bishop also had arranged lodging for Curtiss and his two comrades in the house of a Catholic priest. Accommodations for the "Week of Aviation" were at a premium in the hotels and boardinghouses of Rheims; even tiny bedrooms in humble homes rented for $40 a day. Aristocrats and the wealthy had gobbled up all the choice suites well in advance. The excitement mounting over this event was fantastic.

A complication arose at Le Havre when it developed that the express company could not guarantee delivery of the plane at Rheims in less than a week. Here it was the 12th, and the meet was due to open on the 22nd, allowing Curtiss at most two days to assemble and break in a totally untried machine. It was packed in four long, flattish boxes. A compromise was hastily arranged whereby the railroad allowed the cases aboard as personal baggage, which was fair enough except that it meant sharing a compartment with them and having them privately transported across Paris from the Gare St. Lazare to the Gare de l'Est. This operation created a flurry among cab drivers and an amusing diversion for bystanders. Bishop met Curtiss at the station and hustled him off for an introduction to James Gordon Bennett, who whistled softly, looking out his office window, when informed that the aviator's only emergency equipment was one spare propeller. Bennett made it emphatic that he would relish seeing his trophy won by an American.

During the two hours between trains in Paris, Curtiss was surprised that throngs in the streets knew who he was and shouted vociferous greetings. He refused offers of lavish hospitality if only he would stay longer. A cabled dispatch to New York describing his Paris reception said:

FOR THE TIME, AT LEAST, HE IS QUITE AS POPULAR AS THE WRIGHTS WERE, IF NOT MORE SO, FOR THEY DECLINED THE ISSUE WHEN THEY WERE INVITED TO TAKE PART IN THE GRAND TOURNAMENT, WHILE CURTISS PLUCKILY ACCEPTED IT . . . WHEN THE PARISIANS LEARNED THAT CURTISS HAD COME THERE PRACTICALLY AT HIS OWN EXPENSE, AND THAT HE HAD BEEN DOING A LOT OF HARD WORK IN OBSCURITY WHILE THE WRIGHTS GOT ALL OF AMERICA'S PRAISE, THEY WARMED UP TO HIM MORE THAN EVER, AND IT IS CERTAIN THAT HE WILL BE ONE OF THE FAVORITES IN THE RHEIMS TOURNAMENT.

Rheims: a city so ancient that it was a prosperous market town when Caesar's legions conquered Gaul; a select place of residence for Roman governors; city in whose magnificent cathedral the kings of France were traditionally crowned by the Archbishop of Rheims; before whose portals armies for centuries had surged back and forth across the plains; where Jeanne d'Arc won a famous victory, so that her statue was among its revered monuments. And now Rheims was going to witness a new sort of history being made.

The field of aerial combat had been enlarged from a racetrack on the plain of Bethény not far outside the city, and was surrounded by stout wooden fencing. Four vast grandstands were designed to hold an aggregate 50,000 spectators. The stands were referred to as tribunes, after the Roman style. Ranged along the opposite side of the grounds was "a desolate village of raw pine," a long row of jerry-built sheds for the airplanes; next to these were large tents for dirigibles and spherical balloons. Never before had so many aircraft been assembled in one place. Forty-four of these were aeroplanes, and the scene was already lively when Curtiss arrived, engines spitting fire up and down the line; planes, from the big ungainly Farmans to small, elegant monoplanes, taking off and landing on test runs.

The distance requirement for the Gordon Bennett Trophy was 20 kilometers, which meant twice around a rectangular 10-kilometer. course. Each of the four corners was marked by a conspicuous red-and-white pylon. Near the judges' stand was a tall tower from which vari-colored flags would signal the results of events in a code, the key to which was printed in the programs.

Eight major events were listed on the week's program—seven for airplanes, one for dirigibles—with a total $40,000 in prizes. The Bennett Trophy race was to be the grand climax, reserved for Saturday, the next-to-last day; then on Sunday would come the Prix de Vitesse, a speed test of 30 kilometers for 20,000 francs. With only one plane to gamble, Curtiss steadfastly resisted the urging of Americans in the crowd to enter some of the earlier competitions. In response to such pressure, he set his jaw and said: "I came over to win the Gordon Bennett Cup, and nothing—*nothing* will stop me." But he aimed to enter for the Prix de Vitesse once that was behind him.

At the very outset, he had a dash of cold water to his hopes on learning that his engine was no secret to the opposition. Getting wind of it ahead of time, Blériot had an 8-cylinder motor hurriedly built, and it was reputed to yield 80 horsepower (against Curtiss's 50). After seeing the monoplane in the air with this engine, Curtiss said glumly: "Blériot is faster than we are." Tod Shriver, familiar with his motorcycle racing technique, retorted: "Glenn, I have seen you win many a race on the turns."

Although the feeling was prevalent that Blériot had the trophy as good as clinched, the French were deeply interested in the challenger and his airplane. His lean Yankee appearance and somber reticence, coupled with the goatee on his chin, made him, in their eyes, the living symbol of "l'Oncle Sam." They thought it a very American trait that, instead of sauntering about basking in the public gaze, he spent his time with his mechanic, Shriver, laboring steadily at his machine with greasy hands. They remarked on the oddity of Shriver's working in shirtsleeves; French mechanics traditionally wore smocks. "We must be the most picturesque nation on earth," Tod expostulated after working for hours before a milling audience.

Though Curtiss was assigned an individual hangar, cavernous for the size of his plane, it was like a goldfish bowl as other aviators, mechanics, and paying customers flocked around unabashedly. As the machine was being assembled, watchers voiced astonishment at its smallness. "The Frenchmen were inclined to regard it as a boy's aeroplane," said Curtiss, "but after we got it warmed up it made man's size flights." The airmen were curious about his laminated wooden propellers; their own were either metallic or carved from solid wood. The builder of Blériot's monoplane, M. Chauvière, made Curtiss the gift of one of his propellers (which did not get used).

* * *

The first thing Bishop was anxious to know from Curtiss was his side of the disturbing stories he had heard from the Wright brothers. Doubtless Curtiss gave him a rather different version of the visit to Dayton and of Selfridge's request for advice. On the patent matter itself, according to Curtiss:

"I told him I thought our device was outside the claims of the Wright patents, and that the Wrights were not entitled to a monopoly of flying, and that I thought we had . . . a good chance of winning the suit. Mr. Bishop told me that he didn't want to get into a fight, and I told him that I was on good friendly terms with the Wrights and had talked with them on various occasions, recognizing their great achievements in being the first to fly, and recognizing their patents, as I understood them. But I still contended that our neutral ailerons were outside of their claims and we should continue to use them, and if they brought suit on that we had a fair chance to win."

Bishop felt better about the situation. Still he insisted that he did not wish to be drawn into any litigation with the Wrights, if only for the reason that he must maintain a neutral position as president of the Aero Club.

Another subject of discussion while marking time for the meet to get under way was Augustus Herring, and their comparing of notes was real enlightening to both. They reverted to the beginning, and

Curtiss said that Herring had told him he did not need to talk with Bishop about the organization of the company, as he (Herring) would handle the matter. Bishop replied, "Why, he told me the same thing about you."

As they neared a conclusion that Herring had hoodwinked them both, Curtiss said: "I supposed that you knew and investigated Herring's inventions and patents yourself."

"Why, I supposed you did," Bishop exclaimed.

"How does it happen," Curtiss sensibly inquired, "that we didn't get together?"

The brothers Wright chose a theatrical moment for their crackdown—the eve of the world's first great tourney of the air. The timing was deliberate, for psychological impact. To their way of thinking, every airplane on that field (excepting the five of their own type, produced abroad under franchise) infringed their patent. They did not propose to let this sort of thing continue without payment of royalties to them. The spark which actually touched them off was the sale of the *Golden Flier* to the Aeronautic Society; but Curtiss's going to Rheims to compete for a monetary prize was also a decisive factor.

Five days behind Curtiss, Orville Wright took ship for a series of demonstration flights in Berlin, in an agreement with the German Wright Company, just then organized. Angered at encountering more headlines in New York about the doings of Curtiss, he mailed a letter to Wilbur before embarking. Enclosing a sample clipping, he said:

"I think best plan is to start suit against Curtiss, Aeronautic Society, etc., at once. This will call attention of public to fact that the machine [*Golden Flier*] is an infringement of ours . . . It may be a good idea to resign (or withdraw) our names as honorary members of the Aeronautic Society if suit is brought against it.

"If suit is brought before the races are run at Rheims, the effect will be better than after."

Wilbur hurried east to consult with attorneys and on August 18 filed petitions for injunctions against the Aeronautic Society, the Herring-Curtiss Company, and Glenn H. Curtiss. Since New York City and Hammondsport were in different judicial districts, it was necessary to open proceedings in federal courts of both New York and Buffalo. On August 19 (the day Curtiss first got his plane in the air at Rheims) a lawsuit was launched in the U. S. District Court in New York against the Aeronautic Society, seeking to restrain the society from further exhibition of the *Golden Flier*, to recover damages, and to compel surrender of the plane for destruction. The bill of complaint alleged that, unless the society was stopped from flying, it would "practically destroy" a large source of revenue which was their due. It further alleged that they had earlier notified Curtiss that a machine of his (the *June Bug*) violated their patent, and that he then informed them he did not expect to do exhibition flying, and "sought to make them believe he would not perform such act."

Within a few days, papers were served in Hammondsport on Mrs. Lena Curtiss and Lynn D. Masson, secretary-treasurer of the company. In Bath, County Judge Monroe Wheeler gave out a statement in his capacity as president and counsel of the company: "These suits will be defended, and it will be the policy of the defense to disprove all claims of infringement by showing that many of the infringements alleged were fully covered by patents taken out by Mr. Herring and his associates in the Curtiss-Herring [sic] Company before the Wrights applied for patents. While the plaintiffs in the case are without doubt acting in good faith in their allegations, the records of the patent office, which will be produced by the defense, will easily and satis-factorily adjust what at first was regarded by the public as a stupendous litigation."

The old friend and well-wisher of the brothers, Octave Chanute, did not yet speak out in public, but his disapproval showed in a reply to Ernest L. Jones, editor of *Aeronautics*, who sought his advice on how to handle the case: "I think the Wrights have made a blunder by bringing suit at this time. Not only will this antagonize very many persons but it may disclose some prior patents which will invalidate their more important claims."

The news spread like wildfire among the flyers and through the tribunes at the plain of Bethény. The overwhelming reaction of European airmen and planemakers was antagonistic to the Wrights, whom they viewed as trying to establish a monopoly on flight; they foresaw that their turn would soon come in every country where the Wright patents were registered. Sour comments were heard among spectators, particu-larly the large American contingent, to the effect that it was unsporting of the Wrights to start suit precisely at the opening of the meet in which Curtiss was the sole representative of the United States in a world championship contest which they had refused to enter.

Journalists scurried about the field asking important persons for comment. That Cortlandt Bishop had undergone a change of view is proved by the assertion then of his belief that the infringement claim was invalid because Curtiss did not employ the wing-warping principle. Practically the only remark they squeezed out of Curtiss was his surprise that the Wrights were bringing a separate suit against him personally. He did not seem very worried, and presently wrote home: "Everyone here thinks the Wrights' suit is only bluff. No one thinks there is any infringement."

*   *   *

The number of airplanes entering the week's events was winnowed to thirty-eight, about evenly divided between biplanes and monoplanes, and there were twenty-eight pilots to fly them. Plainly the moth-like monoplanes had captured the popular imagination, and, after Blériot cut some fancy capers, the American's chances looked forlorn to most French beholders; but airmen of experience sensed that the Curtiss machine was fast and not by any means to be discounted.

Near sundown of the first day of his test flying, Curtiss narrowly averted a mid-air collision when three planes were circling the field at the same time (in itself a historic first). The other two were French. As the cables carried the story: ALL WERE FLYING RAPIDLY, WHEN SUDDENLY CURTISS SAW M. DUMAUEST IN AN ANTOINETTE MONOPLANE APPROACHING AT RIGHT ANGLES AND ON THE SAME LEVEL WITH HIM. AS QUICK AS A FLASH CURTISS REALIZED THE DANGER AND, ELEVATING HIS PLANES, HIS MACHINE INSTANTLY SHOT UPWARD AND SOARED OVER THE FRENCHMAN. THOUSANDS OF SPECTATORS APPLAUDED THE AMERICAN WILDLY. At the end of another dry run, his off-track landing carried him into a field of tall grain and he was thrown out, spraining an ankle; during the remainder of the meet he walked with a cane borrowed from the priest who was his landlord.

French aviators kept chalking up records and smashing up airplanes during the week. Dragoons policed the field and fled at a gallop from low-flying planes. Curtiss sandwiched in his test flights as he could, when official events were not in progress. Even so, he tallied an unofficial speed record in one of these forays, without really planning to do so. At the end of the second day, Blériot had just crossed the finish line for a world speed record of 42.87 miles per hour. Suddenly a cry went up: "The American is starting." For practice, at least, but perchance too with the sly motive of showing up the Channel-conquering celebrity who was universally expected to trounce him on Saturday, Curtiss made an 8-second takeoff and passed the tribunes "going at a terrific pace," rounded the pylons and crossed the finish line "majestically," as one awed reporter put it. An instant after the landing, a flag on the tower signaled that he had bettered Blériot's time by 7 seconds for an average speed of 43.38 miles. Overnight, anyhow, he was holder of the world's informal speed record; next morning Blériot went out and canceled it. The multitude realized now that "l'Americain" would bear watching. All he had to say about the episode was that he had not been pushing his plane to its limit, and that the most interesting aspect of the flight was the view it gave him of his fallen rivals strewn around the course. He counted twelve planes on the ground wrecked or disabled, being hauled back to their sheds by horses and by hand. At that moment, all the flyable airplanes existing in the United States did not number a dozen.

Weather was wretched for the first three days of the meet, with drizzling rain and gluey white mud; when it didn't rain, it was chilly, reducing the gate. Despite this bad start, total attendance over the week was reckoned at 500,000, counting royalty and titles of nobility. A glittering ball was held in Rheims the evening of opening day, but Glenn Curtiss was not among those present. Instead, he could have been found at the field fussing over his aircraft.

Naturally, he made the acquaintance of all the currently reigning European flyers of whom he had read so much: Blériot, Latham, Ferber, Eugène LeFébvre, the sculptor Léon Delagrange, Count de Lambert, the Englishman George B. Cockburn, and the rest. Farman he already knew from being on the welcoming committee when he was in New York the year before. One who especially stuck in his memory was the likeable and gallant little Frenchman, Louis Paulhan. Though he had been flying barely three months, Paulhan was distinguishing himself for altitude work as well as distance.

Early in the week, Curtiss found out who his competitors were to be for the Gordon Bennett Trophy. Thirteen Frenchmen wanted to enter but the rules restricted any one country to three entries. An elimination contest was run off and its winners were Blériot, Latham (with his Antoinette), and LeFébvre (with a Wright). LeFébvre, the saying went, had learned flying "in a correspondence school"; he had ordered a Wright plane by mail and instructions came with it. Only one other entrant had to be considered: George Cockburn, Britain's single challenger, flying a Farman.

The Curtiss style soon made itself distinctive. Maximilian Foster wrote for *Everybody's* magazine: "Curtiss one knew from afar by the speed and the light springiness of his biplane, its head-vanes, stretched out in advance, cutting the air like the forebody of a wild fowl homing to its nightly rest . . . His was a sprightly engine of flight; it had an abrupt and startling quickness all its own, so that one never quite overcame the habit of gasping when the intrepid driver cut corners at every pylon." Charles Edward White depicted for *Harper's Weekly* the "grim, lanky American holding a wheel in a network of piano wires"; how he faded into a mere speck, rounded a distant pylon, and came hurtling back: "Here is certainly the quintessence of mechanical efficiency."

Some comparison between Curtiss and the Wrights was inevitable among Europeans who had seen the Dayton pair so lately reaping laurels. A prominent Frenchman sketched a similitude: "These men might be brothers as far as resemblances go. They are all retiring, conservative, sharp-featured, blue-eyed and ambidextrous. They all have bird faces. Look at them as they stand watching the clouds and you will see it. They resemble each other in their manner of speech, their movements and their build."

One by one, the premium events of the week were ticked off, and considerable grumbling was heard among Americans in attendance as Curtiss remained obdurately on the sidelines. The main competition leading up to the Bennett Cup was the Grand Prix de la Champagne for 100,000 francs; spread out over three days, its goal was the greatest distance covered without refueling or touching ground. This was won by Henry Farman, in his clumsy Voisin biplane, who droned on into the dusk as flares were lighted at the pylons and auto headlamps were ignited. He came down after 3 hours, 4 minutes, for a distance of 111.85 miles.

*   *   *

The adversaries for the Gordon Bennett Trophy were each allowed a trial round of the course before notifying the judges' stand of their readiness for official start. They were to fly and be timed individually. Each could choose in advance the hour for his trial, within the limits of 10:00 A.M. and 5:30 P.M. With his earlybird penchant, Curtiss no doubt would have preferred the crack of dawn, but he settled for the 10 o'clock slot. The day turned out ideal, weatherwise —clear, sunny, windless. The tribunes bulged with ardent humanity. Much betting went on, and Blériot, the French hero with the 80-horsepower motor in his monoplane, continued the runaway favorite.

The gold-winged biplane, all that stood between Blériot and the trophy (and $5000), was warming up its engine. Not a breath of air was stirring except the wash of his propeller as Curtiss, in a brown leather jacket and the inevitable visored cap, hitched himself up to the seat and tried the wheel and shoulder-yoke to make sure all was in order. "I expected to have a very calm flight," he said when it was over; but he was in for a rude surprise. Once aloft, he found the atmosphere "boiling" (his word for turbulence). The sun beating on the plain had set thermal updrafts in motion. "It was as if I were riding in a fast automobile and every few minutes struck a bump." On the far leg of the course, opposite the grandstands, was a stretch the pilots had nicknamed the "graveyard," so many crashes had occurred there due to a vortex of turbulence. When he struck this, Curtiss was pitched about so violently that he "mentally resolved if I got out of this alive I would not start again under such conditions for the Coupe or any other event."

Upon landing, he was astonished to hear that his time was his best yet. "I thought the matter over and came to the conclusion that this disturbed condition of the atmosphere without any wind was most conducive to speed. In a perfectly calm atmosphere a vacuum doubtless would have been formed behind the machine. With the broken air currents the propeller always had a fresh mass of air to work on, consequently obtaining great push."

Thus, Curtiss once more reasoning a thing through. Decision: to go for the Coupe Internationale right away, taking advantage of the "boiling" air. The word was sent to the judges. Curtiss had his gas tank replenished, his propeller changed. After takeoff, he circled to gain 500 feet altitude, then dove for the starting line to get a fast start. Tricks learned from motorcycle racing he now adapted to flying. Steep banks on the turns and shaving the pylons so closely that it seemed he would peel the paint. Spectators were dazzled. No man had ever flown like that before. Of course, there had never been racing pylons before to shave. The thermal currents were bad as ever at the "graveyard." "The shocks were so violent indeed that I was lifted completely out of my seat and was able to maintain my position in the aeroplane only by wedging my feet against the framework." When he thought he detected a couple of misfires, he adjusted the mixture with a small wheel he had devised a few days earlier.

Twice around the course, and down. He sat still and watched the time being posted: 15 minutes, 50 seconds; average speed, 46½ miles per hour. Well, for the time being, at least, he was speed champion of the air. What he had really done (if one wished to be gloomy) was to set a mark for Blériot to shoot at. All he could do was sweat out the attempts of his rivals for the remainder of the day. "I felt like a prisoner awaiting the jury's verdict," he recalled.

Bishop, with his brother David, took Curtiss in his automobile around the field and parked near the timers' stand to await the issue. By intervals, Blériot tried three practice laps but touched down each time because he was dissatisfied with the behavior of his plane, and tinkered all afternoon with the engine.

Meanwhile the other entrants made their bids and met with predictable failures. Neither Latham nor LeFébvre even came close to the Curtiss mark. Cockburn was halfway around the field when a wing tip grazed a shock of corn and he was tossed out.

Blériot waited until 5:10 for his official go, just 20 minutes shy of the closing gong. Nobody was tenser than the occupants of Bishop's big red touring car. Blériot's first circuit showed up a trifle faster than Curtiss's, and they figured right off that the race was over; in fact, Curtiss and Bishop talked about building a faster plane and coming back next year while Blériot was doing his second lap, which looked from where they sat as if he was easily hitting 60 miles per hour. Then, suddenly, they wondered why things were so still: the crowd had not broken into a riot of sound at the finish.

Bishop leaped from the car and dashed to the judges' stand. Sprinting back with a broad grin, he shouted: "You win! You beat Blériot by six seconds." Just then the U.S. flag went up the staff and the band struck into *The Star-Spangled Banner*. The tumult came then in waves, beginning among the hundreds of Americans in the audience, spreading to the French thousands as they gradually recovered from their stunned disbelief and paid generous homage to the foreign victor.

Pandemonium churned around the grandstand box reserved for the U. S. Ambassador to France, Henry White, and his party. Mounted dragoons were sorely pressed to keep the ebullient crowd from engulfing the automobile in which the newly crowned king of the air sat unregally beside James Gordon Bennett. Abashed and embarrassed by the demonstration, though inwardly exultant at having achieved what he came to do, Curtiss accepted the compliments and shook the extended hands. He uttered few words in return. One of the first to push through to the red motorcar was Louis Blériot who emotionally congratulated his vanquisher and pledged to be in America to return the trophy to France at the next year's meet (a promise which was unkept). A lane was opened for Ambassador White and his guests. After felicitating Curtiss in the name of the government and people of the United States, he introduced Mrs. Theodore Roosevelt, wife of the ex-President who himself was on a hunting safari in Africa. With her were three of the Roosevelt children, Ethel, Quentin, and Archie. "Bully!" cried Quentin, in the well-known manner of his father.[1]

On behalf of the Aero Club of America, Bishop told the press: "This is the greatest sporting victory the world has seen, and it has been won against heavy odds. America was represented in the contest by one competitor against the combined genius of the world."

The newspapers promptly proclaimed Curtiss "Champion Aviator of the World." (The speed record, of course, did not long stand. Records toppled fast in those days.)

In faraway Hammondsport that Saturday night, joy was unconfined. Flags flew, cannon boomed, champagne flowed, bonfires blazed. A citizens' committee set plans rolling for a welcome-home reception to eclipse any blow-out in the history of the village. A subscription fund was started for the celebration and a gold medal.

*   *   *

Having captured the trophy, Curtiss no longer needed to coddle his plane, so that on Sunday, the windup of the meet, he tackled two additional speed prizes in which the contests were essentially between him and Blériot. In a 10-kilometer dash (one lap of the course), Blériot had a mite of revenge by clipping four seconds off the American's time. Then came the Prix de la Vitesse (thrice around the pylons) for 10,000 francs. Blériot led off, but after one lap he disappeared behind a hillock and a column of smoke arose. A broken something caused him to smack the ground, and he scrambled free to watch his plane burn; luckily his injuries were not serious. Curtiss took the Prix de la Vitesse almost by default, making his total winnings at Rheims $7400 (he was awarded $400 as a quick-starting prize).

From that moment until the hullabaloo subsided, this man who was innately shy and self-effacing was pursued, courted, and quoted as an international celebrity. Reporters lurked in his vicinity with pencils poised. Next day they noted his casual remark: "By the way, I am going to have a look at my cup this afternoon. I have not yet seen it." The Bennett Trophy was on display at a Rheims jewelry shop. In actuality, it was not his to take home, but remained in the custody of the Aero Club of America pending the 1910 race for its possession. That same day he was guest of honor at a big luncheon in the Salons de Germain, of Rheims, with the firm stipulation that he was not to speak; when asked why, he gave the not very clever reply, "Flying is faster than talking," and this too got quoted. Bishop did the speaking for him, and drew applause by referring to Curtiss's origins in a wine growing region where there was a place called Rheims.

Post-mortem analysis of the meet brought comments by reputed experts that the Wright planes did not seem stable enough but flew with "a jerky, bounding motion"; that both the Curtiss and Wright machines "seemed too abrupt in their movements; as if too much were depending on the pilot's skill and faculties—too little on the poise and confidence of the machine itself." Major B. Baden-Powell, secretary of the British Aeronautical Society, wrote: "The Antoinette was certainly the steadiest . . . The Curtiss was also very fairly steady and regular . . . The Wright was distinctly unsteady and continually pitching."

One noticeable aftermath was that a fair percentage of the French aeronauts switched to Curtiss engines. Another was a flurry of orders for Herring-Curtiss airplanes in America—orders that could not readily be filled because of the uncertainty about the Wright suit, besides other troubles which were soon to beset the company.

Whatever the respective merits of the aircraft which had been seen and judged in action, a favored phrase among the writers was that "Rheims had beheld a new age born." Granting that the birth had taken place several years earlier amid the offshore dunes of North Carolina, one scribe amended this to say that the new era had "kicked off its swaddling clothes," or "deplumed itself of its pin feathers." For Rheims it was only too true. Five years later a German warplane flew over that venerable city and dropped explosives . . .

From Rheims to Paris and more adulation for the Champion Aviator of the World. The Aéro Club de France christened its new balloon the *Curtiss Number 1* and invited him to be a passenger on its maiden voyage, along with Blériot, Bishop, and Tod Shriver. This was Curtiss's first ascent in a spherical balloon. The pilot was Edgar W. Mix, noted American balloonist. The bag of hydrogen arose from the Aéro Club's park in the suburb of Saint-Cloud and came down at Courcelles, 80 kilometers from Paris. Bishop's chauffeur trailed it to drive them back to Paris.

That evening, a grand banquet which, as the star guest, he could not avoid. With Ambassador and Mrs. Henry White as hosts, this affair was given in the U. S. Embassy, and 500 elegantly attired people dined off gold plate. An ovation greeted Curtiss when he entered the room arm-in-arm with Louis Blériot. He did not mind the gold dishes so much, but, as he said, "when they wanted me to stand up and make a speech, I was lost."

Wherever he went in Paris, he was in a virtual state of siege. "We stood for more pictures than you can imagine," Ward Fisher remembered. "I didn't know there were so many cameras in the world. Everyone had one and all used them." Curtiss even let himself be persuaded to pose for a photograph beside Anna Held, the famous actress. Knowing that he was supposed to perform for the Hudson-Fulton Celebration, Miss Held offered him $10,000 to fly her from Governors Island to some convenient flat place in Manhattan; she said she wanted to be "the first woman to enter New York in a flying machine." How he evaded that proposition is not recorded.

His sudden renown brought him a deluge of tempting offers for flights in both Europe and America, one even for a lecture tour. The date at Brescia was a contract made by Bishop and had to be fulfilled. His services were in demand in England and Germany, and the sums mentioned were such as to make him reluctant to quit Europe right away. The Hudson-Fulton Commission grew worried, perhaps with some reason. Bishop was quoted as saying that Curtiss had "no definite commitment to fly at the Hudson-Fulton Celebration." This stirred up a teapot tempest. James Beck, chairman of the aeronautic committee, cabled an angry protest to Bishop, saying: IF ANYONE IS INFLUENCING CURTISS TO BREAK FAITH WITH THE PEOPLE OF NEW YORK, KINDLY USE YOUR INFLUENCE TO THE CONTRARY. Bishop retorted that Curtiss had not yet signed the Hudson-Fulton contract; that an unsigned copy had been sent him after he reached France, together with a draft for $1500 as part payment, and both had been returned without signature. William J. Hammer, secretary of the committee under Beck, verified this much, saying Curtiss sent back the contract for a modification in terms. Beck displayed to reporters a copy of an agreement of some sort, signed and notarized on August 4. Curtiss had no intention of backing down on the agreement, as proved when he cabled the factory before going to Brescia, asking if the new machine then under construction could be finished in time for the Hudson-Fulton program. (The explanation for this flap probably lay in certain contracts Herring had signed, without the consent of Curtiss, for public exhibits of the Rheims racer the instant it was back in New York.)

As business partner of the champion, Herring basked in reflected radiance and appointed himself, in effect, his agent in negotiating for future engagements. At the Plaza Hotel, he conferred with two civic emissaries from St. Louis who "offered a very large amount of money" for Curtiss to fly the victory plane at that city's centennial celebration in the forepart of October. Other promoters hastened to New York and sought him out. Chicago, Indianapolis, and Cincinnati begged for Curtiss. Herring cabled him that interest was "stirred to a high pitch" in the Midwest, and urged him to engage Blériot, Latham, and Farman for a joint tour of Western cities. A theatrical manager in Chicago announced that he was in receipt of a cable from Curtiss at Brescia accepting his offer of $8000 for five flights "in the original Rheims machine"; he then boarded a train for New York to finalize details with Herring. A New York firm wished to purchase the plane, and Herring replied that the original was "contracted out," but that they might have a copy. Herring had already sold a replica of the *Golden Flier* with a dummy motor, for $500, to a Mr. Russell who exhibited it on stage in a vaudeville act.

*   *   *

The spotlight now shifted to Brescia, where the Concour Internationale d'Aviation was due to open September 8. For that spectacle, Curtiss was tenfold the attraction he had been when Bishop entered him. Automobile enthusiast that he was, he gladly accepted Bishop's invitation to make the journey with him by motorcar, while Shriver and Fisher escorted the airplane to Italy by train. The Bishop party detoured by way of Frankfurt-am-Main to pause at an aeronautical exhibition there going on, thence followed up the Rhine and crossed into Switzerland. Dizzy Alpine roads frequently had Curtiss keeping one nervous hand on the door, ready to jump, but this was not the reason for his leaving the scenic jaunt at Lucerne and completing the trip by rail; time was short for him to get his plane in tune.

While en route, they heard that Eugène LeFébvre, who was also scheduled to compete at Brescia, had been killed while flying at Juvisy-sur-Orge. He was the second man in the world (next after Selfridge) to lose his life in an airplane crash. Lieutenant Mario Calderara, an Italian flyer whose acquaintance they were soon to make at Brescia, shrugged and said: "It simply proves that the Wright machine is dangerous. Out of six pilots who have learned to use it [i.e., in Europe], three have had accidents." Calderara, whose own plane was a Wright, was one of those three. (Wilbur had taught him to fly the previous spring and held him in some disapproval because he was "a cigarette fiend.")

The welcome awaiting Curtiss was in the bravura style, much warmer than it had been in France. For one thing, Italy had no favorite son to oppose him. At Brescia, whenever he showed, it was "Bravo! . . Viva! . . Curtiss!" Moreover, the attendance was nowhere near as exclusive. The myriads streaming into town came not only in glossy automobiles but in donkey carts and afoot. Those who could not afford grandstand seats shinnied up trees. Carabinièri raised clouds of dust galloping hither and yon to keep the peasants behind the sidelines. The crowds exceeded anticipation and caught the restaurants in short supply. People fought over food, and a contessa stood patiently at a restaurant door for a chicken wing.

Curtiss was much feted by officialdom, but found the flying field too rough for his liking. When, at 4:00 P.M. of opening day, he took his plane up and "executed a maneuver," the throng "went wild." Blériot appeared in spite of his mishap, but was no real threat, bereft of his finest machine and carrying a burned hand in a sling. Except for Calderara and a French airman, M. Rougier, Curtiss was practically the whole show. The paper back home boasted: "Mr. Curtiss was the only aviator to make brilliant flights, and is said to have saved the meeting from failure."

This plane of his was a demon for getting off the ground. He knocked off the quick-starting prize with ease, being airborne in 8⅓ seconds. He refrained from entering the passenger-carrying contest, and Calderara walked off with that.

In his entire career, Curtiss never was much given to altitude flying, but at Brescia he tried it for the first time in competition. A question lingers as to how serious he was about this. He climbed only to 80 meters, whereas M. Rougier went to 116 meters and took the money. Immediately afterward, Rougier ascribed his victory to Curtiss's sportsmanship, saying the American had secretly agreed ahead of time to let him have the altitude prize. "Curtiss is a true gentleman," he declared. "He might have gone higher than I, but he promised to leave me the first prize and he has kept his word. This is real American chivalry."

There just was no contest for the Grand Prix de Brescia, which was 50,000 lire for the best speed over a 50-kilometer course. After Curtiss covered the distance in 49 minutes, 23⅕ seconds, Rougier made a hopeless try.

It was at Brescia that Curtiss accepted his first passenger, and a celebrated one at that. Gabriele D'Annunzio, Italy's admired soldier-author, was in steady attendance upon the meet, taking notes for a novel with an aviation theme. Studiously examining the Curtiss plane, he pronounced it "admirable for its simplicity and the ingenuity of its form of construction . . . It is an aeroplane that I would call instinctive. It seems frail at first sight, but if you look at it closely you will see that all the parts are strong."

D'Annunzio had already flown once, in a Wright plane with Lieutenant Calderara, and desired a second experience. Curtiss promised to give him a ride on Sunday when all contests were over. A wooden slab was wired to the wing beside the pilot, and foot-rests were installed to accommodate the writer's short legs. After a brief spin aloft, D'Annunzio rhapsodized: "Until now I have never really lived! Life on earth is a creeping, crawling business. It is in the air that one feels the glory of being a man and of conquering the elements. There is the exquisite smoothness of motion and the joy of gliding through space—It is wonderful! Can I not express it in poetry? I might try." (Actually, he later put flying into poetry and a little of the vice versa. D'Annunzio was one of Italy's leading and most colorful pilots in World War I.)

A second request was not so easily granted. Princess Letitia of the Royal House of Savoy came around to congratulate Curtiss and asked: "Would you take me with you?" All he could answer was: "I should be delighted if my machine were fitted for carrying passengers." He pointed to the tiny, hard seat, and explained that it would hardly be suited to Her Royal Highness. The Princess confided to him that the King, Victor Emmanuel III, was convinced the Curtiss airplane was "the best and surest in the world."

The reward for Curtiss's flying at Brescia was more than at Rheims; it came to $7600. His total "take" for the European trip was $15,000. No aviator until then had won so much cash in so short a period. Bishop collected the prize money for both meets and later gave Curtiss a check, after taking his travel expense off the top.

Before sailing from Cherbourg on September 15, the triumphant aviator remarked that European flying men had been "not so hard to beat as I had apprehended." As a second observation, he said he was now satisfied that the biplane was superior to the monoplane, "and I think it will hold the supremacy for some time to come."

Finally he gave the reporters an announcement of real import: "Since coming to Europe I have made arrangements to fly in connection with the Hudson-Fulton Celebration." The contract, he informed them, called for a flight from Governors Island up river to the Soldiers' and Sailors' Monument on Riverside Drive and return. It was still unsigned.

13. Fumble at Governors Island

A bedlam of whistles, sirens, bells, and brass bands broke loose in New York Harbor that morning of September 21, 1909, swelling in crescendo until "all the noises in the world were merged into one ear-splitting shriek." The din was triggered when two ocean liners, by the wildest of chances, made the passage of the Narrows in close succession, after pacing each other across the Atlantic on roughly parallel courses. Each vessel bore a conquering hero returning to his homeland, strangers heretofore but soon to be acquaintances through being drawn into the vortex of a simultaneous mad welcoming by the metropolis. Both were quiet, unpretentious men, modest of deportment, who shrank from public display but could not now evade it.

The hero aboard the *Kaiser Wilhelm II*, out of Cherbourg, was Glenn H. Curtiss, anointed "world's champion aviator." A score of notables were on the ship's manifest, yet during the voyage the victor of Rheims was "the most talked about but the least talkative of them all." Leaning on the rail with Shriver and Fisher as the Statue of Liberty hove into view, he was abashed at the uproar. The three proudest battleships of the French fleet had just dropped anchor in the North River, a vanguard of the international naval flotilla gathering for the Hudson-Fulton Celebration, and there could be no mistaking the object of their salvos. Waiting at the gangplank were a delegation from the Aero Club and, more warming to his heart, a trio of greeters from Hammondsport—his wife, Lynn D. Masson, and Alexander Pfitzner.

The *Oscar II*, out of Copenhagen, brought as her suddenly famous passenger Dr. Frederick A. Cook, hailed as the first human being to reach the North Pole. He came fresh from bestowal of the gold medal of the Royal Danish Geographical Society, in the presence of the King of Denmark; and a seven-gun salute ordered by the King of Norway at the port of Christiansand. Now awaiting at quarantine were the embraces of his wife and two young daughters; after which they were taken aboard a chartered excursion steamer for a tour of the harbor and a landing in Brooklyn, where he once practiced medicine. Cook sat in the lead automobile of a triumphal parade through the streets, and was then whisked to a suite in the Waldorf-Astoria on Fifth Avenue at 34th Street. Said the New York *Herald* next morning: "He who first stood on the apex of the world, Dr. Frederick Albert Cook, was welcomed home yesterday amid a demonstration of popular confidence and enthusiasm without a parallel in the history of this city."

It was ironic that the two men who were, for the time being, the most celebrated individuals on Manhattan Island were both poised on the threshold of their lengthy personal ordeals. Curtiss was compelled to gird for battle against the accusation of being an unprincipled infringer of patents. Storm clouds looming up from the north made Dr. Cook out to be a liar and a fraud who had never set foot near the Pole. In the ensuing controversies, both would have their legions of fervid defenders and detractors.

The nascence of aviation vied for public attention with the race for the North Pole. Commander Robert E. Peary, in a series of Arctic thrusts, had espoused the attainment of the Pole as his lifetime goal, a virtual obsession. On an expedition to northern Greenland in 1891, he had taken along Dr. Cook (without recompense) as physician. Cook then made a careful study of the Eskimos, learned their language, won their friendship. In his report to the Philadelphia Academy of Natural Sciences, Peary acknowledged his obligation to Cook, speaking of him as "patient and skillful surgeon, indefatigable worker, earnest student of the peculiar people among whom we lived." Afterward going his separate way, Cook set up his practice in Brooklyn but could not shake off the spell of icy exploration. He turned to the Antarctic, later to Alaska and Mount McKinley. Then, invited to command a schooner for a wealthy big-game hunter in a voyage to Greenland, he was inspired to use that trip as the springboard for taking a crack at the Pole himself, while Peary was raising funds for his final, do-or-die assault.

On March 18, 1908, Cook struck forth over the ice pack from Axel Heiberg Land with dog sleds and four Eskimos, two of whom he sent back with a message after gaining a northward start. No further word came from Cook for more than a year, and he was believed lost. Then, on April 15, 1909, he and his Eskimos, emaciated and near starvation, with no dogs left, came stumbling across the ice back to Annoatok, Greenland, where he had left a cache of food. Greeted and revived by Harry Whitney, a sportsman from New Haven, Connecticut, he learned with dismay that his supplies, along with a store of valuable furs, had been confiscated by Peary and left under guard, while Peary started his own polar dash. Cook now confided in Whitney that he had reached the North Pole on April 21, 1908, and he was seemingly corroborated by his Eskimos.[1]

With a fresh team of dogs and an Eskimo companion, Cook mushed down the Greenland coast until he was able to board a Danish government vessel bound for Copenhagen. During the voyage, he was advised by the inspector of North Greenland to send word of his polar discovery ahead, rather than waiting until arrival in Denmark for the announcement. Accordingly, the ship made an unscheduled stop at Lerwick in the Shetland Islands, which had a cable station. This was on September 1, while Curtiss was being feted in France and heavily publicized by the two *Heralds* of James Gordon Bennett.

Lacking money for his passage home, Cook thought of selling his story to a newspaper. He was aware of the New York *Herald's* long reputation for news of explorations in far places; he may have heard that the New York *Times* was a partial sponsor of Peary's current expedition by purchasing advance rights to his story. The *Times* was striving to undercut the *Herald's* supremacy. In any case, Cook sensed the *Herald* as the best market for his own exclusive and cabled its New York office from Lerwick, offering his initial announcement for $3000. Although Bennett already had one hero on his hands, he was not averse to a second. A chance to offset the *Times'* Peary scoop, whatever that might turn out to be, had dropped providentially in his lap, and Bennett snapped it up. Not only did he gladly pay the $3000, but he signed Cook up for a series of bylined articles, plus exclusive rights to his photographs, for $50,000.

From a wireless station at Indian Harbor, Labrador, on September 6, flashed a message from Peary: STARS AND STRIPES NAILED TO THE POLE. Four days later, Peary cabled the editor of the *Herald:* DO NOT IMAGINE HERALD LIKELY TO BE IMPOSED UPON BY COOK STORY, BUT FOR YOUR INFORMATION COOK HAS SIMPLY HANDED THE PUBLIC A GOLD BRICK. For ensuing weeks, the Cook-Peary debate was mainly a headline battle between two newspapers—and Glenn Curtiss, aviator, was caught in the crossfire. The *Herald,* with its duality of demigods to celebrate, awarded the priority to Cook, splashing daily banners across its front page. Persons who knew the nature of Curtiss would guess that he was as well satisfied with the lesser prominence.

❀   ❀   ❀

The New York State Legislature, at the outset of its 1909 session, created a Hudson-Fulton Commission to prepare a mammoth commemoration of two great episodes in the history of the Hudson River. This was the tercentenary year of Captain Henry Hudson's upstream cruise to the future site of Albany. Although Robert Fulton's retracing of the route by steamboat had occurred in 1807, a delayed centennial of that event was combined into the Hudson-Fulton Celebration, scheduled for late September and early October, the season of Hudson's downriver return and departure. Because of "the extraordinary advance in the science of aerial locomotion," the Commission appointed an Aeronautics Committee "to consider the feasibility of, and, if practicable, arrange for an exhibition of flying machines."

Taking its cue from this proposal, the New York *World,* a paper also alert for promotional gimmicks, announced in February a prize of $10,000 for a flight from New York to Albany during the Hudson-Fulton pageantry. No such princely sum had yet been offered in the United States for an aerial exploit. While the idea may have been incubated in the editorial rooms of the *World,* its sanction surely came from the crusading publisher, Joseph Pulitzer, placing him in a category with Bennett and Lord Northcliffe as a benefactor of fledgling aviation. By that time, the aging Pulitzer, broken in health and totally blind, lived almost continually on his palatial yacht, cruising European waters, at-

tended by a staff of male secretaries who kept him abreast of world
affairs by reading to him. The prize could be won either by an airplane
or a dirigible balloon. Since an airship seemed likeliest to cover the
distance, the Commission fancied having a dirigible soar above the
grand procession of ships which was to climax the festivities by steaming
up the river.

The Aeronautics Committee first tried for a zeppelin, but Count
Ferdinand von Zeppelin responded from Germany that it would not
be practical to send one. The next unfeasible thought was the Signal
Corps dirigible. When the *World* prize was announced, Captain Baldwin
hurried to Hammondsport to begin construction of a different, faster
type of *Arrow* for entry in the contest; he said it would be powered
by a special Curtiss engine designed to run one hundred consecutive
hours.

James M. Beck, chairman of the committee, went abroad in an
effort to corral European aviators for an International Aviation Meet,
interviewing Farman, Blériot, Delagrange, Latham, and Count de
Lambert. They demanded "enormous sums," prohibitive for his budget,
pointing out that aviation meets were springing up all over Europe that
year and large prizes were being offered. Beck came home and opened
negotiations with Curtiss and Wilbur Wright for a few demonstrations
at New York City. It was surprising that Wilbur gave in so quickly, after
the Wrights had said so much against "mountebank" flying; possibly he
decided the time had come to show Curtiss up. Then, too, he drove a
hard bargain with the Commission: $15,000 if, between September 25
and October 9, he should make a flight exceeding 10 miles in length or
of one hour's duration.

This was triple the amount allotted for Curtiss: $5000 for a flight
from Governors Island up the river to a buoy marker near Grant's
Tomb and return (a total distance of about 20 miles); or, if he failed
that, for a number of flights from near Grant's Tomb across the river
to the Palisades and back. Almost the first thing Curtiss did on disembarking from France was to affix his final signature to the Hudson-Fulton
contract, which had been modified, at his insistence, to a duration
between September 25 and October 2; the original time span had
been the same as Wright's, through October 9. Curtiss had agreed, while
in Italy, to a St. Louis engagement starting the 6th and he must allow
time for packing and shipping his plane. Hence, Wright's contract ran
a week longer than his.

A key member of the Hudson-Fulton Commission was Major General Leonard Wood, commanding officer of the Army's Department of the East, and through his influence Governors Island was designated as the base for these exhibitions and the starting point for a New York-to-Albany flight should that be undertaken. Governors Island, then headquarters of the U. S. First Army, sits in the harbor a scant half-mile off Battery Park, the south tip of Manhattan. At that time it was being enlarged with silt and muck dredged from the channel, and a sandy plain of 96 acres so far had been added; this was the area made available for the flights, whereon two "aeroplane sheds" were erected.

Governors Island solved the problem of a New York terminal, but a landing place would also be required at Albany for any attack on the *World* prize. The contest committee of the Aero Club, accompanied by Baldwin, rode a riverboat up to study the course and locate such a spot. In a day's scouting at Albany, they settled upon Van Rensselaer Island, a patch of floodplain on the southerly margin of the city, separated from the mainland only by a narrow creek.[2]

Wilbur Wright appeared in New York while Curtiss was still at sea, and began setting up his machine and catapult derrick on the island. When a reporter asked if the patent action was perhaps only a friendly suit to establish priority of claims, he answered: "It is as friendly as any lawsuit may be, but it is of course for the purpose of preventing Mr. Curtiss from manufacturing machines which harm our patented features . . . Our principal claim rests on the control of the machine, and as that is the fundamental factor of all aeroplanes we are, of course, bound to defend it."

After the futile attempt to snare foreign airmen, the Hudson-Fulton Commission had ended by scoring a master stroke in bringing Curtiss and Wright together on the same program. The two types of airplane which were the symbols in a brewing legalistic fight were to be pitted in aerial combat, so to speak. Although no overt competition was suggested, rivalry was implicit in the situation. One New York paper observed that the aviators were coming not merely for money, or to make commonplace flights, but that: "It is a matter of pride and supremacy with each of them." As things eventuated, this was the only occasion when Curtiss and either of the Wright brothers ever flew in a simultaneous engagement from the same field. It would also mark Wilbur's public debut as a pilot in his own country.

Over and above these exciting factors, the papers were whetting

the popular appetite for the duel of Governors Island with a diversity
of speculations. It was a fact that both aviators were committed by
their contracts to flying over the busiest harbor in the world, which
would be abnormally cluttered by the array of warships. These would
be the first overwater flights in America. But the metropolitan public
was led to anticipate flights above the skyscrapers as well, the obvious
dangers of which lent an added dash of spice. The *Herald* advised
people to "keep an eye on the Statue of Liberty," and predicted that
Curtiss and Wright "will be chasing each other up the rivers and over
the housetops." Subway strap-hangers read that the machines "will
look like huge gulls and will dip and oscillate in their flight very much
like soaring birds."

*　　*　　*

The fact was that Curtiss had grave misgivings about measuring up
to Wright's performance. He was placed at a disadvantage from the
start through being deprived of the plane with which he won the
trophy in France, and which the Hudson-Fulton Commission fully expected him to use. Without consulting his partner, Herring had pre-
sumptuously contracted for its display in department stores for two
months to come. Upon his return, Curtiss told him mildly that it was
"a little inconvenient that the Rheims machine was tied up." The
contracts meant that he would have to rely upon the new plane, as yet
untested, with a 4-cylinder engine. He could discern no good reason
why the 8-cylinder motor might not be borrowed out of the Rheims
racer and a dummy engine substituted while it was merely standing
around in floor exhibits. Such a thing was absolutely out of the question,
retorted Herring, since the contracts called for it to be intact, exactly
as it flew in France.

The individual who had thrown the monkey wrench unwittingly
in the first place was Rodman Wanamaker; and the chances are that,
considering his genuine interest in encouraging aviation, he would have
consented to an engine substitution had he known of the handicap
under which Curtiss was being forced to operate. Rodman was the son
of John Wanamaker, founder of the mercantile empire which embraced
department stores in New York and Philadelphia. As European manager
of the company, he spent much of his time abroad, and it was he who
pioneered the policy of introducing Parisian fashions to New York.
After Blériot flew the Channel, he purchased a twin of the prize-

winning monoplane and shipped it for display in the family emporiums. It had proved a strong customer attraction.

The moment Curtiss won at Rheims, an agent of the Wanamaker firm called on Herring with an offer of $5000 for exhibit of the plane in both the New York and Philadelphia stores, two weeks in each. Herring signed on the dotted line as an officer of the Herring-Curtiss Company, technically the owner of the machine. Next came Edward Filene from Boston, also a department store executive, representing a committee styled "Boston, 1915," whose aim was to drum up an international exposition for that city in 1915. Filene paid $4000 for a four-week exhibit of the plane immediately following its Wanamaker display, with an option to purchase it for an additional $4000 (the option was not exercised). The St. Louis Centennial committee was willing to pay up to $15,000 for a few days' exhibit plus one day of Curtiss flying—provided it could have the original Rheims racer, which Wanamaker had sewed up.

Regardless of how Herring had tied his hands for the Hudson-Fulton show, the commercial prospects of flying now descended upon Curtiss with a rush. A flock of agents with more offers were waiting to pounce in New York, and he received them, one after another, at his suite in the Hotel Astor. Some of the propositions were accepted "because I could not afford to reject them," as he explained. "It required a great deal of money to run the shop, and there was no commercial demand for aeroplanes. They were, as yet, valuable only as 'show machines.'" An unspoken reason was the need he foresaw to build up a financial backlog with which to combat the Wright litigation.

Next day was hectic, beginning with an official City Hall accolade by Mayor George B. McClellan, Jr., son of the famous Civil War general of the Army of the Potomac. After that, he huddled with a delegation from Washington and Baltimore soliciting his support to obtain the 1910 running of the Gordon Bennett Trophy contest for their vicinity. Everyone took it for granted that Curtiss would then be defending the trophy against foreign challengers.

A luncheon and reception by the Aero Club of America ensued at the Lawyers Club, where he was seated alongside Judge Elbert H. Gary and Guglielmo Marconi, the inventor of wireless. Bishop, the president, was not yet back from Europe, but had cabled the club to raise a fund for a gold medal. An introductory speaker said: "Yesterday we welcomed home the American who discovered the North Pole. Today we welcome home the American who won the greatest victory in the history of aerial effort." When the medal was presented, Curtiss, looking stiff and choked in a high white collar, responded: "Gentlemen, I managed to get the cup and win the race in France without any serious blunders, and with your kind indulgence I will leave it to others to interest you, so far as the talking goes." The audience came to its feet as one man and cheered.

Although he was invited, Wilbur Wright was conspicuously absent from this affair sponsored by a club of which he was an honorary member. In his note of refusal, he said that, while "heartily appreciating" the achievements of Curtiss abroad, he could not spare the time from getting his plane ready for the Hudson-Fulton flights. As a matter of fact, Wright pointedly declined invitations to any function at which Curtiss was to appear.

As soon as he could make his escape from the Aero Club reception, Curtiss and his wife ferried to Governors Island to look over the grounds and inspect the shed which was to shelter his airplane. Wright's shed stood nearby, and Curtiss strolled across for a friendly greeting. Wilbur looked up, his hands greasy from working on his engine, and said: "How do you do, Mr. Curtiss? You will excuse me from shaking hands, for you see what they are like."

Curtiss passed it off and Wright inquired: "How are you feeling since your return?"

"Very good."

"Really, you ought to," Wilbur said, in his nearest approach to a compliment; then he asked if Curtiss had made use of "the suggestions" he had given him before his departure for France (possibly they had talked at the Aero Club).

"Some of them," was the rejoinder.

"Yes, you must have followed some of my advice."

This dialogue obviously was not going anywhere, and, after a few remarks about the arrangements at Governors Island, the Curtisses returned to the Astor. The following morning they caught a train for Hammondsport and the welcome-home reception which had originally been planned as a surprise but could not be kept secret.

❂   ❂   ❂

At no time since Lazarus Hammond staked out the location had the village witnessed such a jubilation as now unfolded. More than one

poetaster was impelled into verse. The opening stanza of a so-called
poem which found its way into print ran as follows:

> Ho! for Glenn H. Curtiss,
> A boy that you knew,
> He was born in Steuben;
> It was here that he grew.
> His beginning, though humble,
> Has grown with the years,
> And he stands up today
> With America's peers.
> We admire his pluck,
> And are glad of his luck,
> And we give him due honor today.

The town was bedecked with flags, banners, bunting, colored lights,
transparencies, and signs. An immense stock of fireworks was laid in.
Employees of the Herring-Curtiss works took pride in decorating the
factory grounds. Suspended above an open space between shop buildings was a dummy model of the Rheims plane. Beyond that a speaker's
platform was erected, backed by a large electric sign outlined in red,
white, and blue lights: GHC–WELCOME HOME.

The county seat was hardly less enthusiastic, and, because of the
change of trains there, Bath had the first chance to pay homage.
A special train ran from Hammondsport on the B.&H. short-line,
carrying a citizens' committee, two coaches jammed with Herring-Curtiss
workers, and the Hammondsport Band. Bath mustered its Soldiers'
Home Band and a large percentage of its populace for a vociferous
greeting at the station where Curtiss stepped down from the Lackawanna train at 5:30 P.M. Unhappily, a steady drizzle of rain had set in
at 5 o'clock, and it persisted throughout the evening. An impromptu
reception at the Steuben Club was followed by a small dinner party
at a Bath hotel for the hero and his welcoming committee. It is worthy
of mention that two of the diners were James H. Smellie, the pharma-
cist, and Lew H. Brown, the newspaper editor.

The special train made its 9-mile run through rainy darkness, its
whistle shrilling and bell clanging all the way. The track was illumined
by the red flare of railroad fusees. As the locomotive chuffed past
the tiny depot of Rheims, the sky ahead burst forth with rockets and
bombs. Hand fireworks were freely distributed among people in the
streets. Mayor George Keeler thrust a bundle of Roman candles into

the arms of a boy named Alderman Gleason with the instruction: "Keep them a-popping, only be careful where you shoot."

The main trouble was in keeping the fireworks dry enough to detonate. A huge cask of beer was on tap under cover of the bandstand in the Park Square, its contents free to all who turned the spigot. A circuitous parade route was curtailed to one street because of the weather.

That night, hardly anyone stayed home in Hammondsport, rain and mud notwithstanding. As the train pulled in at the lakefront station, it was engulfed by a milling, cheering multitude. Curtiss was shepherded with difficulty into an open horse carriage which was then hauled up Sheather Street not by horses but by a score of his own employees. The village band led the parade between crowded sidewalks amid a bombardment of Roman candles. The featured float bore thirty of the town's prettiest girls, all gowned in sheer white, getting wet. The destination was the factory on the hill, where Curtiss mounted the platform to accept the plaudits of his fellow townsmen.

The address of fulsome praise and welcome was delivered by Judge Monroe Wheeler, who ended by presenting the gold medal paid for by public subscription. Curtiss was little more voluble on home ground than elsewhere, and his response was simple: "Although I spent a number of years as a student of the Hammondsport school, I never learned words which are adequate to express my appreciation of the reception I have been accorded tonight, or to express my thanks for this medal which has just been presented to me. The last four weeks have been very eventful. I have met with considerable success and have met many notable people, but on no occasion have I experienced the happiness that I do tonight as I look upon this assemblage."

During the interval at home, Glenn made a present to his Lena of the $5000 prize money which came with the Bennett Trophy, and she used a portion of it for the purchase of an electric automobile. A tale survived among the villagers that he also presented $500 to an elderly widow who had once paid $65 express charges for him on a shipment of bicycle parts, when he was broke. (Quite likely, this was Malinda Bennitt.)

*   *   *

During this interlude, the milieu of New York Harbor and the North River had undergone spectacular embellishment. The French

battleships had been followed into the estuary by twenty U.S. dread-
noughts, a squadron of the Royal British Navy, and two Italian
cruisers. Still more naval vessels rendezvoused from Germany, the
Netherlands, Mexico, and Argentina, until the "war fleet" drawn up in
seriate rank with the Palisades cliff for a backdrop extended for 10 miles,
as far up as Spuyten Duyvil. Counting tenders, colliers, and river
craft, the harbor was clogged with no less than 1595 vessels. A special
curiosity attached to two of these: faithful restorations of Henry Hudson's *Half Moon* and Robert Fulton's *Clermont* (a misnomer through
history-book error, its authentic name having been the *North River*).
The crews of all these assorted vessels were as anticipatory as Manhattan's millions of the flying phenomena to come. The Army Signal
Corps arranged a code of flag signals between the island and the
tower of the Singer Building to apprise the public when a flight might
be expected; while Marconi messages were to be flashed to such
men-of-war as carried wireless equipment, they in turn to hoist flag
signals for the others.

The flights were announced to begin on Monday, September 27,
but rain kept Wright on the ground, while Curtiss had yet to put in his
appearance—a tardiness which annoyed the Commission, even though
the weather was unflyable. His plane preceded him and was ready
when he showed up Tuesday morning, but then a brisk wind precluded
any attempts. In reply to reporters' queries, he denied any intention
of tackling the New York-to-Albany prize with the machine then at his
command; and declared emphatically that he was not going to fly above
Manhattan skyscrapers, "not even if the city would deed to him all
the property he passed over." Such a stunt would be "foolhardy at this
stage of aviation." He explained that the new machine was "the
smallest biplane ever built," weighing only 400 pounds, and that its
fuel capacity was limited to four gallons.

Both pilots were forearmed against the danger of coming down in
water. Curtiss had a "boat-shaped device" beneath the center of his craft
and, on the underside of each wing tip, a small metal cylinder filled
with compressed air. Wright had waited until he was in New York to
purchase a canoe for his flotation gear, covering its top with canvas.
They were equally worried about how these devices might behave in
flight.

For once, the monorail takeoff system and landing skids gave Wilbur a distinct advantage. Curtiss discovered that he was under an

additional handicap: the recently dredged soil on Governors Island was rather infirm and his wheels bogged down in the sand.

With his penchant for early-bird flying, Curtiss found sleeping quarters on the island, determined not to miss any opportunty for a flight in the short time at his disposal. (Wright slept at a hotel in the city.) Then, the wind giving no hope of abatement, he crossed to the mainland and rode uptown for a call on Captain Baldwin at the balloon grounds, which were at Riverside Drive and 120th Street. There were two dirigible entrants for the *World's* $10,000 prize: Baldwin and George L. Tomlinson of Johnstown, New York. They were good friends, and Baldwin had sold Tomlinson his airship, almost a duplicate of his own. The dirigibles were tethered on Morningside Heights behind a board fence on which were painted the words: *HUDSON-FULTON FLIGHTS*. Watching the gasbags sway in the wind, Curtiss was reminded of "the ceaseless weaving of a restless elephant." These contestants, too, were waiting for calmer atmosphere.

While in town, Curtiss stopped in at the Wanamaker store to see for himself how the exhibit of his Rheims racer was making out. Inasmuch as he could not have that machine at Governors Island, he was at least gratified to observe that it was a magnetic draw. Thousands of New Yorkers inspected it in a steady stream. He had read with mixed feelings the conspicuous advertisement appearing in the morning papers:

HAVE YOU EVER SEEN
A FLYING MACHINE?

It's here—the very machine that won the Championship.

Today, if conditions are right, those wizards of the air will probably be sailing over New York.

If you would like to see what the machine that rides the air like a bird looks like—come to Wanamaker's today.

And when you gaze on this curious device your pulses will thrill a bit—for you will know that it is the identical machine on which that daring American, Glenn H. Curtiss, won the championship.

o   *   o

Wednesday the 29th dawned as the first decent flying day of the week, and Curtiss was up and astir at 6 o'clock to take advantage of it.

The fact that the hour was "unearthly early" for spectatorship did not disturb him. This, after all, would be his first test flight of the plane, and he did not expect to do much. It was witnessed only by a personal friend and an Army officer. After a slow-motion takeoff in yielding sand, he covered a mere 300 yards and sat down. Perhaps the spare four-bladed propeller would get him airborne faster than the two-bladed one he had on. Leaving orders with his men to switch the props, he started for the Battery to get breakfast. Wright was coming off the ferry and offhandedly asked, "Well, how is it going?"

"Very good, only I made a pretty bad landing."

Wilbur paused to scan the sky and observed: "Looks pretty good. I think I will take a little spin in a few minutes."

Curtiss changed his mind about breakfast and walked back with him. Swinging his catapult monorail around so it would head into the breeze, Wilbur took off with ease and executed a circuit of the island while two passing ferryboats reversed their screws to give their passengers a treat. As he came down, Curtiss hurried over to congratulate him. A squad of Fort Jay soldiers helped hoist his plane back on the rail, and Wright, buttoning his coat around him, was again airborne within an hour. This time he headed purposefully over the water. The steamship *Lusitania* was outward bound and her passengers, mobbing the rails, were all but hysterical at seeing him making for Bedloe's Island, home of the Statue of Liberty. He circled that famous lady at the level of her knees and returned, completing 2½ miles over water. He did not fly again that day.

At about the same hour, the two dirigibles prepared to light out. Tomlinson was off first in his *Galatin* and was almost out of sight before Baldwin, shouting "Albany or bust!," dropped his moorings. Rising over Grant's Tomb, Captain Tom headed straight upstream at mid-channel, pegging along at a 20-mile clip. Off Washington Heights the *Arrow* was buffeted by a gust, straining guy ropes so that a part of the light framework snapped; a piece of broken wood jammed the steering gear. Baldwin descended carefully on the water. Cutters sped from battleships and tossed draglines by which he was towed ashore. Meanwhile Tomlinson had drifted inland as far as White Plains where, with bad leaks of both oil and gasoline and fearing fire, he came down on a farm. Neither balloonist tried again, and the New York *World* announced shortly that the prize offer for a flight to Albany was being extended for one year. Baldwin must get his dirigible packed for shipment to St. Louis, where he had to meet the same exhibition date as Curtiss.

Wind recurred with such persistence that both pilots were held earthbound on Governors Island for the balance of the week, while impatient New Yorkers watched and listened for signals in vain. They sat in great numbers along Riverside Drive awaiting the advertised flight to Grant's Tomb, and pestered policemen with inquiries. One cop complained: "You'd think *I* was keeping 'em back, the way these people go at me. They blame me and not the wind."

Governors Island, as a military preserve, was not thrown open to the public, but some persons with influential connections, such as newsmen, held passes during this unusual episode. Early comers were two New York attorneys: Emerson R. Newell, retained by Curtiss and the Herring-Curtiss Company as defense counsel in the infringement suit; and Thomas A. Hill, representing the Aeronautic Society in the like capacity. Their purpose was a thorough examination of the Curtiss airplane in preparation of the defense arguments. While the elements were preventing further flying activity during four solid days, the U. S. Circuit Court Judge at Buffalo, John R. Hazel, issued a show-cause order as to why a preliminary injunction should not be issued against the defendants. This order was to be argued on October 14.

Perhaps the keenest of the reporters, by virtue of his familiarity with aviation and his prior acquaintance with both Curtiss and the Wright brothers, was the able, youthful Associated Press man, Jerome S. Fanciulli, just twenty-one years of age. As advertising manager for the Jamestown Exposition of 1907, Fanciulli had his first taste of aeronautics with the dirigible ascensions of Beachey and Knabenshue, who were then working for Baldwin. From there he landed a job with the Washington *Post* where he hobnobbed with an older reporter who had covered the hapless trials of the Langley aerodrome and was utterly convinced that it could have flown; this man's eloquent defense of Langley aroused Fanciulli's interest to the extent that he boned up on the subject and was therefore handed the paper's aeronautical assignments. He covered the trials of the Army Signal Corps contract dirigible and airplanes at Fort Myer, thus getting on friendly terms with the Wright brothers and Curtiss. From the *Post* he hopped to the Washington bureau of the AP as its aeronautical specialist and was assigned to Governors Island for the Hudson-Fulton flights, where he had ready access to both airplane sheds. Beyond realizing that Curtiss was "rather naïve and badly needed someone to manage his affairs, especially his public relations," Fanciulli as yet had no thought of an alliance with him. He was fresh in the AP job and eager to advance in it.

Before the week was out, a thing happened to alter the direction of Jerome Fanciulli's life. As he told it, Tom Baldwin put the bee in Curtiss's bonnet. In several discussions on the island, at the Astor Hotel, and at the Aero Club, Curtiss tried to persuade Fanciulli to come to work for him as his personal manager and also to organize the exhibition business for him. He said, in substance, that "there was a tremendous demand from all over the country for exhibition flights and he was anxious to get started . . . He didn't think there was going to be much sale of aeroplanes." Fanciulli's immediate reaction was negative because of the Herring entanglement. In his coverage of the occurrences at Fort Myer, he had seen Herring's "technical delivery" of an airplane in suitcases and observed how he wriggled out of the government contract. He sized Herring up as "a fourflusher and a faker," and bluntly informed Curtiss that he did not wish to be connected with a business in which Herring had any part. As he afterward avowed, he also told Curtiss: "I thought it had been a great mistake for him to have become associated with Mr. Herring; that Mr. Herring had attained a very bad reputation for himself by the manner in which he had taken a contract with the government, and the manner in which he had failed to carry out the provisions of that contract; that I thought Mr. Curtiss would suffer as the result of being associated with Mr. Herring."

Curtiss confessed that he was "greatly disappointed" in his tie-up with Herring; saying that Herring had claimed to possess certain patents and an airplane that had actually flown, "but up to that time he hadn't seen any evidences." He fully realized the "reflection that there might be on him through the manner in which Mr. Herring had handled his business with the government." He confided in the AP reporter that his failure so far to make a satisfactory flight at Governors Island was due to Herring's action in renting out his only 8-cylinder machine for store display. To convince Fanciulli, he assured him "that he thought undoubtedly something could be done whereby he could break away from that connection."

On the promise that he would be working for Curtiss individually, and not for the Herring-Curtiss Company, Fanciulli accepted, went to Hammondsport and "wrote my own contract" with the aid of Monroe Wheeler.

Another promising young man, not a journalist but an engineer, gained access to the island. He was Grover C. Loening, the Columbia student who had haunted the Hempstead Plains the previous summer in his eagerness to see Curtiss flying the *Gold Bug*. Now Loening seems to have gravitated toward the Wright side of the field; at least he made enough impression on Wilbur so that, in a relatively short time, he was on the payroll of the Wright company. In a book of recollections published after he had himself been successful as an aircraft manufacturer, Loening remembered the scene at Governors Island. He said that Wright "openly despised Curtiss, was convinced he was not only faking but doing so with a cheap scheme to hurt the Wrights; and here on this very occasion was the first appearance of that vicious hatred and rivalry between the Wright and the Curtiss camps which was destined to play an important and sometimes tragic role throughout the succeeding five years of aviation development."

Loening wrote that he himself did not believe Curtiss flew at all at Governors Island.

*   *   *

The term of Curtiss's contract was due to expire Saturday night and he had yet to perform a flight which the public could see. He felt crestfallen, as well he might, in the sharp contrast with Wright's Statue of Liberty exploit; in all truth, he had delivered nothing except his presence for the money the Commission was contracted to pay him. When Saturday wasted away without a let-up in the wind, he resolved to stay over Sunday and gamble for a break. Whatever the weather, he was aware that Wright, bound by his religious scruples, would not fly on the Sabbath. Curtiss had a maxim: "Sunday is my lucky day." This was one time when it did not hold.

Again spending the night on the island, he was abroad at daybreak and found the wind still blowing diligently. As it refused to diminish during the forenoon, he took the ferry and whiled away time in the city. Back at the island, he paced about nervously, watching flags on poles and smoke columns from the stacks of boats. At last, in late afternoon, the wind began to subside. People would say, as usual, that he was too timid about wind. In near desperation, at 5:30 when dusk was closing in, he had the plane wheeled out, made a takeoff, climbed to 50 feet, and traversed about a half-mile. The engine coughed and he landed. "It was no fault of the motor," he explained. "I shut it off and descended purposely because I did not like the way the air was boiling." As the Commission reported the flight: ". . . toward sunset, in a fitful wind, he made another and more successful attempt to fly. [He had reached the edge of the island] apparently headed for the Statue of Liberty, when the aeroplane swerved and careened as if it were about to fall. A moment later the aviator, evidently averse to traveling over the water, turned his vertical plane, and sailed around in a graceful semicircle over the Island . . . This was not an official flight and the representatives of the Commission were not present to observe it."[3]

In the gathering twilight, few persons witnessed this flight from Manhattan or the maritime fleet. Ruefully, he informed newsmen: "It is a far greater disappointment to me than to the people, not to have been able to make such flights here last week as I was expected to give . . . Now I feel that I cannot break contracts that I have in St. Louis and elsewhere to remain here longer. I sacrificed many good opportunities on the other side to hurry back to this country in order that I might fly here, and when I made an agreement to do my best between September 27 and October 2, I thought surely there would be good weather during that period." Some friends urged him to stay longer, arguing that a good flight at New York would be more to his advantage than anything he might do at St. Louis; but he insisted that the most important thing was to honor a commitment.

It was perhaps as well that time denied him another day, as he could hardly have matched Wilbur Wright's sensational performance of Monday morning, hence would have suffered still further by comparison. Curtiss was on a train bound for Hammondsport and his airplane was in its boxes being carted to the ferry when Wilbur brilliantly salvaged the drooping Hudson-Fulton aerial program. With a life preserver at his feet, two American flags fluttering from his front elevator and another from the canoe, he flew up the river at an altitude of 200 feet, amid a loud hullabaloo from ships and shore. He went 1000 feet past Grant's Tomb before turning about and retracing the route. While the total distance flown over water was equivalent to that covered by Blériot in crossing the Channel, Wright's feat was the more difficult and perilous because of the crowded surface and thermal drafts. He fully intended a second flight in the afternoon which would have far eclipsed the first: up the East River, beneath the Brooklyn Bridge, following the Harlem River in its curve to join the Hudson at Spuyten Duyvil, thence across the Palisades and returning with a swing over Newark. While his engine was warming for this ambitious itinerary, a cylinder head blew off and Wright did no further flying there.

Learning on his arrival at Hammondsport what Wright had achieved, Curtiss lauded it as "a really magnificent flight." Then he mailed a note to Herring which reflects a caustic undertone: "I am sorry I didn't get any good flights in New York. I might have better stayed away entirely, but it can't be helped now." His remorse was little short of traumatic, and was not to be quickly dismissed from his mind.

Nor did his wretched showing at Governors Island sit well with the Hudson-Fulton Commission. Its report to the Legislature summed up the aviation activities: "The flights by Mr. Wright were very gratifying and met the most sanguine expectations of the Commission." But: "The Commission's experience with Mr. Curtiss was less satisfactory." Without a murmur, Wright was paid the full $15,000 of his contract. Curtiss offered to accept $3500, to compensate him for time and expenses, but the Commission balked at that. Only after he belatedly filed suit to collect was a compromise settlement reached in the amount of $2500.

After just a few hours in Hammondsport, Curtiss set off to fulfill his date at St. Louis, for which he held a guarantee of $6000. This time Lena went with him, as she did thenceforth on nearly all his flying tours. Going from there to Chicago for the next engagement, he consulted with Octave Chanute on the patent litigation. Curtiss later wrote to Alexander Graham Bell: "I spent two evenings in Chicago with Dr. Chanute, and from what he says the Wrights have little prospect of winning."

Chanute dated a letter October 14 to Emerson R. Newell, the Curtiss defense lawyer: "I have your letter of the 8th, and saw Mr. G. H. Curtiss last night relative thereto. I understand from you that you want to find 'some prior art which will show that the warping of the planes themselves was old.' The bare idea of warping and twisting the wings is old, but there are several ways of accomplishing it . . . I do not remember any balancing devices such as Mr. Curtiss used. I dare say, however, that they are quite old."

A few days after his talks with Curtiss, Chanute was writing to Ernest L. Jones, editor of *Aeronautics:* "I learn from good sources that Herring is about played out."

14. Westering Wings

St. Louis was celebrating its centennial as a city, and had succeeded in hooking the "world's champion aviator," yanking him away from the eastern seaboard. Forest Park was the stage for the St. Louis air meet, in which a French pilot, Georges François Osmont, also appeared with a Farman biplane. Three dirigible balloons soared about, directed by Tom Baldwin, Lincoln Beachey, and Roy Knabenshue. Baldwin's *Arrow* proved none the worse for its watery adventure on the Hudson.

When Curtiss took to the air on October 9 for a preliminary two-minute canter around the field, he threw an immense crowd into a frenzy of delight. This was said to be the first time an aeroplane was ever seen more than a few feet off the ground west of the Mississippi. It was also Curtiss's first genuine test of the Hudson-Fulton machine. A woman spectator was injured when her horses, panicked by the apparition in the air, reared and upset the carriage in which she sat. Curtiss enacted a series of good flights, so that the St. Louis committee was amply satisfied.

The prospect was less encouraging at Chicago. Evidently Curtiss had intimations of a financial impasse there before he started west,

as the Hammondsport *Herald* chronicled: ". . . if certain parties in
Chicago put up the necessary money, he will fly in Chicago the week
beginning October 13th, for which he will receive $10,000 and an
additional $10,000 if he flies across Lake Michigan." Thomas W. Ryley,
the theatrical manager who had flaunted a cablegram from Curtiss in
Italy accepting his offer for five flights, had been overly optimistic.
With no sponsor, the week was wide open, the field available, and
Curtiss and Baldwin resolved to take a gamble on running a show for
themselves. "We lost money there," Curtiss confessed. The reason for
the failure was Chicago's decision to live up to its name as the Windy
City. An autumnal blow permitted little flying all week. On only one
day, according to a message reaching Hammondsport, did Curtiss make
"a risky flight full of dips and tilts that startled the crowd."

Chicago was not a total loss, in spite of all. On the plus side of the
ledger were his opportunity to confer with Chanute and the fact that
he latched onto his first exhibition pilot at a moment when he needed
an understudy. More accurately, the embryo pilot latched onto him.

Since riding Israel Ludlow's bucking kites towed behind automobiles, Charles K. Hamilton had risen to being a dirigible jockey and
parachute jumper. Hamilton, a pint-sized, wiry redhead who habitually
behaved as if his mainspring were wound too tight, was ballooning
about Japan when he read of what transpired at Rheims. On the instant,
he decided that was the kind of aeronautics for him. Cutting short his
Oriental tour, he took off in pursuit of Glenn Curtiss, finally catching
up with him in Chicago. One could no more ignore Charley Hamilton
than a hornet in an automobile. He begged and badgered Curtiss to
teach him to fly. At length, having nothing better to do while the wind
kept blowing, Curtiss allowed him to sit at the controls and gave him a
little basic ground instruction. After sizing him up for a day or so,
the maestro asked how much he weighed. One hundred pounds, said
he. "That is a great advantage in flying these small-powered machines,"
Curtiss allowed, with a hint that if he cared to drop in at Hammondsport some day he might be vouchsafed a bit of practice. Hamilton made
a blue streak for Keuka Lake and was there ahead of his preceptor.
Willy-nilly, Curtiss had himself a pupil.

Finishing out the unprofitable week in Chicago, Glenn and Lena
interrupted the homeward journey with a stopover in Detroit, accepting an invitation from R. D. Chapin, general manager of the Chalmers-
Detroit Company. The men had made contact at Rheims and Chapin
was a passenger on the same ship coming back. Entertained by their

host at the Detroit Country Club and the University Club, the couple
boarded a lake steamer for the overnight cruise to Cleveland. They
brought with them a Chalmers-Detroit automobile, fresh from the factory, dustily driving it on from Cleveland to Hammondsport.

*   *   *

Back at Hammondsport business matters of the utmost concern
were clamoring to be dealt with. Topping the pile, naturally, was the
question of what to do about the Wright litigation. Curtiss plunged
into immediate talks with other company officials on this topic. Monroe
Wheeler feared the suit might evolve into a serious threat, and cited a
letter he had at hand from Newell, the patent attorney in New York,
expressing his doubt if further flights ought to be made for the present,
excepting for tests and experiments. To this advice, Curtiss responded
(in substance): "There seemed to be a good deal of exhibition business
in sight, and that if the company's machines were not exhibited they
could not be sold; and that if they were not flown at these meets there
would be little use of continuing in the aeroplane business . . . [That
he was] willing to go on and continue to do that flying on my own
responsibility . . . to take those risks personally."

A dilemma scarcely less demanding was what to do about Mr.
Herring. Since Curtiss's return from Europe, the ill-will between him
and Herring had bloomed into virtually an open breach. The Hammondsport parties to the company were emphatically of the same mind
as Curtiss. They informed him that Herring was primed to make trouble
over the money collected abroad, on the score that it should be paid
in to the company treasury. In fact, there had been merely a verbal
understanding by which Cortlandt Bishop turned over the cash prizes
to the flyer personally. Now the pro-Curtiss directors felt that the time
had come to record it as company policy that he be permitted
to keep for himself whatever winnings and earnings he obtained by
flying, and to make this policy retroactive.

Wheeler, both president and legal counsel of the company, who
drew up a resolution to that effect, afterward clarified his reasoning:
"The position of an aviator at that time was a very dangerous one.
It was a position which was attended with considerable risk and in
which he might be killed or crippled for life at any time he made
a flight. I did not think it was the intention of the parties to the
contract, and that they did not contemplate, as a matter of law, if

he flew he would not have his earnings." Wheeler deemed Curtiss to
be "the prime flyer of this hemisphere," and that the company was
fortunate in having him advertise it by his feats; but considered that
he could not be expected to take the risks without the rewards. Wheeler
doubted that Curtiss would go on flying for exhibition "and take
chances and have a lot of stockholders of the company sit back and
take the winnings of his flights."

Curtiss mailed Herring a short, crisp note: "If it is convenient,
I think it would be a good plan for you to come up Sunday, so
that we can have a little directors' meeting. Mr. Gilbert is going to
be here [Bishop's proxy on the board]. Mr. Baldwin is now here and
will stay over." Herring came, unaware of the motive. The special
session of the board of directors took place on October 25 at Bath,
in Wheeler's law office. The proposed resolution was sprung:

"Resolved: That since the organization of this company, it recognizes that Glenn H. Curtiss has been the manager of said company
and its business; that it is expressly agreed that he is and shall be
employed as the sole manager of said company, and its business, with
authority to him to designate an assistant manager and fix his compensation; and that, whereas the said Glenn H. Curtiss has from time to
time since the organization of the company given exhibition flights
with an aeroplane, now in order that there may be no misunderstanding
between him and the company, it is expressly agreed that all trophies,
medals, prizes and compensation which he has earned or received in
the past in making such flights is and shall be his sole property, and
the company lays no claim thereto; and that in view of the fact that
such exhibition flights are a valuable advertisement to the Company
and its business and products, and involve great risk to his life and
limb, therefore it is agreed that said Curtiss may engage in the business
upon his own account and upon his own behalf in making exhibition
flights by himself or by any substitute or employee, and may also teach
and instruct others in the art of aeroplane flying; this company recognizes that in so doing that the advertisement resulting therefrom is a
benefit to the business of the company, and will more than compensate
for the loss of his immediate services at the offices of the plant in
Hammondsport, N.Y., and the company recognizes that such acts on his
part will be in furtherence of the interests of said company."

Prior to the rollcall, Herring interposed: "Would that resolution
apply to me, also?"

With vitriol on his tongue, Wheeler answered: "Yes, Mr. Herring.

If you can get off the ground, that resolution will also apply to you."[1]

The minutes showed a unanimous yes vote by the five directors. Herring subsequently protested that his vote was negative, and that A. W. Gilbert, an elderly man, was asleep at the time. Even had this been the case, Wheeler, Baldwin, and Curtiss constituted a majority of the board.

Herring would further maintain from a witness stand that no mention was made at this meeting about the employment of Jerome Fanciulli, which had been consummated two days earlier without his knowledge. Fanciulli, having cast the die, traveled to Bath on the 23rd to confer with Curtiss and Wheeler. The contract was drawn up then and there, making it clear that he would work only for Curtiss and not for the Herring-Curtiss Company. The terms provided that he was "to manage the interests of the said Glenn H. Curtiss . . . said interests to include the sale, exhibition, and exploitation of the Curtiss aeroplane, and any other business which the said Glenn H. Curtiss may direct." The contract was signed in privacy, with Monroe Wheeler as witness and notary. Fanciulli was installed in an office at Hammondsport for the time being.

Meanwhile, Curtiss was instructing Charley Hamilton, who turned out to be a phenomenally apt pupil. After a few lessons, he left the young madcap alone with the Hudson-Fulton plane while making a hurried business trip to New York. Upon his return, he was barely inside the house when Harry Champlin telephoned from the racetrack: "Hey, Glenn, you'd better come right over here. Charley Hamilton has your aeroplane in the air. He has flown fifteen times around the field and doesn't know how to get down."

Of course, Hamilton did know how to get down, but nonetheless Curtiss drove fast to Stony Brook Farm, uneasy about the fellow's precocity and the limited fuel capacity. By the time he got there, Charley had completed nineteen circuits and tossed in a couple of cross-country rambles for good measure. Curtiss recognized a natural-born pilot when he saw one, and this chap had the instincts of an uninhibited bird. "I was undertaking the exhibition business," as Curtiss said, "and I needed assistants, and needed another good flyer at least." He and Fanciulli talked it over and decided to hire Hamilton to fill some of the exhibition requests that were piling up.

Monroe Wheeler prepared a tentative contract, but, before it was submitted to Hamilton, Curtiss had second thoughts: "Does not this contract make Mr. Hamilton an employee, and does it not increase my liability for Hamilton's flying? I observe that Mr. Hamilton is a very venturesome flyer, and on account of his light weight is able to do a good deal with the aeroplane. I am afraid, if I have a contract with him where he appears to be my employee, I may assume more responsibility for his flying than it is right that I should do." The lawyer concurred, and drafted a different form of contract which was the basis of the lease system practiced by the Curtiss Exhibition Company as long as it lasted. Although the Exhibition Company had yet to be organized, Hamilton in effect became its charter pilot when he happily grabbed at the deal by which he leased an airplane from Curtiss, paying 60 percent of his net proceeds for its use; repairs to be shared in like proportion. The lessor assumed responsibility for lawsuits or damage incurred by the flyer. Hamilton was quickly on the road, starting to build his fame as the pioneer daredevil of the sky, with bookings at Kansas City and St. Joseph, Missouri. Curtiss himself took on a mid-November engagement at Cincinnati.

Increasingly, the two individuals whose names were linked in the Herring-Curtiss Company were operating at cross-purposes. Herring had independently engaged a New York automobile sales agency (Wyckoff, Church & Partridge) as the New York outlet for Herring-Curtiss airplanes. This agency promptly made a sale to a Chicago sportsman, James E. Plew, for $7500. The so-called "Plew machine" was the second airplane sold privately out of the Hammondsport plant. Orders were accepted from a Mrs. Rathbone of Elmira, sister to the late Matthias Arnot who had been Herring's patron when he claimed to have flown; from Clifford B. Harmon, a wealthy Long Island realtor; and from a San Francisco dealer who wanted eight machines.

Considering that the Wrights already had made a defendant of one purchaser, the Aeronautic Society, such sales were treading on thin ice, unless the planes were to be confined to "sporting" uses. The company might well have to shoulder financial responsibility if they were commercially employed. Moreover, Curtiss thought it unwise to "flood the market" with exhibition flyers while such activity remained the primary source of income. Bypassing Herring as if he did not exist, Curtiss and Fanciulli put into effect a restricted sales contract. Under this policy, a purchaser must agree not to use his machine in public flights "for amusement or advertising purposes"; and not in races or contests unless under auspices of the Aero Club of America or an affiliated club (the Aero Club had appeased the Wrights with a percentage of gate receipts for any event under its jurisdiction in which "infringing" aircraft appeared). As the sales contracts which Herring's agency had negotiated with Harmon and Mrs. Rathbone did not contain this clause, Curtiss halted delivery, even though down payments had been made.

An exception was the case of F. L. D. de Reimsdyck, a Hollander residing in France. Having seen Curtiss fly at Rheims and admired his plane, he jouneyed by sea and land to Hammondsport to purchase a machine like it, saying he intended flying it in Egypt. Since de Reimsdyck would be taking the product immediately out of the country, the sale was accepted without the restrictive clause. This was the first Curtiss-built airplane sold abroad.

During this troubled period, Alexander Pfitzner, the stalwart and personable Hungarian engineer, was putting the finishing touches on his unique monoplane, the project which had brought him to Hammondsport a year earlier. While studying aeronautics, Pfitzner had carved a niche for himself in the community, his tall good looks and courtly manners making him a heart-throb to the fair sex. He was partial to Bertha Mott, daughter of Mrs. Lulu Mott, who conducted the boardinghouse where most transient aviation men stayed while in town. When he squired Bertha to dances, he never failed to send her a corsage for the occasion and called for her punctually in full evening dress. Villagers had it that Bertha was "very much in love."

Pfitzner was an intimate friend and admirer of Curtiss, but was not a regular company employee, though he helped with engines. The monoplane was contrived at his own expense, with parts made to his order by the Curtiss works, including an aluminum motor weighing but 97 pounds. Henry Kleckler termed him "a kind of peculiar cuss—moody —but a smart feller." Instead of ailerons, he invented a device whereby the ends of the wings could be telescoped: that is, one side pushed out while the other was drawn in. Pfitzner made his maiden flight on December 21, damaged the gear and propeller in landing, but felt he had proved his point, and filed for a patent on his original controls. Whatever he had proved, he was the first man in America to fly a monoplane of his own making. That next March, he took the little machine down the lake to Snug Harbor for an attempted takeoff from the ice, broke through, and had a frigid ducking.[2]

* * *

When the Wrights came around to accepting Wall Street financing, they exercised considerably better judgment than Curtiss in the choice of backers. Eight months after the incorporation of Herring-Curtiss, they disposed of their American interests to a group of eastern capitalists, who then incorporated the Wright Company in New York State, while the plant remained at Dayton. On the face of it, they were selling out, but in reality they continued as a potent presence in the company. Among the stockholders were such impressive figures as Cornelius Vanderbilt, August Belmont, and Robert J. Collier. The settlement involved $100,000 in cash, 40 percent of the stock, and a royalty of 10 percent on every machine marketed. Wilbur informed Chanute, in almost the last truly friendly letter that passed between them: "The general supervision of the business will be in our hands though a general manager will be secured to directly have charge. We will devote most of our time to experimental work." As matters turned out, they devoted most of their time instead to prosecuting the patent infringement actions.

On December 12, their venerable father, Bishop Milton Wright, penned an entry in his diary: "Wilbur went to New York to see a photograph of Curtiss machine contradicting his affidavit. Thus the lawyers abuse Curtiss."

On January 3, 1910, Federal Judge John R. Hazel, at Buffalo, granted the temporary injunction for which the Wrights had applied, and the decision was a thunderclap in the aeronautical world. Surprise was voiced in legal circles that the injunction was issued prior to an adjudication of the patent on which it was based. In a statement given the Associated Press, Curtiss said: "In the arguments of their lawyers the Wrights proved theoretically to Judge Hazel . . . that my machines depend on the vertical rudder to maintain equilibrium. I will demonstrate by actual flight that they do not. That will end the action for injunction, for the Wrights' patents hinge on what is called the warping surface. Their machines have to depend on the vertical rudder to help maintain their balance. The warping surface of the planes gives the machines a turning tendency which the rudder has to overcome. The rudders on the Curtiss machines have no such function. This demonstration will prove what I say.

"We are going to take the decision of the judges before the courts."

Just about simultaneously with the ruling of Judge Hazel, Wright attorneys in New York served a paper on the French aviator, Louis Paulhan, as he walked down the gangplank. It was a notification of intent to apply for an injunction to prevent him from flying in the United States. This was the first overt act by the Wrights against a European flyer, and a wave of indignation surged across France, where it was recalled that Wilbur Wright had received his initial popular recognition and acclaim. American newspapers raised a chorus of editorial sympathy for Paulhan, who, as a foreign guest on these shores, was greeted in such a manner.

*   *   *

The primary reason for Paulhan's visit was an International Air Meet which the newly formed Aero Club of California was scheduling at Los Angeles for ten days, commencing January 10, 1910. In fact, it was Paulhan's participation which would make the meet "international." Sixteen aircraft were entered, and this was to be the first confrontation in the Western Hemisphere between French and American planes. The principal native machines were three Curtiss models. Finally the Rheims racer was out of bondage to the department stores, and its proprietor was looking forward eagerly to flying it competitively for the first time since Brescia.

Though Cortlandt Bishop was planning to attend the Los Angeles meet, he had misgivings that Curtiss had agreed to enter, wondering what repercussions might come from the Wrights (who were also invited to take part, but refrained). Curtiss tried to calm Bishop: "I have not contracted to make any exhibition flights and I have merely been guaranteed that my share in the prizes will not be less than $10,000. As my time and my life, as well as the little reputation I have been able to get together, are worth something, I insisted that I could not make the trip on the mere chance of getting a cup or two."

Actually, a Curtiss team of three pilots went to California—his most ambitious showing to date. He already had Hamilton on contract, and Charles Willard was delighted to be a member of the trio with the Aeronautic Society's *Golden Flier*.

Louis Paulhan arrived well equipped with two Farman biplanes and two Blériot monoplanes, intending to stay awhile. His retinue included his wife, two assistant pilots, and five mechanics. Paulhan was under contract to an American promoter, Edwin Cleary, not simply for the Los Angeles meet but for an extensive tour of the United States at the unprecedented fee of $24,000 a month.

With the legalistic shadow hanging over the two major contestants, journalistic fear was outspoken that the Wright actions would force cancellation of the California show for which such elaborate preparations had been made. This did not happen because both defendants were allowed to post bonds and go on flying, pending appeal of the injunction blockages.

For the "flying carnival," Los Angeles developed Aviation Field on an outlying farm. Grandstands were erected to accommodate 25,000 people, and large tents served as hangars. Paulhan lost no time in renewing acquaintance with Curtiss, whom he had met before at Rheims. The "wonderful little Frenchman," as he was often hailed during his performances at Los Angeles, walked smiling into the tent where Curtiss was assembling his planes. Wordlessly, for neither spoke the other's language, they clasped hands warmly, like two knights of the air pledging mutual solidarity in a common cause. Clifford Harmon, who was on the grounds for balloon ascents, was a witness to this rather poignant handshake. Harmon, an exceptionally tall man, remarked to other bystanders: "This is the first time I ever wanted to be small."

With the grandstands packed on opening day, Curtiss was out in front in getting his Rheims racer into the air for a test run, thereby becoming the first man to make a public airplane flight on the Pacific Coast.

Paulhan quickly trotted out one of his Blériots. In a brisk wind, the fragile-looking craft "rolled and careened," as women squealed and shrieked. Watching from below, Curtiss was needled as to why he left all the grandstanding to the Frenchman, and replied: "I am satisfied to let Paulhan have the applause, providing I am able to take the prizes."

Full of confidence again with the championship Rheims plane under him, Curtiss was certain to take the speed prize of $3000. This contest called for ten laps around a measured course, which he reeled off while a band played waltz music. Paulhan made a futile gesture with one of his monoplanes, then retired from the lists.

Having ascertained in Italy that the 8-cylinder machine could perform well with two people aboard, Curtiss went for a second speed prize with a passenger, winning at 55 miles per hour. The lightweight passenger was Jerome Fanciulli, who had come west with his employer to make sure the public relations would be properly handled in this instance. Predictably, Curtiss also pocketed the award for quick takeoff: $6\frac{2}{5}$ seconds in a run of 98 feet.

The priority item on Paulhan's agenda was the recapture of the world's altitude record previously held by him, since wrested away by Hubert Latham. Right after Paulhan's arrival in America, Latham had upped his own mark in France to 3600 feet. As usual, Curtiss had no real interest in the altitude department. Climbing up and up in one of his Farmans until he was "almost out of sight," the "wonderful little Frenchman" established the new record at 4165 feet for a prize of $3000. Paulhan won a like sum for endurance and time aloft. His remaining great ambition was the Michelin Cup for cross-country distance, carrying with it a $10,000 prize (this award, offered by André Michelin in France, was currently held by Henry Farman at 144 miles). When Paulhan captured it with a nonstop flight to the Sierra Madre range, circling the Santa Anita racetrack, and return, it was essentially the climax of the program and enabled him to come away with more prize money than Curtiss.

It remained for the Curtiss trio, however, to supply a circus-like anticlimax so far as sensationalism was concerned. On the final day of the meet, Curtiss, Hamilton, and Willard went into the air together, their aim "to give the crowd something to remember." This they proceeded to do by putting on a free-for-all exhibition, chasing one another around the course with flourishes for a solid half-hour. Their gratuitous performance struck one New York correspondent as being "the most remarkable flying the world has yet seen." Moreover, it left a highly favorable impression of Curtiss and his aircraft in the public mind, which went a long way toward erasing the stigma of Governors Island. Conceivably, that was an underlying motive.

Other extracurricular activities went on during the Los Angeles splurge which helped to make it the most broadly interesting aerial occasion to date, East or West. In accord with his published promise on the eve of the meet, Curtiss seized every opportunity, when the field was free from program events, for demonstrations calculated to disprove the claim of the Wrights that the control of his machines, like theirs, depended on a combination of the rear vertical rudder with the action of the ailerons. Many paying customers lingered around to watch these tests. Hamilton and Willard alternated with Curtiss in flying the experiments. At times the steering wheel was tied; again, both the wheel and the kingpost were sealed, to prove there had been no movement; the rudder thus was fixed in its neutral position and only the ailerons could be operated. The ailerons were moved in diverse ways, sometimes at angles so exaggerated as to violently rock the machine. Augustus Post volunteered as a semi-official observer of these tests; other witnesses were Clifford Harmon and Lieutenant Paul M. Beck of the U. S. Army. The pilots and all three ground observers later swore during the litigation that they were unable to detect any turning tendency whatever resulting from the use of the ailerons alone.

Lieutenant Beck, a Signal Corps officer stationed at Benicia Barracks, California, was detailed by the War Department as the Army's observer at the Los Angeles meet. In the tradition of Tom Selfridge, Beck asked for the assignment, partly because he had improvised a bombsight and hoped to obtain the cooperation of a pilot to try it out. Curtiss flew him several times around the course, at one point of which a target area was marked out. From an altitude of 250 feet, Beck dropped 15-pound sandbags and consistently missed the target, which did not speak very well for his primitive bombsight. Nonetheless these tests were significant as being the earliest attempt by Army personnel to drop projectiles with the aid of a sighting device.

It was during the Los Angeles meet that Charles Willard, without meaning to do so, coined a phrase which was to plague aviation for many years to come. Landing from a bumpy flight, he said offhandedly that the air was "as full of holes as a Swiss cheese." The remark caught the ear of a reporter who wrote it into that day's dispatch. Papers across the nation picked it up, and before long pseudo-scientific articles were being printed on the subject of "holes in the air." The fable about "air pockets" persisted until after World War I, and many a crash was blamed on them.

o   o   o

As the meet came to a close, both the Curtiss and Paulhan camps were flooded with lucrative invitations from other cities, especially in the West and South. Owing to difficulties besetting his company, Curtiss must rush back to Hammondsport, but he turned loose the two Charleys on filling such dates as they could manage. Curtiss himself took on a contract at Phoenix, Arizona, in February, and there observed: "All through this part of the country people are crazy to see flights."

Charley Hamilton was entrusted with the Rheims racer and set off for San Diego via Bakersfield and Fresno. Soon he was building his legend by flitting a dangerous distance out over the Pacific surf from the Coronado Hotel in a 20-mile wind; doing the "highest, longest glide" yet made; and flying after dark.

That Curtiss had not yet abandoned the hope of an amiable compromise with the Wright brothers is indicated by a proposal he apparently then made to Fanciulli to stop off at Dayton on his way home from Los Angeles. Fanciulli later testified that, owing to his good relations with the Wrights, Curtiss wanted him "to see whether the Wrights would be friendly to him." He said Curtiss would have liked very much "to either form a combination with them, or, if they wouldn't consider that, to get someone to make an arrangement with them whereby the patent litigation should be avoided." For some unexplained reason, Fanciulli did not go to Dayton. All he said was that "The Wrights were very bitter"; which could suggest that they refused to see him.[3]

Louis Paulhan entertained at San Francisco, Salt Lake City, Denver, El Paso, and New Orleans. He toured on, unaware that a U.S. deputy marshal was trailing him through Phoenix, Kansas City, and St. Louis. Finally on February 23, at Oklahoma City, where Paulhan was readying for another exhibition, the marshal pounced. On that date, Federal Judge Learned Hand granted the injunction, together with a ruling that Paulhan furnish a bond of $25,000, out of which the Wrights could be indemnified for their percentage of any profits he made. The bond must be posted in cash. The judge suspended the injunction until March 12 to allow attorneys time to prepare an appeal.

When the paper was served on him, Paulhan raised his clenched fists and emitted a stream of French invective. Packing up at once, he quit Oklahoma City in high dudgeon, canceling dates at Dallas, Memphis, and other cities of the South and Midwest. He threatened to sail for France, then decided to stay in order to give the public his side of the case. His four airplanes were taken to the Jamaica, Long Island, racetrack, where he made a few flights without recompense.

Indignation welled up on both sides of the Atlantic. Several newspaper cartoons rang changes on a theme typified by the one which depicted the Wright brothers brandishing their fists at an airplane, shouting: "Keep Out of My Air!" The New York *World* headlined:

FLY NO MORE IF
YOU DO NOT HIRE
WRIGHT'S WINGS

The French people were greatly incensed. The Fédération Aéronautique Internationale notified the Aero Club of America that, unless the Wrights would guarantee not to molest foreign flyers, no European pilots would come to the United States for the next October running of the Gordon Bennett Trophy race, and that the meet might be held a second time in France. The Wrights replied that they did not intend to obstruct the meet, but that a fund must be set aside to compensate them for the use of "infringing" machines. One of France's foremost pilots, Robert Esnault-Pelterie, sounded off: "The judgment given by Judge Hand is iniquitous. Such a decision would be impossible in a European court." He was sarcastic about the Wrights' "kind offer" to permit foreign flyers to compete for the Coupe Internationale.

By now, Paulhan was having trouble with his manager, Edwin Cleary, who did not care to put up the $25,000 bond for his continued flying. Moreover, Paulhan alleged that Cleary was $30,000 in arrears with his contract payments, and renewed his threat to go home. Cleary obtained an injunction to restrain his client from removing the four aircraft. Leaving the planes where they were, Paulhan and his party quietly boarded a ship at New York. Back on familiar soil, he exulted: "I am most happy to be safe in France. I have finally escaped the nightmare of the last few weeks." He branded the Wrights as "veritable birds of prey"; said that Wilbur had appeared with lawyers at his Jamaica hangar and, barely acknowledging his handshake, "hurled himself on my machines."

As for the impounded airplanes, Paulhan had the last chuckle: they never had belonged to him in the first place; he had them on loan from the manufacturers for the publicity value.

15. Herring Non Grata

After comparing notes with Curtiss in France, Cortlandt Field Bishop was aware that all was not well with the company of which he had been the promulgator a scant six months earlier; still he did not rush home to see what might be done about it. When he finally did return on October 23, he found that a meeting of the board of directors was called for the 25th in Monroe Wheeler's law office at Bath. Instead of arranging to be there, he repaired to his summer mansion in the Berkshires, dispatching his secretary, A. W. Gilbert, as his deputy. Not until Gilbert reported back did he begin to realize how sorely the company's affairs had gone awry, and then he was jolted hard. Even so, his concern was mainly for the fate of his investment and that of his brother David.

For so wealthy a man, Bishop's $21,000 plunge into the aviation pond was shallow enough; moreover, the grand talk about formidable Wall Street financing to be lured by him had fizzled like a wet firecracker. Manifestly, the Herring-Curtiss Company stood on shaky fiscal ground from the start, with a mere $38,000 in tangible money from three New York investors, plus the indeterminate amount kicked in by

Augustus M. Herring. Whatever that may have been on paper, Herring rapidly manipulated it down to $7100 in actual cash, then kept on whittling. His ultimate apparent capital investment was $5658, which "mildly speaking, is a conservative amount of working capital for a $360,000 corporation" (to quote a presiding judge in the legal aftermath). Herring's only detectable source of income from his New York machine-shop was the making of toy airplanes.

When the company was incorporated, Wheeler asked Herring: "What are you going to do for working capital—money to run the business?" The reply was that he had "made provision for that": he intended to sell some of his stock to raise it. On the strength of that, and in anticipation of larger orders, the company went ahead and erected new buildings to the tune of $18,000; then the working capital was not forthcoming.

The plain truth was that Glenn Curtiss himself was the major investor in the Herring-Curtiss Company, considering all that he laid on the line. The others, even the Bishops, were riding on his coattails. In the original transaction, Herring was to pay him $55,000 for his properties; plus an additional $5000 if an inventory showed the value of his assets to be in excess of $62,000. An accounting firm appraised the total value at $82,272.11, so that Curtiss received $60,000, of which $15,000 was a mortgage. The difference was represented by his shares of stock in the new company. On top of everything, his career and business reputation (his name being a nationally known trademark) were at stake. A year later, after the company had gone through the wringer, another group of appraisers evaluated the assets, including the Curtiss name and good-will of the motorcycle works, at somewhere between $90,000 and $115,000.

The special board meeting at Bath clearly signaled that the tension between Herring and the rest of the company had reached a snapping point. He still had not revealed to Curtiss or any other company official a single item of his purported inventions, patents, or patent applications, as stipulated in the deal. Reminded several times of this oversight, he had procrastinated "with the plea that, if divulged by him, the information might come to outsiders and the company lose the benefit." Now his fellow directors decided the time had come to crack down. After adopting the retroactive resolution allowing Curtiss to keep for himself the winnings and earnings of his flights, the board took two other actions aimed at Herring.

The first of these was worded: "Resolved, That Mr. Herring turn over to the company all of the patents and patentable rights and inventions which Mr. Curtiss assigned to him and which said Herring agreed to assign to the company."

The second resolution called upon Herring to deliver all of his own "inventions, devices and improvements"; his applications for patents "covering some 51 claims"; all "special jigs and patterns mentioned in his agreement with the company"; and also that he supply the company with a list of the "inventions, devices and improvements mentioned in his contract and the numbers of applications for patents pending for the same."

The "instrument" by which Herring had agreed to surrender his patent claims was couched in such general terms that it did not conform to the requirements of the U. S. Patent Office; consequently the company had been unable to obtain any information about them.

Of course, Herring was present when these resolutions were adopted. By his later testimony, as regards Curtiss inventions or patents (meaning essentially at that time the one-fifth interest in the A.E.A. patent application), Herring denied that any demand had been made on him to turn them over to the company; and said: "I do not remember that there was anything tangible in existence at that time to make a demand for." As for his own patent claims, he recalled his reply to the board as being that he had "only one application in the office and that I was perfectly willing to assign. I thought I had transferred it to the company, but that I was willing to sign any papers that they might prepare that would make the transfer more complete."

In point of fact, Herring never did turn over to the company any patents (they being non-existent), or any listing of patent applications.[1] The overriding purpose for which the directors desired a showdown on these was to ascertain once and for all whether he had any claims to inventions which might be helpful against the Wright suit. Neither did Herring deliver the jigs and patterns from his New York shop; he was correct in saying afterward that these were not really wanted at Hammondsport, as they would have been useless for anything being done there.

*   *   *

If proof of continuing friendly relations between Curtiss and Alexander Graham Bell were needed, it may be seen in a telegram which

Bell sent his erstwhile associate from Washington on October 30, 1909: WISH YOU COULD COME HERE FOR CONFERENCE WITH CHARLES BELL BE-FORE I RETURN BADDECK. WANT TO GO AT ONCE BUT WOULD WAIT A DAY OR TWO FOR YOU. COME RIGHT TO MY HOUSE AND SHAKE A PAW FOR AULD LANG SYNE.

Curtiss was not laggard in accepting this overture. Bell's diary entry for November 2 recorded: "Mr. Curtiss arrived here yesterday morning . . . After lunch, had conference with Charles J. Bell on way to government testing ground. Saw college grounds and Wright machine. Met Wilbur Wright and several officers of Signal Service. Wright has large horizontal tail on machine and two solid looking wheels. Doubt whether wheels are [illegible] up, but did not care to examine the machine too curiously.—Curtiss left by 3 P.M. train for New York to attend meeting of Aero Club."

For the latter, this was his first encounter with Wright since the episode of Governors Island. Wilbur had gone direct from there to College Park, Maryland (site of the University of Maryland), to round out the contract for the Army airplane by teaching two officers to fly it. Presumably Bell was anxious to see a Wright airplane in action.

The talk with Charles J. Bell, the Washington banker who was trustee for the Aerial Experiment Association, was most likely for the purpose of discussing the A.E.A. patent application; potential royalties for its use as between Curtiss and the Canadian Aerodrome Company; and the bearing upon it of the Wright infringement suits.

Bell was keeping a weather eye cocked at the legalistic moves of the Wright brothers. Within a few weeks, Casey Baldwin wired for his opinion on the offer of a large Canadian department store for exhibit of one of the Baddeck aerodromes, and he answered: "Proper place of exhibition of flying machines is the air, not a department store . . . Advise going slowly until Curtiss law suit develops. . . . I will see you through [i.e., in financing the Aerodrome Company] to the end of March—after that, the deluge. Seek only to perfect your machine and demonstrate its capabilities this winter on the ice . . . Then if nothing develops from Canadian or British governments, see no objection to your sending men to exhibit machines to raise money for the aerodrome company; but just as well to go slowly now and let Curtiss law suit develop without any possibility of your being involved."

In all probability, Curtiss would have seen Bishop at the Aero Club meeting and briefed him further on the Herring trouble. At any rate, worry gnawed at Bishop, and letters shuttled between him and Hammondsport. In one case he told Curtiss: "I fear that Herring's interest in the company represents nothing but water, and it should be wrung out if it is possible to do so." From Curtiss, he received this: "[Herring] has always been a failure. He has fooled Mr. Chanute, Hiram Maxim, Professor Langley, and the U.S. government, and has deceived you and me. We cannot afford to take chances with him again . . . Out of consideration for the other stockholders I have about decided to make Herring a proposition to buy or sell."

Bishop's mounting distress prompted him to write the president of the company, Monroe Wheeler, on November 15, pronouncing the situation "intolerable," and insisting that something be done. Now his basic anxiety came into the open, that "myself and my brother, who put in $37,000 in hard cash, are likely to be sacrificed entirely and crushed between the two contending interests, one of which seems to have a majority of the stock and for which he has contributed no real value to the combination." Curtiss took upon himself a reply to that apprehension, saying the only danger was "the probable change of management after March 1st next," and adding:

"There can absolutely be no patching up the matter. It has got to go one way or the other. A temporary management means nothing without control. I must have control or get out."

* * *

Before going to France, Curtiss had been disillusioned with the partner of whom he had expected so much. That was nothing compared to the revelations awaiting him after his homecoming.

Herring's defaulting on his contract with the Army was damaging to the prestige of the company, even though the firm had nothing to do with that contract. The failure was a grievous blow to Curtiss, who had thought himself allied with an aeronautical genius.

Curtiss found himself in not only a humiliating position but a critical business dilemma. If his associate were merely an impostor, it may have been endured; but now there were sinister omens that he might be a scoundrel as well. Rumor told him that Herring was trying to round up proxy votes, to augment the majority stock voting rights he personally held, in a scheme to grab complete control of the company when the first annual meeting of Herring-Curtiss stockholders came up the following January. With incredible naïveté, Curtiss had walked into a trap which made it feasible for Herring to do this. Monroe Wheeler, the hard-headed attorney, had sanctioned a corporate structure so loose that Herring was able to assign himself the controlling stock without putting up anything whatever in return. As an attorney's brief would say in retrospect: "He could oust Curtiss, Wheeler, Baldwin, and everybody at Hammondsport, on the strength of his watered stock, and that was perfectly legitimate. But if the directors . . . sought to prevent it, that was a foul conspiracy."

Curtiss was unable to clarify how it all happened. In an interview for the local paper, he asserted that Herring "has not paid one penny in money or otherwise for the large share of stock which he, as promoter, secured for himself entirely unbeknown to me or the other stockholders."

The 3600 shares of Herring-Curtiss stock were distributed among twenty-one stockholders. Herring held 2015 shares, or a paper value of $201,500 out of a total $360,000. The other shares were apportioned as follows: Curtiss, 505 shares; A. W. Gilbert, for the Bishop and Deering investments, 631 shares; Monroe Wheeler, seven shares; the remaining 442 shares scattered. Curtiss had seen to it that stockholders in his motorcycle company received Herring-Curtiss shares in exchange.

Of lesser significance, but similiarly ominous, were reports that Herring was ready to make trouble over the prizes won by the flyer in Europe, pressing sharp inquiries as to their amount and disposition. He had retained in his possession certain shares of stock earmarked to raise working capital as needed (when Curtiss wrote asking Herring for an accounting on these shares, he got no reply). Lena, of course, would have informed him of Herring's visits to Hammondsport during his absence, expressly to pry into the company's books. On one such visit, he had clouded up at finding no record of payment for the *Golden Flier*, and demanded an explanation of her. According to Herring, Mrs. Curtiss said she would "find out about it." When he looked again after the homecoming celebration, Herring said he had found an entry of $3000.[2]

Weeks dragged past with no response from Herring to the October resolutions, and the directors decided on drastic action to bring him to book. A board meeting was summoned at the company offices in Hammondsport on December 18, and Herring showed up with an attorney, J. John Hassett of Elmira. Without more ado, the board voted to ask an injunction compelling him to turn over the putative patents and other stipulated items to the company, and at the same time to restrain him from disposing of any of his stock.

While the document of formal notification of this action was being drawn up, Herring excused himself from the room. When he did not reappear, his lawyer went out, ostensibly to locate him, and neither came back. Henry Kleckler and Jerome Fanciulli spent a long, cold evening in an open automobile, combing the roads around Hammondsport in a fruitless search for them. The ensuing issue of the *Herald* related a weird tale of Herring's "sensational get away." It seems that Hassett, who was registered at the Wadsworth Hotel in Hammondsport, telephoned a confederate waiting in Bath. This third party hailed a young man passing in an automobile and hired him to drive to Hammondsport, pick up a Mr. Hassett at the hotel, and follow his instructions. The driver, by coincidence, was Rumsey Wheeler, a son of Monroe Wheeler who was presiding at the board meeting. Hassett ordered him to drive along the west shore lake road. After some distance, he was commanded to stop and a hulking man emerged from the shadows of a clump of bushes to be greeted by Hassett. Rumsey Wheeler figured he was mixed up with a gang of criminals, panicked, and drove off, leaving the pair stranded on the highway.

The person who had been hiding in the bushes, of course, was Herring, who, with his attorney, then plodded the road until they reached a lighted house. Telling the occupants that their automobile had broken down, they were given lodging for the night. Next morning they engaged their host to drive them to Savona, a small station on the far side of Bath, where they were able to catch a train for New York without recognition.

The injunction was issued next day by a Supreme Court judge in Bath. Some time later the *Herald* said Herring had been "in hiding for three weeks to prevent the service of injunction papers." The story added: "Meanwhile the works are doing but little, which cannot but hurt the business of the company, as it certainly does the village. Mr. Herring is accounted a man of great genius in aeronautics, and he has thus far in the controversy proved himself an artful dodger and a shrewd manipulator of his affairs. The Curtiss people claim the right of it, however, which view seems to be accepted by the majority of people acquainted with the facts."

Injunctions flew thick and fast. Herring filed a stockholder's action

against his fellow officers and directors to recover losses which he
alleged the company had sustained through mismanagement. On the
29th, he obtained a court order to restrain the majority directors from
"favoring" Curtiss until his suit could be brought to trial. He filed
an affidavit asserting that he was the inventor of the devices which
had made the Herring-Curtiss machines a success, and depicting
Curtiss as merely a skillful "driver" employed by the company at a
salary of $5000. He charged that Curtiss had engaged, without proper
authorization, a personal press agent to promote his reputation. Herring's
injunction was promptly vacated by a justice in Utica who decided
it had been granted without due consideration, and that it was
"so sweeping in its terms as to practically prohibit the company from
the transaction of business."

On January 10, 1910, the company obtained an injunction restraining Herring from voting his shares at the stockholders' meeting scheduled for the 20th. The meeting was thereupon postponed indefinitely.
By this time, Curtiss was at the Los Angeles meet, under bond to fly
pending appeal of the Wright injunction, and the Wrights would
soon have their injunction against Louis Paulhan.

*   *   *

Meanwhile, Dr. Bell had sponsored the election of Curtiss to
honorary membership in the Aero Club of America, thereby giving
him equivalent status with the Wright brothers in that exclusive organization. The Wrights had been "honorary" from the outset, while
Curtiss had been an active member since 1907.

Upon learning of the Herring-Curtiss split, Bell had an inspiration.
Rarely, if ever before or after, did Mabel Bell write anything herself
in his *Home Notes*. On December 27, 1909, the Bells were evidently
having a late evening discussion, as she cited the hour of 11:30 P.M.
when, in her graceful flowing handwriting, she penned this entry:

> Alec much excited over new idea. I have persuaded him
> to dictate letter as follows to Baldwin and McCurdy.
>
> Boys!—an Idea! Why not get Curtiss to come to Canada
> and manufacture engines for the Aerodrome Company? Why
> not take him into the company? He's sold the Hammonds-
> port business to the Herring people—he has received the money
> for it and shares in the Herring company. He has now
> quarreled with Herring and has brought a law suit against

him. If he resigns his position there, there would be nothing to prevent him from coming to Canada. In the event of war between Great Britain and Germany, while it would be quite true that American engines and aerodromes could not be imported into Canada, the war would not prevent Canadian aerodromes from being imported into the United States. The Canadian Aerodrome Company might supply dromes both for the British Empire and for the United States.

Why should not the company replace the old A.E.A.? be organized by the Trustee in Canada and the old associates come together again in a commercial company? We should manufacture the whole thing, engines and all.

A.G.B.

Bell's brainstorm was short-lived, however, as the Herring-Curtiss imbroglio took another course.

A few pages after Mabel Bell registered the great "Idea," Bell wrote his latest thoughts on the Wright lawsuit into his diary:

I have no means of knowing whether Curtiss employs flat or curved surfaces, but the Wright Brothers have made out such a strong prima facie case that the court has granted them a preliminary injunction against Curtiss. It would be a matter of precaution for Baldwin and McCurdy to make quite sure that their *lateral* balancing rudders are aero *planes* pure and simple—flat surfaces, and could not be held to be concave on the underside and convex above.

The brief for the Wright Brothers is a remarkably able document. I am not so well satisfied that the Curtiss Case has been equally well managed.

There is no doubt at all in my mind that however the Curtiss case may be settled the Wright Brothers will be after Baldwin and McCurdy the moment they attempt to make money by their machines.

*   *   *

The Wright case hovered like a gathering storm cloud over all that was transpiring at Hammondsport. Until the tangled affairs of the company were straightened away, it would be in a crippled condition to assume a defensive posture against that menace. It was more than courtroom rhetoric when an attorney in future litigation observed that any attempt to appraise the Herring episode "and leave the Wright case out of the calculation is like the play of *Hamlet* with Hamlet left out." Was this an oblique reference to the role which was being played out by Curtiss against "a sea of troubles?"

During this identical period, the long friendship between the Wrights and Octave Chanute reached overt rupture in what must rank as the most poignant quarrel of aviation history. The brothers had been aware for some time that their old adviser was out of sympathy with the course they were taking, but a façade of amiability had been maintained in the letters. An interview which Chanute granted a reporter for the New York *World* cracked Wilbur's control. Chanute was quoted as saying:

"I admire the Wrights. I feel friendly toward them for the marvels they have achieved; but you can easily gauge how I feel concerning their attitude at present by the remark I made to Wilbur Wright recently. I told him I was sorry to see they were suing other experimenters and abstaining from entering the contests and competitions in which other men are brilliantly winning laurels. I told him that in my opinion they are wasting valuable time over lawsuits which they ought to concentrate in their work. Personally, I do not think that the courts will hold that the principle underlying the warping tips can be patented. They may win on the application of their particular mechanism . . . There is no question that the fundamental principle underlying was well known before the Wrights incorporated it in their machine."

Wilbur Wright caught him up on this in a letter dated January 20, 1910, saying: "As this opinion is quite different from that which you expressed in 1901 when you became acquainted with our methods, I do not know whether it is mere newspaper talk or whether it really represents your present views." If Chanute was cognizant of any proof that their system was known in the art before they developed it, he asked where such documents might be obtained, then went on: "It is our view that morally the world owes its almost universal use of our system of lateral control entirely to us. It is also our opinion that legally it owes it to us. If however there is anything in print which might invalidate our legal rights, it will be to our advantage to know it before spending too much on lawyers."

Chanute replied that the interview was "about as accurate as such things usually are," and said: "I did tell you in 1901 that the mechanism by which your surfaces were warped was original with yourselves. This I adhere to, but it does not follow that it covers the general principle of warping or twisting wings, the proposals for doing this being very ancient . . . When I gave you a copy of the Mouillard patent in 1901 I think I called your attention to his method of twisting the rear of the wings. If the courts will decide that the purpose and results were entirely different and that you were the first to conceive the twisting of the wings, so much the better for you, but my judgment is that you will be restricted to the particular method by which you do it. Therefore it was that I told you in New York that you were making a mistake by abstaining from prize-winning contests while public curiosity is yet so keen, and by bringing suits to prevent others from doing so. This is still my opinion and I am afraid, my friend, that your usually sound judgment has been warped by the desire for great wealth.

"If, as I infer from your letter, my opinions form a grievance in your mind, I am sorry, but this brings me to say that I also have a little grievance against you." In a recent Boston speech, Wilbur had related how Chanute "turned up" at their shop in Dayton in 1901 and they invited him to their Kitty Hawk camp. "This conveyed the impression that I thrust myself upon you at that time and it omitted to state that you were the first to write me, in 1900, asking for information which was gladly furnished, that many letters passed between us, and that both in 1900 and 1901 you had written me to invite me to visit you, before I 'turned up' in 1901." This and other incidents of the sort grated on Chanute, and he wrote: "I hope that, in future, you will not give out the impression that I was the first to seek your acquaintance, or pay me left-handed compliments, such as saying that 'sometimes an experienced person's advice was of great value to younger men.'"

Chanute's dig about money as a motive stung Wilbur to the quick, and he wrote back a lengthy letter, in the course of which he said: "As to inordinate desire for wealth, you are the only person acquainted with us who has ever made such an accusation. We believed that the physical and financial risks which we took, and the value of the service to the world, justified sufficient compensation to enable us to live modestly with enough surplus income to permit the devotion of our future time to scientific experimenting instead of business . . . You apparently concede to us no right to compensation for the solution of a problem ages old except such as is granted to persons who had no part in producing the invention. That is to say, we may compete with mountebanks for a chance to earn money in the mountebank business, but are entitled to nothing whatever for past work as inventors. If holding a different view constitutes us almost criminals, as some seem to think, we are not ashamed. We honestly think that our work of 1900–1906 has been and will be of value to the world, and that the world owes us something as inventors, regardless of whether we personally make Roman holidays for accident-loving crowds."

Speaking of grievances, Wilbur mentioned that he and Orville also held one, dating as far back as 1902: namely, a widespread impression, which they blamed mainly on Chanute, that "we were mere pupils and dependents of yours." Wilbur said he had found this attitude especially in France, where there was a general belief that Chanute had even supplied them with funds—"in short, that you furnished the science and money while we contributed a little mechanical skill, and that when success had been achieved you magnanimously stepped aside and permitted us to enjoy the rewards . . . The difficulty of correcting the errors without seeming to disparage you and hurting your feelings kept me silent, though I sometimes restrained myself with difficulty."

Adverting to another *World* article, which implied that Chanute felt hurt "because we had been silent regarding our indebtedness to you," Wilbur continued: "I confess that I have found it most difficult to formulate a precise statement of what you contributed to our success . . . We on our part have been much hurt by your apparent backwardness in correcting mistaken impressions, but we have assumed that you too have found it difficult to substitute for the erroneous reports a really satisfactory precise statement of the truth. If such a statement could be prepared it would relieve a situation very painful both to you and to us.

"I have written with great frankness because I feel that such frankness is really more healthful to friendship than the secretly nursed bitterness which has been allowed to grow for so long a time . . . We do not insist that friends shall always agree with us . . . We have no wish to quarrel with a man toward whom we ought to preserve a feeling of gratitude."

After digesting this, Chanute wrote to a mutual acquaintance that he had "a violent letter" from Wilbur Wright in which he "disputes my opinion, brings up various grievances and quite loses his temper." He would answer it in a few days, he said, "but the prospects are that we will have a row." Chanute postponed the answer, however, and when three months had elapsed Wilbur wrote again, saying he had no reply as yet and feared that "the frankness with which delicate subjects were treated may have blinded you to the real spirit and purpose of the letter." "My brother and I do not form many intimate friendships," he pursued, "and do not lightly give them up . . . We prize too highly the friendship which meant so much to us in the years of our early struggles to willingly see it worn away by uncorrected misunderstandings, which might be corrected by a frank discussion . . . My object was not to give offense, but to remove it." Again, he suggested that they prepare a joint statement to set the record straight.

Israel Ludlow sent Chanute a copy of Wilbur Wright's latest affidavit in March 1910, with the remark that he felt "much as you do, but even more strongly." Ludlow said that what Wright had written "was mild compared to what he allowed his counsel to say before the Court." He added that it was not pleasant to hear him (Chanute) referred to as "an amiable old gentleman" before a judge of the Court of the United States.

Chanute at last answered Wilbur on May 14, and that letter was destined to be his farewell to the Wrights. Noting that his health was poor and he was threatened with nervous exhaustion, he said he was about to sail for a recuperative trip to Europe. He said Wilbur's last missive was gratifying, "for I own that I felt very much hurt by your letter of January 29th, which I thought both unduly angry and unfair as well as unjust." Ignoring Wilbur's proposal of a joint statement, he wrote: "I have never given out the impression, either in writing or speech, that you had taken up aeronautics at my instance or were, as you put it, pupils of mine. I have always written and spoken of you as original investigators and worthy of the highest respect. How much I may have been of help I do not know . . . The difference in opinion between us, i.e., whether the warping of the wings was in the nature of a discovery by yourselves, or had already been proposed and experimented by others, will have to be passed upon by others, but I have always said that you are entitled to immense credit for devising apparatus by which it has been reduced to successful practice."

Chanute made his European voyage, returned home to Chicago, and breathed his last in November 1910, two months short of his seventy-ninth birthday. He died unreconciled with the Wrights.

*   *   *

With the thorny Herring problem unsolved, the business fell stagnant to the point where Curtiss more than once met the payroll by digging into his own pocket. He and his inner circle cast about for means of salvaging the company after blockading Herring's plan to seize control; no stockholders' meeting could legally be held until that injunction was dismissed. The stickler was that neither he nor his intimates would accept any solution which left Herring entrenched in the company, and Herring would not budge.

The first move by Curtiss, when communication was re-established with Herring or his attorney, was to make him a cash offer of $10,000 for his stock, on condition that he drop all legal action. As an alternative, Curtiss offered to sell his own stock to Herring for $10,000, together with stock held by the Hammondsport people for an additional $3500, on Herring's pledge to forego any further legal proceedings. Herring rejected both proposals. Curtiss doubled the ante with an offer of $20,000 for Herring's stock, with no better result.

Charles L. Kingsley, a stockholder who was a New York Telephone Company executive and kept a summer home at Keuka Lake (owner of the Kingsley Flats), tried to mediate a solution; he suggested the raising of a $50,000 fund by bonds and mortgages with which to reimburse the Bishop group and Herring, "if Herring would get out." Concerning this plan, Curtiss said later: "I believed it was an impractical scheme and did not give it any serious consideration." Bishop then proposed a voting trust with election of a new board of directors of "reputable business men," removing both Curtiss and Herring from positions of active control; Curtiss would not countenance that, believing it was "not free from sinister design against himself and his welfare."

Herring launched into a frenzy of letter writing. To Kingsley he wrote: "If Curtiss wants the law, he shall have his fill of it . . . If he wants fair play he will have to begin by giving it. There is one very simple settlement he can make—drop his suit and concede what I am suing for, and then get together and put the Wright brothers out of business." He turned back to Bishop for support, asking another $20,000 for "properly running the company by taking it out of Curtiss's hands." "Can't I make some arrangement with you to hold the company together," he pleaded, "and properly manage and finance it for a few months? . . . I don't want personal control of the company —but I don't want to lose what I have in it, or be worried for fear of losing it.—I want to have my mind free enough to be able to do some work in developing a better machine." He discovered that Bishop was not so easy a mark as he had been the previous year.

In the financial pinch, the exhibition bookings were a godsend, so that it was desirable to hold onto the few aircraft available and if possible to build more. Above all, if the company was doomed to skid into insolvency Curtiss wished to run no risk of having those planes impounded as assets. At the same time, he had $10,000 of his private securities tied up in the bond required by the Wright injunction to fly them. The release of these securities to meet other contingencies was cited as the reason for a resolution of the Herring-Curtiss directors (minus Herring) in the winter of 1910: "That Mr. Curtiss be authorized to sell the Rheims aeroplane, and the two aeroplanes which were sent to Los Angeles, at the best prices obtainable, and apply the proceeds, up to $10,000 to secure the American Surety Company upon its bonds given in the suit in the U. S. Court of Wright Company vs. Herring-Curtiss Company and Curtiss, and the surplus of such sales to turn over to such company."[3]

Determined not to let those aircraft out of his hands, Curtiss imparted his willingness to purchase them, as an individual, to Wheeler, but the attorney advised that his position in the company precluded that. A rather devious transaction was then arranged whereby Charles Hamilton appeared as the nominal purchaser of the three machines for $10,000. Payment was made with Hamilton's check for $7000, which actually represented Curtiss's 60 percent share of the proceeds of some of Hamilton's flights; together with Curtiss's personal check for $3000. A trial court judge, who was distinctly favorable toward Curtiss, in years to come referred to this deal as "pure subterfuge," and said: "Mr. Curtiss was the real purchaser and his ownership was later confirmed by a bill of sale executed to him from Hamilton." The point at issue when the jurist voiced that opinion was whether the planes might not have brought more than $10,000 on the open market, netting a surplus for the company. At any rate, the aircraft were kept on the road.

At odd times during that winter, Curtiss conducted further experiments from the ice of Keuka Lake, with wheel tied and rudder sealed, to gather evidence against the Wright claim that his controls depended on a combination of ailerons with rudder action.

* * *

In New York's plush Hotel St. Regis, the Aero Club of America held its annual banquet on March 24, 1910. Its theme was the celebration of the American victory at Rheims, and Glenn H. Curtiss was guest of honor. Suspended over the speakers' table was a quarter-sized replica of the Rheims racer.

Uncomfortable in full-dress, Curtiss sat and stared at the burnished silver of the Gordon Bennett Trophy which sat resplendent on the table before him. He had seen it before in the window of a jewelry shop in the ancient city of Rheims. He could not help noticing that the aeroplane adorning its crest was modelled after a Wright machine. Beside it, also reflecting back the lights of the chandeliers, stood the Scientific American Trophy on which he was the holder of two legs. Without the knowledge of his fellow members, plans were secretly spinning in his head to claim its permanent possession in the near future.

The guest list carried two hundred names of distinguished and moneyed men. When Curtiss was introduced for his usual laconic remarks, these two hundred stood up in unison and gave three rousing cheers.

The brothers in Dayton, Ohio, had been sent a special invitation, although, as honorary members of the club, they hardly needed one. They were not among those present.

* * *

A traveling salesman named David Herman, who made frequent calls at the Herring-Curtiss factory, seems to have been the first to broach the bankruptcy idea as one means by which a company might obtain a business divorce from an unwanted official who could not be fired. In discussing the Herring problem with Curtiss and others during a Hammondsport stop in the fall of 1909, Herman mentioned that he knew a lawyer in Detroit, one Oscar M. Springer, who was a specialist in such matters. Nothing indicates that he was encouraged to do so, but in a brief time the salesman was back in town with Springer in tow. Curtiss afterward recalled having talked with such a person, but said he promptly dismissed him. Springer then sent a bill. "We objected to the payment of the bill upon the ground we did not order the services to be rendered, and that we did not engage him to render the services." Later on, the company sent Springer a token payment to be rid of him. But the bankruptcy idea continued to buzz around like a bluebottle fly.

Jerome Fanciulli volunteered to consult a corporation attorney in New York whom he claimed as a personal friend. This was Ormsby McHarg, who had briefly been Assistant Secretary of Commerce and Labor in the Taft administration. According to Fanciulli: "Mr. Curtiss and I discussed the matter of eliminating Mr. Herring, and went to see Judge Wheeler in Bath." They told him that Fanciulli knew a lawyer in New York who could "possibly handle the thing." Wheeler said he was agreeable to asking McHarg's advice, but "didn't wish to personally mix in it." Fanciulli went to New York, where McHarg supposedly told him that "if the company could be shown to be bankrupt, that was the clearest and quickest way to get rid of Mr. Herring."

Fanciulli's story was related in the form of testimony from a witness stand years later, and his credibility was called into question when it was shown that he and Curtiss since had a serious falling-out over money matters, in which Curtiss discharged him. Nonetheless, Curtiss confirmed that he and Fanciulli "had several conversations on the question of what could be done for the purpose of relieving the situation"; and also that Fanciulli did go to see McHarg: "As I recall the matter, Mr. McHarg recommended that we take action against Herring."

At all events, the company's condition slipped from bad to worse, and its credit drooped correspondingly. The Bank of Hammondsport was its main banking repository, and that bank's readiness to lend "up to the legal limit" had indicated its past confidence in the company; now the bank was a creditor "to a very considerable amount." As it happened, Wheeler was one of the bank's directors and also its legal counsel. The bank gradually lost its confidence and began to treat with the company "at arm's length." To quote from a court decision: "Many things which would put a cautious business man upon his guard were apparent, and the bank . . . followed the normal policy adopted by financial institutions toward a shaky customer."

Herring saw how things were drifting, and wrote his lawyer in March that "Bishop has laid down flat"; that "he is working with Curtiss to squeeze me." Hassett circularized the creditors, trying to line them up in Herring's corner by promising that their claims would be fully allowed if they played the game.

One day Curtiss beckoned Martin V. Margeson, a pattern maker who was one of his most trusted employees, to the rear of the plant and confided that "he couldn't do anything with Herring and they would have to put it [the company] in the hands of a receiver." Before this happened, he wanted Margeson to "get out some stuff" and transfer it to a building "down on Pulteney Street." As the machinist told it: "He wanted to get out this stuff and to put up a few machines while they were lying idle." Margeson carried out instructions, presumably with connivance of the entire village, and Captain Baldwin took charge over the Pulteney Street refuge, where planes were turned out at the rate of one a week for a short time.

The Standard Audit Company, of New York, had done the audit of properties and assets at the time of the Herring-Curtiss incorporation and had not yet been paid for the job. Now it fell to the lot of Standard Audit to trigger the downfall of that same company, if unwittingly. During the winter of 1910, it submitted a bill for $1100. The bill remained unpaid and was allowed to go to judgment. To satisfy that judgment, a levy was made against the company's property. At this point, the Bank of Hammondsport strode upon the stage with a claim for $7500, and, joined by two minor Hammondsport creditors, alleged the insolvency of the company and filed a petition of involuntary bankruptcy against it.

This happened on April 1, 1910. The court appointed as receiver Gabriel H. Parkhurst of Bath, brother of a former judge whom he had served as clerk. Parkhurst took de facto possession of the factory, the properties, and assets. One of his first acts was to notify both Curtiss and Herring that their services were no longer needed, and that their salaries ceased as of that date.

Curtiss vowed that no creditors would lose money by the bankruptcy, and that he would reimburse all stockholders of the former G. H. Curtiss Manufacturing Company whose stock had been converted to Herring-Curtiss shares, with 6 percent interest. The day after the filing of the petition he began mailing form letters to customers, of which this one to an Iowa dealer will serve as an example.

Dear Sir:—

Within the past few months you have no doubt heard more or less about the suit of the Wright Brothers against the Herring-Curtiss Company and perhaps you have also heard something of the internal troubles of the Herring-Curtiss Company.

Inasmuch as the Herring-Curtiss Company is owing you for deposits on orders placed with them, I feel that you are entitled to some statement in regard to the financial and other affairs of the company and the cause or causes that have brought us to the present state of embarrassment.

It is generally known to motorcycle manufacturers and dealers who supply such manufacturers that a heavy investment in material and parts is necessary during the late fall and winter months in order to have worked up ready for spring delivery. This heavy investment necessitates the borrowing of large sums of money to tide over the fall and winter months.

However the New York parties who came into the Herring-Curtiss Company and took over the G. H. Curtiss Manufacturing Company (perhaps not fully realizing the necessity of making heavy loans to provide materials to be worked during the winter months) secured a court order restraining the active management from borrowing money.

Then about the same time the Wright Brothers injunction was filed against the Herring-Curtiss Company and the issuing of both injunctions was published, broadcast, and our credit with loaners of substantial sums was gone.

These injunctions were both set aside within a very few days, but this news was not so readily published by the papers and the great damage had been done to us.

Since then we have made a desperate struggle to pull through but I am sorry to say we have been forced into a corner (through a bill contracted by the New York parties) and some of our largest creditors have thought best for the protection of all creditors to face bankruptcy proceedings, which I understand have been started.

Unfortunately this movement on the part of the creditors may delay our deliveries somewhat, but with the cooperation of the credit customers it is possible that our troubles may be cleared up within a short time and deliveries made without much delay through the parties who buy in the business at the bankrupt sale, providing the creditors vote for this plan.

I wish to take this opportunity to personally thank creditors for the favors they have extended in the past and will say that I believe the assets of the company are sufficient, if properly handled by a trustee who is familiar with the motorcycle business, to pay creditors almost in full.

I regret very much the necessity of writing a letter of this kind and wish to assure you that personally I will do anything that lies within my power to hasten the delivery of machines or parts that may be ordered by you.

Very truly yours,

G. H. CURTISS, Manager.

A month later, the Hammondsport *Herald* noted: "There is no material change in the affairs of the Herring-Curtiss Works. An application has been made to the courts for permission to go ahead with the manufacture of motorcycles and fill orders on hand which will assure the plant being kept in operation while the various differences in connection with the bankruptcy and other proceedings are pending."

At the time when that rather somber report appeared, Curtiss was deeply immersed in preparing for another flying exploit which would restore his luster a thousandfold.

*   *   *

On the ground of his status as a director, Herring was refused permission to contest the bankruptcy action. Instead, he intervened as a creditor, thus bringing about "a very active and earnest trial" of the insolvency question. He alleged conspiracy, fraud, and even embezzlement in bringing the company to the verge of bankruptcy. On November 23, he appealed once more to Bishop, saying: "The Referee's report is rabidly pro-Curtiss." His motive in carrying on the litigation "single-handed," he insisted, was that "I do not want the stockholders who invested in the Company on my advice to be plundered." Now, he said, he had "collected the evidence that conclusively proves the wrecking of the company was a prearranged conspiracy"; and went on: "I believe that if you understood the true state of affairs you would not stand idly by to be eventually branded with stigma of having been a passive party to the conspiracy, as having failed to lift a hand to help set things right. You are interested, I know, in seeing fair play." He asked Bishop for a loan of $16,000 with which to buy up enough creditors' claims to elect the trustee in bankruptcy; promising, after such election, to pay him back $32,000 on the investments by him and his brother. Bishop did not sally to the rescue.

A decree in bankruptcy was issued on December 2, 1910, confirmed by the U. S. District Court at Buffalo. The company listed nominal assets of $60,906.42, liabilities of $93,527.54. The receiver, Gabriel Parkhurst, was thereupon appointed as trustee in bankruptcy.

Contrary to Herring's charges, the master in bankruptcy declared his finding that the insolvency was not induced by "fraud or conspiracy"; and summed up what, in his estimation, were its causes:

1. Overcapitalization and lack of working capital. 2. The Wright suit; that is to say, the resultant publicity, loss of credit, and necessity of guarantees to purchasers against damages. 3. The action by Herring charging fraud and embezzlement, with its consequent unfavorable publicity. 4. Delay and inability to complete the Model G motors, owing to litigation and loss of credit. 5. The impossibility of borrowing money.

Thus was Herring exorcized. Although Curtiss had no plant in which to operate, he lost no time in forming a new company. On the day following the decree, the Curtiss Aeroplane Company was registered with the State Department at Albany, its directors being Glenn H. Curtiss, Lena P. Curtiss, and G. Ray Hall. Its purpose was stated to be "for manufacture, lease and sale of aeroplanes, and such other business as can be lawfully transacted." Capital stock was $20,000, in 200 common shares at $100 par value. Curtiss took 195 shares, his wife one share, Hall one share, and Wheeler the balance. It is worthy of notice that the stock was tightly held by the select Hammondsport group, and that the amount of working capital specified with which to commence operating was only $1000.

Production had been steadily decreasing under the receivership, men being laid off, and other businesses in the village suffering commensurately. By year's end, the factory on the hillside was shut

down entirely, and some one hundred men were out of work. Specialized
mechanics left town to accept employment elsewhere. A pall of gloom
settled over Pleasant Valley and the very name of Herring was anathema
to the community.

❂   ❂   ❂

The trustee in bankruptcy advertised a public auction of the
Herring-Curtiss property and assets for January 14, 1911. At the request
of Herring's attorney, who indicated that his client proposed making
a bid but required time to raise money, that date was twice postponed.
Herring utilized the grace period in mailing a circular letter to all
creditors, telling them "it is not probable that when the assets of the
company are sold by the Trustee, it will bring a sufficient price to
pay more than a very small percentage of the face value of the
claims." He offered them 30 percent of their claims, secured by notes,
for their help to bid in the property himself. As a would-be clincher,
he reminded them that "the plant is poorly located, being at the end
of a small town."

Creditors did not rise to the bait, with the result that no bid
was heard from Herring when the trustee's sale took place on February 11. Curtiss was at this time in San Diego, where he had established winter flying operations, leaving his interests in Wheeler's hands.
Wheeler aimed to hold the bid at the "lowest possible figure" and
yet make sure it was adequate to cover a $15,000 purchase-money
mortgage Curtiss held on the real property. In the absence of other
bidding, the auctioneer's gavel fell at Wheeler's bid of $18,418. A
stranger, Charles Marvin, spoke up to brand this as "a grossly inadequate price," and demanded a resale, offering a bond to guarantee
a larger bid. Marvin refused to say whom he represented, but he
proved to be an attorney sent by Herring. The trustee granted a
second auction, with the understanding that the Curtiss mortgage be
paid out of the proceeds, and set the new date for March 4. When
the sale was not confirmed, "There were many anxious people in Hammondsport," the local weekly observed.

Bidding was "quite animated" in the second auction, attended by
the Herring attorney who evidently was not authorized to bid beyond
$25,000. The property was knocked down for $25,100 to Reuben R.
Lyon, acting as agent for Wheeler and Curtiss. Marvin again demanded
that the sale be set aside and another auction be held, advancing

a technical claim that the Curtiss mortgage could not legally be paid in full out of the proceeds, but should be paid pro rata with the other unsecured debts. To erase any lingering doubts, the trustee ordered still a third sale.

At this juncture, the Hammondsport *Herald* fulminated: "There must be a stopping place somewhere in the law which even Herring will be obliged to observe . . . Herring may be the millionaire that he was first reported to be, or he may be one of those who can hide behind the 'blessed be nothing' theory. Nobody here knows much more about him than when he first came here, except that as an obstructionist he is king."

In the third auction, conducted April 15, the Curtiss agent once more entered his bid of $25,100, which nobody topped. The sale was confirmed, and no further protest was raised about the price being "inadequate."

The wheel of fortune turned and Curtiss was back in undisputed possession of his "shop" and his cherished Castle Hill. The fledgling Curtiss Aeroplane Company had a roof over its head, at least, and the economy of Hammondsport showed fresh signs of life.

At the State Department in Albany on December 12, 1911, was incorporated the Curtiss Motor Company, Inc., for the manufacture, sale, or lease of motors, motorcycles, "other self-propelling or horseless motors"; also engines for use in "aeroplanes and hydroaeroplanes." Capital stock in this case was $600,000, of which Curtiss retained half for himself. Officers were: president and general manager, G. H. Curtiss; vice-president, Monroe Wheeler; secretary and treasurer, G. Ray Hall. The board of directors consisted of Wheeler, Hall, Fanciulli, Philip B. Sawyer of Elmira, and Samuel D. French of Bath.

With this dawning of a new day, Curtiss redeemed his pledge to see that creditors were reimbursed and the shares of his original stockholders restored with interest. At the same time, he rewarded four associates who had stuck loyally by him through the struggle. He made an outright gift of 100 shares each of preferred stock in the Curtiss Motor Company to Monroe Wheeler, Ray Hall, Harry Genung, and Henry Kleckler. When asked in future about this burst of generosity, as if there had been something underhanded about it, he said that these men had already paid for it "in the nature of their services." Each recipient profited handsomely on that stock. (He also presented 600 shares of the stock to Lena Curtiss.)

It cannot escape notice that Curtiss omitted the Herring group of investors from his largess. That is, he apparently never reimbursed the two Bishop brothers and James Deering for their losses in the bankrupt company. If one looks around for reasons, let him remember that Bishop made an emphatic point from the outset that he would not supply any funds to help oppose the suit of the Wright brothers. He had not been asked to do so.

About a year after the property auction, another sale was advertised to clean up some odds and ends of paper assets. Herring, the Bishops, and a few remaining creditors were duly notified of this, but none thought enough of these leftovers to put in an appearance. With no competition, Wheeler obtained them with a bid of $10 for the accounts and $5 for everything else. Among the "everything else" was the document attesting Curtiss as the owner of a one-fifth share in the patent of the Aerial Experiment Association, and this was stored away in Wheeler's safe at Bath, and virtually forgotten. Although the patent by now had been allowed, it was being contested.

As Herring's stock fell valueless in the bankruptcy, the suit to force its surrender or cancellation was never brought to trial. Nor did anyone bother to formally get the Herring-Curtiss Company dissolved. While Herring subsided into quiescence, Curtiss had yet to hear the last of him—much to his sorrow.

16. Return to the River

Halley's comet, one of the brightest of celestial wanderers visible to the naked eye, comes around but once in seventy-six years, and is the first comet whose return ever was accurately predicted. The last previous time it had been glimpsed by earthlings was in 1835. Halley's comet put on a dazzling show with its recurrence in May 1910, although people had to get up in the small hours to see it, or stay up. There was probably no connection, but King Edward VII, monarch of Great Britain, died that same month, and King George V ascended the throne.

In New York City, the roofs of hotels and apartment houses were crowded nightly with "comet parties," with express elevators running to the top. At the Hotel Gotham, a man hired an orchestra and was host to a "comet breakfast" on the roof. Newspapers printed timetables of its rising. Guests checking into hotels fought for rooms whose windows commanded a view of the comet, and left calls for 3 A.M. if they decided to catch some sleep. A Wall Street broker chartered a balloon to get a closer look. A rumor circulated that the comet's tail would brush the earth on May 18, and that this cosmic accident would encompass the end of the world. At least one New York suicide was ascribed to worry over the impending fate, and another person went insane. The 18th came and went, and nobody felt a tremor.

New Yorkers fully expected, before that summer was far advanced, to see airplanes winging along their Hudson waterfront in competition for the *World's* $10,000 prize. A temptation of such magnitude would hardly be allowed to dangle for another season. Halley's comet had drawn millions to rooftops, so that the best vantage points from which to watch for flying machines were well staked out.

In stretching the offer for a New York–Albany flight, after the dirigibles of Baldwin and Tomlinson failed, the *World* modified the rules. As the conditions now stood, the award would go to "the first person who makes the Fulton Flight" on or before October 10, 1910, in a machine either lighter or heavier than air; the trip to be completed within 24 consecutive hours. Two very significant changes had been made. Instead of starting from New York and flying north to Albany, the pilot had his choice of either direction. More importantly, he would be allowed two landings en route.

The Army was amenable to having the sandy field on Governors Island used as the southern terminus, and the airplane "sheds" of the Hudson-Fulton Celebration were yet intact. Presumably, Van Rensselaer Island, scouted the year before by the Aero Club committee, was still available at the Albany end. Any intermediate landing fields would be up to the flyer. The distance was reckoned at 152 miles, and its traversing would amount to an American cross-country record. The world's distance record had just been hung up in England by Louis Paulhan, winning Lord Northcliffe's $50,000 prize for the London-to-Manchester flight, 186 miles. Paulhan made it a two-day jaunt, April 27–28, stopping overnight at Lichfield. He followed the tracks of the London & North Western Railway, and was accompanied by a special train which, by spells, he raced. Lord Northcliffe was no piker when it came to aerial prizes. Three years after this, he offered a like sum, £10,000, for a crossing of the Atlantic, and that was ultimately collected in 1919.

*   *   *

Almost certainly, Glenn Curtiss began contemplating a whack at the Hudson River prize as soon as he knew that the *World* had extended its period for another year. Harry Genung was authority for the statement that the flub at Governors Island continued to rankle in his mind; that he deeply resented the imputation that he had not even seriously tried to give the metropolis a decent flight during that bad week. For him, the whole New York episode stood as unfinished business. A better way of vindicating himself could hardly be imagined than a flight between New York and Albany; the $10,000 prize money might be considered a secondary purpose, as far as he was concerned. An additional motive was the fact that, if he succeeded, he would probably knock off the third leg on the Scientific American Trophy at the same time, giving him its permanent possession; it was hardly likely that anyone else would exceed his distance before the end of the year.

Sometime in the 1910 winter the Hudson River flight became an earnest topic of family discussion in the house on Castle Hill. The Genungs, Harry and Martha, were still residing in the Curtiss house, and they took part in these debates. At first, Lena Curtiss argued against the project on the score that it would be too dangerous if he had to make an emergency landing in the river. Glenn and Lena were a well-mated couple, and she was not prone to tossing emotional stumbling-blocks in the way of her husband's admittedly risky flying career. Hence it was an unusual thing to hear her voicing objections, but she probably helped to crystallize his thinking on flotation gear as a precaution. Instead of a hazard, he viewed the stream as a relatively safe place to come down, provided the plane could remain afloat for a reasonable length of time. River traffic was sufficient so that help could quickly reach him, and besides he was a strong swimmer. Thus reassured, Lena gave in.

Curtiss confided the scheme to his two best mechanics, Henry Kleckler and Damon Merrill, who quietly began work on an airplane for the purpose. Top security prevailed for more reasons than one. Curtiss knew full well that other airmen would be hot after the *World* prize that summer, and therefore he did not wish his intention to leak out until the latest possible moment. The Herring mess was coming rapidly to a head, and it would be disastrous for Herring to get wind of what was going on. As the receivership went into effect in April, the machine was assembled in the makeshift Pulteney Street building.

The prime essential was a capable 8-cylindered motor, and this one was a marked improvement over that which went to France. In fact, it could, if pressed, really deliver the 50-horsepower wallop at which it was rated, making it the most potent engine Curtiss had yet produced. The airframe was a larger model of the Rheims racer, with 8 feet more of wing span. The same biplaned front elevator jutted

ahead on bamboo outriggers, and, like the midwing ailerons, was a
trifle bigger. The wing fabric was rubberized silk, like that of the
Silver Dart, which went slack in wet weather and tightened in the
sun. The usual shoulder yoke moved the ailerons, the wheel took
care of rudder and elevator, while the pilot's feet were occupied with
throttle and ignition. The seat was hardly more than a plank at the
leading edge of the wing.

The flotation gear consisted of two airtight metal cylinders slung
beneath the wings, and five inflated air bags of Baldwin's balloon
cloth sewed together in series on a "planing board" which ran lengthwise of the center, just off ground. The board curved upward at the
front as a "hydro-surface." As Curtiss said: "That was really the first
amphibian plane"; the seaplane and flying boat were its lineal descendants. As soon as she could fly, he took her over Keuka Lake and
cautiously came down in the shallows near shore. She landed satisfactorily, floated, but was not constructed for even a try at a water takeoff.

So far, so good, but Curtiss was bent upon giving this aircraft plenty
of advance workout. To that end, he took her south the second week
in April for a series of exhibition flights in concert with Charles Hamilton, Charles Willard, and a new recruit to the team, J. C. (Bud) Mars.
At Memphis, the plane proved its mettle with a fresh world's record
for quick getaway, at 5⅘ seconds; the record Curtiss broke was his
own, 6⅘ seconds, made in January at Los Angeles with the Rheims
racer.

Rejoicing that the machine built for the "Fulton Flight" seemed
another winner, Curtiss now surrendered to his wife's coaxing and took
her up for a spin, her first and only flight in an early plane. She had
now adopted the habit of accompanying him on exhibition forays.
About the Memphis adventure, Lena said: "I enjoyed that immensely.
I wasn't one particle afraid. But Mr. Curtiss does not like to take
passengers. I never urged him to take me again."

Bud Mars, destined to be a luminary as "The Curtiss Daredevil,"
made his public debut at the Memphis meet and promptly distinguished
himself by equaling the quick-start record of his preceptor. Then he
undistinguished himself with a plunge to the infield, landing on a
parked touring car in which were sitting two women and three children.
Luckily the top was up and nobody was much hurt.

From Tennessee, the crew moved on to San Antonio's annual
spring carnival. There they were joined by Captain Baldwin, who
came to baptize his own first plane, the *Red Devil,* built with variations

on the Curtiss pattern. The *Red Devil* performed so well that Baldwin took up airplane showmanship in preference to ballooning. Persistent wind put a crimp in the Texas exhibitions, but Curtiss again lowered his record by getting into the air from a standing start in 5½ seconds.

             ❋   ❋   ❋

Back in Hammondsport, arrangements were seriously begun for the Hudson River enterprise. An inquiry to the U. S. Weather Bureau brought information that winds in the valley were prevailingly from the northwest, and this firmed up the decision to make the flight southward. Curtiss already leaned that way from the sensible view that, with engine trouble more apt to hit soon after takeoff, he would have a choice of open fields at the Albany end.

Doubtless he had heard from Baldwin about the flat platter of Van Rensselaer Island at the south edge of Albany. No move was made to engage its use in advance, as that would have tipped his hand. Better to wait and trust to luck that the farmer would be agreeable. Van Rensselaer Island was a weedy patch of flood plain just outside the city limits; hardly an island at all, separated from the mainland only by a narrow moat called Island Creek. Spring freshets had caused the first Dutch fur traders to abandon it as a post. Now its river side was shielded by dikes, behind which stood a pumphouse and storage tanks of the Standard Oil Company. The rest made fertile soil for truck-garden crops.

On Saturday evening, May 21, his birthday, Curtiss gave the plane a last-minute workout from the field he had developed on the Kingsley Flats. Sunday it was dismantled and packed into its long wooden traveling cases.

The Curtiss party slipped unobtrusively into Albany on Monday, the 23rd, and registered at the Hotel Ten Eyck. Accompanying Glenn and Lena were Jerome Fanciulli, his wife, and three mechanics—Henry Kleckler, Clarence White, and Elmer Robinson. The first order of business was rental of the field. A run to the island disclosed a plot of meadow adjacent to patches of onions, potatoes, corn, and rye. The owner, a man of German extraction, demanded $100 for a few days' lease of the grassland, but let himself be cajoled down to $5. (This minor deal determined the location of one of the earliest municipal airports in the United States.) A tent was raised and the mechanics unpacked the boxes.

That night Curtiss wired the Aero Club that he was going for the prize, then mailed a letter of formal notification to the New York *World*, saying he intended to start from Albany on Thursday morning, the 26th. "For over a year," he wrote, "I have made exhaustive experiments with the object of perfecting a machine that would start from and alight on the water. It was my intention to give such a machine its first practical test by attempting to fly from Albany to New York over the Hudson River, with the hope of obtaining the *World's* most commendable Hudson-Fulton prize.

"While my experiments have proved very successful, they have not been completed. It is my belief that the incentive offered by the *World* to aviators and experimenters has been responsible for considerable activity similar to that in my own case.

"If I should be successful in winning your prize, I would have only one regret; that is, that there would be no further inducement for other aviators to make the same flight."

The Aero Club snapped into action, designating Jacob L. Ten Eyck as official starter. Ten Eyck, a real estate and insurance man, descendant of early Dutch aristocracy, was president of the newly founded Aero Club of Albany. The next day's headlines started a ferment up and down the Hudson valley. Albany newspapers awakened to what was transpiring under their noses and sent reporters scurrying to the South End.

Having put Kleckler and his aides to work assembling the plane, Curtiss took passage Tuesday morning on the Hudson River dayboat, *Albany*, for New York. Methodical as always, he did this for a careful study of the route, especially to gather as much as he could about the air currents. He was accompanied on the pleasant cruise by Lena and the Fanciulli couple. The sidewheeler was not far downstream when Curtiss accosted the first mate with questions about weather and winds, explaining that he proposed flying down the river. The mate led him to the skipper, saying: "Captain, this is Mr. Curtiss, the flying machine man. That's all I know."—in a tone as if to disclaim all responsibility for what might ensue.

The captain courteously invited the foursome to ride in the pilot-house, the better to scan the country. He advised that the trickiest winds were likely to be encountered past the southern Catskills, through the gorge of the Hudson Highlands, and in the vicinity of Peekskill. The only bridge as yet crossing the Hudson between Albany and New York was the Mid-Hudson at Poughkeepsie, a suspension span

212 feet above the water. As the vessel neared it, Curtiss debated with his party whether to pass over or under the bridge. "Then it seemed really to dawn upon the captain for the first time," he recalled, "that I was actually going to fly down the river in an aeroplane. Thereafter his answers were vague and given without interest." Still, the captain was not too skeptical to wish him a safe trip as they debarked at New York, with a promise to blast his whistle if the plane should pass above his boat.

Overnight in the city, the airman conferred with officers of the Aero Club and was glad to hear that his old friend, Augustus Post, would accompany him back to Albany as the club's observer. On Wednesday, they bought railroad tickets for a stopover at Poughkeepsie to reconnoiter a landing place. There was no thought of a nonstop flight; not so much because it was an impossibility, as to avoid the weight of a full fuel load. Besides, it was an unwise chance to take. Poughkeepsie was chosen as the approximate midpoint. Curtiss kept in mind for possible alternates the parade ground at West Point and the drill field of the New York National Guard camp at Peekskill.

A car took them around Poughkeepsie, and the first prospect examined was the campus of Vassar College; it was dismissed as having too many trees. The search progressed to a farm some three miles south of Poughkeepsie, where a large grassy field was found on the hillslope overlooking the river. The area was commonly known as Camelot, although that name, strictly speaking, applied only to a small hamlet and railroad depot at the foot of the hill.[1] The owner of the land, W. F. Gill, was not only willing to permit a landing there—he was "peacock proud" to have his acres selected for such an honor. More, he volunteered to set up a pole with a red flag. By the oddest of coincidences, Gill's place was named Stony Brook Farm. Before leaving, Curtiss spotted another landmark, a short pier jutting into the river below.

Alighting from the train in Albany late that evening, they were greeted by a crashing thunderstorm which afforded Curtiss a handy alibi for announcing cancellation of the Thursday morning start. A hasty check with Kleckler informed him that the airplane was not ready.

The New York *World* launched a publicity buildup for the flight which its prize had fostered, and opened an "aeronautical booth" in the corridor of the Pulitzer Building, displaying airplane models and photographs. Then the rival *Times* moved in and pirated part of the *World's* show. The *Times* chartered a special train on the New York

Central to pace the flight, to carry Mrs. Curtiss and her friends, and to keep that paper's reporters and cameraman abreast of the plane. The *World* could not match such coverage as that. While the charter called only for a fast locomotive and one coach, the railroad added two more coaches and a baggage car for ballast. The train took its position on a siding at the Albany station and kept steam up.

The capital city was having its induction into the air age and its populace was duly responsive. As Curtiss's predilection for early morning flying was well known, crowds began gathering at the island right after dawn. A local paper observed that "comet parties" in Albany gave way to "sunrise aeroplane parties." Automobile loads of people converged from a wide radius, as far away as western Massachusetts, and a few families raised tents and camped on the fringes of the field. Hotels were jammed, and the lobby of the Ten Eyck milled with members of the State Legislature, just winding up a session but lingering for a glimpse of the noted birdman.

The Mayor of Albany, James B. McEwan, dictated a letter to Mayor William J. Gaynor of New York, which he requested Curtiss to carry in his pocket and deliver after his arrival. The letter said:

"On the occasion of the first long flight by aeroplane in this country, I take the opportunity of sending Your Honor greetings and good wishes.

"The great flight, if accomplished, as I hope, will be historic. It is possible, too, that it is but the forerunner of what may in the not too distant future be a commonplace occurrence.

"The speed of this new instrument of locomotion seems to fit it admirably for many purposes of service to humanity, especially in the way of rapid communication. So far, however, no letter has yet been carried by this new means, and I am glad that these greetings between us should be the first."

In other words, Mayor McEwan was heralding the birth of airmail.

*   *   *

Curtiss realized that he had blundered in announcing his start for the 26th; a postponement at the very outset automatically invited comparison with Governors Island. To make matters worse, Thursday turned out to be a beautiful day for flying. Jacob Ten Eyck appeared in the morning at the hotel named for his forebears and drove Curtiss and Post to the island. Clearly, the machine would not be shipshape before late afternoon. The flotation devices had yet to be attached.

Curtiss spent the day coddling the engine and tightening every nut and turnbuckle, painting them with coats of shellac as insurance against their jarring loose. At least the inquisitive public, roaming about, enjoyed a full day of inspecting an airplane at close range and observing its pilot at work. Whenever the propeller whirled, straw hats flew all over the lot.

Everyone noticed the red-and-white enameled trinket which the aviator wore pinned to the visor of his cap. A propeller in its design bisected a circular scroll bearing the words "International School of Aeronautics." When newsmen queried him about it, he said: "I wouldn't part with that pin for all the world." In fact, he was to wear it as a lucky charm throughout his exhibition career. It had been given him while flying the *Gold Bug* at Hempstead Plains, by Lieutenant Anthony Triaca, lately of the Italian Army, who was optimistically founding a flying school at Mineola. Triaca appointed Curtiss a "professor" in the short-lived school.

A liaison was arranged with the Weather Bureau at Albany, and Curtiss and Post went to its office for a personal talk with the meteorologist. The forecast was promising, so that a takeoff was scheduled for Friday morning early. A message went to a Poughkeepsie garage to have a supply of gasoline and oil waiting at the Camelot meadow. Curtiss left a pre-dawn call, and hundreds of Albany citizens woke up sleepy-eyed to be in time at the island.

It was a false alarm. The morning was gusty, and wind was the bugbear of all cautious flyers. Curtiss peeled his jacket and spent the forenoon tinkering with his plane, while onlookers grew restless and Mrs. Curtiss sat waiting, with a few other women, on the packing cases in the tent. At 11 A.M., Post and Fanciulli drove off to find a telephone and check the Weather Bureau. Back they came with a favorable prognosis which they had barely delivered when a gust struck so fiercely that it knocked down two tent poles. Several times later during the day the machine was wheeled out when a freakish puff convinced the airman it was no go. Reporters began dropping sly remarks about Governors Island. Curtiss gave them a lecture:

"Some day the laymen will learn enough of the air game to allow us our leisure in preparing without growing impatient. They don't understand what there is to do, and how tedious and long the task becomes. But if some of them had spent hours planning every precaution they could conceive of, and then in a trial flight had found that they failed totally because some little, insignificant thing they had overlooked went wrong, they would see the need for fussing away as we have day after day in making ready.

"An aeroplane is like a monster violin. It is a work of art, yet not a standardized commercial product. Everything has to be built by hand and adjusted to its duty in the mechanism, and then the whole thing has to be tuned up to work in harmony. It is just a monster instrument of wires and spruce wood braces and bamboo and steel framework . . .

"Of course I have never undergone the strain of so long a flight as I am now called upon to make. It takes both hands and my body all the time to operate the machine, and there is no such thing as taking leisure aloft for such a task, for instance, as putting on a pair of gloves. One can't handle the craft even on the smoothest gliding with a single hand."

Dr. William Greene of Rochester, a balloonist, who claimed to have a self-designed airplane nearly completed to enter for the prize, appeared at the grounds. He had just ridden a steamboat up the river to survey the route. "Hello, old man," a cynical reporter greeted him, "are you up here to get some free advertising, too?" Greene had been a member of the Aeronautic Society when it purchased the *Golden Flier*.

Other aspirants for the $10,000 were making noises. Clifford Harmon, who had imported a Farman biplane and was flying it at Mineola, said he would try for the prize if it were unclaimed within a week. To this threat Curtiss riposted that it was "no job for an amateur." An expatriate Belgian, Romaine Berger, living at Hempstead, was constructing a large monoplane, and he proclaimed: "I'll not only fly to Albany from New York, but I will make the round trip without once coming to ground."

Meanwhile, Charley Hamilton had wirelessed ahead from a ship at sea that he was en route to New York, bringing the Rheims racer, with the intent of going after the prize if Curtiss failed. He had been doing exhibition flights in Florida. Curtiss then explained that he had sent for Hamilton: "I fully realize that this is one of the hardest aerial propositions it is possible to conceive. If I go down in the water, I want another machine to take up the job at once." He wished to make doubly certain the prize would be taken by a Curtiss plane.

Docking at week's end, Hamilton put in a call to Curtiss saying he needed a fresh propeller. Curtiss telephoned Hammondsport to ship him one immediately. Hamilton talked freely to the press, declaring:

"Curtiss does not like to fly in a wind, but I prefer it to calm. If he waits until it is calm at Albany, he will find a wind at this end. It is never calm at both ends of the Hudson Valley at the same time." Should Curtiss fail, he pledged a takeoff for a nonstop flight from Governors Island the following Tuesday.

Having disappointed watchers all day Friday, Curtiss went up in the twilight calm to reward them. A downdraft plummeted him very near to a crash, but he pulled out in time and regained enough altitude for a fair, if hasty, landing. After a late check with the Weather Bureau, he then announced a sunrise start for Saturday morning, left a call at the hotel desk for 3:15 A.M., and instructed Kleckler to have the plane out of the tent and ready to travel by 5 o'clock. Once again many Albanians curtailed their slumber. Between the comet and Curtiss, a lot of sleep was being lost.

So certain was he of a takeoff that Lena Curtiss, others of the official party, and the *Times* staffers went direct from breakfast to the train, which crossed the river and proceeded to the rendezvous point. The main line of the Central to New York hugs the east shore of the river, and the impromptu airfield was on the west side. As plane and train were to start neck-and-neck, and since trees intervened, signals were prearranged. When the locomotive was halted opposite, it was to give three toots of its whistle. The plane's motor would then be cranked, and when it was set for takeoff a white flag would be waved to the engineer from the roof of the Standard Oil warehouse. The special train was given right-of-way on the main southbound track; even crack express trains, if overtaken, were to be sidetracked while it passed.

On this Saturday morning, the locomotive shrilled its whistle. The pilot was on his seat by 5:30, in his "uniform" whose most striking item was a pair of fisherman's rubber-boot waders with tops that pulled up to the armpits. Curtiss had adopted this outfit, not in expectation of wading, but for warmth: "I had found them the best sort of flying suit available." A cork lifejacket was strapped around his midriff. The whistle blew, the propeller was flipped, the engine spoke. But the white flag was not waved from the roof. At the exact wrong moment, a flurry of wind sent whitecaps scudding across the river and the pilot cut the switch. The train backtracked to the Rensselaer switchyard and marked time.

About this time the German farmer, whose ire had been rising as unbidden guests trampled his potatoes and onions, came striding forth with a bullwhip in hand and hailed Curtiss: "You lit in my rye field in that trip you made last night, and you've got to pay the damages." A touch of diplomacy, larded with the promise that his manager would reimburse him amply, mollified the man so that he joined the watchers and forgot his crops.

The hour of 8:00 A.M. was set for the delayed start. Again the train chuffed down the track and whistled. Fanciulli had gone off for a final telephone checkup on weather. He came back with news that a strong wind was working its way up the valley, and this caused a second postponement. At one point, Curtiss "threw himself on the grass in despair at the waste of time." By midforenoon word arrived that all was well in the lower valley, but a twenty-mile wind had sprung up by then at Albany. The airman was heard to say disconsolately: "I've made another mistake. If I had started an hour ago this wind wouldn't have hurt me. Now I can't get up." The day was a washout, and the Curtiss group settled for a tour of the State Capitol.

An atmosphere of disenchantment prevailed, especially downriver where conditions were now ideal. Newspapers spoke of his "wasting golden opportunities" and adding "two more false starts to his record." A Poughkeepsie paper did not hide its disgust: "Curtiss gives us a pain in the neck. All those who are waiting to see him go down the river are wasting their time." Even the New York *Times* wondered if its chartered train was worth the money, and observed: "The fact seems to be that the Hammondsport aviator, after his three days of waiting, is beginning to lose faith in the feasibility of the undertaking."

The chief protagonist himself was "getting as tired of waiting as everyone else," and recollected: "The delay had got somewhat on my nerves and I had determined to make a start [on Sunday] if there was half a chance." The Weather Bureau was highly encouraging, and once more there was the scenario of an announcement, a predawn call left at the desk, orders to mechanics to have the plane ready by sunrise, a telegram to the Poughkeepsie garage. He thought: "It's now or never."

❀   ❀   ❀

Sunday, May 29, 1910. "Sunday always was my lucky day," he had said before.

Piling out of bed at the call, Curtiss drove to the island, sampled the still air, saw a clear sky, and hastened back to the hotel where he phoned the Poughkeepsie police station. "How's the weather down there?"

"Fine," came the reply. "There isn't enough breeze to flap the flag against the Court House pole."

"That's good enough. I'm Glenn Curtiss, and you can say that I have decided to leave Albany right away."

After a hasty breakfast, Lena went straight to the train, with the Fanciullis, Augustus Post, Henry Kleckler, and the *Times* reporter and photographer. (The reactions of newsmen covering the story without benefit of train are mercifully unrecorded.) Two railroad officials rode along, one the division superintendent. For all its four coaches, the train carried only nine passengers, exclusive of crew. With a cleared track ahead, it was assigned the time of the Twentieth Century Limited, which ran on ahead.

No more than one hundred spectators were on hand for the genuine thing when it came. Presumably the transients had run out of patience and the local denizens had heard the wolf cry too many times. Jacob Ten Eyck again drove Curtiss to the field to serve his function as starter. Final preparations consumed two hours. Curtiss made certain the mayor's letter was safely tucked in an inside pocket, and a large case-watch in a pocket that was handier. His flying togs, besides the rubber waders and lifebelt, consisted of a brown leather jacket, gloves, soft visored cap worn backward, and heavy motorcycle goggles. For "instruments," he relied on the flutter of a sleeve as speed indicator, sighted across wings at the horizon to gauge balance, and watched smoke from factory stacks for wind direction.

Wheels left ground at 7:02 A.M., and the white flag alerted the engineer of the train. Island Creek being the city boundary, the pilot circled slightly north across it, to formalize the start from Albany. Wires flashed the tidings down the valley. In Poughkeepsie the City Hall bell clamored. In New York, people began to group around bulletin boards of the *World* and the *Times*, and in front of cigar-store windows where progress of the flight was posted. Rooftops of apartment houses on Washington Heights and bordering Riverside Drive were at a premium, while the waterfront parks were overrun.

Adopting an altitude of 700 feet, Curtiss headed down midstream, noticing that he could see deep beneath the surface of the water. "It was a perfect summer day . . . The air was calm and I felt an immense sense of relief . . . The motor sounded like music." For several miles the aircraft and train were invisible to one another because of woodland.

When the train hove into view, he saw heads in the windows, hats and handkerchiefs being waved. He was able to identify Lena when she unfurled a large American flag brought for the purpose. "It was no effort at all to keep up with the train, which was making 50 miles an hour. It was like a real race and I enjoyed the contest more than anything else during the flight." Sometimes the plane was far out ahead, then the train would catch up on a straightaway stretch.

Clusters of human beings appeared on both shores. River traffic was plentiful and Curtiss could see boatmen waving. White puffs of steam from tugboats hauling strings of barges told him that unheard whistles were being blown in salute. Thirty-three minutes after takeoff he passed Hudson where it seemed that every home had emptied itself onto the docks. At 8:20 the Mid-Hudson Bridge loomed ahead, and he elected to fly over instead of under it. The population of Poughkeepsie looked like "swarms of busy ants, running here and there, waving their hats and hands."

To the considerable distress of the clergy, attendance at Pough-keepsie churches fell off sharply that morning. At least one minister, the Reverend William H. Hubbard of the Mill Hill Baptist Church, was so righteously indignant as to chastise his flock and the aviator for "desecrating the Sabbath." In the sermon he preached to the few faithful, he lamented: "It seems strange to me that this man could not have picked out one of the other six days of the week to make his trip . . . Conditions have come to a pretty pass when church members should so far forget themselves as to allow such a spectacle to draw their thoughts away from God and the proper observance of His day."

Soon picking up the pier which was his Camelot landmark, Curtiss veered inland over a stand of trees, sighted the red flag, and bounced to a landing on the only part of the meadow which, as he knew from prior footwork, was free from furrows and ditches. It was 8:26 A.M. Men came running, among them Mr. Gill. The field was no more than 200 feet from the Albany Post Road, and automobiles pulled off the highway to disgorge their occupants. Curtiss glanced around and asked: "Where is the gasoline and oil that was to be left here for me?"

"It isn't here," replied Gill. "I haven't seen it." Apparently the garage proprietor observed the Sabbath.

"Well, that's too bad," Curtiss said, a bit testily. "I'm rather sorry I stopped. I could have gone on to West Point if I'd known that, or perhaps made New York."

Turning to the bystanders, he shouted: "Perhaps some of you

automobile people can let me have a little gasoline—about five gallons."
At least a dozen responded: "Sure we will." He accepted the offerings
of two New Jersey motorists who, from spare cans in their cars,
replenished his tank with eight gallons (he had three gallons left from
Albany). They also provided him with a gallon and a half of oil.

The train pulled off on the Camelot siding, and soon its passengers
came toiling breathlessly up the slope through grass and shrubbery.
Lena delivered a hug and kiss for her intrepid husband. Kleckler
brought pliers, wrench, and screwdriver, with which he rapidly went
over the machine. The only thing he found to fix was a loosened wire.

During this halt an officer telephoned from the West Point Military
Academy urging Curtiss to make a landing on the parade ground
and allow the cadets an examination of his machine. The aviator
responded that he would gladly have accepted had he been sure his
fuel supply would hold out. In reality, he wanted nothing now to
stand between him and a safe landing within the corporate bounds of
New York City.

An ax was brought to chop a few saplings for takeoff clearance.
He awaited a whistle signal from the train when the passengers
were back aboard, and lifted into the air at 9:26 A.M., having been
grounded exactly one hour.

Twenty miles south of Poughkeepsie the river is pinched off into
a steep-sided defile through the range of the Hudson Highlands. The
portals are rugged Storm King Mountain, 1340 feet high, and Breakneck
Ridge. The 15-mile gorge is a funnel for wind currents, and the flyer
was prepared for these without knowing how bad they would be
aloft. Approaching Storm King, he climbed to 2000 feet. Just past the
mountain's crest, the plane abruptly lurched forward, tilting sidewise
at the same time, and lost a good hundred feet in seconds. Caught by
surprise, Curtiss nearly tumbled out. "It was the worst plunge I ever
got in an aeroplane." Moments later the machine was tossed and
buffeted about, almost beyond control. "My heart was in my mouth.
I thought it was all over." By pushing the post forward, he managed
to regain a semblance of control.

The watchers in the train had a clear view of the ordeal which
the fragile craft was undergoing, and Lena was nearly frantic with
anxiety, while the others shouted "Go it, old boy!" and "She's bucking
like a three-year-old!" Afterward Lena said: "The aeroplane swerved
and dipped and for a minute made my heart stand still, for I knew
this to be a point of danger."

Looking back on this cliffhanger from many years in the future, Beckwith Havens, a later Curtiss exhibition flyer, mused: "How the hell he did it I don't know, with that 'long head.' The only way was on the deck or up good and high."

Storm King, Curtiss reminisced, was "the place I first learned that air went up and down as well as sideways." Figuring to find calmer air near the water, he let down to 40 feet and leveled off. Even then a gust tilted the plane so that a wing almost touched water. "I thought for an instant that my trip was about to end, and made a quick mental calculation as to the length of time it would take a boat to reach me after I should drop in the water." After that, the rock ramparts on either hand seemed to provide shelter, and he breathed easier. Soon he was passing over West Point where the cadets were out in full panoply waving uniform caps in greeting. He was struck with how easy it would be to drop explosives on such a fortress. It was 10:02 A.M.

The engine was kept lubricated by means of a hand-operated oil pump. Ordinarily he gave the oil lever a push about every ten minutes. Going through the Highlands he pumped oil until a long blue veil hung out behind "like a comet's tail." Before emerging past Bear Mountain he checked the oil gauge and found it worrisomely low. "I must have been too enthusiastic with the lever," he thought. Not until the trip was over did he discover that there had been a serious oil leak.

Out of the Highlands trough and skimming above the widewater of the Tappan Zee, he relaxed enough to enjoy the spectacle of the Palisades looming up on his right. Further glances at the oil level, however, increased his uneasiness. At last, in the hazy distance, he could make out the Metropolitan Life tower and the Singer Building. But he knew that Manhattan Island is 13.4 miles long, and that Governors Island is a half-mile beyond its southern end. Dared he chance 14 miles more? The prize might be won by landing anywhere inside the city limits.

As the locomotive crossed the municipal boundary below Yonkers, the engineer yanked down his whistle cord and held it until the train turned away from the Hudson into the Harlem River gorge at Spuyten Duyvil. Curtiss peered into that gorge past the rock bluff of Inwood, which is the northern fingertip of Manhattan. Less than a mile back there he could see a smooth patch of green which looked like a lawn on a small plateau. The oil situation by now was such that he decided he must get down somewhere, and the Inwood neighborhood was inside the city. With a wide swing over toward the Palisades to gain a heading into the Harlem notch, he took the gamble.

The late William B. Isham, a leather merchant and financier, had found a rare seat for his estate. A mesa-like outlier of the Inwood marble rises perhaps a hundred feet above the floor of the Harlem River valley, its top slanting toward the Hudson. There, at the eastern eminence of the small hill, Isham built his abode, whence he could look down upon the less fortunate masses of the Bronx. All the westward slope of his private plateau was a landscaped backyard, and it was this which Curtiss had singled out for his emergency landing.[2]

The mansion was occupied by an Isham daughter and her husband, Minturn Post Collins. That morning Mr. Collins was sitting on his veranda perusing the Sunday paper when he distinctly heard the sound of a motor behind the house. He hurried around the corner and saw an airplane, of all things, which had run up the slope of his lawn. The aeronaut was on the ground holding his machine to keep it from rolling backward. Two young men appeared out of nowhere to help him, and blocks were placed under the wheels. Collins had just been reading about the anticipated flight. He held out his hand and said: "I am certainly delighted to be the first to congratulate you on arriving in the city limits, and I am glad you picked our backyard as the place to land. You are great, there's no doubt of that."

"Thank you," replied Curtiss, "but what's worrying me now is oil and gasoline. Have you any that you can spare?"

Collins had gasoline and sent a servant to fetch it. The oil was obtained from a nearby boatyard. Curtiss found a telephone to call the *World* with the news that he had landed within the city and proposed to continue on to Governors Island as soon as possible. While he might have rested on his laurels right where he was and pocketed the prize, there remained an unresolved chord. "I wanted to wheel my craft back into that old aerodrome on Governors Island." The fact that he did so prompted a magazine writer to term it "a magnificent sportsmanlike thing that won him the unbounded admiration of all New York."

Returning to his plane, he found it a magnet for a stampede of people who had transformed the Isham estate into a fairgrounds. A police patrol drove up to preserve order. A rapid survey showed him that he had flown into a kind of cul-de-sac, and that it was going to be a hairy place to get out of. He would need to take off back down the short slope, drop over the side of the butte and pick up speed with the drop, while steering between the two steep rock walls of the Spuyten Duyvil gorge. Engine failure or a downdraft would plunge him, if he was lucky, into the Harlem River. The self-vindication which was his aim made the risk worth taking. If it worked, New Yorkers could never again impugn his courage.

The Inwood landing had been at 10:25. It was 11:42 when he swooped off from the Isham lawn, gathered altitude, and was shortly again over the open Hudson. Automobiles lit out to attempt pacing him along Riverside Drive but could not keep up. From there on, all was bedlam down the tidal estuary whose margins are among the most populous shores in the world. Water craft of all descriptions cut loose with sirens, whistles, bells. Every ferryboat was jammed to the rails. Passengers and crews of ocean liners at their piers crowded to the sterns.

After circling the Statue of Liberty, he came down at Governors Island almost on the stroke of twelve, where the garrison was abroad and cheering. Total flying time had been 2 hours, 51 minutes, for an average speed of 52 mph. The first hand extended to him was that of the new commanding officer of the Department of the East, Major General Frederick Dent Grant, son of President Ulysses S. Grant above whose tomb Curtiss had just flown. A functionary of the *World* elbowed in to take charge, informing him that a check for $10,000 was being drawn.

Meanwhile, the train had pulled into Grand Central Station, whence Lena encountered some delay in reaching Governors Island. Curtiss was halfway to the ferry when he met her hurrying radiantly from it. An affectionate embrace ensued in view of the soldiery. Then the kiss had to be reenacted "ever so many times" (as she said) for the benefit of news photographers.

After luncheon at the Hotel Astor, Curtiss was escorted to the Pulitzer Building, where the *World* generously invited reporters of other papers and wire services to a press conference. Until this moment the airplane which had flown to fame had been anonymous. Curtiss announced that he was christening it, ex post facto, the *Hudson Flyer*.

The $10,000 check was ceremonially handed over by J. Angus Shaw, vice-president and treasurer of the Press Publishing Company. It was the largest award Curtiss ever received for a flight; he later asserted that no other single prize or fee exceeded $5000. He promptly presented the check in his turn to Mrs. Curtiss who, when asked what she would do with it, replied: "I don't know, unless I buy an automobile. It is the only sport I am really fond of."

*   *   *

In his published utterances, Curtiss indicated that two principal ideas had occupied his thoughts during the flight: the potentiality of the airplane for bombing, and the need for landing fields. "All the great battles of the future," he said, "will be fought in the air. I have demonstrated that it is easy to fly over cities and fortifications. It would be perfectly practical to drop enough dynamite or picric acid down on West Point or a city like New York to destroy it utterly . . . Take my word for it, the days for big warships are numbered." At the gratulatory banquet, he said he had been thinking about "the difficulty of finding suitable landing places for the flying machine in or near the great cities"; and suggested that ordinances might soon have to be adopted to remedy this shortcoming.

A third thought which he did not publicly communicate was later placed on record by him. It was during the Albany–New York flight, he revealed, "that I decided to build an aeroplane that would be available for starting or landing on water."

Thanks to its chartered train, the *Times* was able to give a far more flamboyant spread to the story than the sponsoring *World*. The cameraman had snapped photos like mad from the baggage-car window while someone held him from behind, and these were splashed over eight pages. Editorially, the *Times* avowed that this flight had been "needed to complete the poetic harmonies of Hudson-Fulton Celebration Week."

The following Tuesday night, the *World* was host to a full-dress banquet in Curtiss's honor. The aviator was flanked on the dais by such personages as John Jacob Astor, Hudson Maxim, Don C. Seitz, business manager of the *World*, and Adolph S. Ochs, publisher of the *Times*. He took this occasion to deliver the letter from the Mayor of Albany to the Mayor of New York. In accepting it, Mayor Gaynor remarked that some might think it strange a little town like Hammondsport could produce a man like Curtiss, but the reason was that people in Hammondsport had "more time to think" than New Yorkers. Then he added: "Mr. Curtiss's memorable flight has demonstrated the possibilities of intercity communication by aeroplane."

As a climax to the dinner program, Don Seitz announced that the *World*, in unison with its sister newspaper, the St. Louis *Post-Dispatch*, was offering a new prize: $30,000 for a flight between New York and St. Louis, either way, to be accomplished at any time from August 15, 1910, to January 1, 1911.

Adolph Ochs sat quietly, not presuming to butt in on his competitor's show, but next morning his *Times* hit the streets with the proclamation of a $25,000 prize offered jointly by the *Times* and the Chicago *Evening Post*, for a flight, whether east or west, between New York and Chicago. Curtiss intimated that he might try for this one, and Albany promptly invited him to make that city one of his stops.

At his homecoming this time, while being driven from Bath, his car was halted by a crowd of Hammondsport High School students in a cordon across the street. His captors gave the school yell, then formed a parade to escort him to Castle Hill, where he favored them with "a brief but graceful speech."

As no other airman exceeded his distance before the end of the year, the *Scientific American* announced permanent award of its trophy to Curtiss in its issue of January 14, 1911, for the flight from Albany to Poughkeepsie. The magazine was frank in stating it had expected others to compete, and said: "It is a matter of great regret to us, as indeed it must be to all who are interested in promoting aviation in this country, that upon every occasion the cup was won without any competition." This seemed to prove "a decadence of the true sporting spirit," and that flyers preferred going for large cash prizes; that "the game is governed by the professional."

The trophy was presented at the annual dinner of the Aero Club on March 29 and accepted by Augustus Post as deputy for Curtiss, who was then at his North Island camp in California. Making the presentation, Charles A. Munn, the publisher, said: "Three names will always remain associated with the history of the river—that of Hudson, the explorer; that of Robert Fulton, the introducer of river navigation; and that of Glenn H. Curtiss, the birdman."

The Albany-to-New York flight was the event, more than any other, which marked the birth of practical aviation in America. Up to then, flying had been more an experiment and a sport than an activity to be taken seriously. By achieving the first sustained flight between two major cities, Curtiss had pried off the lid. He had proved that an airplane might dependably start from here and go to there. He had pointed the way to passenger flying, airmail, air express, and all. The excitement kicked up by his deed triggered an outbreak of distance flights which stretched ever longer until they marked out the continental airways.

17. The Exhibitionists

Lightweight, nervy, erratic, and bibulous, Charles K. Hamilton was the hottest plane jockey Curtiss yet had in his stable, and well he knew it. Utterly devoid of fear in the air, refusing to admit limitations on what a plane could do, he was the pioneer of American stunt pilots. At a stage when the mere act of aviating was a stunt in itself, and when most who did it were content to fly "straight" and come safely back to earth, Hamilton invented tricks as he went along. Although Curtiss often voiced his disapproval of stunting, he could not deny that it was lucrative, and he pocketed his percentage from "Charley K's" capers—when and if he could collect it.

The main trouble with Hamilton was that he soon turned into a prima donna. He came to Hammondsport not only to learn flying but in the expectation of buying an airplane with which to hit the show circuits as a free-lance. After signing the lease contract, he grew resentful of the high percentage payments to which he was committed. Quick fame and fat fees only fanned his dissatisfaction.

Elated by its coup with the chartered train, the New York *Times* resolved on an aerial spectacular of its own, in addition to its prize offer for a New York–Chicago flight, while the public mood was still at fever pitch from the Hudson River flight. With an assist from the Philadelphia *Public Ledger,* the paper hatched a project for a round-trip flight between two cities in a single day. Instead of bothering with another prize, the *Times* hired Hamilton outright for the job, at an undisclosed sum. That cutup was "at play in the air" over the Hempstead Plains, where he "played tag" with Harmon and Captain Baldwin. Charley dazzled the crowds with his "high glides" and dives, raced automobiles, and so on. The *Times* proposition called for him to fly nonstop from Governors Island to Philadelphia, refuel, and fly back. He was to follow the tracks of the Pennsylvania Railroad, accompanied by a chartered train. A landing field was found at North Philadelphia. The one-way distance being 86 miles, a round-trip would exceed the Curtiss cross-country record by 20 miles.

Hamilton was to use the modified Rheims racer. The cooperation which Curtiss extended to his protégé in this venture was nothing if not generous. To insure an extra fuel supply, he shipped a 20-gallon tank and sent down two mechanics to install it. Then he returned to Governors Island in person to condition the motor and supervise trials. The propeller was transferred from the *Hudson Flyer.* Success in this endeavor would be another triumph for Curtiss aircraft. Lena was again an interested bystander, and Tom Baldwin came over from Long Island with his man, Tod Shriver, to lend moral support.

Hamilton's grandest day dawned June 13, a fortnight after Curtiss had beaten him to a crack at the *World* prize. Girded with inflated inner-tubes, he took his perch with "careless sangfroid" and was off, picking up the train on the Jersey side and staying ahead of it all the way. This was represented as the first time an airplane ever ran on a time schedule. The return trip was marred by a forced landing at South Amboy where the wheels got mired in a marsh. Hauled out, Hamilton revived the motor and landed back at Governors Island before nightfall. The *Times* lavished even more space on this achievement than it had on the Hudson River flight.

*   *   *

Suspicion of Hamilton's motives had been aroused during the previous winter when he was turned loose in the Southwest following the Los Angeles meet. Curtiss was "very much afraid that Hamilton was trying to get out from us or planning some trick on us"; he said they purposely booked him into San Antonio where they could "pin him down." Fanciulli testified: "We had considerable trouble with Hamilton; couldn't get much information from him as to how much money he was taking in . . . We sent him some rather severe telegrams in an effort to line him up." What they actually feared was that he might hop the border into Mexico, and Fanciulli engaged a Pinkerton detective to keep an eye on him "so that he wouldn't leave the country with his machine."

Between April 25 and June 15, Hamilton turned in no report at all on his earnings, and any prodding by Curtiss "seemed to irritate him." When they were together again at Governors Island, Hamilton asked for release from his contract, saying he wanted to pluck some of the prize money that was growing on trees in Europe. Curtiss refused to let him off the hook, and, right after the Philadelphia flight, assigned him to fill an engagement at Nashville. The exhibition business was really booming by now, and Curtiss set off to fly in some Midwestern meets. At Louisville he had word from Hamilton that he had shipped the plane to Nashville but was not himself going to fly it. Curtiss wired back: YOU AGREED GOING TO NASHVILLE. KEEP YOUR PROMISE, PAY UP, AND WILL RELEASE YOU THEN IF YOU WISH. He followed this up with a letter: "Now that you have proven by your actions that you do not appreciate in the least all that I have done for you, and are unfair and unscrupulous, I believe we will be better off with you out of the country . . . If you go to Nashville, I will know that your refusal was a hold-up to get me to let you go abroad."

Hamilton did go to Nashville, after all, but not to Europe. Although he still refused to pay up, the contract remained in effect and Curtiss seems to have hoped for a rapprochement. At least he prevailed on him to take part in an important Atlantic City meet in July, where Curtiss also was to appear.

The remarks of Curtiss on the possibility of dropping bombs on warships, at the end of the Albany–New York flight, did not escape notice in the Navy Department, where the dreadnought reigned supreme. Following up its advantage, the New York *World* persuaded the aviator to experiment in dropping dummy bombs on nautical targets. On the surface of Keuka Lake, rows of buoyed flags were lined up to simulate the deck of a battleship. With military observers present on June 30, Curtiss flew back and forth dropping 8-inch lengths of lead pipe. Of seventeen "bombs," fifteen landed inside the target; one which was dropped from an altitude of 1000 feet fell seven feet outside. The Navy witness, Rear Admiral W. W. Kimball (Ret.), said: "There was nothing in the trial that would lead one to suppose that in the present state of the art of aviation there is anything in a possible aerial attack to cause the slightest uneasiness to the commanding officer of a well-ordered ship." The admiral bore down on the fact that the airplane signaled its approach by motor noise; also that it would have trouble hitting such a target from a height great enough to give the plane a fighting chance.

The Hammondsport test was a rehearsal, in effect, for a more graphic demonstration being set up for the Atlantic City program—a mimic battle between aircraft and a war vessel to be stationed by the Navy. Three airplanes were to "attack" the ship with make-believe bombs, piloted by Curtiss, Hamilton, and Walter Brookins, star of an exhibition team just fielded by the Wright Company. The sham battle was scrubbed when the Navy withdrew the use of a ship on the ground that foreign agents might be watching. A private owner bravely offered his sloop-yacht as a target, and Curtiss dropped oranges near the hull, trying not to spatter the deck.

The particular event which lured Curtiss to Atlantic City, however, was a 50-mile overwater race for which the Aero Club offered a purse of $5000. He had been experimenting with pontoons on the *Hudson Flyer*, hoping to spring a surprise at the meet with a true hydroplane, but takeoff from water still eluded him. The world's first speed competition above ocean water was a challenge. The course, marked by stake-boats, was 2½ miles around. Using the *Hudson Flyer*, he captured the prize on July 11, setting a new U.S. speed record for 50 miles.

One day during the meet he created a flurry when he flew offshore and vanished into mist. The crowd grew apprehensive as he did not soon reappear and measures were taken to begin a sea search. After an hour he came winging back, casually explaining that a friend had invited him for a social visit, so he had "dropped in on him." The friend was Lieutenant Hugh M. Willoughby of Ventnor, just down the coast, who had asked him to come and look over a plane he was contriving.

The principal reason for which Curtiss had wanted Hamilton with him in Atlantic City was to try for an altitude record against Brookins; in other words, to pit a Curtiss plane against a Wright in high flying. They had angry words again about the overdue lease payments, and Hamilton flew the coop instead, leaving the Rheims plane behind.[1] When reporters asked questions, Curtiss told them frankly he had made a formal demand for the arrears, and added: "Mr. Hamilton is a mere boy, and his sudden rise to fame appears to have been too much for him.

I'm sorry he has acted the way he has, for his place will be hard to fill."
(Curtiss then sued Hamilton for $6513.63, winning a judgment of
$6211 plus costs.)

Providentially, a replacement for Hamilton on the team, if not as a
wild stuntster, turned up in Atlantic City. The Canadian Aerodrome
Company had come to the end of its tether for lack of government
orders; Parliament rejected an appropriation for military aircraft. The
Silver Dart was wrecked at Petawawa and the *Baddeck Number 1* had
cracked up. The Bells were setting forth on a round-the-world cruise,
taking along as their guests Casey Baldwin and his bride. J. A. D.
McCurdy, discouraged and in debt, was sold on flying, much more so
than Baldwin. Of the A.E.A. associates, he had grown closest to Curtiss
in their work together on the *Dart* and the *Loon*. McCurdy now sought
out Curtiss and accepted his invitation to be an exhibition pilot; more
than likely he had come to Atlantic City with that in view.

*   *   *

All during that summer while the cloud of bankruptcy hung over
the plant in Hammondsport, Curtiss poured his energies into flying
and was almost perpetually on the road. It was in his mind to defend
personally the Gordon Bennett Trophy at the next international flying
meet, which was being arranged for Garden City, Long Island, that
October. The board of governors of the Aero Club invited him, as current holder of the cup, to be a member of the three-man American
team for its defense without undergoing the elimination trials required
of others. The location for the meet was later switched to the Belmont
Park racetrack, as having better facilities for planes and people.

For all his modest, seemingly aloof, demeanor, Curtiss was at home
in front of crowds. Without theatricality, he had acquired a certain
sense of showmanship in his motorcycle racing, and Captain Baldwin
taught him more of the art. Actually, he had developed into a skilled
aviator, and a reliable one who did not indulge in needless risks. The
pyrotechnics he left to the daredevils, while reminding them that there
were some limits on what an airplane might be expected to do. As he
said later on in the game: "I do not now, nor ever have encouraged
so-called 'fancy' flying. I regard some of the spectacular gyrations performed by any of a half dozen flyers I know as foolhardy and as taking
unnecessary chances. I do not believe fancy or trick flying demonstrates

anything except an unlimited amount of nerve and skill, and perhaps the possibilities of aerial acrobatics."

Always while aloft, he was studying the conditions of flying and of the atmosphere, absorbing knowledge which he then, without dramatizing or phony mystery, communicated to others. He was graphic and frank in describing his experiences; for example: "When I strike a gust of wind it's like hitting a steep grade on a motorcycle. It's as solid a reality as that."

So far, the exhibition business had been a rather informal affair with Jerome Fanciulli operating a clearinghouse for bookings. By now he had set up an office in New York. In June 1910 Curtiss sent this memorandum to Fanciulli: "If you run across a man with money and a name worth something, or a few of them, who would take stock, we might organize a company. Bishop was a good one—is there any more like him?" Fanciulli did not corral a financier, but the idea took root. In September 1910 the Curtiss Exhibition Company was formed, with Curtiss, Wheeler, and Fanciulli as its incorporators and sole stockholders. The capital stock was $20,000, of which Curtiss subscribed $18,000; the remaining stock was assigned to his two colleagues without cash investment on their part. Thus the Exhibition Company came into being before there was a Curtiss Aeroplane Company.

The percentage basis on which the contract pilots leased their planes evolved into a sliding scale, adjusted to how proficient they became. As Curtiss explained it: "The better class of aviators, and those who were less likely to have smash-ups, received a better percentage of receipts." A beginner might retain 25 percent of his "take," and work his way up to 50 percent or better. Virtuoso pilots, with a stunting reputation, commanded fabulous fees for gambling their lives: $1000 for a day's work was commonplace, but the best of them got as much as $1500 for a single flight, or $5000 a day. According to Fanciulli, the Exhibition Company made over $1,000,000 in three years; Curtiss said the figure, after expenses, was more like $400,000.[2]

*   *   *

From Atlantic City, Curtiss hopped to Omaha to carry out an engagement with Bud Mars, a favorite flying partner. A rash of accidents had occurred all over the country, and when asked at Omaha for comment, Curtiss proposed regular inspection of airplanes. Next on the itinerary was an air meet at Pittsburgh where he and Mars flew a duet over the walls of Western Penitentiary for the entertainment of the prisoners.

Such excursions were all leading up to a major wingding at the Sheepshead Bay racetrack, Brooklyn, which fully merited the label of "Curtiss carnival" which some papers bestowed upon it. Initially scheduled for three days in August, this show drew such eager response that it was extended over two weeks. The cream of Curtiss flyers were brought together, making a crew of six headed by the chief. A promising new recruit, Eugene Ely, was in the lineup. The rest were Willard, Mars, McCurdy, and Augustus Post. The last-named, taught by Curtiss, was the only known bearded exhibitionist. While he flew occasional dates, Post did not get beyond the talented amateur class, and stood in no need of money; still, during this meet, he managed a "bronco-busting flight" over the steeplechase hurdles of the racetrack.

As many as five airplanes were in the air at once, chasing one another, and this was hailed as a record for multiple flights in the New York City area. Once Bud Mars flew daringly far out across Lower New York Bay. But the really significant aspects of Sheepshead Bay were of special interest to the military.

Major Samuel Reber of the Signal Corps came out from Governors Island as a daily observer and it was he who suggested the experiment of rifle fire from the air. This was not as simple as it sounds, when the precariously perched passenger needed both hands for the weapon and a steady aim; moreover, fear was expressed that the bullets might ricochet and hit spectators. Reber arranged the assignment of an expert marksman, Lieutenant Jacob E. Fickel, and Curtiss piloted him. A standard Army target was laid out in the center of the racetrack infield and Fickel used a Springfield rifle. The plane made passes over the target at approximately 100 feet, the officer firing from directly above to guard against ricochet. The test was none too successful, and Curtiss blamed himself for not holding the plane steady enough. Nonetheless, two bullet holes were found in the target after four passes. On the strength of his report, Fickel was ordered to the Remington Arms Company to assist in designing a gunsight that would compensate for speed of an airplane.

On another day, McCurdy won the distinction of sending history's first air-to-ground wireless message. Among his talents was the ability to telegraph Morse code. A sending set was installed in his plane with a key attached to the control wheel and a loose aerial wire trailing beneath. The technician, a former Signal Corps officer, H. M. Horton, placed his receiver atop the grandstand. When McCurdy was 500 feet up and a mile away from the grandstand, Horton was able to read the message he tapped out: ANOTHER CHAPTER IN AERIAL ACHIEVEMENT IS RECORDED IN THE SENDING OF THIS WIRELESS MESSAGE FROM AN AEROPLANE IN FLIGHT. J. A. D. MCCURDY.

The end of August found Curtiss at Cleveland, under auspices of the Aero Club of that city, poised for a fresh sensation: the longest overwater flight on record in the world. The Ohio shore of Lake Erie assumes a bow shape between Cleveland and Sandusky, and it was across the arc of this open water that he had engaged to fly, going and returning. Newspapers gave this undertaking a great buildup, and the lakeshore throngs which congregated at either end of the route were estimated to total 200,000. The Cleveland *Press* informed its readers that "Aviator Curtiss is said to be the most cautious of all birdmen"; asserting that his methods were "like those of the Indian." At Euclid Beach, his takeoff point, he walked out to the end of the pier for a wind observation, but carried no instrument. He merely looked down at his shadow, explaining: "My coat is my wind gauge. When it flaps evenly, I know the wind is steady."

Again it was the trusty *Hudson Flyer* which carried him over water. On August 31, he flew from Euclid Beach to Cedar Point, on Sandusky Bay, a distance of 64¾ miles. Returning next day, he raced informally with the fast Lake Shore mail train, beating it into Cleveland by 17 minutes. The Cleveland Aero Club honored him that night with a banquet.

Next stop Boston. He hastened direct from Ohio to the Atlantic Aviation Field for the Harvard-Boston Aeronautical Meet, opening September 3, upon which he was staking a great deal. Thus far he had postponed a response to the Aero Club's query about defending the Bennett Trophy Cup because there was something he must find out: how serious the foreign competition was going to be, and how well the new racing plane he had been designing might face up to it. He was reasonably sure that the European challenger he would have to beat was Claude Grahame-White, England's speed demon; and Grahame-White was entered for the Harvard-Boston tournament with his Blériot monoplane powered by a Gnôme rotary motor rated at 100-horsepower.

Charley Willard joined Curtiss here, and a couple of Wright exhibitionists were on the field: Brookins and Ralph Johnstone. President William Howard Taft made his rotund appearance. A spectator of greater interest to Curtiss was John T. Trowbridge, the venerable author of *Darius Green and His Flying Machine*. Then aged eighty-two and living in Arlington, a suburb of Boston, Trowbridge wore a flowing white beard which invited comparison to Walt Whitman. He had come to see flying machines in action at last, and it is tempting to guess that he was introduced to Curtiss. Riding the wave of public enthusiasm for aviation, a fresh edition of *Darius Green* was just being published.

Unhappy with his racer in early trials, Curtiss had a substitute propeller shipped from home, and negotiated a swap of engines for a 65-horsepower from a Burgess plane. These measures availed little for the machine which later went on the road as the *Boston Flyer*. Grahame-White romped away with almost every prize and was easily the fair-haired boy of the meet. Curtiss had to content himself with second prize of $2000 for speed, and he was not in the habit of being an also-ran. Still he delayed giving the Aero Club its answer, and turned to the design of a radically different plane for the Belmont meet.

The New York State Fair at Syracuse saw him next, billed as the "world's champion aviator." McCurdy had been booked, but Curtiss decided to take it himself, even agreeing to a race with an automobile.

*   *   *

In the meantime, the reward which might be collected by the airman who first flew the 1000 miles between New York and Chicago had increased to $30,000. Clifford Harmon added $5000 to the $25,000 jointly dangled by the New York *Times* and the Chicago *Evening Post*. The distance must be covered within 168 hours of elapsed time, a full week. A thousand miles would constitute, far and away, the cross-country record of the world, and rivalry for the prize promised to grow into a free-for-all race, with at least eight entrants. Cities along the way vied to be picked as stopovers. A starting date was fixed for October 8, 1910. By general accord, the takeoff would be from Chicago, benefiting from the westerly winds.

While Curtiss changed his mind about personal participation, he formulated plans for a five-man team of his pilots to enter, casting himself in the role of coach. On the first day of October, they were all assembled at Hawthorne Park racetrack, Chicago: Bud Mars, Eugene Ely, John McCurdy, Charley Willard, and Gus Post. A condition of the race was that competitors arrive by October 3 to give daily flights leading up to the start, the profits from which would be added to the prize money.

At a strategy conference of the Curtiss task force around a big table in the LaSalle Hotel, Curtiss drew a laugh by exclaiming: "By George, boys, I'll tell you what. I'll jump the fence with you on Saturday and keep you company a little way just for the sport." (A handicap of the Hawthorne track was a high fence around it.)

The Curtiss men were on hand early enough to provide Chicagoans with a weekend show, attracting 10,000 spectators on Saturday, 20,000 on Sunday. Curtiss sped five times around the field, "making short dips and quick turns, to the amazement of the crowd." Later, with McCurdy and Willard in the air, he zoomed up to join them, and they stacked themselves about 75 feet apart, with Curtiss in the middle. Chicago had never seen three planes up at once; on Sunday they saw four, as Ely entered the act.

Mixed emotions greeted Charley Hamilton when he turned up with a self-made plane entitled the *Hamiltonian* (alias *Black Devil*). Hobbling with a cane, he looked drawn and unwell, and confessed to a crash in California a few days before in which the plane settled on top of him. Hot oil had burned his legs, and his back was sprained; for extra measure he had developed pleurisy on the train to Chicago. After hanging around, he withdrew from the race because of illness, and left for New York to await the Belmont Park meet.

Other potential entrants dropped out until the Curtiss stalwarts were left in the running, and they were winnowed down to three: McCurdy, Willard, and Ely. A route was mapped out, some of the stops being Toledo, Cleveland, Buffalo, Rochester, Syracuse, Utica, Schenectady, Albany, and Poughkeepsie. All those cities began preparing elaborate receptions. The *Times* chartered a train to follow the flight on the Lake Shore Railroad and the New York Central. Progress bulletins were to be tossed off at each telegraph office passed. A "pathfinder" automobile set out to cover the route, with Fanciulli, his wife, and reporters of the sponsoring papers; its function to pin down arrangements and supplies at each stop.

Before week's end it was obvious that repair parts available along the way would be inadequate to service three aircraft, and Curtiss ruled that only one plane should attempt the trip. The three chosen pilots drew straws for the privilege, and Ely won the draw.

The takeoff was delayed to Sunday, October 9. Ely was assigned the *Boston Flyer*, which had proved faster than the *Hudson Flyer*, after all. Curtiss took it up for a final check, landed, and told Ely: "I think the machine will do. Good luck to you." McCurdy and Willard escorted Ely for a few miles, while the Curtisses departed to board the special train which stood panting at Gary, Indiana.

But Ely did not fly far that day. The engine coughed when he was only 11 miles out and he came down at suburban Beverly Shores to fix the trouble, a vibrating needle pin in a new carburetor. This was quickly done, but in his takeoff run in prairie grass the front wheel hit a stone and crumpled. Two mechanics hopped in a car and rushed a new wheel, but it was then too late for a fresh start that night.

Monday morning, 50,000 people awaited at La Porte and 75,000 at South Bend. Ely took off, but the engine sputtered within half a mile and he picked out another field. A deep ditch nearly flopped the plane over and sent the pilot rolling. Curtiss left the train, with mechanics and spare parts, and drove fast to the scene. Returning at 4:00 P.M., he announced that Ely would be along any moment. Came 5:45, and still no Ely. The station agent at Gary got a flash saying: HE'S DROPPED IN EAST CHICAGO. FELL LIKE A BULLET OUT OF THE SKY. Then Ely telephoned Curtiss: "I'm all right. Tell my wife. The machine's smashed, though, and I can't get out of here until tomorrow. Don't know what's the matter, but my engine stopped again."

He was down in a swamp only five miles from Gary. Again Curtiss headed the relief expedition, finding that the plane required more parts than were to be had. On Tuesday, Ely reluctantly gave up, having vanquished 32 miles of the 1000. "But I will do it sometime," he vowed, "as sure as I'm alive here now."

After Ely tossed in the sponge, a mechanic going over the engine made a discovery: the pinhole air vent of the fuel tank was clogged with oily dust. "There's your trouble, Gene," he said.

*   *   *

As the date approached for the Gordon Bennett Cup race at Belmont Park, Curtiss still held the door ajar for defending personally the trophy he brought back from Rheims. On October 18, he notified J. C. McCoy, chairman of the aviation committee, that two men of his staff would operate new racing machines "of the monoplane type" at the meet. This was a real surprise, as he had been an outspoken partisan of the biplane. Actually, he sent four entries to the meet, the other two being regular models.

Fanciulli now confirmed that his employer had been at work for some time on a new type of racer which he preferred to call a "single surface machine." The arrival of the Curtiss "mystery" plane aroused keen speculation at the Belmont track as the first model was whisked into the hangar and uncrated behind closed doors. When it was unveiled, experts found it "almost revolutionary." Not quite a monoplane, it retained the lower wing, with 30-foot span; but it had a small wing "like an awning" overhead the center. The motor was rated at 65-horsepower, and the radiator was right behind the pilot's back. The two models were experimental and had yet to be flown. McCurdy and Ely were elected to initiate them.

The interest was sharpened by the fact that the Wrights were also coming to the meet with a "mystery plane." For them to build a racing machine was news in itself. That the brothers were descending from their pedestal to enter a prize competition was little less than sensational, and a report spread that Orville might even fly for the Bennett Trophy. They arrived at Belmont with a slogan: "The cup will remain in America."

The threat of European flyers to boycott the tournament because of the Wrights' royalty demands had been circumvented by a blanket settlement. The Aero Corporation, managing the meet, signed a contract to pay the Wright Company 25 percent of gate proceeds in return for a pledge of non-interference. This pact was later modified to a flat sum of $25,000, and the Wrights agreed to supply five planes and pilots to the program. In consequence, both France and England were sending three-man teams to challenge for the trophy.

Inquisitive flyers shuttled between the Curtiss hangar and the Wright tent to compare the two "mystery" aircraft. The Wright entry was called the *Baby Grand*, depicted as a "pocket edition" of their standard, with twice the power. The most conspicuous change was elimination of the front elevator (or "long head"); the *Baby Grand* also had wheels in combination with skids. The Wrights had never before used an engine beyond 30-horsepower; this one had 60. When Orville took it up for a swing around the Belmont track, he startled everyone with a speed upwards of 70 miles per hour. Instantly the *Baby Grand* was the favorite to win the cup.

With the exception of Post, who was off on a balloon race, Curtiss had with him the same men as at Chicago: i.e., Ely, McCurdy, Willard, and Mars. From Mineola, Tom Baldwin brought over his *Red Devil*. And Hamilton, in better shape than they saw him last at Chicago, was there with his *Hamiltonian*.

The Gordon Bennett race was scheduled as the climax on Saturday, October 29. Three days prior to that, the personnel of the American defense team had not yet been chosen; windiness kept putting off elimination trials. Curtiss had sized up the competition and decided that either the Wright plane or Grahame-White's Blériot could beat him. He then notified the committee he would not enter. His "single surface" racers were not even put into the air.

Finally the board of governors of the Aero Club, in desperation, resolved to pick the defenders arbitrarily. Both Curtiss and Wilbur Wright attended the meeting. Once more the question was put to Curtiss: would he be one of the three? His final answer was negative. The board then named Walter Brookins, with the *Baby Grand;* Charles Hamilton, with his *Hamiltonian;* and J. Armstrong Drexel, with a Blériot monoplane.

A rumor gained currency that Curtiss was irked because none of his men was selected for the team. Cortlandt Bishop replied to this: "The fact is, Mr. Curtiss assured me himself that he was well content with the selections made, as he did not believe he could win in competition with the 100-horsepower Blériot monoplanes."

At first glance, it makes no sense that a man so highly competitive by nature was so meek about defending the trophy he had won brilliantly just a year earlier. Again, it must be recalled that the Herring-Curtiss bankruptcy had not yet been adjudicated; that the plant in Hammondsport was in receivership and not his property; and that Curtiss, with only a makeshift little shop in another part of town, was in no position to produce a superior racing plane.

In a pre-race trial run, Brookins crashed the Wright entry in front of the grandstand when four of his eight cylinders quit. The chance of keeping the trophy in America was wrecked with the *Baby Grand.* Hamilton was unable to get his engine working right and pulled out. The Gordon Bennett Cup passed into English possession when Grahame-White covered the 100-kilometer course in a minute more than one hour, for a new speed record of 62.1 miles.

A few weeks after the meet, the Wright brothers obtained an injunction to stop the Aero Corporation from distributing $198,000 gate receipts while they strove to collect $15,000 more. They claimed a verbal agreement for additional payment if the proceeds warranted it. Allan A. Ryan, chairman of the arrangements committee, branded the claim "outrageous," and said "it comes with ill grace from a company that has been treated by the Aero Corporation with the consideration and courtesy which has been extended to them."

*   *   *

If Curtiss came away from the Belmont meet crestfallen, he was more than compensated in the long run by a close and very significant friendship which had its beginning on that occasion.

The U. S. Navy was at last warming up to the concept that airplanes might serve some useful purpose as fleet auxiliaries. On October 21, Captain Washington Irving Chambers, a keen-minded naval engineer, was handed orders to represent the Navy Department "in observing everything that will be of use in the study of aviation and its influence upon the problems of naval warfare at the Aviation Tournament to be held at Belmont Park, New York, October 22 to 30, 1910." His opposite number assigned to the meet by the Army Signal Corps was Major Samuel Reber.

The New York *World*, making the most of its $10,000 investment in Curtiss, had cooked up a new feat for him: flying an airplane from the deck of an outbound ocean liner back to land. The point of this trick was to show how transatlantic mail delivery might be speeded by having a plane precede a ship into port. There can be no doubt that Curtiss discussed this proposal with Chambers and Reber at Belmont Park, since they both cooperated with it in their military capacities immediately afterward.

While Ely and Willard went direct to Halethorpe, Maryland, a Baltimore suburb, for exhibition flights, McCurdy drew the choice assignment. The *World* enlisted the collaboration of the Hamburg-American Line whose steamer, the *Kaiserin Auguste Victoria*, was due to sail from New York on November 5. (Some guessed that the German Navy entertained an unusual interest in having the experiment conducted from a German vessel.) The plan was for the liner to proceed 50 miles out to sea, then head into the wind to help McCurdy take to the air off Fire Island. McCurdy would then wing back to Governors Island with a waterproof sack of mail. Two torpedo-boat destroyers

were to attend the ship, carrying reporters and bringing home observers who were aboard the steamer.

Curtiss and McCurdy directed construction of a fan-shaped launching platform over the liner's foredeck. This platform was 85 feet long,
inclined downward at a 10-degree angle over the bow. One of the
new Curtiss biplanes was transported from Belmont Park to the Hoboken
pier of the Hamburg-American Line. The experiment spurred a late
rush of cabin applications on the liner.

On November 4 a terrific gale hit the Eastern Seaboard. It wrecked
planes at Baltimore, including those of Ely and Willard. As the wind
whipped up the coast, Curtiss conferred with the steamship company
and announced a week's postponement of the test, until November
12 when the Hamburg-American liner *Pennsylvania* would be sailing.
McCurdy had to depart for a booking at Charlotte, North Carolina,
and Bud Mars was called in to replace him.

The same preparations were repeated on the *Pennsylvania*, save
for a switch of the launching stage from bow to stern. Curtiss oversaw
lashing of the plane to the platform. The ship was decorated with
gay bunting from truck to keel. Moments before she was due to cast
off, Curtiss and Mars came aboard and started the engine for a last-
minute test. As the propeller whirled, two fragments of wood flew
off at a tangent. A mechanic had left a piece of rubber tubing on
the lower wing and suction drew it into the prop. The steering gear
was crippled and the vessel could not delay for its repair. The plane
was removed to the pier and the liner sailed with the platform still
perched above its stern.

Meanwhile, the Navy had picked up the idea and sought the
cooperation of Curtiss, who assigned Gene Ely to that task while he
and Mars were still occupied with the *Pennsylvania*. Captain Chambers
was ordered to report at Norfolk Navy Yard on November 12 for
temporary duty on the cruiser *Birmingham* "for experimental work on
the practicality of using aeroplanes from vessels in connection with
scouting duty." Ely arrived simultaneously and the *Hudson Flyer*
was ferried in by a Navy tug from the Jamestown racetrack.

The platform constructed over the bow of the *Birmingham* was
83 feet long, 26 feet wide, sloping at 5 degrees with an uptilt at
the end. This trial was set for Monday, the 14th, and Curtiss could
not get there in time to be a witness. The cruiser was anchored
off Fort Monroe, and Ely's stint was to fly 12 miles across Hampton

Roads to the Navy Yard. It was a miserable day for flying. A strong wind drove rain in sheets as the cruiser steamed into the Roads, getting up speed to give him an extra shove. The rain turned to sleet and Ely marked time from 11:30 to 3:30, when the wind abated enough so that he could hop off between showers, preferring that the ship stand still. The plane dropped 37 feet off the bow and seemed headed for a dive before it picked up speed. Actually the propeller tips and rudder splashed water and Ely was drenched. At once he ran into low fog, heading out to sea, then swerved inshore in the wrong direction for the Navy Yard. "I was simply completely lost," he said. He was blinded by spray on his goggles and had no way of ascertaining how badly his prop was damaged (it was bent and a small piece split off). Wisely, he made for shore when he saw it, landing at Willoughby Spit beside the Hampton Roads Yacht Club, only 2½ miles from the cruiser.

Unimpressive though it was, this flight was the first which ever left a ship and came to land. The navies of Europe took interested note. Ely won a $500 prize from the Aeronautical Reserve and another of $5000 from a private donor, John Barry Ryan. Captain Chambers lauded him for succeeding under "very adverse conditions of weather," and urged the Navy to purchase several planes for study and instruction. A second Navy observer, Lieutenant N. H. Wright, made a similar recommendation, while reporting: "This flight from the *Birmingham* was of great service in making a start in naval aviation . . . As a practical naval flight, however, it was not a success . . . No such narrow margin of safety as this flight showed would be permissible . . . Means for rising from the water must be devised and means of hoisting the machine aboard ship in case it should land in the water."

In the immediate aftermath, Curtiss made his celebrated offer of free flight instruction to officers of both Navy and Army. And presently he was setting up winter camp on San Diego Bay to begin solving what the Navy wanted done.

✿   ✿   ✿

After quitting Curtiss, Charley Hamilton grew even more reckless, drank heavily, was a chain smoker, and lived on his nerves. Other flyers said he never took off without a few belts of liquor, and that ultimately mechanics had to help him board his plane. Still, he was "the only man on record who could mix alcohol with altitude and get away with it"; and "he could do things drunk in an airplane which other people couldn't do sober." He was so patched up from wrecks that there was "little left of the original Hamilton." In and out of hospitals, he had two nervous breakdowns. Surprisingly enough. he died in bed: an internal hemorrhage got him in 1914, at the age of thirty-two.

The real replacement for Hamilton, who soon came to excel him and everyone else in the business as a stunt man, crept up on Curtiss unawares in the autumn of 1910. When the Wright Company weaned Roy Knabenshue away from dirigibles to head its exhibition crew, he tried to bring his partner, Lincoln Beachey, with him, but Beachey demanded more money than the Wrights were willing to pay, and he made a beeline for Hammondsport. There he was given a tryout and promptly cracked up the plane. Curtiss was about to dismiss the fellow when Fanciulli interceded. Beachey damaged a second plane, and Fanciulli, who sensed promise in him that Curtiss missed, had to do some fast talking to get him a third chance. This time he clicked, and Curtiss made his all-time best investment in a show pilot. Even Wilbur Wright, watching him fly, conceded: "Beachey is the most wonderful flyer I ever saw and the greatest aviator of all." The Hammondsport *Herald* said: "He is perhaps the most skillful and daring aviator in the world today."

Lincoln Beachey took up where Hamilton left off, inventing ever more hair-raising tricks and becoming a legend of his time. He was blissfully ignorant of the laws of aerodynamics, and Curtiss warned him time and again that the machines he flew were not built to withstand the strains he put upon them. Yet he seemed to lead a charmed life. He beat the fast-climb record, rising 6500 feet in 15 minutes. To set a world's altitude record, he put in 10 gallons of gas and announced he would keep climbing until the fuel ran out; that he did, reaching 11,642 feet (in an era when the pilot sat out in the open air), then made a record volplane coming to earth with a dead stick. An ambition of his was to fly straight up for one mile, and he nagged Curtiss to build him a plane that would rise perpendicularly.

Beachey's best-known stunt was an improvement over Hamilton's long glide—a 90-degree dive after cutting the engine at high altitude. Spectators could hear his wires whining as he descended, and many thought he had genuinely lost control as he neared ground. Women fainted before he leveled off. His bag of tricks also included the Death Dip, the Ocean Wave, the Dutch Roll, the Coney Island Dip, and the Spiral Glide.

A great advantage which Beachey held over Hamilton was his abstemious way of life: he neither drank nor smoked, hence his daring could not be attributed to pot-valiance. A single glass of champagne would "throw him," according to one of his flying pals. Lest he be mistaken for a pillar of virtue, however, it must be recorded that his weakness was the fair sex; Becky Havens avowed that this was a "real strong weakness" with Beachey. His social manners and conduct left much to be desired: he could be stubborn, insolent, moody, arrogant, insulting. "Beachey was a strange, strange character," recalled Havens, one of his rare close friends. The Governor of California once stepped forward to compliment him as he landed from a brilliant performance. Ignoring the proffered hand, Beachey turned on his heel, got back in the plane, and circled over the field, stripping off one garment after another, letting them flutter to earth. When he was down to his undershorts, or less, he landed and snapped to his mechanic: "Let's hear what he has to say about me now."

Beachey's classic deed of derring-do was his flirtation with the Horseshoe Falls at Niagara on June 27, 1911, for which he was amply recompensed by the Niagara International Carnival. His fellow headliners on that program were Harry Houdini, the magician, who slid across the gorge on a wire; and Bobby Leach, who shot the Whirlpool Rapids in a barrel. Taking off from a baseball diamond on the American side, Beachey went up 2000 feet and made a trial pass to test the air currents. Going aloft again, he dove at the perilous center of the Horseshoe, pulling out at 200 feet above the crest, then pitching down through the mist and violent turbulence. The carburetor sucked in so much spray that his engine nearly died. He flew under the steel-arch bridge and on down the gorge almost to the Whirlpool, then shaved the wooded cliff to land on the Canadian side.

Not long after Beachey started flying for Curtiss, he rammed a fence, smashing the front elevator. Ripping off the remnants, he took to the air without the "long head" and found that the plane handled far more easily. When Havens heard about this, he had his mechanic remove the front controls from his machine, and said: "It was just like you'd been shackled all your life and suddenly took the chains off." Curtiss went up without the "head," flew around for half an hour and came back exclaiming: "My God, that's so much better!" Henceforth Curtiss dispensed entirely with the out-front elevator which had for so long been considered obligatory.

*   *   *

Meanwhile, Havana took fire about aviation and Cuba's first air meet was arranged for January 1911, on the polo field of Camp Columbia. Curtiss planes and men, Beachey among them, dominated the activities. For the stellar event, the Havana *Post* offered $5000 and the city of Havana $3000 to the man intrepid enough to fly across the shark-infested waters from Key West, Florida. McCurdy took up this challenge, equipping his plane with flotation gear like that used by Curtiss over the Hudson. The Navy assisted by stationing destroyers 10 miles apart over the 90-mile route.

"I had quite a dashboard," McCurdy recollected. "An Ingersoll dollar watch and a 35-cent compass." It was a fine flight until he was within 10 miles of the Cuban coast and could see Morro Castle ahead. He was the first man ever to fly beyond sight of land. And then a connecting-rod had to poke a hole in the crankcase. Settling calmly down between swells, McCurdy did not even get his feet wet. The nearest destroyer reached him in 4½ minutes, for which he was grateful as he watched shark fins circling.

Havana went wild in its reception, even though he had fallen short of land. McCurdy mounted a flag-bedecked platform and a Cuban government official made an eloquent and laudatory speech, which eventually ended with the presentation of a sealed envelope, ostensibly containing his check for $8000. When he opened the envelope in privacy, he found it empty, as he told the story.

*   *   *

Hammondsport became the mecca for young men smitten with air fever. J. Lansing Callan, for example, lived in the Hudson River town of Valatie, worked for his father's profitable real estate agency in Albany, and presumaby had been a witness to the Albany–New York flight. In December 1910 he wrote to the Curtiss Exhibition Company office, inquiring what dates Curtiss might be in New York or Hammondsport; he held a letter of introduction from Jacob L. Ten Eyck, he mentioned. "I do not hesitate in saying that the object of my asking for these dates is in order to obtain a personal interview with Mr. Curtiss in regard to getting a position with him as an operator of one of his machines."

Jerome Fanciulli replied that Curtiss would not be in this part of the country for some time, as he was just then establishing training and experimental grounds in California; but telling Callan: "It is also our intention to establish such training grounds in the East," and enclosing an information sheet about this plan. The proposition was: "A course in practical flying and practical aeroplane operation." The course was to include a minimum of six lessons in two weeks, for a fee of $500, which would be applied on the purchase of an airplane if the student should decide to buy. A deposit of $500 was required, to cover breakage or damage.

Callan's father was deadset against his taking up flying, and refused to advance him money for lessons. The following summer Lansing (better known as Lanny) went to Hammondsport and made a verbal agreement with Curtiss whereby he might commence lessons for a down payment of $250, the balance to be paid when halfway through the course. A sympathetic uncle lent Callan the money with which he was able to go to San Diego in December 1911. Lanny Callan became one of Curtiss's most useful pilots and instructors.

Beckwith Havens, aged twenty-one, returned to his native New York after trying his hand as an automobile salesman in California, and approached Fanciulli with the novel idea of becoming the world's first airplane salesman. Fanciulli approved it as a good promotion gag, but Havens could find no customers, and next suggested that an agent for airplanes ought at least to be able to fly one. Dispatched to Hammondsport for a talk with Curtiss, he was disconcerted at being told that he must have $500 in advance; as an employee, so to speak, he had expected the lessons to be free. Angrily, he went back to Fanciulli, who said: "Are you willing to sign a note? You can make back the $500 in a few days, and a lot more." Armed with a bank loan, Havens retraced his steps to Hammondsport, learned to fly, and found the pickings so lush on the exhibition circuit that he abandoned the notion of being a salesman; in fact, he never sold a plane.

The Curtiss Exhibition Company contracted the premiere female flyer in the United States. An eighteen-year-old Rochester girl, Blanche Scott, had won celebrity as the first woman to drive an automobile across the continent. Late in 1910, Blanche appeared in Hammondsport and convinced Curtiss of the publicity value in having a she-pilot. He personally gave her instruction and, with some trepidation, entrusted her with a few exhibition dates. One slight problem presented itself in connection with a woman flying an open-air plane: skirts. Blanche solved this by donning full-cut bloomers.

Aside from a couple of minor crackups, Blanche Scott was lucky and retired from flying while her luck held. The second woman pilot to whom Curtiss surrendered was less fortunate. Julia Clarke, twenty-six, of Denver, came to him at San Diego that winter with a wad of inherited money, declared that the Wrights had refused to teach her, and begged him to do so. Curtiss shook his head, fearing an accident. She purchased a plane notwithstanding, and Lanny Callan gave her pointers. Noting her determination, Curtiss, as she told it, went to her and said that "if I had made up my mind to get smashed up and nothing would change my plans, he would teach me the balance of the art of cloud exploring." When she was "flying as well as a man," he permitted her to take the road. In July 1912, while flying at the Illinois State Fair, Julia Clarke clipped a tree and was killed.

A rollcall of the exhibition pilots who flew under the banner of Curtiss would be superfluous, but a few of the others were Hugh Robinson, C. C. Wittmer, C. F. Walsh, R. C. McHenry, and Eugene Godet. It was Hugh Robinson who, in the spring of 1912, made a record airmail flight of 375 miles, hopping down the Mississippi River from Minneapolis to Rock Island. Demonstrations of mail delivery by air were a frequent stunt, encouraged by Curtiss who always kept an eye peeled to future practical uses for aircraft.

By and large, exhibitionists tended to favor the type of plane in which they learned, and there was a distinct cleavage between the partisans of Curtiss and the Wrights. Even allowing for prejudice, however, the majority of flyers deemed the Curtiss type the simplest of all to operate. Curtiss himself asserted in 1912 that almost all the pilots then flying his machines were "practically self-taught." One of the last survivors of the exhibition era was Becky Havens, a Curtiss partisan, to be sure. Not long before his death, he said: "No one ever had a natural control except Curtiss. The Curtiss plane was a hot little devil. The Wright seemed slow-and-easy. The feeling we all had was that the Wright was dangerous in a dive, with all that wing-loading. And that chain drive was an awkward thing, besides."

*   *   *

Curtiss's own career as an exhibition flyer did not extend beyond 1911, when he became deeply preoccupied with the development of hydroplanes. Almost exclusively from then on, such personal flying as he did was for experimental purposes in connection with aircraft for use on water.

His recollection was that he made his farewell exhibition flights in August 1911 at Winona Lake, Indiana. There was something by which to pinpoint this: "I remember at Winona I took Billy Sunday up for a ride." The famous evangelist of the "sawdust trail" had his summer home on Winona Lake, and asked Curtiss to give him his baptism in aviation.

*   *   *

While disapproving stuntsmanship, Curtiss confessed his admiration for Lincoln Beachey: "I consider Lincoln the most daring and skillful aviator under any and all conditions that I have ever seen." Though Beachey graduated from the Exhibition Company's team to become the highest paid of freelance pilots, he remained on excellent terms with Curtiss, continued using Curtiss planes during much of his career, and had a substantial sum of money invested in Curtiss stock. So illustrious was his name that he commanded as much as $5000 for a single performance.

As the exhibition mania spread, crashes took a mounting toll of flyers. "It got so we were losing a pilot a month," Becky Havens estimated. Although Beachey was known as a rough, hardbitten character, he evidently had a soft streak. Several of the killed pilots had been his friends, to whom he had confided secrets of his virtuosity. Remorse crept up on him, mingled perhaps with a hunch that one day his own luck might run out. "I feel as if I had murdered them," he accused himself. "Those boys were like brothers to me."

Abruptly and surprisingly, in March 1913, Beachey publicly announced his retirement, averring that "only at the point of a revolver" could he ever be induced to fly again.

In his renunciation, he said: "I have defied death at every opportunity in the last two years. I have been a bad influence, and
the death of a number of young aviators in this country can be traced,
I believe, to a desire to emulate me in my foolishly daring exploits
in the air." At the same time, he felt disgust with the morbid psychology
of spectator crowds. "They call me the Master Birdman, but they pay
to see me die."

For a substitute source of income, he signed up for a vaudeville
tour. His resolution endured for six months and then was undermined
by a combination of two challenges which he was unable to resist.

In France, a flyer named Adolphe Pegoud achieved the world's
first loop-the-loop, a stunt which had been considered impossible. Becky
Havens read about it in a newspaper and brought it to Beachey's
attention as they were breakfasting together in a New York restaurant.
Beachey flared up and shouted: "If he can do it, so can I."

Beachey was already tempted by a forthcoming race around Manhattan Island, billed as the Times Aerial Derby because the New York
Times was putting up $2250 in prizes, $1000 for the winner. This
race was to be the main event of an air meet centering at Oakwood
Heights field on Staten Island, sponsored by the Aeronautic Society
of New York to commemorate the tenth anniversary of the Wright
brothers' flights at Kitty Hawk. J. R. Hall, the program manager, boasted
that he had talked Beachey into making his return to aviation as a
contestant in the Manhattan race.

One September day, Beachey strode into the Hammondsport plant
and asked Curtiss to build him a plane expressly for looping. It was
to be "more than twice as strong as any of the standard makes,"
with a 100-horsepower engine. It would have a stout harness with
which the pilot could strap himself in. With the new plane assured,
he sent his entry for the Times Aerial Derby and told the press:
"I thought I had given up flying. In a year's time, aviation has
changed from a dangerous sport to a serious business. I believe there
is work for me to do that is worth any man's doing." He promised
Hall to duplicate at the Staten Island meet every stunt Pegoud had
done, including the loop, and do it better. The Frenchman had also
flown upside down. Beachey proposed to top him with a "backward
somersault." He was impatient to get all these tricks accomplished, as
Pegoud was reported coming for an American tour in the near future.
The great Beachey must not be humiliated in his native air!

When the cables brought news that Pegoud had looped four times in succession, Beachey expostulated: "Now I am jealous! I always knew those things could be done. I really built my last machine to do them with, but a year ago aviation in this country was discouraging. Now the advancement in every direction is wonderful, and I intend to prove, to my own satisfaction at least, just what can be done with the aeroplane as it is built today."

On the verge of sailing for Europe when Beachey burst back upon the scene, Curtiss put the special plane into production but was unable to stick around for its test flying. He had a date to keep with the Russian Navy Department.

*   *   *

Four miles down the west side of Keuka Lake were the cellars of the Urbana Wine Company whose president, Walter E. Hildreth, was also president of the American Wine Growers Association and owned a Manhattan hotel. The Hildreth family, New Yorkers by residence, enjoyed summers in a rustic cottage which the winery maintained on the lakeshore. While the parents returned to New York for a few days, the two attractive Hildreth daughters remained at the lake. The sisters—Ruth, 20, and Dorothea, 19—were lively members of the young social set in Hammondsport and popular with the aviators. On the 7th of October, they had as luncheon guests at the cottage two of the dashing naval officers then flying aeroboats on the lake: Lieutenants Holden C. Richardson and Pat Bellinger. The foursome were preparing to attend a lavish "homecoming" dinner party for Beachey which Jim Bauder was throwing that night in Bath.

Some time after lunch, they espied an airplane out over the lake and the men recognized it as Beachey's new "looping" machine. To avoid a crowd, Lincoln had decided to give it a fling without advance notice. On the spur of the moment, the two couples piled into a motorboat and gunned it for Kingsley Field to see the sport.

As Beachey later explained, he wished to make his early tests "privately and quietly" with no audience; he had flown but once in nine months, and this plane incorporated some changes from the standard. "No one was invited to be present . . . After I made my first flight, people began coming from all directions. I made another flight immediately and had much trouble in finding a clear landing space. Then I decided to quit. In the meantime school had let out, hundreds of people had gathered, and I was urged to fly once more and not disappoint them. After several refusals, I finally agreed to take one more flight."

Near the waterfront stood a large tent, serving as hangar for the Navy's flying boats. When the Hildreth girls and their escorts arrived, it was Dorothea who suggested they clamber to the roof of the tent for a better view. Removing shoes, they pulled themselves up by the guy ropes and perched on the ridgepole, a couple at either end. The sisters had a camera which they passed back and forth, snapping pictures as Beachey started his third hop.

At an altitude of no more than 50 feet, he swung out over the lake, veered around and headed toward the tent. All at once the Navy men realized that the plane was coming in too low, and slid down the sloping tent top, reaching to pull the girls after them. The way Beachey figured what happened was this: "Either I encountered a downward trend of air . . . or I had lost so much speed in the quick turn that the machine lost headway and settled. Perhaps it was a combination of the two. I tried in every way to clear the tent but felt the shock of striking the ridgepole. Then the machine seemed to become unmanageable and the next thing I knew I was hanging in the straps head downward in the wreckage."

A wheel fouled the ridgepole and the four people were hurled from the tent-top. Both girls were struck by the airplane. Ruth Hildreth was killed outright, a portion of her skull torn away. Dorothea flung her arms upward and the propeller sliced through one side of her chest; she also sustained a fractured hip and arm. Dorothea was rushed to the hospital in Bath, where she lay in such critical condition that she was not informed of her sister's death. After a year of hospitalization, she recovered. The Navy men were injured, though not seriously, in the fall.

At first the crowd thought Beachey had been killed in the crash, as he hung inertly suspended. In reality, he got off with bruises, sprains, and a finger injury. He walked about the field in a daze, moaning that he wished it had been his life that was forfeit. Afterward he was confined to bed in nervous shock.

During the excitement of the tragedy, a thief had slipped into Beachey's room at Lulu Mott's boarding-house and relieved him of $6000 in cash.

A coroner's jury returned a verdict of accidental death and cleared Beachey of blame. Witnesses testified that he had been no more venturesome than usual; that the field was placarded as private, and spectators had gathered at their own risk. This was the only aviation fatality ever to occur at Hammondsport during the Curtiss years.

Some newspapers were critical of Beachey, hinting that he had been stunting at the time. Perturbed, he issued a statement of self-defense, saying: "Surely I am sick enough at heart, not to mention bodily injuries, without having to suffer from editorial criticism based on untruthful reports of Tuesday's terrible accident. I was not attempting to loop the loop or do any other extraordinary feat at the time . . . When a coroner's jury composed of representative men of the town, some of them friends of the unfortunate young lady and eye witnesses of the accident, exonerates me, it seems hard to me to be berated by some of the press for these untruthful reports."

Sympathetic messages came from other aviators and friends, urging him not to give up flying. While making up his mind, he canceled his entry in the around-Manhattan race, which was won by William S. Luckey, a graduate of the Curtiss school, in a Curtiss plane.

The mother of Ruth Hildreth refused to go near Hammondsport for the rest of her life, and the family never again occupied the cottage. Dorothea did not revisit the village until 1954.[3]

*   *   *

Beachey's decision was to put the accident from his mind and keep on flying. When the plane was rebuilt, he took it out to the winter camp at North Island in California and there, on November 18, performed the first loop in America. Diving from 3500 feet, he lifted the nose at 1000, described the circle, and came out of it at 300 feet. Curtiss, between trips to Europe, was at San Diego to watch this feat, and commented later: "I don't know yet why he didn't set his machine afire when the gas flowed down over the hot engine, but somehow Beachey got away with it."

On Thanksgiving Day he tripled. In a night letter to Curtiss from San Diego, he gloated:

"Exhibition Polo Grounds today four thousand dollars. Flew upside down half mile, loop three times in succession; 800 feet first, 600 second, 500 third. Power on all the time, engine not missing. Leaving tonight for Washington. Invitation Secretary War and Navy to give my ideas aviation in connection with government."

On Christmas day at San Francisco, Beachey looped five times in a row, breaking Pegoud's world record of four. He followed this up with a double loop at 300 feet, which he claimed as the record for low-altitude looping (Pegoud always performed high). On December 28, he looped six times over San Francisco Bay. On January 4, 1914, he made it seven, and then did a "corkscrew twist" while the plane was in vertical position on the up-side of a loop. By this time he had totaled 43 loops, one of which encircled a hydroplane in midair.

* * *

Beachey's guardian angel was vigilant up to a point. While looping at Santa Barbara in 1914, he lost control and plunged 1000 feet. At 400 feet from earth, he managed to right the aircraft enough to crash into the branches of a tree, walking away with minor injuries.

Later that year, he did loops over the Mall in Washington while President Woodrow Wilson watched from a White House window. At the Panama-Pacific Exposition in San Francisco, he flew through the immense Machinery Hall, in at one end and out the other.

And then the luck ran out.

On March 14, 1915, he was putting on a show for a crowd of 50,000 at the Exposition in a new Taube monoplane from Germany. Curtiss had warned him repeatedly about making demands on a plane which were beyond its aerodynamic capabilities. In this instance, he was expecting the monoplane to perform the same stunts he had hitherto done with a biplane. After a series of loops, he cut the motor at 3000 feet and went into his famous "perpendicular drop." When he tried to pull out of it, the wings folded and he dove into San Francisco Bay.

Ironically, he was not killed by the impact. The virtuoso pilot of his era simply drowned. When they recovered the body, the seat harness was partly unfastened. He had attained the ripe age of 31.

Beachey, the inveterate ladies' man, was engaged to be married when it happened.

18. Water Flying

The Navy's sudden flicker of interest was kindled in the fall of the year, and the season had a bearing on what happened next. Ely's saltation from shipboard almost came to grief because of foul November weather. The rugged northern winter to come ruled out flying experiments of any consequence at Hammondsport until the vineyards bloomed again. Aware that the Navy Department was at last in a receptive frame of mind and could probably be won over with an airplane capable of lifting off water, Curtiss had no intention of wasting precious months. Moreover, he had not yet regained possession of his factory.

As chief of the Navy's embryonic flying branch, Captain W. I. Chambers held no very exalted status, consigned to a cramped and dusty office hidden among filing cabinets, with no staff and no clerical help. About all he could do was recommend. Still, he tackled his nebulous task with crusading zeal and an abiding faith that his gold-braid superiors could be shown the light. The singular rapport which sprang up between him and Curtiss was fateful for both of them and for the cause of naval aeronautics. The aviator's practicality was much to his liking, and he found him "always ready to make experiments and as progressive as the Wrights were conservative."[1]

Curtiss confided to Chambers, probably as early as the Belmont meet, his plan to establish winter quarters in a warmer clime and set to work in earnest on the seaplane conundrum, which had so far baffled everyone who attacked it. For his part, Chambers gave his newfound friend all the help and encouragement he had the authority to do, along with advice on what would sway the thinking of the Secretary of the Navy. A steady correspondence flourished between them, and the high opinion which the captain held of his civilian collaborator is reflected in his subsequent words: "I believe that the progress made by the United States Navy in developing aviation during its early and critical period is due to Mr. Curtiss more than to anyone else."

The experience at Los Angeles the preceding January had shown Curtiss the desirability of the Southern California climate for winter flying work. The likeliest alternative, as he knew from motorcycle racing, would be Florida. Presumably the scale was tipped by Chambers, who would have been quick to point out the potentiality of naval collaboration in California harbors, especially that of San Diego. In addition, Chambers already had set machinery in motion for another shipboard experiment in San Francisco Harbor, and Curtiss had a role to play in that. Weather statistics indicated that San Diego afforded minimal wind and maximal sunshine, and the Aero Club of San Diego got busy on influencing the choice.

Curtiss was astute enough to realize that a core of trained pilots in the armed services would help build a military market for aircraft. On November 29, 1910, on the eve of starting west, he sent identical letters to Secretary of the Navy George von L. Meyer and Secretary of War Jacob M. Dickinson. These were open invitations for both the Navy and Army to assign officers to an experimental camp he proposed in California, where he offered to give them flying instruction without charge as a means of "assisting in developing the adaptability of the aeroplane to military purposes."

After preparing incorporation papers for the Curtiss Aeroplane Company, to be filed at Albany as soon as the bankruptcy of Herring-Curtiss was official, Curtiss and wife entrained for Los Angeles, followed by a freight-car load of "experimental material." The decision on where to place the camp could wait until he got there. Also in their wake followed both their mothers.

After a few years at Rock Stream, Glenn's mother had found herself confronted for the second time in her life by an alcoholic problem. J. Charles Adams proved to be quite a consumer of the products of his vineyard. His fortunes deteriorated with his behavior. By 1907, Lua Adams had enough of it, and decamped, taking the ten-year-old son, Carl, with her. She fled to Buffalo, where a sister lived. As Glenn came up in the world, she was a frequent visitor at Hammondsport, and now she decided to leave Buffalo and join him in California. Once there, she affected the name of Lua Curtiss Adams. (As for the abandoned second husband, he lived out the remainder of his life as a semi-recluse in Rock Stream, sometimes voicing mild boasts about the success of his stepson, Glenn.)

On New Year's Day, 1911, Mr. and Mrs. Glenn Curtiss had the honor of riding in the parade of the Pasadena Rose Tournament and Carnival. Their vehicle was an electric Victoria, described by the Pasadena *Daily News* as "one of the most beautiful entries of the parade."

*   *   *

California's second great air meet was scheduled for San Francisco in January 1911, and Captain Chambers had arranged for the cruiser *Pennsylvania* to be anchored in the harbor at that time. The demonstration which he and other Navy officials desired as a sequel to Ely's stunt at Hampton Roads was its reverse: that is, the landing of an airplane on the deck of a ship. Such a maneuver was going to be much trickier, and Curtiss confessed he had "misgivings" about this one. Gene Ely had certainly earned the right to try it, and he was accordingly booked for the San Francisco meet.

Curtiss joined Ely at San Francisco and together they oversaw the construction of a platform above the quarterdeck of the cruiser, sloping toward the stern. Its dimensions were 130 feet by 50 feet. The main problem here was a device to slow the plane before it could plow ahead into the mast. This they solved with the first "arresting gear" ever installed on a ship. A parallel series of twenty-two ropes were stretched athwart the platform, held taut by sandbags tied to either end. Grab-hooks on the belly of the plane caught the ropes. For further safety of the pilot, in case he was pitched out, heavy awning shields flanked the runway.

Meanwhile, Curtiss had been informed by the San Diego Aero Club that a tentative lease was already nailed down for him on North

Island, a scrubby, uninhabited barrier beach between San Diego Bay and the Pacific Ocean. Four miles long, two miles wide, this island belonged to the Coronado Beach Company, which operated the fashionable Hotel del Coronado. It was connected with Coronado Island by a sand spit which cleared water only at low tide. The two islands were separated by a long, shallow embayment known as the Spanish Bight. The location sounded right to Curtiss and he was impatient to look it over.

The Secretary of the Navy was first to respond to the offer of free instruction, and a brawny young officer, Lieutenant Theodore G. Ellyson, was detached from submarine duty at Newport News on December 23 with orders to report to Curtiss wherever he might be. For reasons unknown, Ellyson bore the nickname of Spuds. He found Curtiss in Los Angeles, and, the day after the Pasadena rose parade, they journeyed together to examine the San Diego site. North Island had a number of level spots which could be cleared for fields, but Curtiss especially fancied its firm beaches. An extra dividend, from his viewpoint, was its seclusion from prying crowds. Access could be gained only by boat from across the bay. Curtiss told the Aero Club to go ahead and negotiate the lease.

Lieutenant Ellyson sent a report of the inspection to Captain Chambers, picturing the Spanish Bight as "ideal for water experiments," and remarking: "It is very probable that Mr. Curtiss will establish his permanent headquarters here, or a western station." Ellyson was an immediate convert: "I am a strong Curtiss man as far as the present control is concerned."

Chambers communicated back to Ellyson: "We are all looking for improvements, especially in automatic stability, and if I read Mr. Curtiss correctly he is not too conservative to adopt a good improvement regardless of who owns the patent.

"It may be that we will yet have a machine able to rise from water that is smooth at sea and that can be hoisted out and in like a boat."

The Aero Club concluded a three-year lease for exclusive occupancy of North Island, with a clause that Curtiss could invite the War and Navy Departments to share its use for flying schools. While the carload of "material" from Hammondsport was moved in, Aero Club volunteers slashed brush, put up sheds and shelters, and built a pier for the motor launch which was chartered for transport to and from the city. A defunct haybarn served as the original hangar. Curtiss rented a cottage for Lena and their family entourage on the grounds of the Coronado

Hotel, handy to his work, and assembled the aircraft on which he was determined to try out any and every sort of float device until something worked. Ellyson pitched in and helped, as did the Aero Club amateurs, practically living in bathing suits, often chilled to the marrow. Curtiss hired a skilled machinist, George E. A. Hallett, from the Baker Machine Company on the San Diego waterfront.

In the meantime, the War Department instructed Brigadier General Tasker H. Bliss, commandant of the Department of California, to detail as many men as he could spare for aviation training. As news of Curtiss's open door spread among Army stations of the West, some thirty men applied for the duty. Three were chosen: Lieutenant Paul M. Beck, who had flown with Curtiss at the Los Angeles meet to test his crude bombsight; Lieutenant G. E. M. Kelly and Lieutenant John C. Walker, Jr. Reporting at North Island in January, these young men considered it a rare privilege to take part in experiments leading to a hydroplane, hopefully.

The air meet was to start the second week in January and Curtiss was doubly anxious to be on hand for Ely's shore-to-ship essay, having missed the episode at Hampton Roads. Accompanied by his naval proselyte, he hied to San Francisco, but their hopes were dashed by daily windiness. January 17 was the date for opening the school on North Island. When time ran out, Curtiss and Ellyson returned to San Diego with a promise from the Associated Press to apprise him of the outcome by personal messenger. The wire story was delivered on the 18th, and it was exhilarating.

Ely's takeoff was from the old Presidio parade ground which San Francisco had designated as Selfridge Field in memory of its martyred native son, Tom Selfridge; this coincidence would not have escaped Curtiss's notice. Ship's boats and launches were scattered over the 13 miles of water which had to be traversed. A lookout on the *Pennsylvania* sighted the plane, and her siren roared a blast. Ely circled the fleet, dipping a salute to each ship, then flew in low to the stern of the cruiser, dropping lightly to the platform. Hooks grabbed ropes and stopped him within 60 feet. His wife was waiting on the bridge with Captain C. F. Pond, and the skipper was their host at luncheon. Then Ely winged easily back to Selfridge Field, where soldiers hoisted him on their shoulders and bore him to headquarters. Numerous toasts were drunk.

Exultantly, Curtiss hailed the flight as "probably one of the greatest feats in accurate landing ever performed by an aviator." He said it was a foretaste of what airplanes might do militarily—"joining as nothing else can the two branches of the service."[2]

❋   ❋   ❋

The surprising thing is how quickly a successful seaplane was off water, once Curtiss buckled down to it. The basic machine brought from Hammondsport already had a short, wide pontoon replacing the two rear wheels of the tricycle landing gear, also a small forward pontoon instead of the front wheel. When this was launched on the Spanish Bight, the thrust of the propeller pushed its nose under water. A wooden "planing surface" was added in front, and the outfit could then taxi slowly, with water boiling up over the rear pontoon. To deflect the water, a "snout" of wood and canvas was given to the rear pontoon, and Curtiss could taxi a trifle faster; when the throttle was opened, however, the nose pontoon again went under. They added a wide "planing surface" on bamboo outriggers 6 feet ahead of the forward pontoon. The totality of this unwieldy rig climbed up on the surface and moved along rapidly, but it skidded sidewise and demolished a pontoon on a mud flat.

According to Spuds Ellyson, no less than fifty changes were made in the course of these experiments. "Those of us who did not know Mr. Curtiss well," he said in retrospect, "wondered that he did not give up in despair. Since that time we have learned that anything he says he can do, he always accomplishes, as he always works the problem out in his mind before making any statement." Ellyson revealed more about how he and the Army pupils regarded this man whom they were voluntarily assisting to make a historic breakthrough in aeronautics:

"You see, it was not Curtiss, the genius and inventor, whom we knew. It was 'G.H.,' a comrade and chum, who made us feel that we were all working together, and that our ideas and advice were really of some value. It was never a case of 'do this' or 'do that,' to his amateur or to his regular mechanics, but always, 'What do you think of making this change?' He was always willing to listen to any argument but generally managed to convince you that his plan was best. I could write volumes on Curtiss, the man."

The night after the pontoon was smashed on the mud bar, Curtiss went home and sketched a single pontoon, neat, narrow, and shallow, to supplant what Hallett termed "all the conglomeration we had under the plane." It measured 12 feet long, 2 feet wide, and 1 foot deep, and the front curved upward like the prow of a boat. He took the sketch to the Baker Machine Company where it was detailed by pattern makers and constructed of thin spruce.

On January 26, 1911, the breakthrough happened. As Curtiss told it:

"I had not expected to make a flight . . . only try it on the water to see how the new float acted. It ploughed through the water deeply at first, but gathered speed and rose higher and higher in the water and skipped more and more lightly until the float barely skimmed the surface of the bay. So intent was I in watching the water that I did not notice that I was approaching the shore, and to avoid running aground I tilted the horizontal control and the machine seemed to leap into the air like a frightened gull. So suddenly did it rise that it quite took me by surprise . . . The effect of that first flight on the men who had worked, waited and watched for it was magical. They ran up and down the beach, throwing their hats up into the air and shouting in their enthusiasm."

Still half incredulous that he had actually done it, he swung back and settled on water to try again. When the craft rose just as easily, he knew that he had opened a whole new phase for aviation. Navy vessels anchored in the harbor sensed what was occurring and let loose their whistles in a tumult. Partly as a gesture of pardonable pride, partly to test the plane's behavior in turns, he circled the bay twice.

Once more Glenn Curtiss was front-page news across the land, and he was quoted as saying: "I have succeeded in solving the one problem the Secretary of the Navy regarded as the most difficult, and the one necessary to make the aeroplane of value to the Navy."

The navies of the world had remained lukewarm toward aviation until this positive proof that a hydroplane could be practical. Prior experiments in Europe, notably by Henri Fabre at Marseilles, had been unconvincing. The naval viewpoint changed with startling abruptness when it became manifest that aircraft might serve as a fleet auxiliary. The clincher was the sequel which Curtiss enacted three weeks later.

Soon after Ely's deck landing, the cruiser *Pennsylvania* moved south and stood at anchor in San Diego Bay. In the interim, McCurdy had further caught Navy attention by his lengthy overwater flight from Florida nearly to Havana. Curtiss kept his mind riveted on what Chambers had insinuated about a hydroplane that "can be hoisted in and out like a boat." On February 17, he sent a message out to Captain Pond, on the *Pennsylvania*, saying he "would be pleased to fly over and be hoisted aboard whenever it was convenient to him." The boat brought back Pond's reply: "Come on over." No special preparations were needed. The plane was launched on the Spanish Bight and it took Curtiss less than three minutes to reach the cruiser and sit down on the water alongside. An ordinary crane, used for lifting the ship's launches, lowered a sling which was fastened around the plane. "Not caring to trust too much weight to the untested sling," Curtiss clambered topside and slipped one leg through the big hook of the crane while being lifted to the deck with his machine. After ten minutes aboard, he was lowered and flitted back to the beach hangar. The entire operation consumed less than a half-hour.

Flights with the "water-fowl" were made almost daily from the Spanish Bight, sometimes with Army and Navy men as passengers. Curtiss was enjoying himself immensely during this period: "I will confess that I got more pleasure out of flying the new machine over water than I ever got flying over land." The potentialities of what he had opened up tempted him to prophesy: "Great, powerful hydroaeroplanes may be able to cross the ocean at high speed."

At the same time, he was in a veritable frenzy of experimentation, anxious to explore all avenues as rapidly as possible. A drawback soon encountered was the effect of spray on a propeller: drops of water struck it like bullets, splintering the wood; tin shields for the blades remedied this. When the motor and propeller were shifted to the front, Curtiss disliked the arrangement because the prop blast hit him in the face and the engine obstructed his view. A triplane surface gave "remarkable lifting power" but was dismissed for its less redeeming qualities.

The imagination of Curtiss was working overtime, and the next step beyond a pure hydroplane had to be a hybrid which could function on both land and water: in other words, an amphibian. In a few days he devised a retractable wheeled landing gear, raised and lowered by hand, to supplement the float. George Hallett termed it a "weird contraption," but also "a remarkable piece of experimental engineering and invention." The name, *Triad*, for this pioneer amphibian craft seems to have been Curtiss's own inspiration, signifying the three environments in which it operated—land, sea, and air. On February 26, its inventor took the *Triad* up from the Spanish Bight, lowered its wheels, and landed on the beach of the Coronado Hotel. After lunching in the hotel, he reversed the procedure and was back on the water. Curtiss thought: "It now seems possible to use it to establish communication between the Navy and Army."

As for the platforms used by Ely, any landlubber could see that they were impractical makeshifts. Curtiss and Ellyson set their minds to a solution of this problem, and the officer felt that getting the plane off the ship was the really important angle. A compressed-air catapult seemed too rough. They talked about a slanting cable running down from a ship's superstructure to the bow, with a groove on the underside of the airplane to fit it. They did not get around to trying this idea at North Island, but it would keep.

Meanwhile in Washington, Captain Chambers grew more excited over what his collaboration with Curtiss had produced, and now he had ammunition with which to press for an appropriation. Fanciulli let him know that he and Curtiss had decided on $10,000 as the price for a fully equipped hydroaeroplane.

Chambers had an imagination, too, and asked the aviator in one letter why it would not be possible to apply electric power to flying. He received this reply: "The idea of driving an aeroplane with an electric motor and getting power by wireless has for some time been interesting me. I do not think that with the present storage batteries there would be any chance to use an electric motor economically."

As soon as the lease on North Island was consummated, Curtiss wrote again to the military cabinet officers, inviting the Army and Navy to share the island with him for their respective aviation purposes. The Secretary of the Navy responded that the matter would be considered, and that, for the moment, Ensign Charles F. Pousland was being detached from a destroyer for flying instruction at San Diego.

The training aspect of the camp had not been neglected during the invention of the hydroplane, and two civilian pupils were admitted along with the military enrollees; these were Charles C. Wittmer of Chicago and R. H. St. Henry of San Francisco. The practice machine was a 4-cylinder biplane with truncated wings and a governor on the motor to prevent its getting airborne during basic instruction: hence the expression, "grasscutter," born at San Diego and transferred to Hammondsport. The students affectionately called this original training plane "Lizzie."

In one of his "grasscutter" runs, Lieutenant Kelly forgot how to switch off the engine. "Stop it! Stop it!" Curtiss yelled. When Kelly kept on going, Curtiss ran, crawled up under the moving plane and cut the switch. His coat was torn, his back wrenched, and he was sorely bruised.

Curtiss insisted that the training must be thorough, as the Army and Navy men were in turn to be flying instructors for others. His attitude toward his pupils is revealed in his words: "I have never seen anyone more eager to fly, and to fly as quickly as possible, than were these officers . . . I did not want to force the knowledge of aviation upon the young officers. Rather, I wanted to let them absorb most of it, and to come by the thing naturally and with confidence."

On April 11, 1911, the school turned out its first graduate and the U. S. Navy obtained its first accredited pilot. Curtiss informed Secretary of the Navy Meyer: "I have the honor to report that Lieutenant Ellyson is now competent to care for and operate Curtiss aeroplanes and instruct others in the operation of these machines."

During this interlude, the Curtiss Aeroplane Company delivered its first plane to the War Department, with McCurdy doing the acceptance flight. The machine went to San Antonio for experimental use of the Army. An indication that someone in the War Department thought Curtiss could be lured away from his love affair with the Navy, and that he might be of greater use than merely in supplying aircraft, is seen in a curious rumor which found its way into print. Whether it was a trial balloon or actually had substance, this report stated that the Army was about to brevet Glenn H. Curtiss with the rank of colonel and place him in charge of its aeronautical section.

The townsfolk of Hammondsport, meantime, underwent a jittery winter. As if fretting over the suspenseful auction of the Herring-Curtiss properties were not enough, they read this item in their local paper: "Glenn H. Curtiss has purchased a small island in the bay at Coronado to build a winter home and conduct experimental work in flying machines." Evidently gossip magnified this until the village foresaw the loss of its most illustrious citizen together with his industry. At any rate, Curtiss felt it incumbent on him to calm the fears of his friends and neighbors with a letter to the Herald, explaining that he could not have bought the island had he been ever so inclined: the asking price was $6,000,000. He added a few chatty details:

"Aside from our camp, there is nothing on the island but some sage brush and a million jack rabbits. Rabbits are so numerous that they get in the way of starting and alighting the aeroplanes. Only last week Mr. Harkness [Harry S. Harkness, a New York sportsman] struck one of

them with his propeller in landing, and ruined the propeller as well as
the rabbit . . . We have a delightful combination of sunshine, flowers,
ants and lizards . . . San Diego is like Hammondsport in that you can
get in by one railroad only."

*   *   *

The Curtisses and Jennie Neff returned to Hammondsport on May
1, 1911, leaving Lua Curtiss Adams and her son, Carl, at Coronado.

Except for the ongoing Wright litigation, the clouds had dissipated
and the prospect could hardly have been rosier. Curtiss was supremely
confident that no high court could rule that the aileron was an infringement of the wing-warping patent. The season in California had witnessed a series of phenomenal achievements, and he was now assured of
a Navy order for two machines, presaging a run of future naval business.
Once again he was the rightful owner of Castle Hill and the plant
which was ready to roll into production of aircraft and engines. The
Navy detailed Spuds Ellyson to Hammondsport to continue working
with him, and would soon assign more officers for flight instruction. He
projected a flying school at the head of Keuka Lake. The villagers
sensed the dawning of a new day after the Herring nightmare.

If there was one small flaw in the picture for Curtiss, it was the
personal matter of governing affairs for his mother, who had not only
made herself a complete responsibility but was bent upon bringing her
relatives from Jasper to California as dependents. Lua had a penchant
for dreaming up business enterprises for herself, and Glenn had trouble
keeping her from going off at tangents. It appears that her first brainstorm in California was the marketing of aviation trinkets, trading on
his name, to judge from his admonition soon after his return home:
"I have your letter and sketches. I would not get too deep in the
jewelry business. The man who made the little propellers is not with us
and I cannot furnish them. [At a guess, she wanted imitations of the
enameled gimcrack he wore on his cap visor.] . . . I suggest that you
look for a good place to live somewhere back on the hill. If you could
find a so-called ranch with irrigation rights I think it would be a good
place to take the whole family—sort of turn them out to pasture . . . In
reference to photography, I recommend that Carl experiment a little so
that he can be of some use to us later."

Before long, Lua was complaining of an insect nuisance, and Glenn's
caustic humor shows in the letter he sent back: "The reference to the

fleas don't sound very encouraging, but don't you think that after you have been there a year or so you become distasteful to them? I understand that the natives don't mind them."

Now the hydroplane and flying boat era dawned on Keuka Lake. The villagers were excited afresh by their introduction to an airplane which could fly from water. Curtiss very nearly got the new epoch off to an unhappy start. The float sprang a leak and was partly filled when he took the hydroaeroplane up for its first Hammondsport flight. As he lowered in for a landing, the weight shifting to the prow caused a dive and the machine flipped. The pilot was thrown through the front controls, suffering injuries which were luckily minor. Ellyson reported the incident to Chambers: "If there had been no frontal control, Mr. Curtiss would not have been injured at all, and he expects to do away with it in future hydroaeroplanes." Pontoons would henceforth be divided into compartments, he added.

The impact of San Diego resulted in a Congressional appropriation of $25,000 for the Navy to gain a start in aviation, and Chambers sent specifications, asking Curtiss if he could make delivery by July 1. Chambers wanted, in brief, a de luxe version of the *Triad:* "a hydroaeroplane capable of rising from or landing on either the land or the water, capable of attaining a speed of at least 55 miles an hour, with a fuel supply for four hours' flight. To carry two people and to be so fitted that either person could control the machine."

With an affirmative response, Chambers prepared requisitions for two Curtiss planes: the *Triad,* designated as the Navy A-1; and a 4-cylinder land plane, the A-2, for flight training. An order for a land machine went to the Wright Company.

Since the A-1 must carry two men, it would need extra power. Curtiss called in Kleckler and said: "Henny, you've got to get busy on a bigger engine." The motor eventuating was the prototype of the immortal OX-5, which was to see widespread service in World War I and later. The specifications also demanded quick invention of a system of dual control.

It was only fair that the Navy's initial aircraft be entrusted to its first qualified pilot, who had been present all through its evolutionary stages. Three pilots were needed for the three planes being purchased, and Lieutenant John H. Towers was ordered to Hammondsport to understudy Ellyson. Lieutenant John Rodgers went to Dayton for training in the Wright machine.

More than incidentally, Curtiss had found an order awaiting from the German Imperial Navy for two hydroplanes, along with an invitation to demonstrate them in person at Kiel harbor. This was the harbinger of a flood of European orders, while the Japanese Navy made overtures to dispatch a cadre of officers to Hammondsport for instruction.

In that month of June 1911, the Aero Club of America assumed the function of issuing pilots' licenses under the rules of the Fédération Aéronautique Internationale. The recipient of its License Number 1, after some debate, was Glenn H. Curtiss. This was an honor which might logically have been expected to accrue to Orville Wright. The rationale for its award to Curtiss was the fact that he had made the first public flight in America by a citizen of the United States. (Already he held license Number 2 from France, in tribute to his Rheims flight; Blériot had French license Number 1.) It is worthy of note that, in the near future, a certificate of graduation from the Curtiss Flying School was more highly valued in many quarters than an Aero Club license.

Jack Towers reported for duty on June 27, on which date Curtiss wrote Captain Chambers: "I am very anxious to have you come up here, as I want to talk to you about the future requirements of the Navy. It is my wish to push the manufacture of aeroplanes, and, if possible, secure a large part of the Navy business." Chambers was responsive, arriving on July 1 for the first of several sojourns in Hammondsport, just in time to accept formal delivery of the A-1.

Ellyson maintained a log on flights of the A-1, making an entry that on July 2 he attempted to fly Chambers to Penn Yan but, lacking wind, was unable to get off water; they taxied the entire 22 miles, giving Chambers a scenic tour of the lake, and Ellyson flew back solo. There ensued a good deal of passenger carrying by both Curtiss and Ellyson, the latter taking Chambers up on a later day. Another passenger noted was George Hallett, the mechanic from San Diego, whom Curtiss had found so useful that he brought him to Hammondsport. They had difficulty with radiator leaks and the engine finally had to be rebuilt. All engine repairs and replacements were done by Curtiss "without charge to the government."

By the wane of summer, Jack Towers qualified for his Aero Club pilot's license. Before the A-1 was taken to Greenbury Point, Annapolis, where the Navy was setting up an aerial station, the two officers and Curtiss carried out the long-discussed experiment with the launching wire. A cable 250 feet long was stretched from a 16-foot platform on the lakeshore to an underwater spile; auxiliary wires on either side held the plane on even keel during its toboggan slide. Takeoffs were successful, and Curtiss concluded that this was the "last step" for launching from shipboard. After further trials of the method, however, Ellyson told Chambers: "I would not recommend the use of this device on a ship with rolling motion."

*   *   *

Another exquisite silver trophy was put forth in 1911, proclaimed as the Aero Club of America Trophy (later known as the Collier Trophy). Its donor was Robert J. Collier, president of the Collier publishing empire and one of the charter investors in the Wright Company. The trophy, kept in custody by the Aero Club, was to be given annually for the most significant contribution to the science of aeronautics during the year. Its initial award went to Glenn H. Curtiss for his invention of the hydroplane. The announcement, issued through *Collier's* magazine, said: "No event since the advent of the aeroplane itself has aroused so much interest as the hydroaeroplane."

Never before had Curtiss applied for a patent, excepting as he shared in the A.E.A. patent application. Feeling now that he had so fundamental an invention that it should be recorded, he filed with the U. S. Patent Office on August 22, 1911, an application for a patent on a hydroaeroplane. After presenting his seven claims to "new and useful improvements," the document stated: "I am aware that various modifications may be made in my invention without departing from the spirit of the claims, and I therefore do not desire to be limited to the preferred embodiments herein shown in the drawings." (The application was granted October 12, 1915, as Patent Number 1,156,215.)[3]

So prominent a figure had Curtiss grown to be in the public eye that the Frederick A. Stokes Company asked him to write a book on the general subject: *Curtiss: Story of the Aeroplane.* Confiding this request to Alexander Graham Bell, he said: "Not having the talent or time to get out copy for a book of this kind, I have gotten Mr. Post to take hold of it." Augustus M. Post was to be his ghost writer for the section of the book which would appear under his byline; others, including Post and Spuds Ellyson, contributed passages in their own names. Post suggested to Curtiss that he ask Dr. Bell to write a foreword, and this was the reason for the letter. Bell did not relish the idea, replying: "I would gladly do anything I could to assist you or the cause of aviation, and I trust you realize that I have the keenest appreciation of your great work, and pride in having contributed what I could toward the new art which you have done so much for." Still, Bell felt that the book, as outlined in Post's prospectus, would be a psychological blunder. "I am too proud of you and interested in you to help you make such a mistake."

Nevertheless, the project went forward, and the book appeared in 1912 under the title *The Curtiss Aviation Book*, lacking an introduction. It was dedicated "To Mrs. Mabel G. Bell." In flying circles, it was not much respected for accuracy or style of content. Henry Kleckler said it "didn't sound like Curtiss"; Lincoln Beachey snapped that it would "poison your mind."

In making the request to Bell, in October 1911, Curtiss mentioned that he had been "spending weeks" in the New York offices of Emerson R. Newell, for the recording of testimony in the Wright infringement suit; and remarked: "It proves fair to be almost as lengthy as the famous Bell patent case."

*   *   *

Simultaneously with his return to San Diego for the second winter at North Island, Curtiss planted a flying school at Miami, sending Charles C. Wittmer to take charge. His reasoning was that "this locality was calculated to develop an interest in the utility of the aeroplane, hydroaeroplane and flying boat, in the minds of men of prominence who were accustomed to go to Florida during the winter season."

Miami's mayor, E. G. Sewell, started the ball rolling in 1911 when he besought the Wright brothers to come down and afford that city a glimpse of human flight. They sent Howard Gill, of their exhibition team, who did some flying over the future site of Hialeah for a fee of $7500. Mayor Sewell then tried to persuade them to set up a pilot training school, but they were disinterested. Sewell turned to Curtiss, who accepted for a $1000 guarantee and the gift of a field. The field was on Miami Beach, and from it Wittmer and Beckwith Havens proceeded to fly the first hydroplanes over Biscayne Bay.

In selecting 1912 winter quarters for the Naval Aviation Detachment, the Navy Department considered Guantánamo Bay, but evidently Chambers swung the choice back to North Island; he argued that "we can work with ships there," whereas the Atlantic Fleet was "always busy and rushed." This year the Navy intended to conduct its own camp. Chambers wired Curtiss of the decision after his arrival at San Diego, and Curtiss wrote that the telegram announcing "that the aviators were coming to San Diego was certainy a great joy to us out here . . . We have a fine place here to try out the wire scheme—a cliff near water's edge."

The Navy's tent camp was laid out three-fourths of a mile from the Curtiss establishment, and its occupants jokingly dubbed it "Camp Trouble." Ellyson was back and Towers was initiated to North Island, as these congenial partners kept on working with the A-1. They tested out a new Curtiss double control, with twin steering wheels, and Ellyson logged: "It will be satisfactory for instruction."

A newcomer among the Navy personnel, whose presence may be traced directly to the influence of Captain Chambers, was Naval Constructor Holden C. Richardson, a young man of unusual technical ability. Richardson's specialty was the structure and shaping of hulls, and Chambers schemed to channel this talent into water aircraft. Beyond a doubt, the captain knew of Curtiss's intention to tackle the problem of the flying boat during the 1912 season at North Island. Because of the larger, wider hull involved, this was certain to be a much harder nut to crack than the hydroplane. At any rate, Richardson spent a good portion of his time at the Curtiss camp where he was given basic flight training. In frequent passenger flights with Ellyson and Towers in the *Triad*, he learned more, and by April he had his wings.

The fame of the Curtiss school had spread so that it drew an influx of private pupils. J. Lansing Callan, on borrowed money, was happily realizing his ambition, living at the Club House which had been added to the island's facilities (board and lodging cost him $4 a week). Julia Clarke created a ripple. Then there was a married couple, Mr. and Mrs. W. B. Atwater from New York, who had instruction preparatory to their purchase of a hydroplane. The Atwaters afterward took the machine on an Asiatic tour, and their flights at Tokyo helped to spur Japanese interest in aviation.

The bird population was thick about San Diego Bay, and its human competitors often found the air cluttered with gulls, wild ducks, and pelicans. This gave Curtiss the notion of aerial hunting—that is, chasing birds with a net on the front of the plane. "Perhaps," he mused, "when the killing of wild fowl with guns shall have palled on sportsmen, we shall see the method of 'netting' them with an aeroplane come into use." Mrs. Atwater went so far as to try this dubious sport, but gave it up when her propeller barely missed a fat pelican.

While such things were transpiring on the West Coast, an old friend, Louis Paulhan, put in his appearance at Hammondsport to

obtain a license for European manufacture and sales of Curtiss hydroplanes. Jerome Fanciulli accompanied him back to France with a sample
machine which was demonstrated at Monte Carlo. During a conference
with a business associate of Paulhan's, the two Frenchmen indulged in
side discussions in their own language without realizing that Fanciulli
understood French, and he detected what he judged to be some unscrupulous "conniving." He notified Curtiss of this and the negotiation
was broken off. (Fanciulli booked his return passage on the maiden
voyage of the *Titanic;* an urgent cablegram, however, summoned him
back to New York two weeks ahead of her sailing date. The *Titanic*
sank in April 1912.)

At North Island, all efforts failed to get an experimental aeroboat
hull unglued from the water of the Spanish Bight. Thus it came about,
with some poetic justice, that Keuka Lake saw the world's first flying
boat arise from her bosom in the summer of 1912.

The key to the puzzle was simple enough, but no one had thought
of it before. A contingent of Navy men were again detailed to Hammondsport for the summer, and Chambers himself made another trip of
"inspection." No matter how they shaped a hull, it had too much suction
to quit the water. Curtiss pursued the trial runs in a motorboat,
usually with Richardson, studying the wake. One day, as they pulled
up to the pier after another failure, Curtiss asked the rest what they
would think about putting a jog, or a wedge, on the bottom to break
the suction. All judged it worth a try, and he dispatched Kleckler to saw
some pieces of wood, which were then fastened to the hull like a
shallow step. "As soon as that was done," recalled Kleckler, "they found
they could rise up on top of the water and take off like a flying dog."
From then on, hulls were built with the "step bottom," and also with
ventilating ducts which admitted air behind the step.

*   *   *

A domestic event of some moment coincided almost precisely with
the birth of the flying boat. On June 16, 1912, a son was born.

Over the past ten years, Lena had held to her oath not to bear
another child, so fearful was she of a congenital defect. The sorrow of
losing her firstborn, though subdued, had never left her. The trepidation with which she awaited this confinement may well be surmised. To
her infinite joy, the second baby was normal. Congratulatory messages
poured in from all over, ringing changes on the theme: "Long live the
new aviator."

52. Charles K. Hamilton, the original Curtiss exhibition pilot, learning the game at Hammondsport. FROM THE HENRY KLECKLER ALBUMS.

53. Lincoln Beachey, the most talented flyer and stunt man of his time. J. LANSING CALLAN COLLECTION.

54. Beachey diving under the steel-arch bridge at Niagara after his daring descent over the lip of the Horseshoe Falls. J. LANSING CALLAN COLLECTION.

55. J. Lansing Callan caught the aviation craze from seeing the start of Curtiss's Hudson River flight. On borrowed money, he learned to fly at the Curtiss camp at San Diego. J. LANSING CALLAN COLLECTION.

56. Julia Clarke argued Curtiss into letting her go on the exhibition circuit. She paid with her life. J. LANSING CALLAN COLLECTION.

57. Captain Thomas Baldwin, who built and flew the first successful American dirigible, could not resist building an airplane for himself, after the Curtiss pattern, calling it the *Red Devil*. With it, he did considerable exhibition flying. FROM THE HENRY KLECKLER ALBUMS.

58. A typical handbill of an exhibition meet in which a Curtiss contract flyer appeared. This was at Sarnia, Ontario. COURTESY, OWEN S. BILLMAN.

DAY OF PLEASURE

TUESDAY, JULY 1ST Bayview Park SARNIA

AEROPLANE FLIGHTS

AEROPLANE FLIGHTS

Aviator Beachey in his Curtiss Aeroplane who will do everything that is possible to do with an Aeroplane.

5 Mile Race between Motorcycle and Aeroplane

5 MILE Professional RACE

59. Curtiss did his last exhibition flying at Winona Lake, Indiana, in August 1911. There he departed from custom to take a passenger in a hydroplane: Billy Sunday, the most celebrated evangelist of the time. CULVER PICTURES.

60. The dawn of a new epoch in naval aviation: Eugene Ely's plane after landing aboard the cruiser *Pennsylvania* in San Francisco Harbor, January 1911. J. LANSING CALLAN COLLECTION.

61. Eugene Ely taking off from the *Pennsylvania* for return flight to land. NAVY DEPART-
MENT PHOTO IN THE NATIONAL ARCHIVES.

62. Curtiss with the first hydroplane, about to take off from the Spanish Bight at San
Diego, 1911. NATIONAL AIR AND SPACE MUSEUM.

63. What the Secretary of the Navy asked for: Curtiss on the top wing of his hydroaeroplane about to be hoisted aboard the cruiser *Pennsylvania* in San Diego Harbor. NAVY DEPARTMENT PHOTO IN THE NATIONAL ARCHIVES.

64. The instruction of Navy Pilot No. 1, Lieutenant Theodore (Spuds) Ellyson, at San Diego. Curtiss has just shifted the dual-control wheel to Ellyson. J. LANSING CALLAN COLLECTION.

65. Experiment with a triplane at the North Island Curtiss Aviation Camp. FROM THE
HENRY KLECKLER ALBUMS.

66. The Aero Club of America issued its pilot's license Number 1 to Glenn Curtiss in June 1911. The delicate decision as between Curtiss and Orville Wright for this honor was reached on the basis that he was the first American citizen to make a public flight in this country. COURTESY, GLENN H. CURTISS, JR.

67. Back at Hammondsport (summer 1911), the pioneer amphibian, the *Triad,* was given work-outs. Spuds Ellyson perches beside Curtiss on the wing. The deep notch of the Glen is seen beyond. NATIONAL AIR AND SPACE MUSEUM.

68. At last, water-flying on Keuka Lake. With a Navy order for two planes, Curtiss established lakefront beaching facilities. FROM THE HENRY KLECKLER ALBUMS.

69. The Navy's pilot Number 3, Lieutenant John H. Towers, was assigned to Hammondsport for training in 1911. J. LANSING CALLAN COLLECTION.

70. Curtiss and Ellyson had discussed an inclined wire as a means of launching a plane from a Navy vessel at sea. The experiment was successfully tried on the shore of Keuka Lake in September 1911. NATIONAL AIR AND SPACE MUSEUM.

71. Scene at the Curtiss Aviation School on North Island, San Diego, winter of 1912.
J. LANSING CALLAN COLLECTION.

72. Curtiss finally licked the problem of the flying boat on Keuka Lake in the summer of 1912. Early aeroboats lined up at the waterfront. NATIONAL AIR AND SPACE MUSEUM.

73. The Curtiss Aviation School at Hammondsport was going full-tilt by June 1912. J. LANSING CALLAN COLLECTION.

74. The Navy immediately wanted men trained in the use of flying boats. Here Curtiss discusses dual control with Lieutenant John H. Towers. J. LANSING CALLAN COLLECTION.

75. Proud parents: Glenn H. Curtiss, Jr., was born in June 1912, at almost the same time as the aeroboat. COURTESY, GLENN H. CURTISS, JR.

76. The Smithsonian Institution
awarded the Langley Medal
to Curtiss in 1913 for his invention of the hydroplane and
the flying boat. COURTESY,
GLENN H. CURTISS, JR.

77. Orville and Wilbur Wright
during their attendance at the
Belmont Park international
air meet of 1910.

78. Henry Ford visited
Hammondsport, probably in
1913, judging by the model of
the flying boat Curtiss is showing
him. FROM THE HENRY
KLECKLER ALBUMS.

79. After swearing off flying for a few months, Lincoln Beachey backslid. He had Curtiss build for him this specially reinforced plane for looping. NATIONAL AIR AND SPACE MUSEUM.

80. A split-second of horror: Testing out his new stunt machine, Beachey lost control and fouled the ridgepole of the tent on which two couples were sitting. One of the Hildreth sisters was killed. Their Navy escorts were Lieutenants Bellinger and Richardson. The snapshot was caught by an eight-year-old boy with a box camera. COURTESY, MRS. FREDERICK RUSSELL.

In a letter to his mother, Curtiss said: "The baby is all right and Lena doing well. He got pretty well squeezed 'aborning' but don't look bad today. He weighs 8½ pounds. They all insist on naming him Glenn H."

And so he was christened Glenn Hammond Curtiss, Junior, but commonly called "Baby Glenn," and finally "Babe," during his boyhood. Lena lavished upon him the affection which Carlton had not survived to enjoy. Glenn, Jr., was never informed that he once had a brother until he was old enough to leave home for preparatory school.

During the 1912 stay in California, Curtiss had acquired a piece of land overlooking the Pacific, at Coronado, and engaged a contractor to build a bungalow for his mother. By this time, Lua Curtiss Adams had gathered into her fold one of her sisters, Kate, and her aged father, Henry Andrews. Glenn's letters to her often carried an undertone of vexation, as if he were scolding an unruly child. No sooner was he back in Hammondsport than Lua found fault with the site on which her house was being erected, and he retorted: "I simply agreed to what I understood you wanted. I have remarked several times to Lena that I expected you would be dissatisfied with it after you got it . . . I suppose it is placed now and we will have to leave it there for awhile . . . It is quite possible that the big house will never be built anyway." (Curtiss had contemplated building a home of his own on the property.)

It is perhaps germane to note that the son invariably signed letters to his mother in this fashion: "Yours truly, G. H. Curtiss." When the bungalow was finished, he wrote her a stern lecture:

"I should like to say something to impress upon you how desirous I am to have you get started in the new cottage right. The Andrews family has a reputation of being the poorest housekeepers known, except, perhaps, Mrs. Howe.

"I should like to see you redeem the reputation to a certain extent by getting started right in the cottage and keeping it up in shape if you don't do anything else. It is also good training for Carl. I know that it will be an effort, but I am going to be real mean and disagreeable about it so that you won't forget it.

"I should like to have an expression from you on the subject."

*　　*　　*

Flying boats were placed in production without delay to meet a demand that mushroomed rapidly. Here at last was an aircraft with appeal to the "sportsman" trade; which could be employed with relative safety by private owners who lived beside water. The millionaire who sparked the vogue, coming to Hammondsport to learn how to fly his purchase, was Harold F. McCormick, vice-president of the International Harvester Corporation (he was the son of Cyrus McCormick, inventor of the reaper). His use of the aeroboat to commute 28 miles between his home on Lake Michigan and his Chicago office was widely publicized, giving a valuable boost to the market.

Among customers who followed the example were another Chicago man, L. R. (Jack) Vilas; William B. Scripps, the Detroit publisher; and J. B. R. Verplanck, who resided on the Hudson at Fishkill. When Henry Ford, the motor magnate, appeared in Hammondsport, it was given out that he came as a potential patron for a flying boat; he departed without buying, however, and the presumption is strong that he was there on an entirely different errand, one which related to the Wright suit.[4]

Aside from the outburst of aeroboat activity, the Curtiss Aviation School was going full tilt, with fourteen pupils and two instructors to begin the season. This was the first open flying school in the United States, and not the least of its advantages was the opportunity for practical work on airplanes and engines. Instruction flights, averaging a hundred a day in 1912, were from Kingsley Field, easterly of the village (today the site of Hammondsport High School). Some 50 acres were rented from Charles Kingsley, and his barn served as a workshop; that year Curtiss erected a "shed" as an aeroboat hangar. Often enough, grazing cows were chased from the field to make way for the "grasscutters" in which neophytes scuttled about. On one record day, 240 student flights were counted.

Those were the merriest, maddest years the town had experienced. Budding aviators burned up the dusty highways in rakish automobiles, danced to all hours in pavilions beside the lake, and attended gay parties in the homes of the winemasters. A motto prevailed among the student pilots: "Water for frogs—wine for men." Lulu Mott's boardinghouse, bursting at the seams, came to be known as the "Aviators' Home." Village girls vied for the attentions of the aerial glamor boys. Early graduates of the school fared forth to serve as flying instructors in many parts of the world—in South America, England, Italy, Spain, Russia.

Curtiss forbade any of his pilots or pupils to fly above the village. He feared that parts might fall off the machines.

Broken and discarded propellers were supposed to be chopped up and burned. Some of the factory workmen ran a tidy little racket on the side. Instead of destroying the propellers, they sold splinters as souvenirs to tourists, with a sales palaver about the terrible "wreck" they had gone through.

The Orient came to Hammondsport that summer. The Imperial Japanese Navy placed an order for three hydroaeroplanes and sent as many officers to learn how to fly them. They were escorted to town by Commander Tareuchi, the naval attaché of Japan at Washington. They were joined by a fellow countryman, M. Kondo, who had studied flying at San Diego and who served as their interpreter. Failing to obtain a job at the Curtiss plant, as hoped, Kondo applied to the Kirkham Motor Works in Bath. While displaying his flying ability at Savona in a plane with which the Kirkham brothers were involved, he collided with a windmill. The Nipponese officers went from Hammondsport to conduct his funeral by Japanese ritual.

*　　*　　*

In July of 1912, Curtiss checked out his "Number 2 flying boat" on Keuka Lake, with Captain Chambers as the most interested observer in view of the fact that he had just induced the Navy to spend money on such a craft. Someone nicknamed it the *Flying Fish*. It was a two-passenger machine, in reality an amphibian, equipped with folding wheels. The 26-foot hull was partitioned into watertight compartments.

Now a fresh phase of experiment had engaged the interest of Curtiss. Making the acquaintance of Elmer Sperry, founder of the Sperry Gyroscope Company, some time earlier at the Aero Club, he had been shown the gyro-stabilizer which Sperry was developing for ships. They had some discussion of the possible use of such a device on planes. The emergence of the aeroboat, larger than any previous airplane, invited a full-scale experiment, and Sperry revived contact with Curtiss, who wrote back:

"Recent accidents have caused people to appreciate the dangers of aviation. In some cases accidents could perhaps have been prevented had the machine been equipped with this particular automatic balancer. But, at any rate, this is the psychological moment to demonstrate such a device."

The upshot was that Sperry sent his son, Lawrence, to Hammondsport for a series of experiments which lengthened out over three years and enlisted cooperation from the Navy. Lawrence Sperry already had taught himself to fly in a homemade plane. The "gyrostat" was first tried in a hydroplane, later in an aeroboat, Curtiss personally making repeated test flights. The mechanism consisted of two gyroscopes rotated by electricity. When the plane tilted, the gyros retained their own level, actuating valves in a compressed-air line; the air moved pistons to adjust the plane's controls accordantly.

Curtiss assigned Kleckler to work with Sperry on details of the device, and flights were made over Keuka far into the bitter cold of December. Sperry went west for the winter camp, where tests continued from the Spanish Bight. From Coronado, Curtiss informed Captain Chambers: "I realize that there is considerable more experimenting to do with this gyro, but I expect something will come out of it ultimately."

Back in Hammondsport for the summer of 1913, the gyro-stabilizer was installed in the Navy's flying boat and a new Navy pilot, Lieutenant P. N. L. (Pat) Bellinger, flew the tests.

Curtiss directed Lawrence Sperry's attention to a $10,000 prize offered by the French War Department for the most outstanding improvement in safety for flying; then furnished him with a fresh aeroboat, equipped with the gyro-stabilizer, to compete for it. In 1914, Lawrence demonstrated over the river Seine at Paris, standing upright with arms folded while his mechanic crawled out on the wings. He won the prize.

*   *   *

Curtiss obtained three separate patents pertaining to the flying boat; another on his dual-control system. The patents were all assigned to his company. In no case did he prosecute a patent infringement suit. To illustrate his attitude toward litigation where his own patents were involved, one instance may suffice.

The Wright Company, in alliance with W. Starling Burgess, soon invaded the aeroboat field. In November 1912 Curtiss wrote Chambers that "The Burgess-Wright people" were building a flying boat "practically a duplicate of ours." He went on:

"It is not our desire to monopolize the business, but on such things as we originated we feel that we should at least get a royalty so that, if possible, we may be reimbursed for the money we have spent on patents. I am beginning to think, however, that the best plan is to let the patents go, and go after the business."

In the same letter, he noted that Lieutenant Ellyson had returned to Hammondsport, bringing a bride with him: "Mr. Ellyson gave us a surprise in appearing with his wife . . . I am glad Mr. Ellyson is married, but hope it will not interfere with his work."

In the late summer of 1912, Curtiss revisited Europe for the first time since winning the Gordon Bennett Cup. Now he was on a fishing expedition—angling for hydroplane and aeroboat business. The fishing was good, and, from what he learned, "There is little question about our priority all around." To Captain Chambers, he confided on October 4:

"I have just returned from a very satisfactory trip abroad. Aviation in all its branches, and especially water-flying, is booming all over Europe, and there is a marked contrast when you reach America and find everyone sitting around and wondering what is going to be done." He sold several more hydroplanes to the Russian Navy, and found that the Russians, Germans, and British were much interested in the flying boat. There was universal agreement that "the single central float system is what they must all come to."

The factory put on a night shift and went into 24-hour production. The flying boat hulls were fashioned from spruce, covered with canvas painted battleship gray. Curtiss had purchased in England a supply of duralumin, the light aluminum alloy being employed by the Germans in the framework of zeppelins. (The secret of this alloy was not yet known in America.) The Navy wished him to experiment with a metallic hull, but this did not prove satisfactory.

*   *   *

The maples were decked out in pastel shades, and it was getting on into autumn, when Lieutenant Jerome C. Hunsaker arrived in Hammondsport. This he well remembered because grapes were ripe and because the man he had come to see—an almost legendary figure by now among junior naval officers—took him pheasant hunting.

The mission of Hunsaker, a brilliant engineer attached to the Corps of Naval Constructors, was to familiarize himself with water-flying machines and submit a report on their potential to Rear Admiral David W. Taylor. Hunsaker had graduated from Annapolis in 1908 at the head of his class; after a short tour of sea duty, the Navy sent him to MIT for graduate engineering study in which he won his doctor's degree. He had taught the first college course in aviation science and was soon to organize and direct a trail-blazing department of aeronautical engineering at MIT, while retaining his naval status.

Ushered into "a simple house, simply furnished," Hunsaker found the aeronaut as unpretentious as his home; "a very genial and considerate host . . . generous, friendly, responsive . . . not a reader, but a fellow you liked to sit around and talk to." Similarly lacking in affectation, Lena treated him as one of the family, personally prepared their breakfast, and kept them faithfully supplied with coffee. A small thing he noticed was that no dogs or cats roamed the house. The Curtisses were not pet fanciers. When Hunsaker remarked that perhaps he should keep a parrot for someone to talk to, Curtiss did not think the jest funny enough to warrant a smile.

A long-continued friendship warmed between these two individuals as Hunsaker visited Hammondsport at other times. World War I intervened, and when next they came into close association, it would be in relation to one of the great flying episodes of all time.

*   *   *

The Aero Club-Collier Trophy was awarded Curtiss for the second successive year, in recognition of his development of the flying boat.

The Navy did not go back to San Diego for the winter of 1913, transferring its aviation camp from Annapolis to Guantánamo Bay, Cuba, with Towers as aviator-in-charge. The Army moved in at North Island instead, with its Signal Corps Flying School, paying Curtiss a nominal rent of $25 a month. Although his three-year lease of the island extended until February 1914, Curtiss did not personally return, being on another European business trip as that year opened, while other events crowded in upon him.

In the summer of 1913, he was distressed to hear of serious accidents which befell his two favorite naval protégés. The dangers of flight were of deep concern to him. Elmer Sperry knew this, and Hunsaker quickly found it out.

Jack Towers was passenger with Ensign William D. Billingsley in maneuvers over Chesapeake Bay, in a Wright plane equipped with pontoons. Either a violent gust or a mechanical failure threw the aircraft into a nosedive from 1600 feet, pitching the pilot from his seat in such a way that he disabled the controls. Towers grabbed a strut with an agility born of the fact that he was a trained gymnast, and clung for life while the plane turned a slow somersault. Below, he could see Billingsley tumbling over and over. Towers was seriously injured when the wreck hit the water, but had presence of mind to lash himself to a pontoon and was soon rescued; after four months in the hospital he returned to duty. Billingsley's was the first death in naval aviation.

Spuds Ellyson had become a father and was billeted at Annapolis. Missing the nightboat out of Washington, he was frantic to reach home because his infant daughter was scheduled to undergo surgery next morning. At the Navy Yard, he rousted out mechanics to help him launch a hydroplane and set out to fly to Annapolis. Fog was dense over the bay that night and the plane vanished into its cloak. Ellyson's body was recovered some days later. His shoes were missing, as if he had tried to swim.

19. Feud with the Wrights

It is futile but tempting to speculate upon how much faster and further aviation might have traveled had it not been hobbled by the Wright patent infringement suits. Experiments were discouraged, capital held back, manufacture diminished, flyers divided into factions, just when the pinions were feathering. The technical line of development was obscured for a full five years. Regardless of partisanship, remnants of which lurk in the air to this day, if there is one thing upon which all authorities have agreed it is that the litigations pressed by the recognized pioneers of flight were a grievous setback to its advancement. Historically, it can be argued that World War I may have taken a different course if airplanes had been more mature when it erupted.

An equally provocative "if" to contemplate is how greatly aviation might have benefited had the Wright brothers and Glenn Curtiss joined forces while the science was in its formative stage, instead of slugging each other through the courts. By all logic, this is what should have happened. In personality, temperament, and background, these men had much in common. With roots deep in the soil of provincial America, reared in its solid virtues, they were alike in being self-made engineers of limited education, risen out of the "Yankee tinker" tradition via the bicycle-shop route. The chief difference in the synopses of their careers was that the Wrights skipped over the motorcycle phase and consequently did not delve so deeply into engines. With them, a motor was merely something they needed to power a glider.

The evidence is ample that Curtiss was willing, indeed anxious, to collaborate with the brothers, and in fact made overtures to that effect; also that friends of both parties strove to bring them together. The ultimate irony is that the two mighty companies founded by them did eventually merge. When that occurred, an officer of the Curtiss-Wright Corporation ineptly referred to Hammondsport as "the place where the Curtiss brothers came from."

                              *   *   *

In 1909, the magazine *Aeronautics* asked Thomas A. Hill, a New York attorney specializing on patents, to contribute an article analyzing the basis of the suit (Hill had already been retained by the Aeronautic Society). He wrote that the Wright claims, as he had read them in the file wrapper at the Patent Office, "do not cover supplementary surfaces and it is difficult to understand how supplementary surfaces can be brought within what was intended to be covered by the patent granted to them." Hill predicted that "success by the Wrights is somewhat doubtful," and said: "There is nothing in the Wright patent contained to warrant the inference that they at any time intended to use supplemental surfaces for accomplishing substantially what they accomplish by warping, flexing, bending, twisting, or otherwise distorting the lateral margins of their main plane. From an inspection of the Curtiss machine, it will be seen that it is quite impossible to flex, warp or otherwise bend or move the main planes and that a similar effect to that produced thereby is obtained in the Curtiss machine by supplemental or auxiliary surfaces, planes or rudders, which are pivotally mounted . . . The use of supplemental surfaces appears to be indisputably a public right, and upon this apparently hinges the issues involved in the present suit."

Since *Aeronautics* was the most widely read periodical in the field, Hill's interpretation surely influenced the attitude of flyers toward the case; although many of them probably had their minds made up without it. Grover Loening, who was a Wright champion all the way, said in his memoirs that, by filing suit, the brothers "turned the hand of almost every man in aviation against them"; that: "Orville sued Curtiss for revenge and prestige. But the New York bankers interested in the Wright Company sued Curtiss because they wanted to establish a monopoly."

A fifty-year-old federal jurist named John Raymond Hazel, on January 3, 1910, laid down a precept which proved to be the keynote of future decisions in the war of Wright versus Curtiss. In granting the preliminary injunction to the plaintiffs, Judge Hazel ruled that "the claims in controversy are entitled to a broad and liberal construction." In effect, this was a declaration that the Wright patent on the operating principle of the 1903 glider covered everything in sight, so far as the control of stability in an airplane was concerned. Moreover, it was the first judicial pronouncement in America relating to the science and mechanics of aviation, hence establishing a precedent in law where none had existed.

An opinion of this sort from Justice Hazel was predictable. The same judge had used substantially the same words in 1900 to uphold the claims of George B. Selden in the suit which raised the curtain on the lengthy wrangle over automobile patent rights.

One feels a certain sympathy for a judge, none too erudite, with no grounding at all in the complexities of engineering technology, who (because of the district in which he sat) found himself saddled with the duty of reaching critical decisions on the two most revolutionary inventions of the early twentieth century. Even the "expert" witnesses, whose testimony engulfed him, were uncertain and often diametrically disagreed on technicalities. There were no guideposts for either case, and the maladministration of the patent laws was notorious. The general climate of the judiciary, in those incredible years which turned out miracles ranging from the telephone to wireless, was to regard invention as something akin to divine revelation, and to bestow upon pioneering patents the widest possible latitude. Incidentally, the "broad construction" viewpoint relieved judges of the necessity for dealing with intricate technical details which baffled understanding. About the best a judge could do, when confronted by the mountainous records of a patent litigation, was grope his way to a personal opinion and make it sound as authentic as possible. The fate of industries hinged upon such decisions.

A careful reading of Judge Hazel's two decisions in the case of Wright vs. Curtiss (he handed down another in 1913) leaves small doubt that he was predisposed in favor of the Wrights and swayed by the arguments of their attorneys. The same judge would scarcely be likely, in a second decision, to contradict his own earlier one. In the 1910 injunction ruling, he gave considerable weight to the idea of "public acquiescence" in the pioneering nature of the Wrights' achievement, but was a trifle loose in his facts when he said: "The newspapers of the country heralded as marvelous the success of the patentees, and published wide that human flight had been made possible and that the patentees were the first in the annals of the world to achieve success with a heavier than air flying machine." His memory should have served him better as to the extent of journalistic fanfare in the wake of Kitty Hawk.

In another passage of his reasoning, Judge Hazel implied his acceptance of the piracy charge: that the Aerial Experiment Association had stolen ideas from the Wrights and imitated their machine. He referred pointedly to Tom Selfridge's request for advice on glider construction, and to Herring's visit to Kitty Hawk with Chanute, and stated that both Herring and Curtiss "obtained detailed information prior to the construction of the defendant's machine, as to experiments and pressure of wind on curved and flat planes and mode of maintaining equilibrium in flights." The judge's knowledge of the work of the A.E.A. was manifestly skimpy; and he was far off base in presuming that Herring had anything whatever to do with the design of the Curtiss plane. At all events, the gist of his 1910 decision was this:

"I incline to the view . . . that the claims of the patent in suit should be broadly construed; and when given such construction the elements of the Wright machine are found in defendants' machine performing the same functional result. There are dissimilarities in defendants' structure—changes of form and strengthening of parts—which may be improvements, but such dissimilarities seem to me to have no bearing upon the means adopted to preserve the equilibrium, which means are the equivalent of the claims in suit and attain an identical result . . . The patent in issue does not belong to the class of patents which requires narrowing to the details of construction."

Inasmuch as Judge John R. Hazel cast so long a shadow over the life of Curtiss, a sketch of his background is helpful: Born in Buffalo in 1860, of humble German immigrant parentage, he worked hard for an education and became an attorney by "reading law" in an office. Admitted to practice with a Buffalo law firm, he quickly showed a flair for politics in a club of young Republicans, was a delegate to state conventions, and rose to be chairman of the Erie County

Republican Committee. He was a delegate to both Republican National Conventions which nominated William McKinley for the presidency; indeed, he was credited with swinging the ballot to McKinley, who did not forget the favor.

Because the case load of the U. S. District Court in New York City had grown so heavy, a new district was created in 1900—the U. S. District Court for Western New York, with headquarters in Buffalo. President McKinley rewarded John R. Hazel with the appointment to its bench in June 1900. A storm of public and newspaper criticism ensued over the blatantly political nature of the appointment. Almost the first important case tossed in the lap of this inexperienced judge was the patent infringement suit against the Buffalo Gasolene Motor Company, in which he ruled that the Selden patent was entitled to a broad and liberal construction.

Federal Judge Hazel administered the oath of office to President Theodore Roosevelt after McKinley was assassinated in Buffalo.

*   *   *

As before stated, Curtiss posted a bond of $10,000 to go on flying while the injunction was in process of appeal. Under that bond he was enabled to fly at the Los Angeles meet and to make the Albany-to-New York flight. Then on June 14, 1910, the three judges of the U. S. Circuit Court of Appeals reversed Judge Hazel's action, holding that "infringement was not so clearly established as to justify a preliminary injunction"; furthermore asserting that "the record before us contains numerous affidavits which were not presented until after the original decision," and which were admitted "upon motion for rehearing without discussion of their contents by the court."

With the vacating of the injunction, Curtiss's bond was released, but now the case commenced in earnest, because he chose to fight it through. While the Wrights prosecuted other suits, mainly in Europe, in the last analysis Curtiss stood alone in a one-man battle against odds. In the first instance, this was a battle for business survival, to be sure; but it was also, in large degree, a matter of principle. Had he backed down, the Wright Company's monopoly of the aviation industry doubtless would have succeeded. This stubborn stand was comparable to that of Henry Ford against the Selden combination, which overlapped it timewise.

During this identical period, according to Harry Genung, a merger of Curtiss with the Wrights was being agitated "by people interested in promoting aviation." When the proposal was later "advanced in more earnest," Curtiss's plant manager recalled, the Wright brothers were "so stubborn in their demands for control, etc., as to make the thing ridiculous from our point of view. They had little to offer us beyond a patent truce. We were away out in front in the practical application of the art, but they consistently refused to properly recognize the value of our achievements. In their opinion, they were the 'Seldons' [sic] of aviation and the world should pay them bounty."

Various feelers were put forth in the attempt to reach an accommodation and to stop the case from going the full course with heavy expense to both sides. Jerome Fanciulli arranged a luncheon meeting between his employer and the Wrights at a New York hotel in 1910, and himself sat through it; he remembered the talk as outwardly amiable, but the only agreement at its end was that the matter would have to be left in the hands of the patent attorneys. Roy Knabenshue, managing the Wright exhibition crew, said he tried to bring the two companies into harmony "in every possible manner"; that Curtiss came to Dayton twice; that he "would agree, and then he would change his mind."

An impression of the direct negotiating which went on may be gleaned from an exchange of correspondence during November 1910. Wilbur wrote to Curtiss on the 5th: "Referring to the matter recently discussed between us, I suggest that the following would be satisfactory in all probability to both parties: to wit, you to pay one thousand dollars on each machine manufactured by you, and one hundred dollars for each day the machine makes exhibition flights. The agreement to cover both the past and the future."

On the 23rd, Curtiss made this response:

"I have received the letter that you sent me from New York enclosing a tentative proposition to settle the patent suit. It had been my intention upon receipt of this to make you a counter offer, but in thinking the matter over, it has occurred to me, that to accept a license—even at no cost to us—might not improve our condition. In fact, it had been my idea that the principal advantage in a deal of this kind would be the assistance it afforded to you toward excluding the foreign aviators and those who do use your device.

"I note that Moisant's organization has started out to tour the country with warping wings. If this is permitted, even by giving them a license, I cannot see that we would have improved our position.

"If anything occurs to alter my views on the subject, I will communicate with you further."

Wilbur's tart answer was dated the 30th:

"Your letter of November 23 received. The negotiation was initiated at your request and now seems to be similarly closed by you. As I stated in one of our conferences, any agreement, in order to be effective, must possess sufficient elements of advantage to each party to make both satisfied. If you do not consider that such advantages exist so far as you are concerned, it is well for both parties to revert to the established mode of settlement. We are compelled to push through a test case anyway against someone, and there is nothing in our former affidavits in this case which will do us harm or embarrass us when the case comes up for regular trial.

"Although I entered upon the negotiations without enthusiasm, I have endeavored in good faith to reach a mutually satisfactory basis of settlement and disarranged my plans to give you time to consider the matter carefully, without insisting upon anything definite from you. Now, however, I must consider the negotiations at an end unless you do something at once."

Curtiss did not wholly slam the door, as shown by a letter mailed to Wilbur on December 26 from California, where he had gone to establish the North Island camp:

"I am afraid I deserve to be criticized for pressing the negotiations for a settlement with you, but when I first took it up I did not realize the intricacies of the case. I finally concluded that it would be necessary to go on with the trial, but I assure you that you can count on my cooperation in any matter in which we can get together to cut down the expense of the litigation, or to further the interests of the exhibition or manufacturing business."

Apparently Curtiss was reluctant to abandon hope of a rapprochement. In the course of his return trip from the winter camp of 1911, he wired Orville from St. Louis: WILL STOP OFF DAYTON TOMORROW AFTERNOON. HOPE TO SEE YOU. ALSO PLEASED TO HAVE MISS WRIGHT AND YOURSELF TAKE LUNCH WITH MRS. CURTISS AND I AT ALGONQUIN AT 1 O'CLOCK. The record fails to indicate whether or not this invitation was accepted. (Wilbur was abroad at that moment, hence not invited.)

The Wrights somehow got hold of a Curtiss plane later in that year and conducted flights with it at their old pasture field outside Dayton, studying its controls for purposes of the lawsuit. Their father, Bishop Milton Wright, put these entries in his diary: "The boys try a Curtiss machine, at Simms, and break it" . . . "Orville went, after noon, to Simms Station to try a Curtiss machine" . . . "Wilbur went out to try the Curtiss machine. It is hard to fly with."

The assembling of evidence in this complex case meant delving into the entire science of aeronautics, insofar as it was understood up to then; ransacking the history of attempts to fly, from Leonardo da Vinci down the line. It meant gathering the testimony of virtually every flying man and experimenter who could be rounded up. The task was colossal and time-consuming, and the profession of patent attorney was a lucrative one. Emerson R. Newell continued as chief defense counsel; another New York attorney, Arthur C. Fraser, headed the battery for the Wright Company. The primary case dragged on over four years to a decision, and then the battle was not ended. Orville Wright once told Knabenshue that the cost of the litigation to his side was $152,000; Curtiss said his own costs exceeded $175,000.

Commentators, ex post facto, generally conceded to the Wrights the more capable legal staff. Curtiss himself once admitted this, behind closed doors. In the wisdom of hindsight, he agreed that the defense should have been based on the A.E.A. patent, pure and simple; that is to say, on the aileron. Instead, Newell adopted a four-point strategy: (1) That the Wright patent was not entitled to the broad interpretation. (2) That if it were to be broadly construed, it was invalid because of the prior art. (3) That, if it were properly construed as to its scope, the defendants did not infringe. (4) That in any event the Curtiss mode of flying was on a different principle.

A patent infringement suit was not like a courtroom trial, with a judge on the bench and a jury in the box. No legalistic procedure was so unwieldy, inefficient, and cumbersome. Affidavits, counteraffidavits, and rebuttals were submitted by the principals in the case. Depositions were taken from witnesses wherever might be convenient— often in law offices or hotel rooms. No judicial control was exercised over the line of questioning or in the exclusion of irrelevant or duplicated material. Much of the testimony, it was commonly said among attorneys, would never have been admitted in a court of law. Consequently the records piled up to awesome proportions, ultimately to be shoveled in front of a judge whose duty it was to try to make sense out of them.

A brief sampling from the cross-barrage of affidavits sworn to by Curtiss and the Wrights may suffice to give the flavor of this rigmarole.

The brothers assumed an attitude of superior knowledge, emphasizing their seniority in the field and the comparative brevity of Curtiss's experience. Repeatedly, they injected phrases like: "As persons skilled in the art, we assert"; or "As persons having long experience with flying machines." In one joint affidavit, they said: "Mr. Curtiss's failure to perceive the real conditions cannot overcome the unchangeable laws of nature." Again: "The present affidavit of Mr. Curtiss is a most remarkable one and of itself constitutes an impeachment of his powers of correct observation and shows his incompetence to give expert testimony as to what actually occurs on his machine, and even seems to raise a direct question of veracity."

A note of vexation is discernible in this passage from a Curtiss affidavit:

"The theories which they [the Wrights] have advanced are very misleading, and I know of my own knowledge from my numerous flights . . . that the actual facts which they assert as to the necessary operation of defendants' machines are erroneous . . . The actual facts are as I have set forth, and the actual facts are, I understand, the crux of the matter, and not the theories which may be advanced."

A major issue in the case was whether or not the Curtiss control depended upon a combination of the tail rudder with the action of the ailerons. A great deal of defense testimony was introduced concerning the series of experiments at Hammondsport and San Diego, in which the rudder was immobilized and the steering wheel sealed. Curtiss testified: "I have never detected any turning effect caused by the operation of the ailerons." Statements were sworn by each of the pilots who participated in these tests, including Lieutenant Ellyson, Captain Beck, Charles Willard, and Augustus Post. They all corroborated Curtiss.

The Wrights retorted that these witnesses "were not sufficiently trained in such work to note what was really occurring." They insisted that if the tail rudder were made immovable for such an experiment, the plane would be "absolutely uncontrollable," and said: "We state positively that machines with fixed vertical tails are death traps and of no practical value as flying machines."

And so it went.

In the midst of these proceedings, Curtiss volunteered his views on the case to Captain Chambers, in a letter dated November, 1912:

"In the first place, when the Wright Bros. made their application they found it necessary to confine their claims to just what was new in their machine, otherwise, the patent would not be allowed. The new things in their machine were a combination of the warping and the turning of the rudder to counteract the turning effect caused by the warping. Their success in actual flying led them to try to make their patent cover things which it was not intended to cover, and their exploitation as the first to fly has been used in an effort to get the Court to enlarge the scope of their patent.

"The lawyers have tried to show we copied their machine, purposely making slight changes to avoid infringing the patent, and they now claim that our rudder is in no sense a rudder, but simply a vane used for the purpose of counteracting the turning effect, as in their machine.

"The facts are, the honors bestowed upon the Wrights and the credit which is due them is not because of their patent, but because of their achievement. I hope their patent will be adjudicated and that the machines which operate as their machine does will be adjudged infringements, but all authorities agree that our machines operate on a different principle, and I do not believe a disinterested patent attorney could be found who would allow that our machine infringes their patent. However, the litigation has cost us forty or fifty thousand dollars and the industry—or what there is of it in America—is entirely the result of our taking up this case as we have, single-handed, and fighting it out. Had we not taken this stand, the Wright Co. would have been in position to enjoin all manufacturers and the whole industry would have been monopolized. Not only warping wing machines, but the aileron construction and the Farman construction would have been controlled; in fact, any machine which could fly, including hydro-aeroplanes and all would come under jurisdiction of the Wright patent, so that the trade certainly owes us something."

* * *

Returning home from a business trip in the East, Wilbur Wright came down with typhoid fever at the beginning of May 1912. In a letter written from his sickbed, he complained of delays in the patent suit, which, he felt, had already "destroyed fully three fourths of the value of our patent." "Up to the present time a decision in our favor would have given us a monopoly, but if we wait too long a favorable decision may have little value to us."

Wilbur's illness lasted through the month. After showing marked improvement, he took a turn for the worse and died on May 30. He was forty-five years of age. The shock of this bereavement was almost unendurable to Orville, who brooded and never really regained his former interest in aeronautical research.

The surviving brother made it evident in remarks during the lonely remainder of his life that he blamed Curtiss in some measure for Wilbur's loss; that is to say, if Curtiss had not opposed the lawsuit Wilbur might have recovered. "The death of my brother Wilbur," he said in one widely published statement, "is a thing we must definitely charge to our long struggle . . . The delays were what worried him to his death . . . first into a state of chronic nervousness, and then into a physical fatigue which made him an easy prey for the attack of typhoid which caused his death . . . It wasn't as if we had been fighting a stand-up foe in a square give-and-take fight. We were fighting foes whose strategy was played in the dark."

Grover Loening, who was working for the Wright Company as chief engineer at the time and remained a loyal friend, left it on record that, after Wilbur's death, "Orville and his sister Katharine had, preying on their minds and characters, the one great hate and obsession, the patent fight with Curtiss. It was a constant subject of conversation, and the effort of Curtiss and his group to take credit away from the Wrights was a bitter thing to stand for."

Captain Holden C. Richardson of the Navy, in the years of his retirement, recollected an occasion when, as a young naval constructor, he was an overnight guest in the Wright home at Dayton. "Katharine especially was terribly bitter toward Curtiss," he said. "Couldn't forgive him." As a matter of fact, Katharine could hardly treat Richardson with civility. "She knew I was a friend of Curtiss." In a taped interview, Richardson voiced a few thoughts on the lawsuit: "The Wright battle was a dirty thing . . . The Wrights were gummed up by patent lawyers. The patent was wrong . . . The Wright plane was all wrong . . . It was the lawyers made that mess."

*   *   *

In the Curtiss lore, one comes upon an unverified story that he was lunching with an associate in a New York hotel when a tall, graying man strode up to their table and asked: "You're Glenn Curtiss, aren't you?"

Curtiss acknowledged the identity.

"Well, I see they have you with your back nearly to the wall. When they get you right up against it, come and see me."

The stranger turned abruptly back to his own table. "Who," Curtiss asked his companion, "was that man?"

"You're joking, aren't you? Surely you recognized Henry Ford."

Whatever the circumstances of the original meeting between Ford and Curtiss, this makes a good yarn. Certainly, Ford was at Hammondsport in either 1912 or 1913. Beyond a doubt, Ford was in sympathy with Curtiss in his patent fight, and at the showdown gave him a valuable helping hand. (As a peripheral note, it is of interest that Curtiss had formerly held the Ford automobile agency in Hammondsport.)

Ford nursed a deep distrust of monopolistic practice and Wall Street power. Believing that invention was largely "a matter of evolution," he looked upon the patent system as a necessary evil, if necessary at all. His conflict with the Selden interests left him with a fierce hatred of patent monopoly of any kind. He had just emerged victorious from that ordeal, and stood at the top of the automobile heap, when his relationship with Curtiss began.

Except possibly for Bell's prolonged battle in defense of his telephone rights, no patent litigation had been more vitriolic nor aroused keener public interest than that between the owners of Selden's automobile patent and the Ford Motor Company. George B. Selden, a resident of Rochester, New York, had studied law in his father's office, although his true bent was toward science and technology. Because of his mechanical interest, he specialized in patent law, handling all such cases for his father. When he could afford it, he equipped an experimental shop on the edge of the Genesee gorge at Rochester, hiring a machinist assistant, William Gomm. His great ambition was to invent a "road locomotive," and he began a study of internal combustion engines using liquid and gaseous fuels. Gasoline was not yet known, but the Vacuum Oil Company had recently set up a refinery in Rochester for experiments in "cracking" crude Pennsylvania petroleum into its fractions.

Selden and Gomm developed a primitive 3-cylinder compression engine in which they induced explosions of vaporized hydrocarbon distillates. In May 1878—the very month in which Glenn Curtiss was born—this engine made its first brief and noisy run. Selden turned to his assistant and shouted: "Billy, we have struck a new power." (Of course, internal combustion engines had previously been operated in Europe.)

Without perfecting the motor, Selden drew up his plans for a horseless carriage to be powered by it, and, in May 1879, applied for a patent on a "road engine." He did not actually build such a vehicle, though he made some futile attempts at raising capital to finance its manufacture. With a shrewder knowledge of patent law than of engineering, Selden kept his application in a pending status and bode his time for someone else to produce a practical automobile. As the law existed, he was allowed a two-year grace period within which to file an amendment to his patent, at which time the application would be renewed for another period of grace. He repeated this process every two years. By 1895, he decided that the time was ripe and pushed through his patent, with no intention of making automobiles himself, but with a plan to sue for infringement anyone else who did. There is no question that Selden was the first to *apply* for a patent on the idea of an automobile: that is, on the combination by which a self-propelled vehicle might be put together.

Having obtained the patent, Selden lacked capital to force infringement actions against the many automobile companies which were springing up. In 1899, he sold his patent rights, on a royalty basis, to a company in Hartford, Connecticut, which then joined with a syndicate in New Jersey calling itself the Electric Vehicle Company to exploit the patent. Infringement test cases were promptly filed against the Winton Motor Carriage Company, of Cleveland, and the Buffalo Gasolene Motor Company which was making engines for automobiles. Both defendant companies entered writs of demurrer for dismissal of the suits. It was Federal Judge John R. Hazel's overruling of the demurrer of the Buffalo Gasolene Motor Company which foreshadowed his future attitude on patents.

Selden's patent seemed to have legal validity, and, rather than foot the bill for an endless string of infringement suits, nine automobile companies banded together into the Association of Licensed Automobile Manufacturers, purchasing the right to use the Selden patent for a royalty of 1¼ percent of the retail price of each automobile sold. Selden himself was to receive one-fifth of all royalties collected. Membership in the Association was soon expanded to a score or more. By 1906, Selden was receiving royalties from almost every automobile maker in the United States and their number was legion. He organized the Selden Motor Vehicle Company in Rochester, but still did not produce a successful automobile.

One firm which was not paying royalties was the Ford Motor Company. Henry Ford had applied for a license at the outset, but the A.L.A.M. turned him down on the score that he was a mere "assembler" of cars. This kindled Ford's wrath and stubborn streak. Already he was working out his plan to build low-priced cars in quantity (the "poor man's automobile"), and the Selden patent stood across his path. The Ford Motor Company went ahead independently, and the expected infringement suit resulted.

On September 15, 1909—just before the Wright brothers fired their opening gun—a judge of the U. S. District Court of Southern New York handed down a decision recognizing George B. Selden as the true inventor of the automobile and allowing broad scope to his patent. By this time, more than $2,000,000 in royalties had been paid to the Selden group. If the decision held, no automobile could be manufactured, sold, or driven in the United States without a Selden license and a royalty payment.

Henry Ford refused to accept the decision as final and carried the fight to appeal, posting bonds to protect purchasers of his cars. At this time, W. Benton Crisp, a New York attorney of exceptional talents, had been added to Ford's legal staff. Crisp was the chief strategist in conducting the appeal.

On January 9, 1911, the U. S. Circuit Court of Appeals reversed the earlier verdict in a roundabout way. While deciding that Selden had a valid and true patent, it allowed that the defendants were not guilty of infringement because they were using the Otto four-cycle type of engine (practically all makers were now so doing), instead of the Brayton two-cycle type on which Selden's patent was based. The fine hand of Crisp showed in this technicality. But the decision also avowed that Selden had disclosed "absolutely nothing" of social value; and that "From the point of view of public interest it were even better that the patent had never been granted."

The triumph of Henry Ford was immense, and, to the public mind, he was a knight in shining armor who had raised his lance for the right and won the tourney. The automotive industry, which had sat on its hands while he waged the battle, now paid him unblushing homage. It even gave a banquet in his honor. The A.L.A.M. promptly disbanded and its place was taken by the National Automobile

Chamber of Commerce, which drew up a cross-licensing agreement, pooling patents to get rid of the infringement bugaboo for all time. (Selden's patent expired by limitation a year after the decision.) This development held important implications for the future of the airplane industry.

*　*　*

The initial blow fell on Curtiss while he was at the San Diego camp in the winter of 1913, working with Sperry on the gyro-stabilizer. In the U. S. District Court, Western District of New York, at Buffalo, on the 27th of February, Federal Judge John R. Hazel handed down his decision in favor of the Wright Company. Once again he ruled that the Wright patent was "entitled to a liberal construction," and went on:

"I am of opinion, after complete consideration of the testimony on both sides, that the patentees by their method of securing the equilibrium of the plane made an important advance in an embryonic art. They were not the first to conceive the idea of using monoplane or biplane surfaces for flying, nor the first to support two planes at their margins one above the other, or to use vertical tails, or rudders for steering, or to plane horizontal rudders forward of the machine to guide it upward or downward in its flight. The prior separate use of such elements is freely admitted by the patentees, but they assert, rightly, I think, that the patented combination was a new combination performing a new and novel result . . . Having attained success where others failed, they may rightly be considered pioneer inventors in the aeroplane art. The employment, in a changed form, of the warping feature or its equivalent by another, although better effects or results are obtained, does not avoid infringement . . .

"The witness, Curtiss, frankly testified that the purpose [of the ailerons] is to preserve the lateral balance 'without the use of any other element or part,' it making no difference whether the aeroplane is in a straight or curved flight. Such concession supports the infringement of the claim under consideration . . .

"While it is true . . . that the defendants have constructed their machine somewhat differently from the complainants' and do not at all times and on all occasions operate the same on the Wright principle, yet the changes they have made in their construction relate to the form only . . . The evidence is that on occasions, depending upon aerial conditions or other disturbing causes, they use the vertical rudder not only to steer their machine, but to assist the ailerons in restoring balance."

Appeal was taken to the U. S. Circuit Court of Appeals, Second Circuit, New York. By posting another bond, Curtiss was allowed to continue operations until the final decision was obtained.

*   *   *

While the appeal was in process, Curtiss was notified at San Diego that he had been chosen by the Board of Regents of the Smithsonian Institution to receive the Langley Medal, whose object was to recognize "specially meritorious investigations in connection with the science of aerodromics and its application to aviation." He had been advanced for the honor by Dr. Bell, in reward for development of waterflight craft. Wiring his acceptance, he said: THIS AWARD IS INDEED A SURPRISE TO ME.

The Langley Medal had been bestowed but once before, to the Wright brothers in 1910. Now two medals were being awarded simultaneously, the other recipient being Gustave Eiffel (builder of the Eiffel Tower) for researches relating to the resistance of air to machines in flight.

The Smithsonian created the Langley Medal in 1908, at the instance of Dr. Bell, as a memorial to its late secretary, Dr. Samuel P. Langley. It was also Bell who, at that time, proposed the Wrights as its initial recipients, and who later delivered the speech of presentation to them. Since then, the Aero Club of Washington had designated May 6 as Langley Day, for annual ceremonies in that city; May 6 being the date in 1896 when Langley flew his first steam-driven model above the Potomac River. Langley Day, 1913, was set for presenting the medal, and Curtiss hastened his departure from California to attend. The French Ambassador accepted on behalf of M. Eiffel.

The ceremonies at the Smithsonian began with unveiling of a Langley Memorial Tablet in the entrance foyer. As chairman of the award committee, Bell presented the medal after an address in which he reviewed the milestones of flight, not neglecting the work of the A.E.A. Sketching the career of Curtiss, he said: "By July 1912, he had developed that remarkable machine he calls 'the flying boat,' which represents the greatest advance yet made along these lines. It develops great speed upon the water and also in the air and is equally at home in either element. The world is now following Mr.

348

Curtiss's lead in the development of flying machines of this kind." Handing over the medal, he said it was awarded "for advancing the art of aerodromics by your successful development of a hydro-aerodrome, whereby the safety of the aviator is greatly enhanced."

The models flown by Langley in the late '90s were on display, and Curtiss, in his acceptance remarks, said: "As I look at the Langley models here, it becomes more evident to me than ever before—the merit of these machines and the great work which Mr. Langley did. We now know, as a result of Mr. Eiffel's laboratory experiments, that the flying planes used by Professor Langley had a great deal of efficiency, and it is also generally known that the Langley machines, as he built them, had more inherent stability than the models which those of us who followed after Langley used in our first flights. I cannot say too much in favor and in memory of Professor Langley."

The more spectacular portion of the day's events ensued at the Army War College, with flying by various types of aircraft, including the newer Curtiss models. Lieutenant Jack Towers took the Assistant Secretary of War, Henry T. Breckenridge, for a flight in an aeroboat. That evening Dr. and Mrs. Bell were hosts at a reception in honor of Curtiss at their Washington home. Several hundred guests arrived —government officials, members of the diplomatic corps, high society, and distinguished scientists.

At the same meeting which awarded the medals, the Board of Regents had voted to reopen the Smithsonian's aeronautical laboratory, closed since Langley's death, and to call it the Langley Aerodynamical Laboratory. The wreckage of the Langley "aerodrome" was gathering dust in the building where his workshop had been. An advisory committee was appointed for the revival of the laboratory, and both Curtiss and Orville Wright were among its fourteen members. Dr. Albert F. Zahm, a professor of mechanics at the Catholic University of America who had a special knowledge of aeronautics, was named as its director, and he at once set sail for a study of similar European laboratories, accompanied by Naval Constructor Jerome Hunsaker.

After prolonged contest in the Patent Office, the three A.E.A. patents were finally issued in the latter part of 1913: that is, the joint overall patent, and the two individually granted to Bell and Baldwin. The trustee was still prevented from doing anything with the aileron patent, however, because of a fresh declaration of interference filed with the Patent Office by another obscure claimant to priority.

Noting that a third assessment against the A.E.A. members was necessary to contest this claim, Bell wrote into his diary:
"But patents already granted give us complete control of the flying
machine field exclusive of the Wright patents and everybody is using
our inventions to avoid the Wrights' patents. So the Wright patents
and the A.E.A. patents together control the whole field of aviation
in America. There is no use offering to consolidate with the Wrights
so long as any of our patents are involved in litigation."

The Bells discussed with Casey Baldwin and his wife the idea of
organizing a joint stock company, and if this plan were to be adopted,
Bell speculated: "We should then go first to Mr. Curtiss who is engaged
in the commercial business of manufacturing flying machines and who
is actually using the A.E.A. inventions, and offer to sell out to him.
In the event of his declination, we should next go to Orville Wright
with a proposition to sell out to the Wright Company, which would
give that company complete control of the flying machine field. Should
he decline, then we could make arrangements to manufacture flying
machines under our own patents."

* * *

The prestige of Curtiss abroad was greatly augmented by his conquest of water flying, and several overtures were made for him to
transfer his company to Europe as his patent headaches piled up
in America. The Russian Navy went so far as to select a factory site
near St. Petersburg, and he went there to look it over in the fall
of 1913. The nations of the Old World felt themselves being drawn
helplessly into the vortex of war, and sensed the role which aviation
was destined to play in it. The Curtiss hydros and aeroboats held
much promise as naval auxiliaries in coastal waters.

As the fateful year 1914 opened, Curtiss was once more in Europe,
drumming up business and anticipating a large Italian order. This
time he was accompanied by his family, and rented a pleasant villa
overlooking the Mediterranean at Nice. He was on the verge of making
some demonstration flights with an aeroboat at Venice when crushing
news came: the U. S. Circuit Court of Appeals, on January 14, had
affirmed the decision of Federal Judge Hazel. The three judges of
the higher bench were "in full accord with the reasoning by which
he [Hazel] reached the conclusion that the patent in suit is a valid
one . . . and that the claims should have a liberal interpretation." It

was their opinion that: "A machine that infringes part of the time is an infringement, although it may at other times be so operated as not to infringe."

The villa on the Riviera was plunged in gloom. Its master dispatched a two-word cablegram to Orville Wright in Dayton: CONGRATULATIONS. CURTISS.

Next, he told reporters that he would assuredly carry the case to the U. S. Supreme Court. If the Supreme Court did not topple the decision, he would thenceforth devote himself entirely to flying boats and engines.

A New York newspaper splashed a headline:

WRIGHT, MASTER OF
FLYING IN AMERICA

Curtiss's more considered reaction was expressed in a letter to Captain W. I. Chambers in Washington:

"Needless to say I was greatly surprised at the recent decision in the Wright case. I had fully expected at least a modification of Judge Hazel's opinion. As the patent was not intended to cover neutral ailerons, I feel that the judges were not called upon to broaden it to that extent. We shall carry the case as far as possible, but of course will pay royalties if we have to, and I hope there will be no interruption in our business relations with your department."

Reports were rife that Curtiss might now accept the Russian invitation, and these seem to have caused some concern at the Navy Department. A scrawled page of pencil notes among the Chambers papers appears to have been the draft of a memorandum on this subject: "This looks like a big bluff unless something has gone wrong with the Curtiss interests in that disastrous contest over the Wright patents. Curtiss has ideal conditions for his plant at Hammondsport, the best in the United States, and his organization would make a sorry showing in Russia . . . If this is true it is disgraceful . . . This may be true, and the Wright Company ought to regard the prospect with ghoulish glee, after refusing to approve of water flying until after Curtiss did something worth while, opened the Wright eyes. The patriotic American stockholders of the Wright Company would shed no tears over the departure of Curtiss."

A close liaison existed between Chambers and plant executives at Hammondsport. At this juncture, Lyman J. Seely, a former Rochester newsman who had attained a high rung on the Curtiss ladder in a short time, filled him in a trifle more on the possibility that his employer might expatriate himself: "As to France: We are still at sea. Mr. Curtiss has had what sound like remarkable offers to establish himself in each of three different European countries. One of these, I understand, offers him an initial order equal to just double the best year's business the Curtiss Company ever did in this country.

"Personally I am satisfied that Mr. Curtiss takes more interest in aviation and in maintaining his status in the field in this country than in merely making out of it all he possibly can. This situation, however, leaves him with several strings to his bow and it must be comforting to him to feel that regardless of the eventualities in this country his future in aviation is assured. The decision in the case is, to say the least, exasperating to anyone able to grasp the finer points at issue."

*   *   *

Winding up his European business in a hurry, Curtiss sailed for home to face the music. The omens, he found, were not at all favorable for a compromise with the man who was his embittered nemesis.

The verdict had unlocked the lips of Orville Wright. Abandoning a long-standing habit of public reticence, he now released a lengthy prepared statement to the press in which he openly castigated Curtiss by name. Beyond that, he submitted to interview on his intentions in view of the outcome. His patent rights were now fully validated and an appeal to the U. S. Supreme Court was an impossibility, he declared. He would demand a royalty of 20 percent on every airplane ($1000 on the standard planes then on the market), plus retroactive settlements. He would permit no plane to be manufactured or flown without a license from the Wright Company. He was prepared, however, to adopt, "a policy of leniency" for all manufacturers, with the sole exception of Curtiss. Those who had built planes without deliberately knowing they were infringing would be "dealt with lightly." He said he was not optimistic of collecting much from Curtiss in the way of back claims, for he had "personal knowledge" that this defendant had anticipated the decision by "having all his property put beyond reach of court seizure" (the inference was that he had placed it in his wife's name).

Wright said of the royalty policy: "This is not an act of harshness. It is an act of great benefit to aerial navigation . . . The only advances made in aeroplane construction in the past ten years have been improvements in the motor and not in the dynamic power of the aeroplane itself . . . The methods of control are now just what they were then [i.e., in 1903] . . . What incentive was there to do hard thinking when anyone could loot the thinking that had previously been done? And what incentive was there to announce an improvement when the person making it could know for a certainty that it would be freely adopted by all who cared to use it?

"I want all the inventors who can possibly be brought into the industry to work upon the aeroplane. And let them start with the problem of bringing in something new—beyond the scope of our patents, which will render the patents useless and obsolete. Then we will be glad to retire in their favor . . .

"I hope I am not an oppressor when I say that men who came to our aeroplane sheds at Dayton and pledged to us that they never would fly, and were scientists seeking scientific data, are not entitled today to stand up under the guise of injured innocence when we ask for an accounting on the flying they have done since we gave them free access to our aeroplanes and our patent papers.

"We obtained an injunction against Glenn H. Curtiss four years ago which could have stopped him from flying at that time, and would have compelled him to seek a license under our patents. But Mr. Curtiss made an affidavit on which he obtained the dissolution of this injunction, and before the same judges three years later he was compelled to give testimony which invalidated the contents of his previous affidavit. So that, except for this action, we would have settled the problem we must settle now four years ago. And aviation would be upon a settled and stable basis."

Here he adverted to the death of Wilbur, which he ascribed to the worries and fatigue of the court struggle. Then he related in more detail his version of the 1906 meeting with Curtiss:

"Soon after we had commenced to fly, a very fine man came to Dayton with a balloon and had engine trouble there. This was my good friend, Captain Thomas A. Baldwin. Baldwin sent for Glenn Curtiss, a motor builder, to come and repair his engines. We met Mr. Curtiss and told him—then an incredulous unbeliever—about our flights. We wanted him to know about them as an engine builder, because we needed to have motors of the right kind. We told him all there was to tell. That was before any one had ever flown anywhere in the world, except ourselves.

"Later, when the Aerial Experiment Station was opened, with Mr. Curtiss as a demonstrator, we answered all questions asked us, even a question as to where the center of pressure was and center of gravity in our machine. We were shocked when we found Mr. Curtiss was starting out as an exhibitor, and wrote him to that effect. We received a letter saying that he had no intention of ever becoming an exhibitor or making commercial use of our invention. We offered him a license then, but he thought he could get along without it.

"We have offered to license him twice since then and have agreed upon all the terms, except one, which had nothing to do with the money involved."

Any summary of the aftermath would be remiss if it overlooked the garbled interview with Captain Thomas Baldwin which appeared in the New York *Times;* this was consistently cited by Wright partisans and biographers as supporting Orville's account of the Dayton Fair episode. The article stated in its lead that Baldwin and Curtiss stayed in Dayton six months, and that while there "We both heard for the first time about flying." It quoted Baldwin as saying:

"Many a day I would lie behind a tree on the fairgrounds near Dayton, when neither myself nor the Wrights were working, and would listen to Wilbur and Orville Wright talking to us about aeroplane flight.

"Curtiss and I would ask, for instance, if the Wrights used chains to connect the propellers to the engine. Both brothers would answer at once, without the slightest hesitation: 'Yes, we do!'

"I sometimes suggested to Curtiss that he was asking too many questions, but he kept right on. The Wrights had the frankness of schoolboys in it all, and had a rare confidence in us. I am sure that Curtiss at that time never thought of taking up flying. It came to him later, I am sure. Mr. Curtiss is a friend of mine today, and I have served in his companies as a director. But it is due to the Wrights as a simple matter of justice to have the story of the actual genesis of flight fully established."

Baldwin gave some kind of an interview to the *Times,* but the obvious misstatements of fact make the accuracy of this printed account strongly suspect. In the first place, the Dayton engagement was for a week, not six months. There was not "many a day" to lie behind a tree. It was absurd on the face of it for Baldwin to say "We both heard about flying for the first time"; the letter Curtiss had sent the Wrights four months earlier, with a view to selling them engines for their planes, clearly belies that. Baldwin knew exactly when and how Curtiss took up flying, because he was there through it all; moreover, Baldwin had built a plane of his own on the Curtiss pattern. If the interview proves one thing, it is that the Wrights did not show them their airplane, for all their schoolboy frankness.

*   *   *

On February 28, Curtiss explained in a letter to Captain Chambers that he had not replied to Orville Wright's statement because "I had given my word before I saw the printed articles that I would not be drawn into a controversy at this time." Now he was beginning to feel, however, that it ought to be answered, and "probably will be in time." He told Chambers that he was in receipt of a letter from "a prominent person who is familiar with the patent case from the start," in which that individual wrote: "There is, I regret to say, in Mr. Wright's interview . . . something which is subject to the gravest criticism. I am truly amazed at his unfairness and downright misstatement of facts which are within my own knowledge. It is a shameful attack upon you personally, and he should be made to suffer for it."

Analyzing the passages of Wright's statement reflecting on the character of Curtiss, the facts of which a third party could have had direct knowledge, a reader can only deduce that the unidentified correspondent was either Bell or Captain Baldwin.

In spite of the explicit hostility in the statement, Curtiss tried hard for a contact with Wright, seemingly to discuss a proposal for consolidating their interests. Learning that Orville was about to make a business trip to New York, he wired him at Dayton (February 25) suggesting he travel by way of Buffalo; there Curtiss would meet him and ride the train with him to New York. PLEASE ANSWER COLLECT, the telegram ended. Obviously, the message either miscarried or Wright ignored it, as Curtiss wired him next day at the Hotel Manhattan: IF RETURNING DAYTON THIS WEEK CAN YOU NOT COME VIA LACKAWANNA AND STOP AT HAMMONDSPORT, OR IF YOU CANNOT STOP OFF I SHOULD LIKE TO JOIN YOU AT BATH TO TALK OVER SOME MATTERS WHICH I THINK

COULD BEST BE DISCUSSED PERSONALLY BETWEEN US. KINDLY CALL ME ON
THE TELEPHONE OR TELEGRAPH COLLECT.

Again Wright seems to have snubbed him, for Curtiss wrote him
on March 5:

"I will be glad to come to Dayton next week if I can arrange
for an interview with you. A number of our mutual friends think that
there is an opportunity just now for an organization which will benefit
us both financially. It seems to me that we should talk the matter
over personally. It was for this purpose that I wished to get into
communication with you during your recent visit to New York."

The conjecture is inescapable that Curtiss's pledge not to heat
up the controversy had been given in the hope of having a talk with
Wright. No answer to the letter of March 5 appears in the record.
Finding Wright thus unresponsive, Curtiss resolved not to surrender
without a struggle. On March 8, he gave the press his reply to Wright's
attack:

"In some New York daily papers there have been published certain statements attributed to Mr. Orville Wright, regarding his attitude
in the aeroplane patent situation. Mixed in with these direct quotations
were interpolated insinuations impugning my good faith in the patent
litigation, and carrying suggestions easily interpreted as such untruths
as I cannot believe Mr. Wright, or any other sane man, ever made.

"The idea that any single line or part of my machine was either
copied from the Wright machines, suggested by the Wrights, or
by their machines, is absurd, if not malicious. My first public flights,
as a member of the Aerial Experiment Association, are a matter of
record, and were made months before the Wrights exhibited their
first public flights. I never had an item of information from either
of the Wrights that helped me in designing or constructing my
machines or that I ever consciously used. I believe today, as I always
have believed, that the Curtiss control differs fundamentally from that
employed by the Wrights, and that its superiority to the Wright
system is demonstrated by the records of two machines during the
last five years. That I was unable to satisfactorily demonstrate this
intricate technical point to the court I consider a misfortune largely
due to the fact that our knowledge of aviation was vastly less when
this case went into court several years ago than it is today.

"My feeling with regard to Mr. Wright's declarations of his attitude
in the matter of royalties is well reflected by the attached reprint
from the editorial column of the Boston *Transcript*."

The appended editorial was written by the aviation editor of the Boston *Transcript*, and it said in part:

"America has become a closed book to all makers of aeroplanes based on the Wright principle. So much is clearly evident from the momentous interview given out on Thursday by Orville Wright . . .

"That the Wright Company is entitled to compensation, and that it should reap some benefit from the patent so painstakingly worked out by the brothers no one can deny. But with all due respect to Mr. Wright, he is not adopting a line of action which will result in such benefit. None of the constructors now at work would object to paying a reasonable amount for the right to manufacture, but a royalty of 20 percent is away out of the question. Again, the Wright patent covers merely the controls. The Wrights had very little to do with motor development, and their motor today is inferior for aeronautical work to many others produced in this country. It is a manifest injustice therefore that constructors who go to the expense of importing foreign motors, for instance, shall be forced to pay a royalty of 20 percent on this part of the machine, for which the Wrights can claim no credit whatever . . .

"It is difficult to believe that Mr. Wright is actuated by other than personal animosity. He must see that his course will not pay in a financial sense, for under his terms he can secure no licenses, as he could easily do under a more liberal policy.

"The effect of the Wright decree will beyond question numb what little life remains in aviation in America. One of the most progressive and wide-awake concerns in the country, the Curtiss Aeroplane Company of Hammondsport, N.Y., is virtually forced out of the country, a situation with which Mr. Wright is highly content, as appears from the text of his interview."

*   *   *

On March 30, Curtiss sat in a conference at the Washington home of Alexander Graham Bell, discussing the patent decision. The others were Charles J. Bell, trustee for the A.E.A.; J. A. D. McCurdy; and Sheldon Cameron, the patent attorney of the A.E.A.

Bell gave a résumé of this conference in his *Home Notes:* "Mr. Curtiss consulted Mr. Cameron as to what form of machine he could use with the least chance of being declared an infringer. Mr. Cameron thought that the A.E.A. Patent for a central vertical balancing rudder seemed to afford the best chance of protection. I then directed attention to the fact that this patent stands in my name; and requested Mr. Cameron to have an assignment of this prepared for my signature, transferring the patent to Mr. Charles J. Bell as trustee."

Curtiss spoke of a substitute control device, which he said "could be used on his machines and produce practically as strong a balancing power as the ailerons now employed." Bell thought it would be covered by the A.E.A. patents. "It is the general impression that this is a non-infringing device so far as the Wright patent is concerned . . . Mr. C. J. Bell concluded by saying the only practical means of raising capital to exploit aviation would be for the Wrights and Curtiss to get together in a new company which could control the situation without fear of litigation."

At some point in his quandary, Curtiss availed himself of Henry Ford's proffer of assistance. According to one source, he found a letter from Ford awaiting his return from Europe. The primary step urged by the automobile potentate was a change of attorneys: he arranged for Curtiss to be represented by W. Benton Crisp, who had delivered the coup de grace to the Selden affair. There followed a two-day conference in Ford's office in Detroit, attended by Curtiss, Crisp, and Monroe Wheeler.

Ford reportedly then told Curtiss: "My entire legal staff is at your disposal. Patents should be used to protect the inventor, not to hold back progress."

The idea of appealing to the Supreme Court was considered, but Crisp advised against it, unless a diversionary tactic failed. It was true that the Supreme Court rarely accepted patent cases, since constitutional questions were not usually involved. This did not necessarily mean that a talented lawyer could not have made a constitutional issue of a patent monopoly over the aviation industry; but the Supreme Court's attitude on the Wright decision did not ever come to a test. Crisp advocated the strategy of introducing a different method of using ailerons, thereby forcing Wright to launch a fresh infringement suit. Obligingly, the Wright Company took the bait. With Curtiss once more a beleaguered defendant, Crisp was enabled to obtain a stay of the permanent injunction ordered by the prior decision.

The alternative system, which challenged Wright to prove that it was an infringement, consisted in employing only one aileron at a time—that is, with no simultaneous operation. An interlock prevented the aileron on the opposite side from moving in unison. Presently a new statement was issued to the press, over the signature of G. H. Curtiss, announcing the adoption of this method, with a three-page preamble explaining why it was significant. The legalistic analysis of Judge Hazel's decision, calculated to show where there was a loophole for this device, suggests the hand of Mr. Crisp in preparing the release, which started off:

"Great harm is being done the American aeroplane industry by the public press in its reiteration of statement and suggestion that the court decision in favor of the Wrights gives them practically a monopoly on the manufacture of aeroplanes, and that it places them in position to dictate to the makers and users of aeroplanes ad libitum. This, it seems to me, is a delusion due to a too easy acceptance of conclusions based on gossip and prejudiced claims rather than on the sense and wording of Judge Hazel's decision.

"If every aeroplane manufacturer in America, and every prospective purchaser of an aeroplane, and every man now owning and using an aeroplane, will carefully read Judge Hazel's decision, and then, if necessary, read it through again, they will awake to the fact that it upholds a series of combinations. First, the means for *simultaneously* raising one aileron and depressing the other. Second, in combination with this simultaneous operation of the ailerons or marginal portions, the use of the rudder. Third, in combination with the foregoing, the use of the front elevator.

"In other words, the basic element of the claim as sustained lies in the simultaneous operation of the ailerons or marginal portions. This one word, *simultaneous*, on analysis, makes reasonable and logical the broad support given to the Wright claims by the court . . . This also explains the position of the Court of Appeals in sustaining 'the reasoning' by which Judge Hazel reached his decision.

"Judge Hazel did not find that the Wrights invented or patented any of the individual elements covered by their patent . . . Nor did the court by any means uphold all the claims of the Wright patent . . ."

The statement went on to dissect in some detail the decision of Judge Hazel, and at its ending arrived at the Curtiss announcement:

"I awaited the final decision of the courts before announcing any change, because I felt confident of ultimate success in the litigation and had a system of control that was satisfactory and had been widely advertised. But we have been experimenting for years with an alternate system which is equal to, if not better than the old one, and with which we now equip all Curtiss machines.

"These facts seem entitled to publicity as wide as that given the statements asserting the almost unlimited scope of the decision."

*   *   *

A mystifying and unproductive meeting between Curtiss and Wright finally did take place, seemingly engineered by their legal staffs. This was after war orders from Europe began to inundate the Curtiss Company, and Curtiss had moved his main plant into Buffalo. He wrote Orville on June 11, 1915:

"Through a letter to our Mr. [John P.] Tarbox, from your attorneys some weeks ago, I learned of your willingness to talk over our differences with a view to a possible solution of the matter outside of court. This seems to me a matter which should be handled between principals.

"I believe you and I alone can make more progress than can be made by our representatives, and if you are willing to meet me halfway, I have confidence that we can arrive at a satisfactory arrangement of our mutual troubles.

"Unless I receive word from you not to come, I will be in Dayton on Tuesday morning next, to see you personally."

This time Orville responded: "Your letter received. Will see you Tuesday morning in Dayton."

Whatever transpired at that rendezvous, not very much frost was thawed. Among the Wright papers is found a slightly later inquiry, dated July 2, 1915: "Pursuant to our recent conversation, have you any proposals or suggestions to make? Would it not be convenient for you to come to Buffalo?"

Manifestly, Wright had withdrawn once more into his shell. Curtiss made another attempt on September 15, to which came the brusque reply: "If you desire to have a conference in regard to settling the patent litigation, I would recommend that you see Messrs. Wing & Russell, 14 Wall Street, New York City."

An explanation for this final brush-off was soon apparent: Orville was in the act of selling out his entire interest in the company. During the past year, he had systematically bought up all the outstanding stock, save for 3 percent held by Robert J. Collier. Now he disposed of his holdings, including patents, to a syndicate, headed by William Boyce Thompson, which formed a new corporation. The news announcement of this said that Mr. Wright was being retained as "chief aeronautical engineer, at a large salary," and that the company would continue to prosecute the patent infringement suits. His name was listed among the corporate officials as a director and consulting engineer. For himself, he said he intended to devote his whole time to scientific research with a laboratory in his home. In actuality, he went into retirement from that time forth, emerging rarely into the public eye, treated reverently as the "elder statesman" of aviation.

The amount received by Wright from the sale of his stock and patents was undisclosed, but published estimates ran from $675,000 to $1,500,000. A lifelong bachelor, he resided in a handsome, porticoed mansion, Hawthorn Hill, in a suburb of Dayton, attended by his devoted sister, Katharine, and a housekeeper.[1] But creative energy had drained from him with Wilbur's death. He walked with a slight limp, his souvenir of the crash in which Selfridge was killed, and his health was not robust.

Not until Orville had relinquished all ownership and control in the company was an aileron ever used on a Wright airplane. Toward the end of 1915, ailerons made their debut on the Model K observation seaplane and the Model L military scout.

*   *   *

A small windfall of patents, applied for much earlier, showered on Curtiss during 1916. Early in the year, the Patent Office issued his patent on the flying boat: ". . . a hydroaeroplane comprising a boat structure . . . which at the bow is upwardly inclined to form a broad, laterally extended surface adapted to distribute the shock of impact upon contact with the water." The "stepped bottom" was specified, and a hull divided by bulkheads transversely into two watertight sections. Hulls were 25 to 30 feet long, "and are expected in the future to be of much greater length."

In November came a patent he had applied for way back in 1910, on a biplane with "certain novel parts and combinations of parts"; including the movable shoulder frame for aileron control, together with "a whiffletree or pulley, or other suitable equalizing device . . . so that these forces must always be exactly equal." This patent was already outdated.

Two patents were issued together on the day after Christmas. One related to an exhaust-heater for air inlets, to heat air for the fuel mixture of aircraft engines. The other pertained to a new type of hull for flying boats, characterized by support of the tail controls upon the body of the hull, "and the passengers within it." This design was intended to "provide improvements in carrying capacity, strength and efficiency," and to simplify the structure.

On the basis of these patents, the Curtiss Aeroplane and Motor Corporation notified constructors of water-aircraft that they must obtain licenses; no royalty figure was specified, but manufacturers feared it would be the same as that being exacted by the Wright Company, which had settled down to a flat 5 percent. Smaller firms seeking Army and Navy contracts had to shave their bids close, and the Wright royalty wiped out all profit in many instances; they appealed to the Aero Club of America to exert its influence to help them stay in business.

America's entry into the war, quickly followed by a $640,000,000 appropriation for aircraft, brought the situation to a head. A group of airplane companies borrowed a chapter from the automobile industry, banded together as the Manufacturers Aircraft Association, and adopted a cross-licensing agreement. The chief architect of this pact was W. Benton Crisp, who had drawn up the automobile cross-license plan. The association's president, Frank H. Russell, announced: "All patent litigation relating to airplanes between members of the association ceases automatically." A New York editorial termed the agreement "something between a truce and an alliance," and hailed the end of an industrial war "that has had many unpleasant and distasteful features."[2]

The two giants, the Curtiss and the Wright companies, were those which really mattered. A royalty of $200 (or 1 percent of gross value) was to be paid on each machine; the royalties went into the treasury of the association for distribution to the patentees. It was provided that a total payment of $2,000,000 each be made to the Curtiss and Wright companies for relinquishing their patents to the pool. After they were paid off, royalties were to be siphoned into a fund "for general development of the industry."

While the cross-licensing agreement was ostensibly to prevail only for the duration of the war, in practice it was extended in perpetuity. Thus ended the battle of Wright vs. Curtiss—without a final determination or a rejection by the Supreme Court. Lacking that, the 1913 decision by Judge Hazel, upheld by the Circuit Court of Appeals, was commonly accepted by the laity as the last word. Many students of aeronautical history, however, have expressed doubt that such a decision would have been reached at a later day, in the light of more complete knowledge. Nonetheless, Hazel's decision stood, and Curtiss was stuck with the opprobrious label of "infringer," never abandoned by the Wright partisans.

When Judge Hazel retired from the bench in 1931, he was honored with a testimonial banquet in Buffalo. One of the speakers heaped fulsome praise upon him for wise decisions which, he said, had greatly advanced the development of both the automobile and the airplane industries.

20. Atlantic Fantasy

"The latest thing in aviation is a proposition for a transatlantic flight," Curtiss mentioned to Captain Washington Irving Chambers in November 1913, shortly before embarking afresh to Europe. "I do not know as yet whether it will materialize, but it is assuming a very interesting aspect."

A footnote which he withheld was that a flying boat designed to that end—the largest airplane yet built in the United States—was already under clandestine construction. For the time being this was a secret between himself and Rodman Wanamaker, the mercantile heir who had once exhibited the Rheims racer at the family stores.

Almost from the moment he solved the problem of takeoff from water, Curtiss had been flirting with a conviction that the Atlantic could and would be flown. There had been discussions of the possibility with Wanamaker at the Aero Club, and between him and Lieutenant John Towers at Hammondsport and San Diego. Towers put in his bid for a part in such an adventure if it ever came to pass. In early 1912, Curtiss said:

"Following up the success of my new hydroaeroplane, I have

taken great interest in the idea of a flight across the ocean by aeroplane. I consider the flight possible, and I am willing to undertake the construction of a machine for the purpose . . . Perhaps, backed by government aid and with the cooperation of their naval vessels, a chain of ships could be stretched across the ocean which would make it possible even now to fly with safety over the distance between Nova Scotia and Ireland, about 2000 miles . . . The accomplishment of this great flight over the ocean will no doubt mean great things for the progress of the world but it will require further development along the lines of the flying boat, where a substantial vessel will be provided, able to stand rough seas, and yet able to rise and skim the surface of the water."

The idea was by no means a monopoly. Walter Wellman, a journalist-adventurer, had made the original attempt in a dirigible named the *America*. Accompanied by Melvin Vaniman and a crew of four, he set sail from Atlantic City on October 15, 1910. His wireless messages ceased after reporting that the balloon was down and drifting. Changing winds drove the *America* southward and she tried for Bermuda, not quite making it. A British mail packet rescued the crew on October 18.

An agent for Phil O. Parmelee, a Wright exhibition flyer, wrote the Secretary of the Navy, in 1912, that Parmelee wished to try a flight across the Atlantic, asking for a fast destroyer to pace him. Around the same time, Harry N. Atwood, who had flown from St. Louis to New York, visited the Navy Department with a similar request; he planned to fly from Boston via Newfoundland to Ireland in a Wright land plane. The Navy refused both pleas on the ground that it could not assume even an indirect responsibility for such a gamble.

The emergence of the flying boat persuaded Lord Northcliffe, the London publisher, that the time was ripe to encourage a transatlantic flight. His motive was more serious than the mere promotion of a sensational exploit. He was worried about the German zeppelins and the damage they might inflict on England in the war which now seemed imminent. The aeroboat, if used as a fleet auxiliary in the North Sea, struck him as an effective means of heading them off. Accordingly, on March 31, 1913, Lord Northcliffe proclaimed his offer of the *Daily Mail* prize for a flight across the Atlantic by "hydro-aeroplane," in either direction. The amount was indeed munificent: £10,000, which equaled $50,000 in American currency. The chief condition was that the flight be completed within 72 consecutive hours. It could be made between any point in the United States, Canada, or Newfoundland, and any point in the United Kingdom. The monetary reward was soon augmented by $5000 posted on behalf of the Woman's Aerial League of Great Britain.

In view of this prize, Wanamaker asked Curtiss if he thought it could now actually be done. The reply came that it was only a question of money and mathematics, plus a stronger motor. Wanamaker told him to go to work on designs. In fulfilling orders for Russia and Italy, Curtiss made variations as deliberate experiments for the transatlantic machine; one exact prototype of the tentative hull was shipped to Italy.

* * *

When Curtiss went overseas that September, taking along a demonstrating model of the flying boat, a secondary objective was a study of the problems of an oceanic flight. To that end, he consulted with members of the Aero Club of Great Britain, British meteorologists, and other specialists, regarding weather patterns of the North Atlantic. He also made two new acquaintances who proved significant to his future.

The British agency for his flying boats had recently been acquired by the White & Thompson Company, Ltd., an aeronautical firm for whom Lieutenant John Cyril Porte was a test pilot. When Curtiss made demonstration flights of the aeroboat at Shoreham, Porte was an observer and quite likely a passenger; at any rate, he was a wholehearted convert to both the machine and its inventor. A large, good-humored chap in his early thirties, Porte looked so healthy that it came as a surprise for strangers to learn that he had been invalided out of the submarine service with tuberculosis. Maybe on the theory that higher air would benefit him, he took up flying, and now his lieutenancy was in the Royal Naval Flying Corps. He was one of a handful of pilots in the world who possessed an expert knowledge of navigation, and this fact would have registered with Curtiss.

While in England, the man from Hammondsport hired his first genuine design engineer. This was B. Douglas Thomas, then working for the Sopwith company, and he already had done basic sketches for a tractor biplane. Curtiss was aware that the U. S. Army was about to discard all pusher models in favor of tractors, because of the frequency of smashups. His own experience was entirely with pushers, which he preferred, but he wanted to be ready for the switch to front propellers. Thomas came with him back to Hammondsport.

Wanamaker was keener than ever on the transatlantic scheme. A crusader for peace, he was impressed with the "moral effect" such a flight could exert at a moment when the threat of war hung heavy over the world. Moreover, 1914 was to be celebrated as the centenary of peace between the United States and Great Britain: the Treaty of Ghent had signified the end of the last war between them in 1814. He envisioned the flight as a "fitting climax" of that observance.

As Curtiss and Wanamaker worked it out, this would be a nonstop flight from St. John's, Newfoundland, to Cape Clear at the south tip of Ireland; they figured that, with a good tail wind at 10,000 feet, the distance might be covered between dawn and dusk. Two pilots were mandatory, and both should be naval officers, for their knowledge of navigation. Curtiss made no gesture toward going himself, on the score that he was not a navigator.

It was Wanamaker who proposed that one pilot should be British, to emphasize the durability of Anglo-American friendship. Curtiss already had his own candidate in mind: Lieutenant John Towers. Chances are that he also recommended Porte as the Englishman, having so recently been in contact with him; although a reference says that Wanamaker cabled Sumner R. Hollander, who represented his stores in England, to locate a British pilot for him, and that Porte was his choice.

A number of English and French flyers made tentative announcements about going for the Northcliffe prize, but the Curtiss flying boat was the initial entry. Wanamaker lifted the curtain on February 4, 1914, with a letter to Alan R. Hawley, president of the Aero Club of America:

"In the cause of science and in the interest of world peace, I have the honor to announce first of all to the Aero Club of America my intention to make a purely scientific test of aeronautic powers by crossing the Atlantic by one flight, if possible . . . I sincerely hope that the operators and navigators may be from the Navy of the United States and of Great Britain, because naval aeronauts have the qualifications to navigate this uncharted journey in the air . . . The transatlantic flyer to be used in the journey is now being constructed by Mr. Glenn H. Curtiss, from plans that we have been studying for a long time . . .

"The science of aviation has made great strides within only a few years. It has conquered many of nature's obstacles. It has crossed the

English Channel, so late as 1909, when that accomplishment seemed utterly impossible. It has conquered the Alps. Yet it halts at the great ocean, and until one of our great oceans is crossed in a single flight, aviation will not have met the supreme test.

"The crossing of the Atlantic Ocean in one flight of an aircraft is, to my mind, as important to aerial navigation as was the voyage of Columbus to transportation by water. It will be of far more practical importance than was the successful expedition to the North Pole.

"What man has done before, he can do any number of times. Once the Atlantic is crossed in a single flight of an airship, there will soon follow regular transatlantic trips and a fixed safe transatlantic passenger air line . . . The crossing of the Atlantic by air is not a matter merely of initiative, nor of daring, nor even of skill; it is a problem of science.

"As a scientific and humanitarian undertaking, I venture to ask your cooperation and the cooperation of the governments of the United States and Great Britain."

The Aero Club cabled the entry to the Royal Aero Club of the United Kingdom, in whose hands Northcliffe had placed jurisdiction. This uncorked the news in England that Lieutenant John C. Porte had been selected as chief pilot, to fly with an American airman yet to be designated. Porte said, "It will be a jolly adventure," and sailed for New York not far behind Curtiss, who met him there on February 24. They conferred with Aero Club officers and J. A. D. McCurdy whose advice was sought because of his overwater flight between Florida and Cuba. Then Porte was escorted to Hammondsport.

At this juncture, Orville Wright injected a discordant note, telling reporters that Curtiss would not be allowed to build an airplane for the flight unless he took out a Wright license and settled for all back business. "The Curtiss machine can start from Canada," he said, "as Canada is the only civilized country in which our patents are not recognized. But I have not enough expectation that the craft will ever land near enough to any country where our patents are validated—that is, anywhere in Europe—to make it worth while to tell you what I would do in that case."

Wanamaker immediately made it known that Wright's attitude would have no effect upon his relations with Curtiss, and that preparations for the flight would go forward. He pointed out that his order had been placed before Curtiss went abroad in September 1913, hence prior to the Court of Appeals decision.

Wright was next quoted as saying that Curtiss knew full well that the machine he was building could not cross the ocean. This stung Curtiss into a retort:

"The question as to whether or not I am sincere in this undertaking is answered by the fact that payment for the machine is due only after it has proved itself capable of carrying the load sufficient for the proposed flight. It is obvious that I would not undertake this arrangement unless I was confident of being able to produce the machine. I call attention to the fact that there has been considerable advancement in aviation since the Wrights made their machine. There are many practical engineers, aviators and scientists who believe that the Atlantic will be crossed by an aeroplane this year."

Curtiss went to Washington to seek advice from government and naval authorities, and while there was a dinner guest at the Bell home. Updating Dr. and Mrs. Bell on the transatlantic project, he said that the Wright stumbling-block might compel him to finish the airplane in Canada. Dr. Bell invited him, if it came to that, to use his laboratories at Baddeck, promising to "give him every facility."

Curtiss "drew a very pretty picture" of making an aeroboat flight from New York to Nova Scotia and alighting on the Bras d'Or. The Bell diary recorded him as saying that "we need not be surprised should he appear in the air there during the coming summer." Bell observed: "I do not know whether he was serious in this or only yarning. I am inclined to think, however, that he was serious, and that we may really have a flying visit from him at Beinn Bhreagh . . . I must write to Casey Baldwin about this, and recommend him to invite Curtiss to visit Beinn Breagh at the time of the yacht races . . . The publicity attending such a flight would be good for the yacht club and be good for Baddeck, as many visitors would doubtless appear."

❂   ❂   ❂

As soon as Porte was in this country, Curtiss wired Jack Towers, now in charge of a newly established Naval Flying School at Pensacola, Florida, asking him to come to New York for "a very important conference." Remembering their former talks, Towers guessed the reason and was gripped by excitement as he journeyed north. His surmise was verified when he met with Rodman Wanamaker, who offered him the spot as copilot. His acceptance naturally depended on approval by the Navy Department, where Curtiss's influence still counted although Chambers had just been retired as Chief of Naval Aeronautics.

In the meantime, J. Lansing Callan, stationed at Pensacola also as a civilian instructor, had been ardently pulling strings. Lyman Seely wrote him in mid-February that he would "call Mr. Curtiss's attention once more to your interest in the flight." Evidently Curtiss sympathized with Lanny's ambition and wished to let him down easy, judging from a letter dated after Towers had been summoned: "The arrangements for this flight are entirely up to Mr. Wanamaker, as we are acting only as the builders of the aeroplane. Of course we are interested in the success of the undertaking just the same. I understand that Lieut. Towers has seen Mr. Wanamaker, and perhaps they have come to some understanding. It is rather early to predict whether or not the machine will be capable of carrying fuel enough for the flight, so that there is time to decide about the aviators later. We have a big job to produce a machine which will carry the fuel."

Soon after that, Callan had a telegram from one J. W. Scott of Hammondsport: ACTING ON THE INSTRUCTION OF G.H., WE ARE FORWARDING YOU A CASE OF GREAT WESTERN, BY EXPRESS, PREPAID.

Towers proceeded to Hammondsport on temporary duty, pending the anticipated orders from Washington which would put him on pilot status. The consent was slow in coming, and rumor had it that the Secretary of the Navy was averse to placing an American officer under command of a Britisher as chief pilot. The tight little group consisting of Curtiss, Towers, and Porte agreed upon using two 100-horsepower engines instead of the single 200-horsepower motor originally planned. The cockpit was to be enclosed by a hood with celluloid windows. Since it was unlikely that the craft could rise again if it came down in midocean, there was to be an auxiliary water screw for cruising like a boat. Wings could be jettisoned in such a case. The new English engineer, B. D. Thomas, was drawn in on the structural design.

Porte returned to England for a few weeks to arrange private affairs, and while there conferred with Captain F. Creagh Osborne, superintendent of compasses for the British Admiralty, a foremost authority on navigation. Osborne strongly advised against a nonstop flight to Ireland, suggesting rather a three-stage trip by way of the Azores and Spain. Porte was persuaded, and Osborne promised to meet him in Newfoundland with specially built compasses which he would install at that time.

While Porte was away he lost his prospective copilot. Mexico was in the throes of revolutionary turmoil, and when a party of American sailors were arrested in Tampico the United States dispatched the Atlantic Fleet to Vera Cruz. For the first time in history, naval aircraft were destined to come under fire. The Navy had so small a number of trained pilots that none could be spared, and so Towers was ordered to duty with the fleet. A week before the Tampico incident, Harry Genung had notified Lanny Callan at Pensacola that Curtiss wanted him to return north "right away." This hurried summons makes sense only if Towers was already expecting to be recalled and Callan was in line as his alternate (the Azores plan was not yet known at Hammondsport).

The reshuffle of copilots is a bit confusing. According to George Hallett, the mechanic from San Diego: "I heard Curtiss say that Towers would not be allowed to go, so I said to him: 'What you need is a good engine mechanic who can fly enough to take a trick at the controls.'" Hallett was in charge of mounting and test-running the two OX motors. As Curtiss thought more of the idea, he had Francis (Doc) Wildman, chief instructor for aeroboats, put Hallett through a cram course in their operation.

So many reports of foreign rivalry for the Northcliffe prize cropped up that there was talk of a transatlantic "race." Gustav Hamel, a British citizen, formally entered in May with a Martinsyde monoplane, proposing to start from Newfoundland and drop his undergear on leaving land. Hamel went to Paris to fly back a new plane and was lost enroute in the English Channel. A young Frenchman, Auguste Maicon, was the third to file entry. Curtiss discounted the competition, pointing out that European motors were "great consumers of oil and gasoline"; that the usual foreign engine would burn up 1200 pounds of castor oil. "If we succeed in getting our new motor up to the efficiency we hope to, it will consume only 180 pounds of oil for a distance equal to that across the ocean."

Lloyds of London posted betting odds of 47-to-1 against success of the flight, and Curtiss employees made up a pool of $2000 to cable a wager. Later, they were chagrined to learn that the cable had been delayed in transmission so that the bet was not placed at those high odds. Ultimately the odds were down to 6-to-1.

A sister plane was started in construction as a substitute in case the original was wrecked. Six engines in all were built so that extras would be on hand in Newfoundland. And Rodman Wanamaker took ship for Europe to study the route and initiate arrangements on the other side.

The preparations were all very meticulous. As for the plane itself, a news writer observed that "No more conscientious piece of work has ever been turned out of a factory"; that it was put together "with the care of an artist working on a mosaic." The stress of every nut and piece of wood had been painstakingly calculated.

*   *   *

During that spring, Lincoln Beachey, interviewed as he was boarding ship for Europe, let fall some remarks about the project that were displeasing to Curtiss. "I do not know enough about flying to undertake anything like that," Beachey was quoted. "I am really sorry to see schemes flaunted before the public that are on their face absurd and impossible. The reaction will be inevitable . . . I would urge upon all promoters of oversea flying that they give the entering airmen a tryout in round trips between New York and Albany. Let the transatlantic machine, for instance, grill its way up the Hudson to Albany and back six times without alighting. Then you will begin to know what may be done about the ocean flight."

Touchy on the subject, Curtiss wrote the following letter for forwarding:

Dear Beachey:
I enclose a clipping from a New York paper, printed the day after you sailed. I have noticed that newspaper reporters have a way of taking advantage of the time after a man has sailed to misquote him. I daresay that this was done in your case, because I cannot think of any reason why you should "knock" our transatlantic scheme.

Of course we know it is a big undertaking and do not consider its accomplishment a sure thing by any means, but we have a contract to build the machine and are putting a great deal of time and money into the effort to produce one which will carry the weight. The navigating is up to the operator, but Lieut. Porte has it pretty well planned.

Back at Hammondsport by mid-June, John Cyril Porte had no trouble selling his associates on the piecemeal route via the Azores. Its advantage at the outset was a marked reduction in fuel load: distance to the Azores was around 1100 miles, contrasted with the 1800 to Ireland. A crucial problem was the weight with which the plane must lift off; this was something no aircraft had faced before.

The itinerary was mapped out in three legs: Newfoundland to Ponta Delgada on the island of São Miguel; thence to Vigo Bay, Spain; and the final hop to Plymouth, England. The estimated total flying time was 55 hours, of which 20 hours was allotted for the long first stage. Fuel allowance for the Azores haul was 300 gallons (1900 pounds), so that the basic test which the craft had to meet was a takeoff from Keuka Lake with one ton of ballast.

A Wanamaker agent, W. D. Walker, went to Newfoundland to select a starting place. Under the guidance of W. D. Reid, president of the Reid-Newfoundland Railroad, he chose a fjord with a sheltered beach at Cape Broyle, 33 miles south of St. John's. There he laid in supplies and sat down to wait.

Now the proper role was found for Lanny Callan—one well suited to his handsome looks and charm. He was sent to the Azores to make advance arrangements. His reward would be to step in as relief pilot from Ponta Delgada the rest of the way to England. George Hallett was assigned as copilot and mechanic for the first leg.

A spotlight of world interest was focused upon the little village of Hammondsport. A bevy of city reporters and photographers, some from London, swooped in and camped. Motion picture cameras were perched on the tops of hangars. Automobile tourist parties by the hundreds drove long distances to goggle at the wonder airplane of its era. It was regarded as the last word in mankind's newest science, ensconced in a curiously pastoral setting. A dozen good milch cows grazed tranquilly nearby, contemptuous of the hubbub. Reporters depicted the hillslopes with their crazy-quilt pattern of vineyards, and the forest of green trees muffling the town with two weatherbeaten church steeples rising through. Passenger aeroboats did a rushing business. A baseball game was played between pickup teams of newsmen and aviators (the journalists won).

With the tide of popular enthusiasm running high, Orville Wright relented, giving the word that he would not after all obtain an injunction to prevent the transatlantic flight. A statement issued by the

Wright Company explained that, in the time since he had predicted failure of the flight, both the airplane and its route had been altered. "Mr. Wright's prediction has been repeated over and over again in an unfair way," the release said. If the flight should be successful, "it will not prove that Wright was wrong."

Lieutenant Porte was a gentleman of note around the village, who "will make a popular hero of the right kind," as a reporter wrote. He picked up a cheap, floppy-brimmed straw hat in a local store, and this became his trademark. The son of an Anglican rector, reared in Ireland, he could have donned morning-coat and passed for a cabinet minister. Yet he carried himself with "no airs or attitudes," and was described as "a good-natured, lounging, careless big man with an engaging smile and fine Irish manners. He never looks very serious outside of an airboat."

So revolutionary and hopefully historic a craft must, perforce, be given a christening and launching, and June 22 was the date set for that ritual. Until now her only label was: the Rodman Wanamaker Transatlantic Flyer. Curtiss queried Wanamaker in Paris for a suitable name, and he cabled back AMERICA.

In imitation of a ship's launching, a bottle of champagne was to be broken over the prow. Three village belles drew straws to be queen of the ceremony, and the winner was Miss Katherine Masson, sixteen, daughter of an official in the Pleasant Valley Wine Company. A tripod was reared with the champagne dangling like a pendulum from its apex. The bottle was wired tightly between two horseshoes to facilitate its breakage while also symbolizing good luck. A metal shield protected the delicate nose of the plane from damage and served as a target for Miss Masson when she swung the bottle from the safe distance of a low platform. An American flag unfurled to the breeze above the cabin. The town was combed for a Union Jack, and when none could be found the correspondent of a London newspaper glued a British stamp to the hull.

With an audience of several hundred clustered around, Katherine Masson mounted the platform, virginally gowned in white silk with a picture hat to match, and opened the program by reciting a poem composed for the occasion. The author was Dr. A. F. Zahm, director of the Smithsonian's Langley Aerodynamical Laboratory, who was a transient resident of Hammondsport for quite another reason.

Majestic courser of sea and air,
Within this ample hold
Two navigators bold
The Atlantic main a-bridging are to bear
Glad greetings from the New World to the Old.
Peace herald of the century,
"America" I christen thee.

Proud billows of the imperious ocean
Salute thy bow with gentlest motion;
And while within this double wing
The unerring motors timely sing,
May all the powers of the atmosphere
Sustain and speed thy glorious career.[1]

A champagne bottle should have behaved better for the grand-daughter of Jules Masson, a pioneer French vintner in Hammondsport. Lieutenant Porte stepped up and placed the bottle in her hands. She gave it a swing on its pendulum wire, it struck the bow, but it failed to break. She hurled it again with more vigor and the same result. Now Porte's "English was up" (in the *Herald*'s phrase), and he gave the perdurable quart a couple of yeoman's heaves; at the second one, the bottle slipped out of its horseshoe sling and rolled on the ground. A solemn occasion was degenerating into comedy and people began to laugh. Flushed with anger, Porte picked the bottle up in both hands and stalked menacingly toward the *America*'s nose. Curtiss stopped him before any damage was inflicted. As a last resort, the bottle was trussed to the prow and Porte grimly assaulted it with a sledgehammer. Both the hull and Porte's wearing apparel were doused with foaming champagne, to the "considerable merriment" of the onlookers.

*   *   *

By the time the *America* was reeled from her cradle into shallow water, it was too late for her maiden flight that day. Next morning Curtiss and Porte took her up together for two short circles over the lake, after which the former said that she "surpassed my expectations"; the latter that it was "the finest flying craft I ever sat in—steady as a rock." Far from being sluggish, she was hard to hold down.

The ship was painted a brilliant red, for high visibility at sea. The upper wing span was 72 feet, the lower 46; thus it was more a sesquiplane than a biplane. The skin was varnished Japanese silk. The hull was 32 feet long, structured of white cedar, four feet in the beam and divided into four watertight compartments. The cabin was lined with oiled silk; the full-width pilots' bench was upholstered with a thick corduroy cushion, and in a space behind it life-preservers were spread out as a mattress. Instead of the familiar shoulder-yoke of the Curtiss control, a foot bar operated the ailerons.

Instruments were still rudimentary. A major navigational problem was going to be the lateral drift caused by side winds, and a newly devised Sperry drift indicator was to be given its baptism. Curtiss asked Elmer Sperry for a gyro-stabilizer, only to be told that his full output was tied up in a contract with the Navy. Porte was to carry a sextant, an aneroid barometer, and a speed indicator. Beyond that and the compasses, he planned to stay low and watch for vessels, which he trusted would fly position signals.

*   *   *

After landing U. S. Marines, the naval force was soon withdrawn from Mexican waters and Jack Towers was ordered back to Washington for instructions. There he found that Rear Admiral Bradley A. Fiske had conceived an interest in the Atlantic flight and wished to know more about it. Fiske got Towers reassigned to Hammondsport as an observer. If Towers should decide that the performance of the plane made the flight practicable, then the Admiral would see to it that he went along; promising in that case to do all in his power to arrange the cooperation of Navy ships along the route. Captain Chambers was also in Hammondsport intently watching progress when Towers reappeared. Manifestly, if the *America* proved seaworthy the Navy was going to get involved. Porte wrote instructions to Callan: "In all probability a fast cruiser of the U. S. Navy will arrive at the Azores Islands a few days previous to our start. If so, unless you receive further communication on the subject, give them 100 gallons of gas and 10 gallons of oil. They will await our arrival in the vicinity of Flores, in all probability a hundred miles to the northwest, being in wireless communication with all the three islands . . . I hope you are not finding your sojourn very lonely."

Groups of enthusiasts arranged trips to Newfoundland to bid the *America* bon voyage. A Hammondsport party was organized, including Mr. and Mrs. Glenn Curtiss, Mr. and Mrs. Lyman J. Seely, and Dr.

P. L. Alden. A large delegation from the Aero Club of America planned
to go, headed by its president, Alan R. Hawley. Steamship berths from
New York were booked for July 3.

The original target date for takeoff was the full-moon period of
July, but preliminary load tests were disappointing and a long and
frustrating series of changes began. Sacks of cement were used for
ballast. A pair of side elevators was added beneath the wings, like
thin canoes with blunt sterns, and the risability was somewhat improved.

The daily doings of the *America* made page one news in New
York papers, down to their finest detail. Dramatically, on June 29, it
was elbowed off the front page by the black headlines accompanying
a cable dispatch datelined Sarajevo, Bosnia: "Archduke Francis Ferdinand, heir to the throne of Austria-Hungary, and his wife, the Duchess
of Hohenburg, were shot and killed by a Bosnian student here today." On an inside page of the *Times* might be found a story bearing
the more familiar Hammondsport dateline, telling how the *America*
had narrowly escaped wrecking in a fierce thunderstorm when wind
ripped the plane from her mooring. Lightning had played awesomely
on the hills above Keuka Lake, and hailstones ruined a million dollars
worth of grapes. Henceforward, the *America* was to be anchored with
twenty-four stout ropes.

On July 1, Porte postponed sailing for Newfoundland until the
11th, saying the boat's performance was "not satisfactory." When he
entrained for New York, friends said that the delays had "got on his
nerves" and he needed a rest. In New York he met Captain Osborne,
who was delivering the Admiralty compasses a bit prematurely. The
compass needles rested in horsehair to cushion vibration. Instead of
Newfoundland, Osborne came then to Hammondsport, where they tested
out the instruments in a motorboat on the lake. Osborne also brought
a Union Jack to be carried on the flight.

Porte received mail from food manufacturers, offering to supply
edibles for the journey at no cost; he said the staple diet would
probably be hard-boiled eggs. A decision was made to take along
carrier pigeons. The side elevators didn't pan out well; pontoons were
tried instead but discarded. A larger tail fin was added. Curtiss proved
that the plane could fly and land on one engine alone, by taking it
down the lake and alternating the motors. Still it did not rise too
well with ballast. Steamer reservations were postponed to July 18,
and now the sights were set on the full-moon phase of August 5.

The London *Daily Mail* queried Porte about rumors the flight would be abandoned. He replied: SOLUTION CERTAIN EARLY DATE. WEIGHT CAR-RYING QUALITIES AND BEHAVIOR IN AIR BEYOND EXPECTATION.

Meanwhile, Callan was busy in the Azores. Against the contingency that the plane could not reach Ponta Delgada, he set up alternate supply depots on the islands of Flores and Fayal. In case the arrival were after dark, he had wood heaped for a huge bonfire on a headland of Fayal. The island governor arranged for fishing boats to keep out of the way the day of the flight; also for a government vessel to be anchored in the harbor of Ponta Delgada, on which Porte and Hallett could catch up sleep while Callan went over the engines and fueled up (under the prize rules, the plane must not be moored to a wharf and its crew must not go ashore).

Callan had a handbill printed, in both English and Portuguese, and disseminated through shipping offices. It read:

AEROPLANE AMERICA

NOTICE

To all vessels in Azorean waters, and Portuguese coast

* * *

An aeroplane with boat attached, painted red and named "America," is expected to cross the Atlantic Ocean sometime in July or August by way of St. John's, N.F., Fayal, San Miguel, and Portuguese coast.

In case of accident, it will land on the water where it will float until assistance arrives. If you should see it at any time, please render aid as soon as possible and notify the agent at San Miguel. Your assistance will be appreciated. Ponta Delgada, San Miguel.

* * *

All the while, Curtiss refused to be discouraged, reminding pessimists that his organization was attempting something which never had been done before—that is, lifting an airplane with a heavy load —and that they must grope their way with patient experimenting. He came up with the novel idea of a "sea-sled" bottom, shaped like an inverted V, with a deep groove running lengthwise. A false bottom in that form was attached to the hull, and it seemed to work so well that they decided to rebuild the hull. This meant putting off the shipping date until August 1, and Porte said: "If we had to wait until September, I would make the trip then. September would be better than August in one respect. There would be less danger from tropical storms between the Azores and Spain."

The "sea-sled" bottom fizzled and was removed. Still the *America* was not raising load enough to equal the weight of fuel she must carry to make the Azores. Neither of the engines, rated at 100-horse-power, was developing more than 85. To gain extra power, they installed a third engine, with a three-bladed tractor propeller, cutting away part of the upper wing to mount it over the cabin. Thus the *America* became the first tri-motored airplane. Curtiss tested it with a load of 2600 pounds, taxied back in toward shore and shouted: "I want more ballast. I can't hold her down." Later he exulted: "This is what we have been looking for for a long time."

Because of the excess fuel it would burn, the third engine was intended for use only in takeoffs and emergencies. To measure fuel comsumption, Porte and Hallett next day flew down the lake to Penn Yan and return, finding the rate worrisomely greater than was allowable. They blamed the third engine whose prop windmilled when idle. Hard figures showed they could carry enough fuel for 1200 miles, which would barely reach the Azores in fair weather with no margin for safety.

So intent had they been on grooming the *America* that hardly anyone at Hammondsport had paid much heed to the news from Europe. On July 26, those who saw a Sunday paper read banner headlines such as this:

> AUSTRIA BREAKS WITH SERVIA;
> EUROPEAN WAR NOW LOOKS NEAR;
> RUSSIA TO MOBILIZE HER ARMY

There still remained space on page one of the New York *Times* for a head: OCEAN FLIGHT OFF UNTIL OCTOBER. The article explained that the high rate of gas consumption ended all hope of sailing on August 1, and: "It is problematical now whether the trans-atlantic flight can ever be attempted in the *America*."

The plane was taken to the shop for an overhaul in which Curtiss aimed to knock off 100 pounds, perhaps to resort to a wheeled takeoff. Rather than eliminate the third engine, he guessed it might be run throttled down, which would be more economical than carrying it dead. Porte said: "I wish to state most emphatically there is no idea whatsoever of abandoning the flight this year."

The Aero Club thought it had a solution in a new route which it had mapped, planting a fuel station on Flemish Cap, a shoal of the Newfoundland Banks 420 miles southeast of St. John's.

When a newsman was so tactless as to ask Porte if he had undertaken the flight because doctors warned him he had not long to live, he bridled: "That's all nonsense. There is not a particle of truth in that. My health is all right." Actually his lungs were not as strong as he pretended. He seized the opportunity now for a brief rest at Saranac Lake, a celebrated haven for tuberculosis patients.

On July 28, Austria-Hungary declared war on Servia. On August 1, Germany declared war on Russia, while France ordered general mobilization. The German army smashed across frontiers into Belgium, Luxembourg, and France. On August 4, Great Britain went to war over the violation of Belgian neutrality. Germans promptly shot down a French plane—the first aircraft destroyed in warfare.

Lieutenant John Cyril Porte was on a special aerial reserve list of the British Admiralty; in fact, his was the only name on that list. Rushing down from the Adirondacks, he boarded the *Lusitania* without waiting for military summons.

*   *   *

What about the flight of the *America?* Wanamaker at first stated that it would merely be postponed. Instantly, both Jack Towers and Lanny Callan put in their bids to be Porte's successor. On second thought, it occurred to someone that, with England a belligerent, no landing could be made in the British Isles. After a conference at the Aero Club, the announcement came that no transatlantic flight would be attempted until the war was over, at which time Porte might return and finish the job. Few people expected hostilities to last very long.

On his arrival in England, Porte stepped into uniform as Wing Commander in the Royal Naval Air Service, and one of his first acts was inducing the Admiralty to purchase the *America* and her duplicate. Wanamaker, who had not formally accepted delivery, relinquished his contract, in return for Curtiss's promise to build him another *America* "as soon as feasible."

The two flying boats were shipped to Liverpool aboard the liner *Mauretania* on September 30, amid tight security. The packing cases were addressed to a private individual, as dummy purchaser, invoiced as containing "machinery of some kind." A delicate question confronted the State Department in letting them go: was an airplane to be classed as munitions of war? If so, it was subject to seizure as contraband, and the United States could be held accountable for permitting its shipment. As a matter of fact, it was not long until the German Ambassador, Count Johann-Heinrich von Bernstorff, called at the State Department to protest the shipment. He said it had come to his knowledge that the *America* and five more planes of its type had been delivered in England; furthermore, that England had ordered thirty-six more such machines from Curtiss, and that Russia had also placed an order. Secretary of State William Jennings Bryan held the ambassador at bay with a ruling that airplanes were not contraband of war.

The *America* went into immediate service on anti-submarine patrol and as an escort for troop ships. She was credited with sinking three German U-boats up to September 1915. What was more important, she became the prototype for a long line of flying boats employed by England during World War I, which were designed chiefly by Porte, enlarging and improving on what he had learned at Hammondsport. Most of these were manufactured by Curtiss in the United States and shipped to England. In fact, its very name became a generic title for future models: Porte's H-4 was called the Small America, his H-12 the Large America.

At the outbreak of war, Towers was ordered to London as naval attaché to the U. S. Embassy.[2] He and Porte promptly got together and talked about reviving the ocean flight project when peace came.

Far from abandoning the idea, Rodman Wanamaker in 1916 incorporated the America Transoceanic Company, and notified the Aero Club that this company, "acting for me, has placed an order for a new and larger *America*," then under construction. "When completed and accepted, the new *America* will make the attempt to cross the Atlantic, in which project I again venture to ask the cooperation of the Aero Club of America." Although the entry of the United States as a belligerent in the war effectively killed that project, Wanamaker kept the America Transoceanic Company alive, hoping that it would eventually operate airlines across oceans.[3]

21. Flying the *Langley*

Having invested $50,000 in the dragonfly "aerodrome" of Dr. Samuel P. Langley, the War Department did not intend to consign its crippled carcass to the junk heap nor yet to exalt it into a museum piece. Rather, it was regarded as an incomplete experiment. After the second ignominious dive into the Potomac in 1903, it was locked away in a disused carpenter shop back of the Smithsonian Institution, with a vague notion of some day giving it another chance when public derision would have subsided.

At Langley's death in 1906, Wilbur Wright lamented to Octave Chanute: "It is really pathetic that he should have missed the honor he cared for above all others, merely because he could not launch his machine successfully. If he could only have started it, the chances are that it would have flown sufficiently to have secured to him the name he coveted." In 1907, Wilbur said: "It is reported by Dr. Bell that the Langley machine is to be tried again, but he does not say whether the War Department is to have a hand in it." That Bell's inkling was not without foundation is shown by the hint dropped by General James Allen, Chief Signal Officer, that "the old Langley machine" might be brought forth for experiments, at the time when Army contracts were awarded to the Wright brothers and Herring.

Both Bell and Chanute were consistent advocates of resurrecting the hapless "aerodrome," as was Dr. Charles D. Walcott, Langley's successor as secretary of the Smithsonian. Walcott asked Chanute in 1908 what he thought about having it rebuilt, and the latter replied: "If the Institution does not mind taking this risk and suitable arrangements can be made about the expense, I believe that it would be desirable to make the test, in order to demonstrate that the Langley machine was competent to fly and might have put our government in possession of a type of flying machine, which, although inferior to that of the Wrights, might have been evolved into an effective scouting instrument."

Speaking to the Western Society of Engineers at Chicago in 1909, Chanute said: "There is no doubt . . . that if the machine had been properly launched it would have flown. The machine is still in existence . . . It is most unfortunate that further effort was not then made to launch that machine."

In making the principal address awarding the Langley Medal to the Wright brothers in 1910, Dr. Bell paid homage to Professor Langley and referred to his airplane as "a perfectly good flying machine—excellently constructed and the fruit of years of labor. It was simply never launched into the air, and so has never been given the opportunity of showing what it could do. Who can say what a third trial might have demonstrated?"

Still the relic (nicknamed the *Buzzard*) went on gathering cobwebs. The Smithsonian lacked funds to do anything about it. When the Langley Aerodynamical Laboratory was established in 1913, however, the situation changed. The "aerodrome," wrecked just ten years before, was its choicest possession, and nothing could have been more logical than its rehabilitation.

*   *   *

In January 1914, Lincoln Beachey was flying loops at San Francisco, Curtiss was abroad, and the Court of Appeals rendered its verdict in favor of the Wright patent. Whatever his motive, Beachey chose this moment for a proposition to the Smithsonian: he offered to restore the Langley plane, provide it with a new engine, and fly it. Dr. Walcott responded that it would be inadvisable to take out the original, but that the Smithsonian would afford him "every facility" to make a "perfect reproduction." Beachey garnered publicity and said: "You can fly a kitchen table if your motor is strong enough. This is what I want to show." Then he pursued the matter no further. But the New York *Times* picked it up in an editorial comment:

"People with minds naturally suspicious are likely to look for a connection between certain patent litigation and the announcement by Lincoln Beachey, the aviator, that he is going to prove that if Prof. Langley had been able to put a modern motor in his aeroplane it would have sailed the air as well as those since made.

"However that may be, the proposal has interest, for there is no doubt that Prof. Langley was very close to the solution of the great problem, and his many friends would welcome a vindication of his work. Should this come, it would add a new pathos to the scientist's death so soon after the failure of his machine—a death commonly ascribed to the disappointment of his high hopes."

Evidently Curtiss heard of Beachey's gesture the moment he was home from Europe, if not earlier. Meanwhile, Dr. Walcott had written to the Curtiss Aeroplane Company: "In connection with the reopening and development of work under the Langley Aerodynamical Laboratory, it seems desirable to make a thorough test of the principles involved in the construction of the Langley heavier-than-air, mancarrying, flying machine, especially the question as to tandem arrangement of the planes, and the general stability, especially longitudinal stability."

Walcott afterward said that he asked Curtiss if he would be willing to undertake the tests, and to make an estimate of the cost of restoration.

The steps by which the renewed experiments with the *Langley* came about are highly pertinent, in view of the long and rancorous controversy they kicked up.

Before involving himself, Curtiss sounded out the opinion of Dr. Bell, to whom he wrote on February 16: "There has been some talk of reproducing the old Langley machine and having it flown. I should like to know what you think of this plan, as it would be an easy thing to do, provided it is worthwhile." While Bell's reply is not in evidence, it was almost surely affirmative.

Sometime during March, Curtiss was asked to send a flying boat to Washington for demonstration in the Langley Day program, as he had done the previous year. In his reply he said: "I would like to put the Langley aeroplane itself in the air."

On March 16 Curtiss mailed a letter to Lincoln Beachey: "I am told that you offered at the time of the Wright decision to fly the Langley machine. I believe that this would be a good thing to do and I think I can get permission to rebuild the machine, which would go a long way toward showing that the Wrights did not invent the flying machine as a whole but only a balancing device, and we would get a better decision next time. Let me know if you are serious in this and if so we will take the matter up with the Smithsonian Institution."

Exactly a week later Beachey embarked for Europe, which suggests that he was not overly serious. And two days after that Dr. Bell picked up his invention, talked into it, and made this entry in his *Home Notes:*

"Yesterday, March 25, Secretary Walcott called me up by telephone at the Volta Bureau to let me know that Mr. Glenn H. Curtiss was anxious to make a copy of the Langley Aerodrome. Mr. Walcott said that Curtiss could have it made in time to try it on Langley Day, May 6, 1914, and that Curtiss thought the expense would not exceed about $2000, and Secretary Walcott wanted to know whether I would approve of an appropriation of $2000 from the Smithsonian funds to aid Curtiss to make the experiment.

"I told Secretary Walcott that I should like to see the experiment made but doubt the advisability of the Smithsonian funds being used for the purpose. Secretary Walcott said, 'I was thinking that I might chip in myself personally to the extent of a thousand dollars.' And I replied that I also would be glad to chip in and thought it would be much better to have the experiment made by outside parties at their own expense than to make the Smithsonian responsible for it."

On the morrow, Walcott phoned again. "I expressed the same views but told him I would back him up in whatever he decided was best to be done. He suggested that he had better telegraph Curtiss to come right on and talk the matter over and I agreed to this.

"This is an important matter, and considering my past relations with Curtiss in the A.E.A. and the probability that I may be associated with Curtiss in some way or other should the patents of the A.E.A. be transferred to his company, it may be well for me to be careful about endorsing the proposition that Smithsonian funds should be expended upon this experiment. It would undoubtedly be to the interest of Curtiss and the A.E.A. to have the experiment made, but if I endorsed the proposition that the Smithsonian funds should be used for the purpose, might I not lay myself open to the charge that I had taken advantage of my position as a Regent of the Smithsonian Institution, and a member of its executive committee, to use Smithsonian funds to further my own interests? I think under the circumstances that I had better take the ground that, while I had no objections to the use of the Smithsonian funds for this purpose, if the Regents desire it, *I* should not *vote* upon the matter.

"I propose to write to Secretary Walcott and suggest the propriety of the experiment being made under the auspices of the Aero Club of Washington and at its expense. If the Aero Club chooses to get up a subscription to cover the expenses, I would be glad to contribute personally to the fund. Upon this plan the Smithsonian would only be called on to give its moral support without contributing financially to the experiment."

In another phone talk with Bell, Walcott said it was his thought "to have Curtiss make the experiment quietly at Hammondsport, N.Y., without directing public attention to the matter; and if successful he could repeat it here in public on Langley Day. He stated that, in the opinion of Zahm and himself, that most of the fatalities that have occurred have been due to lack of fore and aft stability, leading to a dive; and that the tandem principle adopted by Langley would remedy this and lessen, if not entirely prevent, a fatal dive." Walcott said he understood Bell's position, and that "it probably would be necessary for him to go ahead on his own responsibility."

Curtiss came to Washington and a conference took place on March 30 at Bell's home. Besides him and Bell, the participants were Walcott, McCurdy, and Sheldon Cameron, the patent attorney. Whereas Curtiss's proposal had been only to construct a replica, Walcott now seemed inclined to use the original. Bell registered his dissent that the original machine ought not to be risked, but that a reproduction should be made. There was unanimous agreement that the initial tests be as private as possible; if these succeeded, then the machine should be returned to Washington for public exhibition on Langley Day.

＊　　＊　　＊

Secretary Walcott prevailed with his plan for repairing the original *Langley*. Undoubtedly, he was motivated in part by a desire to refurbish the luster of the scientist under whom he had worked and whose memory he so much revered. To do this with Langley's own airplane, rather than a facsimile, would make the vindication that much more telling. Walcott had hoped, as far back as 1908, to have the experiment conducted by Langley's assistant, Charles M. Manly, who built the engine and survived the Potomac plunges. Manly was now in private business and had no plant in which to do the reconstruction. Curtiss owned what was probably the best available plant in the country, with a corps of skilled aircraft mechanics. He was a recent recipient of the Langley Medal and a member of the advisory committee of the Langley Laboratory. Certainly Orville Wright would have refused, if asked. Had the Langley "aerodrome" actually been capable of manned flight in 1903, it would antedate the Wright machine as a viable airplane.

Curtiss was not unmindful of this point, as evinced by his letter to Beachey; nor of the bearing which a successful flight with the *Langley* might have on some future court decision. No less was Bell, as his diary proves. It does not necessarily follow that this was Curtiss's real or only motive in taking on the experiment. Nor do the preliminaries suggest a conspiracy between Walcott and Curtiss to discountenance the achievement of the Wright brothers. The *Langley* would not have fulfilled its destiny in aviation if it had been denied the ultimate trial. From a purely practical point of view, Curtiss was the logical man to do it, if anyone did.

At any rate, in the forepart of April, the *Langley* (as it thereafter came to be known) was crated and shipped in a box-car to Hammondsport. As to who paid Curtiss $2000 for the restoration, some question lingers. Walcott afterward stated more than once that the Smithsonian footed the bill; but it is barely possible that he and Bell privately shared it, as they had talked of doing. No such item appears under the detailed "disbursements" in the annual report of the executive committee of the Board of Regents (of which Bell was a member) for the fiscal years 1914 or 1915. An expenditure of $723.73 for the Langley Laboratory was reported for 1914, and one of $418.58 for 1915.

While the work of rehabilitation was done in a segregated part of the plant, the *Langley's* presence was by no means a secret, as so many critical sources would have it. The *Herald* promptly reported its arrival, with the commentary: "We in Hammondsport who have witnessed every conceivable form of aircraft tried out to destruction, failure, or partial success, have grown generous in our judgment of those patient men who labor with transporting enthusiasm to create new means of mastering the wayward, elusive and seductive air."

One must hold in mind that the *Langley* episode coincided partially with the construction and trials of the *America*, and this was a compelling reason why it could not have been kept under wraps. The village was crawling with newsmen and photographers. Inasmuch as the *America* was Curtiss's priority project of the summer, it probably accounts for the fact that the *Langley* was not anywhere near ready in time for Langley Day in Washington.

The Smithsonian assigned Dr. A. F. Zahm as its official representative at Hammondsport[1]; when the time came for the first flight attempts, Dr. Walcott himself appeared. The personal services of Manly were secured in restoring the radial motor which was his handiwork. From being waterlogged and then neglected for ten years in storage, the engine was in deplorable condition; nevertheless, one of the primary aims was to fly the machine at first with its 1903 motor. The best that Manly could do was to doctor it up to two-thirds of its pristine power, but Curtiss gave it a hotter spark, at least, with magneto ignition instead of the previous dry-cell batteries.

The basic objectives of the Aerodynamical Laboratory, as set forth by Dr. Zahm, were twofold: firstly, to show whether the *Langley*, as originally constructed, was capable of sustained free flight with a pilot; secondly, to determine more fully the advantages (and/or disadvantages) of the tandem-winged type of airplane.

Consequently there was to be a dual set of experiments. At the outset the machine would be restored as nearly as feasible to its 1903 condition and briefly tested that way, to see whether it could fly or not. If it flew, then a modern motor would be installed and various changes successively made for a longer series of trials.

The first decision to be made was on method of takeoff: whether by catapult, on wheels, or from water. Curtiss "favorably entertained" the catapult idea, according to Zahm; but, remembering what happened before, dismissed it. Hammondsport terrain afforded no extensive level field, and no one could predict how long a run might be required. Moreover, Langley's models had all been designed for coming down on water. Preoccupied as he was with water aircraft, Curtiss opted for the aquatic means, and pontoons made the *Langley* a hydroplane.

The pontoons were, of course, a radical change, and at the same time a drawback. They increased the weight by 340 pounds and created air resistance. On the other hand, the struts attaching them afforded a certain amount of bracing to the spinal framework, if not to the wings.

Any such bracing was offset, in some degree at least, by elimination
of the stiffening keel which formerly extended underneath. While these
alterations opened the door to carping that it was not the same
machine which Langley tried to launch, they hewed as close to the
line as circumstances would permit, and they were not concealed.
The essential point was not to modify the original flying characteristics
any more than could be helped.

The same two pusher propellers were retained. One smashed wing
was completely rebuilt, and several broken ribs were replaced elsewhere.
The four wings were recovered with cloth and the fabric varnished.
The system of control and balance remained untouched for all the
tests: no ailerons, no wing-warping. The pilot could rely only on the
dihedral angle of the wings, the moving of a vertical rear rudder, and
the shifting of his own weight. Henry Kleckler, engineer in charge of
the repairs, vehemently denied in his later years the accusation that
the plane was basically redesigned at the start. "It wasn't true," he
insisted. "We absolutely restored everything the way it was, as near
as it was possible to do so." Dr. Zahm reported that the work was
done "according to the minute descriptions contained in the Langley
Memoir on Mechanical Flight." Manly, who was present much of the
time, verified these claims to authenticity.

When all the parts had been made ready in the factory, they were
taken down to the lakefront and assembled in full view of the reporters
and flocks of visitors. That no effort was made to deceive the press
concerning the alterations is indicated by this sample description
from one New York newspaper: "The wings had been rebuilt because
the old cloth was torn and useless and many of the ribs were broken
when the machine fell in the Potomac. All of the original ribs that
were intact or could be repaired were used . . . and the missing ribs
were replaced with duplicates of the old ones. The new ones, however,
were made of laminated wood, not hollowed out with the painstaking
care bestowed on the originals . . . Few changes could be made in
the old motor. The carburetor only was changed, and that was because
no one here understood the workings of the original mechanism. Absolutely no changes were made in the system of balance."

At a later date, when Casey Baldwin asked him for a candid statement of the facts, Curtiss replied: "It is true that it was flown without a
single change that could have *improved its flying qualities*. The only
changes were the replacements of the broken parts and the addition

of the floats . . . The addition of the three floats and their supports added 350 pounds of weight to the machine, not to mention the head resistance."

* * *

Curtiss took it upon himself to do the test flying of the opening and crucial phase. On the morning of May 28, a clear day with a light breeze, a dozen men waded into the lake carrying the *Langley* and gently deposited it on the water. Curtiss was sitting in the pilot's car suspended beneath the forward wings. The propellers were spun and the craft gradually gained speed until it raised a few feet clear of the water. Quoting from Dr. Zahm's account in the next annual report of the Smithsonian Institution:

"Many eager witnesses and camera men were at hand, on shore and in boats. The four-winged craft, pointed somewhat across the wind, went skimming over the wavelets, then automatically headed into the wind, rose in level poise, soared gracefully for 150 feet, and landed softly on the water near the shore. Mr. Curtiss asserted that he could have flown further, but, being unused to the machine, imagined the left wings had more resistance than the right."

The New York *Times* reporter made his lead: "'Langley's Folly' flew over Lake Keuka today—approximately 11 years since it caused the country to laugh at its inventor when on its trial flight it fell into the Potomac." Further down in his story, he asserted that "aside from the floats, the machine was almost exactly as it was when the faulty launchings were made over the Potomac River."

Hailing the success editorially, the same newspaper observed that the Wright suit "was won upon the fact that no other aeroplane had ever maintained itself in air with human freight, and inferentially could not. What effect Mr. Curtiss's demonstration with the Langley aerodrome will have in modifying the recent decision of the Circuit Court in favor of the Wrights' contention no one can now tell."

From Washington sped a telegram addressed to G. H. Curtiss: CONGRATULATIONS ON YOUR SUCCESSFUL VINDICATION OF LANGLEY'S DROME. THIS IS REALLY THE CROWNING ACHIEVEMENT OF YOUR CAREER, AT LEAST SO FAR. MY BEST WISHES FOR YOUR CONTINUED SUCCESS. GRAHAM BELL.

In the ensuing days, Curtiss lifted the machine off water for a few more short hops, chiefly to accommodate photographers but also to prove that the first one was not a fluke. Then, deeming that the flyability of the original *Langley* had been proved, Walcott ordered the installation of a Curtiss engine and propeller, and returned to Washington. The second phase of the experiments—to gather data on the potentialities of the tandem-wing type of airplane—was then ushered in.

Beachey, back from his European excursion, let slip a remark to the effect that he might loop the *Langley*. This aroused the editorial ire of the *Times:* "If Lincoln Beachey really intends to 'loop the loop' in the late Prof. Langley's flying machine, public sentiment should stop it. This historic relic ought not to be subjected to any further dangers. Its practicability has been demonstrated, and that is enough. It should now be protected from sensational 'stunts' for advertising purposes . . . It takes rank with Fulton's steamboat and Stephenson's steam engine. It should be guarded reverently as the nation's, and should be vigilantly protected from notoriety seekers."

❂   ❂   ❂

Meanwhile, sitting at home in Dayton, Orville Wright was greatly disturbed by what was going on at Hammondsport. With his deep-seated resentment of Curtiss, he viewed the experiment as a plot hatched between him and Secretary Walcott to diminish the attainments of the Wright brothers and to bolster Curtiss's further defense in the patent suit. Fortuitously for Orville, he received a visitor who held similar ideas.

Griffith Brewer, an English attorney, had met the Wrights in Europe, had learned to fly in a Wright plane, and in 1913 had rounded up financing for the British Wright Company, Ltd., to protect their patent rights and collect past royalties in England. Now he set out to do a book on aerial pioneering and, in his research, was invited to spend three months as a guest at Hawthorn Hill. Upon his arrival in June 1914, by his own account, he was told that there had been "some propaganda in the American press tending to belittle the Wrights' work." In retrospect, he wrote: "It seemed possible that some endeavor was being made to show that the Wrights were not pioneers in flying because of Langley's earlier work." Instead of starting immediately on the book, Orville suggested "that if I wanted to get busy I might do a better work by going to Hammondsport and seeing what they were doing to the Langley machine."

Alighting from the train at Hammondsport, Brewer felt "rather like a detective going into hostile country, where I should get rough handling if my mission were known." Falling in with a correspondent from the London *Daily Chronicle*, he solicited his aid in posing as another reporter from England. Under this incognito, he "watched them changing the camber on the shores of the lake." (By this time, changes in the *Langley* had begun for the second-phase experiments, and it was recognized that the original deep camber of the wings was inefficient. It may be noted that the alterations he saw were being made openly on the lakeshore.)

When the *Langley* was again launched with the 80-horsepower Curtiss engine, its single tractor propeller, the modified camber, and the pilot's seat on top of the machine instead of in the underslung bucket, Brewer was a keen-eyed watcher. He and his journalistic chum rented a boat and rowed down the lake to observe at close range. Their presence was not questioned, he said, because "This was welcome as propaganda of value to the Curtiss organization."

Griffith Brewer not only reported his findings back to Orville Wright, but he wrote to the New York *Times*, declaring that the press had been misled into believing the *Langley* was flown in its original condition. In this published letter, he enumerated various changes which, he charged, had been made before it was ever flown. He concluded: "Why, if such a demonstration was considered desirable, was not the old historic relic left untouched and a copy made to satisfy an insane curiosity? [And why was not some] impartial, unprejudiced person chosen to make the tests, instead of the person who has been found guilty of infringement of the Wright patent?"

Brewer's attack drew an editorial backfire from the *Scientific American*: "The sole purpose of the Hammondsport test is to continue an experiment begun by Langley, but unfortunately terminated by adverse newspaper criticism. In justice to Langley's memory, it is fitting that the machine should be thoroughly tried. Mr. Curtiss has nothing to gain by the experiment. Wing warping is not involved. The success of the Langley machine, decided enough from the standpoint of the patent lawyer, will not help Mr. Curtiss in the least. His is an act of piety which deserves commendation . . .

"Over and over again it is expressly stated that Langley regarded this machine only as an experiment. It was a step from an unmanned to a manned machine."

More was to be heard from both Brewer and Wright on this subject in the years to come.

*　　*　　*

Owing to the preoccupation of Curtiss and his plant with the transatlantic project, while also coping with foreign orders, the *Langley* was shunted aside for the balance of the summer. By September it had the stage to itself. With further alterations, tests were resumed and many flights made during a fortnight. The pilot for these was Elwood (Gink) Doherty, a recent graduate of the Curtiss school.[2] Adequately powered now and reinforced, the craft flew at altitudes up to 30 feet and traversed distances in excess of a half-mile. Some flights were made in a wind that raised whitecaps on the lake.

The Smithsonian was gratified enough to leave the machine at Hammondsport for continued tests in the summer of 1915. Actually, these were resumed in April, before the ice was gone from the lake, with takeoffs on sled runners instead of pontoons. In the summer's activity, Gink Doherty shared the piloting with Walter Johnson, chief instructor of the flying school. One of their forays attained a record distance of ten miles. (Curtiss by now had moved his main plant to Buffalo and was residing there.)

The extension of the experiments into a second season irked Orville Wright more than ever, and he sent another undercover agent to Hammondsport. This emissary was his elder brother, Lorin Wright, who adopted the pseudonym of W. L. Oren while in the locality. Lorin seemed to enjoy his espionage role. Cautiously, he refrained from registering at a hotel in Hammondsport, riding the train back to Bath at night, whence he reported to Orville on the day's events. "I came here as I was afraid to telegraph from Hammondsport," he said.

Seeking out the *Langley* on arrival, Lorin took note of such recent changes as he was able to recognize, but the wind was too strong that day for it to be flown. He roamed at will through the lakefront hangars without interference, taking pictures and carefully examining three aeroboats; he even operated the ailerons on one of these, and informed Orville that "they both move at the same time, one up and the other down." In a special delivery letter to Dayton, he wrote: "It seems everyone here is very loyal and I do not know what to do for confirmation of these points . . . I wish I had someone here who could see and understand. I cannot go away to find anyone from outside as

I want to see who will be here to witness Langley trials and to see it myself. I will get names and addresses of witnesses anyhow whether they are friendly or unfriendly."

By early train next morning, Lorin Wright was back in Hammondsport armed with camera and binoculars. As luck would have it, this was a day when an accident befell the *Langley*. He peered through his glasses as Walter Johnson mounted to the pilot's perch and started a takeoff run. After some 1000 feet, Lorin recounted, "the rear wings broke about midway the length of the spars and folded upwards." The machine was towed back to shore and Lorin began snapping photos, but was discovered in the act. Johnson demanded that he surrender the film, "saying they could not allow any pictures of the wrecked machine to be made." After refusing at first, Lorin finally yielded up his film pack to Henry Weyman, a company executive, who sent a boy uptown on a bicycle to get him a replacement. When this came, Lorin declined to accept it. Weyman laid it on his knee and walked away. Lorin set the film pack down upon the runway and shook the dust of Hammondsport from his feet, with none the wiser as to his identity.

* * *

Following additional test flights, the *Langley* was shipped back to Washington, but not again into a limbo of neglect. Now it had earned its place in the sun as a venerated historic heirloom.

The old "aerodrome" was meticulously restored by R. Luther Reed, a woodworking expert who had been in charge of its initial construction. In 1918, it was suspended in an exhibit hall of the Smithsonian Institution, and the words engraved on its placard were these:

"Original Langley flying machine, 1903. The first man-carrying aeroplane in the history of the world capable of sustained free flight.

"Invented, built, and tested over the Potomac River by Samuel Pierpont Langley in 1903. Successfully flown at Hammondsport, N.Y., June 2, 1914."

22. A Fortune of War

George C. Lehmann, industrial commissioner of Buffalo, was dispirited. His ordinarily booming city of steel mills, grain elevators, and Great Lakes cargo vessels had been in the economic doldrums for months. Hundreds of men were out of jobs, including many expert mechanics, and the Christmas season was coming on. Toward the end of a drab afternoon in early December 1914, the commissioner was minded to close his office early and go home when a surprise caller walked in.

The stranger introduced himself as a scout for Glenn H. Curtiss, and explained that his company was so swamped by war orders that it was casting about for a new location. Mr. Curtiss "looked with favor" on Buffalo because it was a key shipping center; because Lake Erie would be handy for the tryouts of flying boats; because it afforded a good labor market; and because a considerable amount of the materials used in Hammondsport already were derived from Buffalo.

The industrial commissioner suddenly felt better. In years past Buffalo had angled for the Curtiss plant without success, and here it was being handed to him, gift-wrapped. The Chamber of Commerce sprang into action and, within two days, canvassed all available factory space in the city. On the third day Curtiss popped into town, with Harry Genung, to inspect the recommended quarters, which were in a vacant building of the E. R. Thomas Motor Car Company, alongside the Niagara River. Without more ado, he signed a lease and the Chamber of Commerce boasted of "securing for Buffalo an exceptionally fine industry."

By sheer coincidence, the E. R. Thomas Company was the same automotive firm from which Curtiss had purchased the mail-order castings for his first motorcycle engine in 1901.

Consternation reigned in Hammondsport when the news broke. As soon as Curtiss returned from Buffalo, however, he dispelled part of the dismay by announcing that only the Curtiss Aeroplane Company was going elsewhere. The Curtiss Motor Company would remain in Hammondsport, producing engines for shipment to Buffalo. Pumping up optimism, the local weekly advised its readers to "look for the doughnut and not the hole," and sang a paean for the leading citizen who was about to transfer his residence, if not his allegiance:

"We have faith in Curtiss and believe in him more and more. He has a faculty for rising above great and unforeseen obstacles that would crush and discourage the average man, and goes right on undaunted from great to greater things. He bids fair to do for the aero-water navigation what Edison has done for electricity or Ford for motor cars."

* * *

Though Curtiss was well enough aware of a lively European demand for his aeroboats, he had no premonition of the tide which was about to engulf him. When a colleague remarked that the war might mean great fortune for him, he shrugged it off as "much too visionary." Nor did he yet realize that he already had a land plane which was destined to evolve into the most useful and respected training aircraft of the war: the JN type, known to an entire generation of airmen as the Jenny.

Glenn Hammond Curtiss, quondam fixer of doorbells and racer of bicycles, was simply caught up on the crest of a wave and tossed to affluent heights of which he had never dreamed. It happened almost without his volition. In 1914 he passed his thirty-sixth birthday.

The thing about it was that, in a small out-of-the-way village, he chanced to be operating the only manufactory on the American continent which was geared to produce airplanes on a quantity basis at short notice. In that shady town, he had drawn together and nurtured the largest, most competent corps of aeronautical engineers and mechanics to be found in any one spot of the Western Hemisphere. His aviation motors were recognized as the best in the United States. His conquest of water-flight had greatly enhanced his international reputation, and he was already filling contracts with governments which now became the Allies. Above all else, the conflict just beginning was the first war of history in which aircraft emerged as weapons.

The *America* had been unfortunately timed for flying the Atlantic; from another viewpoint, she had been constructed at a most opportune time. England's immediate purchase of the *America* and her twin constituted the first sale by Curtiss to a nation which was an outright belligerent. Wing Commander Porte then made himself the ardent promoter of Curtiss flying boats for war use. Winston Churchill, First Lord of the Admiralty, is reputed to have barked: "Accept everything America can produce to these specifications." Someone in the British Embassy at Washington supposedly told Curtiss: "The British government wants you to build all the planes you can as fast as you can."

Whoever may have said what to whom, Great Britain was Curtiss's largest, most remunerative overseas customer during World War I. The *Wall Street Journal* reported that, during the fiscal year ended October 31, 1915, the Curtiss industry produced more than $6,000,000 worth of airplanes and motors, chiefly for England; and that the company showed profits of $2,500,000 for the year's business. In December of that year, the company received a new $15,000,000 contract from the British government.

When Curtiss awakened to the volume of orders coming his way, he notified Lyman Seely, who had hopped to England as his sales manager, that he could not possibly meet the demand without a rapid plant expansion. British officials asked how much this would cost. He cabled an estimated figure of 75,000, omitting the word "dollars" to conserve space. The Admiralty Board assumed he meant pounds in English currency, and, to make sure he had enough, advanced him $600,000 as a deposit against future orders.

A decisive factor to keep in mind, in appraising what the war did for Curtiss (and what he, in turn, did for the Allies) was the ruling by Secretary of State Bryan that airplanes were not contraband of war. So long as they were unarmed when shipped, they passed for harmless vehicles which might be transported in neutral vessels from neutral ports to any other nation, peaceful or belligerent. (In all fairness, one could hardly begrudge Germany a diplomatic protest.)

Some officers of the British War Mission peeled off and went to Hammondsport in the fall of 1914. Apparently their instant order for 250 JN training planes triggered the decision to move to Buffalo; the necessary labor was not to be found in Hammondsport.

Both Curtiss and Wright were backward about giving up their "pushers," in which the pilot sat out in front and "had to look behind to see whether the aeroplane was coming or not." The feeling was that a pilot's vision would be obscured if the engine and propeller were ahead of him; that he "must be able to see the grass right under him." When Curtiss had his first flight in a tractor, he said he liked his own type better. Still, the Army put out specifications for a trial model of tractor type, and these were tough to meet.

The hiring of B. Douglas Thomas, the young Sopwith engineer, was a foresighted stroke for Curtiss. The "J" model which Thomas soon produced at Hammondsport was Curtiss's first tractor plane. At that point the mid-wing ailerons were discarded in favor of trailing-edge ailerons, initially on the top wing. The best features of the "J" were then combined with the best of the "N" (Curtiss's standard plane), and the JN was the outcome, its prototype sold to the Army for evaluation. Its tandem cockpits made it adaptable both for training and observation. British engineers pronounced it "just about perfect" for a trainer. The letters JN readily invited the affectionate nickname, Jenny. The Jenny became the most universal training plane of both the American and British armies. By the end of the war, it was said that 95 percent of U.S. military pilots had handled the controls of either the Jenny or the Curtiss aeroboat, or both.[1]

Curtiss created positions in Buffalo for several of his closest associates. Harry Genung went along as vice-president and plant manager; Henry Kleckler as a design engineer; Monroe Wheeler as general counsel to the company. The relationship with Charles M. Manly which began during the Langley experiments was intensified, so that Manly was later appointed chief inspection engineer for the Curtiss companies. Another principal in the Langley episode, Dr. A. F. Zahm, became prominent in the Curtiss organization.

Simultaneously with the move to the Niagara Frontier, J. A. D. McCurdy made an overture to the Canadian government relative to a Curtiss branch plant in Toronto. While Ottawa was not yet ready to purchase planes, the British government was willing to divert some of its orders through Canada, and established a flying school at Toronto. Accordingly, the Curtiss Aeroplane and Motor Company, Ltd., was formed in February 1915, opening operations in a large concrete building overlooking Toronto harbor. McCurdy was its secretary-treasurer and managing director. The Toronto plant later produced the Canadian version of the Jenny, famed in song and story as the Canuck.

It has been suggested that one reason for the Canadian branch was to get around the Wright patent stumbling block. Roy Knabenshue, in testimony before a Congressional hearing in after years, stated that Orville Wright sent him to Buffalo on a secret mission to find out whether Curtiss planes being made for England were equipped with ailerons. Knabenshue gained entry to the factory without difficulty. He said: "There was not an aileron in sight. The planes as constructed had no lateral control and did not infringe. Curtiss had a plant over in Toronto where he built ailerons for the ships separately, shipping them to England where they were then assembled."[2]

The rented quarters in Buffalo were swiftly outgrown, and in the spring of 1915 the company put up a large factory structure on Churchill Street within thirty days. The Chamber of Commerce was impressed by its 120,000 square feet of floor space "absolutely free of pillars or obstructions." This became known as the Churchill Plant, headquarters of the company.

A confidential credit report was made on Glenn Curtiss in 1915, rating him as "a man of large means." His worth was estimated at somewhere between $300,000 and $400,000, exclusive of his wife's "substantial" holdings and of outside security investments. The appraisal summed up: "If the European war continues another year and a half, Mr. Curtiss will be a multi-millionaire . . . Personally, he is highly regarded, spoken of as a man of good character and habits, is considered of good integrity, and authorities who are in a position to know him are of the opinion that he would not ask or contract beyond his ability to pay."

*   *   *

From the moment war orders started flowing, Hammondsport took on a military atmosphere. This was not altogether strange for a village accustomed to uniforms, but now the uniforms were of foreign cut. British officers were assigned as inspectors to the Curtiss plants, both in Hammondsport and Buffalo. French, Italian, and Russian officers came and went. Then, too, there was a semi-hysterical undercurrent of fear—fear of spies and saboteurs. The Hammondsport plant was brilliantly floodlighted, its grounds patrolled by armed guards. Espionage rumors floated on the breeze. A tale was spread to the effect that German agents, posing as French, already had tried to buy the whole works, merely to burn its stock and keep it out of production.

Some of the fear seeped into the Curtiss household, where the parents worried for the safety of "Baby Glenn," now in his third year. What they dreaded was kidnapping—either for ransom or for enemy espionage purposes. Glenn, Junior, was never left alone for the duration of the war. A full-time nurse, a strong young woman, was engaged as his bodyguard.

Two buildings were added to the Hammondsport plant to step up its engine production, which went on day and night. The terraced hillside literally shook with the bench-tests of roaring motors. The chronic housing shortage took on the dimensions of a catastrophe. The payroll swelled to 3000, thrice the normal census of the village. Many workmen camped in tents on the outskirts. Curtiss came down from Buffalo, subscribed to 1000 shares in the Savings and Loan Association, and purchased a tract of land on which emergency housing was erected, of the California bungalow style. One week in August employees found double pay in their envelopes, "to show our appreciation of your services during these rush times."

The Curtiss homestead was not deserted. Mr. and Mrs. George Osborne moved in as caretakers, and during the war period it was known as the Club House, where meals were provided for the transient foreign officers. Mrs. Osborne was an aunt of Lena Curtiss, as well as a good cook. In Buffalo, the Curtisses rented a house on a fashionable street and began living on a scale more in keeping with their improved circumstances. Glenn paid better attention to his wardrobe, and substituted a fedora hat for the habitual cap. He indulged his automobile hobby with a Pierce-Arrow car (Pierce-Arrows were made in Buffalo), and personally trained a sixteen-year-old youth to be his chauffeur. Later he acquired a white Cadillac town car, upon which he characteristically had a special body job done. The radiator bore a strong resemblance to that of a Rolls-Royce. Where the insignia "RR" would have been, he placed the initial "C" (for Curtiss, not Cadillac). When baffled passersby asked the chauffeur what make of car it was, he would reply "Complex," and they went away still puzzled.

The old hometown continued to see Curtiss fairly often, in his chauffeured Pierce-Arrow. A few miles up in the hills, on Middle Road, lived Charles C. Potter, a kinsman of Lena's, with whom he liked to hobnob. Potter allowed him to post his farm for a private hunting preserve. This hard-headed countryman held the distinction of having been so skeptical about the future of aviation that he stubbornly refused to buy stock in the Curtiss company. Now, tramping his meadows with gun and dog, Curtiss told him, almost plaintively: "You know, Charley, I've got so much money it makes my head ache."

Glenn's sister, Rutha, had gone on living in Rochester as a teacher in the school for deaf-mutes, but romance had finally touched her restricted life. Unlike him, she had inherited from Grandfather Claudius the tendency to embonpoint, and had grown into a large and decidedly fleshy woman. The man who now proposed marriage was Augustus Hesley, likewise a graduate of the school and a member of its faculty; he was enough older than Rutha to have entered the school before she was born. Curtiss sponsored their wedding party in Buffalo in 1915, located a home for them, and gave Hesley a clerical job in his plant. Alumni of the Rochester School for the Deaf remember Hesley as a rather short, pudgy man with white hair.

A young girl who was a former pupil in Rutha's classes was a house-guest in her Buffalo home. One day while Rutha was dozing, this visitor answered a knock at the back door and saw a slender, unimposing person whom she took to be a salesman. Leaving him standing on the porch, she went to awaken Rutha, saying there was a man outside asking to see her. Going to the door, Rutha turned to Jessie Ramsay and said: "Why, that is Glenn!" When he had gone, Rutha explained to Jessie that her brother often dropped in to see how she was getting along, and that he invariably left a check for a generous amount; she opened a drawer and displayed several such checks which she had not cashed.

Another family tie was reknit in 1916, when Curtiss brought his half brother, G. Carl Adams from California, took him into his home, and made a position for him in the company. Although Carl was but nineteen, he was placed in charge of an experimental department

which Glenn was nursing along. It was not long before Lua Curtiss
Adams also showed up in Buffalo to savor the prosperity.

＊　　＊　　＊

So vastly had the industry grown in a short time that the invasion
of Wall Street capital was inevitable. At the end of the first Buffalo
year, a syndicate formed by William Morris Imbrie & Company
purchased the controlling stock. On January 13, 1916, the Curtiss
Aeroplane and Motor Corporation was organized, combining the two
prior companies. Also gathered into the fold were the Toronto branch,
the Curtiss Exhibition Company (under which training schools were
now being operated), and the Curtiss California Company. A month
later the stock of the Burgess Company, at Marblehead, Massachusetts,
was absorbed, and W. Starling Burgess became a Curtiss executive.

Glenn H. Curtiss was named as president of the new corporation.
Its capital stock was $9,000,000. With this development, Curtiss became
publicly a millionaire. Followers of financial pages could read that he
was paid in cash $2,321,712.50, and that his stock holdings were
valued at $4,534,212.50.

At this juncture, Curtiss remembered how George Keeler, the
hardware merchant and village mayor, had extended him financial
aid when he was starting out in the motorcycle business. Keeler was
surprised to receive a certificate for stock worth $10,000 in the Curtiss
Aeroplane and Motor Corporation.

Curtiss's one-fifth share in the patent of the Aerial Experiment
Association had been locked in Monroe Wheeler's safe since the
auction of the Herring-Curtiss Company assets. It was among the leftover papers which Wheeler had bid in for $15. Now Wheeler re-
stored the share to Curtiss, who transferred it to the company, at
the same time recommending that the corporation purchase the shares
of the other A.E.A. members. A negotiation with Charles J. Bell, the
A.E.A. trustee, resulted in a settlement of 500 shares of stock in the
new company and a trifle over $7900 in cash. In the subsequent
division, Mrs. Bell received 35 percent of the stock.

Regarding this settlement, which was accepted just prior to the
cross-licensing agreement pooling all aircraft patents, Bell afterward
wrote: "The patents were sold to the Curtiss Company for a consideration that did not at all express any estimate of value of the A.E.A.
patents but did express the good will of the Associates toward Mr.

Curtiss personally and the feeling that the patents should belong to the Curtiss Company as Curtiss himself was one of the patentees and a member of the A.E.A."

Shortly after incorporation of the big company, a group of New York bankers attempted to promote a merger between the Curtiss and the Wright companies "for the purpose of stabilizing the aeroplane business in this country" and of putting an end to the old litigation. A financial writer reported that "progress is being made," but then the negotiations fell through, apparently for lack of enthusiasm on the part of the Curtiss people. Wall Street insiders pointed out that the Curtiss company had done far more in manufacture and shipment of aircraft to the Allies, and that its plants had the superior productive capacity and earning power. One analyst speculated that the failure of the merger plan meant that Curtiss would press his appeal to the Supreme Court.

America's entry into the European war in April 1917 was promptly followed by an appropriation of $640,000,000 for military aviation. Brigadier General George O. Squier, Chief of the Signal Corps, said: "The determination of the Allied governments is to enter Germany by the air route—and the United States government is going to provide enough machines to make itself felt in putting this program through." In effect, the U. S. Army and Navy were now competitors of European nations for the Curtiss output. This in turn spelled another major plant expansion and a financial transfusion.

For some time Curtiss had been on intimate terms with John North Willys, president of the Willys-Overland Automobile Company of Toledo and a national figure in finance and industry. The company literature says that he "succeeded in interesting John N. Willys in his plan for a combination of interests." While Willys knew less than little about airplanes, he was deemed an expert on standardized production and marketing. With a fresh supply of capital, Willys moved in and reorganized the Curtiss Corporation in July 1917 with a new set of officers. Curtiss took a more comfortable seat as chairman of the board of directors, while Willys installed himself as president of the corporation. The Willys-Overland Company suspended its manufacture of autos and converted the bulk of its facilities into making airplane engines and parts.

The first thing Willys did at Buffalo was to start construction of the colossal North Elmwood Plant at a cost of $4,000,000. If there had been any question about the Curtiss company's claim to being the largest aviation industry in the world, this settled it. The buildings sprawled over 72 acres and were completed in 90 days, in time to absorb $150,000,000 in new military orders for 1918. At peak production during World War I, the Curtiss plants in Buffalo employed 18,000 workers. They turned out a total of 10,000 airplanes and aeroboats, as many as 112 in a single week, and were aiming for fifty a day when the Armistice put a stop to all that.

*   *   *

An uncomfortable aftermath of the *America* episode cropped out in England during the war. In August 1917 the Crown filed corruption charges against Wing Commander John C. Porte, of the Royal Navy Air Service, and his legal adviser, William A. Casson. In plain words, Porte was accused of receiving indirectly, through Casson's connivance, some $240,000 in commissions on Admiralty contracts with the Curtiss company. The case broke as a considerable shock for the British public, to whom Porte was a war hero. Starting with the *America* type, he had developed almost single-handedly the giant flying boats of England's so-called "Silent Navy" which patrolled the Channel and the North Sea. In 1917 alone, Porte's planes were credited with bombing forty-four German U-boats and bringing down several marauding zeppelins. He had personally taken part in some of the sky patrols and shared in the sinking of at least one U-boat. And all the time he was known to be a sick man.

While at Hammondsport in 1914, Porte had agreed with Curtiss to be his agent for aeroboats in England after the projected ocean flight was done; he was to have received a commission of either 20 or 25 percent on sales. When Porte hastened home to be commissioned by the Admiralty, he ostensibly severed all commercial connections, making over his financial interests to Casson for the duration. Casson, past sixty, a retired civil servant and barrister, was by way of being an adopted father to Porte and had nursed him through some of his sieges with tuberculosis.

About this time, Lyman J. Seely arrived in England as sales manager for the Curtiss company and made contact with Casson. Seely had succeeded Jerome Fanciulli as Curtiss's publicity representative and rose rapidly in his favor. In some obscure manner, a

split of commissions on sales to the Admiralty was arranged between
him and Casson, seemingly without the knowledge of either Curtiss
or Porte. After instructing Porte to purchase the *America* and her
duplicate, the Admiralty counted on his relationship with Curtiss to
facilitate further large orders for flying boats. In 1916, the Admiralty
placed an $11,000,000 order with the Curtiss Aeroplane and Motor
Corporation.

The Crown attorneys alleged that Seely's rate of commission from
his company was 15 percent. It was generally understood in Hammondsport that Seely and his wife lived high and handsomely during
their wartime stay in London. By the time the case opened, they
had returned to America. Although no actual charge was filed
against Seely, the clerk of the court called upon "Lyman J. Seely to
surrender," and received no response. Seely was once referred to in
the proceedings as "a fugitive from justice."

As the charges were being read in the London police court,
preparatory to arraignment, Porte collapsed and the case was postponed for a week. When it resumed, Porte was not well enough to
appear, and a specialist testified that he had "an advanced case of
chronic pulmonary tuberculosis" and must be given several weeks of
complete rest "free from mental or physical strain." The case against
Porte was adjourned *sine die*, while Casson was committed for trial.

Casson pleaded guilty to twelve counts of an indictment charging him with having made a gift to Porte for "showing favor" to the
Curtiss company in business of the Crown. He was fined £6,000 and
made restitution of all moneys he had personally received in commissions.

When Porte was finally arraigned, he was acquitted in a nolle
prosequi. In dismissing the charges, the court went to great lengths
in citing extenuating circumstances. It asserted that he had held a
"very advantageous commercial position" in aeronautics at the outbreak
of the war, abandoning it to offer his services to the King. "He had
left New York hastily, with nothing but his clothing, although in poor
health. From that time on, he had no more concern with commercial
interests. The commissions came into Casson's hands." All but £10,000
of the accumulated commissions was still held in reserve for him, and
he turned over the entire amount to the exchequer. The court felt
that this action would "remove any possible stigma from the name
and reputation of a very useful and distinguished public servant";

pointing out that he was doing "invaluable work" for the Admiralty, which was anxious to retain his services. In conclusion, the court said: "The progress of his malady is such that those services will not be available much longer."

An authoritative British periodical, *The Aeroplane*, carried an analysis of the case, saying the whole affair had grown out of a personal quarrel aimed at someone else who came through unscathed; that Porte, Casson, and Seely were "the victims of a vendetta in which they were not concerned." In defense of Porte, the writer (presumably the editor of the magazine) said that, in working with Curtiss on design of the *America*, he had acquired "a certain definite proprietarial interest" in that type of flying boat, entitling him to a percentage on its future sales; and that he would have been "fully justified in settling down to work as a perfectly good munitions profiteer, running a flying-boat factory of his own, and drawing commission on Curtiss aeroplanes as a side line." All this he had given up in order to render conspicuous war service, "in spite of being in a state of health such as would have caused any ordinary man to become a chronic invalid." The article went so far as to suggest that the officers of the Crown "rather regretted having brought the charges" and were content to divert the money paid by the Curtiss company into the exchequer. "In other words, it seems as if, having been persuaded to bring a bribery charge, the State has accepted a bribe to stop the proceedings." There was a veiled hint in this sentence: "If Mr. Seely cared to come over to this country to fight the case, and could bring Mr. Glenn Curtiss as chief witness, it is probable that he would put quite a different complexion on it."

The article concluded with this statement: "It is noteworthy that at no time in the case has it ever been suggested that the Curtiss Company itself was guilty of any corrupt practice."

To clear the air, a "substituted" contract was written to cover the Admiralty's latest order from the Curtiss company, containing a clause prohibiting the payment of commissions on any work for the Admiralty. Because of the embarrassment caused by the case, Seely was dismissed from the company. Seely was in no financial pain, however, and continued to live in style in his big Hammondsport home; he acquired a chain of weekly newspapers in the region, including the Hammondsport *Herald*.

As for John Cyril Porte, he was commissioned a lieutenant-colonel in the Royal Air Force when it was organized shortly after his acquittal.

In June 1918, King George V decorated him with the Distinguished Order of St. Michael and St. George. The death which had stalked him for so long overtook him at last in the autumn of 1919.

* * *

Meanwhile, Glenn Curtiss was uneasy in the seats of the mighty. He was not cut out to be a titan of industry, and was astray in the mazes of high finance. At heart, he was the Yankee tinker yearning for the freedom of his "shop." His abilities as an administrator were not remarkable, and he disliked the weighty responsibilities which had been thrust upon him. Instinctively, he understood the value of creative activity to the human psyche; the manipulation of vast factories was not his notion of self-expression. He once put into words his philosophy on this score:

"Right at the beginning we learned an invaluable truth. We learned that so long as we were experimenting we never grew tired. Experimenting is never work—it is plain fun. Most of my time I have been able to put in eighteen hours a day when occasion required without feeling any special fatigue, because I never worked more than half the time. The other half was devoted to experimenting in some form or other. That was not tiring but rejuvenating. The man who works himself down can work himself back up if he will develop a turn for experimenting."

In effect, John N. Willys shifted the burden from his shoulders. Fortune's wheel had spun and bestowed upon him the power and the riches with which to establish a tinker's shop on a grandiose scale. For some time he had been dreaming of a plant solely devoted to research and experiment. No such facility had hitherto existed in the realm of aeronautics. Credit is due the company that it was able to see the potential worth of the idea at a period when total energies were being concentrated on war production. The Curtiss Engineering Corporation was organized as a separate entity with Curtiss as its president. The Curtiss Aeroplane and Motor Corporation, however, held 51 percent of the stock.

In choosing a site for this pioneering venture, Curtiss recalled the Hempstead Plains, where he had flown the *Gold Bug*. Since that time, Long Island had burgeoned as aviation territory, and Army pilot training had multiplied its flying fields to a total of eighteen. The near convenience of bays indenting both north and south shores of the island recommended it for aeroboat experimenting. The plant of the Engineering Corporation was completed by the end of 1917 at Garden City, and Curtiss transferred his personal headquarters and a handpicked staff of engineers, among them Manly, Kleckler, Dr. Zahm, and Charles Kirkham (of the Bath Kirkham brothers).[8]

The Garden City plant became virtually a school for young aeronautical engineers—a "university," as it were, for the industry. Aviation officials of Army and Navy resorted to it for advice and consultation. The priority item in its equipment, at Curtiss's insistence, was its wind tunnel, ten feet in diameter, at that time the largest in the United States. Curtiss believed strongly that the future of the science lay in the wind tunnel (of course, this was not an original thought, but the appurtenances of the tunnel at Garden City were said to be the most elaborate yet devised). "We can design streamlines by mathematics and test our work as we go," Curtiss explained. "And incidentally nobody gets killed trying something extraordinary in a wind tunnel."

A dozen types of airplane might be seen being assembled at a given time, no two of them alike. The usual procedure was to build one complete job and fly it; if it looked good enough, several more of the type would be made; then the blueprints went to Buffalo for production. Experiments were conducted with engines and propellers. In the early postwar era, the first practical metal propeller, the Curtiss-Reed, was developed there. So were the famed Curtiss racers, which cracked the 200-mile speed barrier.

The home purchased by the Curtisses at Garden City made some pretension to being an estate. (When they sold it several years later, the price tag was $275,000.) A large, white dwelling, it sat well back from Stewart Avenue, approached by a long driveway between rows of trees. It was surrounded by spacious landscaped grounds encompassing a formal garden, a greenhouse, a semicircular swimming pool, and several practice golf holes.

After the years of single-minded attention to business, Curtiss seems now to have made a conscious effort to unbend, to find different modes of recreation, to mold himself into a more pliable human being. He went so far as to join some clubs. The widened scope of his outdoor exertions bespeaks a resolution to keep himself in physical trim. He resumed bicycling, for example. While cars stood in the garage, he habitually pumped a bicycle the two miles between home and plant. The private pool invited a revival of his early love of swimming. With visitors in the cool of evening, he made good use of a bowling-green on the lawn. Not altogether a novice at golf, he took that game up afresh, if none too conscientiously. Archery, a sport that was new to him, captured his fancy so that he made a serious study of it.

Those who shared his recreations were often amused to discover that he was experimenting in connection with his fun. A business associate one day drove up to his home unexpectedly to find him barefoot in the middle of the lawn, seated on the grass in a most unusual posture. An oversized archery bow was gripped between the toes of his left foot, while his right hand drew back an exceptionally long arrow and let it zip unerringly at a target 60 feet away. The target was stuck full of arrows. Recognizing the technique as one used by certain African tribesmen in hunting large game, the visitor jokingly asked Curtiss if he had "reverted to type." In all seriousness, Curtiss replied: "No. I am only studying flight. I have learned a lot of interesting things this afternoon."

On a hunting trip in the Adirondacks, E. H. (Ned) Ballard recalled, they had a long hike over a rough mountain trail to reach camp, and were footsore on arrival. That night before the campfire, they debated what might be the best footwear for Adirondack tramping. When they started out next morning, Ballard was surprised to notice that Curtiss was wearing unmatched shoes: on one foot was a high leather hunting boot, on the other an ankle-length rubber shoe. "Lost part of your gear?" Ballard asked. Curtiss shook his head. "I just want to find out which is the better one to wear."

*   *   *

With the move to Long Island, Glenn's mother returned to California, taking with her Rutha and Augustus Hesley. Carl Adams went to Garden City, where his half brother promoted him into a higher position. But Carl left his heart behind in Buffalo, and in the spring of 1918 went back to reclaim it. The Curtisses made the trip with him, to attend his marriage to Dorothy McDonald. When the bridal pair began housekeeping in Garden City, Glenn and Lena furnished their home as a wedding gift.

Dorothy Adams (known to all as Dot) became an immediate favorite with Curtiss. She was a recent university graduate, and he boasted of her as "the first member of the family who ever went to college." At his request, she tutored him in English for some time; he wanted to improve his usage in speeches and letters. She kept as a memento the envelope of a letter he once mailed her, addressed to "• Adams."

Lena Curtiss took Dorothy Adams with her when she went shopping in New York. In expensive stores, Dot could not buy, but she "liked to look." Evidently Lena put a bug in her husband's ear. After a couple of these trips, as they were setting out again for Fifth Avenue, Curtiss handed Dot a check for $1000 with the injunction: "Buy something you want but can't afford."

A young Naval Reserve man, Ensign Theodore P. Wright, also a newlywed, was assigned to the Garden City plant at this time. Becoming friendly with the Adams couple, the Wrights were included in a beach party planned by Glenn and Lena. They all drove together to the exclusive north shore of Long Island and located a beach on Sands Point, where a driftwood fire was built for a corn roast. Curtiss found a length of rather large pipe and concocted the idea of feeding ears of corn into it, like ammunition into a gun. The pipe was then laid in the fire and the corn came out nicely steamed.

In the midst of the picnic repast, a self-important and obviously well-heeled citizen came storming down the bluff, averring that they were on his property and would have to remove themselves. Curtiss apologized in a soft-spoken manner, saying they hadn't known it was private property and would leave on the instant. As an afterthought, he mentioned: "By the way, I'm Glenn Curtiss from Garden City." The angry property owner at once changed his attitude, shook hands, and insisted that the apology was his. He said he was honored to have them use his beach, and joined the party.

*   *   *

A frequent visitor at the Garden City estate these days was Commander Jerome C. Hunsaker of the Navy. When last he had been a guest of the Curtisses, it was in the simple house at Hammondsport. While their present dwelling was sumptuous by comparison, he observed that its furnishings displayed no very sophisticated taste or interest in furniture as such. Curtiss still referred to his plant as "the shop." "The word 'factory' was not in his vocabulary," Hunsaker would recall.

Some people at the Curtiss Engineering Corporation, Hunsaker also remarked, would have been as well pleased if their boss had spent more time than he did at archery, golf, or other pastimes. He was prone to come bicycling in Monday morning all charged up with fresh ideas which meant alterations in whatever they were working on, with consequent delays in production.

Curtiss's suggestions were rarely framed as orders. They were usually couched as questions: "Why not do so and so?" or "Could we do it this way?" Once he had put a point across, however, he did not drop it. A week later he was sure to come around and see if it had been done.

The major job going on in the Garden City plant that summer was construction of a gigantic flying boat, the NC-1, for the Navy. It had been conceived as the prototype for a series of such monsters which, the Navy hoped, would be able to deliver themselves across the Atlantic to the war front. This accounted for the presence of Commander Hunsaker at Garden City.

23. Atlantic Reality

German U-boats were sinking Allied ships faster than they could be replaced, and this was the most critical problem facing the Navy when the United States entered the war. From then on, American vessels, too, were their legitimate prey. Enemy subs moved in to prowl the eastern seaboard, and the Navy placed orders with the Curtiss company for the great H-12 and H-16 flying boats developed by Porte as an outgrowth of the *America*, which were giving notable service in anti-submarine patrol off the English Channel and North Sea coasts.

But something even bigger and of longer range was in the mind of Rear Admiral David W. Taylor, commander of the Navy's Bureau of Construction and Repair. The fleets of airplanes promised to the Allies with which to carry the war into Germany could hardly reach the goal if they were sent to the bottom on their way over. Moreover, so acute was the shipping shortage that every available vessel was sorely needed for the transport of troops, munitions, and foodstuffs. For another thing, the Allied high command desired a plane of adequate range to bomb the U-boats nesting in the wide mouth of the Gironde River, bottling up Bordeaux and harrassing the French coast.

Shortly after Congress declared war in April of 1917, Admiral Taylor circulated a memorandum among officers of his Bureau: "The ideal solution [of the submarine problem] would be big flying boats or the equivalent that would be able to keep the sea, if not the air, in any weather, and also be able to fly across the Atlantic to avoid difficulties of delivery." Somewhat later, he sent a memo to Naval Constructor Jerome Hunsaker, who had been recalled from MIT for uniformed duty: "It seems to me the submarine menace could be abated, even if not destroyed, from the air."

Whenever people in Washington talked about huge flying boats, or of crossing the Atlantic by air, they automatically thought of Glenn Curtiss. It was common knowledge that Curtiss had not abandoned his resolution to build an aeroboat which would span the ocean. In an article written for an aviation magazine in 1916, he predicted that the deed would be done "the first fine day that the world is free again to take interest in that side of the development of flying," and that it would not be "a freak performance which might not be repeated in years." He disclosed that he and Rodman Wanamaker planned to mount such a flight in 1917, starting from New York and hopping by way of Newfoundland and the Azores. "Before, we were working experimentally and in doubt and darkness," he wrote. "Now we can work and speak with confidence."

With an odd clairvoyance, Curtiss added: "The second trans-atlantic flight will, I am pretty sure, cover the ocean in all probability without a stop." No prophecy could have turned out more accurately. But the war circumvented a Wanamaker-sponsored flight for the second time.

In early September 1917, Admiral Taylor called in Hunsaker and Naval Constructor G. Conrad Westervelt for a discussion of the U-boat problem. "If we can't get planes over there by sea," he told them, "then we'll have to get them there by air." Adverting to the *America* and how well she had performed on patrol duty for England, Taylor was plainly suggesting her builder for assistance in this case. The plane he wanted must be able to fight submarines and defend itself. "Go ahead, boys," he said. "Build it."

A telegram went straightway to Curtiss in Buffalo: Could he come to Washington in a hurry for consultation on a new design? He was on a train within two hours, bringing with him Henry Kleckler and another topflight engineer, W. L. Gilmore. They found Hunsaker and Westervelt waiting impatiently.

"I don't know exactly how to put this," Hunsaker began, "but Admiral Taylor wants a seaplane that can fly across the Atlantic." Curtiss sat silent for a moment before asking: "By what route?" "Who cares," said Westervelt, "as long as it gets there?" Then from Hunsaker: "Can it be done?" "Of course it can," Curtiss replied. "They don't think so in England and France," Westervelt put in. "I've just come back from Europe and I've talked to the best men in aviation there. They say nobody knows how to build a plane that can make such a trip." "The *America* would have made it if we'd had more time," Curtiss retorted a bit sharply. "What are the specifications for this plane?"

As if on cue, the group was ushered into the offices of Admiral Taylor, who was emphatic but not very specific: the craft would need to be large and strongly powered to carry the fuel for crossing; seaworthy enough to stay afloat if it came down; and adaptable to anti-submarine warfare when it reached Europe. Curtiss agreed to draw up some plans, and he and his engineers caught the next train for Buffalo.

Three days later they were back with preliminary sketches for two alternative designs: a 5-engined machine of 1700-horsepower, and a 3-engined job of 1000-horsepower. The box-type tail was a remarkable innovation. Whereas in previous flying boats the tail had been attached directly to the hull, this one was supported by outrigger booms extending from superstructure and hull, and it rode high above the water. The idea had recently been tried on a small aeroboat at Buffalo. As Curtiss explained the advantages, its height would protect the tail surfaces from breaking waves; it would permit a shorter hull, hence less weight; the short hull would be less vulnerable to damage in a rough sea; the high tail would allow a rearward arc of gunfire. Furthermore, if the ship was hopelessly down at sea, the tail could easily be jettisoned, freeing the hull to be used as a real boat.

While Curtiss indicated his own preference for the triple engines, Admiral Taylor opted for the 5-engined model, and twenty draftsmen in the Bureau of Construction and Repair were put to work on designs. Commander Holden C. Richardson was summoned from instructional duty at the Pensacola training station to take charge of the hull design, a specialty of his. A 3-foot scale model was made and tested by Dr. Zahm in the wind tunnel at Washington Navy Yard.

The one direct specification Admiral Taylor had laid down was the use of the new "U.S. motor." By this he meant the Liberty engine. The 12-cylindered Liberty was a crash project in which an "engine committee," drawing on the best engineering brains of several automobile companies, set out to design a standardized aero motor for mass manufacture in the war effort. Curtiss raised no objection to the Liberties, recognizing their power superiority over his own engines, though they were not yet in production.

On more mature thought, Admiral Taylor was persuaded that the vibration of five engines might tear the ship apart, and switched to the 3-engined design. Instead of assembling the component parts at a naval facility, as first envisioned, it was decided to turn the job over entirely to the Curtiss company, under supervision of the Navy Department. Westervelt and Richardson were assigned to the Buffalo plant. Hunsaker was in over-all charge for the Navy, and he got Professor Charles J. McCarthy down from MIT and "put him in a blue suit." McCarthy was the best man he knew on theory of structures, and the structural picture of the vast wings and the unique tail became his responsibility.

Couriers shuttled between Buffalo and Washington with sketches and drawings as alterations were made almost from day to day. Richardson's hull design was the most debatable thing of all, and Curtiss viewed it with some disfavor. Squadron Commander Porte was enticed over from England to render an opinion, examined the blueprints, said "It is very interesting," and went home. Tests in the wind tunnel and model basin at Washington upheld Richardson. Some argued that the hull should be of aluminum, but Richardson insisted on spruce, and then built it with his own hands, in large part.

The question of an official designation for the aircraft arose, and Westervelt proposed "DWT," the initials of Admiral Taylor. When this suggestion reached the admiral's ears, he vetoed it. Westervelt's second inspiration was "NC," for Navy-Curtiss, and this met with general approbation. Thus the prototype model became the NC-1. Before long it was nicknamed the "Nancy." It seems reasonable to guess that the precedent of the Jenny had some bearing on this sobriquet.

In December 1917 Secretary of the Navy Josephus Daniels signed a contract with the Curtiss Aeroplane and Motor Corporation to construct four machines of the NC type. The company was allowed a profit margin of 10 percent. Because of the many changes as the work went along, the cost of the NC-1 mounted to $150,000. The three additional hulls were farmed out to two New England firms, and sub-contracts were let for various components in order to hasten the job.

As luck would have it, the contract was finalized just as the plant of the Curtiss Engineering Corporation was ready for opening at Garden City. This was within 20 miles of the Naval Air Station at Rockaway Point. The enterprise of the NC-boats was transferred to Garden City, though not in actuality until the spring of 1918, when the hull and other components made at Buffalo were shipped down via the State Barge Canal. A separate NC-boat building was erected in the rear of the main plant. While the NC-1 was still in process, work was commenced on the NC-2. Naturally, the whole deal was hush-hush, and the tightest of security was maintained. Meanwhile, a hangar roomy enough for two of the giants was in preparation at the Rockaway air station.

These aerial behemoths were to be the largest airplanes yet conceived, at least in the United States. The span of the top wing was 126 feet, that of the lower wing 96 feet. The tail alone was bigger than the usual fighting plane, with a span of nearly 38 feet. Over-all length was 68 feet, the height 24 feet and six inches. The hull, which was to carry a crew of six, was 44 feet, nine inches long and 10 feet wide, with cockpits fore and aft. The cruising speed was 75 miles per hour.

Curtiss had a second-floor corner office in the main building but observed no regular office hours; he was "not a nine-to-five man," Hunsaker observed. Periodically, he came around and "stuck his nose in," offering suggestions on this or that detail. The place swarmed with Curtiss "alumni." A British Aviation Commission came out to look the craft over, and its commanding colonel reported to his superiors: "The machine is impossible, and is not likely to be of any use whatever."

In September 1918 the Nancy One was transported piecemeal to Rockaway Point for assembly, and during this operation encountered the first of a series of mishaps that were to plague the NC-boats. A wing, of 12-foot chord, rumbling along on a dolly, took up the width of a narrow highway. A drunken motorist pulled out on the shoulder to pass and wiped off the entire trailing-edge.

Holden Richardson, who had learned to fly under Curtiss some five years earlier, and whose novel hull had raised so many eyebrows, gave the NC-1 her crucial test flight from Jamaica Bay on October 4. Two Curtiss engineers rode in the rear cockpit, while Curtiss watched anxiously from the ramp. She lifted off with no difficulty. While feeling out her characteristics, Richardson kept her airborne only a few seconds at a time for the first several trials. Tests continued all during October as flaws were spotted and corrected. On November 7, Richardson with a full crew took Nancy for a shakedown flight to Washington Navy Yard, where top brass of the Navy came to inspect her.

Four days after that, the Armistice was signed. The military rationale for the NC-boats collapsed like a punctured tire. The NC-2 was uncompleted, the third and fourth Nancies still on the drawing boards. The contract was immediately suspended.

Curtiss's feelings at this juncture are not a matter of record. The onset of the war had ended the transatlantic attempt of the *America*. Now it looked very much as if the war's ending would repeat the story, just when a flying boat with a much better chance was almost ready to take the big jump.

*   *   *

Still, the NC-1, which had cost a good deal of money and effort, was not about to be packed away in mothballs. Besides Admiral Taylor, she had another staunch champion in high place at Washington. The husky young Assistant Secretary of the Navy, Franklin Delano Roosevelt, had adopted the project as his pet. On an inspection visit to the Rockaway Air Station, he had insisted on being taken up for a flight in NC-1, even though a stiff wind was blowing and he was advised against it.

In the letdown after the Armistice, the Navy could well use some recruiting propaganda, and now the security wraps were off the NC-1. One of Britain's "Berlin Bombers," a Handley-Page, had recently garnered headlines by flying with forty people aboard, a world's record. Navy public relations reckoned that the NC-1 could beat that. On November 27, roosts were somehow found for fifty passengers, rounded up from personnel of the naval station and the Curtiss plant. It took some sweat, but the boat lumbered into the air, stayed up two or three minutes, and came down safely. A recount of the passengers was made as they were disembarking. It came out fifty-one. A naval machinist's mate, Harry D. Moulton, had hidden in a dark cranny of the hull and thereby become the world's first aerial stowaway.

But why, after all, must the transatlantic attempt be canceled out simply because peace had dawned? One who asked the question was Commander John H. Towers, who had been keeping a watchful eye on the NC project from his frustrating desk in Naval Operations, while noting with pleasure that the contract had been handed to his old friend Curtiss.

Prior to the Armistice, on October 31, Towers had written a memorandum to the Chief of Naval Operations suggesting that an ocean flight be undertaken by the NC-1 in the spring of 1919, "war or no war"; appending a request that he be given command of the mission. Nothing came of this, and a few weeks later Towers took his proposal higher up the chain of command. He paid a call on the Assistant Secretary of the Navy, a receptive listener. "There are parts of three more NC's in factories all over the country," he reminded Roosevelt, "and they've already been paid for. Why don't we get them to Glenn Curtiss at Garden City and let him assemble them? Then we can make the flight to Europe just for the cost of the gas."

Roosevelt talked to Secretary Daniels and peppered the Navy Department with memos for a month. As a result, a three-man committee was appointed, headed by Naval Constructor Westervelt, to study the proposition; Towers was on the committee. Its report recommended a flight by way of the Azores; that a separate branch be set up in the Navy to handle preparations; that the recent Allies be invited to cooperate. It was suggested that all four NC-boats be flown to Newfoundland as the takeoff point, and that the three which behaved best should then tackle the ocean. The NC-2 was partly completed; the NC-3 could be built by February, the NC-4 by March.

Doubtless it was more than coincidence that the route mapped out for the Nancies was almost identical with that which had been planned for the *America*. The only significant variance was the choice of Lisbon for the continental landfall.

*   *   *

While the Navy's scheme was being developed under a lid of secrecy, Lord Northcliffe revived his £10,000 *Daily Mail* prize, thereby precipitating a scramble in England. No less than nine British entries were registered for attempts in the summer of 1919. Commander John C. Porte re-entered the lists, though not for the prize. He proposed bringing one of his five-engined triplane flying boats, designated as Porte Super-Babies, to Newfoundland for the attempt; it was christened the *Porte*. Since this craft belonged to the Admiralty, he could not rightly employ it to compete for the Northcliffe cash.

Rodman Wanamaker made no move toward entering a plane

this time, presumably because of the Navy's forthcoming multiple flight and Curtiss's deep involvement with that.

Secretary Daniels approved the NC-boat program on February 4, setting up a Transatlantic Flight Section to supervise. The Nancies were not entered for the *Daily Mail* reward; on the contrary, their crews were expressly forbidden to accept any prize money should it be offered. So far as the Navy Department was concerned, this was to be strictly a scientific affair—so it said.

Now Jack Towers was granted his heart's desire: he was appointed to the command of the mission. Inquisitive reporters began snooping to uncover the reason for his abrupt transfer out of the Bureau of Naval Operations to some mysterious new assignment. They found it readily enough. Towers chose the NC-3 for his flagship, possibly because his pilot's license rated him as Naval Aviator Number 3.

For skippers of the other three boats, he named: NC-1, Lieutenant Commander Patrick N. L. Bellinger; NC-2, Lieutenant Commander Marc Mitscher; NC-4, Lieutenant Commander Albert C. (Putty) Read. Then, for his own pilot in the NC-3, he tapped Holden C. Richardson.

Three of the mission's top officers, Towers, Bellinger, and Richardson, were graduates of Curtiss training at Hammondsport, and had their baptism in aeroboats on Keuka Lake. Bellinger and Richardson were the men who had sat on the ridgepole of the tent with the Hildreth sisters that tragic day when Lincoln Beachey lost control of his plane.

The Navy arranged a "bridge" of destroyers along the route at 50-mile intervals. The planes were to carry short-beam radios to maintain contact among themselves, and radio of longer range for communication with the destroyers. As the later NC-boats were launched in early spring, it became obvious that more power was needed to carry the fuel load. The addition of a fourth engine front would mean a major redesigning job. Marc Mitscher suggested a pusher engine in tandem behind the center engine, which was an arrangement tried out on his NC-2 and then adopted for all.

In late March, a destroyer was dispatched to Newfoundland to seek out a takeoff harbor. The spotters aboard were Pat Bellinger and Lieutenant E. F. Stone, pilot of the NC-4. They selected Trepassey Bay, a long, bleak fjord 60 miles south of St. John's, plagued by crosswinds, rough water, and bone-chilling fog.

Gremlins began their dirty work at Rockaway Point. The NC-2 performed none too well in early tests, and then, torn loose from her moorings in a heavy wind, was so severely battered that she was scratched from the mission and cannibalized for the benefit of the others. Mitscher, losing his command, was made executive officer and chief pilot in the NC-1, under Bellinger.[1]

In another gale, the NC-1 dragged her moorings, went aground, stove in her hull, and wrecked a wing. She received a new wing by transplant from the NC-2. A major worry gnawing at everyone was what would really happen to any of the boats if forced down in a heavy sea.

A target date of May 14 was set for the takeoff from Newfoundland because that would be the next time of full moon. Hopefully, this meant starting from Rockaway at least a week earlier. The NC-4 was not delivered until the last day of April. A Navy machinist was working beneath the "Four" while one of her engines was being revved. Impulsively reaching out an arm to point at something, he was surprised to see his hand lying on the ground. The propeller had lopped it off.

In the anxiety to get the mission moving, crews labored far into the night. In the small hours of May 5, workmen were fueling up tanks of the NC-1 and NC-4, berthed in the hangar. Perhaps a spark from an electric pump did it. Suddenly flames were licking the fabric of both aircraft. Luckily a score of men were in the hangar, and their quick action with fire extinguishers nipped an utter catastrophe in the bud. As it was, the NC-1 lost a wing and the NC-4 most of her tail surfaces. Employees of the Curtiss plant were rousted from their slumbers to begin repairs before dawn, using what remained of the NC-2 in the process.

The three Nancies arose from Jamaica Bay on May 8, heading up the coast in V formation for their first pause at Halifax. Off Cape Cod, Read's NC-4 was forced down, taxied through the night to reach Chatham, and was presumed out of the running. Towers and Bellinger proceeded to Trepassey with orders to make for the Azores without the NC-4 if the weather came right. Wind and waves foiled their takeoff attempts, however, until the "lame duck," with a new engine, caught up on May 15. "I think everybody was glad we hadn't succeeded," Towers said.

The outlook brightened on the 16th, and the fishing village of Trepassey was "as empty as an inverted pitcher" when, tossing spray, the trio became airborne just after 6 P.M. There was something remindful of the three caravels of Columbus as the winged boats dwindled to specks in the eastern sky, their initial goal Ponta Delgada in the Azores. At an altitude of 4500 feet, they picked up guideboats visually, one by one; after nightfall, the destroyers fired starshells through the clouds and fingered the sky with searchlight beams. The only disturbing omen was the discovery that their radio compasses were almost useless because of static from the sparkplugs. For that same reason, their wireless could send but not receive.

The NC-4 soon displayed a tendency to forge ahead of the others, and she actually had to be throttled back to stay in formation. The "lame duck" was surprisingly unlimbered. A partial explanation was that she had deliberately taken on a lighter load of fuel. Her commander, Albert C. Read, was an undersized, quiet, but resolute New Hampshire man. His nickname, Putty, dated from student days at Annapolis when he returned from a summer vacation with no trace of sun-tan; a classmate jokingly remarked that his pallor resembled putty.

After dawn, the Nancies ran into squalls of rain. By midforenoon they were wrapped in dense fog, and Towers gave the order to separate to minimize the danger of collision. They lost contact altogether with the destroyers. Towers and Bellinger reached the same decision at approximately the same time—to land and get bearings. It was unsound judgment for both. Waves were higher than they seemed from above, and the NC-1 and NC-3 were crippled by the impact, helplessly adrift. The crew of the NC-1 was soon rescued by a Greek freighter, and a destroyer sent her hulk to the bottom with gunfire, as a menace to navigation. The NC-3 was less fortunate, and unable to give her position by radio. By heroic efforts, Towers and his crew pumped out her leaking hull and kept her afloat. Wafted along by a gale blowing in the right direction, NC-3 covered 205 miles in 52 hours, miraculously reaching her destination as a derelict. When, outside the harbor of Ponta Delgada, a destroyer sped to take her in tow, Jack Towers snapped: "Tell them to stay out of the way. We're going in under our own power." Three engines were started up, and slowly the NC-3 taxied into port while a 21-gun salute was fired.

Meanwhile, Putty Read in the NC-4 had kept his head, although he was as lost in the fog as the others. He had the advantage of a half-hour's lead. At last he caught a glimpse of rip-tide through a hole in the clouds, spiraled down, and there in happy view was the island of Flores. Thence he groped his way to the sheltered harbor of Horta. After being windbound there for two days, he hopped to Ponta Delgada.

31. A family group during the World War I period. At the left are Captain Thomas S. Baldwin and Glenn Curtiss, Jr. The women are: Minnie Hendershot Mitchell, governess and constant bodyguard to Glenn, Jr., when the parents feared his kidnapping; Mrs. Jenny Neff, the widowed mother of Lena Curtiss, who lived with the Curtisses all her later years; and Mrs. Lena Curtiss. Judging by the boy's age, this photograph was probably taken during their residence in Buffalo. COURTESY GLENN H. CURTISS MUSEUM, HAMMONDSPORT, N.Y.

32. Christening of the *America:* Miss Katherine Masson, holding the bottle of champagne that refused to break. From left: Lieutenant John C. Porte; George Hallett, mechanic and co-pilot; Glenn Curtiss. NATIONAL AIR AND SPACE MUSEUM.

83. Glenn Curtiss, Jr., two years old, perches astride the prow of the *America*, under the watchful eye of his father. NEW YORK PUBLIC LIBRARY.

84. The *America* in a trial run on Keuka Lake. FROM THE COLLECTION OF OWEN S. BILLMAN.

5. The Langley aerodrome being assembled at the lakefront. ARMY AIR FORCE PHOTO IN
THE NATIONAL ARCHIVES.

6. The *Langley* ready for launching on Keuka Lake. NATIONAL AIR AND SPACE MUSEUM.

87. Glenn H. Curtiss in the bucket-like cockpit beneath the front wing of the Langley After he had made it fly, the pilot's seat was moved atop the structure. NATIONAL AIR AND SPACE MUSEUM.

88. The *Langley* just free of the water in Curtiss's flight June 2, 1914, with the original Manly motor. The picture is copied from the 1914 annual report of the Smithsonian Institution.

89. One of the many later flights of the *Langley* over Keuka Lake, after numerous changes were made in order to test the practicality of the tandem-wing type airplane. Note that the pilot, Elwood (Gink) Doherty, is seated above the wings. NATIONAL AIR AND SPACE MUSEUM.

90. The Curtiss plant from the hillside above, at about the time war orders began to pour in. Observe the vineyard on the slope in foreground. The square cupola marks the Curtiss home. FROM THE HENRY KLECKLER ALBUMS.

91. A Curtiss JN-4, better known as Jenny, of World War I vintage. WAR DEPARTMENT
GENERAL STAFF PHOTO IN THE NATIONAL ARCHIVES.

92. The Garden City, Long Island, factory of the Curtiss Engineering Corporation, which
Curtiss conceived as the first experimental plant in the history of aviation. NATIONAL AIR
AND SPACE MUSEUM.

93. Living on Long Island, Curtiss habitually rode a bicycle the two miles between home and office. In fact, his was a bicycling family, as this picture proves. COURTESY, GLENN H. CURTISS, JR.

94. Rear elevation of the NC-1, during assembly, showing the remarkable tail structure conceived by Curtiss to survive high seas.

95. The NC-4 after takeoff from the Rockaway Naval Air Station. COURTESY, THEODORE P. WRIGHT.

96. The crippled NC-3, Towers's flagship, limps into the harbor of Ponta Delgada after a 200-mile battle with the waves. NAVY BUREAU OF SHIPS PHOTO IN THE NATIONAL ARCHIVES.

97. Streamlined triplane developed in 1918 at the Curtiss Garden City plant. With it, Roland Rohlfs set a world's altitude record. COURTESY, GLENN H. CURTISS, JR.

98. Mr. and Mrs. Glenn H. Curtiss, photographed on return from a trip to Europe soon after the war. COURTESY, GLENN H. CURTISS, JR.

99. The Florida home, which Curtiss himself designed in pueblo style. The photo was taken when it was just completed, before landscaping. Miami Springs grew up around it.
COURTESY, GLENN H. CURTISS, JR.

100. City hall of Opa-locka, an architect's conception of a palace out of the Arabian Nights.
COURTESY, GLENN H. CURTISS, JR.

101. Curtiss with one of his streamlined Aero-Car trailers. COURTESY, GLENN H. CURTISS, JR.

102. The *Scooter,* a shallow-draft boat with aero propeller, built by Curtiss to get around Florida's grassy inland channels. COURTESY, GLENN H. CURTISS, JR.

103. Glenn Curtiss, Jr., in an
affectionate pose with his father.
COURTESY, GLENN H. CURTISS, JR.

104. The last formal portrait
of Glenn H. Curtiss. This copy
was inscribed to Henry Kleckler.

105. Just before boarding the Condor to retrace the route of the Hudson
River flight on its 20th anniversary. In the group are: Mayor John Boyd
Thacher, II, of Albany; Glenn Curtiss, Jr.; Mrs. Lena Curtiss and her
husband. COURTESY, GLENN H. CURTISS, JR.

Under Navy protocol, a fleet commander who loses his flagship hoists his flag on another vessel and carries on. Towers expected this usage to apply in his case, and was exasperated when Secretary Daniels issued a delicate ruling that the NC-boats did not qualify as a fleet; that Read was to continue in command of the NC-4 and finish out the trip. Any other decision would have set ill with the American public. The rest of the NC-boat personnel approved the verdict.

At dusk on May 27, 1919, guns boomed in the harbor of Lisbon, Portugal, when Putty Read brought the gallant NC-4 down after a flight of nine hours and 43 minutes from Ponta Delgada. For the first time in the annals of mankind, the Atlantic Ocean had been vanquished by air. To the infinite satisfaction of Glenn Curtiss, who had predicted it years before, it had been achieved by a Curtiss-built airplane. Afterward he awarded an NC-4 "diploma" to each of his employees who had worked on the project.

The saga of the NC-4 was completed on May 31 when she landed at Plymouth, England, whence the Pilgrims once fared forth in a vessel called the *Mayflower*.

* * *

At the time when the Nancies showed in Newfoundland, three British land airplanes were poised in the east coastal region of that island, bent on capturing the *Daily Mail* prize. These were: the *Atlantic* (a Sopwith), crewed by Harry G. Hawker and Lieutenant Commander K. Mackenzie Grieve; the *Raymor* (a Martinsyde), manned by Frederick F. Raynham and Captain William F. Morgan; and a Handley-Page bomber, the betting favorite in England, with a five-man crew commanded by Admiral Mark Kerr.

Attrition had reduced the number of contenders to these and a fourth which had not yet put in its appearance. Porte had to confess that his flying boat with the five engines was too unwieldy for the task, and withdrew it.

The teams of the *Atlantic* and *Raymor* had been holed up in a hotel at St. John's since early spring, frustratingly grounded by abominable weather. The goal of both was Ireland, or farther if possible, in a nonstop flight. When the Nancies beat them to the getaway, they were understandably nonplused. Their spirits revived, however, at news that two of the Navy boats were out of the race and that the

NC-4 was pinned down by weather in the Azores. The Handley-Page was delayed, waiting for new radiators to come from England.

In a concerted effort to "head off the Americans," the two teams scheduled takeoffs for Sunday, May 18. Hawker and Grieve got safely away, dropping the Sopwith's undercarriage as they passed the coast. An hour later, Raynham and Morgan started their run, broke a wheel on a spine of rock, groundlooped and were wrecked. The *Atlantic* crew were forced down in midocean, ditching alongside a Danish tramp steamer which picked them up. As the ship carried no wireless, Hawker and Grieve were given up for several days, until the freighter touched at the Hebrides.

Two veterans of the Royal Air Force, John Alcock and Arthur W. Brown, were late arrivals in Newfoundland. On June 14, they went up in their Vickers bomber, and when next they touched earth it was in an Irish bog which had looked solid enough when they spotted it. Although the Vimy was upended in a humiliating posture, Alcock and Brown had made the first nonstop flight of the Atlantic and collected the Northcliffe prize. Incidentally, they fulfilled Curtiss's prediction: that the second crossing would be without a stop.

*   *   *

Coming home by ship, the NC-4 was placed on exhibition in Central Park, New York City. After that, she underwent a facelifting for a Navy recruiting tour, in which the old wing fabric was replaced with new.

Lieutenant Commander Albert C. Read was, for the nonce, a national and world hero. In his particular honor, but also in tribute to all crew members of the NC-boats, Curtiss hosted a banquet on July 10 in New York's Hotel Commodore. The setting was, to say the least, atmospheric. The dining room was transformed, by means of a false inner shell, to represent the cabin of a gigantic seaplane crossing the Atlantic. It was entered by a gangway, beside which a sign read: *THIS PLANE FOR PLYMOUTH, ENGLAND.* The diners looked out through portholes at moving patches of imitation sky, across which searchlights played. A stage entertainment was performed, with Christopher Columbus and King Neptune among the dramatis personae.

Irvin S. Cobb, the humorist, was master of ceremonies. As speakers he introduced Read, Towers, Bellinger, Admiral Taylor, Glenn Curtiss, and John N. Willys.

For souvenirs of the occasion, all guests received square pieces of the weathered wing fabric removed from the NC-4.

Spic and span in her new dress, escorted by Read and those who had flown with him, the celebrated Nancy went on her triumphal 3000-mile journey. Landing for admiration in thirty-nine cities, she traveled down the Atlantic Coast, around Florida to the Gulf Coast, and up the Mississippi Valley to the Great Lakes.[2]

With the NC-4 episode, the career of Glenn H. Curtiss in aeronautics reached its apex.

24. Florida Years

The plan for a winter home on the West Coast had been dropped because of the excessive travel distance from an industry which was growing busier by the hour. Still, the Curtisses craved seasonal escape to a warm climate, all the more so after exposure in Buffalo to the brumal blasts that whip in from Lake Erie. In the winter of 1916 they broke away for a sojourn at the Royal Palm Hotel, adjacent to the Curtiss Flying School on Miami Beach. While there, Glenn gave personal attention to the school, which had contracted with the Army to train recruits. A batch of Harvard volunteers had lately moved in.

Low-flying planes and the incessant throb of motors annoyed the neighbors. The complaints of seaside residents came to a head when a student pilot tied a note to a grapefruit and aimed it at the lawn of a house inhabited by a girl he was courting. Her parents were not amused when the grapefruit crashed through the roof and came to a pulpy repose on the parlor rug. Sympathetically, Curtiss went shopping for a new flying field.

On the mainland across Biscayne Bay, he explored the open reaches north and west of Miami, then a city under 30,000. Delighted to find a level, prairie-like terrain which appeared to be used only for the grazing of livestock, he inquired for the owner. He was directed to James H. Bright, a genial, jockey-sized individual known wide and far as Mister Jimmy. How much would he take for a piece of land for an airfield? Absolutely nothing; so famous an aviator could have it free of charge. Curtiss picked a spot, moved the flying school, and therewith began another friendship fraught with major consequences.

Jimmy Bright had made his pile as a cattle rancher in Missouri. On a Florida vacation, about the time Curtiss was gaining a foothold in aviation, he had sensed in the sawgrass savannas between Miami and the Everglades a potential for rich grazing if they were seeded with the right kind of grass. Buying up 17,000 acres of the cheap land, he introduced ranching and Brahman bulls to southern Florida. He drained marshes and fought cattle ticks. Blue-eyed Mister Jimmy made up in courtly manners for what he lacked in stature. An expert horseman, he loved to spend long days in the saddle, riding his range.

Returning to Miami the following winter, Curtiss approached Bright about a partnership in the ranch. Bright said he already had a partner, his brother Charles, and didn't need another. Curtiss's answer to this was to buy out the share of Charles Bright with a generous offer. In years to come, James Bright would speak of Curtiss as "the finest partner a man could ever have."

Henceforward, when Curtiss came south the two men rode around together purchasing land at $2 and $3 an acre, annexing it to the ranch. Their holdings ultimately totaled more than 120,000 acres. One day they encountered a band of Seminoles and asked what they called the region. "Hi-a-le-ah," replied the Indians, which denoted something like an upland prairie.

For a man whose nearest approach to farming had been the care of vineyards, Curtiss worked up a remarkable enthusiasm for the breeding of livestock. The herds increased with the pastureland. A widely separate parcel of 48,000 acres was acquired by the partners in the area northwest of Lake Okeechobee, and there they established a ranch for agricultural experimentation. Curtiss registered the name of the new community as Brighton, in tribute to James Bright. To help stimulate Brighton as a real estate development, as well, they built a well-appointed hotel, to which were attached a stable of horses and a pack of fox-hounds. Hunting was excellent in the area, for both foxes and bobcats.

Meanwhile, after the United States was at war, military policy ruled out further pilot training at civilian schools. Curtiss donated the Florida field to the Navy for use by the Marines, and it thereby became the birthplace of the Marine Air Corps. Elsewhere on the ranch, he laid out a new private flying field in a flat place which had been Bright's mule pasture. In time this would be given to the city for the original Miami International Airport.

*   *   *

While thus diversifying his interests, Curtiss had by no means withdrawn from industrial activity. He continued as president of the Curtiss Engineering Corporation, and with the dawn of peace channeled his restless energies into the development of civil aviation. The experimental plant created by him could not have been more timely to this purpose. Before the NC-boats were finished, he announced plans for an "aerial taxi service," for intercity travel in small cabin planes. To that end, the *Oriole* was quickly unveiled, and then the tri-motored *Eagle*, which Bert Acosta flew to Washington for a series of demonstrations carrying eight passengers. With an air of some amazement, a writer for the *Scientific American* said:

"Here is a man and a company making machines for sober, private use, much as an automobile manufacturer makes cars. You can buy a plane as you would a car—from a catalog, and for the use you want to make of it. You can have immediate delivery. You can be taught to run it as you would be taught to run a car . . .

"The one man most largely responsible for this state of affairs refuses to come up to the popular idea of the inventor. He has no long hair or wild eyes. He is not difficult to talk to. He is modest beyond belief as to his own attainments."

During the stress of the war years, Curtiss had given up personal flying. Airplanes had simply outgrown him, as he was wont to say. When asked in 1919 if he expected to fly any more, he replied: "I may later, but I will have to learn all over again."

Speed had never ceased to be his fetish, and he considered it the prime desideratum in vehicles of the air. Now it was possible to concentrate on that aim, and his point of attack—with the advantage of the big tunnel—was streamlining; the reduction of air resistance in every conceivable way. W. L. Gilmore was his head engineer in putting such designs into effect; while Charles Kirkham had perfected a 400-

horsepower motor, the K-12, which left the OX-5s in the lurch. The fastest thing on wings with which the company emerged from the war was the *Wasp*, a triplane which had been designed as a two-place fighter for the Army but was not ready when the Armistice was signed.

With further refinements and a K-12 engine, the *Wasp* began trials at Roosevelt Field in the spring of 1919, flown by Roland Rohlfs, chief test pilot of Curtiss Engineering Corporation. Rohlfs, age twenty-seven, was a lucky acquisition from Buffalo, whose mother wrote detective novels. He promptly got a speed of 162 miles out of the *Wasp*, and the plane also showed altitude possibilities. Curtiss encouraged Rohlfs to assail the world's altitude record currently held by Lieutenant Casale in France (33,137 feet). A special model of the *Wasp* was rushed through, and Rohlfs, in a fur-lined hooded suit, made two practice climbs. On the day of the official attempt, Curtiss was tied up in a board meeting while the *Wasp* circled up and up to a record-smashing 34,610 feet. He reached the field in time to watch the landing and congratulate Rohlfs.

The fastest machines in whose designing he ever participated were the illustrious Curtiss Racers of the early '20s, and their success gave immense satisfaction to the man whose career had sprung out of a craving for speed. The Army and Navy, hoping to stimulate production of swifter pursuit craft, schemed an interservice rivalry for the Pulitzer Trophy in 1922. They invited several industries to submit designs for racing planes whose speed must surpass 190 miles per hour. The Garden City company was the only one which had been pursuing a consistent line of development in that very direction. Curtiss's passion for experiment had kept his engineering staff busy refining successive models since the *Wasp*.

One cannot assert that this or the other detail of the Racers was a definite Curtiss touch, but there is no question that he hovered devotedly over their creation. Neat and trim, they are remembered to this day as the "cleanest" biplanes ever made. A striking innovation was their wing radiators: sheets of corrugated brass laid flat across the wing; the water was cooled by flowing through the wrinkles.

Four Curtiss Racers were all-conquering in the Pulitzer Trophy race at the Army's Selfridge Field in October 1922, astounding the aviation world. The winner was Lieutenant Russell Maughan, with an average of 205.8 mph over a closed course. Glenn Curtiss was on hand to see this happen. Doubtless he was thinking, with nobody knows what inward emotions, of the coincidence that the field was named in honor of Tom Selfridge. Across the screen of his memory there must have flickered images of the *Red Wing*, the *White Wing*, the *June Bug*, the *Silver Dart*.

After the meet, Maughan pushed his racer up to an unofficial straightaway record of 248.5 mph, which made him, for that time bracket, the "fastest man in the world." Two days later, General Billy Mitchell flew the same plane for an official record of 224.05 mph. This was the first time that the world's speed record had been held in the United States since Curtiss brought it home from Rheims in 1909.

What Curtiss said for publication was that much greater power might soon be placed in an airplane, and that head resistance would be further reduced. "Each year we learn more about metals and their alloys. There is no telling where the present development will lead us. I cannot see a limit for some time to come."

Two Curtiss Racers, flown by Navy men, repeated the triumph with even greater speed for the National Air Races at St. Louis in 1923. They were forerunners of a long line of Curtiss Hawks, which were the standard military pursuit planes during most of that decade.

While the incomparable Racers were being perfected, Curtiss was conducting some personal experiments on Manhasset Bay with a thing he termed an aquatic glider. He had noted that thermal currents do not rise vertically above water, as they do over land; yet an albatross will take off from a wave and soar. He wished to learn about the air currents over water, and described his 28-foot glider as "a first step in sea soaring." Acting as his own test pilot, he had it towed by a speedboat until it lifted, then dropped the towline. So far as soaring was concerned, these experiments were a washout; he managed to keep the glider in free flight as long as 17 seconds. But then he got the notion of hitching it as a trailer behind a flying boat, and invited Army and Navy officers to watch while this was accomplished. Perhaps it could lead to an "air train," he suggested. The officers were more interested in it as a towed target for aerial gunnery.

*   *   *

With the abrupt cessation of military business, the vast North Elmwood plant in Buffalo lost its usefulness. War contracts amounting to between $50,000,000 and $75,000,000 with the Curtiss company alone were canceled. Congress passed an appropriation bill of more than $6,000,000 with which to make a settlement on the dropped contracts and to take the idled plant off the company's hands for $1,804,300. Leaving some minor production in Buffalo, the corporation transferred its operating headquarters to the Garden City plant, purchasing nearby Hazelhurst Field, which had been under lease to the Army, and renaming it Curtiss Field. The motor plant in Hammondsport was shut down. Still, the company claimed three-fourths of the reduced output of the American air industry.

In September 1920 the Willys-Overland interests sold their control of the Curtiss Aeroplane and Motor Corporation to Clement M. Keys, heretofore a vice-president of the company. John N. Willys decided that airplanes and automobiles had little in common, and reverted to automobiles. In the financial reorganization, Curtiss cashed in an unknown amount of his stock holdings. As Keys afterward stated, Curtiss refused to come in on the purchase of stock in the new set-up, because "he was getting out of aviation, and getting more interested in real estate, and because he was going to live in Florida and would not be around in the North much."

An accurate appraisal of the Curtiss fortune at this juncture is hard to come by. Intimates of the family used to say that he "came out of the aviation business with $32,000,000." Over the years he had made large gifts of cash and securities to his wife, so that Lena Curtiss was mistress of a considerable fortune in her own right. It was she who insisted that they jointly establish a trust fund for Glenn, Junior. Reputedly this was in the amount of $1,000,000, each parent putting up $500,000.

The plight of Hammondsport, coming on the heels of its lush days, was pathetic. The village, in effect, had lost its two sustaining industries at a single blow. The Prohibition Amendment, clamping down in 1920, virtually knocked out the wineries. Curtiss remained loyal to his native town as long as he lived; his signature on hotel registers, when his actual home was elsewhere, always appeared as: *G. H. Curtiss, Hammondsport, N.Y.* Deeply concerned for the economic welfare of the village, he promoted and financed a venture called Keuka Industries, occupying parts of the deserted plant. It began as a jobbing machine-shop business, under Lyman Seely's management, but this did not pan out well. A few former exhibition pilots came temporarily to the rescue. Beckwith Havens and C. C. Wittmer organized Airships, Inc., making rubber life rafts, flotation gear, and safety belts. When they landed a contract to produce the helium gas cells and interior rigging for the Navy's dirigible, *Shenandoah*, most of Hammondsport's labor slack was taken up. J. Lansing Callan later bought out Wittmer's interest in Airships, Inc., but in the end the old Curtiss shops stood idle again.

* * *

Meanwhile, for the second time in his life, Curtiss was being caught up, almost by inadvertence, on the crest of a wave. This time it was the Florida land boom. Neither he nor Bright had been gifted with prescience, and this was not the reason for which they had accumulated all that land. But there it lay when well-heeled Northerners, in the flush of Harding and Coolidge "normalcy," made the discovery of southern Florida.

Apparently, Bright sensed the trend sooner than his partner. The story goes that Bright made a special trip to Garden City with a suggestion that they break up some of the ranch property and sell it for building lots. Curtiss scoffed: "Jimmy, nobody but you would want to live out there." Nonetheless, he had enough respect for Bright's judgment to give it a try, and they formed a Curtiss-Bright Company to deal in real estate.

Starting in with the segment of the ranch nearest the city, they used material from the spoil-banks of the recently dug Miami Canal for grading. Lots sold faster than streets could be laid out. Recalling the Seminole word for the territory, they incorporated the town of Hialeah in 1921, donating parcels for a town hall, schools, churches, a golf course. Scarcely believing what was happening, the partners sold $1,000,000 worth of lots in one ten-day period. At the height of the boom, they hired 250 salesmen. Before long, houses were springing up all over what had been Bright's original 17,000-acre ranch.

Curtiss built his first Florida home in Hialeah, designing it in the so-called pueblo style of architecture. He enticed Carl Adams into quitting Long Island for the warm land of opportunity, and made a place for him in the enterprise. Typically, he wished to gather old friends about him and let them share in the profits. Quite a number from Hammondsport took advantage of his generosity, forming the nucleus of what may best be described as a "Curtiss colony" in Florida. To a former hunting crony, Ira Brundage, he sent word that he was holding three Hialeah lots for him at the bargain price of $500 each; Brundage went down, bought them, resold them, and started a profitable lumber business. Curtiss made a gift of a lot to Henry Kleckler, but

Henry had bought a farm up in Tyrone and refused to leave it for all the citrus in Florida.

The entrepreneurs of Hialeah were receptive to the promoter of a dogtrack, and then to Joseph Widener's project for a highly ornamental horse track. When the Hialeah Race Track opened in 1925, Bright supplied the pink flamingos for its infield. One would never have recognized the old ranch. Attractions of this ilk helped to make Hialeah a jazzy settlement of the prohibition era, a mecca for gamblers, bootleggers, and gangsters. Curtiss had not bargained for such an atmosphere.

Once infected with the real estate fever, he began dreaming of the "residential paradise" he would really like to build, and turned his eye to the south side of the Miami Canal. He had gone along with Hialeah, and now Bright collaborated with him in this. They opened a second development office bearing the sign: Curtiss-Bright Country Estates. Surveyors and engineers laid out, in accordance with Curtiss's plans, a community in sharp contrast with the square-block pattern of Miami and Hialeah. Streets were more like parkways, winding and curving in bewildering mazes. The centerpiece was a beautiful rolling golf course which was, at the same time, a source of limpid fresh water, enough to supply a populous city.

James Bright had long since made a priceless discovery when he drilled for water on his ranch. He had struck an artesian well with no salty taint. The wells of Miami's water supply, near the shore, yielded water so brackish that, it was said, people hated to bathe in it. On the site of the golf course, a well produced water as pure as Bright had found. In 1923, Curtiss and Bright sold the golf course and its water rights to the city of Miami for a token payment of $1. Thus Miami procured its future municipal water supply.

They called their new development the Country Club Estates. From his western travels, Curtiss had imbibed a taste for pueblo architecture, and he wished all the homes in the Country Club Estates to reflect that note. Those which he himself built were pueblo, sure enough, but the style never truly caught on with the customers.

In the midst of this "residential paradise," the Curtisses erected their own dream house, a larger and far more lavish edition of the previous one in Hialeah. Its cost was $150,000, and they paid another $80,000 for its furnishings, which included many antique objets d'art. Curtiss drew the basic plan, engaging an architect only for details. Rooms veered off at interesting angles, and the tall-ceilinged central drawing room was by way of being a palatial salon. In the rear was a large terraced swimming pool, and at one side an artificial lake upon whose surface floated swans, ducks, and flamingos. The grounds were landscaped with exotic trees, flowers, and shrubbery.

The name over the cast-iron gateway was "Dar-err-aha." Lena had come across the word in a book, and an Armenian dressmaker she patronized on Miami Beach had translated it from the Syrian as meaning "House of Happiness."

Curtiss brought logs from Oregon with which to construct a hunting lodge, hidden away in a thicket of woodland which he spared from the ax in laying out the development. This was used as a masculine retreat and a base of operations for guests who hunted with him in the Everglades or Big Cypress Swamp. He was, in his son's phrase, "a great escaper." He had a way of quietly disappearing, especially when social occasions loomed. A small spiral stairway in a corner of the great drawing-room led to a study he used for a retreat.

As in the case of Hialeah, the partners had Country Club Estates incorporated as a town. After the death of Glenn Curtiss, by vote of the residents in a 1930 referendum, the name of the town was changed to Miami Springs.

Still a third city in the Miami complex can claim Curtiss as its founder, and that is Opa-locka. He envisioned a town further afield in the grassland, where people might have room to grow gardens; also, paradoxically, as an industrial center. An imaginative young architect, Bernhardt E. Mueller, sold him on a flamboyant plan for a city on the theme of the Arabian Nights. "Mr. Curtiss was fascinated with my ideas," said Mueller. He must have been, in fact, hypnotized. After giving the go-ahead, Curtiss asserted he was creating the "Baghdad of Dade County." The result resembled a movie set which had been left standing when the picture was done and the actors departed.

The site was some six miles to the northward of Hialeah, and the Seminoles knew it as Opatishchawahalocka ("a high, dry hammock"). Apprehensive that potential residents might not be able to pronounce that name, Curtiss rechristened it by culling out the four middle syllables. The incredible city hall, in pastel shades of white and pink, loosely imitated a mosque, with minarets and spires and balconies, built as a hollow square around an inner courtyard replete with fountain and statuary. The city hall fronted on Sharazad Boulevard. Nearby structures were similar caricatures of Oriental splendor—a hotel, a bank, a golf club, an archery club. Street names were picked straight out of the

Arabian Nights: Aladdin Street, Sinbad Avenue, Sesame Street, Ali Baba Avenue, Caliph Street, Sultan Avenue. A stroller might, by accident, stumble into Curtiss Drive and wonder if he were lost.[1]

Opa-locka had a gala opening in 1926, in connection with which the Seaboard Airline Railroad ran the pioneer trains over its extension to Miami. For some years thereafter, Arabian Nights Pageants were held annually in this city of fantasy with few inhabitants.

* * *

His enjoyment of the affluent life was flawed by the phantoms of two past episodes which arose to haunt and beleaguer him.

Following the bankruptcy of the Herring-Curtiss Company, Curtiss and his associates were so relieved that they left the loose ends dangling. No one troubled to have the defunct company legally dissolved. The action which had been started to compel Herring to surrender his stock was simply dropped when the stock became valueless. The injunction to prevent a stockholders' meeting was put on a shelf and forgotten—but not by Augustus M. Herring.

Herring bode his time in quiet obscurity, watching the Curtiss company grow and prosper, waiting for the injunction to lapse of its own accord, which it did in November 1916. Able then to vote his stock, though it was worthless, he called a meeting of the stockholders of the Herring-Curtiss Company, at which a new board of directors was chosen (some of these directors had never been stockholders). The board then elected officers, with Herring as president. The resurrected company filed suit in Steuben County in October 1918, to recover $5,000,000 from Glenn H. Curtiss "and others." The others were Monroe Wheeler, Thomas S. Baldwin, Cortlandt Field Bishop, Harry C. Genung, G. Ray Hall, Henry L. Kleckler, Gabriel H. Parkhurst, and the Bank of Hammondsport. The suit was based on the charge that the bankruptcy had been "the outcome of a deliberate and premeditated plan arranged by certain of the defendants to so conduct the business affairs of the plaintiff that insolvency must necessarily ensue"; and that "large monetary gains were ultimately derived" by the defendants. Herring demanded "immediate possession of all properties, sales, inventions, patents, discoveries" of the successor company, and a full accounting on back business.

Busily occupied with the NC-boats and other government contract work, Curtiss made an answering deposition before a referee in New

York City. Denying any conspiracy in the bankruptcy, he said it had been "due to other causes and particularly to an action brought by the Wright brothers . . . to restrain the manufacture, sale or exhibition of aeroplanes by this plaintiff." He further denied that Herring ever communicated any "inventions, discoveries, or improvements" either to him or any of his employees.

Three years elapsed before the trial opened in Monroe County Supreme Court, Rochester, whither it had been adjourned from Hornell, Steuben County. The presiding justice was Samuel N. Sawyer, serving the 7th Judicial District which embraced Steuben and its neighbor counties on the north. The trial consumed eighteen weeks, and during its course both Curtiss and Herring spent long hours on the witness stand. At one point under cross-examination, Herring was asked: "You think you are entitled to credit for a great deal that Glenn Curtiss got credit for, don't you?"

"Yes, sir," the witness replied.

As the probing continued, he said he was sure he could build "a better airplane than they are building now" (i.e., in 1921). As for the Wrights, "I built machines that would fly before they commenced to experiment." The value of the patent applications he "contributed" to the Herring-Curtiss Company, he said, had since been appraised at $500,000.

Judge Sawyer delayed his verdict until May 1923, and then it was a complete victory for the Curtiss side. He absolved all defendants from the accusations of fraud and conspiracy. "As is not unusual," he said, "practically everything done by the defendants, then controlling plaintiff corporation, has been seized upon as evidence of wrong-doing . . . In many instances the things pointed out by plaintiff as evidencing bad faith, fraud, and conspiracy seem to have been ordinary transactions had in the usual course of business, with here and there a case of poor judgment, or an erroneous entry in the books, afterwards sought to be corrected, or an entry which, after this lapse of time, cannot be explained . . . It is only by the most strained interpretation that any suspicion of fraud can be drawn therefrom." Letters and telegrams of Curtiss introduced in evidence, the judge concluded, "as a whole, indicate that Mr. Curtiss was then, at least, engaged in an attempt to sustain a falling structure rather than attempting to complete its ruin by dislodging the cornerstone."

But this was far from the end of the story. Herring appealed, and while the appeal was pending he died of a stroke, on July 18, 1926. His heirs and associates carried on the case. The heirs were a son, William, and a daughter, Mrs. Henry H. Mason of Freeport, Long Island. The State of New York got around to formally dissolving the Herring-Curtiss Corporation in 1926.

On March 14, 1928, the Appellate Division of Supreme Court, sitting at Buffalo, reversed the decision of the lower court as far as Curtiss, Wheeler, and Baldwin were concerned; the other defendants were exonerated. Curtiss, Wheeler, and Baldwin were adjudged "guilty of malfeasance and misfeasance in office." Ironically, of that trio Curtiss had to face the decision alone: both Wheeler and Baldwin had died since the trial. The judges of the Appellate bench ruled:

"The evidence shows that Curtiss had difficulty in adjusting his attitude of mind and his conduct of affairs to the requirements of a corporate business which was not solely his own, as his old company had been, but was one in which others had rights and interests which he was bound to protect."

The decision held that "the Curtiss faction was determined upon ousting Herring without payment to him of any substantial sum"; that the three majority directors "acted selfishly and in their own interest, and hence wrongfully and in breach of their duties as directors"; that "The exigencies of the struggle for control led them to lose sight entirely of the interest of the only stockholders who had contributed actual capital to the enterprise." In sum: "Whether Herring was blameworthy or not is not the issue . . . [Necessities of a fight for control] offer no excuse for a breach of fiduciary duties."

The reaction of Curtiss to this scathing verdict was characteristic: he would continue fighting. From here on, it was a matter of stubborn principle. "He never would have settled," persons close to him said afterward. Lena had urged him, ever since the case began, to "pay off Herring and get it over with." The classic mistake of his life, he always felt, was getting involved with Herring. Whatever the demand for settlement might be, to his way of thinking it would be legalized extortion, if not close to blackmail.[2]

*　*　*

Griffith Brewer, the Englishman who went to Hammondsport incognito to spy on the *Langley* tests for Orville Wright, revisited the United States in 1921. In his words, he discovered that "the campaign of belittling the Wrights was still on." Once more a guest at Hawthorn

Hill, he suggested preparing a paper on the *Langley* affair for delivery to the Royal Aeronautical Society, pointing out that he, as a Britisher, "could afford to attack the Smithsonian when prominent Americans could not." Orville was more than willing to cooperate, and they settled down for a solid two months "to a methodical analysis of the differences between the original Langley machine and the machine experimented with at Hammondsport." The finished paper was typed in Orville's laboratory, and copies were mailed to Curtiss, Dr. Walcott, Dr. Zahm, and Charles Manly.

The probability is that Brewer sounded out Orville at this time in regard to depositing the original Kitty Hawk plane in the British Science Museum.

As planned, Brewer read the document at a meeting of the Royal Aeronautical Society, and its contents stirred up "a tremendous commotion in the aeronautical world" (quoting Brewer). Assailing the Hammondsport experiments as having destroyed the plane's identity, he flatly stated that it "did not do a true, free flight." He taxed Zahm with having reported that the tests were made in an "unmodified machine." He went on to enumerate the lengthy list of changes as he and Wright had worked them out. What he omitted to do, as Orville also consistently omitted to do later on, was to differentiate between the few alterations made for the initial test hops by Curtiss and the many changes made for the long series of tandem-wing experiments which ensued.

When the New York *Times* asked Curtiss for comment on Brewer's blast, he said:

"I did fly the *Langley* in its original condition and it more than made good. The facts are these:

"The Smithsonian Institution sent the machine to me at Hammondsport to be tried out. Brewer, who had heard about my intention to fly it, if possible, took a train for Hammondsport, but he came long after I had had the machine in the air. He arrived to see it flown with a larger motor and with other changes. The original *Langley* was capable of flying and did fly . . .

"I do not know why Brewer brings up all this unless it is the question of the bearing on patents."

An angry chorus of Curtiss and Smithsonian supporters rose to the defense. One of these was an aeronautical engineer, Robert Gilbert Ecob, who had witnessed the Hammondsport tests. He wrote the *Times:*

"The outrageous attack by Griffith Brewer . . . may easily be refuted by scientific data which cannot be questioned. The statements that 'no attempt was made at Hammondsport to fly the original Langley machine' and that 'fundamental aerodynamic changes were made to the machine which were not mentioned in the report of Dr. Zahm to the Smithsonian Institution' are entirely false . . .

"While it is true that only short 'hops' were attempted with the original motor, it was clearly demonstrated that the machine was practical and that it could do exactly what Dr. Langley had claimed for it."

Brewer kept kicking the embers of the smoldering controversy. By 1925, he stated in a later book of memoirs, Orville Wright, "recognizing that the exposure I had made was losing its effect," assented to the request of the British Science Museum. Brewer personally "conducted the negotiations" in a repeat visit to Dayton.

As far back as 1910, Secretary Walcott had written Wilbur Wright that the National Museum was endeavoring to enlarge its collections "illustrating the progress of aviation," inviting him to deposit "one of your machines or a model thereof." Wilbur responded: "If you will inform us just what your preference would be in the matter of a flyer for the National Museum, we will see what would be possible in the way of meeting your wishes. At present nothing is in condition for much use." Walcott said the Smithsonian would like a model of the Fort Myer Army plane, a model of the Kitty Hawk plane, and also one fullsized Wright machine. He added: "If, however, the Wright brothers think the Kittyhawk machine would answer the purpose better, their judgment might decide the question."

It appears that the Wrights took umbrage because Walcott asked for a model of the *Kitty Hawk* instead of the original. At any rate, the matter was deferred, and in 1916 Walcott wrote Orville a specific request for the *Kitty Hawk*, saying: "Will you not be so good as to let me know if you have yet decided on the disposition of this machine?" Wright replied: "While I have had several requests for it from other museums, I have not made any definite arrangements in regard to it."

Now, under Brewer's skillful manipulation, Wright let it be known that he would send the Kitty Hawk machine to the British Science Museum at South Kensington, London.[3] This decision, he said, was due to the manner in which the Smithsonian had allowed the *Langley* to be "mutilated for the purpose of private parties to a patent litigation."

"For twenty years," Wright averred, "I have kept possession of the machine in the hope that a suitable home could be found for it in

America. Several American museums have asked for it, but the one institution among these which seemed of a national enough character was one to which I did not care to entrust the machine . . . I could not be sure that our machine, if given to this institution, would be any safer from mutilation than Langley's had been."

Although the threat was not carried out for some time, it touched off a public furor. An Ohio Representative stood up in the House to demand a congressional investigation of Wright's charges. Secretary Walcott gave out a statement in defense of the Smithsonian's role in the tests. Grover Loening,[4] by now a successful airplane manufacturer, appointed himself an intermediary between Wright and the Smithsonian in a vain attempt to keep the *Kitty Hawk* in this country. When he brought Orville's terms to Washington, he found Walcott "pretty bitter and equally fighting mad."

Without benefit of publicity, Curtiss now made a proposition, by letter, to Orville Wright.[5] In order to resolve the question for good and all, he suggested they collaborate in building an exact replica of the *Langley* and giving it a fair trial together. If it flew, Orville was to pay all expenses of the experiment; if it did not fly, Curtiss would pick up the tab. No reply was forthcoming from Dayton.

Charles Manly advanced a somewhat similar proposal to Wright: that each put up $10,000 to cover the costs of taking the restored machine out of the museum and jointly conducting a conclusive test. At least Manly received an answer, which was this: "You do not seem to understand the issues of the controversy."

The reaction of Curtiss during all this squabble was one of bewilderment. He was "simply surprised that the man acted that way," according to Glenn Curtiss, Jr. He scrupulously refrained from any statement, public or private, impugning Wright.

Dr. Walcott died in 1927 and was succeeded as secretary of the Smithsonian by Dr. Charles G. Abbot, a distinguished astrophysicist who had worked under Langley. The *Kitty Hawk* was still at Dayton, and Dr. Abbot hopefully revived overtures to obtain it. A bit later he answered a question from the editor of the Journal of the Royal Aeronautical Society: "If it is insisted that the Smithsonian Institution must confess to knavery before this controversy can be settled, we dismiss the subject."

One of Wright's primary demands was a change in wording of the placard on the Langley machine as it was displayed, contending it was untruthful in saying: "The first man-carrying aeroplane in the history of the world capable of sustained free flight." Abbot replaced the label with this: "Langley Aerodrome. The original Samuel Pierpont Langley flying machine of 1903, restored." Next he published what was intended as a conciliatory pamphlet, expressing "regret" that the Hammondsport experiments had been "conducted and described in a way to give offense to Mr. Orville Wright and his friends." The brochure contained such phrases as these:

"I concede to Mr. Wright that it [the Smithsonian] lacked of consideration to put the tests of the Langley machine into the hands of his opponent, Mr. Curtiss . . . The fact that the results of these tests might prove valuable to Mr. Curtiss in his defense against Mr. Wright's suit, and the unfavorable aspect in which that might put the Smithsonian Institution, if foreseen, might well have deterred from the course of action adopted . . . I feel that it was a pity that Manly, Dr. Langley's colleague, could not have been the man chosen to make them."

Wright was not appeased. At this point he crated up the historic plane and shipped it to England. Publicly, he explained the action as due to "the hostile and unfair attitude shown towards us by the officials of the Smithsonian Institution." He even inserted a clause in his will leaving it to the British Science Museum, "unless, before my decease, I personally in writing have asked its withdrawal from the museum."[6]

*　*　*

The Florida bubble began to deflate in 1925, and a hurricane the following year hastened the bust. At midnight on September 17, 1926, a wind gauge at Miami Beach registered 132 miles per hour, then the gauge blew away. Newspapers throughout the country published a report that Glenn Curtiss was missing in the hurricane. A day or so later, the Curtiss company at Garden City gave out a statement to the press that it had been notified of his safety.

Hialeah was practically flattened by the blow. The damage there was estimated at $1,300,000. Curtiss dug deeply into his own pocket to assist the victims, and made a trip to New York to help in raising a hurricane relief fund.

Although he and Bright had profited handsomely while the boom lasted, the oft-heard remark that Curtiss "made more in Florida real estate than he ever did in aviation" was a gross exaggeration. The fact is that, when the boom collapsed, he was left holding great tracts of land for which there was no longer a market, but which bled him for taxes. Still he had supreme confidence in the ultimate recovery of real estate values, and clung to the land. At the same time, he went steadily ahead with new investments, and the range of his activities in these years—in business ventures, experiments, and outdoor recreations—was fantastic. Quite possibly, he had never been busier in his life. In all, he organized eighteen Florida corporations. One of them was a bank: the Hialeah-Miami Springs Bank, to help finance home builders.

At no time was his connection with the airplane industry entirely severed. His office in the Garden City plant was maintained, and his advice in aeronautical matters was frequently sought. It is of some significance that when, in 1927, he chartered a holding corporation under title of Glenn H. Curtiss Properties, Inc., its president was Clement M. Keys, who was also president of the Curtiss Aeroplane and Motor Corporation. Capitalized at $3,500,000, the holding company's purpose was to centralize control of all Curtiss properties in Florida, some of which were scattered in Fort Lauderdale, the Lake Okeechobee district, Tampa, and Jacksonville.

As an enthusiastic developer of southern Florida, Curtiss was surely struck by another of those odd coincidences which seemed forever cropping up in his path. Henry M. Flagler, his most famous predecessor in opening up the Miami region, had likewise originated in Hammondsport, son of the first pastor of the Presbyterian Church. As one of John D. Rockefeller's earliest associates, Flagler had made an immense fortune in Standard Oil. In his last years, he had organized the Florida East Coast railway and built luxury hotels to lure vacationers. His Florida investments and donations exceeded $40,000,000.

Despite the luxurious character of their new abode, the Curtisses made no great splash as entertainers. Still, as a penalty of his celebrity, they were on the receiving end of countless social invitations, and the compass of their acquaintanceship inevitably widened far beyond the "Curtiss colony" whose company they actually preferred. When James Deering opened his fabulous Miami estate, Villa Viscaya, they were guests at the first dinner party he gave in that palace. (This, it seems, was the same James Deering who had made a small investment, with the Bishops, in the Herring-Curtiss Company.)

At heart, they remained the smalltown couple who shied away from society pretensions and gabby cocktail parties. It wasn't that they were unsociable people. They took part in "progressive dinners" which moved from house to house when the population of Country Club Estates was scarcely worth a census. But their truest social pleasure was enjoyed in the intimacy of the Sunday night suppers which they gave for a select circle of kinfolk and friends of long standing. Around the table would be, for instance, the Genungs; Curtiss had brought Harry Genung to Florida as manager of his enterprises. There would be Carl and Dot Adams, and Tank and Bess Waters. His onetime racing pal, Leonard Waters, was among those he had tempted to join his residential "paradise." Curtiss would say: "Remember, Tank, when we used to sit up all night on the train to New York because we didn't have the money for a Pullman berth?"

Naturally, the years of mingling with men of circumstance and sophistication had polished off the rough edges of the village mechanic who came up in the world. The middle-aged Curtiss was urbane, affable, articulate, and—considering his limited schooling—a fairly literate man. During the 1920s, he was inclined to be fastidious of attire; while also adopting the informal fashion of linen knickers and plus-fours. In conversation, one subject in which he had meager interest was politics. His subdued sense of humor was of the chuckle, rather than the guffaw, and decidedly did not run to risqué stories. When he cracked a sly joke of his own, it was apt to have a sharp edge, which sometimes gave offense where none was intended. If chivalry demanded, he was known to trespass upon a dance floor, and then he "liked to dance fast." Neither liquor nor tobacco tempted him. At parties where bootleg drinks were served, he would carry the same highball around all evening, pretending it was a refill, rather than seem a killjoy. "It is no merit in me that I don't drink," he told friends. "I simply don't like the stuff." On Christmas Eve, he ritualistically puffed a cigarette and "looked pretty silly doing it," his son recollected.

As long as their principal home was on Long Island, Glenn, Jr., attended a public school. As he entered the teen years, he was sent to a novel boys' preparatory school—the Adirondack-Florida School, whose campus shifted with the seasons. A summer term was held near Paul Smith's in the Adirondacks; a winter term in southern Florida. Before long, the son began putting on weight, and it was evident that he had inherited from the Reverend Claudius Curtiss, his great-grandfather, the genes indicating obesity which had shown up in his Aunt Rutha. Not for this reason, but for others, Glenn, Jr., was something of a problem to his father as he grew older.

Curtiss would have liked his son to take an interest in aeronautics, or at least in some kind of an engineering career, and planned on sending him to college. At one time, he fitted up a corner of a reopened plant building in Hammondsport as an experimental shop specifically for Glenn, Jr., and asked Henry Kleckler to take him under his wing. This scheme didn't work. Junior had other things on his mind, such as fun and frolic. One trait he had from his father was an itch for speed, which he indulged when driving automobiles on rural roads. There was an episode of an accident in which a Hammondsport girl was slightly injured; her father sued for damages, and his father made a settlement out of court. The younger Curtiss never learned to fly nor went in for any phase of aeronautics. He was, on the whole, content to be a rich man's son.[7]

The Curtisses returned to Hammondsport every summer after 1925, occupying the homestead on the hill. It was bruited about that Lena raised some objection on the score that the old house was rundown and they could afford more comfort; she agitated for a cottage on the lake. For some peculiar reason, Curtiss never seemed able to locate a rentable cottage, nor did he buy or build one. Did he have a sentimental attachment? Entirely likely.

Lena's mother, Jennie Neff, was still a member of the household. No sooner was the Florida home a reality than Glenn's mother, out in California, decided that the time had come for her to be near him in her declining years. He built a nice, if modest, stucco home for her in Country Club Estates. Hardly had she moved in when she was dissatisfied with it. He built her a second house which was more elaborate, and maintained her in it with servants. At this stage, Lua Curtiss Adams dropped the "Adams" from her name, becoming once again Mrs. Lua Curtiss (her second son, Carl Adams, strongly disapproved of this quirk). She cut quite a figure in Miami as a clubwoman; relatives afterward said she "traded on the name."

Soon Lua induced Rutha Hesley to leave both California and her husband. Curtiss built a stucco bungalow for her and supported her, along with a more or less steady retinue of deaf-mute guests. Rutha followed her mother's example, listing herself in directories as Miss Rutha Curtiss. That she did not divorce her husband is shown by the fact that Curtiss left a small legacy to "my brother-in-law," Augustus Hesley.

*   *   *

As an inveterate outdoorsman, Curtiss retained much of the slender, sinewy physique of his youth. At the age of fifty, he could bend and touch his toes, could put younger men to shame with the number of his push-ups, could swim the length of a pool and back under water. He blamed his vanishing hairline upon the early habit of wearing a cap, and counseled his son never to do so; Glenn, Jr., followed the advice, only to find as the years passed that it made not the slightest difference.

His favorite athletic pastime was archery golf, at which he became adept. Never too keen about golf as such, he went all-out for the combination of his new-found sport of archery with the conventional game. Arrows replaced golf balls in going around the fairways. At the green, the object was to put an arrow through a small iron ring; Curtiss introduced the use of unhusked coconuts instead as the final target. Proselytizing, he organized the Opa-locka Archery Golf Club. As an incentive to novice archers, he fastened 20-dollar gold pieces to trees and awarded them to those who could hit them from a given distance.

As a coach for the archery club, he engaged a youthful and energetic young man named Howard Hill, a recent arrival in Miami who was an expert bow-and-arrow man. Hill, who was proud of the Creek Indian blood in his veins, had grown up in Alabama, where he learned to hunt game with arrows. Curtiss and Carl Adams took him up to Brighton, where the horses and hounds were available, and soon he was organizing bobcat hunts. Hill inducted Curtiss into bow hunting, and on one occasion they took off together for a bear hunt in Georgia's Okefenokee Swamp. Hill afterward wrote of "G. H." as "an archer, a gentleman, and a true sportsman."

The handsomely swarthy archer accompanied the Curtisses to Hammondsport for a summer or two, and villagers got the impression that he was there as a "tutor" for Glenn, Junior.

According to Hill, Curtiss did not care for horseback riding, and rarely accompanied the riding hunts. Curtiss had renewed his interest in photography, and gave Hill an indoctrination in use of the camera. When Hill was later running his own motion picture producing company in Hollywood, specializing in outdoor documentaries, he credited Curtiss with having started him on that path. (Hill coached Errol Flynn for his role in the movie, *Robin Hood.*)

When driving in the back-country, Curtiss carried both a shotgun and an African hunting-bow in the rear seat. He liked to drive where there were no roads, and had an uncanny knack for judging narrow passages between trees without scraping fenders. As a gunner, he hunted bobcats in the Everglades, wild turkey in Big Cypress Swamp, deer in the Adirondacks, moose in Canada. Once he rented a grouse moor in Scotland. There were alligator hunts by boat; the toothy reptiles were not killed, but snared with a noose around the nose and liberated in other areas where the species was scarce. Commander Jerome Hunsaker was his hunting companion from time to time, finding that he kept a fine collection of guns for the use of his guests. Going out after the small deer of the Everglades, they took along no dog, but waded in the channels to scare up game, while keeping a wary eye peeled for water moccasins and rattlesnakes.

Automobiles continued to be a Curtiss hobby, and he was perpetually making them over to suit himself. Returning from a trip to the Pacific Coast, he tired of the rail journey, jumped off the train at a Midwest station, purchased a new automobile and drove the rest of the way home. As streamlining minimized head resistance for airplanes, he felt that automobiles could be improved by the same treatment. Some of the results he got by altering car bodies were astonishing. After he had given an "egg-shaped" body to a new Packard, he presented it as a gift to Jimmy Bright.

On hunting excursions, he often deplored the lack of hotel accommodations in the hinterlands. As a remedy, he built a portable camp, with home comforts, to be hauled behind an automobile. This he called his "motorized gypsy van," or "motorbungalo." It served nicely, too, for a dressing room at beaches. The streamlined body tapered to a V-shaped prow with a gooseneck pivot to fit a coupling in the rear of a roadster or coupé. After making sundry improvements, Curtiss decided to market his trailer under the trademark of Aero-Car. He organized the Aero-Car Company, of Opa-locka, and placed Carl Adams at its head. The vehicle had a considerable vogue for some years.

Then there was the *Scooter*. Curtiss was not a yachtsman, and fishing never had appealed to him, but he saw a need for getting around Florida's grass-filled inland waterways with more celerity. The *Scooter* was a shallow-draft motorboat powered by an airplane engine and aero propeller mounted on the stern, capable of 50 miles an hour. Nor did his restless imagination stop there: he built a small flying boat adapted to the grassy channels, which made 70 miles an hour.

Incurably addicted to the sketching of aircraft designs, he drew them instead of doodles, and was likely as not to pull forth a pencil and sketch a diagram on his hostess's tablecloth. Many offhand drawings were more carefully committed to paper and kept. Some were strongly suggestive of the streamlined monoplanes which were later to revolutionize the airlines. One diagram showed folding pontoons for a seaplane, the floats to be drawn up as part of the fuselage.

It is no exaggeration to speak of Curtiss as the father of municipal aviation at Miami. He foresaw the city's importance as an aerial crossroads. After donating his Hialeah field to the city in 1927, he promptly laid out a new private field adjacent to Opa-locka, stocking it with Curtiss aircraft such as *Orioles* and *Robins*. It was used for charter flights, training, and aerial photography. This was destined to become Opa-locka Airport, one of the busiest general airfields in the world today.

And still the limit of Curtiss's Florida activities had not been reached. The agricultural digression led him into horticulture, thence into a campaign to introduce little-known tropical fruits into the United States. He began the cultivation of avocados and mangoes, but particularly of papaya trees. Convinced that papaya was a healthful fruit which ought to be popularized in the North, he planted a five-acre papaya grove near Opa-locka.

Curtiss had not been exactly a practicing Methodist since boyhood, but in these latter years he turned from the credo of his grandfather to adopt Christian Science. This apostasy did not prevent him from donating a pipe organ to a newly erected Methodist Episcopal Church at Hammondsport, inscribed to the memory of the Reverend Claudius G. Curtiss. Along with Christian Science faith, he became a health-food faddist, though the fads never lasted long. For one spell he chewed seaweed; for another, he drank milk spiked with some kind of "germ," to quote his son.

He was not above consulting a physician when something specific seemed to be wrong. He was bothered now and then by abdominal adhesions from an old motorcycle crackup; and occasionally by a different pang diagnosed as a low-grade chronic appendicitis. When a doctor wrote a prescription, he would get it filled, then neglect to take it. Another minor complaint was jokingly known to the family as his "sensitive nose." Whenever smoke rolled in from a brush fire in the Everglades, he would hastily pack a bag, drive downtown, and take an upper-floor room in the tallest hotel.

In the health-food field, Dr. John Harvey Kellogg, head of the Battle Creek Sanitarium in Michigan, was a celebrated authority. Curtiss spent a fortnight at Battle Creek for a checkup, and discovered that

Kellogg was an advocate of papaya, prescribing it for stomach patients. Curtiss sent samples of his several papaya varieties back to Kellogg with a note: "Doctor, we need you here."

As a matter of fact, Kellogg had been considering a branch sanitarium in Florida. When he turned up in Miami, Curtiss showed him around his developments, including the Pueblo Hotel. In his early overoptimism, Curtiss had put up this fanciful hostelry, to fit into his pueblo architectural scheme, making its motif the mystical thunderbird of the Navajo Indians. An artist imported from the Southwest decorated the beams and pillars of the lobby with inlaid Indian symbolisms. Hand-woven Navajo rugs were scattered helter-skelter. Guests who signed the register of the Pueblo Hotel included Thomas A. Edison, George Bernard Shaw, and Commander Richard E. Byrd. Instead of the thunderbird, however, its motif might more appropriately have been the white elephant. It was altogether too much hotel for its time and place. After admiring its exotic ornamentation, Dr. Kellogg asked his host: "How would you like to have this place taken off your hands and used as a sanitarium?"

Curtiss replied: "I'll think it over and let you know in the morning."

In the morning, Curtiss rang the doorbell of the rented house where Kellogg was writing a medical text. He brought a document for the doctor to sign: a contract to turn over the hotel for a consideration of $1 a year; if at the end of six years the sanitarium was a going concern, Kellogg was to receive title free and clear. "I told him the price was too cheap," Kellogg laughed, "and offered him ten times that amount."

*   *   *

July 4, 1928, was the twentieth anniversary of the *June Bug* trophy flight. Hammondsport celebrated it big. A crowd estimated at near 60,000 thronged into town, and local police called on state troopers for help in controlling it. Airplane motors droned overhead and a giant Navy amphibian landed and arose from Keuka Lake. The Finger Lakes Association was launching a campaign for a Curtiss Commemorative Airport on the flats of Pleasant Valley (not, however, at the site of the Champlin racetrack). The proposed location had been cleared enough —"a smooth grassy carpet"—for visiting planes to land this day.

A reception and banquet in tribute to Curtiss took place in the assembly room of St. James Episcopal Church. The toastmaster, County

Clerk Reuben B. Oldfield from Bath, began the program by asking all persons present who had been connected with aeronautics prior to 1908 to stand up. One man stood: he was Glenn H. Curtiss. He made brief remarks, concluding with the words: "Don't forget the others."

The major speakers were Commander Holden C. Richardson and Augustus Post. The latter emphasized that the name of Curtiss "must not be dimmed" by those of Lindbergh, Chamberlin, and Byrd, whose transatlantic exploits had made them aviation heroes of the moment. "Their great flights have been due in no small measure to his work," Post reminded, since all modern planes were built "according to basic ideas of Mr. Curtiss."

During the festivities, a reporter asked: "When are you going to move back into this country, Mr. Curtiss?"

His reply: "Well, I never really moved away."

25. Keuka Sunset

The dramatic merger which had been so long hinted, rumored, suggested, and fomented, ultimately came to pass. When it did, amid a fanfare of publicity trumpets, it was not a matter of sentiment or historical logic, but of bare-knuckled high finance.

In the late afternoon of June 26, 1929, boardroom doors swung open in a suite of Wall Street offices, and through the portals issued an announcement that the Curtiss Aeroplane and Motor Corporation and the Wright Aeronautical Corporation had been joined together in business matrimony. The new colossus of the aviation industry was the Curtiss-Wright Corporation. In reality, it represented the amalgamation of two powerful clusters of companies: the so-called Curtiss-Keys Group, on the one hand, and the Hoyt Group, on the other. (Richard F. Hoyt was chairman of the board of the Wright Corporation.) The combine raked in eighteen affiliated companies and twenty-nine subsidiaries, and extended tentacles into some nascent airlines. Financial writers estimated the pooled assets at more than $70,000,000 and the paper value of listed stocks within its control at $220,000,000. The latter figure was due for an early tumble.

The Curtiss-Wright Corporation was saluted as the most prodigious aeronautical organization in the world. Wall Street insiders recognized it as throwing down the gauge of battle to the recently formed United Aircraft and Transport Corporation. Next day aviation shares "gyrated wildly" on the New York Stock Exchange.

It goes without saying that neither of the men whose names were thus brought into hyphenated union had any part in what transpired behind the boardroom doors; although many an uninformed reader conjured a vision of their clasping hands and pledging to let bygones be bygones. Curtiss, at any rate, was listed in the new cast of characters: he was appointed to the technical committee of the Curtiss-Wright Corporation.

Through the business grapevine, Curtiss heard that Orville Wright was indignant because the name "Curtiss" had been given precedence in the title of the corporation. One could hardly begrudge him the chuckle with which he relayed this tidbit of intelligence to the family and close friends.

*   *   *

They were spending the summer, as customary, in Hammondsport, where Curtiss had a fresh project going, partly to keep himself occupied but especially to do something to benefit the village. By his instructions, Henry Kleckler had reopened one of the idle plant buildings and hired eight men to work on an experimental automobile with a front-wheel drive. The idea, as Kleckler understood it, was to apply the principle to the Aero-Car, making it self-propelling.

Whenever he was back in town, Curtiss inquired around to ascertain how his former workmen were making out. Those who were not faring so well were likely to find a check in the mail; some received checks regularly from Florida. It was not commonly known that he placed a standing order with a local fuel dealer to keep certain ex-employees supplied with coal and send the bills to him. Kleckler himself, through unwise investments and overgenerous gifts to relatives, had gone through most of the $300,000 he reputedly made from his Curtiss stock. Now Curtiss was funding him with loans, while urging him to accept the lot he wanted to give him in Florida. "Why don't you get Henny off this farm?" he would say to Mrs. Blanche Kleckler when he dropped in for one of his visits at the Tyrone place ("He was never one to telephone before he came," she recalled).

The crusade for a Curtiss Commemorative Airport was receiving a hefty build-up, and he made a donation to help it along, with the comment: "It would be a good thing for the lake region." The Finger Lakes Association brought political pressure to bear at Albany for a legislative appropriation to establish it as a state airport. (When the Legislature appropriated $25,000 for the purchase of the field, Governor Franklin D. Roosevelt vetoed the bill.)

At the same time a civic movement was under way in the village to have one of the vacant Curtiss shops converted into an aeronautical museum, and he was inclined to do this at his own expense. He felt that such a museum could "preserve many things now being scattered and lost . . . and perhaps inspire further invention in this field which holds unlimited possibilities."

He was troubled because so many people seemed to think that, in his partiality for Florida, he had turned his back on Hammondsport, and he went to considerable pains to counteract this belief. In response to an inquiry from a Buffalo newspaper, he wrote: "I want to correct the impression that I ever left Hammondsport permanently, or that I have lost interest in Western New York."

Meanwhile, the Governor of Florida appointed him to the Board of Commissioners of the Okeechobee Flood Control District. Already he was a member of the Florida State Drainage Board, through his activities in promoting drainage of marshy fringe areas of the Everglades.

In May 1930 the president of the University of Miami invited Curtiss to attend the commencement exercises. He was not apprised of the true reason for this invitation, presumably on Lena's advice. The family, who were privy to the secret, felt sure that he would have found an excuse to stay away, had he known. At any rate, he was tricked into a cap-and-gown and seated, as a distinguished guest, on the platform. In the ensuing ceremonies, to his complete surprise, he was awarded an honorary doctorate.

◊   ◊   ◊

Consequently, it was Dr. Glenn Curtiss who wended to Hammondsport soon after receiving the accolade—though he would have winced to hear himself thus addressed.

On May 21, 1930, he observed his fifty-second birthday.

The New York *Times* asked him to write a piece setting forth his views on the current status of aeronautics, for publication under his byline in a Sunday feature section. Before leaving Miami Springs, he fulfilled that assignment, saying in part:

"The outlook for aviation is, in my opinion, about the same as the outlook for the automobile industry thirty years ago. There were some who thought the automobile a rich man's toy, others foresaw a great industry; but, so far as I can recall, no one predicted the immense development which has taken place.

"The expansion of the automobile industry depended largely on the construction of good roads, whereas the future of aviation depends largely upon the development of landing fields . . .

"Saving time is the equivalent of increasing the duration of life. To business men and executives, time used in traveling from point to point is largely wasted. This is where the airplane comes in."

Honors and the anniversaries of his early flying achievements crowded in upon him. The return to Hammondsport this summer was earlier than usual because of the twentieth anniversary of his Hudson River flight. The Aeronautical Chamber of Commerce of America (successor to the Manufacturers Aircraft Association) had prevailed upon him to re-enact that flight—in a manner of speaking. Implicated in the nostalgic event were the Chambers of Commerce of New York City and Albany.

Naturally, there would be some marked departures from the shaky trip of 1910, and these in themselves symbolized the strides aviation had since made. Instead of sitting precariously out in front of an open-air "pusher" with a lifejacket around him, the hero of the occasion would occupy the enclosed cockpit of a new airliner, a Curtiss Condor. The Condor, the civilian version of a two-engined bomber, carried eighteen passengers and was just being introduced on some of the airlines.

The field of takeoff would be a change, indeed, from Van Rensselaer Island. Albany preened itself on its new airport, several miles out on the heights northwest of the city, but traced its ancestry to the river flats which Curtiss had initiated. The precise anniversary date was May 29, but the re-enactment was set for May 30 in order to take advantage of Memorial Day.

The Curtisses checked in at the familiar Hotel Ten Eyck the night before, with their son who was to share in the experience. Glenn, Junior, had not yet turned eighteen. They learned that the Postoffice Department had used a special mail cachet that day to mark the anniversary; all airmail letters posted between Albany and New York bore the commemorative cancellation.

At a pre-flight luncheon, Lieutenant Governor Herbert H. Lehman bespoke the tribute of the State of New York. Curtiss gave his typical brief response: "I am quite overwhelmed by what has been planned here today. We can't question the development aviation has made. We have only to look at one of those giant ships at Albany Airport to know. Nor can we question the future it will have. The next generation will take naturally to the air. Thank you."

The newspapers reported that he sat with eyes modestly glued to his plate during a storm of applause.

Twenty years earlier he had done it alone. In now retracing the route, he was to be accompanied by approximately eighty people in an aerial procession which involved four escort planes: a Keystone Patrician, a Sikorsky S-38 amphibian, an Army transport, and a sister Condor which had carried a New York delegation up from Curtiss Field.

Among the privileged passengers aboard the leading airplane, besides Lena and Glenn, Jr., were Mayor John Boyd Thacher II of Albany; Alan R. Hawley and Augustus Post from the Aero Club of America; Don C. Seitz, who had been business manager of the New York *World* when Curtiss collected the prize; Henry Kleckler; officials of the Curtiss-Wright Corporation; and a sculptor, Charles Andrew Hafner, who was doing a bust of Curtiss.

Needless to say, these people were not entrusting their lives solely to a man who had not flown for years and had never before sat in the cockpit of a modern airliner. The actual pilot was an Englishman, Captain Frank T. Courtney, a veteran of the Royal Air Force, who had recently come to work for the Curtiss-Wright Corporation. Courtney was himself a celebrity of the moment, having made two unsuccessful stabs at a westward crossing of the Atlantic in a Dornier-Wal flying boat; in the second try he got past the Azores when forced down with an engine afire (a steamship rescued the crew).

Courtney took the Condor up to cruising altitude before turning the controls over to Curtiss, whom he had given a quick briefing. Glenn, the younger, was permitted to stand in the rear of the cockpit, noting that Courtney put on a good act of nonchalance. The Britisher calmly stoked up a cigar, relaxed in his seat, and shot pictures of the scenery with a movie camera. Only once did he offer his copilot a piece of advice. The Condor was 3000 feet above Storm King Mountain when it encountered severe turbulence. By reflex action, Curtiss started pushing the nose down. "We don't do that anymore," Courtney mildly admonished him.

Curtiss studied the landscape unrolling below for comparison with how it had looked to him in 1910. The paved highways and the heavy holiday traffic crawling along them were the most noticeable change. He was able to pick out both of the green patches where he had landed before—at Camelot and Isham Park. The thought occurred to him that in some ways it was too bad an airplane could no longer duck into such small places: "In the compromise with speed, we have had to forego the advantages of slow landings."

At New York, Curtiss circled around Governors Island as the final gesture, after which Courtney took over for the landing at Curtiss Field. As Curtiss stepped down, his face was flushed with pleasure and excitement, his eyes twinkled, and he was in a rare mood for chatting with reporters. He said he had been "astounded" at the ease with which so large a plane could be controlled, and that he had been contrasting the steady roar of its motors with the "crackle" of his little 1910 engine. It amused him that he had subconsciously tried to steer with his hands and to correct for lateral stability by moving his shoulders.

Courtney told the press that his copilot had performed remarkably well for a man who had been so long away from flying, and that he still retained the delicate touch needed to keep an airplane from being overcontrolled.

A limousine, under police escort with screaming sirens, sped the Curtiss family into New York, whence they entrained for Washington to attend the annual Curtiss Marine Trophy Race. He had established the Marine Trophy back in 1911 as an incentive to the flying of hydroplanes and aeroboats.

*   *   *

Awaiting him on return to Hammondsport was another chapter in the pestiferous Herring suit.

Following the adverse decision in 1928, the Appellate Division appointed a former Supreme Court judge, William S. Andrews of Syracuse, as referee to adjudicate a settlement with the Herring heirs. Hearings opened at Rochester in mid-June, with the plaintiffs demanding a minimal $1,000,000. The complete records of the case, literally trunkfuls, were heaped in the Supreme Court chambers of the Monroe County Courthouse.

Curtiss was the first witness called, and he spent a solid five days on the stand, subject to recall after other testimony had been taken.

With a chauffeur, he commuted from Hammondsport for the sessions. After the July Fourth weekend, he hit the road again for Rochester on Monday morning. En route, he was suddenly doubled over by sharp abdominal pain. The driver turned around and took him home. A phone call notified Judge Andrews that the defendant was ill and would be unable to appear.

An attorney of the Herring legal battery, Harold H. Corbin, leaped angrily to his feet, accusing Curtiss of feigning illness as a ruse to delay the case. While he was about it, he denounced the defendant as a "perjurer" and a "civil fraud convict," and charged that he had removed pertinent records outside the state. At the defense table, Stephen J. Warren rose to protest this attack as unfair and contemptible, and praised Curtiss as "one of the finest men in America" who had done a great deal for his country in aviation.

Judge Andrews responded to Corbin's diatribe by appointing a panel of three Rochester physicians to go to Hammondsport and conduct an examination of Curtiss. They reported back that he was afflicted with acute appendicitis and would be apt to suffer a relapse at any time unless the appendix were removed. Andrews thereupon excused Curtiss from further appearance, pending surgery, and adjourned the hearings to October 14 for the completion of his testimony.

Meanwhile Dr. Thew Wright, who had been the family physician when they lived in Buffalo, was hurriedly summoned to Hammondsport. He ordered the patient transferred to the Buffalo General Hospital for an immediate operation. A compartment was reserved on a Lackawanna train and Curtiss was taken by ambulance to make the connection, accompanied by Glenn, Jr. During the ride to Bath, he talked to his son about designing an Aero-Car type of ambulance after his recovery; he was sure it would be smoother-riding than this one was.

At the Buffalo station, ambulance attendants boarded the train with a stretcher, but Curtiss stubbornly refused to be carried. Though his face was pale and drawn, and he was obviously weak, he walked under his own power to the waiting ambulance. Next morning he was wheeled into surgery.

Dr. Wright was aware of the old adhesions, and Curtiss asked him not to do anything about them; he objected to having his "insides" tampered with more than necessary. According to relatives, the surgeon nevertheless detached the adhesions while removing the appendix. The operation was a success and convalescence came along normally. Lena was daily at her husband's bedside, staying in a Buffalo hotel.

Curtiss was to have had a prominent part in the annual New York State air tour sponsored by the State Aviation Commission and the National Aeronautical Association. A cavalcade of airplanes was to flit from city to city in furtherance of airfield development. Hammondsport was to be an important stop on the itinerary because of the crusade for a Curtiss Commemorative Airport. The group flight went ahead as scheduled while he was hospitalized. Some forty-five planes took off from Buffalo on July 14. Noted aviation figures participating in the air tour were Captain John H. Towers, by now assistant chief of the Navy's Bureau of Aeronautics; Captain Holden C. Richardson; and Eugene (Smokey) Rhoads, who had been a chief machinist's mate on the transatlantic flight of the NC-4. G. Carl Adams went along as deputy for his half brother. The entourage circled back from Syracuse on the 18th for its Hammondsport visitation. Some of the planes landed on the historic field of Stony Brook Farm, others at the Bath Country Club.

A woman Christian Science practitioner paid visits to Curtiss in the hospital. On the 22nd, he thanked her for the ministrations and said he would not be needing her any more as he was going home the next day. A private railroad coach was reserved for the journey to Bath. That evening he called in Mrs. Florence Illig to take dictation; Florence was a Buffalo girl he had hired as a substitute secretary. She found him propped up in bed drawing sketches for a glider. The letter he dictated was to a Buffalo newspaper, stating the facts about his hunting license. A considerable point had been made in the Rochester hearings as to his legal residence—whether it was in Florida or New York—and the state in which he held a license to hunt was considered important to the issue. "I don't want to let the people of Hammondsport down," he explained to Mrs. Illig, instructing her to type the letter and bring it to him for signature on the morrow.

Around 6:30 in the morning of July 23, he got out of bed to go to the bathroom. Moments later his private nurse entered the room to find him unconscious on the floor. A pulmonary embolism had stilled his heartbeat.

❋   ❋   ❋

Glenn Hammond Curtiss came home to his final rest in the village where he was born. The bier was prepared in the parlor of his boyhood home on Castle Hill. On the day before burial, a steady stream of mourners moved past the casket, from morning until late afternoon. The ground floor rooms of the homestead overflowed with floral offerings. Conspicuous among the pieces banked around the bier was one in which white roses were shaped into a huge propeller with the letters QB (for Quiet Birdmen, a society of pioneer aviators).[1]

A service was conducted at the home by the Reverend Grant P. Sommerville, rector of St. James Episcopal Church. Every store and office in Hammondsport suspended business during the obsequies. The city of Miami observed an hour of official mourning simultaneously, with flags half-staffed, municipal offices and many businesses closed.

The armed forces of the United States designated official representatives to the funeral: Towers for the Navy, and Lieutenant Colonel F. M. Andres for the Army.

The casket was borne by six of Curtiss's closest associates of years past: C. Leonard Waters, Harry Genung, Henry Kleckler, James Bauder, Rumsey Wheeler, and K. B. MacDonald. Among the honorary bearers were Towers, Richardson, and Callan of the Navy; Mayor C. H. Reeder of Miami; H. Sayre Wheeler of Opa-locka; and Lyman J. Seely and J. Seymour Hubbs of Hammondsport.

All through the services, at the home and at Pleasant Valley Cemetery, motors hummed a threnody overhead. Ten airplanes, converging from five cities, circled continuously. During the final scene at the cemetery, the planes swooped low, one by one, scattering flowers over the Curtiss family plot.

The widow knelt at the graveside, supported by Glenn, Jr. She had elected to wear white mourning. The gown and veil were of white chiffon, matching a white lace hat.

Beneath the maples they laid him, beside his grandparents, his father, and the son, Carlton, who died in infancy. A massive rough-hewn block of granite, with the single word CURTISS, carved into either side, marked the plot.

The grave was within a few hundred feet of the meadow in which he came to earth at the end of his first great flight in the *June Bug*.[2]

Appendix

NOTES

CHAPTER 1. SPEED CRAVING

1. Gideon Curtiss, whose father had fought in the Continental Army, migrated from Litchfield, Connecticut, to Niagara County, New York, in 1817. That frontier region was just then opening to settlement in the wake of the War of 1812. Gideon was cited as the first white settler in Ransomville, where he built a log cabin. He was soon joined by a brother, Gilbert, who walked back to Connecticut to fetch his bride and a packet of appleseeds. Gilbert Curtiss opened a tavern in Ransomville and begat progeny, of whom Claudius G. Curtiss, born in 1823, appears to have been one. (Gideon Curtiss was listed as unmarried in the 1830 census.)

A church record says that Claudius "was converted to God in his twentieth year." In 1845, he married Ruth Bramble, eldest daughter in a farm family of ten, native to the Town of Richmond, near Canandaigua. Their first son, Claudius Adelbert, was born in 1847. Along the way, Claudius (the father) became a book salesman, and in that capacity was assigned to Markham, Ontario, in 1854, where the second son, Frank Richmond, was born. During two years of residence at Markham, near Toronto, Claudius was licensed to preach by the Wesleyan Church of Canada. Returning to New York State, he was ordained an elder by the Evangelical Association, and in 1868 was admitted to the ministry of the Methodist Episcopal Church. Prior to the Hammondsport charge, he had filled pulpits in Seneca, Dansville, Cohocton, Savona, and Jasper.

2. Claudius Adelbert Curtiss simplified his name to Claude. He later married and had two children.

3. It may be that the grandmother had a hand in selecting the name Hammond. She had obviously given Frank the middle name of Richmond as a tribute to the township of Richmond, where she grew up.

CHAPTER 2.   THE HELL-RIDER

1. A minor quibble of later years has been raised over the question: Did Curtiss design his own engines? One encounters a factional school of thought which tries to bestow the credit on "the Kirkham brothers." On this score, facts speak for themselves. The three sons of John Kirkham—Charles, Clarence, and Percy—were not yet affiliated with the machine-shop when Curtiss went to him for castings. John Kirkham was apparently far from being an engine-man, or even a skilled machinist; he was primarily a carpenter. Charles Kirkham, eldest of the brothers, informed the present writer that he was away from home, working in Seneca Falls, when John Kirkham made the deal with Curtiss. It was some time after that, he said, when he had a protracted illness and went home to recover. During his convalescence, his father persuaded him to enroll in a correspondence-school course in mechanical engineering. He asserted that he had not met Curtiss before that time. Upon finishing that course, Charles Kirkham took charge of the machine shop and his two younger brothers came in to work under his tutelage. By this account, the engine designing of the Kirkham brothers could hardly have begun much before Curtiss withdrew his business from the Kirkham shop in 1905.

2. Some references suggest that the wine aristocracy, whose reign had been supreme in Hammondsport, resented the intrusion of a crass mechanical industry in their domain. The assistance extended to Curtiss by members of the leading wine families would seem to belie this. Apart from financing, one of his most helpful allies was Harry Champlin, with his racetrack, as will be seen.

3. Claude Jenkins, a Hammondsport barber, staked out one claim to fame: that it was he who, during a brief interval of working for Curtiss, drew the original of the scroll trademark.

CHAPTER 3.   A DALLIANCE WITH DIRIGIBLES

1. The version most often seen in print is that Baldwin saw a Hercules motorcycle roaring up one of San Francisco's hill streets, flagged down the rider, and asked him what kind of engine that was. Baldwin himself, on a

witness stand, said merely that he obtained a catalog from a San Francisco motorcycle agency, saw the picture of Curtiss winning a hill-climbing contest, and wired for an engine.

2. Rare indeed are the inventions that were the work of one man alone, and especially so when they are something as complicated as an internal combustion engine. Of course, others contributed ideas to Curtiss engines as time rolled along: notably, Henry Kleckler and Alexander Pfitzner. But the key brain in the process was unquestionably Curtiss himself.

3. Marvin W. McFarland, editor, *The Papers of Wilbur and Orville Wright.*

4. The oversized motorcycle ultimately found its way into the collections of the Smithsonian Institution.

CHAPTER 4.   CHANUTE AND THE BROTHERS

1. Herring's letter to the Wright brothers was dated from Freeport, Long Island, on December 26, 1903. After congratulating them, he suggested that their work was probably going to result in "interference suits in the patent office," and continued: "I do not think litigation would benefit either of us . . . There will be enough money to be made out of it to satisfy us all. There is also enough of the 1897–98 machine, on which I flew 72 feet, for it to be reconstructed and flown." Herring claimed it was really he who originated Chanute's "Dune Park 2-surface machines" which had contributed to the Wrights' work and which "gave you your interest in the problem, and to a certain extent a starting point."

The letter went on: "Now the point is this: If you turn your invention into a company, I want to be represented in it; not solely because it is to my interests, but because it would probably be actually to yours." He told them he was negotiating with two foreign governments for his patent rights, and concluded: "Would you consider joining forces and acting as one party in order to get best terms, broadest patent claims, and to avoid future litigation? The basis being a two-thirds interest for you and a one-third interest for me."

CHAPTER 5.   "TO GET INTO THE AIR"

1. First Lieutenant Thomas E. Selfridge came of a family bearing a proud military tradition. His great-grandfather was Rear Admiral Thomas Oliver Selfridge, who commanded the Mare Island Navy Yard during

the Civil War. His grandfather, Lieutenant Thomas O. Selfridge, Jr., was in command of the forward gun battery on the frigate *Cumberland*, which took the brunt of the *Merrimac*'s raking fire at Hampton Roads; when the *Cumberland* sank, he barely escaped through a porthole and swam to a lifeboat. Later, as a Lieutenant Commander, that grandfather commanded the gunboat *Cairo* at the siege of Vicksburg. He rose to be an admiral. Lieutenant Thomas E. Selfridge had been a bit of a hero in the San Francisco earthquake of 1906 by leading a rescue detachment of Marines.

2. Alexander Graham Bell went to Paris in 1880 to receive the Volta Prize of 50,000 francs for his invention of the telephone. This prize, which had been awarded only once before, was established by the Emperor Napoleon in honor of the Italian physicist, Alessandro Volta. Bell used the money to establish the Volta Laboratory in Washington, with Chicester Bell (a cousin) and Sumner Tainter as his associates. When the Volta Laboratory's patents on the graphophone were sold for $200,000, Bell put his share of that profit into the Volta Bureau, to increase knowledge relating to the deaf.

3. The charter of the Aerial Experiment Association reads as follows: "Whereas, the undersigned Alexander Graham Bell of Washington, D.C., U.S.A., has for many years past been carrying on experiments relating to aerial locomotion at his summer laboratory in Beinn Bhreagh, near Baddeck, Nova Scotia, and has reached the stage where he believes a practical aerodrome can be built on the tetrahedral principle driven by an engine and carrying a man, and has felt the advisability of securing expert assistance in pursuing the experiments to their logical conclusion, and has called to his aid Mr. G. H. Curtiss of Hammondsport, N.Y., an expert in motor construction, Mr. F. W. Baldwin, and Mr. J. A. D. McCurdy of Toronto, Engineers, and Lieutenant Thomas Selfridge, Fifth Artillery, U.S.A., military expert in aerodynamics, and

"Whereas, the above-named gentlemen have all of them given considerable attention to the subject of aerial locomotion, and have independent ideas of their own which they desire to develop experimentally, and

"Whereas, it has been thought advisable that the undersigned should work together as an association in which all have equal interest, the above-named gentlemen giving the benefit of their assistance in carrying out the ideas of the said Alexander Graham Bell, said Alexander Graham Bell giving his assistance to these gentlemen in carrying out their own independent ideas relating to aerial locomotion, and all working together individually and conjointly in pursuance of their common aim 'to get into the air' upon the construction of a practical aerodrome driven by its own motive power and carrying a man.

"Now therefore we the undersigned, Alexander Graham Bell, Glenn H. Curtiss, F. W. Baldwin, J. A. D. McCurdy, and T. Selfridge, do hereby agree to associate ourselves together under the name of the 'Aerial Experiment Association,' for the purpose of carrying on experiments relating to aerial locomotion with the special object of constructing a successful aerodrome.

"We agree that the 'Aerial Experiment Association' shall be organized on the first day of October 1907, and shall exist for the term of one year from the date of organization unless otherwise determined by the unanimous vote of the members.

"We agree that the inventions relating to aerial locomotion made by the members of the Association during the lifetime of the Association shall belong to the Association; and that any applications for letters patent for such inventions shall be made in the name of all the members as joint inventors.

"We agree that inventions relating to aerial locomotion made by the members of the Association before the organization of the Association shall belong to the inventors, and not to the Association, unless specially assigned; and that only such prior inventions shall be claimed by individual members as shall be substantiated by the production of written memoranda, drawings, photographs or models existent before the date of the organization so that the proofs of prior invention shall not rest on recollection alone, or upon verbal statements unsupported by documentary or tangible evidence of earlier date than the organization of the Association.

"The said Alexander Graham Bell agrees to place his Laboratory at Beinn Bhreagh near Baddeck, Nova Scotia, at the disposal of the Association for the purpose of carrying on experiments relating to aerial locomotion, together with all the buildings, tools, materials, and appurtenances belonging to the Laboratory, without charge, so long as the Association desires to carry on experiments at Beinn Bhreagh: Provided that the running expenses of the Laboratory, including the salaries of the Superintendent and men employed shall be paid by the Association during their use of the said Laboratory, the number of men employed other than the Superintendent to be at the discretion of the Association, and that any new material or apparatus not in the Laboratory at the date of the organization which may be desired for the use of the Association shall be acquired at the expense of the Association.

"We the undersigned agree to appoint one of our number as

Director of Experiments to be our medium of communication with the Laboratory.

"We agree that the Laboratory workmen shall receive their instructions from the Superintendent of the Laboratory alone, that the Superintendent of the Laboratory shall receive his instructions from the Director of Experiments alone, and that the Director of Experiments shall receive his instructions by vote of the Association of which he is a member.

"We agree that the headquarters of the 'Aerial Experiment Association' shall be at Beinn Bhreagh, near Baddeck, Nova Scotia, and that, on or before the first of January 1908, the headquarters of the Association shall be removed to some place yet to be determined within the limits of the United States.

"This agreement can only be modified by unanimous vote of the undersigned.

"Witness our hands and seals at HALIFAX, Nova Scotia, this thirtieth day of September, A. D., 1907.

William L. Payzant
Notary Public

ALEXANDER GRAHAM BELL
G. H. CURTISS
F. W. BALDWIN
J. A. DOUGLAS McCURDY
T. SELFRIDGE
1st Lt. 5th F.A., U.S.A.

Authenticated by David F. Wilder, Consul General of the United States, September 30, 1907.

CHAPTER 6.   RED WING

1. Perhaps the closest resemblance, if any, was to the latest airplane flown in France by Henry Farman, which the Voisin Frères built for him. Carl Dienstbach, a German aviation writer who was much in evidence at Hammondsport, wrote that when the A.E.A. efforts began, "the greatest achievement in power flight before the public was the Voisin-Farman machine." He noted that the *Red Wing* was built along similar lines; that it contained "virtually every part of the Farman," but "was superior." Dienstbach felt that "keen judgment" controlled the Hammondsport experiments, and further remarked, after the second model had flown: "The excellence of the

tip-control . . . and its superiority in not producing any one-sided drift, over the Wright Brothers tip control, is evident."

CHAPTER 7. WHITE WING

1. In a talk to the Aéro Club de France in 1905, Robert Esnault-Pelterie said of the wing-warping that "we consider this system dangerous"; that it may, "in our opinion, cause excessive strains on the wiring, and so we fear breakages in the air." For that reason he abandoned warping. "We then employed at the front two independent horizontal rudders, one placed at each extremity of the aeroplane. These two rudders were each connected to a little steering device within reach of the two hands of the operator . . . This arrangement gave satisfaction, although it was not as powerful as the wing warping."

CHAPTER 8. JUNE BUG

1. The Hammondsport *Herald* ran this commentary on the origin of the name *June Bug:*

"There is no flying creature which the aeroplane so closely resembles as the beetle. Some kinds of birds fly or soar with the wings extended in a fixed position like the aeroplane, but no bird has any other means of propulsion, and depends on rising currents to keep it in the air. The June bug and a number of other species of beetle have rigid shells or wings which are extended and kept in a fixed position. This is its means of support in the air, while it is propelled by a set of small flexible wings working in the rear of the fixed wings. This is identically the same principle that is used in the mechanical flyer. The canvas covered surfaces resemble the fixed wings of the beetle, while the rotating propeller in the rear takes the place of the small beating wings of the insect."

2. Although Henry Farman was born and reared in France, he was a fullblooded Englishman, the son of a British journalist stationed in Paris. This made it rather ironic that France reaped the benefits of his flying activities. His American tour was negotiated by Frank S. Lahm, representative of a U.S. business concern in Paris, the father of Lieutenant Frank P. Lahm who is encountered later in these pages.

3. When the A.E.A. became divided between Hammondsport and Baddeck, after the *June Bug's* success, Dr. Bell, with his passion for accurate records, hatched the plan of a weekly typed publication to keep the separated members informed of what all were doing. This was the *A.E.A. Bulletin,*

the most remarkable documentation of pioneering aviation experiments in existence. Its circulation was limited to the five members, though seven copies were run off, the extras being for office record and deposit in the Smithsonian Institution. Its contents were confidential. All letters and telegrams were included, as well as special reports and opinions expressed by members.

CHAPTER 9.   TOM SELFRIDGE

1. Such was the quotation as Curtiss recalled it. Another version has Holcomb saying to Selfridge: "Be careful or we will be paying money to your heirs."

2. Lieutenant Benjamin Foulois rose to be Chief of the Army Air Corps in the early 1930s, retiring in 1935 as a major general.

3. Lieutenant Frank P. Lahm, one of the first two Army pilots trained by Wilbur Wright, wrote when he was a brigadier general (Retired): "The extent of the Air Corps' loss in the death of Lieutenant Selfridge, at the time its wings were beginning to take definite form, will never be known. We can only surmise. Endowed with the enthusiasm of youth, coupled with a keen mind, he entered his chosen field with a marked scientific interest. Long hours of study and research, technical discussions with those qualified in this aspect of aviation, had given him a basic knowledge which would have proved especially valuable to the new arm, had he lived to give it the benefit of his attainments. He would undoubtedly have served the Air Corps as its first and leading aeronautical engineer and technical expert. The Army lost an exceptionally brilliant officer and the science of aeronautics, one of its most promising devotees."

4. Much speculation ensued as to the underlying cause of the tragedy. Wilbur Wright, in a letter from France to his sister, theorized that Orville had ordered his mechanics to put on the new propellers; and that if he had done it himself "he would have noticed the thing that made the trouble." Said Wilbur: "I cannot help thinking over and over again 'If I had been there, it would not have happened.'" A whisper went the rounds that Orville was unnerved because of his anger at having to take Selfridge as passenger, and this was even recognized by a reverent biographer of the Wrights, if only to negate it: "That his mind was adversely affected and made inattentive by having as companion a man lately connected with a group that sought to rival the invention of the airplane, is a conjecture with scant support." The same author, in editing some of the Wright letters, made a different comment: "Though Orville had his reasons for not fully approving

of Selfridge, probably he never was so eager to have the machine behave well—to demonstrate to a possible infringer the futility of trying to equal it."

5. The Signal Corps log contains these entries:

"October 12, 1908—Mr. A. M. Herring and Mr. B. Clegg arrived. Aeroplane arrived, and started to put the aeroplane together.

"October 13, 1908—Explained parts of machine to Board at 4 p.m. to 7 p.m., and packed machine for shipment and left at 10:30 p.m."

CHAPTER 10.   SILVER DART

1. The Aero Club's basic rollcall consisted of sportsmen-hobbyists who were oriented toward ballooning. The New York *Herald* estimated that an aggregate wealth of $400,000,000 was represented in its membership. A younger, more venturesome clique, dissatisfied with the emphasis on balloons, spun off into the Aeronautic Society to experiment with heavier-than-air craft. Among these were Gutzon Borglum, the sculptor, and Sir Hiram Maxim, the inventor. The name was changed to Aeronautical Society on May 7, 1910. Some member recorded: "It was the first aeronautical body formed to do things, as well as talk things." (This was not precisely correct. What about the Aerial Experiment Association?)

2. Augustus Moore Herring was perhaps the most baffling figure in early American aeronautics. Chanute became disillusioned with him and the Wrights quickly sized him up; and yet many prominent and intelligent people held him in good regard and the U. S. Army awarded him a contract. He was commonly supposed to have built an airplane of great potentiality, but nobody could be found who had ever actually seen it. Herring was born in Georgia in 1867 and attended Stevens Institute of Technology in Hoboken, New Jersey, where he took engineering courses. When he submitted a thesis on "The Flying Machine as an Engineering Problem," it was rejected by the faculty, and he left without graduating. He copied Lilienthal's gliders, worked with Langley and Chanute, and applied for a patent in 1896 on a biplane with wheeled chassis, horizontal and vertical rudder with flexible controls, special curvature of wings—but no trace of ailerons. Though the Patent Office found nearly twenty fresh claims, it refused his application in 1898, the examiner saying: ". . . no power driven aeroplane has yet been raised into the air with the aeronaut or kept its course wholly detached from the earth for such considerable time as to constitute proof of practical usefulness."

Herring wrote articles for newspapers, magazines, and scientific journals. His wife was a Freeport, Long Island, girl, and he made his home there. A Supreme Court Justice was to say, in writing a decision, that Herring had become "well known to many of the foremost investigators of such subjects and seemingly bore among them a good reputation both personally and as a scientific investigator." The Aero Club of America elected him one of its earliest members and he was a frequenter of its headquarters in New York.

3. The village of Baddeck continues to revere the memory of the *Silver Dart* and the Aerial Experiment Association. Its proudest attraction is the superb Alexander Graham Bell Museum, dedicated in 1956 and maintained by the Canadian Government. The unusual architecture took its geometric theme from Bell's tetrahedral kites. Its exhibits, donated by Bell descendants, are much more concerned with his "aerodrome" and later hydrofoil experiments than with the telephone. The name of Glenn H. Curtiss stands second to Bell's on the bronze plaque listing the A.E.A. members just inside the entrance foyer. In an open-air shrine, off to the rear of the Museum building, a metallic model of the *Silver Dart* tops a pillar of masonry. By their wish, both Dr. Bell and Mabel Bell lie buried on the summit of their "mountain beautiful," with a glacial boulder for their monument.

4. Cortlandt Field Bishop, second president of the Aero Club of America, held a considerable reputation as a patron of the arts and of the racing sports. His father had amassed a fortune of $20,000,000 chiefly in real estate, and was a collector of art objects and antiques. The family owned a 700-acre summer estate, "Ananda," valued at $1,000,000, in the exclusive village of Lenox, Massachusetts. As a youth, Bishop brought the first horseless carriage into the Berkshires, a gasoline-propelled tricycle, with which he shattered the hallowed calm of Lenox, whose residents dubbed it "the holy terror." The village council passed an anti-automobile ordinance directed solely at Bishop, limiting the speed of such a vehicle to six miles an hour and requiring it to be driven with one wheel in the gutter. Since that time he had become interested in aeronautics and made several balloon ascents with the Aero Club of France. One news writer designated him "Man of the Hour" for bringing about the Herring-Curtiss combination.

5. James Deering was heir to the International Harvester fortune, and, like Bishop, spent much of his time in France.

CHAPTER 11.   GOLD BUG; ALIAS GOLDEN FLIER

1. Charles F. Willard, the Aeronautic Society member who first learned to fly the *Curtiss No. 1* and took it on exhibition tour as the *Golden Flier*, long resented the persistence of the *Gold Bug* name in flying literature. When Louis S. Casey, curator of aircraft for the National Air and Space Museum, visited Mr. Willard in California, he listened to his protest, decided

that Willard surely ought to know, and prepared a paper on "The Plane that Never Was—The *Gold Bug.*" Indirectly as a result of that, the British writer, Charles H. Gibbs-Smith, put an addendum into the latest revised edition of his authoritative book, *The Aeroplane,* saying:

"It has now been established that the familiar name of *Gold Bug* . . . was never used by Curtiss or his contemporaries; it must therefore be abandoned by historians. It received its subsequent currency from an inaccurate magazine article; there never was an aeroplane named the *Gold Bug* . . . I am indebted to the authorities of the National Air and Space Museum at Washington, D.C., for this information."

Willard was absolutely correct in stating that the plane he flew was named the *Golden Flier,* but wrong in maintaining that it never had been, at least informally, known as the *Gold Bug.* The files of the Hammondsport *Herald* for the spring and summer of 1909 are proof enough, but there is additional documented evidence. The transcript of courtroom testimony in the suit which Herring some years later brought against Curtiss, the Curtiss Aeroplane & Motor Corporation, and others, contains many repetitions of the *Gold Bug* name. It recurs on the tongues of witnesses, attorneys, and even the presiding judge. Among witnesses who spoke of the *Gold Bug* were Glenn H. Curtiss and Augustus M. Herring. In some instances, attorneys asked witnesses outright (specifically Herring and Curtiss) whether the *Gold Bug* and the Aeronautic Society machine were one and the same airplane. Invariably, they testified that *Gold Bug* was another name for the machine.

2. Dr. Bell was advancing money to Baldwin and McCurdy for the building of two airplanes at his Kite House, in the hope of obtaining orders from the Canadian government. The machines, along lines somewhat similar to the *Silver Dart,* were named the *Baddeck Number 1* and *Baddeck Number 2.* The partners planned a factory at Baddeck.

3. The *Silver Dart* met her fate at Petawawa in August 1909, leaving the *June Bug* the only one of the A.E.A. "dromes" which did not end in a smashup. McCurdy and Baldwin were conducting two-man flights with the *Dart* at the military grounds beside the Ottawa River, sitting tandem. The terrain was unfavorable for flying, with rolling ridges. McCurdy was pilot for a series of these hops in the light of early dawn. In the fourth flight, McCurdy was blinded by the rising sun direct in his eyes and misjudged his landing on the flat top of a ridge. The front wheel struck the edge of the knoll and the *Dart* flipped and crumpled. McCurdy and Baldwin untangled themselves from each other and the wreckage, with only minor injuries. In then forbidding any passenger work with the *Baddeck Number 1,* Bell repeated his earlier admonition: "Remember Selfridge!"

CHAPTER 12.   GLORY AT RHEIMS

1. This may have been Quentin Roosevelt's introduction to aviation. He
grew up to be one of the earliest U. S. Air Service pilots in overseas action in
World War I, and was killed flying over the trenches. To memorialize him, the
Hempstead Plains Aviation Field at Mineola was renamed Roosevelt Field; it
was next-door neighbor to Curtiss Field (owned by the Curtiss company),
and won great renown during the transatlantic flying era of the latter '20s.

CHAPTER 13.   FUMBLE AT GOVERNORS ISLAND

1. Long after his death, there is a growing body of belief that Dr. Frederick Cook may have been the victim of one of history's grave miscarriages of
justice. Disturbing evidence adduced in two books of recent years (*The Case
for Doctor Cook* and *The Big Nail*) suggests that he actually did reach the
Pole, or at least got closer to it than Peary did. By his own account, after he
and his Eskimos had spent two days at or near the Pole while he checked
bearings, they began the return march, but progress was slow because of
opening leads. He set the course a trifle westward to compensate for easterly
drift of the icepack. Instead of making the point from which they started,
where they had cached supplies, they hit a small, barren island 50 miles west
of Axel Heiberg Land. By that time, they had eaten nearly all their dogs.
In a gamble to reach Greenland via Jones Sound, Cook freed the remaining
dogs and set out in a canvas boat for a daring 800-mile voyage. Delayed by
storms, he and the two Eskimos got only halfway to their goal by September,
were forced to winter in a cave on Cape Sparbo, North Devon Island, sub-
sisting on musk oxen which they trapped in a rope snare. When the sun
reappeared, they resumed the trek to Annoatok, harnessing themselves to the
sledge, and arrived there 14 months after leaving. It was "a remarkable feat
of human survival," if nothing else.

Denmark in general supported Cook's claim while the Peary Arctic Club
blasted him in America with all its propaganda resources, spearheaded by the
New York *Times* and the National Geographic Society. He became an object
of ridicule and distrust, and took to lecturing in an effort to vindicate himself
and earn a living. The Geographic Society awarded Peary the verdict, but
many questions have dangled ever since. (By coincidence, Alexander Graham
Bell was one of the founders of the National Geographic Society.)

2. Van Rensselaer Island was the site of Fort Nassau, the fur trading
post established by the Dutch in 1614. Today it is occupied by the Port of
Albany, and no longer an island.

3. A canard which was dignified by inclusion in a prior biography said that Jerome Fanciulli, whom Curtiss "had engaged to serve as an intermediary between himself and the press," put out an announcement that Curtiss had made a flight around the Statue of Liberty at 4 o'clock in the morning (in the dark!) and then hastily packed for St. Louis. "The newspapermen were furious," wrote the author, "and felt that whether the flight had actually been made or not, Curtiss had treated them very badly." No such story appeared in any New York paper examined during the present research. Moreover, Fanciulli was working for the Associated Press, not for Curtiss, and was well regarded as an accurate reporter. It was three weeks before he signed the contract at Hammondsport.

CHAPTER 14. WESTERING WINGS

1. In future court testimony, Herring told a radically different version of this exchange: that he interrupted to say that, if Curtiss had to be paid extra compensation, he (Herring) would "undertake to do the flying and demonstrating for the company without such compensation"; that Wheeler then turned to him and said: "We will give you the same privileges." Herring claimed to have replied: "I don't want any privileges that are an imposition on the rights of the stockholders."

2. Pfitzner, aged thirty-five, met a tragic end. He accepted a job in April 1910, with the Burgess Company at Marblehead, Massachusetts, as assistant engineer. He had several mishaps trying to fly Burgess-Herring machines at Plum Island. That July he went out rowing alone in a skiff on Marblehead Harbor. The skiff was later retrieved, empty save for Pfitzner's coat and hat, a revolver, and a note. Though his body was not found, he was believed to have been a suicide. Bertha Mott was reported to have been "broken-hearted."

3. When interviewed during research for this book, Jerome Fanciulli failed to remember the episode of Curtiss asking him to stop at Dayton; consequently he could shed no light on why he did not do so. Though well past eighty, Fanciulli was a keen-minded and active businessman (operating a truck sales agency) in Washington, D.C. The conversation took place at the National Press Club, of which he was the last survivor of the founding group.

CHAPTER 15. HERRING NON GRATA

1. Herring first applied for a patent in 1896 while working on gliders with Chanute. His drawings showed superposed wings, wheeled chassis, horizontal

and vertical rudder with flexible controls, two propellers of opposite pitches, and curvature of the wings (no ailerons). The Patent Office identified nearly twenty fresh claims in the application, but rejected it in 1898 with the opinion: "So far as the examiner is aware, no power driven aeroplane has yet been raised into the air with the aeronaut or kept its course wholly detached from the earth for such considerable time as to constitute proof of practical usefulness."

After that, Herring did no more about a patent until 1909 when he refiled that application. The Patent Office then found his drawing "too diagrammatic." New drawings were sent, and the Patent Office said "the lines are rough and blurred and the paper is poor," and demanded another set. Several of his claims were rejected out of hand, but the rest were "probably allowable." In 1910, the application was rejected altogether, the Commissioner of Patents pointing out that, for longer than three years, the "operativeness of heavier than air machines had been demonstrated"; and declaring Herring "guilty of laches in not moving earlier." As late as 1924, Herring filed a petition for revival of that application and it was denied.

2. For the *Gold Bug*, the Aeronautic Society gave Curtis a down payment of $500 on an agreed price of $5000. When the machine was partly completed, the Herring-Curtiss Company stepped in and technically finished it. For some unexplained reason, perhaps because he had used the plane for the trophy flight before turning it over to the society, he accepted $4000 for the balance of payment, plus $150 for repairs. When he returned from France, he credited $3000 of the payment to the company, retaining $1650 for himself as recompense for the work he had done on it prior to the formation of the company and for making the demonstration flights and giving instruction.

3. The initial Wright injunction was dissolved, on appeal, in June 1910, thus releasing the $10,000 bond.

CHAPTER 16.   RETURN TO THE RIVER

1. Camelot was a temporary and artificial name for the place where Curtiss made his Poughkeepsie landing. One who goes seeking it now will be disappointed. The locality has reverted to its more venerable name of Barnegat. The well-documented story is that a ferry ran between the village of Milton on the west shore and a dock maintained by the Gill family on the east bank. People called the eastern terminal Milton Ferry, and the New York Central depot used that name. Later the West Shore Railroad was built, passing through Milton, and confusion arose in the timetables as between

Milton and Milton Ferry. The simple solution to this, decreed the railroad directors in 1886, was to coin a fresh name for Milton Ferry. Chauncey M. Depew, then president of the railroad, settled it. He arrived at a board meeting direct from a dinner party at which Tennyson's *Idylls of the King*, just published for the first time in completed form, had been the topic of animated conversation; guests had debated whether King Arthur's Court and his castle of Camelot ever really existed. First item on the agenda of the executive board was the renaming of the Milton Ferry station. Depew leaned back in his chair, clasped hands behind his head, and opined: "I guess, gentlemen, we'll call it Camelot."

In modern time, "progress" wiped out the romantic name as easily as Chauncey Depew conferred it. Tough limestone underlay the place by the riverside. A trap-rock company acquired the land, obliterated the hamlet and depot, and opened a quarry. Since then, the field where Curtiss landed has been preempted by a sprawling plant of the International Business Machines Corporation.

2. William Isham was the father of a fairly well-known artist, Samuel Isham. Not long after the Curtiss flight, the Isham heirs donated the estate and its unique hill to the city of New York for a public park, to be administered in connection with nearby Inwood Park. The mansion was subsequently removed, and today Isham Park serves as a green oasis for a densely populated Bronx neighborhood.

CHAPTER 17. THE EXHIBITIONISTS

1. Brookins set a world altitude record of 6175 feet at Atlantic City, and was dubbed "King of the High Flyers." Evidently Curtiss was bothered by the pre-eminence of Wright planes in altitude work.

2. The Curtiss Exhibition Company was incorporated for a term of three years, and Fanciulli's connection with it ended in November 1912, by resignation. Although the cream of the exhibition business had been skimmed by then, the company continued operating for some time, with headquarters in Hammondsport. Show flying having become more commonplace, rates were drastically reduced. A contract form bearing the date 1913 calls for payment of $600 for one day's flights, $900 for two days' flights, $1200 for three, and $1500 for four. The company agreed to provide at least 30 minutes of flying each day, weather permitting. The "party of the first part" covenanted to provide a suitable field, properly policed, and a NIGHT WATCHMAN (this requirement capitalized) as well as a shed for storage of the plane.

3. Dorothea Hildreth later married, bore children, and became a grand-mother. As Mrs. Frederick A. Russell, a gracious lady in her seventies, she was residing in Connecticut at the time this book was in preparation. She readily cooperated in the research by narrating the facts of the accident as she remembered them, and supplying snapshots. She testified that she and Ruth had not been personally acquainted with Beachey, but were looking forward to meeting him at the dinner that evening.

CHAPTER 18.   WATER FLYING

1. The quotation is from *History of United States Naval Aviation*, by Captain Archibald D. Turnbull, USNR, and Lieutenant Commander Clifford L. Lord, USNR.

2. Eugene Ely was another exhibition pilot who paid the supreme penalty for stunting. At the Georgia State Fair in Macon, in October 1911, he misjudged his distance in a low-altitude "dip" and ploughed into the ground.

3. Curtiss did not escape contention over his seaplane patent. On January 26, 1911 (by coincidence, the day Curtiss first got his hydro-aeroplane off water at North Island), Albert S. Janin, a Staten Island cabinetmaker, filed application for a patent on "a land, water and air machine." In reality, Janin had produced no such aircraft, but he submitted drawings of a device consisting of small side floats to keep the wings of a water-plane on an even keel in takeoff. He had failed to raise money with which to construct a machine to test the device, and no patent was granted him.

In 1914, Thomas A. Hill, the New York attorney who had represented the Aeronautic Society, took up Janin's claims. The Examiners of Interference of the Patent Office ruled against Janin, affirming Curtiss's priority, and saying: "While he [Curtiss] was thus engaged, Janin was sleeping on his rights, from which slumber he did not wake until after the achievements of Curtiss had been widely publicized." Hill appealed to the Board of Examiners of the Patent Office, which reversed the decision, holding that Janin had been too poor to do anything with his idea. Hill publicly exulted that this ruling would make Janin a rich man, with war orders piling up; and that the Curtiss company would have to pay royalties to him on every water-plane sold.

Curtiss issued a reply to Hill's boast: "Mr. Janin and his attorney are quite premature in announcing the award of invention of the hydroplane to Mr. Janin. The interference with Mr. Janin involves one claim. The claim involves the use of small side floats which are in use when the machine operates on the surface of the water as a hydroplane. It does not involve the features which made the hydroaeroplane a successful flying machine, or the features of the flying boat." Rightly, he pointed out that this was only a preliminary decision in a Patent Office tribunal, and that the case would be referred to the federal courts.

The patent case of the Curtiss company and Glenn H. Curtiss against Albert S. Janin and the Janin Company, Inc., was decided in favor of Curtiss by the U. S. District Court of Appeals, 2nd District, on December 15, 1921. The judges ruled that Janin's claim had been purely theoretical, existing only on paper; that "the mere description did not constitute a reduction to practice." They held that Curtiss had reduced the theory to practice, entitling him to the broad patent.

4. Both the time and the motive of Henry Ford's trip to Hammondsport have been fuzzy in the prior literature. An alternate version is that he came to investigate the possibility of using Curtiss airplane engines in his Model T automobiles; this seems highly improbable, as Ford took pride in his own motors, and the primary aim of the Model T was economy. A high-powered aero engine would have been preposterous in a car designed for the common man. The visit is authenticated by a photograph showing Curtiss and Ford standing beside an early flying boat with Keuka Lake in the background.

CHAPTER 19.   FEUD WITH THE WRIGHTS

1. The solace which Wright found in the companionship and sympathy of his sister was shattered in 1926 when Katharine deserted him in favor of matrimony. In a late-blooming romance, she married a friend from her student days at Oberlin College, an editor of a Kansas City newspaper. A clue to how this affected her brother is found in a letter she wrote announcing her marriage: "There has been such an upheaval in our world— Orville's and mine." Katharine did not have long to enjoy her wedded happiness: she died in 1929. Orville lived on until 1948.

2. The charter members of the Manufacturers Aircraft Association were: Aeromarine Plane and Motor Company, the Burgess Company, Curtiss Aeroplane and Motor Corporation, L.W.F. Engineering Company, Standard Aircraft Corporation, Sturtevant Aeroplane Company, Thomas-Morse Aircraft Corporation, and Wright-Martin Aircraft Corporation. A few months later the Dayton Wright Airplane Company became a member. Wright-Martin was a consolidation with Glenn F. Martin to manufacture Hispano-Suiza motors for war use.

CHAPTER 20.   ATLANTIC FANTASY

1. The prospective flight stirred the muse in others besides Professor Zahm. For example, *Leslie's Illustrated Weekly* printed a poem, *To the America,* by Minna Irving:

Bold voyager whose planes are bent
Along the boundless sky,
From continent to continent
Above the deep to fly,
The first adventurous Viking ships
That fared to seas unknown
Together made their daring trips,
But thou must go alone.

Between the broad Atlantic's foam
And virgin spaces vast
Where even sea-birds fear to roam,
Behold! thy fate is cast.
America! may wind and wave
Thy silken pinions spare.
God speed thee o'er the ocean, brave
Columbus of the air!

2. J. Lansing Callan went to Italy as Curtiss sales representative for war orders. Presently he cabled Curtiss: CAN I ACCEPT POSITION INSTRUCTOR ITALIAN NAVY, FOUR MONTHS, AFTER BUSINESS FINISHED? MORE CURTISS AVIATORS HERE MEANS MORE BUSINESS. The answer came: YOUR ACCEPTANCE INSTRUCTOR ITALIAN NAVY AGREEABLE US. This experience led to his being Commander of U. S. Naval air forces in Italy during World War I. Advanced in rank to rear admiral in the Naval Reserve, he was naval attaché to the U. S. Embassy in Rome when Italy declared war on the United States in World War II; along with the Embassy staff, he was held as a prisoner of war for a time. After that, he was naval aide to King Peter of Yugoslavia, and naval attaché to the seven European governments-in-exile in London.

3. Rodman Wanamaker finally attained his goal of sponsoring a transatlantic flight in 1927, when he financed Commander Richard E. Byrd. The third *America,* which flew to France, was a Fokker tri-motor. Painted large above its hangar door at Roosevelt Field were the words: AMERICA TRANS-OCEANIC COMPANY.

CHAPTER 21. FLYING THE *LANGLEY*

1. Marvin W. McFarland, who edited *The Papers of Wilbur and Orville Wright*, postulates the existence of a group which he loosely designates as "the friends of Langley." Among its more prominent members he lists Dr. Charles D. Walcott, Dr. Alexander Graham Bell, and General Adolphus Washington Greely, retired Chief Signal Officer of the Army. "On the periphery of this group," he writes in a footnote, "was Albert F. Zahm, professor of mechanics at the Catholic University of America and later 'expert' witness for Curtiss in the patent suits." In the Wright-slanted literature, Zahm is frequently referred to as the "paid witness" of Curtiss. In this connection, it is only fair to point out that it was common practice to pay witnesses in patent suits a per diem stipend, usually $50 or $60. This was an accepted part of the inevitable high expense of a patent litigation. The witness fees added heavily to the suit of Selden vs. Ford. The Wrights also paid witnesses in their suit against Curtiss.

2. Elwood Doherty was a son of the police commissioner of Buffalo. His nickname, Gink, derived from the fact that his hair was curly, so that schoolmates had called him "Kink"; in time, the sobriquet was modified to Gink. He married Gladys Champlin, whose father was president of the Pleasant Valley winery. For a time during World War I, he joined J. Lansing Callan in Italy as an instructor of pilots for the Italian Navy.

CHAPTER 22. A FORTUNE OF WAR

1. The Jenny went through a series of ten or more modifications. The basic "J" tractor model of B. D. Thomas was first flown as a single-float seaplane from Keuka Lake, the field being too small. The overhang of the top wing, a characteristic of all future Jennies, was because of that original float. The U. S. Army ordered ten JN-2s in 1915; these had the typical Curtiss shoulder-yoke aileron control. A large-scale order of ninety-four JN-4s came from the Army in 1916, with wheel control, for use in General John J. Pershing's campaign in Mexico. America's entry into World War I standardized the advanced model, JN-4-H, which thrust its yellow wings across the sky at every training field in the United States. The Jenny had a remarkable double career: first as a war-time training plane, then as a barnstorming favorite. It was used to initiate the government airmail service in 1918.

2. Canada, as before noted, had not recognized the validity of the Wright patents. In order not to impede England's war effort, Orville Wright

made a blanket royalty settlement with the British government in which he released his patent rights to that nation.

3. In the entrance lobby of the Garden City plant, Curtiss enshrined on a pedestal the 8-cylindered motorcycle on which he had become "fastest man in the world" back in 1907. A tablet alongside told its story.

CHAPTER 23.   ATLANTIC REALITY

1. The later careers of some of these NC-boat crew members were noteworthy in naval aviation. In World War II, Admiral John H. Towers was commander of Air Force, Pacific Fleet; while Admiral Marc A. Mitscher earned the title, "Admiral of the Marianas," with the exploits of his Task Force 58. As for Admiral P. N. L. Bellinger, at the time of the Japanese attack on Pearl Harbor he was commander of Patrol Wing 2 of the Pacific Fleet and also commanded the Ford Island facilities. It was Bellinger who broadcast from Ford Island, three minutes after the first bomb fell, the famous message: AIR RAID, PEARL HARBOR—THIS IS NO DRILL! Somewhat later, Admiral Husband E. Kimmel, commander of Pacific Fleet, repeated his words to Washington and all ships at sea. Bellinger later commanded Air Force, Atlantic Fleet.

Incidentally, one of the vessels damaged in the Pearl Harbor attack was the seaplane tender, *Curtiss*. Named in honor of Glenn H. Curtiss, it had been christened at its launching in 1940 by his widow, who had remarried after his death and was then Mrs. H. Sayre Wheeler. A son of Monroe Wheeler, Sayre Wheeler had been placed by Curtiss in one of his Florida enterprises. The U.S.S. *Curtiss* was afterward repaired from its bombing damage and returned to Pacific duty.

2. The NC-4 was subsequently stored away and almost forgotten at the Norfolk Navy Yard. Through the efforts of Paul Garber, as curator of the National Air Museum, it was located and transferred to the custody of the Smithsonian Institution after World War II. Lacking the room in which to exhibit so large an object, the Air Museum kept it under canvas in a warehouse of its preservation and restoration branch at Silver Spring, Maryland. In 1969, the 50th anniversary year of the transatlantic flight, the National Air and Space Museum (as it now is known) restored and displayed it in the open air of the Washington Mall. As cold weather came on, it was again dismantled and returned to the warehouse. It is due for a position of honor in the contemplated new building of the National Air and Space Museum.

CHAPTER 24. FLORIDA YEARS

1. The Opa-locka City Hall was intended by the architect to suggest the palace of the Emperor in the Arabian Nights tale of the talking bird. The Opa-locka Hotel was the setting of Aladdin and his Magic Lamp. The city hall still serves its municipal purpose today. The town's population was just over 300 by 1930, and during the depression years block after block of beautifully landscaped streets lay without a house on them. In World War II the Navy expanded the Opa-locka flying field into the Miami Naval Air Station. Not until 1947 did Curtiss's vision of Opa-locka as a center for industrial development begin to materialize.

2. After Curtiss's death, one of his widow's first moves was to get the Herring case off her back with an out-of-court settlement. While the amount of that settlement was never made public, Glenn Curtiss Jr., understood it to have been in the neighborhood of $500,000. According to him, Harry Genung, who continued to manage financial affairs for his mother, called together the Herring heirs and their co-plaintiffs in the suit, and told them, in effect: "Now look. We have X number of dollars earmarked with which to continue fighting this case, and we are prepared to spend it to the last dime. How about accepting it right now as a settlement in full, instead of piling up further legal costs for both sides?" The heirs agreed to the compromise.

3. The Kitty Hawk airplane required major restoration work, not only by reason of its age but because it had suffered damage in the Dayton flood of 1913. Griffith Brewer was on hand at the British Science Museum to help assemble it when it finally arrived.

4. Grover Loening was president of the Loening Aeronautical Engineering Corporation and had designed the Loening Air Yachts, which had a short career of carrying commuters between New York and Newport, Rhode Island. He was a strong Wright partisan, and wrote that he was "always watchful and suspicious of everything Curtiss did"; while having "a high appreciation of his qualities as a flyer and promoter, far outweighing, I have always felt, his talents as an engineer or scientist." It was Loening's belief that Curtiss was not even his own designer, "excepting in a vague way"; and he cited for evidence of this the time he found him standing beside one of his new planes, asked him the approximate area of the tail surface, and Curtiss replied: "Oh, I don't know, but if it isn't right, the boys will fix it."

5. This letter has not been found among the Wright papers, and there is no organized collection of Curtiss papers. The existence of such a letter

rests upon the word of the late Glenn H. Curtiss, Jr., who declared to this author that he often heard his father tell of it.

6. The *Kitty Hawk* remained in England almost exactly twenty years, and then came to the Smithsonian Institution after all, where today it is suspended just inside the main entrance of the National Air and Space Museum.

As secretary of the Smithsonian, Dr. Charles G. Abbot could not rest while Orville Wright maintained his grudge and the original Kitty Hawk machine was in a foreign land. In 1937, he sent Wright another feeler: "I desire not to die before clearing our situation if possible." There was no reaction from Dayton. Dr. Abbot enlisted the efforts of Colonel Charles A. Lindbergh as a mediator, again to no avail.

When Great Britain went to war in 1939, facing the certainty of bombing by the Luftwaffe, the *Kitty Hawk* was stored for safety in a sub-terranean shelter in the west of England, with many other museum and art treasures.

Abbot finally reopened a channel of communication with Wright in 1940, offering to publish a fresh statement of the case if Orville would specify in writing precisely what were his terms for patching up the quarrel. Wright demanded nothing less than a public apology with inclusion of these words in the statement: "I sincerely regret that the Institution employed to make the tests of 1914 Glenn H. Curtiss, who had just been adjudged an infringer of the Wright patent by the U. S. Court." The renewed negotiation almost foundered on this obstacle, as Abbot replied:

"You, no doubt, see bad motives where I do not . . . Apparently our present stumbling block is your insistence on a particular form of mention of the Wright-Curtiss litigation. To me this litigation appears wholly ex-traneous to all issues between the Smithsonian and the Wrights, except that it seems an indelicacy to have employed Curtiss as the Institution's agent when a successful flight of the Langley machine would have meant so much to the Wrights. For me now to use your language about the court decision pronouncing Curtiss an infringer of your patent in this important proposed paper would seem to me to be setting up the Smithsonian Institution as an historical authority pronouncing the last word about a litigation in which it has no concern, whereas it is my understanding that further litigation was begun but was discontinued under an agreement between the parties."

A compromise was reached when Abbot bent the knee to this extent: "I sincerely regret that the Institution employed to make the tests of 1914 an agent who had been an unsuccessful defendant in patent litigation brought against him by the Wrights . . . I sincerely regret that statements were repeatedly made by officers of the Institution that the Langley machine was flown in 1914 with 'certain changes of the machine necessary to use pontoons,' without mentioning the other changes included in Dr. Wright's list."

Abbot acceded to Wright's insistence on verbatim publication of the lengthy enumeration of all the changes which had been made in the *Langley* during its stay in Hammondsport, as he and Brewer had worked them out in their collaboration at Dayton. In doing so, however, he attributed this to Orville Wright, not to the Smithsonian itself. (Some people around the Smithsonian referred to it as a "laundry list.")

When Dr. Abbot's new pamphlet was published in 1942, it mollified Orville Wright, and shortly afterward he wrote to the director of the British Science Museum: "I have decided to have the Kitty Hawk returned to America when transport hazards are less than at present." He also made a change in his will to that effect. Abbot's paper was widely interpreted as an "apology" by the Smithsonian Institution. Many years later, Dr. Abbot privately told the present author that he did not intend it as an apology, but that: "I wanted to do anything within reason to settle the controversy. I didn't want Orville Wright to die without making peace between him and the Smithsonian."

After the war, the British Science Museum made a precise replica of the machine to keep for itself. The *Kitty Hawk* was finally returned to America in the fall of 1948 aboard a U. S. Navy escort carrier, and ensconced in the position of honor at the Smithsonian with a gala ceremony on December 17, the 45th anniversary of its original flights. Orville Wright had died of a heart attack the previous January.

7. Glenn Curtiss, Jr., afterward showed some talent as an automobile designer. During the 1960s he acquired the Volkswagen agency for the Southeastern United States, later selling it at good profit. An exceedingly fleshy man for much of his adult life, he was said to have weighed somewhere near 300 pounds. By strenuous measures, he reduced this avoirdupois by at least half. The present writer saw him as a slim, almost emaciated person, when he was age 56. He died of cancer in 1969.

CHAPTER 25. KEUKA SUNSET

1. Hundreds of messages of condolence to Mrs. Lena Curtiss inundated the small Hammondsport telegraph office. Charles and Anne Lindbergh wired "deepest sympathy." Juan T. Trippe, president of Pan American Airways, said: "He, more than any other man, blazed the trail of aircraft development in the years between the first flight of the Wright brothers and the World War."

Rear Admiral Richard E. Byrd was recently back from flying over the South Pole. He telegraphed: "My deepest sympathy in which all members of our expedition join. He was my friend and I know what a great loss you have suffered. Every aviator in the country grieves with you."

A cablegram from France was signed by Louis Blériot. Expressions of condolence came from Rear Admiral William A. Moffett, chief of the Naval Bureau of Aeronautics; from Jack Towers, Bud Mars, Beckwith Havens, Lansing Callan, Hugh Robinson, Roland Rohlfs. Even W. J. Maloney, principal attorney for the late Augustus M. Herring and now for the Herring heirs, wired: "Please permit me to extend my sincere sympathy." The signature of Orville Wright was missing among the sheaf of telegrams.

Mayor C. H. Reeder of Miami said: "This is the greatest loss the state has sustained. He was so modest and retiring that few people actually knew what he had done for the state." The Miami City Commission adopted a resolution of "appreciation and gratitude to Glenn H. Curtiss, the man, and benefactor of this community"; voting to send Mayor Reeder as the city's emissary to the funeral.

Governor Doyle E. Carlton of Florida added his encomium: "As a citizen and developer of Florida he was one of the greatest benefactors. I have met no man more optimistic over the future of Florida. He had invested millions here, and his heart as well as his money was in Florida."

From Washington, Captain Washington Irving Chambers voiced his feelings in a letter to Mrs. Curtiss:

"I understand better than any other person in the Navy how much we owe to him for progress in naval aviation through his generous and kindly cooperation with us in the pioneer development of that which is destined to be one of the greatest factors in national defense and future peace.

"But it was his personal characteristics, his personality and understanding more than his remarkable foresight and skill, that endeared him to me in a bond of friendship that is one of the most cherished memories of my life."

In England, the London *Times* commented: "He was probably the best known of the remaining American pioneers, and he had kept his place in the front of the aircraft industry to the end . . . The exploit which earned him the highest admiration was his flight in the Langley 'aerodrome' . . . which critics believed was incapable of flight."

2. A summation of Curtiss's contributions to aviation has been found among the family papers, referring to him as "The Edison of the Aeronautic World." The document is unsigned, and may have been prepared for legalistic use or company purposes; but its points seem tenable enough for inclusion here. The opening premise is that Glenn H. Curtiss was in reality one of the most prolific of inventors, with at least 500 inventions to his credit, any one of which may have been patentable. The main difference between him and most other inventors, the paper goes on to say, was that he knew little of patents and took almost no interest in them, until the Wright suit compelled

him to learn something of patent law. He was wholly absorbed in his work and "generous to a fault with his ideas as well as his purse." Even then, he patented only what he conceived to be his few most significant developments. He never made a move toward patenting any of his motorcycle innovations, obviously in a class by themselves.

For a direct quotation: "He permitted anyone who willed to use the principles used in the inventions he had made, and the aeronautical industry shall forever be in debt to him for his magnanimity. Scores of experimenters and struggling investors would, during the infancy of the art, have been prevented from securing any foothold whatever had Mr. Curtiss insisted upon enforcing his rights. His value was proved by the universality of adoption of his principles."

The document lists as the "Big Five" of Curtiss inventions, the "backbone" of the early aeronautical industry: 1. The Curtiss airplane, as such. 2. The Curtiss motor. 3. The Curtiss control system. 4. The hydroplane, including the amphibian. 5. The flying boat.

The aileron itself, a joint development, was covered in the A.E.A. patent. Curtiss did obtain patents on the hydroplane, amphibian, and flying boat; on his shoulder-yoke control; and on his device for the training dual control.

Among specific examples of consequential but unpatented Curtiss inventions, which he allowed to enter the public domain, the paper cites: sectional wings, which could be "knocked down" for compact stowage; interplane engine mounting; improved wing dope; and the high-pressure, forced-feed lubricating system, along with efficient crank-case drainage, making possible motors of large size and high-speed operation.

CONCERNING SOURCES

First and foremost, the author would acknowledge the generous assistance of Glenn H. Curtiss, Jr., and express regret that he did not live long enough to peruse the result. While the son in no way tried to influence the interpretation of a single fact, he was deeply interested in seeing a biography which would do justice to his father. The doors of his memory were as open as those of his Coral Gables home. He placed at my complete disposal trunkfuls and cartons of family papers, letters, pictures, documents, and mementos, never before available to any writer. Day after day, he set aside a portion of his time to reminisce about his father, answering questions to the best of his knowledge; being too young, of course, to remember anything of the flying years. Incidentally, this author is happy to have had a hand in persuading him to will his collection to the National Air and Space Museum.

Intimate family memories were graciously supplied by Mrs. Dorothy Adams of Coconut Grove, Florida, the widow of G. Carl Adams; and her house-guest, Mrs. Florence Illig, a one-time Curtiss secretary. A meed of thanks is due Andrew H. Heermance of Miami Springs for his personal remembrances and his excellent services as a guide to the realty developments and airfields associated with Curtiss in the Miami area.

Hammondsport, New York, was of necessity a place of basic research and of "soaking up atmosphere." In that locality, the writer acknowledges favors from Otto P. Kohl, president and curator of the Glenn H. Curtiss Museum of Local History; from the Hammondsport Public Library; from Mrs. Laura Swarthout, Hammondsport village clerk; from Mrs. Geraldine Percy, registrar, village of Hammondsport; from Mrs. Blanche Kleckler, widow of Henry Kleckler; from Chilton Latham, editor of the *Steuben Courier & Advocate,* in Bath, New York, for access to one of the rare files of the Hammondsport *Herald;* from the same Mr. Latham, wearing his other hat as county clerk of Steuben County, for aid in ransacking the records of that office. For verbal recollections, special thanks are also extended to these individuals: Mrs. Elwood Doherty (the former Gladys Champlin); Miss Melanie Masson; Greyton H. Taylor, chairman of the board of the Pleasant Valley Wine Company; Alderman Gleason, of Dundee, New York; Captain and Mrs. J. T. Rogerson, of Dundee and Miami; Mr. and Mrs. Harrie Greene of Wayne, New York; William Allen of Rock Stream, New York. At the risk of overlooking some, the author acknowledges the aid of these other Hammondsporters: Richard G. Sherer; Walter S. Taylor, of the Bully Hill Wine Company; Charles Locke; Tony Doherty; F. M. Aulls; U. S. Arland; Mrs. J. Allan Shaw; and Devello Frank, retired district principal, Hammondsport Central School.

The major documentary research was done in Washington, D.C., particularly in these manuscript collections of the Library of Congress: the papers of Wilbur and Orville Wright; the papers of Octave Chanute; the papers of Captain Washington Irving Chambers; and the papers of Rear Admiral J. Lansing Callan. Much important material was obtained from the National Air and Space Museum of the Smithsonian Institution, and the writer wishes especially to acknowledge the assistance of Louis S. Casey, curator of aircraft for that Museum. Invaluable aid was given by Mrs. Vera Cassilly, curator of the Bell Room at the National Geographic Society. For personal recollections, the writer thanks Dr. Charles G. Abbot, Hyattsville, Maryland, retired secretary of the Smithsonian; and Jerome S. Fanciulli, Bluemont, Virginia, original manager of the Curtiss Exhibition Company.

In Nova Scotia, Dr. Melville Bell Grosvenor extended the hospitality of the Beinn Bhreagh estate, along with delightful memories of his grandfather, Alexander Graham Bell. Mrs. Leonard Muller, a Bell granddaughter, was similarly helpful at the Kite House, remodeled as her summer home. Gratitude also goes to the Alexander Graham Bell Museum at Baddeck, Nova Scotia.

Other institutions whose facilities and collections provided thankworthy help were: the New York State Library, Albany, New York; the John M. Olin Research Library, Cornell University; the Miami Memorial Public Library; the Buffalo and Erie County Historical Society; the Buffalo Public Library.

The author is much beholden to Dr. Jerome S. Hunsaker of Cambridge, Massachusetts, and to the late Professor Theodore P. Wright, Ithaca, New York, for intimate memories of Glenn Curtiss, and especially of the NC-boat episode. Owen S. Billman, Mayfield, New York, a dedicated Curtiss hobbyist, proved a godsend with the loan of extensive taped interviews with Curtiss associates who are now among the missing. More than passing mention is due Mrs. Frederick B. Downing, Kinderhook, New York, sister of Lansing

Callan, for remembrances and access to Callan material not elsewhere available.

Further acknowledgments, no less appreciated for the summation, are tendered to: Mrs. Jessie R. deWitt, Rochester, New York; Mrs. Frederick A. Russell, New Haven, Connecticut; K. M. Molson, curator, air and space division, National Museum of Canada; Douglas Anderson, Elmira, New York; the late Beckwith Havens, New York City; Peter M. Bowers, Seattle, Washington; Ira Brundage, Hialeah, Florida; Charles B. Kirkham, Montgomery, New York; Paul Garber, former curator, National Air Museum; Ralph L. Hoag, superintendent, Rochester School for the Deaf; the Rev. Frank J. Mucci, secretary, Western New York Conference of the Methodist Church, Buffalo, New York.

BIBLIOGRAPHY

The Curtiss Aviation Book. Glenn H. Curtiss and Augustus Post. Stokes, 1912.

Sky Storming Yankee: The Life of Glenn Curtiss. Clara Studer. Stackpole, 1937.

Over Land and Sea. Robert Scharff and Walter S. Taylor. McKay, 1968.

Glenn Curtiss: Pioneer of Naval Aviation. Alden Hatch. Messner, 1942.

Flying Pioneers at Hammondsport, N.Y. Lyman J. Seely. Finger Lakes Association and Better Hammondsport Club, 1929.

Alexander Graham Bell. Catherine MacKenzie. Houghton Mifflin, 1928.

Make a Joyful Sound. Helen Elmira Waite. Macrae Smith, 1961.

The Chord of Steel. Thomas B. Costain. Doubleday, 1960.

Bell and Baldwin. J. H. Parkin. University of Toronto Press, 1964.

Knights of the Air. Lieutenant Lester J. Maitland. Doubleday, Doran, 1929.

Santos-Dumont. Peter Wykeham. Harcourt, Brace, 1962.

Flight Into History: The Wright Brothers and the Air Age. Elsbeth E. Freudenthal. University of Oklahoma Press, 1949.

The Wright Brothers. Fred C. Kelly. Harcourt, Brace, 1943.

The Wright Brothers: Fathers of Flight. John R. McMahon. Little, Brown, 1930.

Miracle at Kitty Hawk. Edited by Fred C. Kelly. Farrar, Straus & Young, 1951.

The Papers of Wilbur and Orville Wright. Marvin W. McFarland, Editor. McGraw-Hill, 1953.

The Scandalous Mr. Bennett. Richard O'Connor. Doubleday, 1962.

Northcliffe. Reginald Pound and Geoffrey Harmsworth. Praeger, 1960.

Northcliffe: An Intimate Biography. Hamilton Fyfe. Macmillan, 1930.

490   APPENDIX

The Business Biography of John Wanamaker. Joseph H. Appel. Macmillan, 1930.
Ford. Allan Nevins. Scribner's, 1954.
Monopoly on Wheels: Henry Ford and the Selden Automobile Patent. William Greenleaf. Wayne State University Press, 1961.
The Big Nail. Theon Wright. John Day Co., 1970.
The Case for Doctor Cook. Andrew A. Freeman. Coward-McCann,1961.
Adventures in the World of Science. Dr. Charles Greeley Abbot. Public Affairs Press, 1958.
The Aviation Business. Elsbeth E. Freudenthal. Vanguard, 1940.
The Aeroplane. Charles H. Gibbs-Smith. Her Majesty's Stationery Office, 1960.
United States Military Aircraft Since 1909. F. G. Swanborough. Putnam, 1963.
British Naval Aircraft Since 1912. Owen Thetford. Putnam, London, 1962.
Wings of War. Theodore MacFarlane Knappen. Putnam, 1920.
History of British Aviation: 1908–1914. R. Douglas Brett. The Aviation Book Club, London, 1929.
Fifty Years of Flying. Griffith Brewer. Air League of the British Empire.
The Flight Across the Atlantic. Curtiss Aeroplane and Motor Corporation, 1919.
Triumph. Hy Steirman and Glenn D. Kittler. Harper & Row, 1961.
But Not in Shame. John Toland. Random House, 1961.
The Silver Dart. H. Gordon Green. Brunswick Press, Ltd., 1959.
The Hudson-Fulton Celebration—1909. 4th Annual Report of the Hudson-Fulton Celebration Commission to the Legislature of the State of New York. 1910.
The Finger Lakes Region: Its Origin and Nature. O. D. von Engeln. Cornell University Press, 1961.
Slim Fingers Beckon. Arch Merrill. American Book-Stratford Press, 1951.
Aerial California. Kenneth M. Johnson. Dawson's Book Shop, Los Angeles, 1961.
Jackrabbits to Jets. Elretta Sudsbury. North Island Historical Committee, 1967.
Wings in the Sun: A History of Florida Aviation. William C. Lazarus. Tyn Cobb's Florida Press, 1951.
Hunting the Hard Way. Howard Hill. Wilcox & Follett Co. 1954.
Wild Adventure. Howard Hill. The Stackpole Co., 1954.
How Our Army Grew Wings. Colonel Charles deForest Chandler and Brigadier General Frank O. Lahm. The Ronald Press Co., 1943.
History of United States Naval Aviation. Captain Archibald D. Turnbull, USNR, and Lieutenant Commander Clifford L. Lord, USNR. Yale University Press, 1949.

Aircraft Year Book. Manufacturers Aircraft Association, Inc. 1919–20.

From the Wright Brothers to the Astronauts. Major General Benjamin D. Foulois; with Colonel C. V. Glines, USAF. McGraw-Hill, 1968.

Annual Report of the Board of Regents of the Smithsonian Institution. Government Printing Office. 1914–1915.

Miami, U.S.A. Helen Muir. Henry Holt, 1953.

Bulletins of the Aerial Experiment Association. Microfilm from the original file preserved by J. A. D. McCurdy and presented by him to the National Research Council, Ottawa.

History of Steuben County, New York. Professor W. W. Clayton. Lewis, Peck & Co., Philadelphia, 1879.

Landmarks of Steuben County, New York. Harlo Hakes (ed.). 1896.

Who's Who in Steuben. William N. Stewart. 1935.

Historical Gazetteer of Steuben County, N.Y. Millard F. Roberts (ed.). 1891.

Niagara County, New York. Edward T. Williams, J. H. Beers & Co., Chicago, 1921.

Dictionary of American Biography.

U. S. Circuit Court of Appeals Record.

Records, Steuben County (N.Y.) Surrogate's Court.

INDEX

Abbot, Charles G., 438–39, 480–81
Acosta, Bert, 426
Adams, Dorothy McDonald, 408–9, 440
Adams, G. Carl, 15, 309, 318, 325, 400–1, 408–9, 430, 440, 442, 443, 444
Adams, J. Charles, 11, 14
Adams, Lua Curtiss. See Curtiss, Mrs. Lua Andrews
A.E.A. Bulletin, 97, 116, 117, 126–29, 144–45, 155, 158, 183, 465–66; last issue of, 162
Aerial Experiment Association (A.E.A.), 66, 75–82ff., 119ff., 136–62, 240, 244–45, 260, 335, 339, 347, 355, 384, 462–64 (see also Bell, Alexander Graham; individual members by name); aerodromes (see Aerodromes; specific aircraft); charter of, 462–64; and patent litigation, 335, 339, 348–49, 354, 355, 356–57, 384, 401; and Scientific American Trophy, 168, 170; transfer of headquarters to Hammondsport, New York, 85ff.
Aeroboats, 349, 394ff., 411–23 (see

also Flying boats); and transatlantic flight, 363–80, 411–23
Aero Car, 426, 444, 449, 454
Aero Club, 37
Aero Club of Albany, 266
Aero Club of America, 37, 47–49, 56, 88, 89, 93–94, 106ff., 117, 129–30, 139–40, 149, 153, 155–57, 228–29, 235, 244, 252, 284, 285, 361, 468; and Albany–New York flight, 262, 266, 267, 280; and Belmont Park and Gordon Bennett Cup Race, 288, 289, 291–94; and Collier Trophy, 321, 330; Curtiss elected member of, 117; and death of Selfridge, 129–30; and Gordon Bennett Trophy, 184, 189, 197, 198; and Hudson-Fulton Celebration, 209, 211–12, 262, 266, 267, 280; issues first pilot's license to Curtiss, 320; and Langley plane, 385; and Scientific American Trophy, 103ff., 168, 171–78; and transatlantic flight, 366–67, 379, 380
Aero Club of California, 231
Aero Club of Cleveland, 288
Aero Club of France, 183–84, 198–99
Aero Club of Great Britain, 365, 367

Aero Club of San Diego, 309, 310, 311, 312
Aero Club of Washington, D.C., 347
Aero Corporation, and Belmont Park meet, 292–94
Aerodromes (aircraft), 1, 3, 68, 83ff., 90ff., 120ff., 132–33, 136ff., 140ff., 148, 152–53, 168, 176, 178, 240, 244–45. See also Kites; specific aircraft, developments, individuals
Aeronautical Annual, 146
Aeronautical Board, U. S. War Department, 120–35
Aeronautical Chamber of Commerce, 451
Aeronautical Society of New York, 139–40, 146, 149, 166–68, 228, 303, 333, 467; and Gold Bug (Golden Flier), 166–68, 169, 171, 172, 175, 177, 181, 190–203; and Hudson-Fulton Celebration, 208
Aeronautic Exhibition Company, 181
Aeronautics (magazine), 146, 191, 222, 333
Ailerons, 97–98, 114, 117, 124, 138, 141–42, 164, 168, 170–71, 172, 173, 189, 233–34, 252, 264, 398, 472, 482; and patent litigation, 339–41, 346–47, 348–49, 350, 356–62
Airmail, 268, 279, 280, 294, 301, 451
Air pockets, 234
Airships. See Balloons; Dirigibles
Airships, Inc. 429–30
Albany–New York (Hudson River) flight, 207–8, 209, 215–17, 262–80, 451–53
Alcock, John, 422
Aldan, Dr. P. L., 19, 376
Allen, General James, 82, 88, 120, 123, 139, 146, 180–81, 381–82
America (dirigible), 364
America (transatlantic flyer), 373–80, 387, 396, 403, 405, 412, 413, 417
American Aerodrome Company, 150–53, 155–56, 159, 163–64
American Bell Telephone Company, 73–74

America Transoceanic Company, 380
Amphibian planes, 264, 315–31. See also specific kinds, planes
Andres, F. M., 456
Andrews, Henry B., 5, 325
Andrews, William S., 453–54
Annex, The, 46, 86
Antoinette monoplanes, 178, 192, 198
Aquatic gliders, 428
Army, U. S., 51, 402, 406; Aeronautical Division, Signal Corps, 71, 75–76 (see also Signal Corps, U. S. Army); and aircraft development, 26, 29, 30, 63, 70–71, 73, 75ff., 88–90, 92, 100, 119–35, 234, 287–88; Board of Ordnance and Fortification, 26, 29, 30, 63, 80–90; Curtiss and activity for, 315, 331, 365–66, 397, 427–28; Curtiss and aviation training for, 296, 309, 311, 312, 313, 316–17, 331; Wright brothers and (see under Wright brothers)
Arnot, Matthias C., 60–61, 228
Arrows. See California Arrows
Associated Press, 30, 88, 100, 105, 218–19, 230
Association of Licensed Automobile Manufacturers (A.L.A.M.), 344, 345
Astor, John Jacob, 47, 279
Atlantic (Sopwith plane), 421–22
Atlantic City air meet, 283, 284, 285, 286
Atlantic Ocean aircraft crossings, 262, 363–80, 411–23
Atwater, Mr. and Mrs. W. B., 323
Atwood, Harry N., 364
Automobile Club of America, 47, 56, 139
Automobiles, 33, 51, 56; patents controversy and, 334, 336, 342–46, 362
Automobile Show, New York City: (1903), 23; (1906), 48, 56

Baby Grand (plane), 292, 293
Baddeck (village), 69, 71, 72ff., 77, 80, 81, 114, 126, 143, 144, 148ff., 153–55, 161–62, 175–76, 368, 468

Baddeck aerodromes, 240; *Number 1*, 176, 178, 285, 469; *Number 2*, 469
Baden-Powell, Major B., 198
Baldwin, Frederick W. (Casey), 158, 162; and Aerial Experiment Association, 70, 72, 75, 79, 80, 114, 117, 126, 240, 244, 245, 462–64, 469; and Bell, 70, 137, 141, 160, 162, 240, 244, 245, 285, 368, 469; and Canadian Aerodrome Company, 160; and Curtiss, 368, 388–89; and *June Bug*, 112, 114; and *Langley* plane, 388–89; marriage of, 117, 162; and patents of Aerial Experiment Association, 348–49; and *Red Wing*, 92–93, 94, 96; and *Silver Dart*, 137, 140, 141, 149; and water airplane, 143–44; and *White Wing*, 96–97, 98, 99–101
Baldwin, Mrs. Frederick W., 117, 162
Baldwin, Sam, 36
Baldwin, Thomas Scott (Captain Tom), 35–46, 49–50, 54, 56–57, 58, 77, 78, 80, 82, 103–4, 137, 145, 186, 219; and Army dirigibles, 88, 89, 103–4, 116, 118, 120–23; background and biography of, 36–38; and Curtiss, 36ff., 77, 78, 80–81, 88–89, 153, 156–57, 158, 285, 352–54, 460–61; and exhibition flying, 223, 224, 264–65; and Herring, 153, 156, 158, 227, 242, 254; and Herring-Curtiss Company, 156–57, 159, 164, 169, 170, 171, 352–54, 433, 435; and Hudson-Fulton competition, 208, 216, 217; and patent litigation, 352–54; and St. Louis Exposition, 40–43; and Wright brothers, 52, 352–56
Ballard, E. H. (Ned), 408
Balloons, 467. *See also* Dirigibles
Balzer, Stephen M., 26–28
Balzer-Manly engine, 27–28
Bank of Hammondsport, 22, 433
Bath, New York, 34, 213, 238
Bauder, Jim, 304, 456

Bauder, Lynn, 165–66
Beachey, Lincoln, 43–44, 218, 223, 302–7, 322; death of, 307; and Hildreth tragedy, 304–6, 473; and *Langley* plane, 382–84, 386, 390; and stunt flying, 297–99, 302–7; and transatlantic flight, 371
Beck, James M., 181–82, 199–200, 208, 340
Beck, Lieutenant Paul M., 233–34, 312
Beinn Bhreagh (Alexander Graham Bell estate), 69–78, 80, 84, 85, 119–20, 126, 145, 147–55, 158, 161–62
Bell, Alexander Graham, 9–10, 13–14, 48–49, 67ff., 85ff., 97–98, 117, 137, 141, 160, 285, 368, 462, 468, 470; and Aerial Experiment Association, 125–26, 131–32, 136–62 *passim*, 168–69, 462–64, 465–66, 469 (*see also* Aerial Experiment Association); and American Aerodrome Company, 150–53, 155–56, 158, 159, 163ff.; biography and background of, 68–69; and *Bulletin* (*see* A.E.A. *Bulletin*); and Canadian Aerodrome Company, 160–61; and Curtiss, 49, 51, 52–53, 56, 67–82 *passim*, 126, 132, 138, 141, 143, 144, 147–48, 150–64 *passim*, 175–76, 222, 239–40, 244–45, 321–22, 347, 348–49, 356–57, 368, 383–84, 389; and death of Selfridge, 128, 129–30; and *June Bug*, 103, 104–5, 107, 108, 112–18 *passim*; and *Langley* plane, 381–82, 383, 384–85, 386, 389, 477; and patents, 113–14, 132, 142–43, 150, 164, 222, 348–49, 354, 356–57, 401–2; and *Red Wing*, 85, 86, 90–92, 93–94; and *Scientific American* Trophy, 168–69, 175–76; and *Silver Dart*, 138, 139, 140–43, 145, 147ff., 468; and tetrahedral kites, 48–49, 67ff., 85ff.; and Volta Bureau, 462; and *White Wing*, 96–97, 99, 100; and Wright brothers, 48–49, 71, 86–87, 94, 125, 127–28, 142, 146, 164, 240, 244–45

Bell, Charles J., 131–32, 159, 240, 356–57
Bell, Mabel Hubbard (Mrs. Alexander Graham Bell), 10, 85, 244–45; and Aerial Experiment Association, 67–68, 69, 71, 72, 73, 74, 78–79, 85, 94, 99, 112–13, 114, 117, 118, 126, 131, 137, 146, 150, 162, 244–45, 285, 401, 468; and Curtiss, 322, 348, 368; illness of, 88, 92, 99, 103, 105; and Selfridge, 119–20, 128–29
Bellinger, Patrick N. L. (Pat), 304–5, 328, 418–20, 422, 478
Bell's Boys, 89, 91ff., 98ff., 136ff., 143–62, 175–76, 178, 183, 244–45. See also Aerial Experiment Association; specific individuals by name
Belmont, August, 230
Belmont, O. H. P., 47
Belmont Park meet, 289, 290, 291–94
Bennett, James Gordon, Jr., 184, 187, 196, 206, 207
Bennitt, Mrs. Malinda, 16, 104–5, 214
Berger, Romaine, 270
Bernstorff, Count Joachim-Heinrich von, 380
Bicycles, 2–3, 11–13, 16–17, 18
Billingsley, Ensign William D., 330–31
Biplanes versus monoplanes, competition for superiority between, 186, 192, 203
Birmingham, U.S.S., 295–96
Bishop, Cortlandt Field, 153, 155, 156, 157, 159, 164, 167, 168–71, 176, 177, 184–85, 186–87, 189–92, 196, 199, 200, 203, 225, 231, 237–42 293, 468; biography and background of, 462; and Herring-Curtiss Company, 250–51, 254, 256–57, 260, 433
Bishop, David, 157, 196, 237, 238, 241, 242, 250, 260
Blanchard, H. Percy, 154
Blériot, Louis, 64, 178, 186, 188–89, 192–93, 195–96, 197, 199, 200, 201, 208, 210, 320, 482
Blériot planes, 232, 288, 289, 293
Bliss, Brigadier General Tasker H., 312

Blue Hill (towing vessel), 84
Bombing, use of planes for, 279, 283–84, 312
Boomerang (balloon), 54, 99, 136
Borglum, Gutzon, 467
Boston Flyer, 289, 290
Boston Globe, 32–33
Boston-Harvard Aeronautical Meet, 288–89
Boston Transcript, 356
Box kites, 13–14, 45, 65. See also Kites; Tetrahedral kites
Bras d'Or Lakes, 69, 148, 149–50, 153–55
Breckenridge, Henry T., 348
Brescia, Italy, Curtiss and aerial competition in, 183, 186, 200–3
Brewer, Griffith, 390–92, 435–37, 479, 481
Bright, Charles, 425
Bright, James H., 425–26, 430, 431–32, 439, 444
Brighton, Florida, 425
Brighton Beach, New York, 44, 116–17
British Science Museum, Kitty Hawk plane and, 436–39, 481
Brookins, Walter, 284, 288, 293, 413
Brown, Arthur W., 422
Brown, Llewellyn H. (Lew), 31–32, 34, 42, 213
Brundage, Ira, 430
Bryan, William Jennings, 356, 380
Buffalo, New York, 392, 394ff., 399, 402ff., 412ff., 424, 428–29
Buffalo Bicycle Supply Company, 32
Buffalo Gasolene Motor Company, 344
Burgess, W. Starling, 42, 179, 180, 328, 401
Burgess Company, 401
Burridge, Lee S., 166
Buzzard, The, 123
Byrd, Richard E., 476, 481–82

Calderara, Lieutenant Mario, 201, 202
California, 308–18, 319, 322–24 (see also individual places); air shows, 231–34

California Arrows (dirigibles), 40–43, 44–45, 48, 49, 54, 56, 58, 80–81, 89, 122, 208, 217, 223

Callan, J. Lansing 299–300, 430, 456, 482; in Italy, 476, 477; and transatlantic flight, 323, 369, 370, 372, 375, 377, 379

Cambria, New York, 7

Camelot, Poughkeepsie, New York, 267, 274, 275, 472–73

Cameron, Sheldon, 114, 356–57, 385

Canada, 151, 153–55, 160–61, 178, 240, 244–45, 285, 397–98, 477

Canadian Aerodrome Company, 160–61, 240, 244–45, 285

Canadian Club of Ottawa, Alexander Graham Bell's address to, 161

Cape Breton Island, 69, 71

Casale, Lieutenant, 427

Casey, Louis S., 468–69

Casson, William A., 403–5

Castle Hill, 6, 7–8, 9, 32, 50, 259, 280, 318, 442, 455

Chambers, Captain Washington Irving, 294, 295–96, 308–9, 311, 314–15, 316, 319, 320, 322–23, 324, 327–29; Curtiss correspondence on patent litigation with, 340–41, 349–50, 354; on death and contributions to aviation of Curtiss, 482; and transatlantic flight, 363

Champlin, Gladys (Mrs. Elwood Doherty), 477

Champlin, Harry M., 11–12, 98–99, 111, 138–39, 146, 227, 460, 477

Champlin, Mrs. Harry, 91–92, 111

Chanute, Octave, 14, 48, 52, 82, 85–86, 130–31; and Aerial Experiment Association, 130–31; and Bell, 69; and Curtiss, 222, 224, 246; death of, 250; described, 60; and Herring, 461, 467; and Langley, 60, 61, 382, 467; and Wright brothers, 28–30, 38–40, 52–53, 59–66, 230, 246–50, 335, 461

Chapin, R. D., 224–25

Chauvière, M., 189

Chicago, Illinois: air exhibitions, 223–24; Automobile Show, 57

Chicago–New York flight, 282, 289–91

Churchill, Winston, 396

City of Portland (dirigible), 43–44

Clarke, Julia, 301, 323

Cleary, Edwin, 231, 236

Clermont, 215

Cleveland, Ohio, 288

Cleveland *Press*, 288

Cobb, Irvin S., 422

Cockburn, George B., 193, 196

Collier, Robert J., 230, 359; Trophy, 321

Collins, Minturn Post, 277

Concour Internationale d'Aviation, Brescia, Italy, 200–3

Coney Island, New York, 44, 116–17

Cook, Albert D., 46, 76

Cook, Dr. Frederick A., 205–7, 470

Corbin, Harold H., 454

Corning, New York, 20–21

Country Club Estates, Florida, 431–32, 440, 442

Coupe Internationale des Aeronauts (Gordon Bennett Cup), 184–200

Courtney, Frank T., 452–53

Cox, Charles R., 154, 162

Crisp, W. Benton, 345, 357, 358, 361

Crooked Lake, 3–4. See also Keuka, Lake

Cuba, air flight from Florida to, 299

Curtiss, Carlton, 17, 456

Curtiss, Claudius (Claude) Adelbert, 459

Curtiss, Claudius G., 4–5, 6–7, 445, 459

Curtiss, Frank Richmond, 5–7

Curtiss, Gideon, 459

Curtiss, Gilbert, 459

Curtiss, Glenn H.: and Aerial Experiment Association, 66–82ff., 85ff., 136ff., 161–62, 356–57, 401–2, 462–69 (*see also* Aerial Experiment Association); and Albany–New York flight, 261–80, 451–53, 472–73; and American Aerodrome Company,

498

150–53, 155–56, 159, 163–64; and archery, 443; awarded Langley Medal, 347–48; awarded permanent possession of *Scientific American* Trophy, 280; and Beachey, 302–7; and Bell, 49, 51, 52–53, 56, 67–82 *passim*, 125, 126, 132, 138, 141, 143, 144, 147–48, 150–64 *passim*, 175–76, 227, 239–40, 244–45, 321–22, 347–49, 356–57, 368, 383–84, 389; and Belmont Park meet, 291–94; and bicycles, 2–3, 11–13, 16–17, 18ff.; birth, family, named, early days in Hammondsport, New York, 4ff.; and Brescia (Italy) competition, 200–3; in California, 296, 300, 308–18, 319, 322–29; and Christian Science, 445, 455; competitive instinct in, 12–13; contributions to aviation, listed, 482–83; creativity and innovations of, 45–46, 50, 54–58, 482–83 (*see also* specific aspects, developments); and Curtiss Aeroplane and Motor Corporation organization, 401ff.; and *Cygnet II*, 148, 153–55; death and burial of, 454–56, 481–82; debut as airplane pilot, 100; descriptions of, 16, 25, 47, 165–66, 188, 440, 442–43; and dirigibles, 35–58; early employment, 10ff.; education, 10; and end of Aerial Experiment Association, 161–62; and engine development, 2–3, 18ff., 32, 54–58 (*see also* Engines; specific aspects, developments, engines); establishes motorcycle speed record in Florida, 56–58; and exhibition flying, 285ff. (*see also* specific aircraft, aspects, developments, meets, trophies); fascination with flying, 163ff.; first ascent in dirigible, 58; Florida residence and activity, 424–27, 449ff.; and flying boats, 302, 303–81 (*see also* Flying boats; specific aircraft, aspects, developments); in France, 183–200; and *Gold Bug* (*Golden Flier;* Rheims racer), 168–82; and

Gordon Bennett Trophy, 106–15, 139–40, 149, 155–56, 168–70, 171–78, 291–94; and Hamilton, 282–85; and Henry Ford, 342–46, 357; and Herring and Herring-Curtiss Company, 152–53, 155, 156–60, 163–64, 166–68, 169–71, 173, 175, 178–81, 189–92, 198, 210–11, 222, 237ff., 250–60, 433–35, 453–54 (*see also* Herring, Augustus M.; Herring-Curtiss Company); hobbies and recreations in later life, 407–8, 440, 442ff.; honorary doctorate awarded by University of Miami, 450; and Hudson-Fulton Celebration, 182, 199–200, 203, 204–22, 261–80; and hunting, 443–44, 454; influence of Keuka Lake on career of, 3–4; and *June Bug*, 102–18, 119; and *June Bug* anniversary, 446–47; and *Langley* plane, 381–93, 435–39; on Long Island, 406–10 (*see also* Long Island; specific places); and McCurdy, 136–37, 145–47, 148–50, 154ff. (*see also* under McCurdy, John A.D.); and manufacture of planes for sale, 152–53, 155, 156–60, 163–64, 166–71 (*see also* specific aspects, companies, developments, individuals); married life, 15–16, 24–25 (*see also* Curtiss, Mrs. Glenn H.); merger with Wright Corporation, 448–49; and motorcycles, 16–17, 18ff., 23–24, 31ff., 45–47, 56ff., 76–77, 163, 164, 179 (*see also* Motorcycles); New York *Times* article on status of aeronautics by, 450–51; one and only "Curtiss dirigible," 80–81, 83–84, 88–89; and ownership of first automobile inHammondsport, New York, 23; and patents, 152–53, 164, 174, 218–20, 222, 332–62 (*see also* Patents; specific aspects, developments, individuals); personality and character of, 25; and photography, 10, 15–16; and pilot training, 296, 301ff., 309, 311, 312, 316–17ff., 326ff. (*see also* specific aspects, agencies, organizations); quoted on experimentation and creativity, 406; receives first pilot's license issued, 320; and *Red Wing*, 83–96 *passim;* relations with employees, 32, 55, 77, 165–66 (*see also* specific companies, individuals); *Scientific American* Trophy and, 103–13, 139–40, 149, 155–56, 168–78, 280; and ship-to-shore flights, 294–96; and *Silver Dart*, 136ff.; speed and racing addiction, 1–3ff., 11–13, 18ff., 426; success and wealth of, 398ff., 429ff.; and Tom Baldwin, 36ff., 77, 80–81, 83–84, 88–89, 118, 120–24, 153–57, 158, 285, 352–54, 460–61; and transatlantic flight, 363–80, 411–23; and U. S. War Department and aviation, 283–84, 294–96, 308–31 (*see also* Army, U. S.; Navy, U. S.; Signal Corps, U. S. Army; specific aspects, developments, individuals); and water planes, 143–45, 203, 308–31, 394ff. (*see also* specific kinds, planes); and wind tunnel use, 407, 426; wind-wagon (horse-scarer) invention of, 50; and World War I activity, 394–410; and Wright brothers, 30, 43, 51–54, 81–82, 88, 89–90, 97, 124, 125, 130, 169–70, 174, 189–91 (*see also under* Wright brothers); and Wright brothers and patents controversy, 208, 225–26, 233–36, 245ff., 260, 331, 332–62 (*see also* Patents; specific aspects, developments, individuals)

Curtiss, Glenn H., Jr., 325, 399, 429, 441–42, 443, 451, 452, 454, 456, 485; death of, 481; described, 481; quoted on father, 432, 438, 440–41, 445, 480, 485; relations with father, 441–42

Curtiss, Mrs. Glenn H. (*formerly* Lena Pearl Neff), 15–16, 24–25, 32, 46–47, 76–77, 110, 148, 154, 191, 205, 212, 214, 222, 224–25, 242, 257, 259, 309, 311, 318, 330; birth and death of first son Carlton, 17, 456; birth of son Glenn, Jr., 324–25; and Florida residence, 424, 431, 440, 442; and Herring-Curtiss Company, 435, 479; and husband's Albany to New York flight, 263–66, 268, 271, 273, 275–79; and husband's death, 454, 456, 481–82; married life, 15–16, 24–25

Curtiss, Mrs. Lua Andrews (*later* Mrs. J. Charles Adams), 5–8, 10, 11, 14, 310, 318–19, 325, 401, 408, 442

Curtiss, Ruth Bramble, 4–5, 7–9, 11, 16, 24–25, 32

Curtiss, Rutha Luella (*later* Mrs. Augustus Hesley), 7, 9–10, 14, 67–78, 400, 408, 442

Curtiss: Story of the Aeroplane, 321–22

Curtiss, U.S.S., 478

Curtiss Aeroplane Company, 257, 259, 309ff., 317ff.; at Buffalo, New York, 394ff.; and *Langley* plane, 383–93; and patent litigation, 333–62; and World War I, 394–410

Curtiss Aeroplane and Motor Company, Ltd., 398

Curtiss Aeroplane and Motor Corporation, 332–62, 401–10, 414ff., 428ff.; merger with Wright Corporation, 448–49

Curtiss Aviation Book, The, 322

Curtiss-Bright Company, 430

Curtiss Commemorative Airport, 446–47, 450, 455

Curtiss Condor (plane), 451–53

Curtiss Engineering Corporation, 406–10, 415ff., 426ff.

Curtiss Exhibition Company, 228, 231–36, 237ff., 264ff., 281–307, 401, 473; formation of, 286ff.

Curtiss Field, Long Island, 429

Curtiss Flying School (Curtiss Aviation School), 300ff., 326ff.

Curtiss (G. H.) Manufacturing Company, 22–23, 25, 36, 44, 45ff., 79–

80, 139, 158–60, 164–66, 178ff., 242, 254–56; incorporation of, 34
Curtiss Hawk (plane), 428
Curtiss Marine Trophy Race, 453
Curtiss Motor Company, Inc., 259–60, 395, 429
Curtiss Number 1 (French dirgible), 199
Curtiss Number 1 engine, 70
Curtiss Number 2 engine, 74, 83–84
Curtiss Racer (plane), 427–28
Curtiss-Reed propeller, 407
Curtiss-Wright Corporation, 333, 402, 448–49, 452
Cygnet (aerodrome), 70, 72, 75, 78, 80–82, 83–85
Cygnet II (aerodrome), 85, 103, 148, 153–56

Daniels, Josephus, 414, 417–18, 421
D'Annunzio, Gabriele, 202
Darius Green and His Flying Machine, 8, 13, 48, 289
Dayton, Ohio, 14, 51–54, 60, 171, 230, 234–35, 252, 342, 352–54, 355, 359–60
Dayton Fair, 52–53
Deering, James M., 157, 260, 440, 468
Delagrange, Léon, 138, 193, 208
Depew, Chauncey, M., 473
Detroit Daily News, 61
Dhonna Beag (Drome Number 6), 144–45
Dickinson, Jacob M., 309
Dienstbach, Carl, 137, 146, 464–65
Dirigibles, 35–38, 88–90, 223 (see also specific aspects, developments, dirigibles, individuals, kinds); Army, Curtiss and Baldwin and, 116, 118, 120–23, 124; and Gordon Bennett competition, 188; and Hudson-Fulton competition, 216, 217; and transatlantic flight, 364
Doherty, Elwood (Gink), 392, 477
"Dope," airplane, use of, 137
Doubleday, Frank N., 186

Dover, Strait of, 178. See also English Channel air crossing competition
Downey, Sergeant, 130–31
Drexel, J. Armstrong, 293
Drome Number 1 (Red Wing), 83–96. See also Red Wing
Drome Number 2 (White Wing), 96–101, 102, 103, 104. See also White Wing
Drome Number 3 (June Bug), 102–18, 119, 124, 132–33, 137, 138, 139, 141, 145, 150, 162. See also June Bug (Drome Number 3)
Drome Number 4 (Silver Dart), 117–18, 136–62. See also Silver Dart
Drome Number 5 (Cygnet II), 85, 103, 148, 153–56
Drome Number 6 (Dhonnas Beag), 144–45

Eagle (plane), 426
Eastman, George, 10
Eastman Dry Plate and Film Company (later Eastman Kodak Company), 10
Ecob, Robert Gilbert, 436–37
Eiffel, Gustave, 347–348
Ellyson, Lieutenant Theodore G., 311–12, 313, 317, 318, 319, 320–21, 323, 328–29, 340; disappearance on hydroplane flight, 331
Ely, Eugene, 287, 289, 290–91; and ship-to-shore flight, 292, 293, 294–96; and shore-to-ship landing, 310, 312, 316; stunting and death of, 474
Empire Race Track meet, Yonkers, New York, 24
Engines (engine development and experimentation), 2, 3, 17ff., 27–31, 35ff., 45ff., 52ff., 70ff., 81–82, 83–84, 88–89. See also specific aspects, developments, individuals, kinds
England. See Great Britain and the British
English Channel air crossing competition, 149, 166, 178, 210
Erie Canal, 4

Esnault-Pelterie, Robert, 97, 236, 465
Experiments and Observations in Soaring Flight (Wilbur Wright), 69

Fabre, Henri, 314
Fairchild, Alexander Graham Bell, 70
Fairchild, David, 70, 108–11
Fairchild, Mrs. David (Marian "Daisy" Bell), 70, 108, 111
Fanciulli, Jerome S., 218–19, 227, 232, 234–35, 243, 253, 316, 324, 403; and Curtiss and Albany–New York flight, 265, 266, 272, 471; and Curtiss and exhibition flying, 283, 286, 292, 297, 300, 473; and patent litigation, 337
Farman, Henry, 64, 114, 116–17, 138, 151, 172, 194, 200, 208, 464, 465
Farman airplanes, 188, 223, 233, 341, 464–65
Federation Aèronautique Internationale, 320
Federation of American Motorcyclists, 76
Fickel, Lieutenant Jacob E., 287
Filene, Edward, 211
Finger Lakes, New York, 4, 145–47
Fisher, Ward, 186, 199, 200, 204
Flagler, Henry M., 440
Florida, 322; Curtiss and exhibition flying in, 270, 322; Curtiss and motorcycle racing in, 31, 56, 57; Curtiss residence and activity in, 424–47, 450
Flotation gear, water flying and, 263, 264, 268, 284, 311, 313–14, 474–75. See also Pontoons; specific aspects, developments, kinds, planes
Flying boats, 302, 308–31, 349, 360–61, 394ff., 411–23, 474–75 (see also Hydroplanes); Langley Medal awarded Curtiss for, 347–48; and transatlantic flight, 363–80, 411–23
Flying Fish ("Number 2 flying boat"), 327–28
Forbes, A. Holland, 173
Ford, Henry, 23, 326, 336, 342–46, 357, 475

Ford automobile, 23. See also Ford, Henry
Fort Myer, Virginia, 106, 117, 118, 121ff., 130, 131, 133–35, 174, 180, 219, 437
Foster, Maximilian, 194
Foulois, Benjamin, D., 121, 123, 124, 125, 130
France and the French, 97, 98, 114–15, 116–17, 139, 157, 223, 230–31, 292, 303–4, 323–24, 329, 351, 379, 411, 427 (see also specific individuals); Curtiss and competition in, 183–200; Gordon Bennett air competition and, 166, 170 (see also specific aspects, individuals); Wright brothers and, 63–64, 65–66, 124, 170, 178, 182, 230–31, 235–36, 248
Fraser, Arthur, C., 339
Frayer-Miller automobile, 23, 51
French, Samuel D., 259
Frost, Susan, 70–71
Frost, Walter, 70–71
Frost King (kite), 69–70
Fulton, Robert, 207, 215, 280
"Fulton Flight," 261–80

Galatin (dirgible), 217
Garden City, Long Island, 33, 58, 173, 285, 407–10, 417, 426–28, 429, 430, 440
Gary, Judge Elbert H., 211
Gaynor, William J., 268, 279
Genung, Harry, 47, 163, 164, 259, 262–63, 336–37, 370, 395, 397, 433, 441, 456
Genung, Martha, 263
George V, King, 406
Germany, 123, 128, 161, 294, 320, 364, 379–80, 397, 411. See also World War I
Gibbs-Smith, Charles H., 469
Gilbert, Arthur W., 169–71, 226, 227, 242
Gill, Howard, 322
Gill, W. F., 267, 274
Gilmore, W. L., 412, 426
Gleason, Alderman, 214

Glen, the (Hammondsport, New York)
4, 5, 6, 50
Glenn H. Curtiss Properties, Inc., 440
Gliders, and early aviation experimentation, 14, 29–30, 60–66ff., 85–87ff.,
92ff., 97, 335, 428. See also Kites;
specific aircraft, developments, individuals, kinds
Godet, Eugene, 301
Gold Bug (Curtiss Number 1; Golden
Flier; Rheims racer), 168–82, 183–
203, 210, 216, 231, 232, 234, 242,
251, 263–64, 270, 282, 472; naming
of, 468–69
Gomm, William, 343–44
Gordon Bennett Cup race, Belmont
Park, 291–94
Gordon Bennett Trophy competition,
149, 157, 166, 169, 170, 173–74,
177, 181, 182, 183–200, 252, 285,
288
Governors Island, 282, 453; Hudson-
Fulton Celebration air competition
and, 182, 204–22, 233, 263, 268,
269, 271, 277, 278
Grahame-White, Claude, 288, 289,
293
Grant, Frederick Dent, 278
Grant, Ulysses S., 278
"Grasscutter" ("Lizzie"), training
plane, 316–17
Great American Aeroplane, "June Bug,"
Winning the American Trophy, July
4, 1908 (motion picture), 112
Great Britain and the British, 160, 161,
240, 262, 288, 289, 292, 293, 329
(see also specific individuals); and
flying boats, 364–80, 403–6, 411ff.,
415, 416; and Kitty Hawk plane,
435–39; and transatlantic flight, 417,
421–22; and World War I and aviation, 396–98, 399, 403–6, 411ff.
Greely, Adolphus W., 477
Green, Darius, 13. See also Darius
Green and His Flying Machine
Greenbury Point, Annapolis, Navy aerial station at, 320

Greene, Dr. William, 270
Green Flash, Barney Oldfield's, 33
Grey, Earl, 161
Grieve, K. Mackenzie, 421–22
Guantánamo Bay, 322, 330
Gustafsen, Charles, 23–26
Gyro-stabilizer, 327–28, 375

H-12 flying boat, 411
H-16 flying boat, 411
Haffner, Charles Andrew, 452
Half Moon, 215
Halifax, Nova Scotia, 78, 80
Hall, G. Ray, 34, 257, 259, 433
Hall, J. R., 303
Hallett, George, 312, 315, 320, 370,
372, 377–78
Halley's comet, 261–62, 268
Hamel, Gustave, 370
Hamilton, Charles K., 44–45, 224,
227–28, 231, 233, 234, 264, 270–71,
281–85, 290, 293, 298; recklessness
in stunt flying and death of, 296–97
Hamiltonion (Black Devil) plane, 290,
293
Hammer, William, J., 199–200
Hammond, Lazarus, and founding of
Hammondsport, New York, 4, 6, 212
Hammondsport, New York, 1ff., 165–
66, 317–18, 333, 395ff.; Aerial Experiment Association headquarters
in, 83ff., 136ff.; air fever and activity in, 299, 304–6, 317–18, 326ff.,
395ff. (see also specific developments, individuals, planes); and anniversary of Hudson River flight by
Curtiss, 451–52; Curtiss' concern and
affection for, 429–30, 447, 449–50;
and end of Herring-Curtiss Company, 254–60; founding of, 4, 5,
212; and June Bug anniversary celebration, 446–47; and Langley plane
restoration and flight, 386–93; reception for Curtiss following Rheims
victory, 212–14; Scientific American
Trophy trial in, 107–13; and World
War I aviation activity, 398ff.

Hammondsport Boys, (bicycle racers), 11–12

Hammondsport *Herald*, 6, 16, 20, 21, 22, 24, 25–26, 28, 29, 31, 33, 34, 89, 138, 139, 161, 224, 243, 256, 259, 297, 317–18, 386, 405

Hand, Judge Learned, 235, 236

Handley-Page (British plane), 416, 421–22

"Happy Hooligan" (Curtiss motorized bicycle), 3, 19–20

Harmon, Clifford, 228, 229, 232, 233–34, 270, 282; and Chicago–New York flight, 289

Harvard-Boston Aeronautical Meet, 288–89

Hassett, J. John, 242–43, 250, 254, 258

Havana, Cuba, McCurdy and flight from Florida to, 299

Havens, Beckwith, 165, 276, 298–99, 300, 301, 302, 303, 322, 429, 482

Hawker, Harry G., 421–22

Hawley, Alan R., 108, 109, 173, 366, 452

Hazel, Judge John R.: and Curtiss-Wright brothers airplane patent litigation, 218, 230, 334–36, 346–47, 349–50, 358, 361–62; described, 335–36; and Ford-Selden automobile patent litigation, 344–46, 362

Hedstrom, Oscar, 23–24

Held, Anna, 199

Helicopters, 99, 172

Hempstead Plains, Long Island, 134, 173, 175, 181, 282

Hercules bicycles and motorcycles, 17, 21–24

Herman, David, 252–53

Herring, Augustus M., 14, 60–61, 87, 90, 94–95, 97–98, 108, 175, 200, 219, 222, 237–46, 250–60, 400, 408, 442, 467–68, 471; biography and background of, 467–68; and Chanute, 461, 467; and Curtiss and Herring-Curtiss Company, 152–53, 155, 156–60, 163–64, 166–68, 169–71, 175, 178–81, 185, 189–92, 198,

210–11, 219, 225–28, 237–45ff., 250–60, 263, 433–35, 471–72; death of, 434–35; and patents, 152–53, 158–59, 160, 171, 179, 189–92, 219, 238–39, 242–46ff., 467, 471–72; and U. S. Army plane contract, 120, 121, 123, 131, 133–35, 164, 167

Herring, William, 435

Herring-Burgess (airplane company), 179–80

Herring-Curtiss Company, 152–53, 155, 156–60, 163–64, 166–68, 169–71, 175, 178–81, 185, 189–92, 198, 200, 211, 218, 219, 222, 225–28, 237–45ff., 250ff., 433–35, 453–54, 471–72, 479; end of, 250–60, 263, 435

Hesley, Augustus, 400, 408, 442

Hialeah, Florida, Curtiss and development of, 425, 430–31, 432

Hildreth, Dorothea (*later* Mrs. Frederick A. Russell), 304–6, 474

Hildreth, Ruth, 304–6, 474

Hildreth, Walter E., 304

Hill Howard, 443

Hill, Thomas A., 218, 333, 474–75

Hollander, Sumner R., 366

Horton, H. M., 287–88

Houdini, Harry, 298

Hoyt, Richard F., 448

Hubbard, Reverend William H., 274

Hubbs, J. Seymour, 22, 33, 51, 456

Hudson, Henry, 207, 215, 280

Hudson Flyer (plane), 278, 282, 284, 288, 295. See also Albany–New York (Hudson River) flight

Hudson-Fulton Celebration, 149, 182, 199–200, 203, 204–22. See also Hudson River (Albany–New York) flight

Hudson River (Albany–New York) flight, 207–8, 209, 215–17, 262–80, 451–53

Hudson River Valley, 4

Hunsaker, Jerome C., 329–30, 348, 409–10, 412–14, 415, 444

Hydrofoils, 144, 145

Hydroplanes, 144, 145, 264, 349, 360–61, 474–75 (*see also* Flying boats); and transatlantic flight, 363–80, 411–23

Illig, Mrs. Florence, 455
Indian motorcycles, 23–24, 46
Ingraham, Kenneth, 138
Internal combustion engines. *See* Engines (engine development and experimentation); specific aspects, developments, individuals, engines
International School of Aeronautics, 269
Inwood, Manhattan, 276–78
Irving, Minna, 476
Isham, Samuel, 473
Isham, William B., 277, 473
Isham Park, New York City, 277, 473
Italy, 200–3

Jamestown Tercentenary Exposition, 50
Janin, Albert S., 474–75
Japanese Navy, 320, 327
Jasper, New York, 5
Jennies (JN type aircraft), 395, 397, 398, 477
JN aircraft. *See* Jennies (JN type aircraft)
Johnson, Walter, 392, 393
Johnstone, Ralph, 288
Jones, Charles Oliver, 53, 54–55, 99, 136
Jones, Ernest L., 146, 191, 222
June Bug (*Drome Number 3*), 102–18, 119, 124, 132–33, 137, 138, 139, 141, 145, 150, 162, 167–68, 191, 465–66; anniversary of *Scientific American* Trophy flight of, 446–47; naming of, 104–5, 465; and *Scientific American* Trophy flight, 102–18, 446–47

K-12 engine, 427
Keeler, George H., 22, 213–14, 401
Kellogg, John Harvey, 445–46

Kelly, Lieutenant G. E. M., 312, 316–17
Kerr, General Francis, 37
Kerr, Mark, 421
Keuka, Lake, 1, 3ff., 50, 86, 92, 99, 112, 145, 146, 147, 148, 224, 252, 264, 283, 304, 318, 319, 324, 327–28, 372, 376, 389, 392, 446; influence on Curtiss' career of, 3–4
Keuka Industries, 429
Keys, Clement M., 429, 440, 448
Kill Devil Hill, Wright brothers experiments at, 29–30, 61
Kimball, Rear-Admiral W. W., 283–84
Kimball, Wilbur R., 146, 172–73
Kimmell, Husband E., 478
Kingsley, Charles L., 250–51, 326
Kingsley Field, 326
Kingsley Flats, 265
Kirkham, Charles, 34, 407, 426–27, 460
Kirkham, Clarence, 34, 460
Kirkham, John, 20, 23, 460
Kirkham, Percy, 34, 460
Kirkham brothers (Kirkham Motor Works), 21, 34, 327, 407, 460. *See also* individual brothers
Kite House, 72, 469
Kites, 45, 48–49, 56, 65, 67ff., 224. *See also* Box kites; Gliders; Tetrahedral kites; specific craft, developments, individuals
Kitty Hawk, North Carolina, 28, 29, 60–66, 69, 87, 247, 303; patent litigation and, 335
Kitty Hawk plane, disposition of, 436–39, 479, 480–81
Kleckler, Henry C., 77, 92, 167, 172, 179, 186, 229, 243, 259, 319, 407, 442, 449, 456, 461; and Albany-New York flight, 263, 265, 266, 267, 271, 273, 275, 452; and Curtiss in Florida, 430–31; and flying boats, 319, 322, 324, 328, 397, 407, 412; and Herring-Curtiss Company, 433; and *Langley* plane, 388
Kleckler, Mrs. Henry C. (Blanche), 449

Knabenshue, A. Roy, 41–42, 43, 44, 55, 89, 218, 223, 297, 339, 398
Kondo, M., 327

Lahm, Frank P., 123, 124–25, 127, 130, 465
Lahm, Frank S., 465
Lambert, Count Charles de, 178, 193, 208
Langley, Dr. Samuel P., 13–14, 26–31, 48, 60, 103, 123, 218, 347–48, 381–93; and aerodromes, 26–31, 48, 62, 348, 381–93, 435–39, 477; Chanute and, 60, 61, 382, 467; Curtiss and, 347–48, 381–93, 435–39; death of, 31, 63, 381; Medal, 146, 171, 347–48, 382, 386; restoration and flight of his original plane, 381–93; Wright brothers and, 28–30, 63, 381, 382, 390–93, 435–39
Langley Aerodynamical Laboratory, 348, 382, 387
Langley Medal, 146, 171, 382, 386; awarded to Curtiss, 347–48; awarded to Wright brothers, 146, 171
Langley plane, 381–93, 435–39, 477
Lateral rudders, 142–43, 230, 233–34, 245, 252, 333, 340–47, 356–62. See also Ailerons; Lateral stability; Patents; Wing warping system
Lateral stability, 96–97, 115, 138, 141–43, 230. See also Ailerons; Lateral rudders; Patents; Wing warping system
Latham, Hubert, 178, 186, 193, 196, 200, 208, 232–33
Laurier, Sir Wilfrid, 161
Leach, Bobby, 298
LeFébvre, Eugene, 193, 196, 201
Lehman, Herbert H., 452
Lehmann, George C., 394–95
Letitia, Princess of Savoy, 202
Lewis and Clark Exposition (1905), 43–44
Liberty engine, 414
Lilienthal, Gustave and Otto, 14, 60

Lindbergh, Charles A., 480, 481
Loening, Grover Cleveland, 171, 219–20; and Kitty Hawk plane 438; and patent litigation, 333–34, 342, 479
London Daily Mail: transatlantic flight prize, 364–65, 366, 377, 417–18, 421–22; trans-English Channel prize, 149, 166, 178, 210
London–Manchester flight, 262
Long Island, 173, 175, 178–79, 181, 182, 282, 285, 429. See also specific airfields, locations
Loon (water plane), 145–47
Looping, aerial stunting and, 303–7
Los Angeles, California, International Air Meet at, 231–34, 244, 264
Louisiana Purchase Exposition, St. Louis, Missouri (1903), 38–43
Luckey, William S., 306
Ludlow, Israel, 44–45, 172, 224, 249; and box kite model number 19, 45
Lusitania, 217
Lyon, George, 12
Lyon, Reuben R., 258–59
LZ-1 (zeppelin), 37

McCarthy, Charles J., 414
McClellan, George B., Jr., 211
McCormick, Cyrus, 326
McCormick, Harold F., 326
McCoy, J. C., 291–92
McCurdy, Arthur, 69–70
McCurdy, John A. D. (Douglas), 70, 314, 317, 469; and Aerial Experiment Association, 70, 72, 74, 75, 117–18, 129, 145–47, 148, 154–56, 162, 244, 462–64, 469; and Canadian Aerodrome Company, 160; and Curtiss, 136–37, 145–47, 148–50, 154–56, 162, 165, 168, 244, 245, 285, 317, 367, 397; and Curtiss and flying boats, 367, 397 (see also specific aspects, craft); and Cygnet II, 154–56; and exhibition flying, 285, 287–88, 289, 290, 291, 292, 293, 294–95, 299; and Florida–Cuba flight, 314; and June Bug, 102, 105,

107, 112, 113–14, 117, 118, 119; and *Langley* plane, 385; and patents, 356; and *Red Wing*, 92–93, 94; and *Silver Dart*, 136–37, 143, 145–47, 148–50, 154–56, 168; and transatlantic flight, 367; and water airplane, 143–45

McCurdy, Lucien, 70

McCurdy, Mabel, 162

MacDonald, K. B., 456

McEwan, James B., 268, 279

McFarland, Marvin W., 477

McHarg, Ormsby, 253

McHenry, R. C., 301

McIver, Dr., 150

McKinley, William, 26, 336

Maicon, Auguste, 370

Mail delivery by air. See Airmail

Maine, U.S.S., 26

Maloney, W. J., 482

Manhattan Island, 276–80, 303. See also Albany–New York (Hudson River) flight; Chicago–New York flight; Governors Island; New York–Philadelphia flight; New York–St. Louis flight

Manly, Charles M., 176, 397, 407, 436, 438; and Curtiss and *Scientific American* Trophy, 108, 109, 110, 140, 176; and *Langley* plane, 27–28, 29, 386, 397, 436, 438

Manufacturers Aircraft Association, 361, 451

Marconi Guglielmo, 211, 215

Margeson, Martin V., 254

Marine Corps, U. S., 426

Marmon automobile, 56

Mars, J. C., (Bud), 264, 286, 287, 293, 295

Marvel Motorcycle Company, 179

Marvin, Charles, 258–59

Mason, Mrs. Henry H., 435

Masson, Jules, 22, 374

Masson, Katherine, 373–74

Masson, Lynn D., 22, 23, 34, 159, 191, 205

Masson, Victor, 22

Mattery, Captain, 55, 57

Maughan, Russell, 427–28

Maxim, Hudson, 279

Maxim, Sir Hiram, 467

Means, James, 146

Memphis, Tennessee, Curtiss and exhibition flights at, 264

Merrill, Damon, 263

Meyer, George von L., Secretary of U. S. Navy, 309, 311, 314, 317

Miami, Florida, Curtiss and residence and activity in, 322, 424ff., 439ff., 450, 456

Michelin (André) Cup, 233

Mineola, Long Island, 173, 174–78, 182, 269

Mitchell, General Billy, 428

Mitscher, Marc, and transatlantic flight, 418–19, 478

Model K observation seaplane, 360

Model L military scout plane, 360

Monoplanes versus biplanes. See Biplanes versus monoplanes

Morgan, William F., 421–22

Morris Park, New York City, Curtiss and *Scientific American* Trophy competition and, 139–40, 159, 166, 171–73, 174

Morse, Samuel F. B., 5

Motorcycles, Curtiss and racing and manufacture of, 18–23ff., 45–47, 56–58, 76–77, 163, 164, 179, 242, 256, 259, 333

Mott Bertha, 229, 471

Mott, Lulu, 229

Moulton, Harry D., 416

Mueller, Bernhardt E., 432

Munn, Charles A., 106–7, 280

Nashville, Tennessee, 283

National Automobile Chamber of Commerce, 345–46

National Cycle Association, 24

National Museum (*later* National Air and Space Museum), U. S., 437–39, 478, 479

Naval Aviation Detachment, U. S., 322ff.
Navy, U. S., and aerial development and experimentation, 45, 76, 283–84, 294–96, 402, 426–28 (see also specific aircraft, aspects, developments, individuals); Curtiss and pilot training and, 296, 309, 311, 316–17, 322ff.; Curtiss and water flying and, 308–31; flying boats and transatlantic flight and, 364, 368–69, 370, 375, 411–23; and Pulitzer Trophy (1922), 427–28
Navy A-1 (plane), 319, 320–21
Navy A-2 (plane), 319
NC (Nancy) flying boats, 410, 414–23, 478; NC-1, 410, 414–21; NC-2, 415, 416, 417–21; NC-3, 417, 418–21; NC-4, 418–23, 478
Neff, Frank F., 19–20
Neff, Lena Pearl (later Mrs. Glenn H. Curtiss), 15–16. See also Curtiss, Mrs. Glenn H.
Neff, Mr. and Mrs. Guy L., 15, 25, 46, 318, 442
"New and Useful Improvement in Flying Machines, A" (patent No. 1,011,106), 143
Newell, Emerson R., 218, 222, 322, 338
New York–Albany (Hudson River) flight, 207–8, 209, 215–17, 262–80, 451–53
New York–Chicago flight, 282, 289–91
New York Herald, 29, 134, 149, 184, 206–7, 210
New York Motorcycle Club, 22; Riverdale Park (New York City) meet (1903), 23ff.
New York–Philadelphia flight, 282
New York–St. Louis flight, 279–80
New York State Fair, Syracuse, 18–19, 33
New York Times, 175, 206, 353, 436–37, 450; and Albany–New York (Hudson River) flight, 267–68, 271,

272, 273, 279; and Chicago–New York flight, 281–82, 290; and Langley plane, 383, 389, 390, 391; and Manhattan Island Aerial Derby, 303
New York Tribune, 30
New York World, 112, 207–8, 216, 217, 235; and New York–Albany flight, 262–80; and New York–St. Louis flight, 279–80; and ship-to-shore flights, 294–96
Niagara Falls, New York, Beachey's aerial stunting at, 298
Northcliffe, Lord: and English Channel crossing prize, 149, 178, 207; and London-Manchester prize, 262; and transatlantic flight prize, 364–80, 417, 421–22
North Island, California, Curtiss and U. S. Navy aviation training at, 310–11, 312, 316, 322–24, 338
North Pole, Cook-Peary controversy and, 205–7, 470
Nova Scotia, 13, 48, 67ff., 78, 103, 137, 148, 153. See also specific locations

Ochs, Adolph S., 279, 280
Oldfield, Barney, 33
Oldfield, Reuben B., 447
Oliver, Robert Shaw, 133
Omaha, Nebraska, 286
Opa-locka, Florida, Curtiss and development of, 432–33, 443, 444, 445, 479
Orient Motor Buckboard, 23
Oriole (plane), 426, 445
Ormond Beach, Florida, 31, 56–57
Osborne, Captain F. Creagh, 369–70, 376
Osborne, Mr. and Mrs. George, 399
Osmont, Georges François, 223
Oswego, New York, 31
OX-5 engine, 319, 427

Pan-American Exposition, Buffalo, New York (1901), 18
Parachutes (parachuting), 37, 43, 80

Paris, France, Curtiss in, 183–84, 198–99

Parkhurst, Gabriel H., 254, 257, 433

Parmelee, Phil O., 364

Patents (and patent litigation), 62–63, 87, 97, 101, 115, 116, 142–43, 152–53, 164, 189–92, 218–20, 222, 225–36 passim, 238–39, 240, 242–44ff., 260, 318, 321, 322, 328, 398, 401–2, 471–72, 474–75 (see also Ailerons; Engines; Lateral rudders; Lateral stability; Rudders; Wing warping system; specific aircraft, companies, individuals); Curtiss and Wright brothers feud, 332–62

Paulhan, Louis, 193, 230–33, 234, 235–36, 244, 262, 323–24

Peary, Commander Robert E., 205–7, 470

Pegoud, Adolphe, 303–4, 307

Pennsylvania (Hamburg-American liner), 295

Pennsylvania, U.S.S., 310, 312, 315

Petawawa, Ontario, 176, 178

Pfitzner, Alexander L., 99, 156, 185, 205, 229, 461; death of, 471

Philadelphia–New York flight, 282

Pittsburgh, Pennsylvania, exhibition flights, 286–87

Pleasant Valley, New York, 4, 12, 22, 50, 98ff., 107ff., 258, 446–47, 456

Pleasant Valley Wine Company, 4, 21, 108, 111

Plew, James E., 228

"Plew machine," 228

Pond, Captain C. F., 312, 314, 315

Pontoons, development and use of, 284, 313–14, 387–88, 389, 445

Popular Mechanics magazine, 9

Porte, Lieutenant John Cyril, and flying boats, 396, 403–6, 411, 414; and transatlantic flight, 365–80, 414, 417

Portland, Oregon, Lewis and Clark Exposition at, 43–44

Post, Augustus M., 88, 108, 140, 169, 233, 287, 292, 321, 447; and Albany–New York flight, 267, 268, 269, 273, 280, 452; and Chicago–

New York flight, 289; and patents, 340

Potomac River: Langley aerial experiments and, 26; U. S. Signal Corps test of Dirigible No. 1 and, 121–22

Potter, Charles C., 400

Poughkeepsie, New York, Curtiss and Albany–New York flight and, 267, 272, 273–75

Pousland, Ensign Charles F., 316

Pratt, Aaron G., 34

Progress in Flying Machines (Chanute), 41

Propellers, development and use of, 50, 54, 70, 104, 120, 125, 127–28, 137–38, 156, 189, 407

Pueblo Hotel Miami, Florida, 446

Pulitzer, Joseph, 207–8

Pulitzer Trophy competition (1922), 427–28

Pulteney Park (Park Square), Hammondsport, New York, 2ff.

Ramsay, Jessie, 400

Rathbone, Mrs., 228, 229

Raymor (British plane), 421–22

Raynham, Frederick F., 421–22

Read, Albert C. (Putty), 418–19, 420–21, 422–23

Reber, Major Samuel, 287, 294

Red Devil (plane), 264–65

Red Wing (Drome Number 1), 83–96, 464–65

Reed, R. Luther, 393

Reeder, C. H., 456, 482

Reid, W. D., 372

Reimsdyck, F. L. D. de, 229

Rheims, France, Curtiss and Gordon Bennett Trophy air competition in, 174, 177, 181, 182, 183–200

Rheims, New York, 108, 185, 213

Rheims racer. See Gold Bug (Curtiss Number 1; Golden Flyer; Rheims racer)

Rhoads, Eugene (Smokey), 455

Richardson, Holden C., 304–5, 323, 324, 342, 413–14, 415–16, 418, 447,

455, 456; put in charge of hull design at Pensacola, Florida, Naval Training Station, 413–14; and transatlantic flight, 413–14, 415–16, 418
Robinson, Elmer, 265
Robinson, Hugh, 301, 482
Rochester, New York, Curtiss in, 9–11, 33–34, 46
Rochester Motor Club motorcycle race, Curtiss victory in, 46
Rockaway Point, U. S. Naval Air Station at, 415, 416, 418–19
Rock Stream, New York, 11
Rodgers, Lieutenant John, 319
Rohlfs, Roland, 427, 482
Rolls-Royce automobile engine, 56
Roosevelt, Franklin D., 416, 417, 450
Roosevelt, Quentin, 197, 470
Roosevelt, Mrs. Theodore, 197
Roosevelt, Theodore, 71, 76, 129, 197, 336
Roosevelt Field, Long Island, 427, 470
Rougier, M., 201–2
Rudders (and rudder development), patent litigation and, 142–43, 333, 340–47, 456–57. See also Lateral rudders; specific aspects, developments, individuals
Russell, Frank H., 361
Russia (Russian Navy), 304, 329, 349, 350, 380
Ryan, Allan A., 294
Ryan, John Barry, 296
Ryley, Thomas W., 224

St. Henry, R. H., 316
St. Louis, Missouri: air meets, 38–43, 80–81, 88, 200, 208, 211, 217, 222, 223; Exposition (1903), 38–43
St. Louis–New York flight, 279–80
San Antonio, Texas, exhibition flights at, 264–65
San Diego, California, 296, 300, 309–18, 319, 322–24, 330
San Francisco, California, 310–312

Santos-Dumont, Alberto, 37–38, 39, 42, 64, 65, 97, 117; Dirigible Number 6 of, 37, 39; Dirigible Number 7 of, 39; Dirigible 14 bis of, 65, 97
Sawyer, Philip B., 259
Sawyer, Samuel N., 434
Scientific American magazine, 93, 280, 391. See also Scientific American Trophy
Scientific American Trophy, 103ff., 106–15, 139–40, 149, 155–56, 168–70, 171–78, 252, 263, 280
Scooter (Curtiss motorboat), 444
Scott, Blanche, 301
Scott, J. W., 369
Scott, James F., 90
Scripps, William B., 326
Seaplanes, 143–45, 203, 318–31. See also specific aspects, craft, developments, individuals, kinds
Seely, Lyman J., 350–51, 369, 375, 396, 403–6, 429, 456
Seitz, Don C., 279–80, 452
Selden, George B., 334, 336, 343–46, 357
Selfridge, Edward A., 131
Selfridge, Thomas E. (Tom), 71, 72, 73, 75–76, 79ff., 85, 86–87, 117, 119–35, 234, 312, 428, 461–62ff., 466; and Cygnet, 84–85; death of, 127–31, 466–67; first Army pilot to fly an airplane, 100; and June Bug, 104, 105–6, 107, 112, 115, 117, 118, 119; and patents, 335; and Red Wing, 84–87, 90–95; and Wright brothers, 115, 124–30, 136, 138, 335, 466–67; and White Wing, 98, 100, 101, 138
Selfridge, Thomas O., Jr., 462
Selfridge Air Force Base, Mount Clemens, Michigan, 128, 427–28
Selfridge Field, San Francisco, 312
Seneca Lake, New York, 4, 11
Sewell, E. G., 322
Shaw, J. Angus, 278
Sheepshead Bay, Brooklyn, air exhibition at, 287–88

Shenandoah (Navy dirigible), 429–30
Ship-to-shore flights, 294–96
Shore-to-ship plane landings, 310–13, 316, 321
Shriver, Tod, 186, 188–89, 199, 200, 204, 282
Signal Corps, U. S. Army, and aerial development and experimentation, 71, 75–76, 89–90, 120, 121, 123–35, 139, 146, 167, 180–81, 215, 233–34, 287–88, 294, 402 (*see also* specific aspects, developments, individuals); and Dirigible Number 1, 88–90, 120ff.; and World War I planes, 402
Signal Corps Flying School, North Island, California, 330
Silver Dart (*Drome Number 4*), 117–18, 132–33, 136–62, 167–68, 169, 178, 264, 285, 467–68, 469
Smellie, James H. (Jim), 11, 12, 16, 17, 213
Smithsonian Institution, 6, 13, 14, 26, 27, 30, 63, 123, 146, 162; and *Kitty Hawk* plane, 436–39, 479, 480–81; and *Langley* plane, 347–48, 381–93, 435–39; and Wright brothers, 435–39, 479, 480–81
Sommerville, Grant P., 456
Spanish-American War, 26; Langley and aircraft development and, 26
Spanish Bight, California, Curtiss and aeronautical development for U. S. Navy at, 311, 313, 315, 324, 328
Sparta, Livingston County, New York, 7
Sperry, Elmer, Curtiss and hydroplane "gyrostat" and, 327–28, 330, 375
Sperry, Lawrence, 327–28
Sperry Gyroscope Company, 327
Springer, Oscar M., and Herring-Curtiss Company bankruptcy plan, 253
Springstead (towboat), 92
Squier, Brigadier General George O.: and U. S. Army Signal Corps aeronautical development in World War I, 402; and Wright brothers and

plane contract for Signal Corps, 127, 131
Stability in aircraft, patent litigation and, 334–62. *See also* Ailerons; Lateral rudders; Lateral stability; Patents (and patent litigation); Wing warping system; specific aircraft, individuals
Stanton, A. W., and Curtiss on "first motorcycle tandem trip," 20–21
Staten Island, Aeronautical Society air meet at, 303
Statue of Liberty, 210, 217, 220, 221; Curtiss and Albany–New York flight and, 378; Curtiss and Wilbur Wright and flight competition and, 210, 217, 220, 221, 471
Stearns motor-bicycle, 12, 19
Steuben County, New York, 1–2, 5, 20, 213, 433–35
Stevens, Leo, and dirigible flight at Coney Island, New York, 44
Stoddard-Dayton automobile, 104
Stone, E. F., and first transatlantic flight, 418
Stony Brook Farm, Hammondsport, New York, 11–12, 92, 99, 104, 119, 139, 146, 227, 267, 455
Storm King Mountain, New York, 275, 276, 452
Stunt pilots and stunting, 281, 285–86, 297–99, 302–7. *See also* specific aspects, pilots
Sunday, Billy, baptized in aviation by Curtiss, 302
Syracuse, New York, Curtiss billed as "world's champion aviator" at State Fair air meet, 289
Syracuse *Post-Standard*, 33

Taft, William Howard, 26, 158, 288
Taggart's machine shop, 20
Tail rudders. *See* Rudders (and rudder development)
Tareuchi, Commander, and Curtiss and hydroplanes for Japanese Navy, 327

Taylor, Rear Admiral David W., and development of water airplanes for Navy, 329, 411–12, 413–14, 416, 422

Ten Eyck, Jacob L., 300; and Albany–New York flight by Curtiss, 266, 268, 273

Tetrahedral kites (tetrahedral aerodromes), 48–49, 56, 67ff., 74ff., 84ff., 103, 117, 132, 140, 144ff., 148–50, 156, 164. See also Box kites; Kites

Thacher, John Boyd II, 452

Thomas, B. Doublas, hired by Curtiss as plane design engineer, 365, 397, 477

Thomas Auto-Bi, 18–20

Thomas (E. R.) Company, 18–20, 395

Thompson, Charles F., reports in Associated Press of Curtiss flights by, 100, 105

Thompson, William Boyce, 359

Times Aerial Derby, Beachey's stunt looping at, 303

Titanic, 324

Tomlinson, George L., Baldwin and Albany–New York dirigible flight and, 216, 217

Towers, John H. (Jack), 319, 320–21, 323, 330–31, 348, 455, 456, 482; accident in Wright plane of, 330–31; and death of Curtiss, 455, 456, 482; qualifies for Aero Club license, 320; and transatlantic flight, 363–64, 366, 368–70, 375, 379, 380, 416–17, 418–20, 422, 478

Transatlantic flight, Curtiss and development of flying boats and 363–80, 411–23. See also specific aircraft, aspects, developments, individuals

Triad (amphibious aircraft), 315–16, 319, 323

Tricia, Lieutenant Anthony, and Curtiss and "International School of Aeronautics," 269

Trippe, Juan T., quoted on role of Curtiss in aircraft development, 481

Trowbridge, John T., Curtiss and his poem, Darius Green and His Flying Machine, 8, 289

20th Century (dirigible), Curtiss and origination of 4-cylinder motor for, 49–50

Ugly Duckling, use of "Curtiss Number 1" motor and, 70, 72, 84

United Aircraft and Transport Corporation, 449

United States government, and aeronautical development and experimentation (see also Army, U. S.; Navy, U. S.; Signal Corps, U. S. Army; Smithsonian Institution; specific agencies, aspects, developments, individuals): and World War I, 396, 411ff.

Vanderbilt, Cornelius, and incorporation of Wright Corporation, 236

Vanderbilt, William K., Jr., and Aero Club of America, 47

Vaniman, Melvin, and attempt at transatlantic flight in dirigible America, 364

Van Rensselaer Island, Albany–New York flight by Curtiss and use of, 262, 266, 268, 272, 273, 470

Vaulx, Count Henri de la, 184

Verplanck, J. B. R., use of Curtiss aeroboat for commutation by, 326

Victor Emmanuel III, King of Italy, praise for Curtiss airplane by, 202

Vilas, L. J. (Jack), use of Curtiss flying boat by, 326

Volta Laboratory Association (Volta Laboratory and Bureau), 73, 462; Alexander Graham Bell and formation of, 73

Volta Prize, 462

Walcott, Dr. Charles D., 146, 382–86, 387, 436–38, 477; and award to

Wright brothers of Langley Medal, 146; and restoration and flight of Langley plane, 382–86, 387, 436–38
Walker, Lieutenant John C., Jr., and Curtiss and hydroplane experiments for U. S. Navy, 312
Walker, W. D., and transatlantic flight, 372
Walsh, C. F., 301
Waltham, Massachusetts, Curtiss and handicap road race at, 32–33
Wanamaker, John, 210
Wanamaker, Rodman: and Byrd and transatlantic flight, 476; and Curtiss and transatlantic flight, 363, 365, 366–68, 371, 372, 373, 379, 381, 412, 417–18; and display of Curtiss' Rheims racer, 210–11, 216
War Department, U. S., and aeronautical development and experimentation. See Army, U. S.; Navy, U. S.; Signal Corps, U. S. Army; specific aircraft, aspects, developments, individuals
Warren, Stephen J., and Herring-Curtiss Company litigation, 454
Washington, Mount, 23, 86
Washington Post, 218
Washington Star, and Silver Dart experiments, 154, 162
Wasp (triplane), Curtiss Engineering Corporation and development of, 427
Water-cooled engine development, Curtiss and, 88–89, 104, 106, 118, 122, 137, 167
Water flying (water planes), 143–45, 203, 308–31 (see also specific aircraft, aspects, developments, individuals, kinds); and transatlantic flight, 363–80 (see also Transatlantic flight)
Waters, C. Leonard (Tank), 12, 32, 56–57, 92, 179; and Curtiss at Florida Speed Carnival, 56–57, 440, 456; and formation of Marvel Motorcycle Company with Curtiss, 179
Waters, Mrs. C. Leonard (Bess), 440

Watkins Glen, New York, 4, 11
Watson, Thomas A., quoted on aerial experimentation by Alexander Graham Bell, 69
Wellman, Walter, and attempt to cross the Atlantic in dirigible America, 364
Western New York Institution for Deaf Mutes, 9–10
Western Society of Engineers, Wilbur Wright's lecture on gliding experiments to, 69
Westervelt, G. Conrad, and transatlantic seaplanes, 412, 414, 417
Westervelt, Zenas F., and teaching of the deaf, 9–10
Weyman, Henry, and Lorin Wright and Langley plane, 393
Wheeler, H. Sayre, and death and burial of Curtiss, 456, 478
Wheeler, Monroe M., 22, 34, 170–71, 179, 214, 225–28, 397, 478; and Curtiss and G. H. Curtiss Manufacturing Company, 22, 34, 397; and Curtiss in Buffalo, New York, 397; and Curtiss and exhibition flights, 286; and Curtiss and air competition in France, 170–71, 214; and end of Herring-Curtiss Company, 253–54, 258–59, 260; and Herring, 225–28, 237–39, 242, 243; and Herring-Curtiss Company, 159, 170–71, 179, 191, 225–28, 237–39, 242, 243, 357, 401, 433, 435; and patents, 191, 237–39, 357, 401
Wheeler, Rumsey, and death and burial of Curtiss, 243, 456
Wheels, early aeronautical development and use of, 98, 106–7, 114, 125
White, Charles Edward, description in Harper's Weekly of Curtiss by, 194
White, Clarence, and Curtiss and Albany–New York flight, 265
White, Harry, and Baldwin and Curtiss motorcycle engine, 35–36
White, Henry, U. S. Ambassador to France, and Gordon Bennett Trophy

victory for Curtiss in France, 196, 197, 199

White Wing (Drome Number 2), 96–101, 102, 103, 104, 124, 465; as first airplane in America controlled by ailerons, 98

Whitney, Harry, and Cook's North Pole race with Peary, 206

Whitney, Harry Payne, 47; and organization of Aero Club of America, 47

Widener, Joseph, and Curtiss and Hialeah Race Track, 431

Wilder, David F., and witnessing of organization of Aerial Experiment Association, 78

Wildman, Francis (Doc), and transatlantic flight, 370

Wilhelm II, Kaiser, 128, 161; condolences on death of Selfridge expressed by, 128; and start of World War I, 161

Willard, Charles F., 287, 288, 340; and Aeronautic Society's Golden Flier, 181, 231, 233, 234, 264, 468–69; and Belmont Park Gordon Bennett Cup race, 291, 293, 294–95; and Chicago–New York flight, 289, 290, 291; and Curtiss and exhibition flying, 287, 288, 289, 291, 293, 294–95, 340; and Silver Dart, 264

Williams, I. Newton, and helicopter experimentation, 99

Willoughby, Lieutenant Hugh M., and Curtiss in Atlantic City air show, 284

Willys, John, and Curtiss and Curtiss Corporation, 402–3, 406, 422, 429

Willys-Overland Automobile Company, 402, 429

Wilson, Woodrow, 307

Wind-wagon (horse-scarer), Curtiss and invention of, 50

Wing warping system, Wright brothers and, 62, 86–87, 97, 124, 142, 168, 170–71, 189–92, 222, 225–28, 230–31, 233–36, 246–50, 318, 332–62; and Curtiss-Wright brothers patent

litigation, 318, 332–62 (see also Patents)

Wireless messages, first sent from air to ground, 287–88

Wittmer, Charles C., 301, 316, 322, 429–30; and Airships, Inc., 429–30; and exhibition flying with Curtiss, 301; and first hydroplane flight over Biscayne Bay, Florida, 322

Women exhibition flyers, Curtiss and, 300–1

Wood, Major General Leonard, and New York–Albany flight, 209

World's fairs, and aeronautics, 50. See also specific aspects, events, individuals, places

World War I, aeronautical development and experimentation and, 161, 319, 329, 330, 364, 376, 378–80, 394–410, 411ff. See also specific aircraft, aspects, countries, developments, individuals

Wright, Bishop Milton, 230, 338–39

Wright, Dr. Thew, 454

Wright, Ensign Theodore P., 409

Wright, Katharine, 124–25, 130–31, 342, 360, 475

Wright, Lieutenant N. H., 296

Wright, Lorin, 392–93

Wright Aeronautical Corporation, 301–2, 319, 328, 332, 364, 372–73, 397; and exhibition flying, 248, 288–89, 292–94, 297, 364; and merger with Curtiss Corporation, 448–49; and patent litigation, 332–62, 475–76

Wright brothers, Orville and Wilbur, 14, 59–66, 71, 81–82, 86–87, 142, 143, 149, 320, 322, 448–49; and Aerial Experiment Association, 86–87, 89–90, 93, 101 (see also specific aspects, developments, individuals); and Alexander Graham Bell, 48–49, 71, 86–87, 94, 125, 127–28, 138, 142, 146, 164, 240, 244–45; and Belmont Park air meet, 292–94; and Chanute, 28–30, 38–40, 59–66, 230, 246, 247–50 (see also under Cha-

nute, Octave); and Curtiss, 43, 51–
54, 81–82, 89–90, 115–16, 212, 218–
22, 225–26, 228, 230–31, 233, 245ff.,
251, 252, 318, 332–62, 448–49, 482;
and Curtiss and Langley plane, 381,
386, 389, 390–92, 435–39, 480–81;
and Curtiss and patent litigation,
318, 320, 332–62 (see also Patents);
and Curtiss and transatlantic flight,
367–68, 372–73; and early aeronautical experimentation and developments, 28–30, 38–40, 42, 48–49,
51–55, 59–66, 69 (see also specific
aircraft, aspects, developments);
and exhibition flying, 284, 288–89,
292–94, 301–2, 322, 364; Experiments and Observations in Soaring
Flight (Wilbur Wright), 69; and
France and the French, 63–64, 65–
66, 124, 170, 178, 182, 187, 194,
230–31, 235–36, 248 (see also specific aspects, individuals); and Gordon Bennett Trophy, 169; and Herring, 133, 134–35, 157, 171; and
Herring-Curtiss Company, 218–20,
225–26, 228, 230–31, 233, 245ff.,
255; and Hudson-Fulton Celebration
air competition, 208, 209–10, 212,
215–22; illness and death of Wilbur,
341–42, 352, 360; injury to Orville
and death of Selfridge in air crash,
127–31, 466–67; and June Bug, 103,
106–7, 114–16; and Kitty Hawk
plane disposition, 436–39, 480–81;
and Langley and early aeronautical
experiments, 28–30; and merger of
Wright Aeronautical Corporation
with Curtiss, 448–49; and patents,
62–63, 87, 97, 101, 115–16, 142–43,
164, 168, 170–71, 174, 189–92, 209–
10, 218–20, 222, 225–28, 230–31,
233–36, 240, 244ff., 318, 332–62,
389–391 (see also specific aspects,
developments, individuals); and

Paulhan, 235–36; praise for Beachey's flying by, 297; and Red Wing,
101; and Scientific American Trophy, 103, 106–7, 114–16; secrecy of,
86–87, 94, 97, 124–25; and Selfridge, 124–31, 466–67; and Smithsonian Institution, 146, 171, 435–39,
480–81; and Smithsonian Institution
award of Langley Medal to, 146,
171; and U. S. Army plane ("flyer"),
89–90, 120, 121, 122–23, 133, 134–
35, 137, 151, 174, 180, 240; and U.
S. Navy aviation, 309, 319; and use
of tracks for launching aircraft, 98,
125; and White Wing, 101; and wing
warping system, 62, 86–87, 97, 124,
142, 168, 170–71, 189–92, 222, 225–
28, 230–31, 233–36, 246–50, 332–
62; and Wright Company airplanes,
166, 186, 190, 193, 198, 230ff., 251ff.
(see also Wright Aeronautical Corporation; Wright Company airplanes
Wright Company airplanes, 166, 186,
190, 193, 198, 230ff., 251ff. See also
specific planes
Wright Cycle Company, 53

Zahm, Dr. Albert F., 348, 373–74, 385,
387, 388, 389, 397, 407, 413, 436–
437, 476, 477; composes poem for
launching of transatlantic plane,
America, 373–74, 476; and Curtiss
Engineering Corporation, 397, 407;
and Curtiss-Wright brothers patent
litigation, 477; and Langley plane
restoration and flight, 387, 388, 389,
436–37, 477 ; named director of
Langley Aerodynamical Laboratory,
348; and transatlantic flight, 373–74,
413
Zeppelin, Count Ferdinand von, 37–38,
208. See also Zeppelins
Zeppelins, 37–38, 208, 329